S0-AUS-464

PERSONAL FINANCE

Sixth Edition

PERSONAL FINANCE

Harold A. Wolf

University of Texas

ALLYN AND BACON, INC.
Boston, London, Sydney, Toronto

to my parents

Cover Designer: Christy Rosso
Series Editor: Richard Carle

Copyright © 1981, 1978, 1975, 1972, 1968, 1964 by Allyn and Bacon, Inc., 470 Atlantic Avenue, Boston, Massachusetts 02210.

All rights reserved. No part of the material protected by this copyright notice may be reproduced or utilized in any form or by any means, electronic or mechanical, including photocopying, recording, or by any information storage and retrieval system, without written permission from the copyright owner.

The third edition of this book was authored by Maurice A. Unger and Harold A. Wolf.

Library of Congress Cataloging in Publication Data

Wolf, Harold Arthur, 1923–
  Personal finance.

  Includes bibliographies and index.
  1. Finance, Personal. I. Title.
HG179.U48 1981   332.024   80-27967
ISBN 0-205-07298-4

Printed in the United States of America

10 9 8 7 6 5 4 3   85 84 83 82

Contents

Preface   ix

PART ONE   ***Budgeting, Buying, Borrowing, and Saving***   **1**

Chapter One   **The Role of Personal Finance**   **2**

Introduction   2/   The Purpose of Personal Finance   2/   The Current Economic
Environment   4/   The Individual and His or Her Income   10/   Society and
National Income   16/   Questions for Review   20/   Cases   20/   Suggested
Readings   21

Chapter Two   **Record-Keeping and Budgeting**   **23**

The Tools of Financial Planning   24/   The Personal Budget   27/   Taking a
Financial Inventory   44/   Questions for Review   44/   Cases   44/   Suggested
Readings   46

Chapter Three   **Caveat Venditor: Caveat Emptor**   **47**

Preliminary Comments on Consumerism   47/   Pre-Purchase Analysis—
Prevention   49/   Making Purchases   54/   Post-Purchase Redress Procedures:
How to Recover Your Losses   68/   Consumer Protection Agencies   71/
Questions for Review   72/   Cases   73/   Suggested Readings   74

Chapter Four   **Banks and the Services They Provide**   **75**

Checks and Checking Accounts   75/   Other Services Banks Provide   89/
Depository Institutions Deregulations Act of 1980   92/   Money Orders and
Travelers Checks   92/   Questions for Review   93/   Cases   93/   Suggested
Readings   94

Chapter Five   **The Role of Consumer Credit**   **95**

The Classification of Consumer Credit   96/   Why Consumers Borrow   98/
Benefits and Dangers of Consumer Credit   99/   How Much Do You Pay?   101

Sources of Consumer Credit 107/ Other Things You Should Know
about Consumer Credit and Consumerism 118/ Financial Documents
Accompanying Consumer Loans 128/ Some Do's and Don'ts of Consumer
Credit 131/ Questions for Review 133/ Cases 134/ Suggested
Readings 135

Chapter Six **Consumer Laws and Protection Agencies** **137**

Introduction 137/ Federal Consumer Protection Laws 138/ Enforcing
Agencies 146/ Questions for Review 150/ Cases 150/ Suggested
Readings 150

Chapter Seven **Savings through Thrift Institutions** **152**

Personal Savings in the United States 153/ Thrift Institutions 155/ Some
Notes on Interest 168/ Questions for Review 172/ Cases 172/ Suggested
Readings 173

APPENDIX A7 Present and Future Values 173

PART TWO *Your Insurance and Annuity Program* **183**

Chapter Eight **Life Insurance** **184**

Some General Insurance Concepts and Principles 185/ Classification of Life
Insurance Policies 193/ Ordinary Life Insurance 194/ Other Types of Life
Insurance 201/ What You Should Know About Buying Life Insurance 204/
Other Things You Should Know About Life Insurance 218/ The Seven Don'ts
of Life Insurance 225/ Questions for Review 226/ Cases 226/ Suggested
Readings 228

Chapter Nine **Health Care and Health Insurance** **229**

Types of Health Insurance Coverage 231/ Other Important Things about
Health Insurance 237/ Nonprofit Health Insurance Plans 239/ How Much
Health Insurance to Buy 243/ Questions for Review 246/ Cases 246/
Suggested Readings 247

APPENDIX A9 Medicare 248

APPENDIX B9 Medicaid 250

Chapter Ten **Property and Liability Insurance** **251**

Insurance on the Home 252/ Other Aspects of Home Insurance 257/ A
Home Insurance Program 259/ Automobile Insurance 260/ Other Aspects
of Automobile Insurance 265/ Miscellaneous and Specialty Insurance 269/
Questions for Review 271/ Cases 271/ Suggested Readings 272

Chapter Eleven **Social Security, Annuities, and Other Pension Plans 273**

Introduction 273/ Social Security 273/ Private (Life Insurance) Annuities 281/ Private (and Government) Pension Plans 288/ Individual Tax-Sheltered Retirement (Pension) Plans 292/ Summary of Your Retirement Program 298/ Questions for Review 299/ Cases 299/ Suggested Readings 300

PART THREE *Investments*   **303**

Chapter Twelve **Some Fundamentals of Direct Investments 304**

Forms of Business Organization 304/ Investment Objectives 307/ Investment Risks 310/ Reducing the Risk of Investments 314/ Sources of Investment Information 315/ Questions for Review 323/ Cases 323/ Suggested Readings 324

Chapter Thirteen **The Array of Securities 326**

The Array of Stock and General Comments 326/ The Array of Bonds and General Comments 337/ Questions for Review 350/ Cases 351/ Suggested Readings 352

Chapter Fourteen **The Investor and the Securities Market 353**

Introduction 353/ Securities Exchanges, Brokers, and Dealers 354/ Quoting Securities 360/ Buying and Selling Securities 367/ Distribution of Earnings from Stocks 369/ Investment Strategies: Timing of Investment Decisions, or When to Buy What 371/ Questions for Review 379/ Cases 379/ Suggested Readings 380

APPENDIX A14 Supplementary Material on Common Stock 381

Chapter Fifteen **Investment Companies (Mutual Funds) and Other Outlets for Surplus Funds 391**

The Classification of Investment Companies 392/ Objectives of Investment Companies 393/ Other Things You Should Know about Investment Companies 396/ Introduction to Other Outlets for Surplus Funds 406/ Commodity Markets 406/ Financial Real Estate Investments 407/ Direct Real Estate Investments 412/ Other (Unusual) Investment Opportunities 418/ Questions for Review 422/ Cases 422/ Suggested Readings 424

APPENDIX A15 Building a Portfolio; the Order of Priorities in Acquiring Assets 425

APPENDIX B15: Diamond Investments 426

PART FOUR **Home Ownership, Taxes, Estate Planning** **433**

Chapter Sixteen **Home Ownership** **434**

Introduction to Home Ownership 434/ Factors to Consider in Buying or Building a Home 439/ How Much is a Home Worth? 446/ Home Financing 448/ Questions for Review 468/ Cases 468/ Suggested Readings 469

Chapter Seventeen **Taxes** **470**

Introduction to Taxes and Expenditures 470/ State and Local Taxes 473/ Federal Personal Income Taxes 475/ Adjusted Gross Income: Page 1 Deductions 487/ Itemized Deductions 487/ Tax Credits 492/ Capital Gains and Losses 495/ Other Things You Should Know about Taxes 497/ Questions for Review 506/ Cases 507/ Suggested Readings 508

Chapter Eighteen **The Tools of Estate Planning** **509**

Gathering the Facts 510/ The Balance Sheet 510/ Modern Wills 512/ The Letter of Last Instructions 521/ Transfer in the Absence of a Will 522/ Trusts 523/ Gift and Estate Taxes 529/ Questions for Review 536/ Cases 537/ Suggested Readings 538

APPENDIX A18 540

Glossary 542

Index 546

Preface

This edition of PERSONAL FINANCE represents a significant and substantial revision in response to the increasing complexity and rapid change taking place in today's economic environment. Personal financial planning was complex enough in 1964 when the first edition was published; it is infinitely more so today.

Inflation is one of the major reasons for this situation. Not too many years ago it was not as difficult as today to keep ahead of inflation and maintain and even increase your standard of living. In 1964 the Consumer Price Index stood at 92.9 (the base year of 1967 being 100); in September 1980 it stood at 251.7. In 1964 the inflation rate was 1.7%; in March, 1980 the figure was 18% per year. The total amount of inflation during this book's life so far has been 163%!

It is obvious that whatever one's individual life-style and goals are, a better understanding of the principles of personal finance is absolutely vital today. The goal of this book remains the same: to provide the reader the necessary information to obtain an understanding of these principles, and to help the reader develop better skill in making financial decisions that will bring the most personal satisfaction.

ORGANIZATION AND APPROACH

All individuals are consumers. As such, they are almost constantly engaged in spending money for all kinds of things; spending on food takes place almost daily, expenditures on big items like a car or household furniture less frequently.

People are also constantly engaged in borrowing money, using credit cards, investing savings, paying taxes, buying houses and life, home, and auto insurance, and many other activities that may involve some financial pitfalls. I hope this book will help the reader avoid some of these pitfalls.

As people grow older their income and patterns of expenditures change. Many young couples just starting out are heavy consumers and light savers. Not only is their income lower, but they are (or soon will be) buying housing and household furniture. With the coming of children, consumption will remain high. However, as income rises, savings hopefully will grow. Later, after a house full of furniture is acquired, and the children are through college, savings should rise further as the heavy consuming years are behind.

This changing pattern of expenditures may be thought of as the family financial cycle. This cycle includes earning income, the need for borrowing, making many different types of expenditures, acquiring earning as well as consumer assets, making plans for retirement, and planning an estate. In the process of going through the financial cycle many complex situations may arise.

The book is divided into 4 parts, comprising 18 chapters. However, almost any chapter can be read out of sequence, and the topics can be studied in any order.

Part one, the Budgeting of Income and Purchases, has seven chapters. Chapter 1, The Role of Personal Finance, begins with a discussion of the purpose of personal finance and the economic environment in which we must live. It then discusses individual income, what determines income, and introduces aggregate income. Chapter 2 deals with record keeping and budgeting. Analysis is made of funds flowing into the budget in the form of income and then an analysis of funds flowing out of the budget in the form of expenditures. This sets the stage for what is to come.

Next there is a chapter on consumerism (Chapter 3) that discusses how to get more utility from consumer expenditure; as such it discusses buying strategies and consumer protection. This is where the consuming side (as opposed to the savings side) of the individual's income is discussed. This is followed by a chapter on banks and the services they provide, and then one on the role of consumer credit. This latter chapter covers the sources of consumer credit as well as the interest one must pay when using it. This chapter is the result of rewriting, reducing, and combining the material in Chapters 5 and 6 in the previous edition.

Next, Chapter 6 presents all of the various consumer protection laws and consumer protection agencies in one chapter rather than at various points in several chapters as in previous editions. Part one ends with Chapter 7 which discusses investing personal savings in thrift institutions.

Part two deals with all types of insurance, annuities, and retirement plans. First, life insurance, health insurance, and property and casualty insurance are examined in separate chapters. In each of the chapters an attempt is made to shed some light on the question of how much and what kind of insurance to buy as well as when to buy it. The final chapter of part two introduces the reader to both private (corporate) and public (social security) pension plans. Individual annuities sold by life insurance companies are also discussed, and then the chapter ends with some material on individual retirement programs that have special tax benefits.

Part three covers investments. If a budget calls for savings, the individual must decide where to invest them. Thrift institutions, which are discussed in part one, may be selected as an investment medium, in which case one invests in fixed assets, and does so indirectly through these institutions. However, many individuals invest directly in corporate stocks and bonds. When investing directly, the individual must still choose between investing in fixed assets (bonds) and variable assets such as stock. Consequently, several chapters on securities are presented. Mutual funds are also presented for those who would like to invest in common stock, but indirectly, not directly. I hope the material will aid investment decision making.

The last chapter in part three, which is Chapter 15, includes some material on other (non security) outlets for saving. This includes investing directly in rental income producing property such as duplexes or apartment buildings. However, also covered in this chapter are unusual (exotic) investment outlets such as gold and silver, antiques, paintings, works of art, and the like.

Part four deals with taxes, homeownership, and estate planning. Home ownership, which represents the largest investment and the largest asset for most individuals, is examined in some detail. We must render unto Caesar the things that are Caesar's; and hence the entire complex area of personal income taxes is examined in part four.

The book ends with a chapter on estate planning or what might be called preservation of accumulated assets as well as the allocation of assets to specific individuals after death. This chapter includes a discussion of trust, and gift and estate taxes. Trusts are one means of reducing taxes, but there are others as well. There is no reason for you to let the government have all of your accumulated assets, just because you are dead.

CHANGES IN THE SIXTH EDITION

In response to many recent developments in the economic and financial world that affect personal finance, and after securing the comments and suggestions of many users of the book, it was decided that a thorough revision of the book was necessary. Major portions of the text were completely reorganized and rewritten.

The reorganization has resulted in the elimination of two chapters. Chapter 11 now covers social security together with other pension plans, rather than in a separate chapter; the investments area is now covered in 4 chapters rather than in 5. Another major change resulted in presenting in one chapter (6) all the material on consumer protection laws and agencies which previously had been scattered throughout several chapters in previous editions.

The chapters on insurance have also been extensively rewritten, with additional material on how much and when to purchase it.

The goal in this revision was to provide the most up-to-date discussion of personal finance topics possible, given the almost daily changes in today's world. The data, statistics, and details concerning inflation, prices, interest rates, and innumerable other information was current when this book went to press.

Many new questions and cases have been added to the end of each chapter, and the list of suggested readings at the end of each chapter has been thoroughly revised and expanded.

ACKNOWLEDGEMENTS

In the preparation of any project of this nature there are many who need to be thanked for having so graciously given of their time and encouragement.

Particular credit is due Professor Lee Richardson formerly of Louisiana State University, who made many valuable contributions throughout the manuscript and who authored Chapter 3. I also wish to single out for special recognition Professor Patricia Tengel of Carnegie Mellon University and Gerry Georginson of the University of Utah for their valuable aid. Bette Grubbs of the Social Security District Office, Austin, Texas, was helpful in the ever changing field of social security. Dick Dexter, agent for Penn. Mutual, and Morgan Brenner of the Educational Training Department at the Penn. Mutual home office were advisors for the chapters on Insurance. Professor Grant J. Wells, of Ball State University, must be cited for graciously giving his time and energy in thoroughly critiquing the manuscript.

The following individuals have made a real contribution, through their thoughtful comments on either various portions of the manuscript or on the previous edition:

Professor Sam Andrews
University of Southern Maine

Professor Sheldon Balbirer
School of Business
University of North Carolina—Greensboro

Professor Robert Berry
Department of Business
Mt. San Antonio College

Professor Margaret A. Charters
Director of Consumer Studies
Syracuse University

Professor Ginny Dickinson
Department of Family Resource
  Management
Oregon State University

Professor Sue A. Greninger
Department of Home Economics
University of Texas at Austin

Professor Jim Hill
Vincennes University

Professor K. P. Hill
School of Business
Wichita State University

Professor Delmar Hylton
School of Business
Wake Forest University

Professor Ralph Marini
School of Business
St. Joseph's College

Professor Cynthia Needles
Family Department
Iowa State University

Professor Sue Peterson
Department of Home Economics
Northern Illinois University

Professor Joseph Samprone
Department of Consumer Sciences and
  Retailing
Purdue University

Professor Grant J. Wells
Department of Finance
College of Business
Ball State University

Professor Esther Williams
Department of Economics
Idaho State University

Arv Vilutis
William C. Heath and Associates, Inc.

In writing a book covering such a wide range of related but somewhat different areas it was necessary to consult various experts on the firing line in the business and financial community. They are too numerous for all of them to be mentioned here, but I do wish to specifically cite the following:

Charles Meek and Randall H. Robinson of Merrill Lynch Pierce Fenner & Smith, Inc.; Dr. William L. Anthes, President, College of Financial Planning, Denver, Colorado; Scott L. Sptizer of the American Stock Exchange; Dick Perkins of E. F. Hutton and Co.; Anne Stanford of North Austin State Bank; John Wolf, John Onken, John Eccles, and William Armer of City National Bank of Austin, Texas; Leona Paycen of the Austin National Bank; Linda Arnold of the Dow Jones and Company, Inc.; Charles Preston of Cartoon Features Syndicate; Jack Rubinson, Director, Department of Research and Economics, National Association of Mutual Savings Banks; Howard Cosgrove of the Credit Union National Association, Inc.; S. Lee Booth, Senior Vice President, National Consumer Finance Association; Jack Lewis, Regional Sales Manager, Farmers Insurance Group; Barbara Wheeler of the New York Stock Exchange; Suzanne K. Stemnock of the American Council of Life Insurance; Harry J. Guinivan of the Investment Company Institute; Fred C. Cohn, President and Editor, Johnson's Charts, Inc.; Judy Dunn of Stewart Title Co.; Loretta Shinder of the Texas State Bank; Jack L. Gardner, Director, Office of Communications, The Council of State Governments; David K. Fortt, Executive Vice President, Vernon Publishing Services, Inc.; Thomas J. Wolff, C.L.U., Vernon, Connecticut; Stephen Sanborn, Vice President, Standard and Poor's Corporation; Paul A. Johnston of Wiesenberger Investment Service; Joseph J. McAlinden, Executive Vice President, Argus Research Corporation; and Melitta Hartung of the American Automobile Association.

In addition, I wish to acknowledge the many students who have made valuable criticisms while using the book and my colleagues at colleges throughout the country who have shared their experience with the book in the classroom. While the full list of those to whom I am in debt is too lengthy to be spelled out here, a number of them must be mentioned. They include Professors Eugene Nelson and Ray Sommerfield of the University of Texas at Austin; Professors Helen N. Goety and E. M. Minter of the University of Alabama; Professors Tim Grady and Joy Haas of the University of Iowa; Professors Craig C. Milnot of Clark College; William J. Klaudt, of Jamestown College; Rodney Wissman of Bakersfield College; Nellie Amondson of Mesa College; Gilbert Fritzler of Warner Pacific College; Dawn Tuttle of the University of Arizona; Edna B. Villar of Pan American University at Edinburg, Texas; Talma B. Hupfield of California State College at Long Beach; John C. Redman of the University of Kentucky; Mary Flournoy of Grambling College; Berneice D. Melton of Eastern New Mexico University; E. W. Green of the University of Texas at El Paso; James D. Mason of Mesa College; Bill Claushan and Carole Makela of Colorado State University; Mary Jaequalin Buckley of Mount Mary College; R. H. Hall of Gulf Coast College; Irwin Harvey of the University of Georgia; Keith L. Keel of Stephens College; Robert S. Livingston of Biola College; Robert Lurensky of Southeastern University; Pauline H. Nelson of Southern Utah State College; Leslie Small of the University of South Florida; Axel W. Swang of David Lipscomb College; R. W. Greenleaf of Indiana University; Doris Beuttenmuller of Maryville College; M. Bridget of Livonia College; J. W. Fleenor of Southern Seminary College; J. H. Hellums of the University of Mississippi; M. Janice Hogan of Arizona State University; Sara Burton Jenkins of the University of Georgia; T. T. Lutz of the University of Evansville; Robert L. Martin of Middle Tenn. State University; Patricia Robbins of Kansas State University; Nell B. Robinson of Texas Christian University; Joseph S. Rowland of the University of Alabama; H. Seeberger of Heidelberg College; Isabell L. Smith of Western Michigan University; and Hannah H. Wells of Dixie College.

Also included are Earl W. Baggerly, Jr., of Merces University in Atlanta; Allan Bloomquest of Indiana University, South Bend; Richard Corbett of Southern Illinois University; Boyd Fuller of the University of Minnesota; Edward L. Grieges III of Florida Junior College; Ray D. Hedges of Western Kentucky University; Mary E. Holder of the University of New Hampshire; Robert A. Hoskins of the College of the Kiskiyous; Stephen Klepper of North Texas State University; Duane R. Johnson of Everett Community College; Mrs. Shirley Kolberg of North Dakota State University; John W. Kreitz of Lane Community College; Ann Langenfeld of the University of Delaware; Helen Paznaean of the University of Massachusetts; W. S. Phillips of Memphis State University; John A. Reynolds of Rio Grande College; Alfredo Romero of Penn State University; Lucile Sales of Western Kentucky University; Juan Steinberg of Jersey City State; Alan Shuart of the University of North Carolina; Auda M. Tatum of Ventura College; Esther Williams of Idaho State University; and Robert E. Wong of the University of Southern California.

Last but not least I give credit to my typists, who have labored over the manuscript. Judy Brown, Andrea Cunningham, Joan Dana, Sharen Lackey, Kathleen Middleton, Leona Sparks, and Mary Wingo deserve special recognition.

PART ONE

Budgeting, Buying, Borrowing, and Saving

In the seven chapters that make up Part I of this book, I shall examine the fundamentals of money management. This will set the stage for a discussion of all the other aspects of personal finance which follow.

Chapter 1 discusses the role of personal finance and the economic environment in which we all must live. It also covers individual income and the factors that help to determine income.

Chapter 2 covers record keeping and personal budgeting. In order to budget more effectively it is helpful first to draw up a personal balance sheet and income statement, and material on that is presented. A budget is essentially a device to help stretch income. If you possess a set of priorities and if a budget tells you where income goes, it is easier to see where it is possible to try to cut expenditures. If saving is one of your goals and you find it difficult to save, perhaps a budget will help.

Chapter 3 deals with consumerism. "Caveat venditor" and "Caveat emptor" are Latin phrases that mean respectively "let the seller beware" and "let the buyer beware." I hope the chapter provides some useful hints and helps the reader obtain more consumer satisfaction per dollar of expenditures. The emphasis is on prevention by wise shopping, but there is some information on how to recover losses as well.

In Chapter 4 the reader is introduced to commercial banks and the services they provide. The most important of these services is the checking account and it is thoroughly explored. But other services such as the savings account, automatic funds transfer, and a number of others are also covered.

Chapter 5 deals with the role of consumer credit. It covers the various types of credit, why it is often necessary to borrow, the benefits and dangers of consumer credit, how much it costs to borrow, and where to go if you need to borrow.

Consumer credit can be a treacherous pitfall and rather expensive if the buyer is not careful; there are ways, with which every buyer should be familiar, to minimize the cost of credit. The secret is to shop around when borrowing money; not all lenders charge the same rate of interest. The purchase of large consumer items such as automobiles and refrigerators takes a lot of money. There is no reason why the buyer should pay what may be needless financing charges that would make these items even more expensive.

In Chapter 6 you are introduced to your rights as a consumer. In recent years a number of federal laws have been passed to protect the consumer and these are all discussed. There are also some state laws. In addition, the federal and state enforcing agencies are presented.

Chapter 7 deals with where to invest the savings which your wise money management and personal budgeting have helped you to achieve. The chapter covers a number of thrift institutions that will accept savings and pay an interest return.

Chapter One

The Role of Personal Finance

"A fool and his money are soon parted."
ANONYMOUS

The objectives of this chapter are to

1   Outline the purpose of personal finance

2   Describe the current economic environment in which personal finance must operate

3   Present some pertinent information on personal income

4   Make a few suggestions regarding improving your income

5   Introduce some data and sources on career opportunities

6   Explore our standard of living

7   Describe briefly what is to come in the rest of the book

INTRODUCTION

Broadly defined, personal finance has to do with the allocation of scarce resources (money income) among alternative and competing ends. Human wants are virtually unlimited, while money income, the means to satisfy these wants, is limited. A dollar spent on clothing cannot be spent on food. Consequently, choices must be made and priorities established.

For a few wealthy individuals almost any and all conceivable wants can be satisfied, although even such cases must be qualified because a vast fortune could be dissipated quickly. For most of us, however, we must manage our personal financial affairs, and if we do this wisely we can accomplish several things: enlarge our income; improve the mileage we get out of each dollar of expenditures; and protect that which we already have.

THE PURPOSE OF PERSONAL FINANCE

Personal finance is intended to help people to plan their financial affairs more intelligently. People are consumers, and personal finance is the finance of and for the consumer. However, it is more than that. People are also producers (by participating in the labor market or by household activities) and hence income earners, savers, and investors. Hence, personal finance must also take cognizance of money income, savings, and investments. Nor does the list end there.

You will from time to time engage in borrowing money, using credit cards, investing your savings, paying taxes, buying insurance, automobiles, houses, furniture, and many other things. You may also be planning your retirement. Carrying out these activities well requires technical knowledge, and the study of personal finance is intended to provide you with this knowledge. These activities may also expose you to some financial pitfalls; once more, knowledge about personal finance will enable you to cope and to achieve many of the goals you set for yourself.

Maximizing Satisfaction

When talking about the "good life" most people have in mind the standard of living, which in turn is determined, in large part, by their purchasing power. They also think about consumption. We are a hedonistic people living in a materialistic age. Generally speaking, we like to enjoy good food, nice clothes, automobiles, fine homes, and many other things. We also enjoy leisure, travel, and entertainment. To be sure, tastes vary and different people want different combinations of a variety of goods and services. Some would consume a larger part of a given income and save less than others. Nevertheless it is probably safe to say that most of us strive to maximize personal satisfaction by applying our own set of values, and we generally associate the degree of satisfaction as positively related to our level of income.

In recent years, a new term, measure of economic welfare (MEW), has come into use. MEW is an attempt to refine income into a more meaningful concept of how well off we are. In the process of earning our income, certain social costs are created that cannot always be measured. They include such things as pollution, congestion, and noise, which reduce the quality of life. Economists refer to these social costs as negative externalities, i.e., costs generated by some but borne by all. Therefore, while our money income is a measure of our standard of living it is an imperfect gauge of the quality of life.

It has been suggested that MEW is equal to income adjusted for a number of things. First, it would be reduced by the cost of maintaining clean air and water. Also subtracted would be the estimated costs of noise and urban congestion, both money costs if available and an estimate of the value of the psychological pain caused by noise and congestion. To this reduced figure would be added an estimate of the value of household activities for which there is no market value and also an estimate of the value of leisure time. This would be MEW. When this is first done, MEW is an abstraction that means little. However, comparing MEW from one year to the next could be a better indication of how life is improving. It could be that income is growing and MEW is declining. If so, this really suggests that the amenities of life are worth more than additional material things and that amenities perhaps are being reduced by population and economic growth.

The difficulty with MEW, of course, is that it must be an estimate. True measures of the cost of pollution cannot always be obtained. The value of increased leisure must also be an estimate. The same is true of noise and congestion. In addition, not only must some of the concepts be estimates, but the value judgments of the estimator are crucial in determining the final figure. For this reason, one cannot cite valid figures for MEW. Nevertheless, it is an interesting and thought-provoking concept.

Consumer Spending

Generally, we maximize our satisfaction by spending our income on a variety of goods and services. Financial experts refer to this as consumption and to expenditures on consumer items as consumption expenditures. We must differentiate between consumer expenditures and other expenditures, which consist of investment expenditures and government expenditures made on our behalf with our tax dollars by the various levels of government. Expenditures, therefore, can be broken down into (1) consumption expenditures, (2) investment expenditures, and (3) government expenditures.

Consumption expenditures are expenditures by individuals on final goods and services.

Investment Expenditures or Wealth Accumulation

Investment expenditures are for the most part made by business, but if you save part of your income (do not spend it on consumption items), you may still spend it on an investment item. That portion of your income that is spent on acquiring a home, a life insurance policy, stocks and bonds, and even a savings deposit in a bank is still spent. But it is spent on acquiring investments which in turn may yield an interest (or investment) return. That is why such expenditures are called investment expenditures.

Government Expenditures

The federal government spends on our behalf billions of dollars. State and local governments spend billions more. They provide us primarily with services: law and order, education, national defense, mail services, roads, etc. But they too are part of overall expenditures, which benefit us and which we pay for with our taxes. Our taxes then are also spending on the services of governments.

Money in the Scheme of Things

Money is the name of the game. You earn your income in the form of money; you make your consumption and investment expenditures (wealth or asset accumulating expenditures); and you pay your taxes in the form of money. Money, therefore, is a medium of exchange. Money is used in virtually all transactions because it is much more convenient than barter; hence, it is also a standard of value. The value of everything is stated in money terms. The third function of money is that it is a store of value. You can convert your work effort into money, store (save) it, and later use the money for personal consumption expenditures.

THE CURRENT ECONOMIC ENVIRONMENT

The trinity of groups that make up most of the U.S. economy consists of governments, businesses, and consumer-producers.[1]

1. To be sure there are others: for example, churches, various nonprofit institutions, farmers, self-employed professionals, and labor unions, to mention only the most obvious. However, farmers and self-employed professionals are really businesses, and the members of labor unions are also part of the consumer-producers. Churches and certain nonprofit organizations, while important, account for only a small part of the total output of goods and services.

Government

At one time it was believed that the government's main role was that of umpire. It was to see that the law was carried out and it enforced contracts between individuals. In addition, it provided for the national defense. In order to carry out its function, the government levied taxes and made certain expenditures.

Today the role of the government has been expanded to include regulation of businesses and even individuals. More restrictions are imposed than formerly to protect the public and the environment. The philosophy is that the government is to do those things that citizens cannot do for themselves, or cannot do as well. The government has more of a welfare function now than in the past.

As the government's role has expanded so has its size, and the dollars in taxes it needs to carry out its role. While the government itself produces very little in the way of goods, it is inexorably wrapped up in the productive process via taxes and regulations. In the process it produces a service.

Businesses

Most of the goods and services produced in the United States today are produced by the business sector. There are hundreds of thousands of business firms; some large like General Motors, some small like many one- or two-owner corner grocery stores.

Business firms employ the majority of the labor force and are the means through which most of the income of the American people is earned. In short, business entities are probably the most important single factor in the economic environment.

Consumers-Producers

As noted above, everyone is a consumer to a greater or lesser extent. However, every consumer who is in the labor force is also a producer. Many consumers thus serve in a dual capacity in our economy; they buy goods and services and sell their labor services. Consumers are demanders of output and suppliers of labor to produce it. To enjoy the good life you have to earn an income. In the short run you have to operate within a given economic environment. But as a group (for example, through unions or consumers groups) you can also affect, to some extent, the economic environment.

The economic environment then consists of an interrelationship between the governments, businesses, and consumer-producers. This is illustrated in Figure 1–1.

The figure shows consumer-producers providing labor services to business firms in exchange for money incomes. These money incomes are then used to make money payments to business firms in exchange for goods and services, which are purchased. These are the consumption expenditures noted above. The diagram shows the circular flow of money represented by the outside arrows which finances the flow of real goods and services depicted by the arrows on the inside. The diagram also shows the payments of taxes on the part of businesses and consumer-producers (individuals) to governments in return for the services supplied by various levels of government. Also shown is a withdrawal in the form of savings from this income stream. Although not shown, these savings will flow back into the system when you buy bonds or stock, or deposit money in a savings account. In doing this, you are making an investment expenditure, or what is the same thing, accumulating wealth in the form of earnings assets. Money, then, is the oil in the system, which is necessary for the interrelationships and permits the production and exchange of real goods and services.

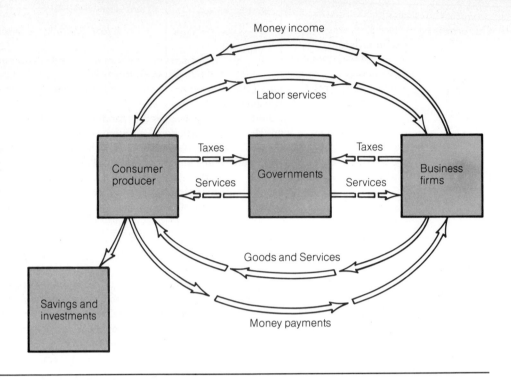

FIGURE 1–1. *The economic environment.*

Inflation

Inflation is also part of the economic environment, and it can affect your "well-being," or your "standard of living" because it can affect how much your income can purchase. Inflation may be defined as a continuous increase in the overall price level; many prices must be considered, not just a few. During periods of inflation the dollar purchases less and less; its value declines. Inflation, then, can be defined in two ways: a rise in the overall price level, or a decline in the value of the dollar. Deflation, or an appreciation in the value of the dollar, is exactly the opposite—a continuous decrease in the overall price level. But deflation happens less frequently than inflation, and in recent years it has not happened at all.

During periods of inflation, those having fixed incomes find themselves with less and less buying power while those whose income rises more rapidly than prices are better off. Inflation is inequitable since it harms some and benefits others.

Adjusting money income to take into account the effects of inflation provides what is known as real income. If prices are rising by 5 percent per year, an individual must obtain a 5 percent annual increase in income just to stay even; real income will then remain the same. If the person's income is fixed, he or she is about 5 percent worse off every year in the above situation. Over the years, this has happened to some. Others, however, have had wage and salary increases that have more than offset inflation in real terms.

A person earning $20,000 in 1970 and still earning that today would have had a real income reduction equivalent to $9,385 by the end of July, 1980.

In 1970 average family money income in the United States was about $10,000; by 1980 this had grown to about $21,000. However, most of this was due to inflation. In real terms, average family income had only increased to about $10,500; it barely kept pace with inflation.

Even persons whose income keeps pace with inflation become worse off as time passes because they move into a higher marginal tax bracket. For example, a person earning $20,000 in 1970 whose income had just kept pace with inflation would be earning $42,620 in 1980. Table 1–1 summarizes this. It shows money income, real income, taxes, after-tax money income, after-tax real income, and economic deterioration for such a hypothetical person. It also shows the same things for a person whose income has remained constant over these years. The person whose income kept up with inflation earned $42,620 (up from $20,000 in 1970), but after-tax real income declined by $2,567 due to higher taxes. The person whose income remained at $20,000 over the period suffered a loss in real income due to inflation of $8,488 ($15,993−$7,505).

In addition to changing people's incomes in real terms, inflation erodes savings held in the form of fixed assets. The dollars held in bank accounts, bonds, and insurance policies will buy less and less as prices rise. Even the interest earned by these investments must be adjusted to take inflation into account. For example, if savings accounts can earn 5 percent interest and prices rise (inflation) at a rate of 3 percent per year, the real interest rate is only 2 percent per year. In some years, the rate of inflation has been higher than the money interest rate, making the real return on fixed investment negative.

Inflation also changes the debtor-creditor relationship. For example, if an individual assumes a $40,000 mortgage in 1980 at the 1980 price level, and if prices then double, the mortgage is paid off in dollars of only one-half the purchasing power of the dollars originally borrowed. The debtor (borrower) benefits from this situation, while the creditor's position is worsened.

Finally, inflation, if it is rapid and continues for a long enough period of time, may produce undesirable psychological and political effects. People may come to expect inflation to continue and spend energy attempting to hedge it rather than in productive activities. If

TABLE 1–1. *How inflation affects income*

	1970	1980	1980
	A AND B	PERSON A	PERSON B
Money income	$20,000	$42,620	$20,000
Real income	$20,000	$20,000	$ 9,385
Taxes*	$ 4,007*	$14,008	$ 4,007*
After-tax money income	$15,993	$28,612	$15,993
After-tax real income	$15,993	$13,426	$ 7,505
Economic deterioration	———	$ 2,567	$ 8,488

Note: The calculations in the table assume that Persons A and B are both single and do not itemize deductions, and that 1979 taxes apply in both years.

*This tax liability will vary by a few dollars depending upon whether it is calculated by using the tax tables or rate schedules. We are ignoring all taxes except the federal personal income tax. People living in states that have personal income taxes may be doing even more poorly than this table suggests.

enough people are aroused, it may even affect their action at the polls, the results of which may or may not be beneficial.

There are many causes of inflation. One is a situation where there are too few goods and a great demand for those goods that forces prices up. This is commonly called "demand-pull" inflation. This was the situation immediately following World War II. During the 1950s and 1960s this factor disappeared but in the 1970s shortages (especially in energy, food, and commodities) again became a factor in driving up prices.

A second factor causing inflation is the easy availability of credit, resulting in an over-supply of money. If there is a large increase in the quantity of money without a concomitant increase in production, prices are bid up.

A third factor could be a rise in the costs of production to a point where manufacturers or producers of goods see their profits threatened, in which case they might raise the price of their product. This is called "cost-push" inflation.

Fourth, inflation may be caused by excessive government expenditures, especially if financed via a deficit in the national budget. This government demand adds to aggregate demand and pulls prices up.

Government regulations are a fifth cause. Not only do the regulations cost the government money to enforce but they also impose additional costs on business in meeting the regulatory requirements.

Institutional factors are a sixth cause of inflation. By this we mean that some businesses and unions have such market power that they can often impose wage and price increases not warranted by market considerations.

Recently some economists have cited a new cause of inflation. It is that both taxes and inflation discriminate against the saver and investor, and in favor of consumption. This causes savings and hence investment capital to dry up, which in turn forces the economy to grow more slowly. This in turn, after a lag, causes the supply of goods and services to be less than it otherwise would have been.

An eighth cause of inflation has to do with foreign trade and the international value of the dollar. If the international value of the dollar declines as it has lately, imports cost more, and this by itself adds to inflation. The mere fact that imports cost more makes it easier for domestic suppliers of like goods to raise their prices, causing a secondary inflationary jolt from this source. Finally, widespread expectations that inflation will continue may contribute to its continuation as people react in ways calculated to protect themselves or to minimize the harm they will suffer. "Buy now before the prices rise" represents this attitude.

Some of the causes of inflation are noted above. These should suggest what we as a nation might do to control or halt inflation. If we have expanded the money supply and credit excessively, this can be halted. If the government taxes and spends too much, this can be stopped. If business and labor contribute to inflation, greater restraint by these groups can lessen upward price movements. If taxes discriminate against savers, changes can be made in the tax laws to remedy this. If government regulations have now gone too far, this can be changed. If the dollar is too weak internationally, it can be strengthened by importing less. We as individuals can do little to control inflation, but as a group we can do a great deal.

Consumer Price Index

The method used to measure the degree to which prices have risen is the statistical device known as index numbers. The Department of Labor calculates and publishes what it calls "the consumer price index," a barometer of inflation. If the worker's wages do not keep

FIGURE 1–2. *Price inflation has worsened during the last few years. Data are expressed as the percentage change from twelve months earlier. (Source: Federal Reserve Bank of New York Quarterly Review, Spring 1980, p. 29.)*

up with a rise in this index, it suggests that the individual is falling behind in terms of what income will purchase. This consumer price index is commonly called the cost of living index. More technically, it is an index issued monthly by the United States Department of Labor's Bureau of Labor Statistics, the full title being "Consumer Price Index for All Urban Consumers."

To construct this index, the prices of some four hundred goods and services are gathered in 85 cities. The index, according to the Bureau of Labor Statistics, covers

> prices of everything people buy for living—food, clothing, automobiles, homes, house furnishings, household supplies, fuel, drugs, and recreational goods; fees to doctors, lawyers, beauty shops; rent, repairs costs, transportation fares, public utility rates, etc. It deals with prices actually charged to consumers, including sales and excise taxes. It also includes real estate taxes in owned homes, but does not include income or social security taxes.[2]

The prices are weighted and averaged. Actually, the index is now figured on a base period of 1967 as being equal to 100. In short, if the base period is 100 and the index is now (July 1980) 247.8, the cost of living has risen 247.8 percent since the base period. By the same token, the same number of dollars now will purchase 59.6 percent less than it would have during the base period. This calculation measures the degree of inflation and the reduction in the purchasing power of the dollar.[3]

Figure 1–3 shows how prices have risen over the past few years' base period. Note that the cost of living can be classified into food items, nonfood items, and services such as medical services; and a composite can be made up of all these items.

2. U.S. Department of Labor, Bureau of Labor Statistics, *Supplement to Economic Indicators* (Rev. January 1967), Washington: U.S. Government Printing Office, 1967, p. 94.

3. When prices rise, the value of the dollar falls but not by the same amount. The value of the dollar falls reciprocally. For example, if prices rise by 100 percent, say from an index of 100 to 200, obviously the value of money cannot fall 100 percent to zero. In this case the value of money fell by 50

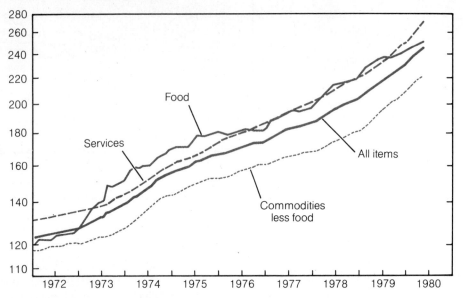

Index, 1967 = 100 (ratio scale)

In May, the consumer price index for all urban consumers rose 1.0 percent percent (0.9 percent seasonally adjusted). Food prices rose 0.5 percent (0.3 percent seasonally adjusted). Nonfood commodity prices rose 0.7 percent (0.4 percent seasonally adjusted) and services prices were up 1.5 percent (1.6 percent seasonally adjusted).

FIGURE 1–3. *Consumer prices.* (*Source:* Economic Indicators, June 1980, Council of Economic Advisers, U.S. Department of Commerce, p. 23.)

THE INDIVIDUAL AND HIS OR HER INCOME

As noted above, your money income will in large part determine your "standard of living." A few people inherit great wealth, but most of us do not. The amount that an individual earns is directly related to education, occupation, age, property ownership, where you live, ability, drive, family connections, and plain luck.

percent. In order to calculate how much the value of money has declined with a given increase in prices, we use the following formula:

$$\frac{\text{Base year prices}}{\text{Current year prices}} = \frac{\text{Value of money in current year}}{\text{Value of money in base year}}$$

or, in the illustration,

$$\frac{100}{247.8} = \frac{X}{100} \text{ or } 247.8X = 10,000, X = 40.4$$

Then 100−40.4 gives us 59.6, which is the decline in the value of money.

Part 1 / Budgeting, Buying, Borrowing, and Saving

Income and Education

Many studies indicate that over a lifetime persons with more schooling tend to earn more money. In general, it may be said that the time, effort, and money invested in education increase the productivity of the individual and yield a return in the form of additional compensation. An alternative explanation, however, is that in acquiring an education a person invests a great deal in what has been called human capital. Just as ordinary capital (plant and equipment) yields a return called interest and profit because it is productive, so too does human capital. According to this theory, part of the high wages and salaries made by the highly educated is a return on human capital and is analogous to interest and profit.

Some experts have expressed concern that colleges are turning out too many graduates who expect elite occupations but who are really not prepared for them. There may not ever be enough elite occupations to go around. Generally in such a case, it would be expected that many of these individuals would enter other less prestigious occupations. Some might even become skilled craftspersons and work with their hands.

Income and Occupation

The income of individuals also varies greatly with occupations. However, there is also a high correlation between higher-income jobs and level of education. For example, professional and managerial workers have the highest incomes and these people, generally speaking, are also college graduates. Private domestic household servants, on the other hand, have the lowest income and are usually the most poorly educated. Many occupations require a college education or a lengthy training period for a person to be qualified for admittance; others do not. However, for any given level of education a number of different occupations are possible, and earnings within these occupations vary substantially. Many high school graduates can choose between more highly paid clerical and sales occupations and more poorly paid service and laborer occupations. Or if they are willing to spend a rather lengthy period as relatively low paid apprentices, they may enter the ranks of the highly skilled, highly paid building trade craft occupations.

Income and Age

Generally speaking, the low-income groups are concentrated among the very young and the very old. The young have low incomes because they have not yet learned a skilled trade or worked their way up the ladder; the old are either retired or hold only part-time jobs. In 1978, for example, families whose head was in the forty-five to fifty-four-year-old bracket earned an average of $23,698, the highest average income of any age classification.

Most family heads reach their maximum earning capacity between the ages of thirty-five and fifty-four. The greatest percentage of those with incomes of $50,000 a year or over are the forty-five to fifty-four-year-olds. As an observer put it: "The trouble is you don't get into the really high income group until you're too old to carry your suitcase."

Income and Property Ownership

The Internal Revenue Service (IRS) classifies income into earned and the so-called unearned. According to their definition, earned income consists solely of wages and salaries; it is a payment made in return for services rendered by individuals. This service is called work. The so-called unearned income consists of income derived from property.

Although precise statistics are unavailable, economists have long known that there is a positive correlation between property ownership and income because most property yields a return. Indeed, nearly all of the truly high incomes in the United States today are derived from property. Real estate yields rent; stocks and bonds yield dividends or interest; oil wells yield royalties; and a theater yields income in the form of revenue from ticket sales.

Two ways of acquiring income-yielding property are inheritance, or saving current income and using it to acquire property. One who inherits property benefits from the savings of a previous generation. One who acquires property makes a sacrifice today by investing current savings (giving up consumption) in order to enjoy a higher income and higher consumption in the future.

While it is true that the more property you own, the more income you receive, it is also true that the more income you receive, the more you are able to save and the more property you are able to acquire. This will enhance your income even more in the future. Low-income groups find it difficult to save and acquire property to increase their future income. High-income groups, on the other hand, are more likely to save and acquire property and to enjoy an even higher income in the future. However, it should be explained that even higher income groups do not find it easy or painless to save and acquire assets. Real effort is usually involved; it means giving up current consumptions, saving money, and buying assets.

"His peak earning years came and went without a ripple." (Drawing by Geo. Price; © 1980 The New Yorker Magazine Inc.)

Part 1 / Budgeting, Buying, Borrowing, and Saving

It is also true that property is even more unequally distributed than income, and this contributes further to inequality of income. Nevertheless, most people are able to save some, and everyone should consciously try to do so. Obtaining property income via saving is both painful and time consuming for most wage earners; but the reward is greater future income.

Regional Differences in Income

Horace Greeley's admonition, "Go West, young man, go West," is still valid insofar as earnings are concerned. Assuming that two persons equal in all respects (such as age and education) are working in the same occupation, but one works in the northern or western part of the United States and the other in the South, the person in the North or West will earn more. It should be noted, however, that incomes are growing more rapidly in the South than in the rest of the country.

Other Factors Affecting Your Income

While the list of other factors that might have an impact upon your income might be quite lengthy, we will note only the more obvious ones.

Luck
Being in the right place at the right time often determines a difference in income between people of equal ability. One of the richest silver strikes in the state of Idaho resulted from a jackass taking the wrong trail and by pure chance knocking off a piece of outcropping that turned out to be high-grade silver ore.

Talent and Brains
Some people are born with talent and "brains"; others are born with just talent and others just "brains"; some have ability, others little or none. A low I.Q. may force a person into jobs that are in the nature of menial labor. Some with talent are able to rise to the top of the income heap through just pure natural ability. A few noted actors and actresses have been known to get by on less. On the other hand, unfortunately, a number of persons have talents that never see the light of day. Still others have physical handicaps that may decrease their earning power, or mental infirmities may equally decrease an individual's earning power.

Hard Work
There is little doubt that some people are more industrious than others. Some people will only do enough to get by; others will do more in the hope that their hard work and energy will win them a promotion to a better paying job. Related to hard work is "incentive." Without an incentive to succeed, people will not work hard. One of the most powerful incentives to work hard is the monetary reward that hard work brings, but different people respond to it with different levels of work intensity.

Family Connections
One way to get ahead might be to marry the boss's daughter—or son! Or if you are just out of law school and the member of a socially prominent family, the latter factor might get you employment in the most prestigious law firm in town. If so, your income is likely to be higher than if you are the son or daughter of an average family and hang out your own shingle.

"I still can't get over it. Me, a poor immigrant boy achieving all this by marrying the boss's daughter." (Permission Cartoon Features Syndicate; from the Wall Street Journal.)

Discrimination

Discrimination has historically been one of the chief causes of inequality of income. The two major groups that were discriminated against insofar as jobs were concerned were minority groups and women. This is now changing. There is very little overt discrimination based on race or sex today; subtle forms still exist, however. Also the results of past discrimination may still affect income today because certain groups have not yet had time to develop the skills needed to compete effectively for better-paying jobs.

The differences in income between white families and those from minority groups, while lessening, are still substantial. In late 1978, median family income in the United States was $15,064. The median income of white families was $15,660, but for nonwhite families the median was $10,130, or only about 65 percent of that of white families.[4]

Improving Your Income; Choosing a Career

Since income is determined in large part by ability, drive, education, and chosen occupation, the individual has some control over it. This is particularly true if the individual is

4. U.S. Department of Commerce, Bureau of the Census, Series P–60, No. 105, June, 1977, p. 120.

young. There are also non-money rewards in many occupations. Therefore, the choice of a vocation is not usually made on the basis of money income alone.

Another factor that must be given some weight in choosing a career is aptitude. Not many can choose a career as a concert pianist. This takes a rare talent and only a few have it. The same may be said of certain other so-called glamorous vocations such as acting or professional athletics. While a good many people would like to make careers in these areas, and many even try to do so, only a few succeed. However, there is nothing wrong with testing talents in these areas at the amateur level (often in high school and college) in order to see whether enough talent exists to warrant professional training. Moreover, one does not need acting talent to go into radio and television. There is room for producers, directors, technicians, and various other behind-the-scene jobs. If one has a liking and an aptitude for this kind of work, it can be a rewarding career.

College students have many options open to them and they often make commitments when selecting a major. The student can choose to be prepared for a career in engineering, law, medicine, accounting, and a wide variety of other professions. It is in the professions that particular care should be given to aptitude. Even a bright student should not go into engineering if an aptitude for mathematics and technology is lacking. Various aptitude tests can determine the likelihood of success in a number of different professions such as law, medicine, and accounting. Information on these tests can be obtained at the counseling and guidance centers that most colleges and universities maintain.

Before finally choosing a career (and an employer), college students should also touch base with their college placement center. These centers are constantly receiving information about various careers as well as various companies. In many cases, the placement centers work with the counseling and guidance centers in career counseling.

Students should also become familiar with four publications on career opportunities. First, there is *The Occupational Outlook for College Graduates,* compiled by the U.S. Department of Labor and published by the U.S. Government Printing Office, Washington, D.C. This publication surveys the general outlook of the job market for college graduates and discusses various professions such as accounting, engineering, and actuarial sciences. It describes each of these professions with respect to the nature of the work, the training required, salaries and working conditions, and the employment outlook.

The second publication that should be examined is the *College Placement Annual.* This is a yearly publication of the College Placement Council, Incorporated (P.O. Box 2263, Bethlehem, Pennsylvania). This council is the official placement organization serving various college placement centers throughout the United States and Canada. The publication gives some general information for college graduates, and it provides an alphabetical list of all the major private employers in the United States as well as all government agencies. It also contains an employment index in which all employers are listed by the occupations they need and the region they serve.

The Occupational Thesaurus is a two-volume work that lists various areas of employment for which college majors would be qualified. It describes the various industries that have a need for people with specific job skills. This publication can be obtained from Everett A. Teal of Lehigh University (Bethlehem, Pennsylvania), or, like the others noted above, it is most likely available at your college placement center or library.

Finally, the student should become familiar with *The Encyclopedia of Careers and Vocational Guidance,* a two-volume work published by J. G. Ferguson Co. of Chicago, Illinois (distributed by Doubleday and Company). It provides some general information about how to find a job, interviewing, and vocational testing. This publication covers all possible jobs and professions, not only those requiring college training. It should be available in your library.

Nonpecuniary Income

Some jobs are more pleasant than others, and the degree of pleasure—or unpleasantness—provided by any given job varies from individual to individual. So there is often an element of nonpecuniary (or psychic) income involved. Some people are willing to accept a lower money income for the prestige attached to a given job. Other people may prefer to live in sunny Florida or California and attach some return for being able to do so. Or a person who wants to live in the crisp cool air of Colorado and be within a few miles of the fine skiing slopes might be willing to sacrifice some money income. Not everyone attempts to maximize money income.

Fringe Benefits

Statistics on money income usually exclude fringe benefits, even though their monetary value can be calculated in many cases. Such things as free—or reduced cost—health insurance, sick leave, paid vacation, and retirement benefits often vary from one job to another. Employers view these costs as legitimate costs of obtaining labor. Employees should also include them in their total income.

SOCIETY AND NATIONAL INCOME

We have examined some of the factors that will influence individual personal income. If we put all of the millions of individuals' incomes together, we have the nation's income. Some knowledge of the nation's income is important in studying personal finance because it will give you a feeling for the overall economy and help you to understand how it is behaving. You will need to have an understanding of two terms that economists and businesspersons use in analyzing what is happening to the entire economy. They are: *national income* and *gross national product*.

National income is merely the sum total of all the *income* of all the people in the United States for a given accounting period. It tells how well off we are as a group; individual income is the individual's share of national income. We shall examine national income in detail, but first we must understand Gross National Product. It is somewhat larger than national income because the government takes something off of the top (excise taxes) and because machinery, plant, and equipment used by industry wear out and must be replaced. *Gross National Product* (usually referred to simply as GNP) is the market value of all final goods and services produced in the United States per year. It is the dollar sum of all Tootsie Rolls, all Ford cars, all tomatoes, and all of the thousands of other products. To this figure must be added the cost of the services of doctors, lawyers, government workers, ministers, and all others who do not make goods but render services.

In 1971 GNP reached over $1 trillion for the first time (it was $1,063.4 billion). By late 1979 it had grown to $2,368.8 billion. Figure 1-4 illustrates the growth in GNP since 1960.

As noted previously, national income is somewhat smaller than GNP (about $444 billion smaller in 1979) because national income does not include the annual replacement of worn-out machinery or certain other items such as the various federal excise taxes. National income has been defined as the return (or income) to all of the various factors of production.

The factors of production produce output and are paid an income to do so. There are essentially four factors of production:

1. Land
2. Labor
3. Capital
4. Ownership or risk assumption

Each of the four factors of production gets a return and this return respectively is

1. Rent to the owners of land
2. Wages and salaries to labor
3. Interest to lenders of capital
4. Profit to owners who assume the risk of business failure

These four types of income are the only kind anyone can possibly earn. Labor and wages and salaries are broadly defined. Salaries include the incomes made by the managers and

FIGURE 1–4. *Gross national product.* (*Source:* Economic Indicators, June 1980, Council of Economic Advisers, U.S. Department of Commerce, p. 1.)

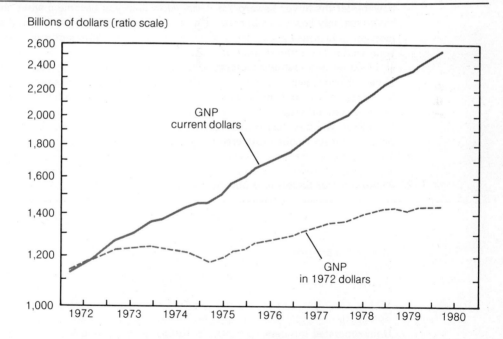

Billions of dollars (ratio scale)

According to revised estimates for the first quarter, gross national product rose $63.9 billion or 10.8 percent, both at annual rates. Real output (GNP adjusted for price changes) rose 1.2 percent from the fourth quarter level and the implicit price deflator rose at a 9.5 percent annual rate.

executives of all business firms. Labor includes all human effort, not just the work of blue-collar employees. The phrase "wages and salaries," then, includes the salary of the president of General Motors as well as that of the president of the United States. They are only specialized and highly skilled workers. The table below illustrates the distribution of the four basic types of income earned by the American people in 1979.

Note that the total return of the four factors of production in Table 1–2 comes to only $1,794.0 billion, whereas national income amounted to $1,924.8 billion in 1979. How do we explain the difference? A fifth category includes a mixture of all four of the above-mentioned types of income: farm income and the income of the self-employed. Their income cannot be separated into wages and salaries, rent, profit, and the like and is lumped togeth-er. It was $130.8 billion in 1979 which, if added to the $1,794.0 billion in Table 1–2, gives us $1,924.8 billion.

WHAT IS TO COME IN THE BOOK

We stated at the beginning of this chapter that the purpose of *Personal Finance* is to help you plan your financial affairs more intelligently. The following chapters will discuss in more detail how to become a better "money manager."

The first step toward intelligent personal financial management is to get a clear idea of where you are and where you want to go. The next chapter discusses record-keeping and budgeting, two skills which will help greatly in achieving these goals.

Chapter 3, "Caveat Venditor; Caveat Emptor" (literally translated, "let the seller beware; let the buyer beware") is designed to help you become a wiser shopper. It dis-cusses not only how to avoid certain pitfalls by sophisticated shopping and how to get the most for your consumer dollar, but also how to obtain redress of grievances if you have been victimized in the marketplace.

You will soon establish a relationship with a bank (or already have done so). You will have a checking account and use certain other services that banks provide. Chapter 4 will introduce you to the (what may seem mysterious but really isn't) world of banks and the services they provide.

When you buy "big ticket" items (cars, household furniture, and the like), you will probably borrow money (use credit) and when doing so, you should shop around. Not all

TABLE 1–2. *Return on four factors of production—1979*

	DOLLARS IN BILLIONS	PERCENT
Wages and salaries	$1,459.2	75.8
Rent	26.9	1.4
Interest	129.7	6.7
Profit	178.2	9.3
Total	$1,794.0	93.2
Unincorporated business and farm income	130.8	6.8
Total	$1,924.8	100.0%

Source: Economic Indicators, Council of Economic Advisers, U.S. De-partment of Commerce, August 1979, p. 4.

lenders will give you the same "deal." Chapter 5 deals with the "Role of Consumer Credit" and with "Shopping for Money," and is designed to help you do just that. Chapter 6 discusses the various laws designed to protect the consumer.

Savings institutions are introduced next because the first surplus you accumulate should probably be invested in a depository (also called thrift) institution. There are a number of these institutions and their differences and similarities are explained. However, only a relatively small number of dollars, for emergency or nest-egg purposes, should be kept in a depository institution because, while they are easily accessible, they do not earn much interest. This is why you will also explore other types of investment outlets in future chapters. You will also want to protect what you have, and hence all of the various types of insurance will be presented. Chapter 8 begins this discussion: it deals with life insurance, which in a sense protects your income stream for your beneficiaries. We will provide guidelines and step-by-step suggestions to help you determine your insurance needs both as to the amount and the type. It is here that we will explore insurance as a savings vehicle as well as a means of protecting the income stream.

Then in Chapter 9 health insurance, the modern way of financing medical needs, is introduced. Since you no doubt drive a car, you will need to know about protection for yourself and your assets in the event of an accident. You will also need to protect your home and personal belongings from all kinds of hazards. Consequently, a chapter on property and liability insurance is included in Part II which deals with insurance.

Related to insurance is the entire area of retirement: therefore, a chapter on social security is presented. In addition, annuities (a vehicle for retirement planning) and other retirement plans are explored because they may be used to supplement social security.

You will also no doubt want to increase your income and build up a portfolio of securities. Therefore, you will need to learn about investment. Part III (Chapters 12, 13, 14, and 15) deals with direct investments. Chapter 7, you will recall, deals with indirect investment via thrift institutions. Now you will be introduced to stocks, bonds, and rental real estate and how to own them directly.

The book concludes with a section on taxes and assets. Home ownership is a good investment. Increasing your assets via home ownership is also a means whereby you may hedge inflation, and home ownership will be presented in Chapter 16 following the chapters on investments. Another way of increasing your assets (and stretching your income) is by minimizing your taxes, and in Chapter 17 material on that is developed. While many students are too young to give serious thought to retirement and estate planning, before too many years pass, you should develop a plan to supplement social security payments. This is especially true because there are numerous methods of doing this and reducing your personal income taxes simultaneously. The final chapter (Chapter 18) introduces the complex area of wills, estate trusts, and estate planning. It deals with keeping what you have earned.

Your personal finance problems and needs will change as the years pass (you may need more or less insurance as you grow older). Because personal financial needs vary over the life cycle, personal financial planning is a permanent task.

We have one final suggestion. You may find it useful to retain the text as a handy reference after the semester is over. While the data and statistics presented will change, the principles and concepts of personal financial management are likely to endure.

QUESTIONS FOR REVIEW

1. How can personal finance help you to manage your financial affairs?

2. How is the degree of satisfaction related to the level of income?

3. What is meant by the measure of economic welfare)?

4. How do consumption expenditures differ from investment expenditures?

5. What is meant by the term "consumer-producer"?

6. What is inflation? How would you expect inflation to affect those on fixed incomes?

7. What does it mean to state that the cost of living index has gone from 100 to 210?

8. How is the cost of living index a barometer of inflation?

9. Are an increase in prices and a decline in the value of money the same thing?

10. How do you calculate how much the value of money has declined from a given increase in prices?

11. What is meant by the phrase "human capital"?

12. In terms of occupational groupings, where does it appear that the opportunity for highest personal income lies? What does your answer suggest in terms of education?

13. If your career follows the expected norm, what can you expect regarding your income as you pass through the various age groups?

14. What is the relationship between income and property ownership?

15. How can the place in which one happens to live affect one's income?

16. How is it that a woman with ability is frequently unable to earn as much on the same job as a man?

17. What aid can you obtain in choosing a career?

18. What is the difference between national income and GNP?

19. What are the four different sources of income?

CASES

1. John Brown is twenty years old and has just completed his military service. He has a high school education but no college, and he has two career alternatives in his uncle's trucking firm. An offer to drive a truck will pay him $300 per week to start and will provide for periodic increase to a maximum salary of $450 per week after five years; moreover, if he can educate himself at night, he will be given an opportunity to move into a managerial position with the firm. The other possibility is to go to the state university and get a degree in business administration. This will take him four years, during which he will probably have to go into debt. At the end of four years, his uncle has promised him a job in the management training program at $400 per week.

   John thinks it would be unwise to forego over $75,000 of income over the four years, especially since he believes he can educate himself at night. Hence he is contemplating taking the truck driving job. Do you agree? Why?

2. Betty Balinski, age twenty-two, has just received her degree from a large midwestern university and has several offers of teaching jobs. She would like your help in deciding which to accept. One is the school system in a midwestern metropolitan area that includes her hometown. It pays $16,000, and she could live at home and save considerably on her expenses. Another job is in a smaller town in the South at a salary of $13,500, but she has heard that the cost of living is much lower there. Finally, she could go to California and accept a job at $17,000.

   In two years, Betty's fiancé will be discharged from the Navy and they plan to marry. She would like to save as much as possible during those two years. Which job should Betty accept and why?

3. Tom Doley has just graduated from high school with better than average grades and has been accepted as a freshman at the college of his choice. Although he has very little

money, he has two alternatives for financing his education. By working part-time during the summer, and perhaps dropping out of school for a semester to work occasionally, he could finish his education in five to six years. The other possibility would be to accept the offer of his uncle, Bruce Gelt, who is willing to lend him the money to enable him to finish college in four years. Tom does not care whether he finishes in four or in six years, but he wants to do what is financially most advantageous for himself. He knows that his income will be greater after he receives his B.A. degree, but is not sure that receiving it one or two years earlier would offset being in debt. What should he do?

4. Albert Buckboard, who has just graduated from a large eastern law school, has two job opportunities: (1) to work for the United States government in Washington, D.C., or (2) a job with a law firm in New Jersey. Albert does not care where he lives but is concerned about the income he can earn. He requests your advice with respect to the advantages and disadvantages of the two positions.

5. Sally Hollsack is about to graduate from college with a degree in accounting. She has been offered a job with a CPA firm and would like your advice whether to accept it or go on and get her MBA.

SUGGESTED READINGS

Baehr, Maureen. *The Job Book*. Old Greenwich, CT: Mind Designs, 1975.

Bolles, Richard. *What Color Is Your Parachute? A Practical Manual for Job Hunters* (revised). Berkeley, CA: Ten Speed Press, 1979.

Bostwick, Burdette. *Finding the Job You've Always Wanted*. New York: John Wiley and Sons, 1977.

College Placement Annual, 1980. Bethlehem, PA: The College Placement Council, Inc., P.O. Box 2263, Bethlehem, PA.

Crystal, John, and Bolles, Richard. *Where Do I Go From Here With My Life?* New York: Seabury Press, 1974.

Economic Indicators. Washington, D.C. A monthly publication by the Council of Economic Advisors for the Joint Economic Committee.

The Encyclopedia of Careers and Vocational Guidance, two vols. Chicago: J. G. Ferguson Publishing Co., 1975.

Figler, Howard. *The Complete Job Search Handbook*. New York: Holt, Rinehart and Winston, 1979.

File, Norman, and Howroyd, Bernard. *How to Beat the Establishment and Get That Job*. Los Angeles, CA: Apple/One Publishing Co., 1971.

Gootnick, David. *Getting A Better Job*. New York: McGraw-Hill, 1978.

Gramm, Philip. "Inflation: Its Cause and Cure." *Federal Reserve Bank of St. Louis Review*, February, 1975.

Hawver, Carl F. *Basic Principles in Family Money and Credit Management* (revised). Washington, D.C.: Educational Services Division, National Consumer Finance Association, 1974.

Hecht, Miriam, and Traub, Lillian. *Alternatives to College*. New York: Macmillan Information, 1974.

Hoppock, Robert. *Occupational Information*. New York: McGraw-Hill Book Co., 1976.

Jackson, Tom, and Mayleas, Davidyne. *The Hidden Job Market*. New York: New York Times Book Company, 1976.

Kocher, Eric. *International Jobs: Where They Are, How to Get Them; A Handbook for Over 500 Career Opportunities Around the World*. Reading, MA: Addison-Wesley, 1979.

Loore, Charles. *The Career Game*. New York: National Institute for Career Planning, 1976.

Malnig, Lawrence R., and Morrow, Sandra. *What Can I Do With A Major in . . . ?* Jersey City, N.J.: St. Peter's College Press, 1975.

Mitchell, Joyce Slayton. *I Can Be Anything: Careers and Colleges for Young Women*. New York: College Entrance Examination Board, 1978.

National Consumer Finance Association. Finance Facts Yearbook. Wasington, D.C. An annual publication.

Samuelson, Paul A. *Economics: An Introductory Analysis*, 11 th ed. New York: McGraw-Hill, 1980, chs. 4, 5, 9, and 10.

Schill, William J., and Nichols, Harold E. *Career Choice and Career Preparation*. Danville, IL: Interstate Printers & Publishers, Inc., 1979.

Thompson, Melvin R. *Why Should I Hire You?* San Diego, CA: Venture Press, 1977.

U.S. Census. *Income of Families and Individuals in the U.S. in Current Population Reports; Consumer Income*. Series P-60. Get latest series of this quarterly publication.

U.S. Department of Labor, Bureau of Labor Statistics. *The Occupational Outlook Handbook, 1979–80 Edition*. Washington, D. C.: U.S. Government Printing Office, 1980.

Chapter Two

Record-Keeping and Budgeting

> "Now! Now!" cried the Queen, "Faster! Faster!" And they went so fast that at last they seemed to skim through the air, hardly touching the ground with their feet . . . "Now, here, you see, it takes all the running you can do, to keep in the same place. If you want to get somewhere else, you must run at least twice as fast as that!"
>
> LEWIS CARROLL, *Alice Through the Looking-Glass*

The objectives of this chapter are to

1   Underline the importance of keeping good records

2   Analyze the two major financial statements (the balance sheet and the income statement) which are important for budgeting

3   Show the benefits and the form of the budget

4   Present some general rules of budgeting

5   Go over the major items in a budget

6   Make a suggestion regarding a periodic family inventory

With today's inflation it seems as if one must indeed run as fast as one can just to stay in the same place. In this regard a budget can help and to budget properly a person must keep adequate financial records and understand the basics involving financial statements.

Most people have to live within their income. While this is not completely true in any one year (for example, a person may borrow to finance a large item such as a car), it is true for most people most of the time. A person who consumes more than his or her income in one year will probably be forced to consume less while repaying the next year what was borrowed. Certainly over a lifetime one can only consume what one has earned or inherited; what has been borrowed must be paid back. The one exception to this is if a person files bankruptcy. Then one can consume more than one's income and get out from under debts through court action.

While persons have command over their money income, they have only two main alternatives as to what to do with it: consume it or save it. Most people divide their income, and while they consume most of it, they save some. Once they have committed a part of their income to consumption, they must make further decisions regarding what type of consumption items to buy. By the same token, once a person has decided to save, say 20 percent of his or her income, a second decision regarding where and how to invest it must be made. In this process, a person must constantly choose between alternatives. A limited income can never stretch over all the alternatives, so priorities must be assigned and choices made.

THE TOOLS OF FINANCIAL PLANNING

Business firms as well as the various levels of government keep financial records and develop financial statements to aid them in their planning, and you can too. The government and many businesses have full-time planning and budgeting staffs, but at the personal level, only a few minutes per day is needed for financial planning once a system is set up. After making a few suggestions regarding record keeping we shall examine the two financial statements that are useful: the balance sheet and the income statement.

Record-Keeping

Record-keeping is necessary for tax purposes as well as for planning your financial affairs. All cancelled checks should be retained for a time. Cancelled checks and receipts for items that are tax deductible should be filed separately so that they will be easily accessible at tax time. After your taxes have been paid, keep these receipts and checks as well as other checks for large amounts for four years because that is the time before the statutes of limitations run out. Less important checks can be destroyed once a year during spring housecleaning. If items are charged on a credit card, and one check pays for many purchases, separate the charge receipts and treat them just like the checks discussed above. In short, learn which items are tax deductible and keep records of these items to the penny. Unhappily, many people, fearful of the Internal Revenue Service, have consistently overpaid their taxes. If you keep adequate records, you may take all of your legal deductions without fear.

Keeping records, paying bills, and reconciling the monthly bank statement is something in which both members of a married couple should be involved. The same is true regarding all major financial decisions. Then in the event one (or both) of the partners is left alone in the future, he or she will not be inexperienced in these matters. One way this could be done is for the husband to keep the books one month and the wife the next.

You should keep a file of manila folders. Classify the major items such as taxes, insurance, investments, household expenditures, and the like. It would probably be worthwhile to purchase a small filing cabinet where all the papers could be kept in one place.

The Personal Balance Sheet

A balance sheet is a financial statement that depicts your financial position at a particular moment in time. It is like a photograph. Its three main components are assets, liabilities, and the difference between the two, called net worth.

Assets

The terms *wealth* and *assets* mean essentially the same thing; anything of value is wealth and can also be looked upon as an asset. Moreover, something of value to you may not be of value to somebody else and therefore is not wealth to that person. Assets, then, are the good things you own. Assets in turn can be broken down into earning and non-earning assets.

1. Earning assets are those that yield a return. Stocks, bonds, savings accounts, and real estate that you can rent out are earning assets in that they yield a return in the form of interest, dividends, or rental income.

2. Non-earning assets consist of personal automobiles, clothing, jewelry, household furniture, and the like. They yield no money return, but they are valuable and are wealth or assets.

Assets can also be classified as financial and nonfinancial.

1. Financial assets include such things as stocks, bonds, bank accounts, and cash or currency.

2. Nonfinancial assets include clothes, real estate, automobiles, etc.

There is some overlap between these classifications. For example, all financial assets except checking accounts and idle currency are also earning assets. Most non-earning assets are also nonfinancial assets, but there are exceptions. For example, a cattle ranch or a wheat farm is an earning asset, but it is not a financial asset. However, the piece of paper proving ownership of the ranch or farm can be considered a financial asset. The largest single asset for most families is their home, and the largest single liability is the mortgage on it.

When you construct your personal balance sheet, list your assets on the left and attach a dollar value to them which reflects their fair market value. You should list and value all of your assets even though you may not have fully paid for some of them; the amount that you still owe will be listed later under your liabilities.

Liabilities

Liabilities are the debts you owe others. The amount you still owe on your car, the sum you have run up on your gasoline credit card, and other charge accounts are examples. The unpaid balance (mortgage) on your family home is another example. Generally speaking, you will have to pay interest on the debts you owe.

Net Worth

Net worth is equal to total assets minus total liabilities. As such, it is the truest reflection of what the person for whom the balance sheet has been drawn up is actually worth. If you were to sell all of your assets and pay off all of your debts, that is what would remain. Assets are nearly always greater than liabilities, but in those relatively rare cases where they are not, the person is technically speaking bankrupt. We will examine bankruptcy below. The following exhibit shows a balance sheet for a hypothetical person. The financial assets are the ones listed first through life insurance. The earning assets have been given an estimated percentage return.

The Personal Income Statement

The income statement is another important financial tool which is useful in planning your personal financial affairs. The balance sheet, you will recall, is a statement that depicts your financial condition as of a given point in time; the income statement shows what has happened to your financial position over a period of time, say a year. It is a flow concept. It can be compared to a stream of water that is measured in terms of flow: so many gallons of water per minute. The income statement measures dollar income inflows and dollar expenditure outflows. In the case of business income statements, sales usually measure gross

TABLE 2–1. *Balance sheet*

ASSETS	EXAMPLE	YOUR PERSONAL ENTRY	% RETURN	LIABILITIES AND NET WORTH	YOUR PERSONAL ENTRY AND % COST
Cash				Unpaid Bills	
Currency	$ 50	_____	0	Bank Credit	
Checking Account	250	_____	0	Card	$ 150 _____
Savings Deposit	1,000	_____	6%	Other Charge	
				Cards	75 _____
Investments				Repair Bill on	
				Car	125 _____
Government Bonds	400	_____	6.5%	Telephone Bill	
				Outstanding	12 _____
Corporate Bonds	1,000	_____	9%	Installment Loan	800 _____
Corporate Stock	500	_____	10%		
Mutual Funds	200	_____	8%	Mortgage Loan	
Cash Value of Life Insurance	300	_____	7%	Owner	
				Occupied	30,000 _____
				Other Rental	25,000 _____
				Total Liabilities	$56,162 _____
Real Estate					
Owner Occupied	40,000	_____			
Rental Property	30,000	_____	12%		
Personal Property					
Automobile	3,000	_____			
Household Furniture	2,000	_____		Net Worth	$23,338
Clothes	500	_____			
Jewelry	200	_____			
Other Assets	100	_____			
Total Assets	$79,500	_____			

inflows and the various expenses (labor costs, raw material costs, etc.) indicate the outflows. The difference between the two represents profits. Your personal income statement measures your salary and other income inflows and your "cost of living" outflows. The difference between the two is called savings and may be looked upon as your yearly surplus or something similar to business profits.

Income

The income statement, then, has three main parts: income, expenditures, and savings. Your income includes not only wages and salaries but all investment income such as interest and dividends. It should also include gifts, inheritance and any other cash inflow.

Outgo—Expenditures

Expenditures consist of all the various items on which you spend your money. Obviously you should develop a number of major categories and keep track of them, but it is not necessary to account separately for every penny spent. There should be a category for food, clothing, transportation, and the like.

Savings

Finally, the income statement should have an item called savings. This item should be planned for; if you assume savings will emerge as a residual, you will often end up with nothing. To be sure, savings are not held in the form of idle cash but are invested, and in that sense they flow out of the income statement. Nevertheless, they are different from other outflows which are mostly consumption items. Two very simple annual and monthly income statements are shown below. You should develop your income statement on either a monthly or annual basis, and multiply or divide in order to obtain the second one.

THE PERSONAL BUDGET

The budget is really a type of income statement. However, while many business income statements represent a look back to see what has happened, a budget is a look forward to allocate expected future income among alternative expenditures. A budget is a financial plan in the form of an income statement which uses current and future operations to achieve certain goals which might otherwise be beyond one's reach. A budget must often be an estimate of future receipts and disbursements.

Benefits of a Budget

Since a budget is a financial guide to spending, it will enable one to run one's personal financial affairs better than those who fail to keep a budget. By using the budget, one can make a real attempt to live within one's income.

TABLE 2–2. *Income statement*

	ANNUAL	MONTHLY	YOUR PERSONAL INCOME STATEMENT
Income			
Wages and Salaries	$15,000	$1,250.00	_____
Interest	200	16.66	_____
Dividends	100	8.33	_____
Christmas Bonus	500	41.67	_____
Other	—	—	_____
Total	$15,800	$1,316.67	_____
Expenditures			
Food	$3,800	$ 316.67	_____
Clothing	900	75.00	_____
Transportation	1,150	95.83	_____
Housing	3,400	283.33	_____
Medical Care	1,050	87.50	_____
Recreation	700	58.33	_____
Other	330	27.50	_____
Taxes			
Social Security	920	76.67	_____
Personal Income tax	2,950	245.83	_____
Savings and Investments	600	50.00	_____

TABLE 2–3. *Yearly income flow*

	JAN.	FEB.	MARCH	APRIL	MAY	JUNE	JULY	AUG.	SEPT.	OCT.	NOV.	DEC.*	ANNUAL
After tax wages or salary of breadwinner	$1,250	$1,250	$1,250	$1,250	$1,250	$1,250	$1,250	$1,250	$1,250	$1,250	$1,250	$1,750	$15,500
Dividend	$25			$25			$25			$25			$ 100
Interest income	$50			$50			$50			$50			$ 200
Other possible income													
Total	$1,325	$1,250	$1,250	$1,325	$1,250	$1,250	$1,325	$1,250	$1,250	$1,325	$1,250	$1,750	$15,800

*Includes Christmas bonus.

A budget will also enable an individual to estimate more effectively his or her income than a person who does not use a budget. It will force the individual into a more acute consciousness of the sums that must be set aside to meet future expenses. The individual will learn to allocate available funds among specific expenses and to estimate what may be left over for savings. Sometimes, through good habits, savings are voluntarily set aside; sometimes they are forced, as when one purchases a home or life insurance. In either case, a budget makes the situation clear. Furthermore, a budget may help you identify alternative ways of spending that can lead to additional savings and concomitant financial security.

If the budget is for a family rather than an individual, the entire family should be brought into the budgetary process. The budget now becomes a group budget. While some members of the family may not contribute much to family income or be directly involved in making expenditures, they should nevertheless be brought into the decision-making process. Expenditures are made on behalf of all members of the family. All members should have input in setting goals and establishing priorities. If it is decided that certain items are to be cut, this can be done more effectively if all members of the family are consulted. Disagreements may exist among family members. There may be different priorities, and compromises will have to be made by all members. There may be a number of different trade-offs, but if agreements can be reached and differences hammered out, all members of the family are more likely to accept any sacrifices necessary to live within the budget.

The Form of the Budget

The form of the budget is not critical, for almost any type can be used. Table 2–4 may serve as a budget. It was left blank so that you may develop a personal budget. Many financial institutions have variations of similar forms and will be delighted to furnish a copy. Remember a budget has two main parts, income and expenditures.

A person can plan a budget on weekly, monthly, or annual bases. Some experts feel it is best to plan a budget period equal to the period between income receipts—a weekly budget if one is paid weekly, and a monthly budget if one is paid monthly. Others feel this can lead to problems if the pay period (and hence the budget) is less than one month because some monthly expenses are greater than the weekly take-home pay. A person in this situation might want to budget monthly and also break the budget down weekly in order to set aside some money each week to meet large expenditures on a monthly basis. Some people, however, have a yearly and a monthly budget as well as the pay-period budget; and for those whose income does not come in uniform amounts at regular intervals, the monthly or yearly budget is probably best. People who have a fluctuating income will find a budget particularly useful, since they may have a problem estimating their income accurately over whatever time period they select.

Some General Rules of Budgeting

No budget will be the same for any two families or any two individuals, even assuming that both have the same income. There is no magic formula for budgeting; however, there are some rules of thumb:

1. Set your goals. The budget should be reasonable and planned toward a reasonable goal. For example, if savings must be increased in order to provide funds for a child's education, other items must be trimmed. Different preferences, income, age, and size of a family will result in different goals for different families.
2. The fixed items of expenditure must be provided for first; such items as rent or mortgage payments, life insurance premiums, and installment loan repayments are

first priority "must" items. Only after these items are included can luxuries and other "comforts" be planned.

3. Big expense items paid less frequently than the budget period have to be spread so that each income period bears a share of these expenses. For example, property taxes, not included in monthly mortgage payments, must be set aside monthly.

4. A major expense cannot necessarily be cut just because it is large. For example, food may take a sizable part of the budget, and that item may appear easy to cut—on paper. However, it should be scrutinized carefully.

5. A budget should help to develop a set of priorities with respect to general items of expenditure, but it need not consist of a detailed set of accounts indicating where every penny is spent. While there are some rules of thumb with respect to major items in a budget, as we shall see below, there are also value judgments involved in choosing among different items. One person or family, because of different preferences, will spend more on clothes and less on housing than another similar family.

6. Adequate records are important. As noted above, a detailed set of accounts is not necessary, but records should be kept indicating how much has been spent on each category.

TABLE 2–4. *A budget plan*

ITEM	AMOUNT
Money income after taxes	$_____
Savings:	
Future goals and emergencies	$_____
Seasonal and large irregular expenses	_____
Regular monthly expenses:	
Rent or mortgage payment	$_____
Utilities	_____
Installment payments	_____
Other	_____
Total	_____
Day-to-day expenses:	
Food and beverages	$_____
Household operation and maintenance	_____
House furnishings and equipment	_____
Clothing	_____
Transportation	_____
Medical care	_____
Education and reading	_____
Recreation	_____
Personal and miscellaneous	_____
Gifts and contributions	_____
Total	_____
Total	$_____

Every budget begins with income. If the only source of income is in the form of salary or wages earned by the head of the family, then there is no real problem except to make a realistic estimate of the income available to the individual. Just because the head of the family is employed at $16,000 per year does not necessarily mean that income can be listed as $16,000. Instead, you might want to list take-home income after all deductions have been made, such as withholding taxes, social security, and any health insurance premiums that are withheld at the source, and the like. On the other hand, if you are self-employed you might want to take your gross income and budget your taxes and social security payments.

If both spouses work, another question arises in planning the budget. Should both spouses' incomes be included as permanent "family" income? Some families treat the lesser income as permanently built into the budget; other families treat it as transitory income and do not include the additional income in the budget. Such families would live on the greater salary and the lower salary could all be saved or used to purchase specific items periodically that the family could not otherwise afford.

If income derives from a business or profession, a more difficult problem arises. Frequently the breadwinner's annual or weekly income can be estimated, based on the volume of business the previous week, month, or year. However, there are some types of businesses that might be called "feast or famine" businesses. In some months or even certain years, income is exceedingly high, and in other months or years, very low. If this is the case, it is probably best to make a low estimate and attempt to live within that amount.

"I now pronounce you a two-spouse working household." (Source: Permission Cartoon Features Syndicate; from *The Wall Street Journal.)*

THE WALL STREET JOURNAL

Expenditures

The reverse side of the budget coin is the expenditures side. Any budget has a number of major expenditures. There are certain "must" items over which the individual has little control, such as rent or mortgage payments. In the long run you can move to a cheaper apartment or sell your home and reduce these payments; nevertheless, in the short run these expenditures are fixed. Certain other expenditures such as food and clothing outlays can be controlled more readily. While it is difficult to reduce the food item in a budget, some reductions can be made by wiser shopping and by buying less expensive grades of food. It is also true that different families will spend different amounts on the same items. Family size differs, and some families (and some individuals) will have different sets of priorities. For example, some will be satisfied with a smaller wardrobe and will desire small luxuries in, perhaps, food. Other families will eat plain food and perhaps splurge a bit on clothing. Priorities are partly personal.

Another problem arising in budgeting concerns large annual or semiannual expenditures. If all expenditures were neatly broken down into monthly bills and if all paychecks were received monthly, one of the biggest problems of budgeting would be eliminated. Unfortunately, necessary payments are frequently not so easily broken down. For example, one might have to pay an insurance premium of $500 every September. (It should perhaps be noted here that semiannual or annual insurance premiums are less costly than paying on a monthly basis, and consequently one might well decide to take advantage of this saving. The budgeting problem, however, becomes a bit more difficult.) It is necessary to set aside a sum each month so that the funds are available to meet the payment when due. A sound psychological reason for this is that many people tend to allow the future to take care of itself and, in the case of insurance premiums, to hope that somehow the money will be available. Some individuals authorize their bank to deduct one-twelfth of their annual insurance premium from their checking account and automatically put it into a special savings account. Then at the end of the year, the premium dollars are available and in the meantime a few dollars of interest will have been earned.

Savings

Finally, in addition to consumption expenditures, a budget should contain an item to assure that the individual (or family) will have some savings. Not all income should be consumed. In the absence of a carefully planned savings program, all too often savings will not materialize. Many people feel that they can budget their expenditures and generate savings as a residual. But conscious effort is usually required to generate savings.

Sample Budgets

Shown below are some sample budgets developed by the Bureau of Labor Statistics for a four-person family; there is a budget for a lower, intermediate, and a higher income family. Each budget applies to the urban United States as a whole. Also shown are some total budget figures developed specifically for a number of different cities which have different costs of living. Anchorage, Alaska, is the most expensive of all U.S. cities according to the Bureau's figures. It should be noted that these budgets reflect a certain level of well-being but this should not be taken as a minimum level set by the government as desirable. You will note that the budgets contain only consumption items and social security and personal income taxes. You should allow for savings as an additional item in your personal budget. Also shown is a blank worksheet on which you can calculate your personal spending and savings.

TABLE 2–5. *Annual budgets for a four-person family at three levels of living in the urban United States; Autumn, 1979.*

	LOWER BUDGET	INTERMEDIATE BUDGET	HIGHER BUDGET
Total budget	$12,585	$20,517	$30,317
Total Consumption	10,234	15,353	21,069
Total Food	3,911	5,044	6,360
At Home	3,364	4,223	5,034
Away From Home	547	821	1,326
Total Housing	2,409	4,594	6,971
Shelter	1,810	3,573	4,801
House Furnishings & Operations	599	1,021	1,931
Transportation	1,004	1,851	2,411
Clothing	866	1,235	1,804
Personal Care	323	433	613
Medical Care	1,171	1,176	1,227
Other Family Consumption	550	1,021	1,684
Other Items	539	877	1,478
Social Security Payments	781	1,256	1,413
Personal Income Taxes	1,032	3,031	6,357

Source: Bureau of Labor Statistics, *News,* April, 1980, U.S. Department of Labor.

Budgetary Variations Over the Life Cycle

It was noted previously that expenditures vary somewhat from family to family because of differences in family sizes, tastes, priorities, and preferences. Expenditures also vary substantially for any given family as the years pass. To some extent, income, too, varies for any given family over the years. This variation in both income and expenditures is reflected in the budget and it is referred to as *life cycle variation*.

When persons reach their peak earning period, income will vary with the job or profession they choose. A person employed as an unskilled or semiskilled worker will reach the maximum within a year or two of initial employment. Unskilled or semiskilled laborers who go to work at age eighteen or twenty will have achieved their maximum income by their early twenties. This maximum (or ceiling) will rise a little bit each year as the union wins cost-of-living wage increases, as well as increases based upon additional productivity (better tools and machinery will permit workers to produce more), and workers will remain at their rising ceiling until they retire.

Skilled laborers like carpenters or electricians will reach their maximum income somewhat later in life. They have long apprenticeships to serve at a relatively low income. They will achieve their maximum income in anywhere from four to six years, and sometimes even longer. (Again, this maximum ceiling rises as the years pass.) For example, pilots who bring supertankers into Houston harbor have to serve an apprenticeship of fourteen years.

Professional people like doctors, lawyers, and corporate executives generally have the longest training period of all. Doctors and lawyers are usually about thirty years old before they can practice, and then it takes additional years before they develop a clientele. Doctors

TABLE 2–6. *Annual budget for four-person family at three levels of living in various cities*

	LOWER	INTERMEDIATE	HIGHER
Boston	$13,623	$24,381	$36,891
New York	12,949	23,856	37,823
Philadelphia	12,861	21,436	31,352
Chicago	12,885	20,564	29,890
Cleveland	12,534	20,868	30,116
Detroit	12,582	20,821	30,668
St. Louis	12,436	19,963	29,008
Atlanta	11,622	18,821	27,673
Baltimore	12,772	20,316	30,110
Dallas	11,687	18,301	27,004
Washington, D.C.	13,631	22,206	32,636
Denver	12,517	20,468	29,976
Los Angeles	13,399	19,871	30,083
Seattle	13,914	20,719	29,583
Honolulu	16,507	25,799	39,689
Anchorage	19,694	27,933	40,785
U.S.	12,585	20,517	30,317

Source: Bureau of Labor Statistics, *News,* April 1980, U.S. Department of Labor.

and lawyers generally achieve their maximum income during their fifties. This is also generally true of corporate executives. These professional people's income often declines a bit during the last few years before they retire. This is especially true of the self-employed.

People's expenditures also follow a life cycle pattern. Young, single adults generally have no real responsibilities and usually save little. While they consume most of their income, it tends to be relatively low. Later, as these people marry and start to raise families, they will begin to save as they build up an equity in houses and life insurance. However, the years between the late twenties and about forty or forty-five are also years of heavy consumption. This is because the family is growing up and needs to acquire durable consumer goods to fill the house they are buying. By this time incomes usually have risen substantially. After about age forty-five, consumption (certainly as a percentage of income, and perhaps absolutely) may begin to decline and savings rise. This is because by now the children are on their own and the house is nearly paid for and is stocked with paid-for furniture and appliances. The years of heavy forced consumption are over. Individuals at this stage may begin to consume more of services like travel, but they also can save more and they will have an incentive to do so because of the approaching retirement years.

During the retirement stage of the life cycle, both income and expenditures usually decline. This does not mean that the standard of living must necessarily decline. Often retired couples move to a less expensive section of the country to live. Also, certain payments need no longer be made. For example, the house should be fully paid for and life insurance is no longer needed. Older people also receive a double tax exemption. On the other hand, people over sixty-five have higher medical expenses than younger people. Not

FIGURE 2–1. *Worksheets for family spending*

See item-by-item explanation accompanying this worksheet.

To convert weekly figures into monthly figures, multiply by 4.33.

Name: _____

Date: _____

LINE NO.		COL. #1 "CASH WEEKLY"	COL. #2 "OTHER MONTHLY"	LINE NO.		COL. #1 "CASH WEEKLY"	COL. #2 "OTHER MONTHLY"
1.	FOOD			51.	SHELTER		
2.	Grocery store			52.	Rent or mortgage		
3.	School lunches			53.	Maintenance on home		
4.	Lunches for working hus. & w.			54.	Property taxes		
5.				55.	Home insurance		
6.				56.			
7.	Total			57.			
8.	HOUSE OPERATION			58.	Total		
9.	Electricity			59.	TRANSPORTATION		
10.	Gas			60.	Auto pyts. (or saving for new car)		
11.	Heating fuel			61.	Bus, taxi or train		
12.	Telephone			62.	Gas & oil for car		
13.	Water			63.	Auto tires & repair		
14.	Household help			64.	Auto insurance		
15.	Furniture and equipment			65.			
16.	Children's allowances			66.			
17.	Newspapers & magazines			67.	Total		
18.	Dues & fees			68.	PERSONAL		
19.	Payments on old bills			69.	Personal allowances (hus. & w.)		
20.				70.	Family entertainment		
21.				71.	Vacation fund		
22.				72.	Education		
23.	Total			73.	Medicine & medical care		
24.	CLOTHING			74.	All insurance (health, life, etc.)		
25.	Clothes for all family			75.	Dues and fees		
26.	Cleaning & laundry			76.	Income taxes not deducted		
27.				77.	Payments on old bills		
28.	Total			78.			
29.	CONTRIBUTIONS			79.			
30.	Holiday gifts			80.	Total		
31.	Non-family gifts			81.	SAVINGS & INVESTMENTS		
32.	Family gifts			82.	Savings		
33.	Charities, Church, Synagogue			83.	Regular investments		
34.				84.	Self-paid retirement plan		
35.				85.			
36.	Total			86.	Total		
37.	SUMMARY: EXPENSE			87.	SUMMARY: EXPENSE		
38.	Food			88.	Shelter		
39.	House operation			89.	Transportation		
40.	Clothing			90.	Personal		
41.	Contributions			91.	Savings and Investment		

		COL. #1	COL. #2
92.	Total expense		
93.	Total cash × 4.33		
94.	Total monthly expense		
95.	Plus monthly expense		
96.	Average monthly expense		
97.	Average monthly income		

only is their budget lower, it also contains different items. However, if they budgeted properly and were able to make substantial savings during the heavy savings years (age forty-five to sixty-five) of the life cycle, their retirement years can be pleasant.

We will now examine some major items in any budget. We should remember that these expenditures will vary in size not only with income but also with respect to family size, the stage of the life cycle, and personal preferences.

Housing

In general, it can be said that low-income groups tend to spend a greater percentage of their income for housing than high-income groups. Extremely low income groups spend between 25 and 35 percent of their incomes for housing, while many very high income groups spend less than 10 percent. Interestingly enough, there is a considerable variation in money spent on housing within any income group, for the following reasons:

1. The size of the family. Within any income group, large families tend to spend a smaller percentage of their incomes for housing than do smaller families. This is probably due to the fact that large families have to spend more on food, clothing, and other necessities than do smaller families.
2. Scales of preference. Some people prefer to spend more on housing than do others within the same income group.
3. The wealth of the family. Some families within any one income group can afford to spend more for housing than others because of their ability to draw from savings and other assets.
4. Length of time that families have been in any one income group. There is frequently a time lag in the adjustment of housing expenditure to change in income.

Whether renting or purchasing a home under the terms of a mortgage, the important thing to remember is that this is a fixed or "must" payment, for which money must be set aside. The mortgage payments always include interest and an item called reduction of principal. The payments may or may not include an item for taxes and insurance. If, in the case of purchasing a home, provision is not made for annual tax payments or insurance protection, then a sum should be set aside each month to take care of this yearly payment.

The person who rents, of course, also pays these four items indirectly because they are included in rental payments. That portion of the mortgage payment that consists of interest is a deductible item on your federal income tax form. However, the renter who pays interest indirectly cannot take this deduction. The same is true of the property tax payment on a home. Therefore, there is a tax advantage to home ownership. It should also be noted that that portion of the mortgage payment that is reduction of principal is really a savings. This is generally referred to as building an equity in a house.

There are some rules suggesting what the expenditures on housing should be. Some bankers suggest that the monthly mortgage payment be no more than 25 percent of the person's monthly income. With respect to rent, the suggestion is that a monthly rent equal to about one week's take-home pay is probably right. These rules of thumb, however, are not sacred, and they can be modified in accordance with one's priorities. This is especially true today because the rapid inflation during the last half of the 1970s caused housing costs to rise more rapidly than the average level of prices.

Household Operations

Household operations consist of such services as fuel, water, electricity, gas, and telephone. Naturally these items vary from family to family, to a large degree depending upon geographical location. In most cases such items as the phone bill are fairly uniform from month to month. Fuel bills, on the other hand, are higher during the winter months. The family may better budget for this type of item by setting aside funds during the summer to pay the higher bills during the winter.

Food

Since food is a major item of the family budget, estimates should be made not only for food consumed at home, but also for meals that are to be eaten out. In practice, individual and family expenditures for food will vary, depending to a great degree on differences in income and tastes. In addition, the size of the family will have a major bearing on what proportion of any budget will be devoted to food.

As food prices rise, those on fixed incomes are forced to spend a larger portion of their budget on this item. And in recent years, food price increases have been among the most rapid. While incomes have also risen, expenditures on food are nevertheless the largest single item in most budgets.

"Yes, I think I can get along on this budget for food. But how are you going to eat?" (Source: Permission Cartoon Features Syndicate; from *The Wall Street Journal.)*

THE WALL STREET JOURNAL

Life Insurance

Nearly all adults in the United States have some form of life insurance. As far as the budget is concerned, life insurance constitutes a necessary fixed cost. Where possible, it is desirable to pay the premiums on an annual basis because this will result in a modest savings in the form of reduced premiums of from 2 to 6 percent.[1] Where this is not practical and premiums have to be paid on a semiannual, quarterly, or monthly basis, a smaller amount of the monthly premiums can often be saved by giving the company permission to withdraw the monthly premium from the premium holder's checking account. This can be done by signing a form supplied by the insurance company. As long as the premium has to be paid anyway, this is a painless way of reducing the cost of the insurance.

Other Insurance

Other fixed items in the budget may include health insurance, property and casualty insurance, personal property insurance, and possibly specialty insurance such as malpractice insurance for professional people. If some of these items are deducted from the paycheck, they don't have to be taken into the budget as fixed expenses. But if they are not automatically deducted, they must be budgeted for; one-twelfth of the annual premium should be set aside each month in order to make these annual payments when they are due.

Regular Payments

Such items as regular payments on loans and furniture and other installment payments should be regarded as fixed expenditures until paid. These expenditures will be discussed in greater detail in Chapters 5 and 6. Here merely note that one who must make such weekly or monthly payments should take them into account in the budget.

Medical Care

The American people spend billions of dollars on health care every year, and the amount is rising rapidly. This figure includes not only health insurance premiums and physicians' services but also dental care, drugs and medicines, eyeglasses, and hospital accommodations. Women spend somewhat more than men for medical services, and, as might be expected, medical expenses tend to rise with age. Medical expense varies greatly from person to person, and it becomes difficult to set aside arbitrarily a sum in the family budget to provide for this sort of expense. Health insurance costs, on the other hand, are readily determinable and constitute a fixed item in the budget.

Frequently physicians and dentists have no objection to being paid on budget terms after an expense has occurred. For example, if a dental bill amounts to $100, many dentists would be only too happy to have the patient make arrangements to pay them at the rate of $20 per month.

Health insurance, however, is the modern method of paying medical bills. Over 180 million Americans had some form of private health insurance in 1978. The total figure is doubtless higher because of Medicare.

Transportation

A recent study showed that, on the average, about 13 percent of personal consumption expenditures went for transportation, most of it in owning and operating the family automobile. Furthermore, with the growth of suburbia, many families find two cars a necessity.

---

1. Technically speaking, premiums are not reduced when they are paid annually. Rather, a service charge of from 2 to 6 percent is added for monthly premiums.

Part 1 / Budgeting, Buying, Borrowing, and Saving

If you own or partially own an automobile, you must take into account in the budget the monthly payments, which may or may not include the insurance. If insurance is not included, you must set aside an amount each month or week to take care of the annual premium. Furthermore, as the car depreciates with age, new tires and other repairs will become necessary. The budget should take care of these items. The weekly or monthly amount spent for gas and oil must also be taken into account.

The American Automobile Association, in a study of the cost of running a car, broke the costs into variable costs (those that vary with the number of miles driven) and fixed costs (those that do not vary with the number of miles driven). The study was made on a 1980 Chevrolet Malibu four-door sedan with a 6 cylinder engine, automatic transmission, and power steering. Table 2-7 summarizes the results of the AAA's findings.

With gasoline becoming more and more expensive, it may be well to remember that for every 10 cents per gallon increase in the price of gas, the per mile cost of running a car

TABLE 2–7. *The cost of driving*

VARIABLE COSTS	AVERAGE PER MILE
Gasoline (unleaded) and oil	5.86 cents
Maintenance	1.12 cents
Tires	.64 cents
	7.62 cents

FIXED COSTS	ANNUALLY
Comprehensive insurance ($100 ded.)	$ 70.00
$250 ded. collision insurance	172.00
Property damage and liability	
($100/300/50M)	248.00
License, registration, taxes	82.00
Depreciation	1,038.00
Finance charge	
(20% down; loan @ 15%/4 yrs.)	423.00
	$2,033.00
	(or $5.57 per day)

AVERAGE ANNUAL DRIVING COSTS

Based on the figures above, the motorist driving 15,000 miles a year would pay:

15,000 miles @ 7.62 cents	$1,143.00
365 days @ $5.57	2,033.00
	$3,176.00
	(or 21.2 cents per mile)

The same person driving 10,000 miles a year would pay:

10,000 miles @ 7.62 cents	$ 762.00
365 days @ $5.57	2,033.00
	$2,795.00
	(or 28 cents per mile)

Source: Your Driving Costs, 1980 Edition, American Automobile Association.

increases by one cent, if the car delivers 10 miles per gallon, or one-half cent if the car delivers 20 miles per gallon.[2]

Clothing

Expenditures for clothing, according to a recent study by the Department of Commerce, amount to about 6.9 percent of total consumption expenditures. Generally, the large expenditures for clothing are seasonal; for example, every family with children is faced with expenditures for clothing during the fall. The ideal way to handle this expense is to set something aside monthly in anticipation of the expenditures. Some stores have a charge account that enables large purchases to be paid off monthly without a service charge. This service will, in effect, cause the family to budget, but unfortunately it prevents them from taking advantage of sales that might occur in other stores.

Savings

No family budget would be complete without an item for savings. In early 1980 aggregate personal savings in the United States were running just under $70 billion, or about 4 percent of disposable personal income which is personal income after taxes. Percentagewise, this is the lowest rate in thirty years. Savings fluctuate substantially. Since 1970, they have fluctuated from $49.4 billion to $83.6 billion, or in percentage terms, from 4 to 7.8 percent of after-tax income. Aggregate savings, of course, are merely the sum total of all individual savings.

A budget should assist in stabilizing savings more effectively. Moreover, a savings feature built into a budget will assure that a person ends up a net saver; relying upon savings to develop as a residual often results in no savings. While the volume of savings is influenced, to a large extent, by the size of a person's income, a budget will also enhance savings, except possibly at the very highest income levels. Possible uses for savings will be discussed in detail in subsequent chapters of this text. Developing a budget will show you whether your savings are too low. If they are and if you find it difficult to save, you can make arrangements with your bank to have a specific amount transferred automatically from your checking to your savings account.

Contributions

Contributions consist of monies given to church, charities, and certain civic groups, the amount varying with the desires of the individual. In some cases, the contribution is a weekly affair and can be easily budgeted. In other cases, the contribution is annual and money should be set aside monthly to take care of it. In cases where pledges are made to charities, arrangements can be made to pay over a period of time in order to make budgeting easy. A later chapter on taxes will point out that contributions made to certain specific organizations are tax deductible within certain limitations.

Gifts, Entertainment, and Recreation

This category includes sums set aside for birthday and holiday gifts for family and friends. Included here should be a reserve for those having children in the family, for sooner or later they will be invited to birthday parties given by their friends, and over a year's time the amount spent on this item is likely to be a bit startling.

On the average, the American family spends about six percent of its income for entertainment and recreation. Although some may regard this as an unnecessary cost, recreation

---

2. From *Your Driving Costs*, 1980 Edition, American Automobile Association.

may be important for health and in the long run save physicians' bills. Recreation relaxes one and tends to release tension; certain types of recreation also give release to hostilities that, if repressed, might lead to the psychiatrist's couch.

Education

Since taxes finance public education, the personal budget need not make an additional allowance for it. However, colleges are not entirely financed with tax funds; if there is a college-aged boy or girl in the family, parents may need to budget for college expenses. Indeed, the budget should probably reflect this expectation before the person reaches college age so that the funds will be available when needed.

Some of the more expensive private colleges now charge tuition and fees in excess of $4,000 per year. In addition to tuition, another $2500 or so is required for room, board, and personal expenses. A year of college can cost as much as $7,000. If a state university is selected, the tuition cost is greatly reduced. Nevertheless, a college education can easily cost in excess of $4000 per year even at a state university. Because of these high costs, it is suggested that a college fund be started for each child at birth. Your personal budget will then contain a monthly item for college for about eighteen years for each child. If $20 per month is put into a college fund at a bank or savings and loan association at 5 percent interest, in eighteen years it will amount to about $7,000. While this sum is hardly enough for four years of college at most schools, it will help. It is possible for the boy or girl to help pay for part of college expenses by taking part-time jobs and by working in the summer.

Progress to graduate school or to some professional school requires even more funds. Moreover, for certain careers, graduate or professional school is absolutely mandatory. Of these schools, medical schools in general are the most costly. Tuition and other fees in more expensive private medical schools can run about $5000 per year, and in private law schools as high as $4000. State-run law and medical schools generally have somewhat lower tuition but it too can run up to $4000 for nonresidents and about half that for residents in medical schools. State-financed law schools generally have tuition charges that are close to or only slightly lower than those of their medical schools.

Other Personal and Miscellaneous Expenses

Anything that cannot be budgeted for as a specific item can be included under "other expenses," and perhaps here one might put something aside as a cushion in the event of an emergency. A special savings account might be set aside and, in the fortunate event that the emergency does not arise, this amount could be added to the permanent savings account.

Certain budgetary items are often forgotten—bank service charges, legal fees, investment counseling fees, and interest on personal debts. From the point of view of budgeting, some of these costs, such as interest payments, are included in fixed items like installment payments. If such expenditures are not fixed and can be foreseen, however, they should be taken into account in the budget.

A Budget and Personal Bankruptcies

A budget may also help you to avoid bankruptcies. There has been a growing trend to bankruptcies over the past twenty years. If you should ever be so unfortunate as to have to declare bankruptcy, there is a regular procedure to follow that I will outline below.

Bankruptcies can be classified into business and personal bankruptcies. Each in turn can be broken down into voluntary and involuntary bankruptcies; involuntary are forced upon a person by creditors. Bankruptcy proceedings are conducted under federal law, but this law does allow for some variations from state to state. Nevertheless, a good deal of uniformity exists. The first step in filing for bankruptcy is to buy a bankruptcy kit, available for a few dollars at any store handling legal papers. This kit contains forms on which must be listed all assets, liabilities, and the creditors; the forms are then filed in federal district court. A $50 per person fee must be paid to the court upon filing. If the case appears to be complex, an attorney should be retained. After the filing, all the creditors are notified and a hearing is held before a bankruptcy referee who is acting under the jurisdiction of the federal court. While the creditors can contest the bankruptcy, it is virtually impossible to prevent a personal bankruptcy from being made effective.

After the bankruptcy is granted, a trustee usually is appointed to take over what assets remain and pay off those debts that can be paid. The debts are classified into an order of priorities; the administrative costs of handling the bankruptcy have first priority. They are followed by wage claims, up to a point, and then taxes. These debts are paid first and then if any assets are left, general claims receive a prorated payment.

In October, 1979 the new federal bankruptcy law went into effect. It significantly changed the relationship between the creditor and the debtor filing for bankruptcy. It did this by making the federal law more sympathetic toward the debtor. There are now certain assets which the federal law protects from seizure to satisfy creditors' claims. The federal law also provides that if the state law is more lenient in the state where the bankruptcy is filed than the federal law in protecting assets from seizure, the person filing bankruptcy may choose the state exemptions if he or she wishes to do so. In effect, then, the federally protected assets become the starting point and establish a minimum on the assets which are protected.

Federally exempt assets include up to $7,500 equity in homestead property, $1,200 in a motor vehicle, and $300 each in furniture, clothing, and other household goods. At the state

Drawing by Mort Gerberg; © 1979 The New Yorker Magazine, Inc.

Part 1 / Budgeting, Buying, Borrowing, and Saving

level, exempt assets vary from state to state, but generally they include the homestead, a car (in some states two cars) regardless of its value, and the "tools of your trade." A house or car, however, are not protected if they have been pledged to pay off a specific debt. Therefore, a house can be seized to pay off a mortgage or a car to pay off the loan which financed the car.

There used to be a stigma attached to personal bankruptcies, but this is less true today. Bankruptcy relieves the person of all debts, and the logic behind this is that a person who has too many debts becomes economically unproductive. Relieving the individual makes him/her productive again, and hence benefits society as well as the individual. While many lenders no doubt would not lend to anyone who has ever declared bankruptcy, the person is not as bad a credit risk as one might imagine. The bankrupt person is debt-free and the law does not permit bankruptcy to be filed again for six years.

While some people have, no doubt, deliberately run up large debts and then taken the easy way out, most bankruptcies appear to be due to poor planning and poor budgeting. In 1979 about two hundred thousand personal bankruptcies were filed in the United States and about the same the year before.[3]

"I've found enlightenment, and I still pull down my 85,000 per. What more can I ask?" (*Source:* Permission Cartoon Features Syndicate; from *The Wall Street Journal.*)

3. *Finance Facts Yearbook,* 1980, p. 53.

TAKING A FINANCIAL INVENTORY

All competent businesspersons take a periodic inventory of their assets, liabilities, and net worth. In this way they are able to tell from year to year whether their financial position is improved. If net worth has increased, they know that they are going forward.

With the rising cost of living, most families feel that everything is going out and nothing is coming in; but this is not necessarily the case. The only way to tell is to make a family balance sheet and compare present status with that of a year ago or five years ago, or any other period, for that matter. A family balance sheet can be used to plan ahead, especially in the purchase of big items such as automobiles, homes, and life insurance. A balance sheet can, for example, provide clues as to whether new life insurance is needed, whether a larger home is within a family's financial means, and whether it would be desirable to increase savings. You were introduced to a balance sheet early in this chapter. You may wish to review it. There are some blank spaces you may use to fill in your personal entries. It also has a column to show the return you are earning on your various assets. You can then compare them and determine which ones appear to be the better investments.

The assets (shown on the left) may be looked on as plus items; they represent property that has value. The items on the right (called liabilities) may be looked on as negative items; they represent debts that you eventually will have to pay. The difference between the two is referred to as net worth, and it is the best measure of what you are actually worth.

QUESTIONS FOR REVIEW

1. Why is it important to keep good financial records?

2. What is a balance sheet? Why is it important?

3. What is an income statement? Why is it important?

4. Discuss briefly a personal budget and the real purpose of a budget.

5. Should you have a weekly, monthly, or annual budget?

6. Comment on the statement that everyone must live within his or her income.

7. Discuss the guidelines or rules of thumb that you believe can be followed when preparing a budget.

8. What are some of the problems that occur when preparing the income side of the budget?

9. Why are some items in a budget fixed and some variable?

10. Discuss the personal budget and the life cycle.

11. Discuss food in the family budget.

12. Discuss briefly why life insurance premiums must be budgeted.

13. Discuss the importance of savings in a budget.

14. Should an allowance be made in the budget for taxes if your employer withholds taxes from your weekly salary? Explain.

15. What role can the budget play in financing a college education?

16. Why is the tuition charged by professional schools like law and medical schools generally higher than that charged by undergraduate colleges?

CASES

1. John and Betty Simpson, who are in their early thirties, have two children, a boy of five and a girl of three. John works for Exxon and earns $15,000 per year after taxes. Having recently discovered that they are saving very little, they have decided to go on a budget.

John would like to buy at least $10,000 more of life insurance, which would cost them $222.30 per year. This would amount to a total life insurance premium payment of $444.60 per year because John already has $10,000 of life insurance. In addition, they would like to save part of their income for the purpose of financing their children's college education and for a nest egg for themselves.

Prepare a budget to help them achieve their goal.

2. Louise and Archibald Rutledge are looking forward to Archie's retirement next year from Ford Motor Company's River Rouge plant, where he has worked on the assembly line for forty years. The company will provide him with a pension of $400 per month. In addition, he will receive social security payments of $910 per month, and he has a contract with a life insurance company that will pay them $200 per month for as long as they both live. This represents their total retirement income.

They have no dependents, and they own a modest home, fully paid for, in a pleasant Detroit suburb. The taxes on their home are $916 per year.

They request your help in planning a budget for their retirement.

3. Joan Rider and Mary Lou Miller, both twenty-five years old, are United Airlines flight attendants flying the Denver-to-Newark run. They share an apartment in Ivy Hill in Newark that costs them $350 per month. They each make $1,200 per month take-home pay plus an allowance for uniforms. Joan has an old Ford that is fully paid for, but Mary has payments of $220 per month to make on her new car. They have agreed to share the common expenses of keeping up the apartment, including the food consumed there.

Prepare a joint budget for Joan and Mary Lou and then a separate personal budget for each of the women for the income they will have left over after meeting their joint expenses.

4. Captain Bob Warning, the pilot of the Boeing 707 on which Joan and Mary Lou fly, has seen the budget you prepared for them and is so impressed he requests your help on a bud-

get for his family. He is forty years old, has been flying with United for thirteen years, and as first pilot is making $70,000 per year. His take-home pay, however, is only $50,000. Bob is married and has four children: two girls aged two and six and two boys aged twelve and ten.

Bob also lives in New Jersey and is buying a house in South Orange on which the payments are $650 per month (including interest, reduction of principal, taxes, and insurance). He has a monthly life insurance premium of $150 he must pay but no other fixed expenses.

5. Mary Rivers has just graduated from Odessa High School in Odessa, Texas. She is going to the university next fall on a full-tuition scholarship. She will, however, have to pay her room and board, buy her own clothes and books, and meet other personal expenses. Mary has decided to live in the dormitories, where she pays a flat fee of $1,500 for room and board for the entire academic year. She can pay this sum in three equal installments, which are due on September 30, October 31, and November 30. Mary has saved up $2,400 from various summer jobs, and she will use that money to help finance her education. She would like to stretch it as far as possible. Also, her uncle has agreed to pay one-half of her room and board fees. Prepare a budget for Ms. Rivers that will minimize her expenses.

6. Sally Holsack is a twenty-two-year-old New Jersey woman who has just graduated from Wesleyan College with a B.A. in chemistry. This morning a letter informed her that she has won a scholarship to the University of Texas Medical School starting next fall. The scholarship will pay only her tuition; she will have to pay her own lab fees and her room and board and miscellaneous expenses. Sally has some money saved, but not a great deal. Her parents have promised to help her with a loan if needed, but Sally would like to minimize her indebtedness when she graduates. Therefore, she would like a bare bones budget to get her through four years of medical school. Can you prepare a hypothetical budget for her?

SUGGESTED READINGS

Automobile Facts and Figures. Detroit, Michigan: Automobile Manufacturers Association, Inc., 1977.

Basic Principles in Family Money and Credit Management. Washington, D.C.: Educational Services Division, National Consumer Finance Association, 1974.

Bohn, Robert F. *A Budget Book and Much More.* Provo, Utah: Brigham Young University, 1978.

The Buying Guide—Consumer Reports. Consumers Union, Mt. Vernon, NY. A monthly publication.

Finance Facts Yearbook, 1980. Published annually by Research Services Division, National Consumer Finance Association, Washington, D.C.

International Credit Union Yearbook. Madison, Wisconsin: Concentration of Credit Union Members, International, Inc., 1980. Published annually.

Juster, F. Thomas (ed.). *The Distribution of Economic Well-Being.* National Bureau of Economic Research, Studies in Income and Wealth. Cambridge, MA: Ballinger Publishing Co., 1977.

The Kiplinger Washington Letter, Washington, D.C. A weekly newsletter with a good deal of material on business and finance.

Money Management. A series of pamphlets published by the Household Finance Corporation. Topics include (1) your food dollar; (2) your clothing dollar; (3) your housing dollar; (4) your home furnishing dollar; (5) your equipment dollar; (6) your shopping dollar; (7) your automobile dollar; (8) your recreation dollar; and (9) your savings and investment dollar. Contact your local Household Finance Company Office for more information on these booklets.

Morgan, James N. (ed.), and the staff of the Economic Behavior Program. *Five Thousand American Families—Patterns of Economic Progress, 1974–77.* Ann Arbor: University of Michigan, Institute for Social Research, 1978.

"1979 Gas Mileage Guide," EPA Fuel Economy Estimates. Consumer Information Center, Pueblo, CO.

U.S. Department of Agriculture. *Family Economics Review.* Washington, D.C.: published quarterly by the Consumer and Food Economic Research Division, U.S. Department of Agriculture.

———. *A Guide to Budgeting for the Family.* Home and Garden Bull. Washington, D.C.: U.S. Government Printing Office, Superintendent of Documents.

———. *National Food Review.* A quarterly publication.

———. *National Food Situation.* Washington, D.C.: published quarterly by the Economic Research Service of the U.S. Department of Agriculture.

U.S. Department of Labor, Bureau of Labor Statistics. *News.* An annual publication on budgeting.

Your Driving Costs, 1981. American Automobile Association, 8111 Gatehouse Road, Falls Church, VA. An annual publication.

Chapter Three

Caveat Venditor: Caveat Emptor

I never saw a purple cow, I never hope to see one; but I can tell you anyhow, I'd rather see than be one.

GELETT BURGESS

The objectives of this chapter are to

1 Emphasize the importance of keeping receipts for goods and services purchased

2 Introduce pre-purchase analysis in order to make the buyer more alert when making purchases

3 Help the reader to avoid certain pitfalls when making purchases

4 Convince the reader that an ounce of prevention is worth a pound of cure

5 Examine common deceptive practices

6 Present some helpful money saving tips

7 Introduce post-purchase redress procedures, which should be helpful in recovering any losses

8 Introduce the various governmental and private consumer protection agencies

PRELIMINARY COMMENTS ON CONSUMERISM

While new legislation and business self-regulation now work to improve the bargaining position of the consumer in the marketplace, consumers must still use good judgment and be able to handle their money armed primarily with their own knowledge. If shoppers cannot solve their problems on their own, at least they should know where to get some help and how to complain and get results. *Caveat venditor* means "Let the seller beware." Persons who can enter the marketplace with the confidence that sellers of goods and providers of services should fear their presence are in a state of mind that few—if any—consumers can legiti-

Grateful acknowledgment is extended to Lee Richardson, formerly Director for Education and Finance, Office of Consumer Affairs, HEW, Washington, D.C.

mately attain. Nonetheless, buyers should constantly seek to have knowledge equal to or better than their seller counterparts if they are to obtain adequate value for their limited dollars. *Caveat emptor,* "Let the buyer beware," is the traditional view taken of the buyer (by many sellers) in American popular culture. Its literal application could result in worthless medicines, dangerous cosmetics, and sky-high prices in those instances where the buyer is uninformed. Occasionally those are the results. Legislation, business self-regulation, high ethical standards of American businesses, and competition serve to prevent many of the hazards of pure *caveat emptor.* Still, within the rules of law, there is much latitude for the consumer to waste money or cause serious physical or psychological injury to self, family, or others as a result of ignorance. All is fair in love, war, and—to some extent—the market-place.

The consumer's arsenal of knowledge and tactics can be divided into three areas: (1) pre-purchase decision-making activities, which consist of analysis before making purchases; (2) making actual purchases, which requires some care; (3) post-purchase redress proce-dures, which deal with how to recover any losses. Customers must think of their financial position, budget, and priorities as well as the tactics of choosing brands, comparing prices, and avoiding deceptive practices before spending any money. In the long run, successful prevention of difficulties through pre-purchase decisions and then making wise purchases will save more time, money, and sorrow than post-purchase redress treatment later, even if successful. Those who buy now and think later are blissfully ignorant of whether they correctly managed their money and got value received for value spent. Sometimes buyers who depend on treatment instead of prevention can only hope for satisfaction in the event they were legally wronged—often at the cost of legal assistance and considerable time and effort.

We Have Met the Enemy, and He Is Us

The critics of the "consumer movement" say it has gone too far, that often its adherents' complaints are not legitimate. Their complaints, it is alleged, often stem from the fact that something costs too much. The critics maintain that high costs are the results of inflation and not something over which businesses have any control. While this may be true at times, it is not at other times. Sometimes the consumer has legitimate complaints. Sometimes shoppers can also avoid problems by wise shopping. But if they cannot, they should know where to get help, or how to complain and get results.

We should remember that in many cases the consumer is also a producer. As consumers we demand perfection; we want good quality products. As producers we are careless and often provide shoddy work. These are the opposite sides of the same coin. It is not the corporate entity or the corporate stockholders of the firm that makes the product, or even necessarily the corporate executives, who are at fault. It might well be shoddy work on the assembly line—that is, other consumers.

Consumer Education

Educating the general public on consumer economics and finance is in its infancy. Various voluntary consumer organizations throughout the country are supporting education-al efforts in consumerism both in and out of the public schools. Nevertheless, the level of sophistication among the general public on consumer finance is not great, and therein lies part of the problem. A more informed consumer is a wiser consumer, and that is what you should strive to become.

Keeping Records (Receipts)

In chapter 2 I stressed the importance of keeping records, for tax as well as other reasons. This is also important when you have a grievance with a merchant. Keep your purchase receipts. On big ticket items especially, keep them for a year or two, or at least until the warranty has expired. On smaller items, or if there is no warranty, use your own good judgment. But keep your receipts at least until you have used the item for a time and know it to be functioning properly. One small manila folder will provide space for all of your receipts.

PRE–PURCHASE ANALYSIS—PREVENTION

Consumers may feel that good buying habits consist of bargaining for the lowest price on a stereo system or finding a sale on a pants suit. Probably the most significant decisions about priorities and life-style are made with less conscious thinking effort than decisions about the details of the product or its price. For example, a family may argue more about the make of an automobile or which accessories to purchase than about its size or whether they need a new car or any car at all. These latter decisions are sometimes made with little regard to cost. A family may purchase a camper when it could save considerably by renting one for the few occasions they will use the vehicle. A parent may worry about the best buy in asparagus when the children would get by on highly nutritious spinach at one-third the price.

When buying services, the consumer must be even more wary because it is often even more difficult to judge quality. This is particularly true of professional services.

Incompetent and Shoddy Workmanship

When you buy services, you may come directly in contact with incompetent or shoddy workmanship. Of course when you buy an auto, TV set, or any other item, you may obtain a product that has had shoddy workmanship embodied in it at the factory, and you have a lemon. But in such a case you must deal with the seller, and you have no direct control over poor workmanship as you do when you buy services.

Most repair services, whether for autos, household appliances, or general home repairs, are provided by small businesses. Not much capital is needed to open a repair shop, and consequently new firms are constantly entering this field. Therefore, the casualty or failure rate is also high and firms from which to choose are in a constant state of flux. There are two dangers to guard against when dealing with repair firms: first, shoddy workmanship by people who don't care and, second, people who are simply incompetent, or a combination of the two. In many cases a person wishing to become an artisan will work for an established shop for a year or two and then strike out on his own, long before he is ready.

To avoid incompetent and shoddy workmanship you should find out how long the business has been in existence and how many years' experience the individual workers have had. Often those firms that have ads as well as listings in the yellow pages of the telephone directory will indicate how long they have been in existence. You can also call your local Better Business Bureau.

When it comes to home repair services, often a realtor is a good source of information because they deal with these people a good deal. Another source could be insurance adjusters, since they deal with roofers, plumbers, tile installers, and the like when they pay damage claims. The only other way to ascertain which firms provide quality services is from personal experience and the experiences of friends and acquaintances.

How to Pick a Professional

In the case of a professional like a lawyer, doctor, or accountant, no one but another professional in the same field really knows how good any given individual is. A friend in any of these professions can help you in the selection process. Or you can ask a professional in a related field who may have some knowledge. If, for example, you ask your banker to recommend a lawyer, he or she will probably recommend three or four to avoid being accused of being partial, but probably all will be at least reasonably competent. Finally, friends and acquaintances who have had an occasion to use these experts can be of some help.

Choosing a Brand

When buying goods, consumers frequently and incorrectly equate brand image with quality. If a product is well known, they presume it will have met the test of previous consumer satisfaction, but that is not necessarily the case. The "name" brand or well-known brand may simply be the most heavily advertised and promoted brand rather than a superior product. Particularly where taste is a matter of individual preference or stylish products have different appeals to different individuals, the brand image may be an unreliable guide.

Brands have different values to different people. Every buyer should know the particular significance of a brand being considered for purchase instead of just relying on an intuitive feeling about the product. The following guidelines will help clarify vague feelings. Buyers should take time to question themselves.

1. Guide to popularity of the product. What is the significance of popularity? Is it important to the buyer to use a popular deodorant?
2. Guide to quality. What quality features are important to the buyer, and does this brand have them? Does the buyer want comfort or gasoline economy in a car?
3. Guide to style. Does the buyer want the stylish features represented by this brand? Is the furniture style important for a television set in the living room?
4. Guide to service and follow-up by the maker. Does the foreign make of automobile have adequate parts and service facilities where the buyer plans to drive?
5. Guide to price. Does the product represent a high-priced or a moderately priced line? Does this brand of coffee or detergent have a discount reputation because it is constantly being sold at "cents-off" prices or because it is consistently lower in price?
6. Guide to prestige. Does the choice of watches make the buyer appear affluent or successful or does it represent the buyer as a penny-pinching bargain hunter? Is prestige or the time of day more important in a watch?
7. Guide to status. Does the choice of a certain living room suite appropriately represent the buyer's occupation, social class, or general standing in the community? Does the appearance of middle-class social status symbols or the pleasure of a "hot tub" count more?

Consumers base some choices between brands on poor information. Of the hundreds of brands found in a supermarket, consumers will be unable to do much more than merely recognize some proportion of them. While recognition at least means that the consumer has run into the brand some time in the past through experience, conversation, advertising, or other promotion, familiarity with the brand alone doesn't make a logical argument for purchase.

The brand problem is not completely understood without an investigation of the private label brand. The national or regional manufacturers' brands are usually the better-known ones; however, the consumer will benefit from lower prices and comparable qualities in certain private labels or a store's own brands. Today, chain department, general merchandise, food, and specialty stores have excellent values in their own lines of goods, made by the retailer's own plants or more often to specification in the factories of other nationally known name brand companies. On frequently purchased products such as food, over-the-counter drugs, and toiletries, a consumer should experiment in the hopes of finding an adequate brand that could result in savings of as much as 50 percent on all future purchases. Aspirin, canned fruits and vegetables, toothpastes, mouthwash, facial tissues, and laundry soaps are good beginning points for inexpensive experiments.

Choosing the Store or Vendor

Often the food buyer's first question in a discussion of saving money in the supermarket is, "Which store has the lowest prices?" The question reveals a major gap in consumer understanding of good spending habits because the questions of product choice and brand choice should be given some weight in the budget. Other pertinent questions about the store or vendor include the varieties and qualities of the products, the types of sales, various services such as delivery and credit, and the convenience of shopping.

The discount store is deceptively labeled in those instances where product quality is inferior to that in higher-priced stores. Regular department stores and discount stores have in many cases evolved to the point where only their names distinguish them. Some discount stores have legitimate overall savings opportunities, while the same is true of discount departments in otherwise higher priced department stores. Knowledgeable shoppers will find good values and lower prices on particular items in any store except those in Alaskan mining towns, isolated tourist souvenir shops, or railroad car dining rooms.

Sources of Information

The following are some sources of information to help persons buy goods more intelligently.

Newspaper Advertising

This is a staple and low-cost source of information for price-conscious buyers because of the frequent use of price advertising and sales information. Department stores, drug chains, and grocers have regular advertisements on a daily, weekly, or other schedule that customers can expect. Wednesday or Thursday grocery advertisements and Sunday department store advertisements are reliable recurrent events in large and small cities. End-of-month, semiannual, and annual sales are common to other stores. Seasonal and holiday sales and advertising are expected from such merchants as sporting goods stores, clothiers, toy stores, and personal finance companies. The January white sales, George Washington Birthday sales, Labor Day sales, and day-after-Christmas sales are well known to American consumers. Each of the seasonal sales provides an opportunity to those who plan purchases for them; on the other hand, they can be financial disasters for persons who make unplanned and unnecessary purchases even at low, low prices. A $150 lawn mower purchased for $100 can be either a $50 savings or a $100 violation of a tight budget. Too, some merchants seem to advertise one gigantic sale after another, leaving the false impression that they never sell at regular prices.

Special Directories

The telephone directory's Yellow Pages provide names of many services and retail businesses, particularly those that the consumer does not visit often. For someone needing to call a plumber, electrician, or photographer, the Yellow Pages provide a reasonably current and complete listing. Unfortunately for consumers, unreliable dealers and professional services are listed side by side with reputable firms, although as noted above sometimes the ads will indicate when the business was established.

Another special directory is the classified newspaper section. Besides its role as intermediary between consumers and businesses selling particular items, classified newspaper advertising provides a forum for consumers to buy and sell goods among themselves. *Caveat emptor* is the rule of classified selling because its advertising carries no guarantees of reliability and fair dealing and to some extent is similar to a laundromat bulletin board. Only a few other special directories exist in retail selling. Some large cities have specialized entertainment, restaurant, or tourist guides of varying quality. Many guides recommend all of their advertisers; the more independent gourmet guides—which may carry no advertising—feel free to criticize the biggest restaurants in town. Newspapers and magazines published for residents of certain cities contain information about current entertainment options.

Better Business Bureaus

Found in more than 140 U.S. cities, semiautonomous BBBs have unique resources in their permanent files to assist consumers before they make their purchases. Consumers generally expect BBBs to assist them in times of trouble after unwise purchases, whereas BBBs emphasize preventative inquiries from potential buyers, both to benefit the consumer and to protect honest merchants from sales lost to disreputable sellers. BBBs can provide both prevention and treatment for consumer problems of certain types. Moderate-sized BBBs in smaller cities record tens of thousands of instances of service or service requests. Some bureaus serve one-hundred-thousand or more requests each year. Most of the work of the bureaus is taken up by the handling of phone, letter, and personal-visit inquiries directly from consumers who want to know whether they can rely upon a particular merchant, product, charity, service company, repairman, etc. Because of various legal complications, BBBs do not directly recommend or condemn a business or other organization. However, consumers can accurately interpret a BBB statement such as "We suggest you contact an attorney before doing business with ABC company" or "We have no cases of unresolved complaints against the firm."

BBB educational work is extensive. Free pamphlets are provided on an assortment of subjects ranging from the purchase of carpets to participation in multilevel sales organizations. BBBs also use newspaper publicity, mobile van exhibits, and other means of reaching people to educate, alert, and warn them about consumer subjects. BBBs are not exclusively concerned with assisting persons in selecting merchants, but their local orientation makes them especially expert in this area of consumer concerns. Some BBBs are well-informed, professionally managed organizations that attempt to serve legitimate businesses and consumers at the same time. Business and consumer interests coincide on many issues, and the BBBs' primary energy is devoted to maintaining minimum ethical standards in the business community. The fact that their financial support comes heavily from local business establishments serves to limit the BBBs from undertaking programs that could serve all legitimate consumer needs concerning the choice of merchants and other problems.

Another possible limitation of BBBs stems from their frequent tie-in with local chambers of commerce, with a consequent reluctance to follow up on complaints against fellow merchants.

Private Industry's Rating and Evaluation Systems

Rating systems such as Underwriter's Laboratories, National Electrical Manufacturers Association, Society of Automotive Engineers, and Good Housekeeping's seal can be useful aids in their particular areas of concern. These evaluators also have limitations: There are too few of these systems, and they tend to evaluate only a limited amount of information, such as UL's electrical safety standards, NEMA's electrical input and output, or SAE's service qualities for motor oil. They do not directly compare all brands, and sometimes their standards of acceptability represent only minimum satisfactory performance. These sources are not of uniform quality, and their ratings may have been influenced by the industries that pay for their services. These private industry sources may provide little assurance of quality or reliability even where they appear to offer general blanket endorsement. Good Housekeeping's seal, for example, does not actually give unqualified approval to products.

Nonprofit Rating Organizations

Consumers Union and Consumers Research, both magazine publishers, are trustworthy and reliable. These organizations use valid tests in most cases and make competent recommendations directly measuring and comparing brand performances. But these organizations have limited applications: While they make tests of many appliances and other major purchases such as cars, their coverage of most other products such as foods, medicines, clothes, or furniture is very spotty. These sources evaluate factors they consider important, such as quality, safety, and convenience, but rarely style and other factors of varying importance to consumers.

Labels and Packages

The consumer has an opportunity to evaluate the qualities of products through information obtained from examination of the package or the product itself. Information content of packages varies widely between classes of products, and much of it is required by federal and state law. Bear in mind these facts when looking at products and labels:

Inspection of products, often indicated by labels or stamping marks, is required of some food and nonfood products. Grade, quality, and condition must be all certified in some instances. Eggs, for example, are graded for age, sorted by size, checked for other qualities and the quantity contained in the package, and sometimes are required to show the name and address of the packer. Fresh produce labels show weights, grades, and specific varieties of vegetables and fruits. "U.S. No. 1 red potatoes" is a typical designation on a ten-pound sack of potatoes.

Listing of ingredients for prepackaged food, drug, and certain chemical products is required. The amount of each ingredient is not usually shown, but the ingredients are listed in descending order of amount on the labels. Confusion may result in cases where "beef and pork" is listed as one ingredient because the relative proportions of each are not clear. Such a list must include special additives like artificial color, artificial flavor, preservatives, and other chemicals. Some food products do not list ingredients because a special exemption has been granted. Cola drinks fall into this category. Minimum standards must be met for standardized products like ice cream, strawberry jam, and mayonnaise, but ingredients are not required to be shown. Imitation products such as nondairy coffee creamer or imitation cream cheese must be so labeled.

A description of nutritional qualities is missing from most food product labels. Pet foods labels usually give percentages for each nutrient, but processors of human foods have begun adding nutritional information more frequently.

Labels sometimes show cost per unit of measure or weight. Unit pricing, increasingly found in large supermarket chains, gives the cost per ounce, pound, quart, or other measure for certain varieties of products regardless of the size of the package. For example, if a six-pack of twelve-ounce bottles of soft drinks costs $.96 and an eight-pack of sixteen-ounce bottles costs $1.44, the cost per ounce is $.013 in the first case and $.011 in the second. Unit pricing shows the cost per ounce so that the consumer will not have to be a mathematical wizard.

Standardized packaging helps consumers make better price comparisons if the weight or other measure of two packages is identical. If two packages of similar toothpaste brands are 6¾ ounces each, then a $.79 purchase is better than an $.83 one. When two sizes or more are found, the consumer then must make the calculation per unit of measure.

Some packages are too big for the product. While standards for size and slack fill allowed in many food and nonfood products have been established, the consumer is better advised to read the label for the weight rather than judge volume by the size of the carton, can, or bottle.

Packages containing hazardous ingredients or having hazardous uses are normally labeled to that effect. Some advise remedies in case of misuse or swallowing and others have prominent warnings on proper handling.

Labels contain information on the use of the product. A lawnmower may have permanent metal plates showing how to start it. A prescription label has the dosage directions. Some labels exaggerate ease of use. Most consumers are familiar with the "easy open" carton or can that requires pliers and ice pick. Other examples of suggested uses that appear on labels are recipes for foods and ideas for applications of glue. The over-the-counter medicine with the label promising cures for cancer, gout, and insomnia fortunately is disappearing.

MAKING PURCHASES

When making purchases, you should exercise care so as not to be deceived and to get the most for your money. People are constantly being subjected to false and misleading advertising, deceptive trade practices, and other pitfalls. You should guard against these. In addition, there are also some money-saving tips with which you should be familiar.

Common Deceptive Practices and Other Pitfalls

The more common deceptive practices and other pitfalls to be avoided are noted briefly below.

"Wholesale Prices" Ads

Many retailers advertise items at "wholesale prices." Retail establishments cannot sell you merchandise at wholesale prices, by definition. There is no standard to determine a true "wholesale price."

"Free Encyclopedias"

Encyclopedias are by no means "free" if customers buy a set of other books at inflated prices equal to that of the regular price of the encyclopedias plus the normal cost of the other books.

Improvements and Repairs

Homeowners are annually bilked out of thousands of dollars by con men with phony "improvements" to homes or property. Often itinerant peddlers will claim expensive repairs are necessary to prevent furnace explosions or termite damage.

Free Merchandise with a Redemption Coupon

The offer of "free" merchandise with a redemption coupon is often a trap baited with low-quality merchandise, such as plastic steak knives. Such gimmicks bring customers face to face with a salesperson, where they may obligate themselves for costly and unneeded merchandise, such as a sewing machine.

Close-out Sales

There are fire sales, water-damage sales, going-out-of-business sales, removal sales, lost-our-lease sales, and other dubious reasons for holding sales. Some of these types of sales are legitimate, while others are not.

Charity Promotions

Promoters often prey upon sympathies of citizens to raise funds for charities. While the charity may be legitimate, the fund-raising expense or promotion fees may consume as much as 90 percent of the gifts. Penny bubble gum machines sometimes are touted as charities.

Vanity Biographical Listings

There are several publications of famous-person reference books that charge listed consumers by requiring them to purchase a copy of the publication in order to be listed.

Illegitimate Training Schools

Many individuals with modest savings are induced to buy a correspondence course to become a writer or artist or to enroll in a school that trains truck drivers. Some of these courses will not improve the income of the student but will enrich the school.

Private Sale Offers

Dealers may use classified ads without identifying themselves and offer overpriced used furniture or even jewelry and furs.

Obituary Exploiters

A con artist may send bills to the bereaved family for nonexistent obligations or purchases.

Pigeon Drop

Incredible numbers of persons still meet strangers who offer to share a large cash treasure they have found if the dupe will put up "good faith" money until the treasure is delivered to be divided among the lucky group. The good faith money is never seen again.

Neighbor's Deliveries

Don't pay for products sent to a neighbor who isn't home. The neighbor may not have ordered them.

Unordered Merchandise

Generally, unsolicited mail orders or other unwanted deliveries of products do not have to be paid for in spite of the repeated bills and collection notices that may follow. Check with a lawyer or post office when in doubt.

Auto Gas Mileage Saver

The thousands of special additives and assorted devices sold to improve auto performance are almost all useless or unproven.

Inheritance Search

The person who claims to be able to help locate deceased wealthy relatives is operating a service for a fee. The fee becomes a means of increasing the wealth of the fee collector.

Health Cures

Numerous persons are subject to chronic illness or the fear of major disease and disability and become the object of quack medicine men. Mexican cancer cure resorts and the fountain of youth are sad illusions to those who turn to them for help. Hair restorers, bust developers, and weight-reducing creams are minor, but more common forms of health quackery.

Referral Sales

It makes little sense to spend $300 for an $80 vacuum cleaner in the hopes of securing $10 payments for each of the persons who are referred to the salesperson and also decide to buy. It still happens.

Chain Letters

Many people don't mind sending $1 to the person whose name is on top of a list of persons, if $10,000 may be forthcoming someday. Supposedly, the $1 contributor's name will rise to the top of the list that he or she is asked to reproduce and mail to ten friends with similar instructions. While illegal, chain letter games still flourish.

Debt Poolers

Some firms will offer to negotiate with creditors of individuals deep in debt in order to help avoid collectors and eventual bankruptcy, but often they will only collect their fees and fail to complete successful negotiations.

Vacation Dream Resorts

Expensive brochures with artists' conceptions of future development may create illusions of Shangri-La. It is obviously unwise to invest in undeveloped, unseen property sold by unproven promoters; but it is easy.

Dancing Instructions

Lonely men and women desire companionship, and persuasive salespersons are aware of this frailty of human nature. As a result, the prospective dancer is swept into two years and $1,800 worth of unnecessary lessons.

Multilevel Marketing Pyramids

Some high-pressure sales organizations offer unwary buyers of distributorships an opportunity to sell cosmetics, wigs, taped self-improvement courses, or almost anything at big discounts if they invest heavily. Unfortunately no one buys the products.

The Psychological Price

A price of $4.95 appears smaller than $5.00, but the difference is minute; $4.73 appears to be a carefully cut price that was shaved to the lowest penny. Possibly the $4.73 item will be a $4.00 value rather than a $5.00 value.

The Inflated List Price

Far too many merchants use artificial prices—often stated as regular or list prices—that were not the prevailing price for the product at any time in the past. The list price becomes the basis of discount price claims. Very few automobiles are sold at the list or "sticker" prices that must be shown on the windows of new cars. Superinflated list or suggested prices are common in the markets and bazaars of foreign countries, where the customer is expected to pay as little as 25 percent of the original price after a round of haggling.

"Harris, I understand you've been telling people to go out and compare." (Source: Drawing by Stevenson; © 1980 The New Yorker Magazine, Inc.)

The Oversold Discount

Furniture and appliance stores may spend more time explaining the money buyers are saving rather than the money they are spending. A consumer may enjoy saving $30 from the original price, but the $199 remaining price on a refrigerator is the price to evaluate more closely and compare to prices of other refrigerators.

Multiple Pricing

Items are difficult to compare if one brand of canned applesauce is $.27 and three of another similar-sized can sell for $.83. Another temptation is to buy three because of the suggestion of the pricing method.

Trade-in Price

Automobiles are easy to trade to a dealer. The important figure in a trade is the difference between the sale price and the trade-in price. A dealer who gives $300 more discount on a new car but a trade-in price of $400 less on the trade is not offering as good a value as a competitor. Some appliance sellers offer trade-ins on worthless used appliances as disguised price discounts.

Slightly-used-product Discounts

The demonstrator car with a few miles of dealer use or the floor sample stove with a slight scratch may both possibly be sold at significant discounts. Sometimes, however, "like new" products have been badly abused and repaired.

Repossessions

Some stores frequently reclaim merchandise from debtors who cannot pay for it and, for surprising discounts, will resell the merchandise in very good condition. Customers should wonder about both the physical condition of the product as well as their own financing arrangements with the dealer who has many repossessed goods for sale.

"Loss Leader" Pricing

Stores use considerable amounts of price discounting but they also expect to make a profit. There may be adequate profit even in a discounted item; but more than likely the seller expects to sell other products at regular, profitable prices to persons who come to the store to buy the special leader items.

Bait-and-switch Pricing

Unethical dealers will try to persuade the customer to buy other products rather than the specially priced one. A "bait and switch" prospect is told that the bait is very poor, out-of-stock, or difficult to show. Furniture dealers may place their special bait in a fourth-floor storage room. A carpet salesperson may arrive for a home demonstration without samples of the bait item but well stocked with expensive substitutes.

There are many new schemes being invented each year to lure the unwary consumer. The only solution is to investigate thoroughly before spending money on any unusual opportunity or offer. So often a simple investigation resulting from a single moment of lucid thinking could save hundreds and thousands of dollars for a consumer who makes a mistake under pressure or false impression.

Money-saving Tips

The tips one can receive from various sources to stretch buying power are endless in quantity. Extensive literature from public and private sources must be culled to obtain useful facts on the great variety of products available to American consumers. Some of the more common tips on frequently purchased products are listed below.

To cut down on the food bill requires a lot of common sense. Families can save as much as 25 percent on their food spending by using common sense alone. If a family is really interested in conserving its dollars, then even more substantial reductions can be made in the food bill.

Consider the nutritional aspects of your food.

- Look at the calorie count of the foods that you're eating. Most middle-income Americans can do without a lot of the foods that they eat, but their problem is that they refuse to even consider doing it.
- Eliminate unnecessary snack foods such as cookies, candy, and potato chips that are generally expensive and are nutritionally deficient. A nutritionally deficient food simply does not have to be eaten unless nothing else is available to stop that old hunger pang.
- Cut down on expensive beverages such as soft drinks of extremely doubtful nutritional values. The only nutritional defense for some soft drinks is that they contain water, an essential in human diets.

Examine your needs for meats, especially expensive beef, lamb, and pork; you may be able to make substantial savings in just this type of food.

- Buy some of the different lower cost cuts and learn ways of cooking them that most persons simply do not bother with. Laziness can be a barrier to sensible food spending.
- Switch your meat buying to cheaper fish and poultry and organ meats, which have generally good nutritional value and may be liked if cooked properly by families who may now think they do not like this type of food.
- Avoid convenient quick-service stores unless the extra 5 to 20 percent cost of foods in these stores is really worth it to you. Surveys show some items in these quick-service stores can cost 50 percent over supermarket prices, and these stores rarely have good sale prices.

All consumers need to discover among the various stores where they shop which of the important items on the shopping list are available in those stores at good bargain prices.

- Do not waste money going all over town every week, but shop one or two different stores each week, alternating among the several stores with which you are familiar. You do not want to waste precious gas, but on the other hand you will miss bargains if you do not vary your stores every now and then.
- Select a particular store or stores to shop in each week, primarily on the basis of major bargains you will be able to stock up on during that week. Use weekly or semiweekly newspaper ads to make your decisions. Do not count on a store that does not advertise to have the bargain that you need.
- When real bargains come along, be ready to spend over your budget. Even if it is going to take another $5, $10, or even $25 for a particular week to take advantage of a few unusually good bargains, you should violate your budget in order to take advantage. After stocking up on some of these key items, your future budgets are going to be much easier to meet because you are living off the stocked-up items that

you bought on good sales. The principle is not to miss bargains that will save you a lot of money just because you have some artificial limit on how much you spend at the grocery store each week.

- Do not be embarrassed or afraid to ask for huge quantities of bargain items when they are available. There is really not too much loss in the minor embarrassment that you may think you are suffering by buying a case or fifty cans or twelve chickens when the price is unusually good.

- Buy as much as you can store or freeze until the next bargain comes along. For example, chicken sales are quite regular, and you do not need to stock up for as many weeks' supply of chicken as you would for items such as canned asparagus, which is rarely put on sale. If you estimate that the next bargain will come along in one or two months, then buy enough at a sale price to carry you through until the next sale comes along.

- In season, buy annual quantities of seasonal fruits and vegetables where possible if you are able to can or freeze them. If you do not like to can or freeze items because it takes you a certain amount of time to do it, reconsider.

- Invest in a freezer to save money only after a realistic look at the operating and depreciation costs of a freezer. Usually you will not save money unless you have a large family. Consider also if you want to pay a little more for the convenience that you get for the extra $10 to $15 a month that the freezer and electricity are going to cost you.

In trying to choose between different brands of foods, consider the following principles:

- Be willing to switch brands when prices shift up and down. Do not lazily get into a habit of buying the same old brand. Many widely used products change prices regularly due to special promotion, sales, and other factors that the alert consumer can take advantage of.

- Do not judge a bargain by the fact that it is an advertised price. In supermarket ads, there are more regular prices being advertised than there are sale prices. Check it out if you want. You will see that many of the advertisements carry only 10 percent of items that are on sale; the rest are just advertised regular prices.

Here are some hints on drug store and prescription prices:

- Some identical prescriptions are sold at different prices by the same drug store— price is at the druggist's discretion. The druggist may lower the price to help the poor, but don't count on it.

- Do not be afraid to ask your doctor to prescribe generic products. Often the generic equivalent can save you a great deal compared to the brand name.

- Pharmacies may tell you whether a prescription can be purchased more cheaply off the shelf without going through the process of having the prescription filled. In other words, not every prescribed item has to be prescribed.

- If a drug store says it "will not be undersold," make the druggist meet the price that you pay at other drug stores. The same principle applies to other types of merchants with the same claim.

- Learn some home remedies, like salt gargle, and ask your doctor whether the claims of the TV commercial for mouthwash and other modern concoctions are really valid.

Among many suggestions that have been offered to energy consumers (households and others) are the following:

- Use one large bulb rather than smaller ones. For example, one 100-watt incandescent lamp produces more light than two 60-watt lamps.
- Turn off lights, heat, and air conditioning in unoccupied storerooms and closets.
- Provide manually wound clocks in lieu of electric clocks.
- Weatherstrip and caulk all houses.
- Plant deciduous trees and vines on south and west sides of homes to provide protective shade against summer sun.
- Service oil burners regularly to improve efficiency.
- Shut off furnace pilots in summer.
- Wash dishes by hand in lieu of using a dishwasher.
- Use washing machines and dishwashers only when a full load has accumulated.
- Eliminate gas yard lights.
- Select more efficient appliances for purchase.
- Install radial tires on all automobiles.
- Do not fill gas tanks on cars over one-half full.
- Drive at a steady, moderate speed.

"We're out of sugar—just sprinkle some of this cereal in your coffee."
(*Permission Cartoon Features Syndicate; from* The Wall Street Journal.)

- Buy products made of recycled materials wherever possible.
- Buy articles made of those materials that present best opportunities for recycling.
- Ban smoking in public buildings so that the amount of fresh air intake can be reduced.

Some observers claim that methods of energy conservation and population control will ease our energy deficit and lessen the world's energy and population problems.

Miscellaneous Tips For Consumers

- Watch for people in your town who are selling second-hand items in garage sales. Many people are in a hurry to move out of town and have to get rid of items that may be useful to you.
- Be on the lookout for white elephant sales and similar sales of schools and civic groups that will have many bargains.
- Buy a cheap postage scale; one that sells for about $1 is a bargain. With today's postal prices, you can't afford to overestimate.
- Special delivery is only a help when you send mail to regular addresses. There is nothing gained when mailing special delivery to a post office box number.
- Do not ever pay postage due unless you know what you are paying for. You are under no obligation to pay postage due unless you want to accept the letter or package.
- Do not spend extra on gasoline grades; on the other hand, do not spend too little when it may damage your engine. Follow the car manufacturer's recommendations.
- Cars with manual gear shifts can be real gasoline wasters if you insist on driving in a low gear. Automatic shifts use 7 percent more gasoline on the average.
- Considering the labor costs of rotating your tires, you may often find that it is cheaper and just as safe not to have your automobile tires rotated every few thousand miles.
- Check chain outlets for blemished tires sold at much lower prices due to minor imperfections.
- Save coupons that give you a few cents off on purchases. Keep an envelope available and start collecting them when you receive them in newspapers, magazines, and in the mail. Merchants will be happy to take them on any of the products they sell.
- When a special is out of stock, insist that the merchant give you the right to come back and purchase it later at the sale price. Even if they do not usually offer a so-called rain check, they will probably give you one anyway if you insist on fair play.
- Standardization in clothing sizes is yet to come. When comparing sizes in different brands, do not assume that the sizes are going to be identical to those of another brand of clothing.
- As soon as you get home change out of your good clothes. They wear out quickly and it would be more economical to wear cheaper house clothes.
- Learn how to shop a sale. At the beginning of the sale, you get a better selection, but at the end you may get further markdowns on the sales items that are moving too slowly.

- During party season, run your parties back to back, in order to take advantage of the leftovers from previous parties.

- Why be extravagant when you wrap gifts? Consider that white tissue may be adequate for certain small gifts or children's gifts at any time of the year.

- To avoid paying a surcharge every month for an unlisted phone number, use a special name of your own choosing and give it out only to close friends.

- Just as a combination lunch of sandwich and drink may be less expensive than each ordered separately, the prices on several major complementary items will be less than their individual prices added together. Rooms of furniture, place settings of silverware, or stereo component collections may be sold at combination prices. It is common to find a minor accessory given away to the buyer of a major product. Ice trays given to refrigerator buyers or batteries with a radio are common examples.

- Fashion goods or overstocked items are severely cut by many merchants in order to free capital for other purchases or to clear out products that are becoming worthless. Some stores specialize in buying markdowns from better, well-known stores that do not want to gain the reputation of being price cutters themselves. Styles may change, but consumers who do not worry about style in clothes or other merchandise can find 30 to 75 percent savings. Christmas cards may be stored for 11½ months, and 50 percent savings on December 26 makes their purchase so far in advance quite worthwhile.

- Some firms will give an immediate discount to a customer who shows any interest in a product. This discount price is perhaps only the beginning of the bargaining. Small, owner-managed firms are good places to attempt to bargain. Owners may bargain whereas hired employees are usually not authorized to negotiate prices.

- While a retailer may offer only one price, another firm of a different type will sell the same item at a much lower price because it pays a wholesaler's price to the manufacturer. Building supply houses, among others, may sell to other retail dealers or even consumers at a discount because of their status as wholesalers. Farmers' prices may vary from those of retailers, and by buying fertilizer from the farmers' supply store instead of a city hardware store, significant savings can be realized.

Other Things You Should Know About Consumerism

There are a number of other things about consumerism with which you should be familiar. The more important of these are discussed below.

The Discount House; Cash Discounts

While cash discounts are difficult to obtain, in recent years the discount house store has developed and in many cases better bargains can be obtained in the discount house than in the more traditional stores. There are several reasons for these savings.

First, in many cases these stores are located in the suburbs or outlying areas and in plain buildings. This may result in lower land and construction costs than the traditional store has even if it moves to the suburbs.

Second, the discount house relies on "self-service" to a greater extent than the traditional store; this reduces its labor costs. The discount house tries to lower costs even more by hiring more part-time help such as students and others whom they pay less. The lower wages result in more labor turnover, but the stores do not mind this. Indeed, this turnover may reduce costs more because a larger proportion of the employees are at the starting and hence minimum wage than is the case in a traditional store. The employees in a discount house are trained to do only a very few things, so the service is generally of a slightly lower quality, but it is usually adequate. Finally, discount houses often carry fewer lines of big items such as refrigerators, which they can buy in larger lots, which reduces their costs further. Because of their lower costs, discount houses can pass some of their savings on to the consumer. By careful shopping one can often find better bargains there.

Warranties

Warranties are usually granted by the manufacturer, not the retailer or the lender. The retailer, however, is usually the one who will repair (or occasionally replace) a defective product. For example, automobile dealers are the agents through which the manufacturers make the warranty good. However, some of the large retailers like Sears Roebuck and Company provide their own guarantee, or warranty. Sometimes the warranty provides only for the replacement of defective parts and does not cover the labor costs of doing so. In other cases both labor and parts are covered.

Retailers and lenders are, technically speaking, not liable for warranties granted by the manufacturer. But they do have to cooperate to make the manufacturer's warranty viable, and usually they do. Consumers may now also legally withhold future payments for defective goods until they are replaced or repaired. See Chapter 6 for a more detailed discussion of the legal aspects of this.

Service Contracts

Many durable goods retailers are now offering service contracts which normally begin after the warranty expires. That is, for a yearly fee the seller will repair the item covered without further charges. Some of these contracts cover both labor and parts, others only parts. Generally, the annual fee is determined by the age of the appliance and the historical repair record of the retailer on that particular item. It is because of the historical repair record that the annual service fee for a $300 item, say a washing machine, may be higher than for another $500 item, say a refrigerator. It is generally true that the fee is the same on two different models of the same item such as a $500 color TV set and a $300 set. However, there are exceptions to this generalization.

If the service contract is renewed at the end of a year, the fee is, of course, increased. It is difficult to generalize as to whether these service contracts are a good buy; some fees seem excessive to this writer, others do not. Since the fees vary a good deal from retailer to retailer and, of course, from item to item sold by the same retailer, you should examine very closely any contract you are considering. Remember, a new item built properly and working correctly should not need repair for some time.

The Cash Discount

Years ago many merchants would grant a 2 to 3 percent cash discount because it saved them paper work and they got their money immediately. Sometimes the cash discount applied if the person paid within ten days rather than the traditional thirty. A 2 percent cash discount for payment within ten days (rather than the traditional payment within thirty days) means one is saving 2 percent over a twenty-day period. This amounts to about 35 percent if converted to an annual basis.

There are two reasons why fewer and fewer retailers will give a cash discount. First, they are geared to handle credit sales and cash sales save them few, if any, expenses. Second, if they are engaged in the financing process, they actually earn a substantial amount (interest) in the financing operation. The common interest that retailers charge is 18 percent. This may well be as much or more than their profit margin. Indeed, one wit once remarked he would gladly sell merchandise at cost if he could finance it on his terms. While cash discounts are difficult to obtain, one should nevertheless (after the final price has been agreed upon) ask for one. Occasionally it might be granted.

The one disadvantage of a cash discount is that it is more difficult to bring pressure on a merchant to correct a defective product if you have already paid him. See the chapter on consumer legal protection for the current legal status of cash discounts.

The Acceleration and Balloon Clauses

The acceleration clause states that if one payment is missed, all remaining payments are immediately due and payable. In the absence of the accelerator clause, the creditor often could only sue monthly as each payment came due. Typically an installment purchaser signs the *note,* which is the promise to pay, and a *security agreement* under the Uniform Commercial Code, which makes the merchandise collateral for the purchase. Unscrupulous dealers can take advantage of the acceleration clause and repossess an item even if only one payment has been missed.

The balloon clause is designed to mislead buyers into thinking they are paying less than they really are and to keep them on the hook longer, to get them to pay more interest. For example, the contract may call for the payment of $50 per month for six months and then a single seventh payment of $300 more. When the seventh payment comes due, the buyer cannot pay and either has to refinance or may even lose the item. If, on the other hand, the contract had called for six monthly payments of $100 each, the buyer may well have been able to afford the payments.

Assigning Wage Clause

It is possible in some states for the creditor to get a court order garnisheeing the wages of a debtor. Then the employer must pay the lender so much per month directly. However, there are limits to how large a portion of a person's wages may be garnisheed and often it is bothersome to get the court order. Therefore, some dealers and financial institutions have inserted wage assignment clauses in their contracts. In such a case, the creditor can go directly to the employer and get a portion of the debtor's wages without first having to obtain a court order.

The Add-on Clause

The add-on clause ties several different sales together. For example, if you purchased a TV set, the seller would retain title until it was paid for. But if you had only one more payment left to make on the TV set when you purchased a refrigerator, the dealer would retain the title of both items until you had paid for both of them. If then, still later (when the TV set was fully paid for and you only had one or two payments left on the refrigerator) you purchased a sofa, all three items would be tied together; the dealer would retain title to all three. If afterward, when you only owed a few more payments on the sofa (and the TV set and the refrigerator were fully paid for), you missed a payment because of an emergency, all three items could be repossessed.

Reputable dealers would not do something like this, but some unscrupulous ones might. Obviously you should be very careful and not let them put an add-on clause in your contract.

Trade-ins, Price Packing, and Dealer Participation

Trade-ins and price packing are related to the amount of the down payment and frequently cause the consumer to pay more for the product than he or she should. Price packing means jacking up the price in excess of what is expected in order to be able to reduce it later during a bargaining session or to enable the dealer to give an unusually large trade-in allowance.

Historically, price packing was resorted to most frequently by automobile and appliance dealers in order to impress the customer with large and unrealistic discounts or trade-in allowances. One of the evils of price packing most common among automobile dealers is the practice of charging different prices for the same autos on the same day. However, since 1958 an effort has been made to eliminate this evil; dealers are now required by law to place a list price tag on the auto. This is only the legally required "suggested list price." There is still room for bargaining and almost no one pays the list price. Moreover, this bargaining can take place in the form of getting more for your trade-in or in getting the list price reduced.

An example of the way the down payment is related to a packed price and the trade-in allowance runs something like this "deal." Suppose an item has a "true" price of $1,000. The dealer may pack it an additional $500, giving it a price of $1,500. The dealer allows the buyers $1,000 trade-in on an item worth $500, and there remains a balance to pay of $500. It could be said that the down payment is then 66.6 percent. If the dealer were realistic and did not pack the price and allowed a $500 trade-in and if this were the "true" worth of the item being traded, then the balance owed is still $500 but the down payment would be only 50 percent. Consequently the down payment can be misleading. Moreover, sometimes the price packing is greater than the added trade-in allowed, and the consumer ends by paying more.

In the automobile business the consumer should be aware of what is called "dealer participation," "dealer reserve," or "dealer bonus." Sometimes an auto dealer will attempt to persuade you to finance the purchase of your auto with a particular finance company. You will have to pay a finance charge on the loan, plus interest. The interest is paid to the financial institution making the loan, while the finance charge is split between the dealer and the financial institution that has purchased the installment paper. From the consumer's viewpoint, it is frequently more desirable to arrange for a bank or credit union loan before attempting to purchase a new car in order to avoid having to pay the additional dealer participation finance charges.

When buying a new car, the buyer is aware of the "suggested list price," but does not know the dealer's cost. So the buyer does not know really how much bargaining room exists. There are a number of car buying guides that attempt to publish the FOB factory price and estimated freight costs. This information is enough to enable the potential buyer to estimate the dealer's cost. However, these published figures are only estimates; often they contain errors or may not take into account dealer's make-ready costs. Sometimes as much as $100 is spent by a dealer in getting a newly received car in full running condition.

On the other hand, sometimes there are sales contests and the auto manufacturers reduce the price of their products if dealers meet their sales quota. This can result in the opposite kind of error from the one noted above and dealers' costs would be below the person's estimate.

When buying a car, two well-known guides which you should consult are:

1. NADA. This is the "blue book" and is published by National Auto Dealers Used Car Guide Co., 8400 Westpark Dr., McLean, VA 22101.
2. *New Car Cost Guide,* published by Auto Invoice Service, Division of Gousha (a Times Mirror Company), 2001 Alameda (or P.O. Box 6227), San Jose, CA 95150.

Most financial institutions that finance cars have these books.

Auto Repair Protection—Coming Soon?

Many consumers have long complained that auto repair is one of the biggest consumer "rip offs" around. The most frequent complaints concern repairs not made, not made properly, and charges made for work not done or if done, not needed. Some experts believe that about $20 billion per year is wasted due to faulty and unnecessary auto repairs. In a survey made by the U.S. Department of Transportation in 1979, it was found that $.53 of each repair dollar was wasted.

Many states and localities have taken steps to provide the public with some protection from unscrupulous or incompetent auto repair shops. Many states have established an "Autocap" panel. This is a committee made up of car dealers and consumers which tries to resolve auto repair complaints. Some states have gone further. California has established a bureau of automotive repair within its Department of Consumer Affairs. Among other things, it has over a dozen "rigged" test cars constantly checking the competency and honesty of repair shops. In New York the Motor Vehicles Department is charged with monitoring repair shops. These activities are designed to keep the repair shops on their toes. If you have an actual complaint which you cannot resolve, check to see if your state or community has an Autocap Panel.

If You Move, What Will It Cost?

Since moving companies which transport household goods across state lines are regulated by the Interstate Commerce Commission (ICC), one would think that their rates are all about the same; but this is not the case. The ICC only sets maximum rates. Some companies are more reliable than others in the quality (and speed) of the service they render. Also some are less honest than others.

Before moving, you should get the rate schedule from several different companies. The cost of any move is based upon the weight of the goods shipped and the distance. It is important that you get an honest accounting of the weight. The truck is weighed both before and after loading, and you are entitled to a ticket showing the weight in each case. If you have any doubt about the honesty of the company, be at the scales when the loaded truck is weighed. Make sure that only the weight of your goods is added to the final amount. Dis-

FIGURE 3-1.

DEFECTIVE MERCHANDISE OR SERVICES	The law now provides that you may withhold payment of any balance due on defective merchandise or services purchased with a credit card, provided you have made a good-faith effort to return the goods or resolve the problem with the merchant from whom you made the purchase.

If the store that honored the credit card was not also the issuer of the card, two limitations apply to this right:

☐ The original amount of the purchase must have exceeded $50; and

☐ The sale must have taken place in your state or within 100 miles of your current address.

Source: Board of Governors of the Federal Reserve System, Washington, D.C. 20551. (December 1976)

honest crewmen may add things on the way to the scale. Also make sure the weight of the loading crew is not added to your bill. Your shipping ticket should, in addition to the weight, also include a list of all the items shipped. Don't misplace this because it will be needed for insurance claims should some items be lost or damaged. Before selecting a mover you should also try to find out the number of claims filed against the companies (the lower the better) and the frequency with which the truck arrives at its destination on time.

POST-PURCHASE REDRESS PROCEDURES: HOW TO RECOVER YOUR LOSSES

In spite of education and other preventive measures, consumers will make mistakes. Fortunately, many problems can be partially or fully resolved by a variety of techniques and actions. Ethical businesses do not want dissatisfied customers to hurt their reputations. Various government agencies can also offer help when the customer has a problem. Some of the principal problems and their remedies are presented below. The National Association of Manufacturers advises that when a complaint is made, it is helpful to the seller or any other party contacted in behalf of the consumer if the buyer follows these procedures.[1]

- Make a habit of keeping receipts, hangtags, warranties, care labels, etc., in one convenient place so they are readily available in case you need to return the merchandise.
- Read and follow instructions carefully as to using, washing, oiling, or other general care. This may eliminate the need for a return.
- If you find it necessary to return an item or make a complaint, think through the reasons why you are dissatisfied so that you can present your case well.

When You Want a Refund

Some sellers will provide 100 percent satisfaction to consumers who desire to return merchandise. They may even bend over backward to avoid embarrassing the customer even if the customer brings in soiled clothes ("too small"!?), half of a ham ("odd taste"!?), or a nonfunctioning radio ("my wife already had bought one"), and a thinly veiled excuse for the refund request. It is unfair to the seller for the buyer to request refunds on some things that have been already used or misused, but many customers often fail to make requests for refunds when they would be welcomed. The National Association of Manufacturers makes the following suggestions when returning merchandise to a store.[2]

- Return merchandise to the store where you bought it and to the department where it was purchased.
- Avoid making returns near closing time or during rush hours, when you may not get to see the person who can do the most for you. If the person has no authority to service your complaint to your satisfaction, ask to see a person higher in authority.
- If you are leaving the item for repair or if a refund will be mailed to you, be sure to obtain a receipt for the item.

1. "The Concern For Quality," National Association of Manufacturers. Undated pamphlet.
2. ibid. "The Concern For Quality."

When You Get the Clerk's Runaround

If an employee fails to offer a refund, provide a service, or give necessary information, the best rule is to go right to the top of the organization. The manager of a store, rather than the public relations manager, personnel manager, or assistant manager, can usually break red tape better than anyone else in the establishment. Otherwise the customer may be frustrated by advancing slowly up the chain of command in a large store.

When You Can't Get Local Satisfaction

If the local sales representatives or local store will not resolve the problem, the top management of a large business will sometimes act. Customers may get satisfaction plus bonus gift packages, samples, or other bonuses from the well-intentioned home office.

A little detective work may be necessary to find the higher authorities. The local representatives of a store may give you their own company's home office and names of key executives; but if the problem centers around a faulty product, they may not be able to supply this information.

Manufacturer addresses can be found on labels and packages of many products. Zip codes are required by law on labels in some cases. Local stockbrokers will have corporation home office addresses in their investment literature. These and other reference books with the pertinent information may be found in any good library. When writing to a company without the name of a particular officer, the president should be addressed. The National Association of Manufacturers advises that when writing a company or returning a purchase by mail, a consumer should do the following:

- Try to find the proper name of the company, the right department, address, and zip code. Improperly addressed letters get delayed. (The librarian in your local library will be able to help you.)

- Write a businesslike letter. Keep a carbon copy, even if the letter is handwritten. Write legibly. This will save time in the long run.

- Give brand name, model number, size, color, and any other information that will help to identify the product.

- Try to explain exactly what is wrong. If you are returning a product, send it in the original package if possible. If the product is small, send the letter with the package and insure it. With certified mail, you can specify a return receipt so you will know it was received. Include your name, address, zip code, and telephone number on your correspondence.

- If you should not hear from the company, send a second letter. Most companies try to acknowledge complaint letters within two or three weeks.

When the Merchant or Manufacturer Won't Help: Voluntary Action

If the problem is quite serious or the firm cannot or will not resolve the situation, the consumer faces a multitude of possible actions—sometimes none of which is satisfactory. There are legal actions as well as other avenues open to the customer, depending upon the particular nature of the complaint.

The independent Better Business Bureaus in more than 140 communities remain the leading complaint-handling agencies. BBBs try to resolve disputes between business and a consumer in a variety of ways but primarily by trying to present to each side the views of the other. A cooperative merchant may resolve a complaint quickly because of the intervention of the influential BBB in a particular case rather than because of the merits of the consumer's complaints. Few merchants will totally ignore the BBB's request for the company's reaction to a complaint. The BBB will not arbitrate a case or attempt to negotiate a settlement between two parties in the complaint situation, but it will undertake stronger measures where the facts warrant.

BBBs release bulletins to their business members to alert them to specific frauds, dubious business practices, deceptive advertising, and other concerns that affect the business world. In some instances, disreputable firms will be specifically named and charges against them from the BBB will be explicitly defined. As necessary, BBBs supply information to law enforcement officials in their pursuit of materials for prosecution under city, state, and federal laws. The BBB will also take legal action to stop certain practices by signing complaints against firms allegedly violating laws. As some BBBs determine that certain practices are undesirable, they may undertake concerted educational and legal activities, including legislative lobbying, to correct situations on a local, statewide, or even nationwide level. Various BBBs work together and exchange much information among themselves for purposes such as tracking the movements of intinerant peddlers or fast-moving fraud artists and developing complete records of the activities of firms doing business in several areas or nationwide.

Business and trade associations are increasingly becoming involved in complaint handling for their members or an entire industry. The Major Appliance Consumer Action Panel (MACAP), primarily supported by the Association of Home Appliance Manufacturers (AHAM), is a leading example of an industry response to consumer complaints. Member companies of AHAM let the consumer-operated but AHAM-sponsored MACAP group resolve the more difficult individual cases as well as advise AHAM members of general consumer problems. The Gas Appliance Manufacturers Association and American Retail Federation also participate in the MACAP program. Industrywide complaint systems are quite rare, but new ones exist in furniture (FICAP), autos (AUTOCAP), and carpets (CRI-CAP).

Finally, if your complaint is not taken care of, you may go to one of the consumer protection agencies described below or take legal action against the business establishment (these could be governmental or private consumer protection agencies). Obviously, it would not be worthwhile for an individual to sue in most cases, but in a few as, for example, if a major defect exists in a car, it might be. Consumer groups or public interest law firms may sometimes take legal action on behalf of consumers. Moreover, in recent years courts have leaned more in the direction of favoring the consumer if there is a legitimate complaint. Some consumer groups or law firms may choose to sue, even if the amount involved in the specific case is too small to warrant the action, on the grounds that such a suit will encourage the retailer and manufacturer to be more responsible in the future. Any publicity that may be generated by a lawsuit or by government action may also serve to increase the responsibility of the seller.

Small Claims Courts

Legal action should probably be limited to a measure of the last resort. In most cases, such action should be taken through a small claims court. Often small claims courts are able to handle claims effectively, quickly, and at a much lower cost than regular legal action. However, the amount of damages for which a person may sue is limited in a small claims court. In most states this is about $500. If you have suffered damages (and would like to collect) in excess of that amount, you would probably have to hire an attorney and go to a regular court. The effectiveness of a small claims court depends on particular state laws and the availability of the courts in particular locations. But you do not need a lawyer. Procedures are usually handled in an informal manner and the legal rules of evidence and procedure are often waived. This means you simply tell the magistrate what happened in your own words.

In some states the small claims courts are under the jurisdiction of the justices of the peace (J.P.), and in others under the alderman. Both of these are elected officials at the lowest (precinct) political subdivision.

The cost of filing a claim in a small claims court is only a few dollars. The actual court costs are also modest, and as a rule are paid by the loser. If you need more information about the small claims court in your area, call your county clerk. The number will be found in the telephone directory. Or you may call the justice of the peace or alderman for your precinct whose numbers, too, will be found in the directory.

CONSUMER PROTECTION AGENCIES

There are a number of federal as well as many state and local consumer protection agencies. In addition, there are some private voluntary consumer protection groups, which have enjoyed varying degrees of success.

Federal Consumer Protection Agencies

While more than forty separate federal agencies perform significant consumer functions, few of them are easily accessible to ordinary citizens seeking information and assistance. Most of these agencies assist consumers without the necessity of consumer participation because they are given specific authority to regulate the actions of business and professional groups. In other words, while they are charged with protecting the consumer interest, they need only to work with groups they can regulate. Critics such as Ralph Nader charge that the constant contact between regulators and the regulated has caused regulators to lose sight of their objectives to serve the consumers they rarely meet.

In any event, consumers seeking assistance from federal agencies should recognize that the agencies serve many individuals and groups in the nation. They cannot be expected to fulfill all demands of individual consumers; they do work with organized groups such as labor, agriculture, and commerce. See Chapter 6, which discusses consumer protection laws, for a further comment on the federal protection agencies as well as a table showing which ones do what and which one you should contact if you have a legitimate grievance.

State and Local Consumer Protection Agencies

In extreme cases of fraud, individuals and groups of consumers can often obtain assistance from agencies of their state government. In rural areas of any state and in many smaller states, however, the limited resources of state consumer protection activities are not conveniently available except by telephone or mail or are missing altogether. All states now claim to have some type of consumer protection bureau, agency, or other unit. Some of these agencies are considered ineffective or are just beginning to breathe some life into their activities.

The absence of consumer protection agencies with notable staff or budget does not mean that *caveat emptor* rages totally unchecked in a state. Many of the agencies of all state governments have partial responsibilities in consumer affairs, and they have had these assignments for many years. For example, advertising, personal selling, door-to-door sales, packaging, and other business practices affecting consumers are regulated to a limited extent by the states. Local district attorneys and state attorneys general rarely consider consumer cases as primary responsibilities, however, except where the specific responsibilities are assigned to an assistant attorney in charge of consumer affairs. A number of states have "little FTC" laws resembling the Federal Trade Commission regulations on deceptive practices.

Some of the recent state emphasis has been to consolidate consumer protection activities under fewer administrators or a single administration more directly responsible to consumer interests. Often this is in some consumer protection division in the Attorney General's Office. Others, however, have only increased the proliferation of administrators by adding another consumer agency or bureau to their existing structure. The major value of these agencies is to focus attention on consumer problems and provide a central service center to assist individuals. Consumers get major frustrations trying to utilize the vast, usually unknown resources of their states to handle their inquiries and complaints.

Voluntary Consumer Organizations

In most states and many communities, voluntary groups of consumers have developed various programs to help themselves and advance their version of the consumers' cause. These groups generally have been assisted in their growth and activities by the Consumer Federation of America, a Washington, D.C. based coalition of over two hundred national, state, and local organizations. CFA's affiliates have their own memberships of more than thirty million persons in consumer, farmer, cooperative, labor, and other endeavors. The National Consumers League, the National Consumer Information Center, National Consumers Congress, and the Congress of Consumer Organizations are other well-known consumer groups on the national level.

Consumer groups developed rapidly following the activities of homemakers a few years ago in a well-publicized eruption of sentiment, pickets, and boycotts of supermarkets over rising prices. The activities of the groups that emerged basically reflect particular interests and special conditions of the urban, suburban, or rural areas in which they flourish.

Some groups do frequent statewide and local area comparisons of store prices for drugs, household items, and food. Others demand financial settlement for its members who have received poor treatment. Generally speaking, however, voluntary consumer organizations do three things: (1) they engage in lobbying at all levels of government to obtain stronger consumer protection laws; (2) they engage in consumer education by sponsoring seminars and lectures on many topics of interest to consumers; (3) they provide consumer counseling. For example, if you have a legitimate complaint, they will explain to you what your legal rights are and how you might go about obtaining relief.

QUESTIONS FOR REVIEW

1. Explain "Caveat emptor" and "Caveat venditor," emphasizing which is justifiable and why.

2. Does "Caveat venditor" mean consumers will always get their money's worth?

3. Why is prevention of consumer problems more desirable for consumers than treatment?

4. Discuss brand name products, pointing out why they are or are not superior to less well known products.

5. Discuss the relative merits of the "brand name" product and the "private label" product.

Part 1 / Budgeting, Buying, Borrowing, and Saving

6. Discuss how a consumer should choose a store or vendor.

7. Better Business Bureaus can be helpful before the purchase or after the purchase. Contrast these two categories of services of BBBs.

8. Contrast bait pricing with loss leader pricing.

9. When is a trade-in just a price discount?

10. Explain how different-sized packages can be confusing. What can be done to overcome this problem?

11. What is meant by the psychological price? The inflated list price?

12. Why do some merchants engage in deceptive practices? How would you define a deceptive practice?

13. Why can discount houses sometimes sell items at a lower price than conventional stores?

14. Discuss briefly the add-on clause and the balloon clause.

15. Explain in detail some of the intricacies of trade-ins, price packing, and dealer participation.

16. Explain how a rigid adherence to a weekly or monthly budget can be unwise.

17. Explain why, in your opinion, it is better to shop wisely than to develop skills at recovering any losses you may have suffered.

18. What strategy would you employ if a clerk were deliberately trying to prevent you from getting a complaint adjudicated?

19. What would you do if you could not get a dispute settled with the management of a local or a national chain?

20. Discuss the conditions under which it might be worthwhile to sue a store to settle a dispute.

21. The rising concern for "consumer protection" seems to be emanating from many sources and for many reasons. Discuss some of these sources and reasons for development.

22. Explain why the consumer does or does not, in your opinion, need protection.

23. What state agencies might a consumer in need of information or action appeal to? Do you think such agencies could do more than they presently do?

24. What possible problems do you see in the doctrine of "Let the Buyer Be Informed"?

25. Why is the consumer generally at a disadvantage when dealing with business firms?

26. Why have most legislative acts relating to consumer protection been at best only partially effective?

27. What types of activities do voluntary consumer organizations perform?

28. How can consumer education help in providing consumer protection?

CASES

1. Visit several supermarkets and compare their prices for common food products. Visit several department stores and discount houses and compare the prices of identical or similar products. What might account for some of the price differentials?

2. Watch newspaper ads for one week and note all of the deceptive or misleading advertising that you can find.

3. John and Jean Sargeant bought a set of four new radial tires for their station wagon recently at a price of $210.50 excluding tax. They were guaranteed against blowout for the life of the tire and for thirty thousand miles tread wear. After one year with just less than ten thousand miles on them, Jean hit a chunk of ice in the road and blew out one of the tires. What kind of settlement are they likely to get? What can they do if the dealer refuses to settle?

4. Make a list of the things you have purchased recently and then make a second list of those things you have purchased but really didn't need. What were the subconscious reasons for buying these products? Were you influenced either directly or indirectly by advertising? Would you buy these products again?

5. Hi and Harriett Hansen were debating the value of their new automobile's brand name. She said it was worthless to her because she

couldn't drive anywhere just because of the product name. Hi said that he felt the brand was valuable because their position in the community as upstanding citizens was enhanced by the purchase. Who was right? Were either or both right?

6. Florence argues that anything selling for $17.73 is bound to be cheap-quality merchandise since it is discounted. Ferdinand argues that such prices often turn out to be inflated. Fitzhugh feels that this price is a typical cut-rate discount price for a $20 item. Evaluate each argument.

7. Ask a large store in your area to indicate how it takes care of customer complaints. Does the store work with the Better Business Bureau, trade associations, voluntary consumer organizations, or government agencies in resolving any customer complaints?

8. Investigate and report on any consumer organization in your area.

9. Jan Burk recently had a problem with the front of his car and took it to the dealer for repairs. The mechanic aligned the front end, performed other work, and pronounced the car fit. On his way home, Jan tested the car at high speed and found the malfunction was still present. Jan took the car back again without explaining what had happened; the repair shop once more aligned his front end and performed other work and pronounced the car fit. This time the repairs actually were made, and the car functioned properly at high speed. A short time later Jan received two bills from the car dealer that were similar but not identical. How should Jan handle the matter?

SUGGESTED READINGS

Aaker, David A., and Day, George S. *Consumerism: Search for the Consumer Interest*. New York: The Free Press, 1978.

Annual Buying Guide, Consumer Reports. Published in December of each year by Consumers Union of the United States, Mount Vernon, New York.

Changing Times, The Kiplinger Magazine. A weekly publication with a good deal of material of interest to the consumer.

Consumer Information Catalog. Consumer Information Center, Pueblo, Colorado; published quarterly.

Consumer News. Office of Consumer Affairs, Washington, D.C.

Consumer Newsweek. A weekly magazine published by Consumer News, Inc., 601 National Press Building, Washington, D.C.

Consumer Reports. Consumer's Union of the U.S., Inc., 256 Washington St., Mt. Vernon, N.Y.

Consumers Bulletin. Consumer's Research, Inc., Washington, N.J.

Cross, Jennifer. *The Supermarket Trap—The Consumer and the Food Industry*. Bloomington: Indiana University Press, 1976.

Epstein, David G. *Consumer Protection*. St. Paul, Minn.: West Publishing Co., 1976.

Everybody's Money. Quarterly. CUNA International, Box 431, Madison, WI 53201.

Federal Trade Commission. *FTC News Summary*. Available from the Commission, Washington, D.C. 20580.

Ford Motor Company. *Car Buying Made Easier*. Annual edition free by writing to Ford Motor Company, Dearborn, MI 48121.

Myerson, Bess. *Consumer Guidelines to Shopping by Mail*. New York: Direct Mail Marketing Association, 6 East 43rd St., New York, N.Y. 10017.

Richardson, Lee. *Consumer Newsletter*. 10465 Waterfowl Terrace, Columbia, MD 21044.

Rosenbloom, Joseph. *Consumer Complaint Guide*. New York: Macmillan, 1978.

———. *Consumer Protection Guide*. New York: Macmillan, 1978.

U.S. Office of Consumer Affairs. *A Consumer's Shopping List of Inflation-Fighting Ideas*. Pueblo, CO., Information Center, 1978.

Warmke, Roman F., Wyllie, Eugene D., and Sellers, Beulah E. *Consumer Decision Making, Guides to Better Living*. Cincinnati: Southwestern Publishing Co., 1977.

———. *Consumer Guides for Buying*. Cincinnati: Southwestern Publishing Co., 1977.

Chapter Four

Banks and the Services They Provide

Neither a borrower nor a lender be; for loan oft loses both itself and friend.

SHAKESPEARE

The objectives of this chapter are to

1   Present checking accounts and explain how they work

2   Introduce the monthly bank statement and show its reconciliation

3   Explain other things banks do

4   Present certain proposed financial reforms

CHECKS AND CHECKING ACCOUNTS

Most adults have checking accounts and use them almost daily. Checks are a convenient means of making payments. A check can be written for any amount, large or small. Until very recently, only commercial banks were permitted to issue checking accounts. Now, however, other institutions may issue NOW accounts, which are similar to checks. However, the bulk of all checks are still drawn on commercial banks.

Banks

The financial institutions we call banks are technically defined as commercial banks to differentiate them from more specialized savings banks that exist in some states. Commercial banks have been called the department stores of financial institutions because they can do under one roof almost everything that the more specialized financial institutions do all together. Generally, banks make loans to businesses, farmers and ranchers, individuals, and all levels of government. Banks perform the role of the trustee, make available strongboxes for safekeeping valuables, and administer the nationwide credit card system that some of them have developed. But the most important role of banks as far as the general public is concerned is to establish and service checking accounts. This service includes clearing checks, which in turn permits our complex society to function.

Since banks perform a fiduciary function and are depositories of other people's monies, they are rather closely regulated by the government. This regulatory power includes the

"Oh yes, the check is signed—look closely there between the setting sun and the lonesome pine." (Permission Cartoon Features Syndicate; from The Wall Street Journal.)

ability to grant bank charters. A bank cannot be established by anyone wishing to do so as is the case with most businesses. In order to obtain a charter and go into the banking business, the group wishing to do so must first prove to the satisfaction of the regulatory agencies that the establishment of the proposed bank would serve the convenience and need of the public and that it would not unduly harm an existing bank.

Checks and Bills of Exchange

A check is classified technically as a bill of exchange. A *bill of exchange* is defined as "an unconditional order in writing addressed by one person to another, signed by the person giving it, requiring the person to whom it is addressed to pay on demand, a sum certain in money to order or to bearer." The Uniform Commercial Code defines the check more precisely. It is a written order, drawn on a bank by a depositor, ordering the bank to pay on demand, and unconditionally, a definite amount of money to bearer or to the order of a specified person. Funds in checking accounts are called "demand deposits." Checks are always payable on demand and you must demand payment (or cash your check) within a reasonable length to time. The code states in effect that a check is not to be paid by a bank after six months have elapsed since its issue.

There are three parties to the bill of exchange. The person drawing the instrument is called the *drawer;* the party requested to pay the stated amount is known as the *drawee;* and the person to whom the instrument is made payable is known as the *payee.*

There are two broad categories of bills of exchange, namely, *checks* and *drafts.* Drafts are specialized checks written by one bank on its account in another bank. They are usually sold to a person who wishes to pay someone in a different section of the country. For example, a person in Denver might buy a draft written on a New York bank from a Denver bank and use it to pay for purchases in New York. A bank draft can be a *sight draft* (payable on demand) or a *time draft* (payable at some predetermined future time).

Opening a Checking Account

Opening a checking account is a simple procedure. The new customer is given a card on which to fill in his or her name, address, phone number, occupation, employer, and signature. The signature on the card is identical to that to be later used on the checks. A specimen signature card is shown in Figure 4-1.

The new customer is assigned a number and given a checkbook with the customer's account number and name and perhaps address and phone number printed on each check. The customer is also given some deposit slips with the same account number on them. Usually when the account is opened an initial deposit is made. When future deposits are made, two deposit slips are filled out, one for the bank and one that is kept by the depositor and serves as a receipt.

When an account is opened, the bank will explain the service charges to the new customer. These may vary somewhat from bank to bank, but there is enough similarity to enable me to generalize. These charges usually vary depending on whether or not the checking account is classified as a regular checking account or a special checking account. On regular accounts many banks provide the customer with personalized checks free of charge. Many others charge a few dollars per two hundred checks. Generally speaking, no service charges are assessed if the minimum monthly balance does not decline below a certain level (usually $300, but sometimes $500). If the account falls below the minimum, there is a service charge, usually a flat fee of $1 or $2. In some cases if the minimum balance falls even lower, say below $200, this flat fee may rise to $2 or $3, and if the minimum balance declines to below $100, the flat fee may rise to $3 or $4. Some banks also add five cents per check to their flat fee service charge if the balance falls below the specified minimum.

Some banks also have special checking accounts. There are no regular service charges and no minimum balance is required. Rather the bank sells the depositor a book of checks at a per check fee (say ten cents for each check), and the depositor is required merely to have on deposit sufficient funds to cover the checks as they are cashed. Generally speaking, special accounts are not very popular, but they do appeal to certain groups such as students who write few checks and whose balance is either low all the time or fluctuates a great deal.

In recent years, some banks have developed a third type of checking account. To obtain it you must usually join a "bank club" or some other arrangement. This usually costs $3, $4, or $5 per month; it varies from bank to bank. But if you join this club, you then have free checking privileges. You get your checks free and there are never any service charges. Belonging to such a club may also provide a few other benefits such as free travelers' checks. Some banks even throw in a few thousand dollars of life insurance. Whether this is worth the $4 or $5 per month, of course, is a matter of individual opinion. Since there are two or three different types of checking accounts to choose from and since service charges vary somewhat from bank to bank, you might wish to shop around before opening an account. Then you can obtain the type of account you want and minimize the cost.

Clearing Checks

Virtually all checks in the United States are now cleared by computer, using "magnetic ink character recognition" (MICR). This is possible because each customer has an account

Account No._____

Account Name _____

No. of Signatures

Required _____

TEXAS STATE BANK
AUSTIN, TEXAS

All the conditions on the reverse side of this card pertaining to this agreement have been read and agreed to by the undersigned. The Texas State Bank is authorized to recognize the following signatures in the payment of funds and all other transactions dealing with this account.

1._____ Soc. Sec. No. _____

2._____ Soc. Sec. No. _____

3._____ Soc. Sec. No. _____

4._____ Soc. Sec. No. _____

| Res. Address _____ | Res. Phone _____ |
| City _____ State _____ | Zip Code _____ |

Employer _____

| Bus. Address _____ | Bus. Phone _____ |

| Perm. Address _____ | City _____ |

| Prev. Bank _____ | City _____ |

Identification _____

| New A/C Clerk _____ Date _____ | Initial Deposit _____ |

Type Account   ☐ Comm   ☐ Reg   ☐ Tex   ☐ 2 + Ck
                ☐ Reg Sav   ☐ S/I Sav   ☐ 2 + Sav

Corresponding 2 + No. _____

Checks Ordered _____ Passbook Issued _____

Comments: _____

JOINT ACCOUNT BECOMING PROPERTY OF SURVIVOR UPON DEATH OF OTHER PARTY

We agree and declare that all funds now, or hereafter, deposited in this account are, and shall be, our joint property and owned by us as joint depositors with right of survivorship, and not as tenants in common; and upon the death of either of us any balance in said account shall become the absolute property of the survivor. The entire account or any part thereof may be withdrawn by, or upon the order of, either of us or the survivor and the bank shall have the right to pay the entire balance to said survivor and upon such payment shall be discharged of all liability.

NOTICE: This agreement is not effective between a husband and wife as to community funds.

_____   _____

NOTICE: Read Additional Terms and Conditions on Reverse Side

FIGURE 4–1 *Example of a signature card.* (Source: Texas Bank of Austin.)

number on his or her checks. It is printed with special ink and characters so that a computer can read it. When the customer writes a check, the bank deducts that amount from the account, and the person receiving the check has that sum added to his or her account. If two different banks are involved, then one bank has a claim on the other. Since hundreds of checks are presented for payment each day, all banks have funds flowing both in and out. Hence in net terms, a bank will lose (or gain) very little on any given day. The clearing of checks is usually carried out by a clearinghouse association or by the Federal Reserve System. It nets the checks and then debits and credits the accounts of the proper bank.

Clearing checks takes time; the period can range from one day if the banks are in the same city to several days or longer if they are on opposite sides of the country. One should be

FIGURE 4-2 *Smith pays Jones some money owed with a check drawn on Bank A. Jones deposits it in Bank B.*

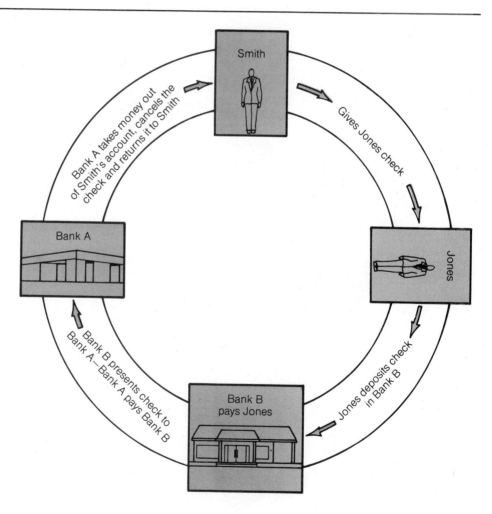

careful not to write checks against a deposited check until sufficient time has elapsed for the first check to clear. Otherwise the written one may clear before the deposited one.

Figures 4-2 and 4-3 show how clearing works. Sometimes the banks involved are in two different cities, perhaps many miles apart. In such a case, a third institution is involved and the clearing process is a little more complicated. This third institution is the Federal Reserve System. The Federal Reserve System was established by the U.S. Congress in 1913 and as such is a federal banking institution. This federal bank does not deal directly with the public, however. It clears checks for banks if they are in different cities. Figure 4-3 illustrates this intercity check clearing process. It is much like the illustration involving only bank A and B, but there is one additional step.

FIGURE 4–3 *Smith pays Jones, who lives and banks in another city.*

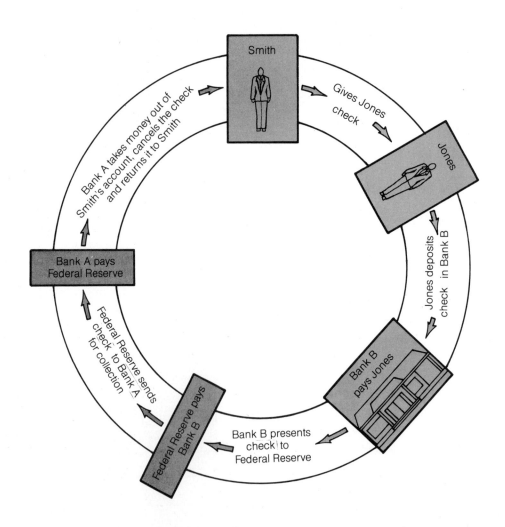

Part 1 / Budgeting, Buying, Borrowing, and Saving

It is often desirable for a married couple to open a joint account. To do this, both individuals must endorse the signature card. A specimen of this type of card is shown in Figure 4-1. Once the account is opened, both persons may write checks or, more precisely, draw against the account.

There are a number of advantages in opening a joint account. The bank regards it as one account; therefore, the service charges are less than they would be if the husband and wife had separate accounts. The most important advantage, however, arises in the event of the death of one of the parties. If the husband has an individual account and the wife has an individual account and the husband dies, then, until the estate of the deceased is probated, the bank will refuse to honor any checks drawn against the husband's account by the man's wife. However, when the husband and wife have a joint account, because of the nature of a joint tenancy with the right of survivorship, title to the fund passes immediately upon death to the survivor. The practical effect is that the wife can draw checks on the joint account after having obtained a release from the tax commission in those states having state inheritance taxes. The release can be arranged by a bank for the survivor within a few days.

The major disadvantage to a joint account is the fact that neither party knows what checks the other has drawn, and the account might be overdrawn. The second disadvantage is that if one of the partners is "flighty," it is not altogether impossible that he or she might clean out the account and take off for places unknown. But this is a personal matter into which we need make no further inquiry.

Certified Checks

Contracts frequently call for payment by certified check. A *certified check* is one signed by the drawer and made payable to the payee in the same way any other check is drawn; however, the drawer takes the check to his or her bank and asks to have it "certified." At this point the cashier or some other employee of the bank takes the check to the bank's bookkeeping department, and right then and there the amount of the check is subtracted from the balance of the drawer's account. The bank employee then stamps the check "certified." The bank is substituting its credit for that of the drawer, so that even if the drawer attempts subsequently to withdraw the amount from the account, he or she cannot. Furthermore, the payee of an uncertified check may have the check certified by requesting that the bank do so. Certified checks are a means of assuring the payee that the check is good in those cases where he or she lacks confidence in the drawer.

Cashier's Checks

A cashier's check is drawn by a bank on its own order to a designated payee or to his or her order. It differs from the certified check in that it is a liability of the bank, not of an individual. A person wishing to buy a cashier's check goes to the bank and pays the face value of the check, which the bank will write on itself. There is an additional small fee for this service. For all practical purposes, the cashier's check serves the same purpose as the certified check. It gives the payee absolute assurance that the check can be converted into cash. However, a cashier's check can be bought from a bank by a nondepositor, whereas certified checks can be obtained only by a depositor.

It should be noted that some banks will sell only cashier's checks and not certified checks. Since these two devices serve the same purpose, many banks do not wish to be bothered with both of them. Figure 4–4 shows a cashier's check.

FIGURE 4–4 *A cashier's check.* (*Source:* Texas Bank of Austin.)

Using a Checking Account

All checks must be written clearly and legibly. The uppermost line on a check is for the date. Immediately below this is a line for the name of the person to whom the check is written and a place to put the dollar amount of the check in figures. Below is a third line to write out the dollar amount of the check in words. The dollar amount expressed in figures and in words must agree. Then the check is signed on the line at the lower righthand corner. The signature there must agree with the signature on the signature card given the bank when the account was opened. For example, a person who sometimes uses the middle initial and sometimes does not will be in trouble. Each check must be signed the same way and precisely as on the signature card. Checks can, of course, be typed, with the exception of the signature. Some checks have another line to the left of the signature. On it can be written for what purpose the check was made out.

Some checks have stubs; some do not. If they do not, records regarding checks must be kept separately. But a person can get checks with stubs. A carefully filled-out stub will provide a record of all checks written. Each check has a number and this same number is on the stub. In addition, the stub has lines for the date, to whom the check was paid, for what purpose, the dollar amount, and the balance remaining in the account. Some people use a transaction register instead of check stubs. This is a little booklet furnished by banks that has space for the same things as the check stub. A sample check and deposit slip are shown in Figure 4-5.

Monthly Bank Statements

Most banks send monthly statements to their depositors indicating the balance at that time. These statements show all deposits and withdrawals during the month, the balance at the beginning and at the end of the month, and the service charges, if any. The cancelled checks are returned at the same time. Although such statements are usually sent toward the end of the month, some banks send them out over several days or even weeks to spread the work of preparing them. These monthly statements can be used by the depositors to reconcile their balance. This requires first an analysis of all checks written but not yet cleared as well as all deposits made but not yet shown.

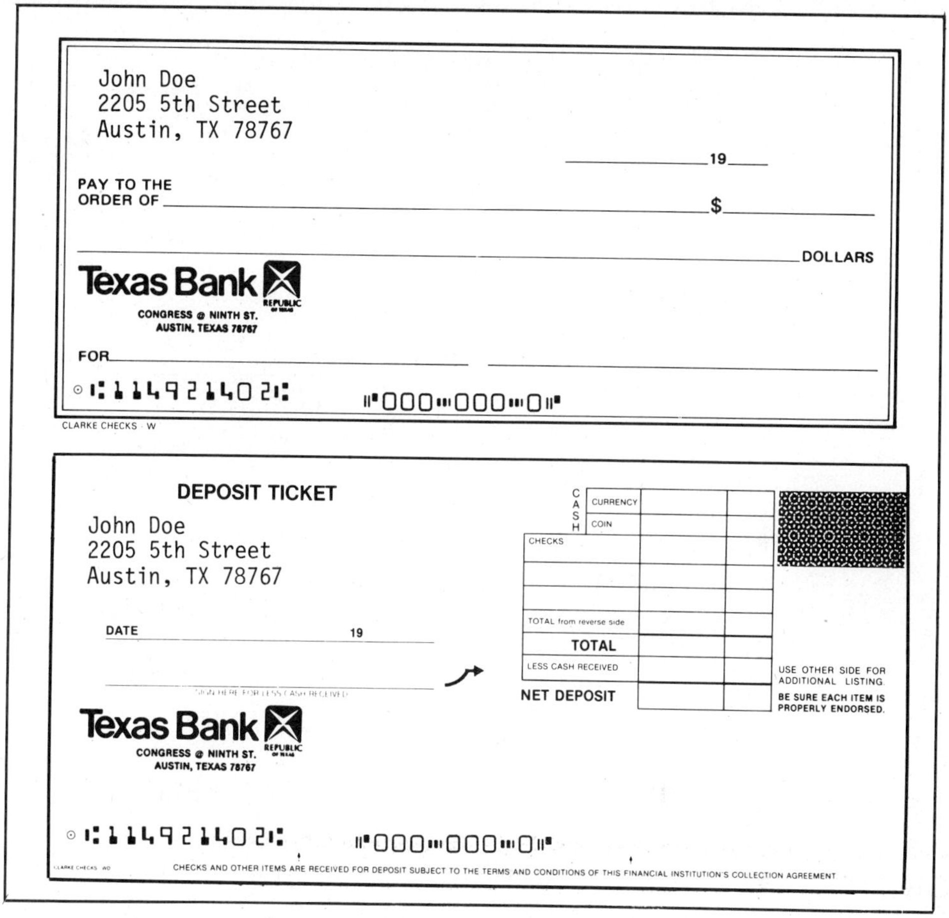

John Doe
2205 5th Street
Austin, TX 78767

19

PAY TO THE
ORDER OF $

DOLLARS

Texas Bank
REPUBLIC
CONGRESS @ NINTH ST.
AUSTIN, TEXAS 78767

FOR

CLARKE CHECKS W

DEPOSIT TICKET

John Doe
2205 5th Street
Austin, TX 78767

DATE 19

CASH CURRENCY
COIN
CHECKS
TOTAL from reverse side
TOTAL
LESS CASH RECEIVED
NET DEPOSIT

USE OTHER SIDE FOR ADDITIONAL LISTING.
BE SURE EACH ITEM IS PROPERLY ENDORSED.

Texas Bank
REPUBLIC
CONGRESS @ NINTH ST.
AUSTIN, TEXAS 78767

CHECKS AND OTHER ITEMS ARE RECEIVED FOR DEPOSIT SUBJECT TO THE TERMS AND CONDITIONS OF THIS FINANCIAL INSTITUTION'S COLLECTION AGREEMENT

FIGURE 4–5 *A check and a deposit slip.* (*Source:* Texas Bank of Austin.)

Reconciliation of Bank Statements

A reconciliation form is often provided on the back of the bank statement. To reconcile a statement, use the following steps. First, enter the ending bank balance that appears on the front of the statement. Next, all checks that have been written but not yet cleared must be added together. Third, subtract this amount from the balance. Fourth, add to the balance any deposits that have been made but do not appear on the statement. This should then be the true balance, which should be reconciled with the checkbook stub balance. To do this, subtract any service charges on the statement from the checkbook stub balance. The check stub balance and the bank statement balance should now agree. If they do not, there has been an error. Go over all calculations again. The cancelled checks should be compared to the check records to make sure the amounts agree. If the bank has made an error (and banks do make errors occasionally), the bank should be notified to correct it. Figure 4-6 is an example of a monthly bank statement.

Texas Bank
REPUBLIC
OF TEXAS

AREA CODE 512   PHONE: 476-6711
P.O. BOX 1328   •   AUSTIN, TEXAS 78767

Statement

ACCOUNT NUMBER		
000-000-0		
2	10 81	DATE

John Doe
2205 5th Street
Austin, TX 78767

IN ACCOUNT WITH

BEGINNING BALANCE	NO. OF CHECKS	TOTAL AMOUNT OF CHECKS PAID	NO OF DEPOSITS	TOTAL AMOUNT OF DEPOSITS	OUT OF TOWN CHECKS DEP	BALANCE FOR SERVICE CHARGE	SERVICE CHARGE
891.09	36	1,531.39	2	918.22		70	5.00

DATE	CHECK	CHECK	DEPOSIT	BALANCE
7-23		BALANCE FORWARD		891.09
7-24	20.00	40.00		
7-24	171.58			659.51
7-25	40.00	160.00		459.51
7-28	8.66	21.00		
7-28	73.73			356.12
7-29	40.00			316.12
7-31	20.00			296.12
8-1	20.00			276.12
8-4	10.11	20.00		
8-4	33.00			213.01
8-5	20.00	40.00		153.01
8-6	40.00			113.01
8-7	40.00			73.01
8-8			469.77	542.78
8-11	58.70			484.08
8-12	6.70	25.00		
8-12	40.00	44.25		368.13
8-14	40.00			328.13
8-18	8.15	13.51		
8-18	50.00			256.47
8-19	4.00	20.00		232.47
8-20	110.00			122.47
8-21	20.00		448.45	550.92
8-25	6.30	8.00		
8-25	40.00	58.70		
8-25	160.00	5.00 SC		272.92

REPUBLIC
OF TEXAS

AT	AUTOMATIC PAYMENT	DM	DEBIT MEMO	LP	LOAN PAYMENT	PR	PAYMENT REVERSAL
BC	BANK CLUB	EC	ERROR CORRECTION	MD	MAIL DEPOSIT	RT	RETURNED CHECK
CR	DEPOSIT OR CREDIT	FC	FINANCE CHARGE	MP	MANUAL PAYMENT	SC	SERVICE CHARGE
DC	DEPOSIT CORRECTION	GA	GENERATED ADVANCE	OD	OVERDRAWN	TR	TRANSFER
DD	DIRECT DEPOSIT						

FIGURE 4–6 *A monthly bank statement.* (*Source:* Texas Bank of Austin.)

Truncation—Coming Soon?

Truncation is a system where cancelled checks are not returned to the drawer with the monthly bank statement. Rather the statement consists of a computer printout which lists each check, its number, the dollar amount, and to whom paid. This statement would serve as proof of payment. The checks would be retained by the bank for a time. Later they would be microfilmed and the actual checks destroyed. Approximately 40,000 checks can be stored on a cassette tape 4 inches in diameter. It is estimated that stopping this avalanche of paper would save financial institutions several billion dollars per year.

A few banks and savings and loan associations (those with NOW accounts which are described below) are experimenting with truncation, and it is being used successfully in a number of European countries. Some experts have expressed concern over whether or not the American people will except truncation. Others point to Europe, and note that truncation will also save the public a good deal of time. Over 30 billion checks are expected to be written this year (1979) and the figure is expected to rise to over 50 billion per year by 1985. With such a volume of paperwork, the public will either have to accept truncation or greatly increased service charges for their checking accounts.

Making Deposits

Deposits can be made in person or by mail. All banks have a special deposit slip bearing the customer's name, address, and account number. It has a spot on which to list all checks (or currency) being deposited. The amount should be totaled on the bottom. The depositor should make out two deposit slips, one for the bank and one that is stamped and returned to the depositor and becomes the receipt until the monthly bank statement is issued.

A word of caution to the mail depositor: currency for deposit should not be sent through the mail and checks should be deposited promptly. If not, death of the drawee may delay collection or the drawer may not have the funds available later for some reason. Finally, there is a time limit; after about six months banks do not have to honor checks.

Overdrafts

Sometimes checks are written for which there are insufficient funds. If the amount is small and the drawer is a good customer of the bank, the check will usually be paid and the drawer notified so he or she can deposit the needed funds. Banks charge a fee for this service ranging from $3 to $5 for each overdraft. If the amount of money involved is relatively large or the drawer is not a valued customer, the bank may refuse to pay the check. In such a case, the check is stamped "insufficient funds" and returned to the payee. Most overdrafts are innocent and come about due to clerical errors; a few are the results of fraud and may involve criminal action.

Endorsing Checks

Checks are transferred from one person to another by means of endorsement. (It might be added here that promissory notes or any other negotiable instrument dealt with in the chapter on shopping for money can be transferred by the same type of endorsements discussed here.) Section 3-202(2) of the Uniform Commercial Code states, "An endorsement must be written by or on behalf of the holder and on the instrument or on a paper so firmly affixed thereto as to become a part thereof." Typically the writing is placed on the back of the instrument. However, if it is clear that the writing is an endorsement, it may be placed anywhere on the instrument or even on a separate piece of paper attached to the instrument.

There are five kinds of endorsements. One of the most common is called an endorsement in blank. The endorser merely signs his or her name on the back of the instrument. This makes the instrument legally payable to the bearer, and if it happens to be a check, anyone can cash it. A thief or a finder of a check endorsed in blank has no legal right to cash the check, but if he or she succeeds in doing so, the person who has endorsed it in blank has no rights against anyone except the person who has unlawfully cashed the check.

Thus the blank endorsement is the name only:

J. J. DeFoe

The special endorsement names the person to whom the instrument is endorsed, for example, "Pay to the order of John Smith" (signed) "J. J. DeFoe." This means that only Smith can endorse the instrument to pass it to someone else or to collect on it. The special endorsement reads as follows:

Pay to the order of John Smith.
J. J. DeFoe

The third kind of endorsement, the restrictive endorsement, prevents further negotiation of the paper. For example, an endorsement stating "Pay to John Smith, only" (signed) "J. J. DeFoe," means exactly that. A better illustration is, "Pay to John Smith, for collection only" (signed) "J. J. DeFoe," or it may read, "For deposit only" (signed) "J. J. DeFoe." When one cashes a check in a supermarket, the clerk immediately stamps the check "For deposit only." One of the reasons for this practice is that if the store is robbed and the checks stolen, there is no financial institution that will cash the check; and if the thief happens to bring the check to the institution carrying the account of the supermarket, the only thing he or she will accomplish is to deposit the check to the market's account. The restrictive endorsement also prevents the finder of a lost check from cashing it. The restrictive endorsement would read as follows:

Pay to the order of John Smith, only.
J. J. DeFoe
or
For deposit only
J. J. DeFoe

The fourth variety, the conditional endorsement, places a condition to the endorsement—for example, "Pay to John Smith after he completes painting my house" (signed) "J. J. DeFoe." Legally the condition is not binding on the person paying the instrument. For example, if the endorsement is on a check and the bank cashes the check before the condition has been complied with, the bank is not liable to DeFoe in the illustration given above. However, Smith would be liable to DeFoe for having violated the condition. It should be noted that the condition makes further negotiation impossible. The conditional endorsement would say the following:

Pay to the order of John Smith when he completes painting my house.
J. J. DeFoe

Finally, a qualified endorsement is an endorsement that limits the liability of the endorser. If a person endorses a promissory note in blank and the maker fails to pay the note when the third party who has legal possession of it demands payment, the original payee is liable. Such a situation would typically arise in this manner: A signs a note promising to pay B. B endorses the note in blank to C. A fails to pay C upon proper demand. C may then collect from B. B as the endorser is said to be secondarily liable on the note. However, it may be that B wishes to limit his or her liability, and in this case, when passing the note to C, B may make a qualified endorsement. This B does by endorsing the note, signing on the back, "Pay to the order of C, without recourse" (signed) "B". The qualified endorsement is illustrated below:

Pay to the order of John Smith without recourse.
J. J. DeFoe

The meaning of this qualified endorsement is that in the event A, the maker, fails to pay C, then B is not liable to C, with the following exceptions:

1. B still guarantees that the instrument is genuine in all respects in what it purports to be.
2. B guarantees that all prior signers have contractual ability.
3. B has good title to the instrument.
4. B guarantees that at the time of the endorsement the instrument was valid.

In practice, the qualified endorsement is generally used by businesspersons, and often is applied to drafts as well as checks. For example, if A purchases a washing machine from B and signs a promissory note in part payment of the machine, B, in order to have cash in hand, may sell the note—or discount the note, as it is said—to a financial institution. If it is endorsed "without recourse," this means that if A fails to pay for the machine, the financial institution cannot go against B. Thus with the qualified endorsement the financial institution is subject to greater risk of loss. The financial institution, therefore, will pay B less for a note with a qualified endorsement than for a note without the qualified endorsement. The reason is obvious; someone must pay for the greater risk.

Stopping Payment on a Check

If for some reason one wishes to stop a check from being collected after it has already been given to someone, one need merely notify the bank upon which it is drawn and the bank will refuse to honor it. There are a number of reasons one might wish to do this. If the check is lost or stolen, a stop order should be given the bank. Or if the check was given for defective merchandise or if some other part of a contract by the payee was not carried out, payment may be stopped.

The bank generally requires that a form be filled out giving the pertinent data regarding the check, such as the date, the check number, the amount of the check, and the payee, in order to put a stop order on a check. Such a stop order is depicted in Figure 4-7.

Some banks have a clause in their stop order relieving them of any liability in the event that they pay a check by mistake that has a stop order on it. In addition, some banks charge a small fee of a few dollars for a stop order. Whether or not a fee is charged usually depends

STOP PAYMENT					

STOP PAYMENT

Texas Bank REPUBLIC OF TEXAS

P. O. BOX 1328 • AUSTIN, TEXAS 78767

FILE COPY

19

Please stop payment on check described below:

CHECK NO.	DATE	AMOUNT	PAYEE	REASON

DUPLICATE CHECK HAS BEEN ISSUED { Yes_____ Ck #_____ Dtd_____ } No_____.

Account No._____

Taken By_____ Dept._____, Time_____

The bank accepts this stop payment order subject to the provisions contained in the Uniform Commercial Code as adopted in Texas. The customer must describe the item with certainty and allow the bank reasonable time to act on the order. This order will automatically become void at the end of six month from date hereof unless renewed in writing.

_____
CUSTOMER'S SIGNATURE

THE BANK ASSUMES NO RESPONSIBILITY IF THE DESCRIPTION OF THE ABOVE CHECK IS INACCURATE OR INCOMPLETE

LITHOPRINT CO., AUSTIN, TEXAS

FIGURE 4–7 *Sample stop payment order form.* (*Source:* Texas Bank of Austin.)

upon how many stop orders a bank has. Many small town banks, where few stop orders are issued, do not charge a fee for this service.

With today's computerized operations, a stopped check is seldom paid due to error. The computer can read both the account number and the dollar amount of the check, which is stamped next to the account number, and it will be programmed to kick out the stopped check. In addition, all tellers are notified that this account has a stop order in it. They scrutinize all checks from that account that are presented for payment at the window. Some banks will even take stop orders over the phone; they only ask that some reasonable time be allowed after the order is given for the bank to program the computer and notify all the tellers.

Drive-In Banking

Most banks have drive-up windows where deposits and withdrawals may be made from within a car as a convenience to the bank's customers. Often these drive-in windows are open later than the regular banking hours. This permits people to meet most of their banking needs on their way home from work. However, a loan cannot be negotiated at a drive-in window; for this a trip to the bank and a meeting with the loan officer is required.

Automated Teller

In recent years, some banks have installed a fully automated twenty-four-hour-a-day teller. It is a machine that will accept deposits or allow withdrawals. One of the more widely used is the "Docutel System," which works with the use of a special mastercharge card. This special card has a magnetic strip on the back on which the customer's bank account number has been placed. The card is placed into a slot, and the machine is activated by three different numbers: the mastercharge number, the customer's bank account number (both on the card), and a special six-digit number that must be punched on a keyboard. The amount of money to be withdrawn (or deposited) is then punched on a panel and the automated teller carries out the transaction. The special six-digit number is a safeguard. If it is given incorrectly, the machine tells the customer to try again. But if the number is given incorrectly three times, the machine keeps the card. The machine can also be programmed to keep lost or stolen cards. These automated tellers are placed outside of the regular bank building and are accessible at all times.

Deposit Safety

What would happen to a depositor's money if a bank should fail? In nearly all cases depositors are protected against such possibilities. The Federal Deposit Insurance Corporation (FDIC), a federal agency, insures deposits up to $100,000 against such loss. All banks in the United States are eligible for FDIC membership.

Of the approximately fourteen thousand banks in the country, all but about four hundred and fifty of the very smallest ones are members. Banks that are members have metal signs indicating this displayed in prominent places or near the tellers' counters. If an insured bank should fail, depositors would get their money back from an agency of the U.S. government. Even if a bank is robbed or burns down, depositors do not lose their money because banks carry private insurance against losses from such risks.

OTHER SERVICES BANKS PROVIDE

There are a number of other services provided by commercial banks with which you should be familiar.[1] They are (1) accepting savings accounts, (2) accepting NOW accounts, (3) providing safety deposit boxes, (4) providing trustee services, which will be discussed in greater detail in chapter 18, (5) nighttime depository lock box, and (6) automatic funds transfer. Each of these will now be examined briefly.

Savings Accounts

Although savings deposits in banks are discussed in greater detail in chapter 7, on thrift institutions, a note is in order at this point. Savings accounts are not as liquid as checking accounts and consist, in general, of funds that can be invested by the banks for the long run.[2] For this reason, banks pay interest on savings deposits rather than charge service fees, as in the case of checking accounts. Savings accounts are also sometimes called time deposits because they cannot be withdrawn by the depositor without prior notice. Technically, notice of thirty days must be given to the bank before the passbook savings funds can be withdrawn. This requirement is nearly always waived by the bank and in fact savings deposits are highly liquid. Recall that earlier we referred to checking account deposits as "demand deposits." Checks cannot be written on savings accounts. In order to make a withdrawal it is

---

1. Loans are not included in this discussion. Banks make all kinds of loans, and they are discussed in the chapter on the role of consumer credit (ch. 5)

2. Liquidity is a relative term, but it refers to how close something is to money; that is, how easily and quickly it can be converted to money. While anything of value can be sold and converted into money, some things can be converted more quickly and easily than others, hence they are more liquid. Money itself is the most liquid commodity of all.

sometimes necessary to make a trip to the bank, although most banks provide for both deposits and withdrawals by mail and even by telephone.

The NOW Account

A NOW account (Negotiated Order of Withdrawal) is another innovative banking service; it is a specialized checking account that bears interest. Some banks have referred to it as a specialized savings account on which checks can be written. In any event, it has some of the attributes of each. It is different from most checking accounts since there are generally no service charges per item. It pays interest at the passbook rate. Some banks, however, require a minimum balance to avoid service charges. Originally, the NOW account was authorized in 1972 only for mutual savings banks in Massachusetts and New Hampshire. In March, 1980 a federal law was passed which makes them legal in all depository institutions throughout the United States.

Automatic Funds Transfer (AFT)

In 1978 the Federal Reserve authorized all national banks to transfer funds automatically from passbook savings accounts to checking accounts. Since then, some states have also permitted state banks to provide this service for their customers. In essence this permits a person to hold the bulk of his or her money in a savings account, where it will earn interest, and minimize the amount of money in a non-interest-bearing checking account. Then as checks are written and come into the bank for clearing, the needed funds are transferred into the checking account by computer.

An agreement is made with the bank that the checking account is not to fall below a certain minimum. This minimum will vary according to the desires and needs of the customer, and some banks permit it to be zero. Then when checks come in which reduce the checking account below the minimum, funds are transferred. Some banks will also provide two-way transfers. That is, if your checking account climbs above the minimum (which may be zero), the computer transfers funds from it to your savings account.

The banks charge varying fees for these services. Some charge a few dollars a month, others charge $.50 or $1 for every day a transfer is made (but not per transfer); others use some combination of the two. Some banks also provide the entire AFT service free of charge if a certain minimum (often $5,000) is kept in the passbook savings account. Some also assess no service charge on the checking account if it never falls below say $300. In these banks if your savings account never falls below $5,000 and your checking account never falls below $300, you could get all of these services free of charge. The AFT system then provides overdraft protection, and is also a means of keeping most of your deposits in interest-bearing accounts.

One word of warning: if you have an AFT system, your bank statement may be more difficult to reconcile. This is because most banks send a monthly statement in the case of the checking account, but only a quarterly statement in the case of the savings account.

Automatic (Computer Assisted) Payment of Bills

In those cases where you have a regular monthly bill of a uniform size (like a mortgage or rent payment) you may authorize the payee to write a draft on your checking account on a certain day. All you need do is sign a card, and the bank will honor the draft and send a receipt to you indicating the bill has been paid.

More recently some banks and savings and loan associations have gone one step further and have developed computer-assisted check writing and bill payment systems. Sometimes these are also tied in with the automatic funds transfer system discussed above, and hence most of your funds can be kept in an interest-bearing savings account until your bills are due. These systems work as follows: You must furnish the financial institution with the names and addresses of all vendors whose bills you want them to pay. Each of these vendors is then given a number by the institution. You are given a secret code number which in addition to your account number enables you, but no one else, to talk to the bank's computer, if you have a 12-key touch tone phone. All you do is call a special number, punch in your secret code number, your account number, the vendor's number, and the amount of money to be paid. The computer writes a check, your account is charged, and the check is mailed for you. Often you may do this 24 hours a day. If you have an old-fashioned telephone you must call the personnel at the bank and they will punch the data into the computer for you. Often the fee for this is less ($.10-$.12 per check) than the postage required to send the check. The institution can still make money because their postage costs are small; they send one check (with one $.15 stamp) to pay hundreds and even thousands of people's bills to certain vendors, like the various credit card issuers, utilities, local governments, and the like.

Safety Deposit Box

Safety deposit boxes are heavy steel boxes inside a special walk-in vault. The vault door is, of course, locked when the bank is closed. Inside the walk-in vault are individual boxes, each with its own separate lock, that may be rented by the bank's customers. These boxes come in several sizes, and rental fees vary with the size and range from about five dollars to about sixty dollars per year. Each customer has a key to the box he or she rents and the bank has a second key; both are needed to open the box. The safety deposit boxes are protected by alarms, heavy metal, and are fireproof insofar as possible. All valuables that could be lost by fire or burglary and that are compact should be kept in a safety deposit box. Certainly this would include such things as stock certificates, bonds, wills, insurance policies, and savings account passbooks. One must be careful where one keeps the key, however; for if it is lost, the box must be opened by drilling through the lock because no other key exists. These boxes should be in the joint name of the husband and wife so that if one dies, the other can enter the box. Otherwise it is sealed until the estate is probated.

Trustee Services

Commercial banks are authorized by law to perform the role of a trustee. This involves managing the assets of someone else. Sometimes a will of a deceased person will set up an estate for the heirs. The trust department of a bank can manage the estate. The bank will look after the financial affairs of a minor. Large banks have well-established trust departments that invest billions of dollars of other people's money. If you need trustee service, go to a large bank. This is a highly specialized service and only large banks are able to do a truly fine job in providing it. The trustee service is discussed in greater detail in Chapter 18.

Nighttime Depository Lock

Most banks also have a nighttime depository lock box. These are built into the wall of the bank. The box can be used from outside the building. A special key opens the door. These are used primarily by business firms that may make deposits after banking hours.

These boxes are not needed if the bank has a fully automated teller, which was discussed above, unless the deposits are too bulky to fit into a legal-size envelope.

DEPOSITORY INSTITUTIONS DEREGULATIONS ACT OF 1980

In March 1980 a federal act (Public Law 96-221) was signed into law by the president. Its provisions go into effect at various times in the future. Its main impact, however, will be to eliminate many of the current differences between commercial banks and other depository institutions. Generally speaking the act provided for the following:

1. Authority for all depository institutions throughout the U.S. to establish NOW accounts for their individual (but not corporate) customers.
2. The automatic transfer of funds from savings to checking accounts.
3. Permit depositor institutions to provide for overdraft protection. That is, an automatic loan would be granted if a check were written in excess of the amount of funds a depositor had in his or her account.
4. Increased insurance on deposits from $40,000 to $100,000.
5. Permit federal savings and loan associations to make consumer loans.
6. Authority for federal savings and loan associations to issue credit cards.
7. Federal savings and loan associations to exercise trust and fiduciary powers.
8. Authority for mutual savings banks to make some commercial loans and to provide checking accounts for these corporate customers.
9. Preempted state usury laws on mortgage loans made by financial institutions. However, the federal law does provide that the various states have until April 1, 1983, to reimpose their ceilings.
10. The phasing out over the next 9 years of the legal ceilings on the interest rate that financial institutions pay on all savings deposits.

Some of the above provisions had been granted piecemeal before in some or all states. The 1980 act provided for more uniform treatment of all institutions throughout the United States. Some observers believe that as time passes the new NOW account will replace both the checking account and the passbook savings account. This is unlikely. First of all the NOW account is not for everybody. The service charges and/or minimum balances may be such that some people will not find them useful. They will continue to need regular checking accounts. Also with the elimination of regulation Q and the freeing of interest rates on savings deposits, the interest which will be paid on NOW accounts may very well turn out to be somewhat lower than on all other interest bearing accounts. The 1980 act will, however, as noted above, lessen the differences among the various depository institutions and in so doing increase competition in the industry.

MONEY ORDERS AND TRAVELER'S CHECKS

Although in terms of dollar volume these instruments rank low compared with checks, they should be mentioned briefly because some disbursements are made in this way. Money orders are a means of transmitting funds and serve much the same function as checks. There are three parties to the money order: the payer, who buys the money order; the payee, who receives it; and the drawee, who is the institution ordered to make the payment. One such institution is the U.S. Post Office. Postal money orders, which are purchased for a small fee from any United States Post Office, permit only one endorsement and are collected by presentation at either a post office or a commercial bank. Although postal money orders are very safe, they are not as convenient to use in paying bills as checks because they require a trip to the post office.

The express money order is issued by the American Express Company, a private corporation. Generally referred to as traveler's checks, they are issued much in the same manner as postal money orders; the basic difference between the two is the fact that the express money order can pass from hand to hand by continuous endorsement. Traveler's checks are sold by many commercial banks, most travel agencies, and at the offices of the American Express Company, which can be found in any large city. They come in denominations of $10; $20; $50; $100; and $500. The fee charged is $1 per $100 of checks purchased. They are often used by people who travel, since they are universally known and accepted almost everywhere just like money itself. They are, however, safer than money because they must be endorsed before they can be exchanged. If they are lost or stolen, American Express will replace them. The checks are numbered and the buyer should make a separate copy of these numbers since they will be needed if a lost or stolen claim is to be filed.

The American Express Company has offices in most foreign countries and their checks are widely accepted abroad. In recent years a number of competitors (mostly large city banks) have entered this field. The Bank of America now has its own negotiable and nearly universally accepted money order. The First National City Bank of New York and a number of other large city banks now also provide this service. These traveler's checks are sold to the public nationally by banks and travel agencies having ties to the issuing banks. The purchase and use conditions of the American Express traveler's checks apply to these competitors' checks.

QUESTIONS FOR REVIEW

1. How do you go about opening a checking account? What are service charges?

2. How do banks clear checks?

3. What are the advantages of a joint checking account between husband and wife?

4. How does a certified check differ from a cashier's check?

5. What is likely to happen if your account has insufficient funds to clear a check?

6. Explain the five different kinds of endorsements found mainly on checks.

7. How do you stop payment on a check?

8. Explain the value of a safety deposit box.

9. Explain the NOW account.

10. How does the automatic funds transfer work?

11. How does an express money order differ from a postal money order?

CASES

1. Bill and Betty Davis are newly married and up to now have been paying their bills in cash. They feel now, however, that the convenience of a checking account is worthwhile. They believe that they will write on the average about fifteen checks per month and that their account, although modest, will not fall below the bank's minimum requirements.

They are uncertain whether to open a regular or a special checking account but do want to minimize the service charges. Can you advise them?

2. Jim and Jill Gorden are a young couple who have recently moved to town. They have decided to open a checking account but are undecided whether they should open a joint account or whether each should have a separate account. Can you outline the advantages and disadvantages of each?

3. Wilfred and Dorothea Brown have just moved to Omaha, Nebraska, and their furniture is due tomorrow. The truck driver has phoned them explaining he will have to be paid $510 before he can unload it and that an ordinary check will not do. He has agreed, however, to accept either a cashier's check or a certified check. What is the difference between an ordinary check, a cashier's check, and a certified check?

4. Alfred White works in a supermarket and one of his duties is to deposit the numerous checks

in the bank handling the store's account. He notices that they are all stamped on the back "For deposit only." The bank clerk told him this was a restrictive endorsement and prevented someone else from cashing the check if it were lost. Can you explain the various other types of endorsements?

5. Rebecca Ann Wagoner has both a savings account and a checking account at the First National Bank, and transfers funds from one to the other as needed. She would like to minimize her checking account balance and maximize her savings deposit balance so as to maximize her interest yield. Recently she learned about the NOW account which has been described as both an interest-bearing checking account and a savings account on which checks can be written. Ann is a bit confused. Could you explain the difference between a savings account, a checking account, and a NOW account?

SUGGESTED READINGS

Bankers Magazine. Boston: Warren, Gorham and Lamont, Inc., Publishers. This journal is published every other month.

Baryman, Sol. *Everyday Credit Checking; A Practical Guide.* New York: Crowell, in Association with the National Association of Credit Management, 1973.

Electronic Fund Transfer and the Public Interest. A Report of the National Commission on Electronic Fund Transfers. Superintendent of Documents, U.S. Government Printing Office, Washington, D.C., February, 1977.

The Electronic Fund Transfer Commission and Finance Companies: Report of the NCFA Task Force. National Consumer Finance Association, 1978.

"Electronic Money . . . and the Payments Mechanism." Boston, MA: Federal Reserve Bank of Boston, 1973.

"Finance Facts Yearbook." Published annually by Research Services Division, National Consumer Finance Association, Washington, D.C.

Gup, Benton E. *Financial Intermediaries,* 2nd ed. Boston: Houghton Mifflin Company, 1980.

Hutchinson, Harry D. *Money, Banking, and the U.S. Economy.* Englewood Cliffs, N.J.: Prentice-Hall, 1980.

Journal of Bank Research. Published quarterly by the Bank Administration Institute, 303 South Northwest Highway, Park Ridge, IL.

Money and Credit Management Education: A Descriptive Catalogue of Educational Materials for the Classroom Teacher or Counselor 1972-73. Washington, D.C.: National Consumer Finance Association, 1977.

Money and Your Marriage. Educational Services Division, National Consumer Finance Association. Washington, D.C. 1977.

Nelson, Paula. *The Joy of Money.* New York: Bantam Books, 1977.

Wyatt, John W., and Wyatt, Madie B. *Business Law,* 4th ed. New York: McGraw-Hill, 1979.

Chapter Five

The Role of Consumer Credit

Ah take the cash and let the credit go.
OMAR KHAYYAM, THE RUBAIYAT

The objectives of this chapter are to

1　Explain the types of consumer credit

2　Throw some light on why consumers borrow

3　Point out the benefits and dangers of consumer credit

4　Show how the dollar amount and the percentage rate of interest paid on consumer credit can be calculated

5　Point out where to go to obtain consumer credit

6　Introduce a number of other things you should know about consumer credit

Why do people buy on the installment plan? It would be cheaper to pay cash for all items because interest and service charges would be eliminated. The same is true when you borrow money at a bank in order to buy an expensive item. The interest cost makes it more expensive. Why is it then that most people do not save enough money through a budget to pay cash for large items like cars or household furniture? There are at least two reasons: First, they are impatient. The money for a car would probably take several years to save and they want the car now. The second reason has to do with the discipline to save. Some people, even if they had a budget, would never be able to save enough to pay cash for a car. So they go into debt, buy the car, and then engage in a negative form of savings when liquidating the debt.

To be sure, some people's income is so high that they can easily pay cash for any purchase. This group borrows little money. At the other extreme are the very low income groups who are unable to borrow much money because their credit rating is such that lenders are hesitant to lend to them. The great bulk of consumer credit, as it is called, is extended to the middle class, those whose incomes are high enough to give them a good credit rating and enable them to borrow but too low to pay cash.

THE CLASSIFICATION OF CONSUMER CREDIT

Consumer credit, as the term implies, is credit extended to individuals for the purchase of final consumer items. Consumer credit is sometimes classified into *sales credit* and *loan credit*. *Sales credit* is extended by a merchant, and the person gets goods and promises to pay later. *Loan credit* is extended by a financial institution, and the person gets money (credit) with which to buy something and must then repay the loan.

A second classification is perhaps superior; it is used by the Federal Reserve Board and consists of (1) installment credit and (2) noninstallment credit.

Installment Credit

Installment credit consists of all credit extended to individuals which is to be repaid in two or more installments. It in turn can be broken down into the type of product that it finances. Such as:

1. Automobile Loans
2. Revolving Charge Accounts
3. Mobile Homes
4. Other

Credit extended for the purchase of autos is the largest single category. Most automobiles sold in the United States are financed through the use of installment credit. Revolving consumer credit is that which is extended through the use of credit cards. Only a portion of the balance need be paid every month and it finances a wide variety of goods such as gasoline, clothing, and some household items.

Credit extended for the purchase of mobile homes is self-explanatory. Most of this credit is extended by commercial banks and finance companies, but in some states savings and loan associations also make it available.

Other consumer credit finances all other durable goods such as TV sets, all household appliances, home improvements, and many other items. It also includes personal loans which may be made to individuals to purchase a wide variety of other goods and services, even a vacation. The following table shows these classifications, the dollar amounts, and the institutions that extended the credit, over the past few years.

Noninstallment Credit

Noninstallment credit consists primarily of single repayment loans and service credit. It also, however, consists of those few remaining old-fashioned charge accounts in which the entire sum charged was due and payable at the end of each month (there are very few of these left in the U.S. today).

Single Repayment Loans

Many upper income and even upper middle income groups are able to borrow money to purchase durable consumer goods on their personal signature. They may, for example, borrow several thousand dollars to buy home household furniture, and then repay the entire amount in one lump sum, say six months later, together with the interest. They will have to do their own budgeting in the meantime and set aside a portion of the loan each month in order to have the wherewithal to liquidate the loan when it comes due.

TABLE 5–1. *Consumer installment credit total outstanding (millions of dollars)*

HOLDER, AND TYPE OF CREDIT	1977	1978	1979	1979		1980				
				NOV.	DEC.	JAN.	FEB.	MAR.	APR.	MAY
				Amounts outstanding (end of period)						
1 Total	230,829	275,629	311,122	307,641	311,122	308,984	308,190	307,621	306,131	303,759
By major holder										
2 Commercial banks	112,373	136,189	149,604	149,057	149,604	148,868	148,249	147,315	145,405	143,174
3 Finance companies	44,868	54,298	68,318	67,164	68,318	68,724	69,545	70,421	71,545	72,101
4 Credit unions	37,605	45,939	48,186	48,673	48,186	47,270	46,707	46,521	45,731	44,907
5 Retailers[2]	23,490	24,876	27,916	25,732	27,916	26,985	26,309	25,841	25,746	25,792
6 Savings and loans	7,354	8,394	10,361	10,241	10,361	10,320	10,543	10,755	10,887	10,930
7 Gasoline companies	2,963	3,240	4,316	4,281	4,316	4,433	4,467	4,421	4,503	4,581
8 Mutual savings banks	2,176	2,693	2,421	2,493	2,421	2,384	2,370	2,347	2,314	2,274
By major type of credit										
9 Automobile	82,911	102,468	115,022	115,121	115,022	114,761	115,007	115,281	115,014	114,318
10 Commercial banks	49,577	60,564	65,229	65,646	65,229	64,824	64,544	64,047	62,978	61,928
11 Indirect paper	27,379	33,850	37,209	37,334	37,209	37,020	36,949	36,821	36,325	35,791
12 Direct loans	22,198	26,714	28,020	28,312	28,020	27,804	27,595	27,226	26,653	26,137
13 Credit unions	18,099	21,967	23,042	23,275	23,042	22,604	22,335	22,246	21,868	21,474
14 Finance companies	15,235	19,937	26,751	26,200	26,751	27,333	28,128	28,988	30,168	30,916
15 Revolving	39,274	47,051	55,330	52,060	55,330	54,420	53,522	52,662	52,217	51,823
16 Commercial banks	18,374	24,434	28,954	27,827	28,954	28,841	28,575	28,241	27,889	27,456
17 Retailers	17,937	19,377	22,060	19,952	22,060	21,146	20,480	20,000	19,825	19,786
18 Gasoline companies	2,963	3,240	4,316	4,281	4,316	4,433	4,467	4,421	4,503	4,581
19 Mobile home	15,141	16,042	17,409	17,349	17,409	17,387	17,476	17,596	17,668	17,642
20 Commercial banks	9,124	9,553	9,991	10,036	9,991	9,968	9,974	9,978	9,965	9,927
21 Finance companies	3,077	3,152	3,390	3,321	3,390	3,415	3,428	3,475	3,523	3,529
22 Savings and loans	2,538	2,848	3,516	3,475	3,516	3,502	3,578	3,650	3,694	3,709
23 Credit unions	402	489	512	517	512	502	496	494	486	477
24 Other	93,503	110,068	123,361	123,111	123,361	122,416	122,185	122,082	121,232	119,976
25 Commercial banks	35,298	41,638	45,430	45,548	45,430	45,235	45,156	45,049	44,573	43,863
26 Finance companies	26,556	31,209	38,177	37,643	38,177	37,976	37,989	37,958	37,854	37,656
27 Credit unions	19,104	23,483	24,632	24,881	24,632	24,164	23,876	23,781	23,377	22,956
28 Retailers	5,553	5,499	5,856	5,780	5,856	5,839	5,829	5,841	5,921	6,006
29 Savings and loans	4,816	5,546	6,845	6,766	6,845	6,818	6,965	7,106	7,193	7,221
30 Mutual savings banks	2,176	2,693	2,421	2,493	2,421	2,384	2,370	2,347	2,314	2,274

Note. Total consumer noninstallment credit outstanding—credit scheduled to be repaid in a lump sum, including single-payment loans, charge accounts, and service credit—amounted to $70.9 billion at the end of 1979, $64.7 billion at the end of 1978, $58.6 billion at the end of 1977, and $55.4 billion at the end of 1976. The Board's series cover most short- and intermediate-term credit extended to individuals through regular business channels, usually to finance the purchase of consumer goods and services or to refinance debts incurred for such purposes, and scheduled to be repaid (or with the option of repayment) in two or more installments.

Source: Federal Reserve Bulletin, July 1980, Board of Governors of the Federal Reserve System, p. A42.

Service Credit

Service credit is that which is extended by professional practitioners and some establishments such as hospitals. Because of the growing use of medical insurance this type of credit is not as important as it once was, but it includes unpaid medical and dental bills, monies owed to hospitals or to the accountant who prepared your tax returns, and that unpaid bill of the plumber who unstopped your sink last week. The amounts owed to utilities after deducting deposits are also part of the statistics of service credit. The figure below shows how consumer installment debt (as well as that repaid) has risen over the last few years.

WHY CONSUMERS BORROW

Consumers borrow or use consumer credit for different reasons just as savers save for different reasons. One individual may save to pay her son's tuition, while another may have to borrow to pay the tuition. Some people pay cash while on vacation; others use credit cards.

High Cost of Durables

A main reason for the use of consumer credit is the high unit cost of durable consumer goods. A *consumer durable* is a durable good having a relatively long life, such as a TV set, household appliances of all kinds, or an automobile. Of the $308 billion consumer debt in March 1980, about $115 billion or approximately 37 percent resulted from the extension of automobile credit. The cheapest and possibly the best way to buy this type of durable good would, of course, be to save and pay cash. But to save, one must abstain from present consumption. However willing the spirit may be, for most of us unfortunately (when it comes to saving) the flesh is weak. Suppose, for example, that we planned to save to buy an auto priced at $7,500; we would have to defer the use of the car and put aside, say, $1,500 per year for five years before we would be able to buy the car. For most of us, saving $1,500 per year for five years for the purpose of buying a car appears a formidable task. Indeed, it is. Once we have part of it saved, as the economists say, our consumption function tilts. This is another way of saying that most of us tend to increase our cash-consumption expenditures if we feel we have a reserve to fall back on. Finally, we find that we are not saving, but are even tapping the funds we have already saved. So we find that when it comes to high unit cost durable goods, most of us buy on time. We are able to use the product immediately instead of having to defer its use until a future date and perhaps not get it at all. For this current use we are willing to pay interest and carrying charges.

Financial Emergencies

Unfortunately, many of us frequently are forced to borrow because of unforeseen emergencies. An individual rushed to the hospital for an appendectomy may have to borrow to pay the surgical bill. A second-guesser might add that it serves the person right for not having the proper hospitalization insurance; but second-guessing is beside the point and the fact still remains that many people are unable to cope with such a situation without a consumer loan. The student should be able to think of dozens of types of emergencies and other reasons for which consumer loans may be necessary.

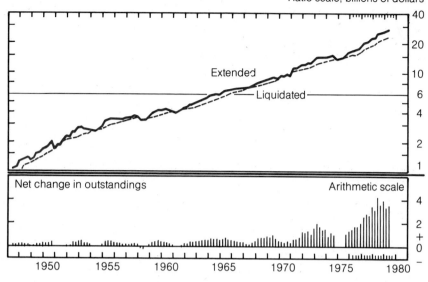

Ratio scale, billions of dollars

FIGURE 5-1. *Total consumer installment credit; seasonally adjusted, quarterly averages. (Source: 1979 Historical Chart Book,* Board of Governors of the Federal Reserve System, p. 65.)

Convenient Form of Payment

Another reason, which from the economist's viewpoint may not be a very good reason for consumer credit, is that it constitutes a convenient and easy method of paying for goods. A dollar down and a dollar a week appears very attractive to many. The terms appear easy enough, and the individual may enjoy consuming the good at the present time. The same is true of the use of credit cards. Charging things and then later paying one bill is more convenient than writing a separate check for each item.

Travel and Vacation

Many people finance their vacations with consumer credit. Not only do they make extensive use of credit cards while on their trips, but often they borrow money at a financial institution to spend at their destination and to finance their transportation costs. This is a growing segment of consumer credit. Ten or fifteen years ago very little consumer credit was used to finance vacations other than through credit cards. Now it is quite common.

BENEFITS AND DANGERS OF CONSUMER CREDIT

There are essentially three groups who are benefited by the extension of consumer credit. These are the savers (who are also the lenders); the borrowers; and society as a whole. There are, of course, dangers as well; and these will be dealt with later.

The Savers

The accumulations of many individual savers make up total national savings. In 1980, for example, total personal income amounted to about $2,000 billion. After taxes and consumption expenditure, there remained a residual of about $84 billion in personal savings.

These thrifty individuals make their money available for borrowers. These savers (lenders) receive the benefit of interest on their loans and thus derive additional income. In short, if it were not for borrowers, the savers would have no place in which to invest their savings and add to them through additional interest income. It is the borrowers who keep the savings institutions in business and keep money out of old socks and mattresses.

Not all individuals borrow to purchase final consumer goods. Business firms borrow an even larger amount than do consumers—they borrow to expand their business. In this way they bring about economic growth. Nevertheless, individual consumers make up an important part of total borrowings, which in turn must be large enough to provide an outlet for total savings.

The Borrowers

Consumer credit will enable the borrowers to consume certain items more quickly than otherwise would be the case. If you go into debt to buy an automobile, you are then forced to save out of future income to repay the loan. Without consumer credit you might end up with neither savings nor the car. With consumer credit you at least have the car.

Society as a Whole

Society as a whole may benefit from consumer credit provided that those granting it do not overdo it. Credit extension may lead to increased demand and hence increased production of goods and services, helping to maintain full employment. It may also be argued that the extension of consumer credit can lead to a lower unit cost of goods. For example, as a result of increased effective demand created by the extension of credit, certain firms are led to large-scale production. To a point, large-scale production brings about certain efficiencies that result in lower costs, and in a competitive economy these savings are frequently passed on to the consumer.

Economic Instability

One of the dangers of consumer credit is economic instability. Some years ago when the Federal Reserve Board concluded and published a monumental study on consumer credit, some controversial questions were left unanswered. One was whether the granting of consumer credit contributed to economic instability. Some economists feel that if the economy is operating at or near capacity, consumer credit must take something away from investment spending or consumer spending on nondurable consumer goods, thus perhaps contributing to economic instability and to a lower rate of economic growth.

Some economists also feel that overextension of credit has lead to inflation, extravagance, and general lack of prudence. Consumer credit increases the demand for goods and services. If this demand is sufficiently strong, it can pull up prices. The demand on the part of individual consumers is by far the largest in our economy. It is really this consumer demand plus business demand for investment expenditures on new plant and equipment plus government demand (expenditures) that together may be excessive and cause inflation. Since consumer demand is the largest of these three, however, it is often singled out for special treatment.

Higher Cost of Goods and Services

One argument against extension of consumer credit is that the resultant interest costs actually reduce the amount of consumer goods that persons might have purchased had they saved the money in the first place. As has been previously pointed out, however, it may be that the cost of borrowing is offset because credit extension increases sales and consequently has a tendency to lower unit costs as a result of mass production. This depends to some extent on the amount of competition involving a particular product and on whether or not any cost savings are actually passed on to the consumer in the form of lower prices.

Getting in Over Your Head

When you borrow money, you take on an obligation of making a fixed payment on a time schedule. This payment is interest and repayment of the principal. I already noted that such a fixed payment comes off the top of the budget before allocating income among alternative wants. How large a fixed payment an individual can accept is determined largely by his or her income. But if credit is easy to obtain and a person lacks discipline, it is possible that he or she will have so many debts that it becomes impossible to meet the fixed monthly payments because they take too large a portion of income. Those who miss a payment or two may have their car or furniture repossessed. Worse still, they may be forced into bankruptcy. This is not really a danger of consumer credit but rather a danger that comes from *abusing* consumer credit. It is the unwise and excessive use of consumer credit that gets people in over their heads. Frequently, this may be just as much the lender's fault as the borrower's. Do not be afraid of consumer credit. Use it when needed, but only wisely and after careful planning. Use it only if you are sure you can take on the additional fixed payment required. This is one of the reasons for a budget, which was discussed in an earlier chapter. A budget can help you avoid getting "in over your head."

HOW MUCH DO YOU PAY?

When one borrows money or buys something on the installment plan, it is wise to take time and shop around. One should not buy the first item one sees from the first dealer one visits. Instead, visit several dealers who are selling the item and compare prices. Or if borrowing money from a lending institution, do not agree to the first terms that are offered but rather visit a number of lending institutions and compare their interest rates and the other terms of the loan. Remember that the item to be purchased or the money to be borrowed will still be there tomorrow. Do not be stampeded into a quick deal.

It is often less costly for consumers to purchase those items of merchandise they need for cash; however, for most of us, installment purchases or cash borrowing are often the alternatives. The difficulty most consumers have when they wish to borrow money is that they are suddenly overcome by a strong sense of inferiority. The first tendency is to feel that the loan will not be granted, and the second—because they frequently need the loan badly—to feel that they must take the first offer that comes along. Individuals would benefit if they would adopt the attitude that money is a commodity like beans and that financial institutions are in business much as are grocery or department stores, so that they often compete with each other in terms of cost. In short, the careful shopper can go from institution to institution and sometimes come up with a bargain.

Interest Rate Calculations

One of the fundamental problems of borrowing is to determine just how much interest is being charged. The borrower should be able to answer the question: What is the effective rate of interest that I must pay? or What is the real cost in terms of the percentage of interest charged?

Although the mathematics of obtaining a precise answer to "How much interest am I paying?" is complex, here is an adequate approximation formula

$$R = \frac{2 \times m \times I}{P(n+1)} \text{ or, transposed, } I = \frac{R \times P(n+1)}{2 \times m}$$

In the above formula:

R = annual simple interest rate in decimal form
I = dollar cost of the credit
m = the number of payment periods in a year (twelve if paying monthly and fifty-two if weekly)
n = the number of payments scheduled in total
P = the net amount of credit or principal advanced

Basically, the individual will be involved in what is called either a "discount" loan or an "add-on" transaction, the latter applying if goods are being purchased on the installment plan. A discounted loan is one in which the interest is taken out in advance. For example, if you borrow $1,000 discounted at 10 percent, the lender takes $100 out in advance, lends you $900, and you repay $1,000.

Suppose in the first instance that Ms. Stein applies for a loan of $100. She is told that the discount charge is $6 and that there is an additional service fee of $2. She is to repay $100 over a one-year period by twelve monthly installments. The total cost is $8; actually she will be receiving $92, but she must pay back $100. Substituting these figures in the formula above:

$$
\begin{aligned}
I &= \$\ 8 \\
m &= \ 12 \\
n &= \ 12 \\
P &= \$92
\end{aligned}
$$

Thus:

$$R = \frac{2 \times 12 \times \$8}{\$92 \times (12+1)} = 0.1605 = 16.05 \text{ percent}$$

Suppose Mr. Muller is buying something on the installment plan that costs $100, that $6 interest is added, and that he is to pay this sum in twelve equal installments for a total of $106. What is his rate of interest? Again using the above formula:

$$
\begin{aligned}
I &= \$\ 6 \\
m &= \ 12 \\
n &= \ 12 \\
P &= \$100
\end{aligned}
$$

Part 1 / Budgeting, Buying, Borrowing, and Saving

Thus:

$$R = \frac{2 \times 12 \times \$6}{\$100 \times (12 + 1)} = 11 \text{ percent}$$

One reason interest rates are higher on consumer loans than on other loans is that usually one is required to pay interest on the original balance throughout the entire period of the loan. Any time loans are repaid on the installment basis, the amount of money actually owed declines with each repayment. In order to calculate the true interest rate, one must take into account this declining balance; otherwise the borrower is paying interest on money even after he/she has already repaid it.

When you borrow money that is repaid on an installment basis, there are three balances: an original balance, a declining balance, and an average balance. We can illustrate this system with another method of calculating the true interest rate. Remember, however, that this second method of calculating the interest rate is somewhat cruder and hence a little less accurate than the formula explained above.

Let us assume that you borrow $1,200 from a bank to purchase a used automobile and agree to repay it in twelve equal monthly installments of $106. You will pay back a total of $1,272; $72 of that total is interest (the I in the formula above); the original balance you owe is $1,200. After one month you make your first payment and you still owe $1,100; a month later you again repay $100 and owe $1,000, and so on. The balance you owe declines each month, as shown in Table 5–2.

At the end of six months, you have repaid $600 and owe only $600; yet you are still paying 6 percent interest on the full $1,200. If you were to calculate and pay interest monthly, you could take 6 percent of the declining balance and divide it by twelve to get the true interest cost at 6 percent. But to approximate what rate you are actually paying, get the average balance over the year (the first and last month's balance divided by two, or $650) and calculate the interest rate on it. Since interest charges are $72 and you have really borrowed only $650, the interest rate is 11.07 percent.

Let us take another case in which you borrow $1,800 at 6 percent add on, to be repaid in eighteen equal monthly installments. Six percent of $1,800 is $108 per year, but since

TABLE 5–2. *Estimating interest costs*

ORIGINAL BALANCE: THE AMOUNT ORIGINALLY BORROWED	MONTH	BALANCE	AVERAGE BALANCE: THE AMOUNT OF MONEY YOU ACTUALLY HAVE ON THE AVERAGE FOR THE FULL YEAR
$1200	1	$1,200	
	2	1,100	
	3	1,000	
	4	900	
	5	800	$650.00
	6	700	
	7	600	
	8	500	
	9	400	
	10	300	
	11	200	
	12	100	

your loan is for a year and a half, an additional interest payment of $54 is called for. Your total interest cost, dollarwise, is $162. You could calculate an average balance for the first year and again for the next 6 months and get the true interest rate, but the formula introduced above provides us with an easier way.

$$I = \$\ 162$$
$$m = \quad 12$$
$$n = \quad 18$$
$$P = \$1800$$

Thus:

$$\frac{24 \times 162}{1800 \times 19} = \frac{3888}{34200} = 11.37 \text{ percent}$$

The terms *add-on interest* and *simple interest* are two technical terms employed in the finance industry. Simple interest (also called true or actuarial interest) is what the actual interest rate, as it has been understood through the ages, really is. It is the interest as applied to a declining or average balance. Add-on interest, however, is the rate that is associated with the original balance even though the balance is declining. When one is discussing finance charges and interest rates, one must be sure to make clear to the lender one's awareness of the difference between add-on and simple interest.

In the past, lenders and merchants offering installment contracts found all kinds of devious ways of disguising the true interest rates. Often they would merely say, "so much down and so much per month," and the true interest cost (the I in the formula) or the net amount of credit advanced (the P in the formula) could not always be ascertained. If asked what the interest rate amounted to, lenders would often become evasive and sometimes even tell outright lies. In many cases, the borrower paid 12, 30, 42 percent or even more without knowing it. All of this changed with the passage of the federal truth in lending law in 1968 (the Consumer Credit Protection Act). This law does not limit the rate that may be charged; it merely requires that the lender tell the borrowers what they are paying, both dollarwise and as a percentage of the loan. (A number of different agencies enforce truth in lending. See chapter 6 for a complete list.) Most lenders use tables that have been worked out in advance to tell the buyer the dollar amount of the finance charge and the annual percentage rate (APR) of these charges. These tables are an alternative to the formulas previously discussed as a method of calculating the true interest cost (APR). Table 5–3 is such a table that can be used to obtain the true interest cost of any add-on rate. The various add-on rates are shown in the first column; then to the right are shown the true rates for the various installment loans repaid monthly. For example, a 10 percent add-on rate is really 14.94 percent if paid back in three installments; 17.97 percent if paid back in twelve; and 17.92 percent if repaid in thirty-six months.

Interest Rates and Consumer Loans

State laws set the maximum rates that may be charged on consumer loans; hence there is some variation from state to state. Some states have a number of different laws, each one applying to a specific lending institution. Others have only one or two laws which regulate all consumer lenders. The laws also allow for different rates for different items. For example, automobiles are generally financed at lower rates than other consumer goods. Also new autos are usually financed at lower rates than used autos. Rates on auto loans generally run from 12 percent all the way up to 30 percent depending upon the lender, the credit rating of

TABLE 5-3. *Actuarial equivalents of add-on rates. The annual add-on rate is shown as the left hand index. If this rate is applied to the original amount for the full term and the loan is repaid monthly, then the body of the table shows the actuarial rate of return on the money actually outstanding.*

Add-on Rate Per Year	Term-Months																	
	3 Mo.	6 Mo.	9 Mo.	12 Mo.	15 Mo.	18 Mo.	24 Mo.	30 Mo.	36 Mo.	42 Mo.	48 Mo.	54 Mo.	60 Mo.	72 Mo.	84 Mo.	96 Mo.	108 Mo.	120 Mo.
1.00	1.50	1.71	1.80	1.84	1.87	1.89	1.91	1.92	1.93	1.93	1.93	1.94	1.94	1.94	1.93	1.93	1.93	1.92
2.00	3.00	3.42	3.59	3.67	3.72	3.76	3.79	3.81	3.82	3.82	3.82	3.82	3.82	3.80	3.79	3.77	3.75	3.74
3.00	4.49	5.12	5.37	5.49	5.56	5.61	5.66	5.68	5.68	5.68	5.67	5.66	5.64	5.61	5.57	5.54	5.50	5.46
3.50	5.24	5.98	6.26	6.40	6.48	6.53	6.58	6.60	6.60	6.59	6.58	6.56	6.54	6.49	6.44	6.39	6.34	6.29
4.00	5.99	6.82	7.14	7.30	7.39	7.45	7.50	7.52	7.51	7.50	7.47	7.45	7.42	7.36	7.30	7.23	7.17	7.11
4.25	6.36	7.25	7.59	7.75	7.85	7.91	7.96	7.97	7.96	7.94	7.92	7.89	7.86	7.79	7.72	7.65	7.58	7.51
4.50	6.74	7.67	8.03	8.21	8.30	8.36	8.41	8.42	8.41	8.39	8.36	8.33	8.29	8.22	8.14	8.06	7.98	7.91
4.75	7.11	8.10	8.47	8.66	8.76	8.82	8.87	8.88	8.86	8.84	8.80	8.77	8.72	8.64	8.55	8.47	8.38	8.30
5.00	7.48	8.52	8.91	9.10	9.21	9.27	9.32	9.33	9.31	9.28	9.24	9.20	9.15	9.06	8.97	8.87	8.78	8.69
5.25	7.86	8.94	9.36	9.55	9.66	9.73	9.78	9.78	9.76	9.72	9.68	9.63	9.58	9.48	9.37	9.27	9.17	9.08
5.50	8.23	9.37	9.79	10.00	10.11	10.18	10.23	10.23	10.20	10.16	10.11	10.06	10.01	9.89	9.78	9.67	9.56	9.46
5.75	8.60	9.79	10.23	10.45	10.57	10.63	10.68	10.67	10.64	10.60	10.54	10.49	10.43	10.31	10.18	10.06	9.95	9.84
6.00	8.98	10.21	10.67	10.90	11.02	11.08	11.13	11.12	11.08	11.03	10.97	10.91	10.85	10.72	10.58	10.46	10.33	10.21
6.25	9.35	10.64	11.11	11.34	11.45	11.53	11.57	11.56	11.52	11.47	11.40	11.34	11.27	11.12	10.98	10.85	10.71	10.59
6.50	9.72	11.06	11.55	11.79	11.91	11.98	12.02	12.00	11.96	11.90	11.83	11.76	11.68	11.53	11.38	11.23	11.09	10.96
6.75	10.10	11.48	11.99	12.23	12.36	12.43	12.47	12.44	12.39	12.33	12.25	12.17	12.09	11.93	11.77	11.61	11.47	11.32
7.00	10.47	11.90	12.43	12.68	12.81	12.87	12.91	12.88	12.83	12.76	12.68	12.59	12.50	12.33	12.16	11.99	11.84	11.69
7.25	10.84	12.32	12.87	13.12	13.25	13.32	13.35	13.32	13.26	13.18	13.10	13.01	12.91	12.73	12.55	12.37	12.21	12.05
7.50	11.22	12.74	13.30	13.57	13.70	13.77	13.80	13.76	13.69	13.61	13.51	13.42	13.32	13.12	12.93	12.75	12.57	12.41
7.75	11.59	13.17	13.74	14.01	14.14	14.21	14.24	14.19	14.12	14.03	13.93	13.83	13.72	13.52	13.31	13.12	12.94	12.76
8.00	11.96	13.59	14.18	14.45	14.59	14.65	14.68	14.63	14.55	14.45	14.35	14.24	14.13	13.91	13.69	13.49	13.30	13.12
8.25	12.33	14.01	14.61	14.89	15.03	15.10	15.12	15.06	14.97	14.87	14.76	14.64	14.53	14.29	14.07	13.86	13.66	13.47
8.50	12.71	14.43	15.05	15.34	15.48	15.54	15.55	15.49	15.40	15.29	15.17	15.05	14.92	14.68	14.45	14.23	14.02	13.82
8.75	13.08	14.85	15.49	15.78	15.92	15.98	15.99	15.92	15.82	15.70	15.58	15.45	15.32	15.07	14.82	14.59	14.37	14.16
9.00	13.45	15.27	15.92	16.22	16.36	16.42	16.43	16.35	16.24	16.12	15.99	15.85	15.71	15.45	15.19	14.95	14.72	14.51
9.25	13.82	15.69	16.35	16.66	16.80	16.86	16.86	16.78	16.66	16.53	16.39	16.25	16.11	15.83	15.56	15.31	15.07	14.85
9.50	14.19	16.11	16.79	17.10	17.24	17.30	17.29	17.21	17.08	16.94	16.80	16.65	16.50	16.21	15.93	15.67	15.42	15.19
9.75	14.57	16.53	17.22	17.53	17.68	17.74	17.73	17.63	17.50	17.35	17.20	17.04	16.89	16.58	16.29	16.02	15.77	15.53
→10.00	14.94	16.94	17.66	17.97	18.12	18.17	18.16	18.06	17.92	17.76	17.60	17.44	17.27	16.96	16.66	16.38	16.11	15.86
10.25	15.31	17.36	18.09	18.41	18.56	18.61	18.59	18.48	18.33	18.17	18.00	17.83	17.66	17.33	17.02	16.73	16.45	16.20
10.50	15.68	17.78	18.52	18.85	18.99	19.05	19.02	18.90	18.75	18.58	18.40	18.22	18.04	17.70	17.38	17.08	16.79	16.53
10.75	16.05	18.20	18.95	19.28	19.43	19.48	19.44	19.32	19.16	18.98	18.79	18.61	18.42	18.07	17.74	17.42	17.13	16.86
11.00	16.43	18.62	19.39	19.72	19.36	19.91	19.87	19.74	19.57	19.38	19.19	19.00	18.80	18.44	18.09	17.77	17.47	17.19
11.25	16.80	19.04	19.82	20.15	20.30	20.35	20.30	20.16	19.98	19.78	19.58	19.38	19.18	18.80	18.45	18.11	17.80	17.52
11.50	17.17	19.45	20.25	20.59	20.73	20.78	20.72	20.57	20.39	20.18	19.97	19.77	19.56	19.17	18.80	18.46	18.14	17.84
11.75	17.54	19.87	20.68	21.02	21.17	21.21	21.15	20.99	20.79	20.58	20.36	20.15	19.94	19.53	19.15	18.80	18.47	18.17
12.00	17.91	20.29	21.11	21.46	21.60	21.64	21.57	21.41	21.20	20.98	20.75	20.53	20.31	19.89	19.50	19.13	18.80	18.49
12.25	18.28	20.70	21.54	21.89	22.03	22.07	21.99	21.82	21.60	21.37	21.14	20.91	20.68	20.25	19.85	19.47	19.13	18.81
12.50	18.65	21.12	21.97	22.32	22.47	22.50	22.42	22.23	22.01	21.77	21.53	21.29	21.05	20.61	20.19	19.81	19.45	19.13
12.75	19.03	21.54	22.40	22.76	22.90	22.93	22.84	22.64	22.41	22.16	21.91	21.66	21.42	20.96	20.54	20.14	19.78	19.44
13.00	19.40	21.95	22.83	23.19	23.33	23.36	23.26	23.05	22.81	22.55	22.30	22.04	21.79	21.32	20.88	20.47	20.10	19.76
13.50	20.14	22.79	23.68	24.05	24.19	24.21	24.09	23.87	23.61	23.33	23.06	22.79	22.52	22.02	21.56	21.14	20.75	20.39
14.00	20.88	23.62	24.54	24.91	25.04	25.06	24.92	24.68	24.40	24.11	23.82	23.53	23.25	22.72	22.24	21.79	21.38	21.01
14.50	21.62	24.45	25.39	25.77	25.90	25.91	25.75	25.49	25.19	24.88	24.57	24.26	23.97	23.41	22.91	22.44	22.02	21.63
15.00	22.36	25.28	26.24	26.62	26.75	26.75	26.58	26.30	25.98	25.64	25.32	24.99	24.68	24.10	23.57	23.09	22.64	22.24
15.50	23.10	26.10	27.09	27.48	27.60	27.60	27.40	27.10	26.76	26.41	26.06	25.72	25.39	24.79	24.23	23.73	23.27	22.85
16.00	23.84	26.93	27.94	28.33	28.45	28.43	28.22	27.89	27.53	27.16	26.80	26.44	26.10	25.46	24.88	24.36	23.88	23.45
16.50	24.58	27.76	28.79	29.18	29.29	29.27	29.03	28.69	28.30	27.91	27.53	27.16	26.80	26.14	25.54	24.99	24.50	24.05
17.00	25.32	28.58	29.64	30.03	30.14	30.10	29.85	29.48	29.07	28.66	28.26	27.87	27.50	26.81	26.18	25.62	25.11	24.65
18.00	26.80	30.23	31.32	31.72	31.81	31.76	31.46	31.04	30.59	30.14	29.70	29.28	28.88	28.13	27.46	26.86	26.31	25.82
19.00	28.28	31.88	33.01	33.40	33.48	33.41	33.06	32.60	32.10	31.61	31.13	30.67	30.24	29.44	28.72	28.08	27.51	26.99
20.00	29.76	33.52	34.68	35.07	35.14	35.05	34.65	34.14	33.60	33.06	32.54	32.05	31.58	30.73	29.97	29.29	28.69	28.14

the borrower, and the age and condition of the auto. The average, however, and the age and condition of the auto. The average, however, is probably about 13 or 14 percent on new autos and 17 to 18 percent on used.

Rates may be calculated on a per monthly basis on the unpaid balance; say 1 to 3 percent, which of course is 12 to 36 percent per year. On very small loans for short periods of time, say of $100 or $200 for 1 month, some states allow rates in excess of 100 percent on an annual basis. For example, if you were to borrow $100 for 30 days there may be a minimum charge of say $10. You would pay back $110 in 30 days for a monthly rate of 10 percent. This amounts to 120 percent if annualized.

Loans to consumers may be secured or unsecured. If the loan is secured, something of value is pledged as collateral such as an automobile or household furniture. This is accomplished by having the borrower give a security agreement to the lender. (See the end of the chapter for an example of a security agreement.) An unsecured loan is called a signature loan; no collateral is pledged and the borrower has a good enough credit rating to obtain the loan by merely signing a promissory note promising to repay it.

The maximum loan which may be made under the various consumer finance laws varies from state to state. This ceiling is under $2,000 in some states and as high as $25,000 in a few. However, with the exception of loans on automobiles and mobile homes very few consumer loans are in excess of $2,000. Figures 5–2 and 5–3 illustrate average loan size and the dollar ceilings on loans in the various states.

A typical consumer loan might work this way. The personable young TV announcer informs you that you can borrow $600 for twenty-four months and repay it in monthly installments of *only* $32 per month. In terms of actual interest what does this mean? First, it means that the total amount you pay back is $768, of which $600 is principal and $168 is interest. It also means that, on the average, you owe the company over the twenty-four-month period about $300—because you are making monthly payments and constantly reducing the debt. Thus on the average unpaid balance of $300, which you had over two years, you are paying $168 in interest, or slightly over 27 percent interest on the average

FIGURE 5–2. *Average loan size, finance companies, selected years 1970–78.* (*Source: 1980 Finance Facts Yearbook,* National Consumer Finance Association, p. 59.)

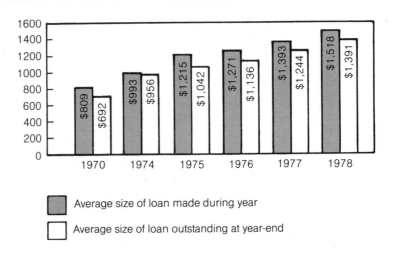

◼ Average size of loan made during year

☐ Average size of loan outstanding at year-end

Part 1 / Budgeting, Buying, Borrowing, and Saving

15 states Less than $2,000

34 states + $2,000 or over

*These eight states permit loans of over $2,000
by finance companies under other laws.
**Arkansas has no consumer finance law.

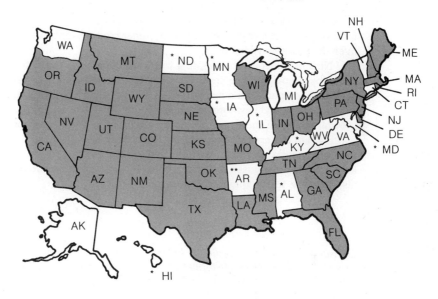

FIGURE 5–3. *Loan ceilings under consumer finance laws, January 1977.* (*Source:*
1979 Finance Facts Yearbook, National Consumer Finance
Association, p. 64.)

unpaid balance of your loan. This figure can be calculated using the formula described
above, as follows:

$$\frac{2mI}{P(N+1)} = \frac{24 \times 168}{600 \times 25} = \frac{4,032}{15,000} = 27 \text{ percent}$$

The same young announcer will also say that there will be no additional handling
charges and this is true. Most state laws prohibit any additional charges in the way of fees,
fines, or other handling charges.

SOURCES OF CONSUMER CREDIT

Consumer credit is made available by a number of financial institutions either directly or
indirectly. It is made available directly when you go to an institution and borrow money. It is
made available indirectly when you go to a merchant and buy something on the installment

Chapter 5 / The Role of Consumer Credit   **107**

plan and the merchant arranges the financing. Sometimes this happens without your knowledge until after it takes place. For example, you sign the papers promising to pay so much per month for so many months. Then, the merchant will take this paper to a financial institution, turn it over to them, and get his money, all at once. This is called selling the paper or more properly discounting it. The institution gets the interest as the monthly payments come in. You are then informed to make the monthly payments to the institution.

Financial institutions may also be extending credit indirectly when you use your credit card. This is because some banks are involved in credit cards, and also because the merchant who has issued the credit card (e.g., Sears or a gasoline company) must borrow more money at, say, a bank to carry you until you pay the bills you have run up on your card. The following chart shows the amount of consumer credit extended by the four main institutions over the past few years.

Nine financial institutions deal with consumer credit in the form of cash. They are the small loan company, the credit union, the industrial bank, the remedial loan society, life insurance companies, commercial banks, savings and loan institutions, mutual savings banks in some states, and pawnbrokers. In addition, I shall discuss credit cards because they are a growing source of short-term consumer credit. Moreover, in recent years *banks* have been moving into the area of *credit cards*. Some people think that this will lead to a *checkless society* some day and that computers will do our banking for us. In addition, an institution known as credit counselors or advisors has sprung up in recent years in some states. I will also examine the unique role of credit counselors.

FIGURE 5–4. *Consumer installment credit, by holder; amount outstanding, end of quarter. (Source: 1979 Historical Chart Book,* Board of Governors of the Federal Reserve System, p. 67.)

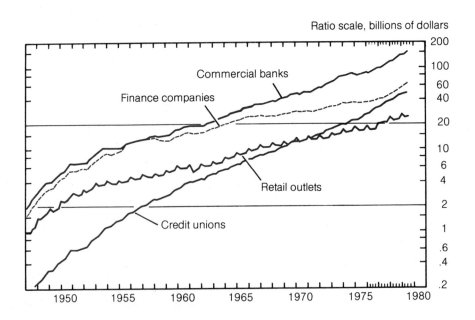

Part 1 / Budgeting, Buying, Borrowing, and Saving

Small Loan Companies

The small loan company, also known as the consumer finance company or personal finance company, is a firm specializing in loans to consumers. Interest rates charged by finance companies are, generally speaking, a bit higher than those charged by some other lenders, because their loans are often smaller and they lend to poorer credit risks than many other lenders. These companies make loans for almost any conceivable purpose, but personal loans and automobile loans constitute the bulk of their business. The pie chart below illustrates the credit outstanding of finance companies.

In 1911, the state of Massachusetts passed the first legislation enabling the operation of small loan companies. The other states gradually followed. Today forty-nine states and the District of Columbia have consumer finance laws; and only one state, Arkansas, has no similar legislation. On small loans, a higher than normal rate of interest is actually necessary. The cost of servicing a small loan is frequently greater than that of servicing a large loan. At 8 or 9 percent interest, for example, it would be impossible for a small loan company to show a profit.

Credit Unions

The credit union is a cooperative type of financial institution designed to make loans to its members for any reasonable purpose. The credit union began in Germany and was introduced into the United States in 1909. Today all states have legislation providing for credit unions, and in 1934 Congress adopted the Federal Credit Union Act enabling a credit union to operate under a federal charter. Hence all credit unions are supervised by either a federal or state regulatory body. Federal credit unions are supervised by the National

FIGURE 5–5. *Consumer installment credit outstanding at finance companies at year end. (Source: 1980 Finance Facts Yearbook,* National Consumer Finance Association, p. 58.)

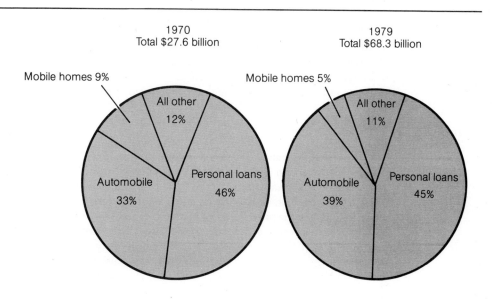

1970
Total $27.6 billion

Mobile homes 9%

All other 12%

Automobile 33%

Personal loans 46%

1979
Total $68.3 billion

Mobile homes 5%

All other 11%

Automobile 39%

Personal loans 45%

Credit Union Administration and state credit unions by the State Credit Union Commission or some other designated state body.

Credit unions have grown very rapidly in recent years largely because many people have discovered them to be an excellent source of funds.

Generally, credit unions charge between 9 and 15 percent on consumer loans, depending upon the size of the loan and the collateral offered. No federally chartered credit union may charge more than 15 percent on any loan. Until recently credit unions could make only consumer loans. But recently federal credit unions (and some state chartered ones) have been given permission to make mortgage loans. Some are slowly moving into this new area.

Because a borrower must be a shareholder in a credit union, the borrower must purchase a share before a loan will be made. Suppose a person working for a firm where there is a credit union desires to borrow $200 to get through some emergency. The person files a credit application, purchases a $5 share in the credit union, and pays a $.25 membership fee. The credit committee passes on the application and the $200 loan is made. When the individual repays the loan, he or she can withdraw the $5 share. More often than not, it will remain on deposit with the credit union, where it earns interest. If one is a lender rather than a borrower, money can be put into a credit union instead of a bank.

Industrial Banks

Industrial banks are also called "Morris Plan" banks. They all operate under a state charter and are found in only twenty states. The first "Morris Plan" was organized in 1910 by Arthur Morris, and it became the first industrial bank. Within a short time, the idea spread to the major cities of the country, where other Morris Plan banks were organized under local ownership. Historically, the Morris Plan specialized in making loans to industrial wage earners; hence the name, industrial bank. The plan provided that the maximum legal rate would be charged for the length of the loan. In addition, there were frequently extra charges for credit reports and recording fees for legal documents where necessary. Under the terms of the plan, the borrower was obligated to make regular deposits in a non-interest-bearing savings account scheduled so that, at the maturity date of the loan, the borrower would have on deposit a sum sufficient to pay the loan.

Today most of them have dropped the name "Morris Plan" and simply call themselves industrial banks. They no longer restrict their loans to industrial workers but make loans to all kinds of people. Moreover, they make all kinds of loans; consumer loans, both first and second mortgage loans, and even business loans. Generally, interest charges on consumer loans range from 10 to 20 percent, although some loans are made above 20 percent.

Remedial Loan Societies

The remedial loan society is basically a pawnshop with a difference of intent. It is a nonprofit organization designed to loan cash on the pledge of watches, diamonds, and other articles that one typically finds in a pawnshop. Historically, these societies were organized through the sale of stock bearing a limited return of 6 percent on the par value of stock. Since 1915, when the peak in the number of societies reached forty-one, they have steadily declined, partly because of the fact that they are strictly nonprofit organizations and lack the aggressiveness of their competitors. In addition, since commercial banks and credit unions have grown rapidly in the field of granting consumer cash loans, the need for such a financial institution has all but disappeared.

Yet there are still a number of these organizations in some of the nation's larger cities. They grant loans rapidly on the pledge of personal property and without credit investigation. Their rates are comparable with bank rates, averaging 1 percent on the unpaid balance of the loan or 12 percent per year. The loans are generally made for a year, but they may frequently be renewed on request. If the loan is not repaid, the article pledged is sold at public auction. If the auctioned chattel brings more than the amount pledged, the surplus is given back to the borrower. If the amount received by the society is less than the loan granted, the loss is borne by the society.

Life Insurance Companies

An individual with a savings type of insurance policy (which will be detailed in Chapter 8) may borrow the cash surrender value from the life insurance company or use the policy as security for a loan with a commercial bank. Generally after a policy has been in force a minimum of two or three years, the insured builds up a "cash surrender value" in the policy. This means that if the holder wishes, he or she may give up the policy and be paid a sum in cash or may borrow an equivalent sum from the insurance company and permit the policy to remain in force. It would appear better to borrow against the policy than to cash it in.

As an alternative, the prospective borrower may use the policy as collateral for a loan with another financial institution. Under these conditions, in the event the borrower fails to meet this obligation, the institution may cash the policy and pay off the loan, returning any surplus to the borrower. If the borrower should die prior to payment, the institution is paid the amount of the debt by the insurance company, any balance being paid to the beneficiaries.

Under the law, the insurance company *must* lend the cash surrender value to the insured if the latter so desires. From the viewpoint of the consumer, this sort of loan has a psychological drawback because one does not *have* to pay back the loan. Consequently, some people just ignore repayment and continue paying the interest. Upon the death of the insured, however, the beneficiary of the policy will receive the face value less the amount of loan outstanding.

Insurance companies generally charge about 8 percent interest per annum on the loan. This is a flat rate, which means that on a loan of $100 at 8 percent, the cost to the borrower is $8 per year, a true 8 percent per year. Many consumers object to the interest payment because they are, in effect, paying it on their own money. The companies are quick to point out, however, that the premiums are based on the assumption that the company will have the use of the premium money for investment and, unless the premiums are to be raised, such a charge is necessary.

Before borrowing on a policy, it is often advisable to shop around at other financial institutions to determine the interest rate that can be obtained there if the policy is used as security. Some people feel that even if another financial institution charges the same rate as the insurance company, it is better to borrow from the other type of financial institution because there is a sense of obligation to repay the loan.

Table 5-4 lists policy loans made by life insurance companies to policyholders over the years.

Commercial Banks

Commercial banks make all kinds of loans including consumer loans. The cost of borrowing from commercial banks compares most favorably with other financial institutions. On a flat basis, or what is also called simple or true interest, the rate generally begins at

TABLE 5–4. *Policy loans, U.S. life insurance companies (000,000 omitted)*

YEAR	AMOUNT	% OF ASSETS	YEAR	AMOUNT	% OF ASSETS
1890	$ 20	2.6	1965	$ 7,678	4.8
1895	36	3.1	1966	9,117	5.5
1900	89	5.1	1967	10,059	5.7
1905	226	8.3	1968	11,306	6.0
1910	495	12.8	1969	13,825	7.0
1915	780	15.0	1970	16,064	7.8
1920	859	11.7	1971	17,065	7.7
1925	1,446	12.5	1972	18,003	7.5
1930	2,807	14.9	1973	20,199	8.0
1935	3,540	15.2	1974	22,862	8.7
1940	3,091	10.0	1975	24,467	8.5
1945	1,962	4.4	1976	25,834	8.0
1950	2,413	3.8	1977	27,556	7.8
1955	3,290	3.6	1978	30,146	7.8
1960	5,231	4.4			

Source: *1979 Life Insurance Fact Book,* American Council of Life Insurance, p. 85.

about 10 percent per year. Usually, however, collateral is needed to get a loan at this rate and it must be a single-payment loan. On installment loans, higher clerical and administrative costs are involved and higher rates are charged. Most consumer loans are installment loans and only about one-half of the entire loan is usually borrowed for the entire period so the effective rate of interest ranges from 11 to 15 percent per year. In addition, in some commercial banks, there is a life insurance policy on the loan, in most cases a type of term insurance that carries an abnormally high rate. Some commercial banks also charge for a credit report and for various filing fees.

Generally speaking, interest rates charged by banks are below those charged by finance companies and many other lenders. It has been alleged that banks "skim the cream" from the borrowing public. They make loans to lower-risk borrowers so their losses and repossession rate are lower, and they can afford to charge a lower interest rate.

Savings and Loan Associations

Savings and loan associations are in the business of accepting deposits and making mortgage loans. However, in some states they have long been permitted to make consumer loans if they are operating under a state charter (like commercial banks, savings and loan associations can operate under a federal or a state charter). Then, in 1980, federal legislation was passed which permitted federally chartered institutions to make consumer loans. They make both installment and single-payment loans. The interest they charge ranges from 6 to 8 percent "add on" if it's an installment loan (making the true or simple interest about 11.5 to 15 percent per annum) and about 10 to 12 percent simple (or true) if it's a single-payment loan. Within these ranges, the actual interest charged on a given loan is determined by the size of the loan and the credit worthiness of the borrower. These rates generally are lower than those charged by finance companies but slightly higher than those charged by credit unions and even some commercial banks.

Mutual Savings Banks

Everything we have said about savings and loan associations in terms of consumer loans applies to mutual savings banks. Mutual savings banks are found only in seventeen states. They may make a limited number of consumer loans in some states, and the rates they charge are comparable to those charged by savings and loan associations.

Pawnbrokers

Pawnbrokers are generally affable individuals about whose signs that mysterious figure in American literature, Ambrose Bierce, had much to say. They will accept nearly anything from pistols to guitars as collateral for loans. Upon failure to repay the loan, the pledged article is sold, thereby creating a marketplace in which young hopefuls may purchase guitars so that they may emulate our great national folk heroes.

The legal key to the pawnshop operation is the fact that personal property is "pledged" as the security for the loan. Under the law, the pawnshop is bound to return the same property as that put up for security. In practice, the pawnshop owner promptly appraises the value of the property to be pledged, and the loan is immediately consummated. The loans are usually granted, however, only in amounts ranging from 20 to 50 percent of the value of the property. The borrower receives a pawn ticket and under the terms of the loan has a stated time period—generally a few months—in which to redeem the pledged object. If the borrower fails to redeem the property within this time, the pawnshop owner is free to sell it, either at public auction or private sale. The interest rate charged varies from about 24 percent to 42 percent a year. While this is a rather high rate for a secured loan, the pawnshops provide an immediate source of money. In addition, there is a handling fee of a few dollars on items left at the pawnshop for over thirty days and on which a loan of $30 or more was made. For the most part, their customers are people in low-income groups who are frequently unable to borrow elsewhere. During periods of depression or recession, there is more activity in the pawnshop business than during periods of prosperity.

Sales Finance Companies

Sales finance companies are an indirect source of funds. They handle many billions of dollars' worth of installment credit a year. Such companies are primarily engaged in the purchase of dealers' time-sales contracts arising out of the sale of goods to consumers. For example, when you buy something on an installment basis, you receive the merchandise while the merchant is in possession of the papers you sign. Because merchants must meet their own financial commitments and are frequently not in a position to do so on a cash basis, they "sell the paper" to the sales finance company.

This transfer of the "paper," as it is called in the trade, is done either on a *recourse* or *without recourse* basis. If the paper is sold without recourse, the finance company bears the risk of loss.

Individuals who deal with merchants using sales finance companies generally pay a higher rate of interest than if they dealt directly with banks or certain other lenders. So the prospective purchaser of an automobile should at least attempt to deal directly with a commercial bank. Moreover, if the individual is a member of a credit union, it might pay to compare the rates of the commercial bank on a new car loan with those of a credit union.

"Getting back to those interest rates, could you be a little more specific than 'it's going to cost a pretty penny'?" (*Source:* Permission Cartoon Features Syndicate; from *The Wall Street Journal.*)

Regrettably, in many instances the time buyer has no choice but to be content to deal with the sales finance company used by the merchant.

Credit Cards

No discussion of consumer credit is complete without some comments about credit cards. We are all familiar with gasoline credit cards and the credit charge plates of the major department stores; nearly all of us use them. Most of us are also familiar with national credit cards like American Express, Diners Club, Visa, Master Card and Carte Blanche, although fewer of us use these.

Traditionally, the credit card permitted consumers to obtain merchandise without paying and then at the end of the month they were sent one bill for all purchases. Credit was extended for a few weeks at most. More and more department stores are using what is referred to as a rotating or revolving charge account. Under a rotating charge account, the buyer is still permitted to liquidate the bill monthly but need not do this. Those who choose not to, move into an automatic monthly payment plan. While these plans vary somewhat from merchant to merchant, they all have a similar structure. They require a minimum monthly payment (usually $10 or 10 percent of the total amount due). They also have a maximum amount (usually $500 to $3,000) beyond which credit will not be extended unless special arrangements are made. Under these rotating charge accounts consumers need never liquidate their total bill. The only requirement is that they make the minimum monthly payment and do not exceed the maximum.

For this extension of credit, merchants charge an interest rate on the unpaid balance. This rate varies somewhat typically; it is 1.5 percent per month on the first $500 and 1 percent per month on the amount in excess of $500. This of course adds up to 18 percent and 12 percent per year. In other cases it is 1.5 percent per month on the first $1,200 or even $1,500 and 1 percent on the excess of that. Some credit cards, especially those administered by banks, have a third step in which interest of about .8 per cent per month is charged on accounts in excess of, say, $2,500. In addition, in some cases, the interest is calculated not on the unpaid balance, but rather on the average daily balance from closing date to closing date. This has the effect of charging interest on future purchases. For example, suppose you are billed $200 on your credit card and pay $100. Then during the next time period you charge another $200. The interest you are charged is then calculated by taking into account the newest $200 as well as the outstanding $100, or on $300.

Regardless of how interest charges are calculated, until recently they were not assessed if the entire bill were liquidated each month. But beginning in 1980 more and more credit card issuers started charging interest regardless of whether or not the bill were liquidated each month. Generally speaking, under this system interest charges are assessed on the average daily balance from billing date to billing date.

Many people believe that if they pay the entire bill monthly (and aren't billed for interest) they obtain an interest-free loan for a few weeks. This is not true. There is no service charge or interest added to the bill, but the price of the goods purchased is slightly higher than it would be in the absence of credit cards. This is true for two reasons. First, there is the extra cost of bookkeeping necessitated by credit cards. Second, since the merchant receives the money a few weeks later, he or she often has to borrow more at a bank to pay bills.[3]

In the case of certain national credit cards such as American Express, Diners Club, and Carte Blanche, the credit card holder pays an annual fee of about $25. The credit card holder is billed monthly and must liquidate the bill monthly except for bills for airline tickets, where a twelve-month payoff is permitted. If a twelve-month payoff is chosen, an additional 1 percent per month interest on the declining balance is added.

In addition to the $25 annual fees paid by the card holder, the national credit card firms receive about 5 or 6 percent of the amount collected from the merchant for whom they collect it. This is their service charge and should be looked upon as a cost of credit. This fee is included in the price of the final goods and services, and again, to a slight extent, those who do not have these credit cards subsidize those of us who do.

Two national credit cards have been developed by the commercial banking system: Visa, issued by the Bank of America, and Master Card issued by the old First National City Bank (now called CitiBank) of New York. Various banks throughout the country have entered into an agreement with one of the two banks and are responsible for the credit cards within their region.

The holders of Master Card or Visa are billed monthly but need not liquidate the debt; all they must do is pay a minimum amount each month and the credit card operates like the revolving charge account discussed above. There is no uniform interest on these nationwide bank credit cards because the sponsoring banks lease their name and credit card system to various local banks throughout the country. And these local banks collect the bills and determine, within limits, the interest or service charges, which are then shared with the home bank. However, a typical rate would be the 1½ percent per month on the 1st $1,200, 1 percent on the balance from $1,200 to $2,500, and .82 or .83 percent on the balance in

---

3. As this book went to press, a few credit cards were experimenting with a service charge for those who liquidate their entire bill each month.

excess of $2,500. This makes the annual rate 18 percent, 12 percent, and about 9 percent, respectively. In addition, the banks receive 5 or 6 percent of the amount collected from the merchants, just as in the case of Diners and American Express cards.

All of these credit cards have a maximum limit on the amount of credit extended that varies with the income of the credit card holder. At one time credit cards were sent to people on an unsolicited basis, but this is no longer the case. Now persons who want a credit card not only must apply, but must qualify. The criterion used to determine whether a person qualifies is primarily income; however, nearly anyone who has an annual income of $10,000 or more can obtain a national credit card upon application.

Summary of the Lenders

We have discussed a number of different sources of consumer credit, and the various rates which they charge. These rates can vary considerably, and therefore, you should shop around and compare rates when you borrow money. The following table summarizes the interest rate range which the major lenders typically charge.

The Checkless Society or Electronic Funds Transfer System

Now that banks have developed national credit cards and they have been widely accepted, the next step will be to use the electronic computers of these banks to pay bills automatically. The result will be to do away with checks almost completely.

Under the present system a bank does the bookkeeping and bill collecting. If you hold one of these cards, all participating merchants send your bills to the bank. The bank adds them up and sends you one monthly bill. You need to write only one check to the bank, which pays all your bills. In the event that you do not have the money to pay the bill, the

TABLE 5–5. *Borrowing table (rates typically charged)*

LENDING INSTITUTIONS	INTEREST RATES APR.
Commercial banks	10–14%
Savings and loan associations	10–14%
Mutual savings banks	10–14%
Credit unions	9–15%
Life insurance co.	8%
Finance co.	12–30%
Credit cards	3 steps 18%
	12%
	and 8.5%

Note: The above rates are generalizations. In some states they may be somewhat above or below those shown in the table; this is particularly true of the finance company rates, which have a very wide range. The rates in the 30 percent area are usually on smaller loans made to higher risk borrowers. The latest figures show that the average annual rate for new autos financed by finance companies was 13.5 percent and for used cars 18 percent. For mobile homes this same rate was 13.64 percent and for other items 19.1 percent.

Part 1 / Budgeting, Buying, Borrowing, and Saving

"Let me assure you that to us here at First National, you're not just a number. You're two numbers, a dash, three more numbers, another dash, and another number." (*Source:* Permission Cartoon Features Syndicate; from *The Wall Street Journal.*)

bank will automatically make you a loan up to a predetermined maximum, if you have authorized this.

The next step, when it comes, will eliminate the need for you ever to write checks or make deposits in your bank account. One little credit card is all you will need. It will work like this. Your weekly or monthly paychecks will be deposited automatically into your bank account by your employer. The bank will automatically pay your regular fixed monthly bills like your mortgage or the payment on your car. This will be done by a computer. When you make any purchases, your credit card will be put into a special machine that all, or nearly all, merchants will have. This machine will be tied to the computer of your bank and the merchant's bank. When you make a purchase, the computer will automatically transfer the amount out of your bank account and into the merchant's bank account. The computer can do this immediately upon the purchase or at the end of the month in accordance with whatever arrangement is made. The computer, through the merchant's machine, will give you a receipt and a bank statement. You will get a bank statement each time you make a purchase (use your bank) rather than monthly. If the transfer of accounts is made at the end of the month rather than when purchases are made, you will still get a monthly statement rather than a statement with each purchase.

Automatic loans will be granted by the computer as needed, in accordance with predetermined maximums. The computer will refuse to let us buy things if we don't have the money in the bank or are ineligible for a loan. The need for checks will virtually be over.

Why is all this likely to come about? Because of convenience. The number of checks being written daily (over one hundred million) is growing so large that the banking system is about to be buried in paper. It is also much more convenient for the public to be relieved of the necessity of writing checks and keeping records.

What will all this checkless money cost? If the bank makes you a loan, its regular interest rate of from 10 to 15 percent will be charged. The rate will vary with your credit standing.

What will the banks charge for the bill collecting process? Presumably they will get about 4 or 5 percent of the bills they process and collect for a merchant. This 5 percent will be included in the final price of the goods. But that is the case now, too. If we use credit cards now, the final price of the goods must be higher.

Recently critics have raised some concerns over this Electronic Funds Transfer System (EFTS). For example, how could a consumer do the equivalent of stopping the payment of a check if purchased goods were defective? Some mechanism would have to be built into the system to permit consumers retrieval of any fund transfer for a period of time. This problem has not be solved.

Then too there is the problem of the monthly bank statement and cancelled check. The computer could no doubt be programmed to provide for a periodic account to serve as a bank statement, but some critics feel persons could lose some degree of control over their bank transactions. If no cancelled checks are available, what legal proof would there be that consumers had paid their bills?

Other critics are concerned about electronic fraud. Someone might be able to manipulate the master computer and steal perhaps almost limitless funds. While the new voice print and finger print systems might stop such fraud, the cost and inconvenience of this might be prohibitive. Finally, some are concerned about the possible invasion of privacy that EFTS would bring about. All of a person's financial transactions would be recorded for possible scrutiny by unauthorized individuals. Perhaps legislation could be enacted to control this and to prevent the widespread dissemination of personal financial data. Nevertheless, many groups are concerned about these problems.

It should be noted that the checkless society is different from the automatic funds transfer (AFT) system discussed in the previous chapter which merely transfers funds from your savings to your checking account or vice versa. It is also different from truncation (discussed in the previous chapter) which merely gives you a computer printout record of your cancelled checks, but does not return them.

OTHER THINGS YOU SHOULD KNOW ABOUT CONSUMER CREDIT AND CONSUMERISM

There are a number of other useful and important things about consumer credit with which you should be familiar. Each of these will be discussed below.

The Credit Application

Whether one is going to open a charge account or is making application for any other type of installment loan, one must make an application for credit. Basically the credit application is a request for information concerning place of employment, address, size of income, bank account, assets and liabilities, and whether or not one has ever had credit. An example of a credit application is shown in Figure 5–6. From this information, the credit investigation is made.

The Credit Bureau's Report

After one has applied for credit, the information is generally forwarded to a local credit bureau for verification. Every credit bureau maintains records containing information on many individuals, much of it obtained from the office of the clerk of the county in which one lives. For example, the fact that any judgments have been recorded against one is entered in the record. In addition, home ownership and all existing mortgages and recorded bills of sale are included.

Credit bureaus also keep records of all previous credit extended going back generally seven years. Credit bureaus are the "middle men"; they receive information from all merchants and institutions that extend credit, store it, and then sell it to any legitimate third party. A legitimate third party is anyone entering into a business transaction involving credit with the person on whom a credit report is requested. If the person requesting credit has established credit elsewhere locally, generally a phone call to the credit bureau is all that is necessary. The bureau will give the merchant the necessary information over the phone, and the fee for this service is only a few dollars. If the person requesting credit is newly arrived in town, it may be necessary for the credit bureau to telephone a bureau in some other town. In such cases, the cost of a credit report can run up fairly fast.

When a credit bureau receives a request from a merchant or lending institution, it will pass on what information it has gathered; but the bureau usually will not assign a credit rating such as poor, fair, good, or excellent. Generally, the information the credit bureau will pass on includes the following:

1. The person's place of employment
2. Length of time with employer
3. Position with the firm
4. Income
5. Husband or wife's income, if any
6. All credit extended over the past seven years and the date it was extended
7. The dollar amount of the extension
8. How the loan was paid off (whether in accordance with the agreement)
9. What kind of security, if any, was required on past loans
10. Whether the person rents or owns his or her own home
11. Judgments, if any, recorded against the person
12. Bankruptcies, if any, that the person has filed

In the case of a young person requesting credit for the first time, no record exists and the credit bureau cannot help as much. The merchant must make a decision based upon the person's place of employment, position, income, and any other information the merchant

LOAN APPLICATION

Texas Bank Austin
900 Congress
Austin, Texas 78767
REPUBLIC

IMPORTANT: Read these directions before completing this Application.

Check Appropriate Box

☐ If you are applying for individual credit in your own name, are not married, and are not relying on alimony, child support, or separate maintenance payments or on the income or assets of another person as the basis for repayment of the credit requested, complete only Sections A and D.

☐ In all other situations, complete all Sections to the extent possible, providing information in B about your spouse or the person on whose alimony, support or maintenance payments or income or assets you are relying.

AMOUNT REQUESTED	NO. OF MONTHS	PURPOSE OF LOAN
	PAYMENT DATE DESIRED	

SECTION A — INFORMATION REGARDING APPLICANT

APPLICANT'S NAME	BIRTHDATE (MO./DAY/YR.)	NO. OF DEPENDENTS (Including Self)	PHONE (Area Code & No.)

ADDRESS	APT. NO.	CITY	STATE	ZIP CODE	HOW LONG? YR. MO.

PREVIOUS ADDRESS (If at Above Less than 5 Years)		CITY		STATE	HOW LONG? YR. MO.

BUSINESS EMPLOYER	GROSS MONTHLY SALARY $	POSITION	HOW LONG? YR. MO.

BUSINESS ADDRESS	CITY	STATE	BUSINESS PHONE

PREVIOUS EMPLOYER (If on Present Job Less than 5 Years)	CITY	STATE	HOW LONG? YR. MO

CHECKING ACCOUNT - NUMBER - NAME OF BANK ☐ NO ☐ YES	SAVINGS ACCOUNT - NUMBER - NAME OF BANK ☐ NO ☐ YES

Alimony, child support, or separate maintenance income need not be revealed if you do not wish to have it considered as a basis for repaying this obligation.

ALIMONY, CHILD SUPPORT, SEPARATE MAINTENANCE RECEIVED UNDER
☐ COURT ORDER   ☐ WRITTEN AGREEMENT   ☐ ORAL UNDERSTANDING

SOURCE OF OTHER INCOME	NET AMT. YEARLY $	NET AMT. MONTHLY $

IS ANY INCOME LISTED IN THIS SECTION LIKELY TO BE REDUCED IN THE NEXT TWO YEARS OR BEFORE THE CREDIT REQUESTED IS PAID OFF?
☐ YES (Explain in detail on a separate sheet)   ☐ NO

NAME OF NEAREST RELATIVE, NOT LIVING WITH YOU	RELATIONSHIP	MOTHER'S MAIDEN NAME

ADDRESS OF NEAREST RELATIVE, NOT LIVING WITH YOU	CITY	STATE	PHONE

SECTION B — INFORMATION REGARDING SPOUSE OR OTHER PARTY *(Use separate sheet if necessary)*

FULL NAME	RELATIONSHIP TO APPLICANT	BIRTHDATE (M/D/Y)	PHONE

ADDRESS	APT. NO.	CITY	STATE	ZIP CODE	HOW LONG? YR. MO.

BUSINESS EMPLOYER	GROSS MONTHLY SALARY $	POSITION	HOW LONG? YR. MO.

BUSINESS ADDRESS	CITY	STATE	BUSINESS PHONE

Alimony, child support, or separate maintenance income need not be revealed if you do not wish to have it considered as a basis for repaying this obligation.

ALIMONY, CHILD SUPPORT, SEPARATE MAINTENANCE RECEIVED UNDER
☐ COURT ORDER   ☐ WRITTEN AGREEMENT   ☐ ORAL UNDERSTANDING

SOURCE OF OTHER INCOME	NET AMT. YEARLY $	NET AMT. MONTHLY $

SECTION C — MARITAL STATUS

APPLICANT
☐ MARRIED   ☐ SEPARATED   ☐ UNMARRIED (Including Single, Divorced or Widowed)

OTHER PARTY
☐ MARRIED   ☐ SEPARATED   ☐ UNMARRIED (Including Single, Divorced or Widowed)

SECTION D — DEBT INFORMATION

(If Section B has been completed, this Section should be completed giving information about both the Applicant and Spouse, or Other Person. Please mark Applicant related information with an "A". If Section B was not completed, only give information about the Applicant in this Section.)

OUTSTANDING DEBTS (Include all charge accounts, instalment contracts, credit cards, etc. Use separate sheet if necessary.)

TYPE	NAME AND ADDRESS OF COMPANY	ACCOUNT NO.	NAME IN WHICH ACCT. CARRIED	BALANCE	MO. PMT.
AUTOMOBILE LOAN					
MASTER CHARGE					
VISA					
INSTALMENT LOAN OR ACCOUNT					
INSTALMENT LOAN OR ACCOUNT					
REVOLVING ACCOUNT					
REVOLVING ACCOUNT					
☐ BUYING HOME ☐ RENT	NAME OF LANDLORD OR MORTGAGE COMPANY				

ARE YOU A CO-MAKER, ENDORSER OR GUARANTOR ON ANY LOAN OR CONTRACT? ☐ YES ☐ NO	HAVE YOU BEEN DECLARED BANKRUPT IN THE LAST 14 YEARS? ☐ YES ☐ NO	ARE THERE ANY UNSATISFIED JUDGEMENTS AGAINST YOU? ☐ YES ☐ NO

Everything that I have stated in this application is correct to the best of my knowledge. I understand that you will retain this application whether or not it is approved. You are authorized to check my credit and employment history and to answer questions about your credit experience with me.

SIGNATURE OF APPLICANT	SOCIAL SECURITY NO.	DRIVER'S LICENSE NO.	DATE

SIGNATURE OF SPOUSE OR OTHER PARTY (Where Applicable)	SOCIAL SECURITY NO.	DRIVER'S LICENSE NO.	DATE

FIGURE 5–6. *Example of a credit application. (Source: Texas Bank of Austin.)*

can obtain. Generally, if the person has a responsible position and is not asking for more credit than his or her income warrants, it will be granted. Then a person begins to build a "track record"; if he or she repays credit in accordance with the agreement, these regular payments will be reported by the merchant and recorded by the credit bureau.

Generally, a credit investigation is made only the first time one applies for credit. Once one has used credit one will have established what is known as a "line of credit." The lending institution and merchants keep their own records and will extend credit up to a maximum amount almost routinely. In such cases, one may still have to fill out an application form but will not have to wait for a credit investigation.

Credit Scoring

Credit scoring is a method of appraising the credit worthiness of potential borrowers. Numerical values are assigned to various factors. It is believed that good credit risks share certain characteristics and poor credit risks share other characteristics and that by analyzing these with a credit scoring report card, better decisions can be made regarding the granting of consumer credit.

Home ownership is a plus factor and a homeowner may receive, say, 20 points. A renter will receive less, but will receive some points for having lived at his or her present address for a certain number of years or more. A person will receive a certain number of points for the job he or she holds (say, for example, a supervisor 25 and a clerk 5), and some more for having held it five years or more. The level of income, assets, other debts outstanding, and marital status will all generate additional points. The total number of points will then be used to help determine whether or not credit will be granted. The credit scoring systems must ignore race, sex, and where a person lives, but can analyze his or her economic and financial strengths. Lenders give various weights to credit characteristics and they have their cutoff point at various total points. A hypothetical credit score and the probability of repaying a loan are shown below. Using such a system, loan officers must now make decisions as to where to draw the line. To help them do this, they may personally interview the prospective borrower.

Credit Life Insurance

Sometimes the lender will insist that the installment buyer purchase life insurance in an amount equal to the debt. The lender is the beneficiary; and in the event of the death of the buyer, the balance of the debt is paid off by the insurance company. The cost of this life insurance is, of course, passed on to the installment buyer. In the case of lending institutions, this cost often shows up in the form of an extra 0.5 percent interest per month. In arrangements made with merchants, it either shows up as an added service charge or is included in the price of the item. In some cases, the lender actually keeps a portion of the insurance premiums; only part of them is necessary to buy insurance. This is another illustration of a price pack to enhance the return of the lender or dealer.

Not all lenders and dealers will insist that the buyer take the credit life insurance. In some states, it is against the law to require that the installment buyer buy credit life insurance as part of the package. However, the buyer seldom knows this, and the law is very difficult to enforce. The lender can simply let it be known that the credit life insurance will have to be purchased as a condition to granting the loan.

Consumers who don't need or want the credit life insurance should try to negotiate it out of the package when discussing the terms of the contract. Showing evidence of knowledge of

TABLE 5-6. *Credit scoring*

CREDIT SCORE	PROBABILITY OF LOAN REPAYMENT
Below 60	.0
60–64	.0
65–69	7.9
70–74	15.2
75–79	20.3
80–84	33.0
85–89	34.2
90–94	45.4
95–99	45.9
100–104	61.9
105–109	70.4
110–114	73.5
115–119	76.0
120–124	80.6
125–129	82.3
130–134	89.5
135–139	92.6
140–144	91.8
145–149	94.5
150–154	96.0
155–159	97.9
160–164	98.4
170 and up	100.0

the subject being negotiated makes it more likely one will be successful in achieving one's goals.

Credit Card Abuse

All credit cards should perhaps have printed on them the warning, "financial experts have determined that credit cards are dangerous to your financial health." They are, if you abuse or overuse them. Then you can get in over your head and your income might be inadequate to liquidate the debt. One cardinal rule of thumb should be, use your credit card as a convenience and not as a source of funds. That is, never use your credit card if you could not immediately write a check for your purchase. Then when you are billed, liquidate your entire credit card charge each month. In this way you never build up an unpaid balance, and your credit card is not a source of borrowed funds for more than a few weeks. It is a convenience in that you need only write one check. You might also consider limiting the number of credit cards you own. Remember, if you need to borrow, go to a financial institution.

Unsolicited credit cards

It is illegal for a card issuer to send you a credit card unless you ask or apply for one. However, a card issuer may send you, without your request, a new card to replace an expired one. You may also be sent an application for a card in the mail or be asked to apply by phone.

Lost or stolen credit cards

Your risk on lost or stolen credit cards is limited.
You do not have to pay for **any** unauthorized charges made **after** you notify the card company of loss or theft of your card. So keep a list of your credit card numbers and notify card issuers immediately if your card is lost or stolen. The most you will have to pay for unauthorized charges is $50 on each card—even if someone runs up several hundred dollars worth of charges before you report a card missing.

Prompt credit for payments

If you can avoid finance charges on your credit card account by paying within a certain time, it is obviously important that you get your bills, and get credit for paying them, promptly. Check your statements to make sure your creditor follows these rules:

   —Prompt billing. Look at the date on the postmark. If your account is one on which no finance charge is added before a certain due date, then creditors must mail their statements at least 14 days before payment is due.
   —Prompt crediting. Look at the payment date entered on the statement. In most cases creditors must credit payments on the day received.

Refunds for overpayments

If you overpay on your credit card account by $1.00 or more, a creditor must give you a refund at your request. Overpayments can occur when, for example, you overlook a return of merchandise to be credited to your account.

Discounts for cash payments

It is illegal for credit card companies to prohibit stores from offering discounts to people who pay by cash or check. Stores that do offer cash discounts must make this fact clear to all buyers. They may not add an extra charge (above the regular price) for those customers choosing to use credit cards.
   For example, suppose you want to buy an item regularly

priced at $50. The store offers discounts for cash of 5 per cent. If you pay in cash, your price should be:

$$\begin{array}{r} \$50.00 \\ -2.50 \text{ (5\% of \$50)} \\ \hline \$47.50 \end{array}$$

If you use a credit card, the price is $50.

Credit card costs

How much you pay for the use of a credit card depends on three important terms of the credit card arrangement, which differ for cards issued by banks, by retail stores, or for travel and entertainment. Creditors must tell you:

1. The annual percentage rate (APR).
2. The method of calculating the finance charge.
3. When finance charges begin to be charged to your credit account.

Some creditors also charge a flat annual membership fee for use of their card.

Federal law does not set rates or tell the creditor how to calculate finance charges—it requires only that the creditor tell you the method. Be sure to ask for an explanation of any terms you don't understand.

Tips on Credit Cards

—Shop around for the best terms. Remember that finance charges may differ depending on the method the creditor uses to assess them.

—Make sure you understand all the terms of your credit card agreement before you sign.

—Pay bills promptly to keep up your good credit rating and to avoid high finance charges.

—Keep a list of all your credit card numbers in case of loss or theft, and keep a good record of your purchases and payments.

Source: Board of Governors of the Federal Reserve System, Washington, D.C. 20551—April 1979

Why Interest Rates Vary

Why do interest rates on consumer loans vary from one institution to another? Aside from reasons involving legislative permissions enabling the various institutions to charge different rates for small loans, there are other considerations. Management expenses tend to vary greatly among the lending institutions. For a small loan company, for example, management expenses tend to be fairly high. This is because many of their loans are small dollarwise. And it costs just as much to manage a $200 or $300 loan as it does for a $2,000 or $3,000 loan. In addition, small loan companies also make loans to people who are poorer credit risks. Because of this greater risk, they charge higher interest rates.

The management costs of the credit unions are low. Because they are mutual organizations, they have very little overhead; often they are given rent-free office space by their employers. Their record of losses is very low, and they are given a tax advantage over the commercial banks.

The insurance company suffers no risk of loss when making a policy loan, and its cost of collection is very low because these loans are single-payment loans that in many instances are never repaid.

Commercial banks, generally speaking, make loans only to the better credit risks. Because of this circumstance, their loss record is low, a fact that their interest charges reflect. Savings and loan associations also accept only the better risks. Hence their rates are usually below those of finance companies and are comparable to those of commercial banks.

Industrial banks, on the other hand, accept more risk and charge higher rates than commercial banks. Also, industrial banks make more extremely small loans—$50 to $100 and even less—that result in high administrative cost per dollar loaned.

As a general rule, when borrowing money, first try a commercial bank, credit union, or insurance company. Usually they charge less than other lending institutions. One should also know that the maximum interest rate permitted on small loans (consumer loans) is higher than the rate permitted under the general usury laws. There are basically three reasons for this difference in interest rates:

1. Usually the cost of the credit investigation is higher per dollar lent. It takes just as much time to run a credit check and determine the credit worthiness of a person borrowing $100 or $1,000 as it does of a person borrowing $10,000 or $20,000.

2. The bookkeeping and record-keeping costs are higher on a small loan than on a larger loan per dollar loaned.

3. There is often more risk to the lender because of the credit rating of many of the people borrowing from small loan companies. Because of the higher risk of default, the lender insists upon a higher rate of interest as compensation for assuming the greater risk.

This third point, high risk, is not always present, however, which is why, if your credit rating is good, it is ridiculous to pay more than 12 or 15 percent on consumer credit. Certain lending institutions such as commercial banks will lend only to those with solid credit ratings, so they are taking a relatively low risk. Personal finance companies will lend to those with poor credit ratings; they take more risk and charge higher rates of interest. While most interest charges, even those going up as high as 30 or 40 percent, are perfectly legal, there are a few lenders who break the law; they are the illegal "loan sharks."

Small loan laws attempt to protect both the borrower and the lender. The lender is permitted to charge higher rates to compensate for the credit investigation, bookkeeping, and risks. Borrowers receive some protection in that while they pay what may be a relatively high rate in some cases, there is a ceiling on the rate they may be charged. If it were not for the legal ceiling, they might fall into the hands of an unscrupulous lender who might charge even more. The unwary consumer should note that where money has been lent at a usurious rate, most states provide for the forfeiture of the principal or interest or both.

Single Repayment Loans

You may enjoy substantial interest savings when you borrow if you agree to repay the loan in one lump sum at a specific future time. You will then, of course, need to do your own budgeting and set aside a certain amount each week or month in order to have the wherewithal to liquidate the loan when due. The major reason why a person can obtain a much lower rate on a noninstallment type consumer loan is because the lender incurs fewer bookkeeping, record-keeping, and collection costs. If you borrow from an insurance company on a noninstallment basis, the annual percentage rate will be about 8 percent. If you then set aside a sum every week or month in a passbook savings account, you will earn anywhere from $5\frac{1}{4}$ to 6 percent for a net cost of about 2 or 3 percent. A single repayment loan from a bank, savings and loan association, mutual savings bank, or credit union will cost about 9 to 10 percent depending upon the size of the loan and your credit rating. This amounts to a net cost of about 4 to 6 percent if you use a passbook savings account to budget the repayment. It should be noted that in order to borrow from many lenders on a noninstallment basis, your credit rating must be better than that of many installment borrowers.

The Family Life Cycle and Installment Credit

A definite pattern of installment debt depends upon the life cycle of the family. Relatively speaking, the young, the old, and, to a lesser extent, the unmarried make little use of installment credit. With marriage and young children comes installment debt. As one wag put it, the finance company holds hands with the bride and the groom as they slowly wend their way from the altar.

Seventy percent of those spending units under the age of forty-five and with the youngest children age six or older have some installment debt. As the children grow up, the installment debt of the spending unit decreases. The years from twenty-five to about forty-five are the years when most of us accumulate our durable consumer goods and raise our families. After that, when we have a household of durables and the children have "flown the coop," we need only make replacements and there is less need for debt.

The family life cycle in relation to age and statistics on installment debt shows this pattern to be consistent. For example, a recent study indicates that 12 percent of those under twenty-five had $2,000 or more of consumer debt. At twenty-five to thirty-four years old, this figure was 19 percent; at thirty-five to forty-four, it was 15 percent; at forty-five to fifty-four, it was 20 percent; for ages fifty-five to sixty-four, it was 8 percent; and for those over sixty-five it was only 3 percent.

Early Repays: The Rule of 78

Supposing that sometime soon after assuming some consumer debt, a consumer experiences good fortune and discovers that she is able to repay it far in advance of the installment schedule. The real question is, if she pays off the debt in advance, is an interest rebate given? The answer is yes, in most cases. Generally the method used to calculate this rebate is referred to as the *rule of 78*, but this figure is misleading. It could just as well be called the rule of 21 or the rule of 171. A few examples will make this clear.

Suppose that Mr. Wilson borrowed $1,200 to be paid off in twelve equal monthly installments at 6 percent add-on interest. This makes his true interest rate just over 11 percent over the entire twelve months and his monthly payments $106. Then, when the third monthly payment is due he decides to liquidate the entire debt. How is the interest recalculated?

First, take the sum of all numbers from 1 to 12; they equal 78. If the loan is repaid in full after one month, the lenders receive $12/78$ of the interest that they would have received had the loan been outstanding the entire year; if it is liquidated after two months, the lenders receive 12 + 11 or $23/78$; if after three months, 12 + 11 + 10 or $33/78$ and so on. Only if the loan is outstanding the full twelve months does the lender receive the full $78/78$ of the agreed-upon interest. Calculating the interest for early repays by this method results in the lender getting somewhat more than a strictly pro rata distribution of interest. For example, after three months on a pro rata basis, the lender would only get one-fourth of the total interest, which would be $19.5/78$ in the example used above. This would be a true interest rate of about 6.5 percent for these three months. It is less than the annual 11 percent that would have applied if the loan had been amortized normally because the declining balance (and hence the average balance) is relatively high during the early months of the loan. But because of the sum-of-the-digits method, the lender gets $33/78$, which in our example is $33/78$ of $72 or a total interest payment of $30.45. This is about 11 percent per year simple interest over these three months. What the sum of the digits does, then, is to increase the interest rate on installment loans to put it back up where it would have been had the loan been amortized normally.

Suppose that in another case $900 is borrowed to be paid back in six monthly install-ments of $150, but after two months the entire loan is liquidated. This could be called the rule of 21 (the sum of the digits from 1 to 6 = 21). The lenders would receive $11/21$ of the total interest if the loan is repaid after two months. The sum of the digits is the rule and it can be used to calculate the interest on an early repay for a loan of any length. All that is needed is to know the total number of payments and the total interest, in dollars, that would be paid if the loan were not liquidated early.

Assume, for example, that an eighteen-month installment loan is repaid in full after six months. The sum of the digits here gives us 171 (18 + 17 + 16 + 15, etc.). Since six months have elapsed, the lender receives $93/171$ (18 + 17 + 16 + 15 + 14 + 13 = 93) of the interest that would have been received had the loan been outstanding the entire eighteen months.

To be sure, lenders do not calculate these rebates in this manner because tables have been prepared and the lender merely looks up the rebate from the tables. These tables have been prepared, however, by using the sum-of-the-digits method described here.

Credit Counselors

In recent years, an additional service has been developed in some states that some borrowers have found useful. It is a service known as *credit advisors* or *credit counselors*. Credit advisors are not a source of credit; they do not lend any money. They do provide two useful services, however.

First, they help a person to manage his or her personal affairs; they may set up a budget and persuade the client to live within it. For example, if a person has monthly payments in excess of his or her ability to pay, the credit counselor will attempt to stretch out the debt over a longer time period and in this way reduce the monthly payments. Second, after having worked out a new payment plan that the individual can meet, the credit advisor will act as the middleman and attempt to persuade the lender to accept the new reduced monthly payments. As a disinterested third party, they can often do this more easily than the person involved.

No one who is capable of budgeting and managing his or her own financial affairs should have to use credit counselors. However, the growth of this group indicates that some people either cannot or will not do this for themselves.

Credit counselors charge a fee for their services, which is generally 12 percent of the outstanding debts (negotiated by them). This then is the fee one pays for not capably planning one's own affairs. It should be noted that most lenders will act as credit counselors for the borrower and, in most cases, will stretch out payments to keep the borrower afloat.

Certified Financial Planners

In recent years a somewhat more sophisticated personal financial planner and advisor has emerged. The certified financial planner (CFP) is able to assist the individual in virtually all aspects of personal financial affairs, including budgeting, restructuring excessive debt, insurance, investments, problems of home ownership, taxes, and even, in some cases, estate planning. Remember that if the CFP is not an attorney, he or she cannot legally draw up a will. Many CFPs are also either accountants, securities brokers, insurance agents, real estate brokers, or attorneys. They have, in a sense, broadened the scope of their services.

Some of the planners have kept their former specialty and will aid the individual in financial planning for little or no fee, earning a commission by selling securities, insurance, real estate, etc. to the person. Other planners charge a fee for their services; it can either be a flat fee or a percentage of the assets involved.

The concept of the certified financial planner was originally developed by the College of Financial Planning in Colorado, which was established by a group of financial planners. There is also an International Association of Financial Planners headquartered in Atlanta, Georgia.

FINANCIAL DOCUMENTS ACCOMPANYING CONSUMER LOANS

A Typical Installment Contract

When you buy something or borrow money on the installment plan, you must sign some papers. The same is true when you borrow on a single repayment loan. The three illustrations below show this. The first is a typical security agreement and installment contract. It is the type generally used to finance the purchase of new automobiles in Texas, but it is drawn up in accordance with the Uniform Commercial Code and also conforms to the federal truth-in-lending law. Consequently, with slight variations, contracts similar to it are used for new cars throughout the United States. This type of contract is also employed to finance other durable goods.

Note that this contract shows (as required by the truth-in-lending law) the number of payments, the fact that they are equal in dollar amounts, the total interest cost dollarwise as well as the true annual percentage rate (APR), and a number of other pertinent facts.

It also has a default and delinquency clause, which spells out certain conditions of the agreement. It provides that the borrower pay all court and attorney's fees if they are necessary to collect payments. It also stipulates the penalty for late payments. The second document is a note for a 90-day single repayment loan. It is very much like the first document. The third item is for a $200 dollar 30-day loan. In this case there is a $15 minimum fee. Over the 30 days this amounts to 90 percent.

Texas Bank
Austin REPUBLIC OF TEXAS   6209990

**LOAN DISCLOSURE STATEMENT,
SECURITY AGREEMENT AND INSTALLMENT NOTE**

DISCLOSURES MADE UNDER FEDERAL LAW

Customer	Date of Loan
Doe, John	FEBRUARY 10th, 1981

Customer's Address	Customer's Home Phone	Total of Payments
2205 5th street	4589211	10,123.92
Austin, Tex 78767	Customer's Business Phone 3212245	Texas

Creditor	Creditor's Address (Street, Town, County, State)
Texas Bank	**900 Congress, Austin, Texas 78767**

LOAN DISCLOSURE STATEMENT AND SECURITY AGREEMENT

Check Applicable Boxes. All statements in which no box is present apply to this loan.

A. **REQUIRED INSURANCE.** PHYSICAL DAMAGE INSURANCE ON THE PROPERTY FOR THE FULL TERM OF THE NOTE IS REQUIRED AS CHECKED BELOW. CUSTOMER HAS OPTION OF FURNISHING THE REQUIRED INSURANCE EITHER THROUGH EXISTING POLICIES OF INSURANCE OWNED OR CONTROLLED BY HIM OR OF PROCURING AND FURNISHING EQUIVALENT INSURANCE COVERAGES THROUGH ANY INSURANCE COMPANY AUTHORIZED TO TRANSACT BUSINESS IN TEXAS. IF OBTAINED FROM OR THROUGH CREDITOR OR IF A CHARGE THEREFOR, IS INCLUDED HEREIN THE CHARGE FOR SUCH INSURANCE SHOWN BELOW IS FOR A TERM OF ___N/A___ MONTHS. ☐ IF CHECKED HERE, THE INSURANCE IS SOLD FOR A PREMIUM NOT FIXED OR APPROVED BY THE STATE BOARD OF INSURANCE, AND CUSTOMER MAY CANCEL SUCH INSURANCE WITHOUT CHARGE FOR **5** DAYS FROM THE DATE OF THIS CONTRACT AND SUBSTITUTE OTHER EQUIVALENT COVERAGE IN THE MANNER ABOVE DESCRIBED. ☐ UNLESS CHECKED HERE, THE REQUIRED INSURANCE IS NOT AVAILABLE FROM OR THROUGH CREDITOR, AND ANY PREMIUMS SHOWN BELOW ARE FOR A TERM REPORTED BY CUSTOMER AND ARE BASED ON INFORMATION SUPPLIED BY CUSTOMER.

TYPE OF PHYSICAL DAMAGE INSURANCE   CHARGE

☐ Collision $ ___N/A___
☐ Comprehensive $ ___N/A___
☐ Fire, Theft and Additional $ ___N/A___
☐ Fire and Extended Coverage $ ___N/A___
Total Physical Damage Insurance Charge $ ___N/A___ (3)

B. OPTIONAL CREDIT LIFE OR CREDIT LIFE AND CREDIT ACCIDENT AND HEALTH (CREDIT A & H INSURANCE). This insurance is not required but is available for the full term of The Note at a charge of $ **170.08** for Credit Life and $ ___N/A___ for Credit Life and Credit A & H. This insurance is subject to the conditions in Paragraph 23(G) on the reverse side, and is not provided unless Customer signs in the box below.

OPTIONAL INSURANCE ELECTION
Customer desires:
☒ Optional Credit Life Insurance
☐ Optional Credit Life and Credit A & H Insurance.
DATE _____
CUSTOMER SIGNATURE

$ **170.08** (4)
Charge for Credit Life or Credit Life and Credit A & H Insurance

C. Proceeds of any insurance, whether paid by return of premiums or otherwise may be applied by Creditor toward repair of the Collateral or payment of the Obligation at its option as set forth in Paragraph 20(G) on the reverse side.

1. **Loan Proceeds:** Amounts paid to Customer or to others on his behalf (other than Items 2, 3, and 4 below)
   A. $ __8,000.00__
   B. $ __N/A__
   C. $ __N/A__
   Total Proceeds $ __8,000.00__ (1)

2. **Fees Prescribed by Law**
   A. Filing Fee $ __N/A__
   B. Release Fee $ __N/A__
   C. Registration Fee $ __N/A__
   D. Certificate of Title Fee $ __N/A__
   Total Fees $ __N/A__ (2)

3. Physical Damage Insurance Charge $ __N/A__ (3)

4. Credit Life or Credit Life and Credit A & H Insurance Charge $ __170.08__ (4)

5. Total Authorized Charges (2+3+4) $ __170.08__ (5)

6. Amount Financed (1+5) $ __8,170.08__ (6)

7. **FINANCE CHARGE** $ __1,953.84__ (7)

8. Total of Payments (6+7) $ __10,123.92__ (8)

9. **ANNUAL PERCENTAGE RATE**   __14.50__ % (9)

10. The Finance Charge accrues from the Date of Loan unless this box is checked ☐ in which case it accrues from __N/A__

11. The date of distribution of the proceeds is estimated to be on or about the date specified in Item 10.

12. **PAYMENT SCHEDULE.** The Total of Payments is payable in __35__ installments of $ __281.22__ each, and one final installment of $ __281.22__. The first installment is due and payable on the __10th__ day of __MARCH__, 19 __81__, and the remaining installments are due and payable on the same day of each succeeding __MONTHLY__ period thereafter until the Note is paid in full.

13. **BALLOON PAYMENT.** If this box is checked ☐, the final installment of $ __N/A__ in Paragraph 12 is more than twice the average of prior installments and such balloon payments may be renewed at Creditor's sole discretion.

14. **ACCELERATION CLAUSE.** Upon failure of Customer to perform any of his obligations hereunder or if Creditor in good faith believes that the prospect of payment of the Obligation is impaired, the amount of the Note legally collectible shall become immediately due and payable at the election of the holder hereof, without notice, and in such event the owner and holder hereof may exercise any of the rights of a secured party after default granted by the Texas Uniform Commercial Code and not prohibited by the Texas Credit Code. In the event of acceleration of maturity, the unearned portion of the FINANCE CHARGE shall be calculated by the method described in Paragraph 16 below and necessary credits will be given, provided that in no event shall the amount of FINANCE CHARGE contracted for, charged or collected hereon exceed the maximum FINANCE CHARGE permitted by law. Upon such occurence, Customer agrees to pay attorney's fees assessed by a court and court costs as well as the reasonable cost for repossession, storing, preparing for sale, or selling any security. After acceleration of maturity, unless prohibited by either Chapter 3 or 4 of the Texas Credit Code as designated on the bottom line of this page, the amount legally owed shall bear interest at the rate of **10%** per annum.

15. **SECURITY INTEREST.** Subject to the terms hereof and of the Texas Uniform Commercial Code, Customer hereby grants to Creditor a security interest in (i) the following described property (herein called "the Property"):

1981 Buick Regal
Ser-#123456789

(ii) all the equipment and accessories thereon, and after-acquired property only to the extent of accessions added thereto, and (iii) all proceeds thereof, including insurance proceeds payable by reason of loss or damage to the Property or return of premiums (all 3 of which are herein collectively called "the Collateral") to secure the payment of (i) the Note, (ii) all other and future debt of Customer to Creditor now existing or hereafter incurred, and (iii) all Reimbursable Costs incurred by Creditor in connection with the Collateral as defined on the reverse side in Paragraph 19(d) (all 3 classes of such debt are herein called jointly "the Obligation"). Collateral will be used for _____

PERSONAL USE _____ and will be located _____ 2205 5th street, Austin 78767 _____

_____ If this box is checked ☐, the security interest in the Collateral to secure the Obligation is also granted pursuant to the terms of a Security Agreement between Customer and Creditor of even date herewith and in the event of any conflict between the terms thereof and hereof, the terms hereof shall prevail. Creditor will have an equitable right to set off any debt owed by Creditor to Customer against the Obligation upon maturity of the Obligation (whether by acceleration or otherwise).

16. REFUND UPON PREPAYMENT. Customer may pay the Note in full at any time during regular business hours, and a refund of the FINANCE CHARGE will be made in accordance with the "Sum of Periodic Balances Method" if payments in Paragraph 12 are substantially equal, successive monthly installments beginning within **1** month plus **15** days after the date of this Contract. In all other cases, the refund will be made under the "Actuarial Method employing the United States rule." Both methods are set out in full in Paragraph 24 on the reverse side. No refund shall be required for partial prepayments and no refund of less than **$1.00** need be made.

17. CHARGE FOR LATE PAYMENT. Customer agrees to pay a charge of **5c** for each **$1.00** of any scheduled installment when any portion of such installment continues unpaid for **10** days or more following the date such payment is due, including Sundays and holidays, and if any installment is deferred as of an installment date for **1** or more full months with the consent of Creditor, Customer agrees to pay deferment interest equal to the difference between the refund which would be required for prepayment in full as of the date of deferment and the refund which would be required for prepayment in full **1** month prior to such date, multiplied by the number of months in the deferment period. If payments in Paragraph 12 are other than substantially equal, successive monthly installments, no late charge shall be collected but Customer agrees to pay interest from the maturity date of any installment until paid at a rate not exceeding the highest lawful contract rate (which is presently **10**% per annum).

Please Charge My Checking Account for the Monthly Installments	Account Number	Account Name	Customer's Signature
	N/A	N/A	

INSTALLMENT NOTE [THE NOTE]

For Value Received, the undersigned Customer and any Co-Signer (herein jointly called "Makers") jointly and severally promise to pay to the order of Creditor at its above address the Total of Payments in paragraph 8 payable as set out in Paragraph 12 pursuant to the terms above and on the reverse side.

NOTICE: SEE OTHER SIDE FOR IMPORTANT INFORMATION. The terms and conditions on the reverse side are made a part hereof and are incorporated herein by reference. **CUSTOMER ACKNOWLEDGES RECEIPT OF A FULLY COMPLETED COPY OF THIS CONTRACT WITH ALL BLANKS COMPLETED, TOGETHER WITH A COPY OF ALL DOCUMENTS SIGNED BY CUSTOMER IN CONNECTION WITH THIS LOAN.**

Customer	Co-Signer
Creditor **Texas Bank**	Co-Signer Name and Address N/A
BY	
CHAPTER 4 OF THE TEXAS CREDIT CODE	Co-Signer's Home Phone N/A / Co-Signer's Business Phone

RPT 77-250-0014

FIGURE 5-7. *Typical security agreement.* (*Source:* Texas Bank of Austin.)

FIGURE 5-8. *Ninety-day single-repayment note.* (*Source:* Texas Bank of Austin.)

LENDER **Texas Bank** Austin	☒ PROMISSORY NOTE (Single Maturity)	NOTE NUMBER 9999	ACCOUNT NUMBER 1111-11-1

| OFFICER 00 | DATE 2-10-81 | MATURITY DATE 5-11-81 | AMOUNT OF NOTE 2000.00 | ANNUAL RATE OF INTEREST (AR) FIXED RATE OF 10 % or LENDER'S PRIME PLUS | PERCENT-AGE POINTS | DAILY RATE 1/365 of AR |

Terms used in this note shall have the meanings indicated in the boxes above. ON DEMAND, or if no demand is made then on or before Maturity Date, for value received, Maker promises to pay to the order of Lender at Lender's address shown above the Amount of Note plus interest on unpaid Amount of Note from Date at the AR. Unpaid and past due Amount of Note and interest shall bear interest at the highest rate Lender lawfully may charge on this note. Until the earlier to occur of Demand or Maturity Date, interest shall be computed at the Daily Rate. If the AR is stated in terms of Lender's prime rate, the AR shall change with each change in such prime rate as of the date of any such change, but shall not exceed the highest rate Lender lawfully may charge on this note.

Each Maker, guarantor, surety and indorser waives demand, presentment, notice of dishonor, protest and diligence in collecting sums due hereunder; agrees to application of any debt of Lender to the payment hereof; agrees that extensions and renewals without limit as to number, acceptance of any number of partial payments, releases of any party liable hereon, and releases or substitutions of collateral, before or after maturity, shall not release or discharge his obligation under this note; and agrees to pay in addition to all other sums due hereunder reasonable attorney's fees if this note is placed in the hands of an attorney for collection or if it is collected through probate, bankruptcy, or other judicial proceeding. Reasonable attorney's fees shall be ten per cent (10%) of the unpaid balance unless either party shall plead and prove otherwise. The holder may accelerate the Maturity Date without prior notice to any party at any time he shall deem himself insecure, if Maker shall fail to pay any other debt to Lender when due, or if any default or event of default shall occur under any agreement securing, evidencing, guaranteeing, or providing for, debt of Maker to Lender. As used herein, where appropriate, the masculine gender includes the feminine and neuter and the singular number includes the plural.

Payment hereof is secured by:

Mr. John Doe
2205 5th Street
Austin, Texas 78767

MAKER

```
NOTE (SERVICE CHARGE)                                          Note No. _____

┌─────────────────────────────────────┬──────────────────────────────────────────┐
│ Name(s) and Address(es) of Borrower(s)│ Name and Address of Bank                   │
│                                      │      State Bank of Allston                 │
│      John Doe                        │      7600 Brighton Road                    │
│      458 West Rd.                    │      Harbor City, AN  068501               │
│      Harbor City, AN  068501         ├─────────────┬──────────────────┬──────────┤
│                                      │ Date of Note │ Total of Payments│ Officer  │
│                                      │   8-10-79    │ $ 215.00         │   AB     │
└─────────────────────────────────────┴─────────────┴──────────────────┴──────────┘
```

For value received, Borrower(s) whose name(s) and address(es) appear above (hereinafter called "Borrower") hereby promises to pay to the order of the Bank whose name and address appear above (hereinafter called "Bank") at Bank's address shown above the Total of Payments shown below in a single payment due _____9-9-79_____

No default, delinquency or similar charges may be charged or received by Bank in connection with this Note.

In the event of prepayment of this Note in full or in part, Bank will **not** refund or credit to Borrower any of the Finance Charge.

1. Cash Advanced or Credit Extended $ 200.00	4. Service Charge $ 15.00
2. Prev. Bal. Renewed (Note # n/a) $ -0-	5. **FINANCE CHARGE** (same as 4) $ 15.00
3. Total Amount of Credit/ Amount Financed (1 + 2) $ 200.00	6. Total of Payments (3 + 5) $ 215.00
	7. **ANNUAL PERCENTAGE RATE** 90.00 %

All parties to this Note including endorsers and guarantors severally waive presentment for payment, notice of nonpayment, protest, notice of protest, demand, notice of dishonor, diligence in enforcement and indulgences of every kind.

Borrower agrees that the service charge disclosed above represents the reasonable value of the services rendered by Bank in connection with the loan evidenced by this Note.

I (We) acknowledge receipt of a copy of this Note executed on the Date of Note above written and completed as to all essential provisions and agree to its terms as set forth above.

Borrower: John Doe   Borrower:

   (X)

FIGURE 5-9. *Thirty-day note.*

SOME DOS AND DON'TS OF CONSUMER CREDIT

The main advice we can provide when you use consumer credit is: "be careful." We can also summarize the things to do and not to do when using consumer credit, as follows:

Dos

1. Before you sign any credit application, decide how you are going to meet the payments when due.
2. Find how much you have left after all your necessary expenses and payments are taken out.
3. Remember that credit costs money. Renting money is like renting a house or a car—you have to pay for its use. This means that an item bought on credit costs more than if it is bought for cash.
4. Be sure you find out how much more an item bought on credit will cost you. Insist that the salesperson give you a written statement showing all costs and charges BEFORE you decide whether or not you want to buy this item.

5. Be a good shopper. Compare cash and "on time" prices for the same item in different stores.

6. If you get careless with credit and find your payments, when added to your necessary living expenses, are more than your paycheck, don't try to hide from your creditors. Ask about consolidating your debts. The lender may be able to lend you enough to pay up the bills and to stretch out the payments so your monthly payments will be reduced to where you can handle them. But, remember, extra time costs extra money; so don't do it unless it is the only way you can pay your debts.

7. Analyze the deal before you sign for it. Look at total cost (purchase price plus interest) of the item you are considering. Would you pay that much in cash for it if you had the cash in your pocket? Would a cheaper model do just as well? Do you really need the item at all?

Don'ts

1. Don't let a smooth-talking sales representative pressure you into a final sale on credit to take advantage of a special bargain. If the "special bargain" is only going to last a few hours, it may not be so special.

2. Don't be a soft touch for a smooth salesperson who uses an emotional approach. *Example:* "You owe it to your kiddies to buy this set of encyclopedias (only $400)." By the time your kiddies are old enough to use them, the books will be outdated and worthless—and you will probably be in a much better position to afford the set they need than you are now.

3. Don't fall for the old sales gag about the "other buyer who is going to snap this bargain up" if you don't get on the dotted line at once. If Salesman Sam really had a customer that eager, he wouldn't be trying so hard to sell you.

4. Don't buy anything—for cash or credit—that you don't really want or need just because it is cheap. *Example:* One eager customer signed up for a $260 super-duper model sweeper. Later, when creditors came around to see why he was behind in his payments, they found he didn't even own a rug. Of course, few people are this eager to buy, but far too many seem unwilling to match their wants and needs with a realistic understanding of their ability to pay.

5. Don't buy anything just because you can get it on credit—or because no down payment is required or because payments are small. Remember, you will have to pay the full price in the end—plus the cost of credit, which is higher if no down payment is made or if payments are stretched over a long period of time to keep them low.

6. Don't count on a supplementary salary in any long-range credit plans (over six months). Layoffs may occur or a wife may become pregnant; then earnings may be cut off.

7. Don't take unnecessary chances. Buy from dealers in whom you have confidence. When you pledge a part of your earnings for the next several months, you want at least to know that you are dealing with a reputable businessperson who has an established place of business and one you can find in case the merchandise is faulty.

8. Don't expect to erase your debt by returning the merchandise. In most cases you have signed two contracts: one for the purchase of the goods and one for the loan of

funds. In many cases, your loan contract will be sold to a bank or finance company at once and you will owe them instead of the dealer. Dealers should stand behind the goods they sell, but you still have to pay the loan in full, even if the car you bought won't run.

9. Don't sign a contract that a salesperson offers to "hold" until you make up your mind. Chances are it will be executed before you are out of sight. *Example:* A woman wanted to try out a used car and the obliging salesman agreed to let her use it for the weekend but "for her protection, insurance, etc." he insisted on having a contract signed that he promised to hold. When the woman took the clunker back on Monday and said she wouldn't buy it, she found she already had.

10. Don't sign your name to anything you have not read completely and carefully and that you do not understand fully. If a salesperson says the contract is standard and doesn't let you read it at your own pace, watch out.

11. Don't sign a contract that seems to be different from what the salesperson told you. In case of doubt, have the salesperson write out what he or she promises, sign it, and give it to you as a part of the agreement. If the salesperson refuses, take yourself away before this person takes you.

12. Don't let a smooth salesperson "switch contracts" so you read one and sign another. If the contract is taken away (for an OK) after you have read it, read it again when it is brought back to be sure it is the same one. Watch for different wording on carbons and for "short sheets" where you read one short page and actually sign a longer one hidden beneath it.

13. Don't overlook the fact that in some states you can't take mortgaged goods across the state line without permission of the mortgage holder. If you might be moving before a major purchase is paid for, check this point before you sign on the dotted line.

QUESTIONS FOR REVIEW

1. How is consumer credit classified for statistical purposes by the Federal Reserve Board?

2. Distinguish between an installment loan and a "single-payment" loan.

3. Distinguish between a charge account and what has been commonly labeled "service credit."

4. The text gives a number of reasons for consumer borrowing; list three and explain each in detail.

5. How do individual savers benefit by consumer borrowing?

6. It is said that society as a whole may benefit from consumer credit. Rationalize this statement.

7. Explain how easy credit and the careless use of it may actually wreck your budget.

8. Is consumer credit growing, staying the same, or declining?

9. Explain in detail whether consumer credit "costs" anything.

10. What are the underlying reasons for permitting small loan companies to charge as high a rate of interest as they do?

11. Explain the manner in which credit unions are organized.

12. What is the difference between the "industrial" bank and a "commercial" bank?

13. Differentiate between the remedial loan society and the pawnshop.

14. How may it be said that borrowing on a life insurance policy has a psychological drawback for many consumers?

15. In order of the lowest cost of borrowing, list the seven financial institutions discussed in the text.

16. What are sales finance companies and what is their relationship to consumer lending?

17. Explain in detail the workings of the "revolving credit plan."

18. Do you think the checkless society will be a reality soon? What are your views regarding it?

19. What is credit life insurance?

20. Aside from permissive legislation, discuss the reasons for variations in loan charges among the various financial institutions that grant consumer loans.

21. How does the family life cycle relate to the volume of the family's installment debt?

22. What are credit counselors and how do they differ from sales finance companies?

23. Discuss the dos and don'ts of credit.

CASES

1. Louise Adams recently opened a revolving charge account at a large department store. The clerk told her she could always have some balance outstanding. However, every month she is billed for her entire account. She cannot reconcile these two facts. Can you help her?

2. In order to obtain consumer credit, it is generally necessary to make an application and undergo a credit investigation. What is the information for which you will be asked when you apply for credit? What will the credit investigation attempt to reveal?

3. Bob and Patricia Snelling, a young married couple, are recent arrivals in town. They rented a small apartment and have little savings left. Bob has a job at which he makes $300 per week and Patricia is seeking employment.

   Joe and Ellen Worth, on the other hand, have lived in the same community for twenty years. The Worths are in their forties, and Joe is a foreman at a local plant where his weekly salary is $500. Moreover, the Worths have a $20,000 mortgage on a $50,000 house.

   Both couples apply for a loan at the local finance company in order to buy a new car. Which applicant is more likely to receive a loan? Why?

4. Bill Brown has found a used car priced at $1,500 that he would like to buy. He has $1,000 in the bank and he can save $50 per month. Should he wait until he has saved $500 and pay cash for the car, or should he borrow $500? What are advantages of waiting and paying cash? What are the advantages of borrowing and financing the car? Can you think of any disadvantages in borrowing the money?

5. Bill Hardy bought a used Ford valued at $2,400 and used his older car as a down payment. He agreed to pay off the balance of $1,600 over two years in twenty-four equal monthly installments of $79.50. What is the true interest rate on the loan?

6. Betty Canfield bought a used car valued at $1,800. The terms of the agreement provided that she make a down payment of $600 and pay the balance at $109 per month over twelve months. What is the actual dollar cost of the credit? What is the true interest rate she is paying for the use of the credit?

7. Helen Walker has decided to buy some new furniture for her apartment. One store has offered to finance it on the basis of $100 down and $20 a week for sixty-five weeks. Another store has offered her the same furniture at $100 per month for fourteen months with no down payment. The furniture is priced at $1,200 if sold for cash. Which of the two stores is offering Helen the better deal? What is the effective interest rate in both cases? Can you offer any suggestions that may save Ms. Walker some money?

8. Bob and Virginia, a young married couple, have decided to buy a TV set on the installment plan. The set they want costs $225 if

bought outright for cash. The dealer has offered it to them for $20 down and $5 per week for fifty weeks. They think this makes the set rather expensive. Calculate what the set will cost them and what proportion of it is interest in absolute dollars. What is the true interest rate?

9. Jean and Dick are a young couple who recently purchased a color TV set on the following terms. They paid $50 down and are paying $50 per month. They are to make ten payments. Yet the sum total which they must pay is $800. They don't understand how they can pay the total sum in ten payments. Can you explain it to them? If they had been able to pay cash, they could have obtained the set for $700. What interest rate are they paying?

10. Jim Hoffman earns $200 per week take-home pay. He has the following installment loans to pay off:

car $75 per month for ten months

refrigerator $25 per month for eight months

furniture $30 per month for twelve months

loan from bank $30 per month for six months

Jim's budget cannot meet these payments. Can you prepare a plan whereby Jim can pay off his debts? The most he can pay is $80 per month. Where can he go for such service?

11. Dorothy Jenkins is a young schoolteacher in Santa Ana, California, who borrowed $600 to repair her car after an accident and to meet other expenses. She agreed to pay it back in nine monthly installments of $74.70. What interest rate is this? However, after two months, Dorothy was reimbursed by an insurance company and was able to liquidate the entire loan. Calculate the actual dollar amount of interest Dorothy paid. What true annual percentage rate is this?

SUGGESTED READINGS

Banking Journal of the American Banker's Association. Published monthly by the American Bankers Association, New York, N.Y.

"Careers in Consumer Finance." National Consumer Finance Association, revised 1970.

Cole, Robert H. *Consumer and Commercial Credit Management,* 4th ed. Homewood, Il.: R. D. Irwin, 1980.

Consumer Credit and You. Greenfield, Massachusetts: Channing L. Bete Company, Inc., no date.

Consumer Finance News. Published monthly by the National Consumer Finance Association, Washington, D.C.

Consumer Finance Rate and Regulation Chart. Compiled by National Consumer Finance Association. Revised annually.

Consumer Loan and Sales Finance Rate and Regulation Chart. Compiled by National Consumer Finance Association. Revised annually.

Consumer Reports. A monthly publication of the Consumers Union of the United States, 256 Washington Street, Mt. Vernon, New York.

Cost of Personal Borrowing in the United States.

Published annually by the Financial Publishing Company, Boston, MA.

Credit. Published bimonthly by the National Consumer Finance Association.

"Credit Research Center Working Papers." A series of research studies on topics significant to consumer credit; published by the Credit Research Center, Purdue University, West Lafayette, IN.

A Date With Your Future. New York: Educational Division, Institute of Life Insurance, undated.

"Electronic Money . . . and the Payments Mechanism." Boston, Massachusetts: Federal Reserve Bank of Boston, 1973.

Family Budget Guide. Washington, D.C.: National Consumer Finance Association.

Finance Facts Yearbook. Published annually by the National Consumer Finance Association, Washington, D.C.

Hawyer, Carl F. *Basic Principles in Family Money and Credit Management.* Educational Services Division, National Consumer Finance Association, 1974.

The Industrial Banker, and Time Sales Financing. A monthly publication of the American Industrial Bankers Association, Washington, D.C.

International Credit Union Yearbook, 1980. Madison, WI: CUNA International, Inc. Published annually.

Let's Learn About Consumer Finance. Washington, D.C.: National Consumer Finance Association.

NCFA Research Report on Finance Companies. Published annually by Research Services Division, National Consumer Finance Association.

"Personal Finance: The Debtor Executive." *Sales Management,* June 1, 1970.

U.S. Department of Agriculture, *Consumers All, The Yearbook on Agriculture.* Published annually by the U.S. Department of Agriculture, Washington, D.C.

Chapter Six

Consumer Laws and Protection Agencies

Thou hast eyes with which to see, but seeth not. In other words read the fine print.

ANONYMOUS

The objectives of this chapter are to

1   Point out that consumers do have some legal protection, because of laws passed on both the federal and state levels

2   Note that there are also private voluntary consumer organizations that can sometimes help, especially in giving advice

3   Introduce the various federal consumer protection laws and explain what they do

4   Indicate to which federal agency you should go if you feel a federal law has been violated

INTRODUCTION

In recent years a good deal of legislation has been passed in an attempt to protect the consumer. There are state laws and state agencies and federal laws and federal agencies. There is no uniformity among the various states so only general comments will be made. Many states have usury laws which have been on the books for years. In some states these usury laws apply to consumer credit, and in some they do not, and special laws have been passed which set the upper limits on consumer credit interest rates. The regular usury laws do, however, usually apply to mortgage loans made to individuals, and to business loans.

In most states there is a consumer credit commission or a similar office which regulates consumer credit lenders and enforces state laws. These laws cover, among other things, the maximum interest rate that may be charged. In a few states this office may listen to consumer complaints and even take action if the complaint is legitimate. But an official state agency to help the consumer is the exception rather than the rule, and generally an individual must take legal action on his or her own unless a federal or state statute has been violated.

Private voluntary consumer organizations also exist in some areas. These groups may aid an individual and bring strength of numbers to bear, or they may provide financial and legal aid in the event of a lawsuit. They may also lobby for stronger consumer protection laws. But unless a law has been violated there is often little that can be done, even if you have been shabbily treated. Consequently, you should read very carefully any installment contract before signing it.

Nevertheless, consumer organizations can help sometimes. If there are none in your area and you wish to start one, contact the Consumer Federation of America. It is a Washington, D.C.-based coalition of seven hundred state and local consumer organizations and will assist other state and local groups in getting started.

FEDERAL CONSUMER PROTECTION LAWS[1]

When you borrow money or buy something on the installment plan there are certain federal laws which protect you to some extent. You should be familiar with this protection and know where you can go if a law has been broken. Currently, federal legislation covers the following general areas, each of which will be discussed in turn:

"Federal labeling laws don't apply to homemade meat loaf." (Source: Permission Cartoon Features Syndicate; from *The Wall Street Journal*.)

1. This material is drawn from Wolf and Associates, "Financial Seminars." Copyright, 1976 by Harold A. Wolf. Used by permission.

Truth in Lending
Fair Credit Reporting
Equal Credit Opportunity
Fair Credit Billing
Consumer Leasing
Fair Debt Collection Practices

Truth in Lending

Officially known as the Consumer Credit Protection Act, the federal truth-in-lending law was passed in 1968 and has been amended several times since then. "Truth in Lending" does essentially what its title suggests: it requires that certain facts be disclosed when consumer loans are made.

Interest Costs

The lender must inform the borrower of the "true" or actuarially correct percentage interest rate that he or she is paying. As pointed out in a previous chapter, this is called the annual percentage rate (APR) and must be distinguished from the so-called add-on interest rate. The add-on rate is misleading because it is calculated on the original balance, which is actually declining if paid off in installments. The borrower must also be told the total dollar amount of interest together with any service charges, extra loading fees, and points. If a product is being financed (rather than money being borrowed, say, at a bank), the cash price as well as credit price must be spelled out.

Balloon Clause and Credit Life

If there is a balloon clause in the contract, this must be disclosed. The cost of any credit life insurance must be explained; the same is true of accident, health, or loss of income insurance written in connection with any credit transactions.

Right of Rescission

The truth-in-lending law also requires that the "right of rescission" clause be inserted into every contract in which the borrower's home is used as collateral (including mobile homes). This gives the borrower three business days in which to nullify any such contract. The borrower's home is frequently used as collateral when a major repair or remodeling job is being done. In such a case, work may not begin until the three days are up unless you, in writing, waive the right of rescission. If you cancel during the three days, you must also do this in writing.

Lost or Stolen Credit Cards

This law also protects the borrower in the event a credit card is lost or stolen. Once the missing card has been reported, the cardholder is not liable for bills stemming from its unauthorized use. It is up to the issuer to block its illegal use. Even if the missing card is not reported, the maximum liability is $50.00 per card. Consequently, report any missing cards immediately, first by telephone and then by registered letter. To do this you will need to know the number of the card; it is suggested that you keep a record of all your credit card numbers. Some credit card issuers have a special form which you may use to report a missing card, or you may report it in an ordinary letter. In any event, treat your credit card like money; never take it out of your purse or wallet except when using it.

Garnishment of Wages

In 1970 an amendment to the truth-in-lending law spelled out the maximum amount of a person's income that may be garnished to meet unpaid debts. This maximum is now either 25 percent of a person's weekly take-home pay or the amount by which his or her weekly take-home pay exceeds 30 times the minimum hourly wage, whichever is the smaller.

The federal law then sets the maximum severity with respect to garnisheeing wages. Moreover, it provides that in those states that have a garnisheeing law more lenient to the debtor than the federal law, the state law shall prevail. The law also prohibits an employer from firing an employee whose wages were garnisheed to satisfy any one debt. Formerly, this was done frequently because garnisheeing wages meant extra bookwork for the employer.

Fair Credit Reporting Act

This act guarantees certain consumer rights in the reporting of credit information about consumers to credit granters. For example, it gives you the right to see your credit file. As noted above, all cities of any size have professional credit bureaus which collect and store pertinent financial data on virtually all individuals in the community. They then sell this data to institutions and individuals who extend credit. They also sell reports to prospective employers and life insurance companies which are considering you for life insurance. Your credit file includes personal data as well as data on where you work, your position, how long you were in that position, your annual income, spouse's income, assets, whether you rent or own your home, previous job and address, number of dependents, your credit history and experience, and any judgments which may have been recorded against you.

Checking Your File

If you merely wish to check your credit file routinely, you will have to pay the regular fees a lender pays—a few dollars. If you have been denied credit because of a credit report, the lender or merchant must tell you this. In such a case you have thirty days during which you may see your credit report free of charge; all data in it must be revealed and its source disclosed. Any errors you find must be corrected, and any falsehoods deleted. If your file contains information subject to two or more interpretations, your interpretation must be added and included in all future reports. The corrected version must also be sent to all possible creditors who have received a report on you during the last six months, and all prospective employers who have received a report during the past two years, at no cost to you.

Adverse Information Limitation

The limits to how long adverse information in your credit file may be made available in a credit report are as follows:

Information on bankruptcies—14 years,
Suits and judgments against you—7 years or until the statute of limitations has expired, whichever is the longer.
Paid tax liens, collection accounts, accounts charged to bad debts, arrests, indictments, convictions, and other damaging information—7 years.

However, none of these limitations apply if the credit reports are to be used in connection with a credit or life insurance transaction involving $50,000 or more, or employment involving an annual salary of $20,000 or more.

Who May See Your File

Although you may see your credit file, it is strictly confidential to almost all others. Those who have a legitimate need may see a credit report as may those whom you authorize. Those who may receive a report without your authorization because they have a legitimate need are:

prospective creditors
creditors or their agents trying to collect past debts

SUMMARY OF CONSUMER CREDIT LAWS

The Federal Consumer credit laws offer you these major protections:

1. The *Truth In Lending Act* requires disclosure of the "finance charge" and the "annual percentage rate"—and certain other costs and terms of credit—so that you can compare the prices of credit from different sources. It also limits your liability on lost or stolen credit cards.

2. The *Equal Credit Opportunity Act* prohibits discrimination against an applicant for credit because of age, sex, marital status, race, color, religion, national origin, or receipt of public assistance. It also prohibits discrimination because you have made a good faith exercise of any of your rights under the Federal consumer credit laws. If you've been denied credit, the law requires that you be notified in writing and gives you the right to request the reason for the denial.

3. The *Fair Credit Billing Act* sets up a procedure for the prompt correction of errors on a credit account and prevents damage to your credit rating while you're settling a dispute.

4. The *Fair Credit Reporting Act* sets up a procedure for correcting mistakes on your credit record and requires that the record be kept confidential.

5. The *Consumer Leasing Act* requires disclosure of information that helps you compare the cost and terms of one lease with another and with the cost and terms of buying on credit or with cash.

6. The *Real Estate Settlement Procedures Act* requires that you be given information about the services and costs involved at "settlement," when real property transfers from seller to buyer.

7. The *Home Mortgage Disclosure Act* requires most lending institutions in metropolitan areas to let the public know where they make their mortgage and home improvement loans.

Pamphlets describing some of these laws in more detail are available from the Board of Governors or from the Federal Reserve Bank in your District.

Source: Board of Governors of the Federal Reserve System, July, 1978.

prospective employers

employees of life insurance companies considering you for life insurance

For anyone else a court order is needed. Even the government cannot see your file or receive a report unless it is considering employing you, granting you a license of some kind, considering you for security clearance, or thinks you owe back taxes. For the IRS to receive a report on you, it must have a legitimate case; it cannot go on a fishing expedition.

Equal Credit Opportunity Act

The Equal Credit Opportunity Act (ECOA) became effective in October, 1975, and it banned discrimination in the granting of credit on the basis of sex or marital status. In 1976 this act was amended so that it now also prohibits discrimination on the basis of race, color, religion, and age. The act also bans discrimination against welfare or other public assistance recipients and borrowers who exercise their rights under consumer protection laws. Moreover, it provides that if people are denied credit, they must be told why in writing.

Women and Credit

Prior to the passage of ECOA, women had more difficulty getting credit than men. A married woman often had to rely on her husband's credit. In addition, singles and divorced people often had a more difficult time getting credit than married couples. Now these as well as other types of credit discrimination are unlawful.

Women should establish credit in their own name if they have an income, even if they are married. If a woman relies upon her husband's credit, then upon death or divorce she may be without it temporarily. To be sure, ECOA will permit her to establish credit in her own name in such a case, but this takes time.

Age and Credit

Prior to the passage of ECOA, it was alleged that lenders sometimes refused to grant credit to older people. This act prevents the arbitrary denial of credit to the elderly, who for the purpose of the provision in this act are defined as persons 62 and older.

Credit may still be denied on the basis of inadequate income, excessive debts, a person's credit record, and the like, but the reason for refusing credit must be spelled out in writing.

Fair Credit Billing Act

The Fair Credit Billing Act (FCBA) does essentially three things. It permits merchants who so desire to grant cash discounts, it permits you to withhold payments for defective merchandise purchased with credit cards, and it provides some safeguards in the case of billing errors.

Cash Discounts

Twenty or thirty years ago cash discounts were often granted by merchants to people who paid cash on the barrelhead. This practice had all but ceased until very recently, when there has been a reemergence of the cash discount. Because of this, some major credit card companies included a provision in their contract with retail merchants prohibiting cash discounts. The FCBA prohibits such "no cash discounts" provisions. The act does not require cash discounts; it merely says that merchants may grant them if they wish. Consequently, if you pay cash rather than use your credit card, you should ask for a discount. This discount is limited to five percent because otherwise it would be in violation of the truth-in-lending law.[2]

Merchants granting cash discounts must have signs so stating in clear sight and in places where they are most likely to be seen, such as near cash registers or on doors at entrances. Moreover, merchants granting cash discounts must grant them to all buyers, not just to credit card holders.

Withholding Payments

The FCBA permits the consumer to stop making payments for defective merchandise or service purchased with credit cards. If the merchant who sold you the merchandise is also the issuer of the credit card, all you need first do is make a good faith effort to return the

---

WHAT IS EQUAL CREDIT OPPORTUNITY?

The law says that a creditor may not discriminate against you—treat you less favorably than another applicant for credit—because of your sex or marital status.

Just because you are a woman, or single, or married, a creditor may not turn you down for a loan.

The rules that follow are designed to stop specific abuses that have limited women's ability to get credit.

The most important rules

☐ You can't be refused credit just because you're a woman.

☐ You can't be refused credit just because you're single, married, separated, divorced, or widowed.

☐ You can't be refused credit because a creditor decides you're of child-bearing age and, as a consequence, won't count your income.

☐ You can't be refused credit because a creditor won't count income you receive regularly from alimony or child support.

☐ You can have credit in your own name if you're creditworthy.

☐ When you apply for your own credit and rely on your own income, information about your spouse or his co-signature can be required only under certain circumstances.

☐ You can keep your own accounts and your own credit history if your marital status changes.

☐ You can build up your own credit record because new accounts must be carried in the names of husband and wife if both use the account or are liable on it.

☐ If you are denied credit, you can find out why.

Source: Board of Governors of the Federal Reserve System, May 1977.

---

2. Discounts in excess of five percent would constitute a finance charge under the truth-in-lending law and hence would necessitate further regulations and red tape.

merchandise or resolve the problem by having the merchant replace or repair the item. In the event that a third party issued the credit card (for example, Visa or Master Card), you may still withhold payment, but now there are two additional restrictions. First, the purchase must have exceeded $50, and, second, it must have taken place in your state or within 100 miles of your current address.

By withholding payments you can generate pressure to have the grievance resolved. If a third party's credit card is involved, you can, by withholding payment, enlist that party as an ally in bringing pressure on the retailer.

Billing Errors

In some cases you may be billed incorrectly because of accounting errors, goods that were delivered to the wrong address, returned, or not accepted, or other reasons. The FCBA makes it easier to settle such disputes. You have sixty days after receiving such a bill to report an error. This must be done in writing and the nature of the dispute explained. The creditor has thirty days in which to send you a written reply. While the dispute is being settled, the creditor may not collect any disputed amount, nor add interest charges on it. During this time the creditor may not close your account nor give you a bad credit rating because of your claim.

This provision of the law also spells out the time period during which a legitimate bill may be paid without an additional finance charge. Generally this so-called free ride (between when a bill is received and must be paid without incurring additional charges) is now fourteen days.

What these provisions of the FCBA have done is to make the creditor more cooperative in settling disputes; complaints must now be investigated. Even though legally complaints must be in writing, in many cases disputes can be settled on the telephone. The national credit card companies have established regional offices throughout the country with full-time people who handle only complaints. Often the address and phone numbers for complaints are on the monthly bills and the numbers are sometimes toll-free.

Consumer Leasing Act

While fewer consumers are involved in leasing than in purchasing, there is some legal protection for those who do lease automobiles, furniture, and other items. The leasing act covers only goods leased for personal, family, or household use; it does not cover goods leased to businesses. The act essentially requires full disclosure. It also is applicable in only those cases where the lessee either must buy or has the option to buy after a specific period of time. The act requires that all payments including official fees be spelled out in advance. In addition, the lessee must be told the market price and the appraised price of the leased item at the end of the lease. The act does not cover lease or rental agreements of less than four months.

Fair Debt Collection Practices Act

The Fair Debt Collection Practices Act (FDCPA) became effective in March, 1978. It spells out the maximum amount of harassment that may be used to collect bills. It limits the number of phone calls that may be made and the time of day during which they may be made. Phone calls must be made at convenient times, which generally are defined as between 8:00 A.M. and 9:00 P.M. The debtor, however, cannot be contacted at his or her place of employment, if it is known that the employer prohibits or discourages this. The total amount of contacts of any sort is fixed, and of course threats, overt or implied, are prohibited.

This act, however, has one loophole. It does not apply to the lenders directly, but only to third parties collecting for them. A creditor can call you anytime, but a collection agency cannot.

Holder-in-Due-Course Doctrine

The Federal Trade Commission (FTC), which enforces many of the federal consumer protection laws, has by means of regulations weakened (but not completely eliminated) the holder-in-due-course doctrine. Holder-in-due-course is the legal concept that, if a merchant entered into a credit relationship with a consumer to finance, say, a refrigerator and then sold the installment contract to a third party (say, a finance company), a legally binding contract existed between the consumer and the finance company. The payments were then made to the finance company which bought the paper on good faith and was not a party to the agreement. In short, under the old holder-in-due-course doctrine you had to pay for the refrigerator even if it was defective. Normally you can generate great pressure to have a defective item repaired or replaced by withholding payments, but this was not possible formerly if a third party was involved.

"It says, 'This is your final notice. If you do not pay immediately, we will destroy your credit and have you thrown in jail. Have a happy day.'" (Source: Permission Cartoon Features Syndicate; from The Wall Street Journal.)

FTC regulations now permit the consumer to stop making payments to third parties (even if a credit card is not involved) for defective merchandise or services. Both the seller and the third party may now be held partly liable. This, of course, permits the consumer to generate greater pressure. If it comes to legal court action, she or he can go after both the seller and the financial institution, since both are equally liable.

While the FCBA strengthens the hand of the consumer somewhat by permitting payments to be withheld, if it comes to a legal battle, sellers and creditors are often not liable. This is because often the warranty is granted by the manufacturer, not the seller. While the lender and the retailer share any warranty granted at that level, neither is liable if it is granted by the manufacturer. This is especially true if a disclaimer clause is inserted into a contract. The retailer and creditor are then freed of liability for defective products if it goes down to the wire in a court case. Nevertheless, the new law is a plus for the consumer because he or she can now withhold payments, generate some additional pressure on the retailer and creditor, and enlist them as allies against the manufacturer.

The FTC's regulations now also prohibit the waiver of defense clauses in installment contracts. These were formerly used by some retailers and protected them against action on the part of the consumer.

ENFORCING AGENCIES

There are a number of federal and state enforcing agencies, which we will now examine. As you can see, if you have a complaint and the law has been violated, the correct agency to use depends on the creditor involved.

Federal Agencies

The federal laws are enforced by the agencies summarized below:

CREDITOR	FEDERAL AGENCY
National commercial banks	The Comptroller of the Currency United States Treasury Department Washington, D.C. The Comptroller has regional offices in a number of major cities. Check the telephone directory.
State banks which are members of the Federal Reserve System	The Federal Reserve Bank serving the area in which the bank is located
State nonmember banks which are insured by the Federal Deposit Insurance Corporation	The Federal Deposit Insurance Corporation Washington, D.C. The FDIC has regional offices in a number of major cities. Look in the telephone directory.
State nonmember noninsured banks	Division of Consumer Credit The Federal Trade Commission Washington, D.C.

	The Federal Trade Commission has regional offices in a number of major cities. There are very few such noninsured banks, however
Federal savings and loan associations	The Federal Home Loan Bank Board Washington, D.C. The FHLBB has regional offices in a number of major cities.
State savings and loans associations insured by the Federal Savings and Loan Insurance Corporation	The Federal Savings and Loan Insurance Corporation Washington, D.C. The FSLIC has regional offices in a number of major cities.
State savings and loan associations which are not insured	Division of Consumer Credit The Federal Trade Commission Washington, D.C. The FTC has regional offices in a number of major cities. Look in the telephone directory. There are very few such noninsured savings associations.
Mutual savings banks	The Federal Deposit Insurance Corporation Washington, D.C. The FDIC has regional offices in a number of major cities. Virtually all mutual savings banks are insured by the FDIC and hence regulated by them.
Federally chartered credit unions and insured state-chartered credit unions	The National Credit Union Administration Washington, D.C. The NCUA has regional offices in a number of major cities.
State-chartered non-insured credit unions	Division of Consumer Credit The Federal Trade Commission Washington, D.C. The FTC has a number of regional offices. There are very few noninsured credit unions.
Retail merchants, including department stores, finance companies, non-bank credit card issuers, and most others	Division of Consumer Credit The Federal Trade Commission Washington, D.C. The FTC has a number of regional offices.
Airlines and other creditors subject to Civil Aeronautics Board	Director, Bureau of Enforcement Civil Aeronautics Board

CREDITOR	FEDERAL AGENCY
Meat packers, poultry processors, and other creditors subject to Packers and Stockyards Act	Nearest Packers and Stockyards Administration area supervisor.
Creditors subject to Interstate Commerce Commission	Office of Proceedings Interstate Commerce Commission Washington, D.C.

The Federal Reserve System and the Comptroller of the Currency have established an Office of Consumer Affairs at all of their regional offices, as have many of the other federal agencies, and that is where you should take your complaints. Moreover, you may do this by mail. Write the Office of Consumer Affairs at the Regional Federal Reserve Bank of your district of the Federal Reserve System. They will send you a complaint form which you can fill out and return to them. A sample of such a complaint form is shown below.

The Department of Health, Education and Welfare (HEW) has also established an Office of Consumer Affairs. Although this office has no power of enforcement, it does listen to complaints from consumer organizations. It plays the role of advocate and will report any violations of federal law to the proper enforcement agencies.

FIGURE 6–1.

COMPLAINT FORM   Federal Reserve System

Name _____   Name of bank _____

Address _____   Address _____
            Street   City   State   Zip

City   State   Zip

Daytime telephone _____   Account number (if applicable)
    (include area code)   _____

The complaint involves the following service:

Checking account ☐   Savings account ☐   Loan ☐

    Other: Please specify _____

I have attempted to resolve this complaint directly with the bank:

No ☐   Yes ☐

    If "No", an attempt should be made to contact the bank and resolve the complaint.

    If "Yes", name of person or department contacted is _____

Date _____

MY COMPLAINT IS AS FOLLOWS (Briefly describe the events in the order in which they happened, including specific dates and the bank's actions to which you object. Enclose copies of any pertinent information or correspondence that may be helpful. Do not send us your only copy of any document.):

_____
_____
_____
_____
_____
_____
_____
_____
_____
_____

This information is solicited under the Federal Trade Commission Improvement Act. Providing the information is voluntary; complete information is necessary to expedite investigation of your complaint. Routine use of the information may include disclosing it to bank(s) or others involved or to other governmental agencies as deemed appropriate.

Date _____   Signatures _____
                                     _____

  If you have a complaint about a bank, you can get help from the Federal Reserve. You may complain about a possible violation of any of the Federal consumer credit laws or about any bank that you think has been unfair or deceptive in any business you have conducted with it. You don't need to have an account at the bank to file a complaint.
Please mail your complaint to the Director, Division of Consumer Affairs, Board of Governors of the Federal Reserve System, Washington, D.C. 20551.

Source: Board of Governors of the Federal Reserve System, July 1978.

State Agencies

At the state level there are state agencies to enforce state laws. All states have banking commissioners by that or some other name. Some have credit union commissioners, savings and loan commissioners, and consumer credit commissioners. Those that do not have a similar state agency to enforce all state laws dealing with consumer credit including the maximum interest rates that may be charged. Some states also have deceptive trade legislation on the books, and some have established offices of consumer protection or consumer affairs, either within the Attorney General's office or elsewhere. Look in the telephone book of your state's capital city to find the proper state agency to which you may take a complaint.

QUESTIONS FOR REVIEW

1. Does the federal law or state law govern the maximum interest rate that may be charged on consumer loans?

2. What do private voluntary consumer organizations do? Are there any in your area?

3. Discuss the truth-in-lending law. What is its purpose?

4. What does the truth-in-lending law say about credit life insurance?

5. What is meant by the right of rescission? What law grants it?

6. What should you do if your credit card is lost or stolen?

7. Which federal law deals with garnishment of wage? Summarize briefly what it provides.

8. What does the Fair Credit Reporting Act do?

9. How long may adverse information be kept in your credit file?

10. Who besides yourself may obtain a credit report on you without a court order?

11. What happens if a woman relies upon her husband's credit, and they then separate?

12. Which law covers cash discounts? What does it provide?

13. What is the holder-in-due-course doctrine?

14. What groups are covered by the Fair Debt Collection Practices Act? Which groups are not covered?

CASES

1. Barbara Hudson applied for a loan at a bank so that she could buy a car. If the loan is granted, what information must the bank provide Barbara? If Barbara is turned down, what must the bank do?

2. Philip and Virginia Kidd recently purchased a new Cadillac. One day while Virginia was driving it, the motor literally exploded. Upon examination the dealer discovered a push rod had come through the block and the motor was damaged beyond repair. What recourse does Virginia have?

3. Dee Van Antwerp of Ogallala, Nebraska has been admitted to the Nebraska bar and has joined her husband in the practice of law. Dee doesn't have any credit cards of her own but uses her husband's. She feels perhaps she should get some cards in her own name, and seeks your advice.

4. Anita Garcia had a flight reservation from Austin, Texas to New Orleans via Dallas. But the flight to Dallas was late, so to avoid missing her connection there she purchased a ticket from another airline via Houston. There was not time to cancel her flight via Dallas at the time but she did so later. She had charged all these flights on her Visa card and later both airlines billed her. What should Anita do?

5. Rusty Snow lost her purse, which had little of value in it except three credit cards. Rusty is concerned that someone might find them and run up a lot of bills. What should she do?

6. Blanche Wright wanted to buy some furniture for her apartment, but the store would not sell it to her on the installment plan because of an unfavorable report from the credit bureau. What are Blanche's rights?

SUGGESTED READINGS

Consumer Handbook to Credit Protection Laws. Board of Governors of the Federal Reserve System, Washington, D.C. 20551, December, 1978.

Consumers, Credit Bureaus, and the Fair Credit Reporting Act. Associated Credit Bureaus, Inc., 6767 Southwest Freeway, Houston, Texas, no date. Check with your local credit bureaus; they may have similar publications by credit bureaus near you.

The Equal Credit Opportunity Act . . . and Age. Board of Governors of the Federal Reserve System, Washington, D.C. 20551, May, 1977.

The Equal Credit Opportunity Act and . . . Credit Rights in Housing. Board of Governors of the Federal Reserve System, Washington, D.C. 20551, January, 1978.

The Equal Credit Opportunity Act and . . . Doctors, Lawyers, Small Retailers, and Others Who May Provide Incidental Credit. Board of Governors of the Federal Reserve System, Washington, D.C. 20551, May, 1977.

The Equal Credit Opportunity Act and . . . Women. Board of Governors of the Federal Reserve System, Washington, D.C. 20551, May, 1977.

Fair Credit Billing. Board of Governors of the Federal Reserve System, Washington, D.C. 20551, December, 1976.

How to File a Consumer Credit Complaint. Board of Governors of the Federal Reserve System, Washington, D.C. 20551, July, 1978.

If You Borrow to Buy Stock. Board of Governors of the Federal Reserve System, Washington, D.C. 20551, no date.

If You Use A Credit Card. Board of Governors of the Federal Reserve System, Washington, D.C. 20551, December, 1978.

Staff Guidelines on Trade Regulations Rule Concerning Preservation of Consumers' Claims and Defenses. Federal Trade Commission, Bureau of Consumer Protection, Washington, D.C., 1976.

Truth in Leasing. Prepared jointly by the Federal Trade Commission and the Board of Governors of the Federal Reserve System, March, 1978.

What Truth in Lending Means to You. Board of Governors of the Federal Reserve System, Washington, D.C. 20551. Revised April, 1978.

Chapter Seven

Savings Through Thrift Institutions

A penny saved is a penny earned.
BENJAMIN FRANKLIN

The objectives of the chapter are to

1 Introduce personal savings in the United States

2 Explain who the savers are, why they save, and the volume of savings

3 Introduce the various thrift institutions through which one might save

4 Illustrate some of the differences among these various thrift institutions

5 Introduce the various types of deposits

6 Examine the yield on various types of deposits at various institutions

7 Note the penalties that must be paid on early withdrawals of certain deposits

8 Look at the safety and liquidity of the deposits

9 Explain the theory of interest and how interest is calculated and compounded by thrift institutions

10 Introduce some supplementary material on interest rates

Persons who manage their personal affairs well will probably have some savings each month. Some of us have savings that appear as a residual after all our expenditures have been made. Others have to budget and really plan for savings or they will not materialize. Once we have put aside some money, we question what to do with our savings. The answer, of course, is that they should be put to work so they will earn interest or dividends. They could be held in the form of idle cash in a mattress, but then they would not be working. Doing this is referred to as hoarding. Individuals who put their savings into hoards are irrational because they forego investment income that is received by those who invest their savings. In part three I will discuss investing in securities; this is commonly known as direct investing. In this chapter I will discuss putting savings in a thrift institution and letting someone else invest them for us. This is referred to as indirect investing or earning interest via an institution.

PERSONAL SAVINGS IN THE UNITED STATES

Savings come from earned income, and they represent that portion of income that individuals do not spend on consumption items. The flow of savings from many small savers through thrift institutions, becoming indirect investments in American business (and governments), is depicted graphically in Figure 7-1. Thrift institutions serve as a channel into which driblets of small savings flow from many individuals and out of which a large dollar volume of savings flows to the legitimate users of savings. Personal or individual savings were 73.8 billion in 1979 and many of these funds were channeled through thrift institutions.

Who Are the U.S. Savers?

Economists generally agree that there is a positive correlation between income and savings; the higher a person's income, the higher is the dollar volume of his or her savings. There may also be a slight correlation between interest rate and savings; if interest rates are higher, there is a greater reward and greater incentive to save. But this theory is more controversial and harder to prove. Studies at the University of Michigan Survey Research Center and elsewhere have suggested that there are a number of other factors influencing savings such as past income, direction of change in income, size of family, and age; but the effects of these variables are more difficult to measure.

Generally, then, we can say that most savings are generated by those whose income is high enough and who are over forty-five years of age. While many low-income groups save some money, their dollar volume is small. High savings among those over forty-five is related to the life cycle variation in the budget, which was discussed in Chapter 2. Up to about age forty-five or fifty are the high consumption years. Then after the children have flown the coop and the house is paid for and full of furniture and other consumer durable goods, more savings are generated out of any given budget.

FIGURE 7-1. *Dollar flows through the economy*

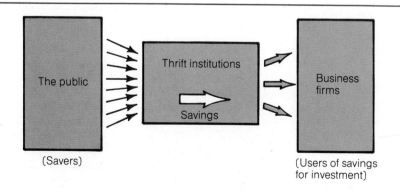

People save for all kinds of different reasons. Many save to supplement their social security and other retirement plans. Some save for possible emergencies and the greater peace of mind savings provide. Others save for some specific purpose: to send a child to college or for a future trip around the world. Still others save to acquire the down payment to buy a home or start a business. Some of the savings earmarked for a specific purpose, such as a college education or a vacation trip, will not become a permanent supply of capital for American business but rather will be liquidated and used for their intended purpose some day. The bulk of individual savings, however, can be looked upon as having been made for purposes of retirement or to provide greater security and peace of mind. They are not likely to be completely liquidated even after retirement and hence can be looked upon as semi-permanent sources of capital by American business firms. Moreover, much of this capital is made available for use through thrift institutions.

Volume and Classification of Savings

Individual (or personal) savings fluctuate greatly from year to year. Since 1970 they fluctuated from a high in 1971 of 7.7 percent to a 1979 low of 4.5 percent of after tax income. Today's current low savings rate is often explained by the rapid rate of inflation. Inflation erodes savings and destroys the incentive to save. Also inflation creates a "buy now before prices rise" attitude. Many economic experts feel today's low rate of saving is dangerous because it starves the economy of capital with which to grow. See Table 7-1.

The savings that you do generate can be classified as "nest egg" or emergency funds, and other savings. The first savings generated should be considered emergency or "nest egg" and should be salted away in a safe place where they can be easily and quickly obtained; a thrift institution would be an ideal place. How large your emergency supply of savings should be would depend upon your age, number of dependents, etc., and is a personal value judgment. Other savings may be invested differently than emergency savings, and how to do that will be covered in future chapters. In order to be easily accessible, your first emergency or "nest egg" funds should be placed in a thrift institution, and the various thrift institutions will be discussed next.

TABLE 7–1. *Personal savings*

YEAR	DOLLAR SAVINGS IN BILLIONS	SAVINGS AS % OF INCOME
1971	57.3	7.7%
1972	49.4	6.2
1973	70.3	7.8
1974	71.7	7.3
1975	83.6	7.7
1976	68.6	5.8
1977	65.0	5.0
1978	72.0	4.9
1979	73.8	4.5

Source: Economic Indicators, June 1980, Council of Economic Advisers, p. 6.

THRIFT INSTITUTIONS

A thrift institution may be defined as one "designed either as repositories of assets used for short-term liquidity purposes or for accumulation of a fund of investment proportions.[1] The following institutions can be classified as thrift institutions:

1. Savings departments of commercial banks
2. Mutual savings banks
3. Savings and loan associations
4. Credit unions
5. Industrial banks
6. U.S. Series E and H savings bonds (since 1980 series EE and HH)[2]
7. Life insurance companies
8. Private pension plans

It should also be noted that the first five institutions mentioned above are also called depository institutions, because they serve as a depository for the public's savings. The first six institutions will be discussed in detail in this chapter; life insurance companies and pension plans will be discussed in separate chapters. While it might appear to many that U.S. savings bonds are not institutions, they are obligations of the U.S. government and they provide an outlet for individual savings. Indeed, from the point of view of the individual, they are safe and highly liquid and perform the same functions as institutions; hence logically they may be treated as such. However, this applies only to Series E and Series H bonds (and EE and HH), and not to other U.S. government bonds or to U.S. government securities that are not bonds.

There are a number of reasons why individuals place not only their nest egg but other surplus funds in thrift institutions.

1. The average person may have neither the skill nor the time to invest in other types of savings media, such as security markets.
2. Many savers want their savings to remain highly liquid, and feel—and rightly so—that thrift institutions are the most liquid type of such media.
3. Many savers feel they have insufficient funds to place in some other investment form, such as the stock market.
4. Most savers feel that the institutions can supply the investment judgment that they lack.
5. These institutions provide an extremely safe place to invest savings.
6. Most people do not wish to hold their savings in the form of idle cash (hoards).

Savings Departments of Commercial Banks

There are four major categories of deposits in commercial banks: demand deposits, savings deposits, time deposits, and the negotiable orders of withdrawal (the NOW account). The demand deposit, legally withdrawable on demand, is commonly referred to as a check-

---

1. Donald P. Jacobs et al., *Financial Institutions*, 5th ed. Homewood, Ill.: Irwin, 1972, p. 220.

2. In January, 1980 the Treasury stopped issuing series E and H bonds, and came out with series EE and HH. Of course, there are still a good many series E and H bonds outstanding.

ing account, and was discussed in a previous chapter. About 30 percent of the deposits in commercial banks are in the form of demand deposits. Savings deposits are the so-called passbook savings accounts, and time deposits consist of the various types of certificates of deposit (called CDs for short) which will be explained below. Savings deposits and time deposits together account for the other 70 percent of bank deposits. Figure 7-2 shows the growth in these deposits at commercial banks over the past few years. The negotiable order of withdrawal (the NOW account) has been available in a few states for a number of years, but throughout the U.S. only since January, 1981. Hence, national figures were not available as this book went to press. Savings deposits, time deposits, and the NOW account earn interest and demand deposits do not.

When opening a passbook savings account deposit in a commercial bank, the depositor is given a passbook upon making the initial deposit. The amount of the initial deposit is noted in the passbook, and any subsequent deposits or withdrawals will also be entered in the book. Passbook savings accounts are very liquid and may be withdrawn at any time without notice. However, while on deposit they earn interest. This is where you should keep your nest egg or emergency funds.

Certificates of deposit or CDs (sometimes called time deposits) are issued by commercial banks to individuals as well as corporations and to state and local governments. If state and local governments or corporations have temporarily idle funds, they invest them for a specific period of time until they are needed. The same is true of individual CDs. They come in various denominations and are pledged for various periods of time. They also earn a higher rate of interest than passbook deposits.

The NOW accounts are a combination of savings accounts and checking accounts. They

FIGURE 7–2. *Principal liabilities of commercial banks, 1926–1979. (Source: 1979 Historical Chart Book, Board of Governors of the Federal Reserve System, p. 79.)*

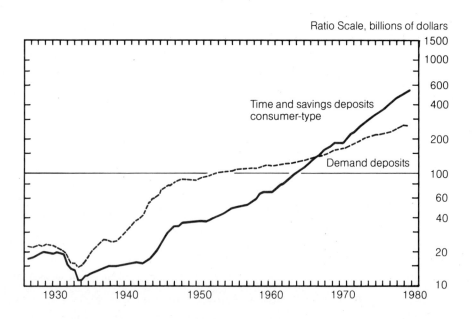

Part 1 / Budgeting, Buying, Borrowing, and Saving

earn interest at just below the passbook rate, and checks (orders of withdrawal) can be written on them. They may also be withdrawn upon demand.

Mutual Savings Banks

Mutual savings banks do primarily two things: they accept savings, time, and NOW deposits and they make mortgage loans, although they also make a few consumer loans. They are nonstock corporations chartered by the states in which they are located. As nonstock corporations, they are owned by their depositors in proportion to each individual's deposit. While, in 1978, federal legislation was passed allowing federally chartered mutual savings banks, there are as yet few operating under a federal charter. The operations of the state-chartered MSBs differ somewhat from state to state, but they do have some uniform characteristics. Mutual savings banks are located primarily in New England, the Middle Atlantic states, and on the West Coast. They are found in only seventeen of the fifty states and in Puerto Rico, but almost five hundred exist in these seventeen states. Ninety percent of their total assets are concentrated in five states, and about 60 percent of their deposits are in the state of New York. In the states of New York, Massachusetts, and Connecticut, they are permitted to issue mutual savings bank life insurance.

Mutual savings banks are run by a board of directors who appoint replacements rather than have them elected by depositors.

When opening an account, a depositor is given a passbook in which entries are made. In the event a depositor wishes to withdraw the funds, this transaction too is entered in the passbook. In eight of the states having mutual savings banks, the maximum size of deposits is limited by law; and in the other nine states and Puerto Rico, it is set by policy of the board of directors. In all states, however, a depositor may have more than one account in a bank. Consequently depositors may deposit just about as much as they wish.

The passbook deposits at mutual savings banks are almost exactly like those at commercial banks, except that MSBs pay ¼ of 1 percent more interest on passbook accounts than do commercial banks. Just as in the case of a commercial bank, these deposits are highly liquid because they can be withdrawn at any time. Consequently, your "nest egg" savings could go in here.

Mutual savings banks also accept various certificates of deposit (CDs), just like commercial banks, and generally pay ¼ of 1 percent higher rates of interest on these as well. Mutual savings banks may also offer the NOW account, but on these they may not pay a higher rate of interest than commercial banks. The reason why savings banks may pay one-quarter percent more than do commercial banks on certain accounts is because the maximum rate which may be paid is set by law. The law allows MSBs this slight interest differential on the theory that they need it to attract savings. Commercial banks, you will recall, are full-service banks, which means they provide a variety of services—savings accounts, checking accounts, consumer loans, business loans, etc. Mutual savings banks, on the other hand, are specialized and make only mortgage loans. Since people could satisfy all of their needs at a commercial bank, they would engage in one-stop banking and save there, if the MSBs didn't pay a bit more interest. It should be noted that this interest rate differential will be eliminated in six more years. In March, 1980, the President signed a new law that phases out over six years the interest rate differential that savings and loan associations and MSBs enjoy over commercial banks.

Savings and Loan Associations

Savings and loan associations, also called building and loan associations, are a highly specialized form of savings and home financing institutions. Like mutual savings banks, they accept savings, time, and NOW deposits and make mostly mortgage loans, although some make a few consumer loans. In aggregate terms, savings and loan associations are the second largest financial institutions; only commercial banks have greater assets. Savings and loan associations are also among the fastest growing of the financial institutions. Moreover, these institutions are found in all fifty states, in the District of Columbia, Guam, and Puerto Rico.

Savings and loan associations can operate under a state or a federal charter. State-chartered associations are regulated by the state savings and loan commissioner, and federal associations are regulated by the Federal Home Loan Bank. State-chartered associations may be mutual organizations in the sense that they have no stockholders, and in some states they may be organized as true stock associations in which they have voting stockholders who are not necessarily depositors. Federally chartered associations are presently not permitted to be organized as true stock associations and, hence, are all mutuals. However, a movement is afoot to permit federally chartered stock associations. At year end 1979 there were almost five thousand savings and loan associations in the United States; about two thousand of these were operating under a federal charter and about three thousand under state authorization.

Many people confuse mutual savings banks and savings and loan associations, but technically there is a slight difference. Savings banks are banks with depositors to whom they pay interest. The deposits are a liability to the bank. At one time savings and loan associations could not call their savings accounts deposits. Rather, they were share accounts and the payment on them was called a dividend rather than interest. This has been changed and now savings and loans do have deposits and the payment on them is called interest.

There are some savings and loan associations that have stockholders and some that are true mutuals that do not have stockholders. Mutual savings banks never have stockholders and they are regulated by the banking authorities; whereas savings and loan associations are regulated by a separate savings and loan commissioner, if they are operating under a state charter, and by the Federal Home Loan Bank Board (FHLBB) if they are operating under a federal charter.

Just like commercial banks and mutual savings banks, the savings and loan associations offer passbook savings deposits, NOW accounts, and a number of different certificates of deposit, which are discussed more fully below. Their passbook deposits and NOW accounts may be withdrawn at any time; and like mutual savings banks, they may pay ¼ of 1 percent higher interest than commercial banks on all of their deposits except the NOW account, and for the same reason.

Credit Unions

The credit union is a cooperative type of financial institution designed to make loans to its members primarily for consumer purchases. The credit union also accepts deposits from members and offers the passbook account, the NOW account, and share certificates, which are similar to certificates of deposit. Credit unions can operate under a federal or under a state charter. Federally chartered credit unions can now invest some of their funds in mortgages; some states allow mortgage investments, while others do not. At the end of 1979 there were approximately 23,000 credit unions in the United States with total assets of over $55 billion.

The credit union is ordinarily organized around a business firm, a union, or a fraternal organization. One may be started by as few as seven employees of a firm who agree to join the credit union once it starts. The members buy shares, which are generally $5 each; but regardless of the number of shares owned, each individual is entitled to only one vote. Each member is given a passbook similar to a savings bank passbook, and the number of shares in terms of dollars is indicated therein. In addition, each member pays a twenty-five-cent membership fee that is used to help defray expenses. The shareholders elect a board of trustees, and the board appoints a president, vice-president, secretary, and treasurer. They then hire whatever other employees are needed. The board generally serves without salary. The shareholders also elect a credit committee whose duty it is to pass upon applications for loans.

Not everyone may purchase shares in or join a credit union. A person cannot just walk in, as in the case of a savings and loan association, and purchase shares. One must ordinarily be an employee of the firm sponsoring the credit union or a relative of an employee. Credit unions also restrict their loans to members; therefore, generally speaking the borrower must also be an employee of the sponsoring firm. Some credit unions, however, while having employment requirements for joining, permit members to remain members after they terminate their employment with the firm in question.

Industrial Banks

Industrial banks are another type of thrift institution; they are found in about 20 states and accept both passbook savings and CDs. At the outset it should be emphasized that there is a dearth of national statistics on industrial banks so that most of what can be said is only a generalization.

In general, industrial banks are regulated by state banking commissions and to a degree the regulations vary from state to state. In most states the only accounts that can be handled by the industrial banks are savings accounts. They are specifically forbidden to handle demand deposit accounts or to act as a trustee. Frequently they are required to establish reserve accounts, often as high as 15 percent of their savings deposits. In some states the law prohibits borrowing by any of the bank's officers or stockholders, and usually the state banking commissioner conducts periodic examinations of the bank. Finally, it should be noted that industrial banks do not even exist in many states.

Types of Deposits

I noted above that there are three types of interest-bearing deposits: passbook deposits, certificates of deposit (CDs), and the NOW accounts. Passbook deposits are offered by all five of the above-discussed depository institutions. They are very liquid and for all practical purposes can be withdrawn without notice at any time, and with no penalty. Technically speaking, however, the institution may require a 30-day written notice before withdrawal. This is because the institution's funds are tied up in long-term investment, and they may need some time to liquidate their investments and raise the funds. However, this 30-day written notice is virtually always waived.

The NOW accounts may also be withdrawn at any time without a penalty. All depository institutions, except industrial banks, may issue NOW accounts.

Certificates of deposit, on the other hand, are pledged for a specific period of time and cannot be withdrawn early without a penalty. The time period (maturity dates) for CDs varies from 30 days to 8 years or more. There are, then, a number of different certificates to choose from. Commercial banks, mutual savings banks, and savings and loan associations are all subject to the same restrictions and may all offer the same type of CDs. From time to time the government imposes a minimum of $1,000 on some of these CDs.

Credit unions and industrial banks, while they can offer CDs, are subject to different laws and they may issue fewer varieties of CDs.

The table below shows the various CDs that commercial banks, savings and loans, and mutual savings banks may offer. Note that the table shows what they *may* offer. Some institutions do not offer all of them; and the table, then, is really the permissible range of offerings the institutions may choose to offer.

There is also the so-called jumbo CD which is not shown in the table. This is a CD in excess of $100,000; and on such a CD, there are no legal restrictions on the maximum interest rate nor on its maturity. These are both subject to negotiation between the institution and the depositor.

Credit unions are permitted to issue share certificates (these are similar to CDs) in any denomination and with various periods of maturity up to six years. In effect, however, many credit unions impose $500 or $1,000 minimums on some of their share certificates.

Industrial banks also issue CDs. However, industrial banks are not regulated by the federal government but only by the states in which they do business. Consequently, the type of CDs they may offer varies from state to state; but, generally speaking, they are competitive with the other depository institutions.

There are two other CDs which require a special explanation. They are the money market CD and the 30-month Treasury note CD. The money market CD must be pledged for six months, and the minimum amount is $10,000. The 30-month Treasury note CD, as the term implies, has a maturity of 30 months, and the minimum amount is only $100. This 30-month CD was designed for the small investor who cannot raise the $10,000 necessary to buy a money market CD. All of the depository institutions may provide these two CDs. It should be noted, however, that in the case of a credit union, they may issue a Treasury note CD for only 18 months rather than 30, which is the requirement for the other institutions.

If you don't wish to tie your money up for 18 months or 30 months, but you have less

TABLE 7–2. *Maximum interest that commercial banks, savings and loan associations, and mutual savings banks may pay on deposits*

MATURITY	COM. BANKS MAXIMUM PERCENT	S&Ls AND MSBs MAXIMUM PERCENT
Passbook	5¼	5½
NOW Account[1]	5	5
90 days to 1 year	5½	5¾
2 to 2½ years	6	6¼
2½ to 4 years	6½	6¾
4 to 6 years	7¼	7½
6 to 8 years	7½	7¾
8 years or more	7¾	8
money market (6 mo.)	Treasury Bill Discount Rate[2]	
Treasury Note (30 mo.)	Treasury Note Rate[3]	

Source: Federal Reserve Bulletin, March 1980, Board of Governors of the Federal Reserve System, p. 10.

1. Savings and Loan Associations and Mutual Savings Banks do not enjoy a ¼ of 1 percent interest differential on the NOW Account.

2. When the Treasury Note rate is below 8¾ percent S&Ls and MSBs may pay ¼ of one per cent above that rate on the 6 months money market certificate. Commercial banks may not do this.

3. This rate is ½ of 1 per cent below the average rate of Treasury notes sold the previous month. As of early 1980 a cap of 12 percent was placed on this CD.

than $10,000, you can also obtain a 6-month money market CD, in some cases, by borrowing the difference between the cash you do have and $10,000 from a financial institution, which will then issue you a certificate. Six months later the institution will return to you the proceeds after taking back their share of the principal and interest. Some banks will loan up to $9,000. The interest you pay on the borrowed funds is usually about equal to (or just slightly above) the money market CD rate, and the interest you receive is also about equal to the CD rates. Another method by which the small investor may participate in the money market CD is to pool funds with trusted friends in order to accumulate $10,000.

Interest Yields on Deposits

Regulation Q is the federal regulation that sets the maximum limit on the interest rate certain institutions may pay on various deposits. However, only commercial banks, savings and loans, and mutual savings banks are subject to it; credit unions and industrial banks are subject to different regulations. On March 31, 1980, the President signed an act that will abolish regulation Q by phasing it out over the next six years. However, the discussion below will still be valid for a few more years.

You will note that Table 7–2 above shows that interest rates vary from a low of 5 percent on a NOW account deposit to a high of 8 percent on a regular CD issued for 8 years or more by a savings and loan association or a mutual savings bank. The two special CDs (the money market CD and the Treasury note CD) have a rate that fluctuates a good deal as will be explained below.

You will also note that SLAs and MSBs enjoy a ¼ of 1 percent preferential interest rate ceiling on most deposits; that is, generally speaking, they pay that much more on most deposits than do commercial banks. The exceptions are the NOW account, the money market certificate, and the Treasury note certificate, as will be explained below. One reason for this preference is to encourage inflows of savings into these institutions because they are heavy suppliers of mortgage money. Mortgage lending, which finances home ownership, has long been encouraged by the U.S. Congress.

Another reason often cited for the SLA and MSB interest preference is to offset their other competitive disadvantage in acquiring deposits. This arises because SLAs and MSBs are specialized lending institutions rather than full-service institutions like commercial banks. If rates were the same, people could satisfy all their financial needs at a one-stop full-service commercial bank and might never develop a relationship with a SLA or a MSB, according to this argument.

The money market CD draws an interest rate that is tied to the rate paid by the U.S. government when it borrows on a short-term basis. That is, the money market CD yields an interest rate equal to the 6-month Treasury bill rate.[3] In early 1980 this got as high as 15 percent. The Treasury bill rate fluctuates a good deal, and consequently, the rate on money market CDs will change, often on a weekly basis. However, once a money market CD is issued, its rate remains constant until it matures.

When the Treasury bill rate is below 9 percent, savings and loan associations and mutual savings banks are permitted to add up to ¼ of 1 percent more to the rate they pay on money market CDs. The rate on these CDs, then, is sometimes higher than the Treasury bill rate. However, commercial banks may not do this. Therefore, the ¼ of 1 percent differential noted above applies to the money market CD when the Treasury bill rate declines to 8¾ percent or lower.

---

3. Treasury bills are securities that the U.S. Treasury uses when it borrows on a short-term basis. They are discussed in Chapter 13 below.

The 30-month Treasury note CD interest rate is tied to the rate on Treasury notes.[4] This CD carries an interest rate that is ½ of 1 percent below the average yield on 30-month Treasury notes sold the previous month. The yield on Treasury notes also fluctuates a great deal. A Treasury note CD issued in July would have a rate of ½ of 1 percent below the average yield on Treasury notes sold during June. However, in March, 1980, when the interest rate on Treasury notes rose above 12 percent, the government put a cap or ceiling of 12 percent on rates that may be paid on Treasury note CDs. It should also be noted that all depository institutions are on an even footing concerning the issuance of these CDs; savings and loan associations and mutual savings banks do not enjoy their usual ¼ of 1 percent advantage.

The interest received on passbook accounts and on virtually all CDs is now compounded daily by most institutions. This is referred to as day-in-to-day-out interest compounding. Daily compounding is permitted on all deposits except the six-month money market CD, which draws only simple interest. Daily compounding increases the effective yield. For example, an 8 percent CD compounded daily results in an annual yield of 8.33 percent. The table below shows the rates by various institutions and the effective yield due to compounding.

As noted above, the jumbo CD (over $100,000) is not subject to regulation, and both the yield and the length of time to maturity is determined by negotiations between the institution and the depositor.

The interest that credit unions and industrial banks may pay is regulated by separate laws. Compared with commercial banks and savings banks and even savings and loan associations, the return on credit union passbook shares tends to be higher. In 1980 most credit unions paid returns of 6 percent or higher on passbook savings. No federal credit union may pay more than a 7 percent dividend on passbook savings because this is the maximum legal

TABLE 7-3. *Lending table for various savings deposits*

| TYPE | INTEREST RATE | | REAL YIELD | |
	COMMERCIAL BANK	SAVINGS & LOAN	COMMERCIAL BANK	SAVINGS & LOAN
Passbook	5¼%	5½%	5.39%	5.65%
NOW accounts	5	5	5.13	5.13
90 day–1 year	5½	5¾	5.65	5.92
1 yr.–2½ years	6	6½	6.18	6.72
2½–4 years	6½	6¾	6.72	6.98
4–6 years	7¼	7½	7.52	7.79
6–8 years	7½	7¾	7.79	8.06
8 or more years	7¾	8	8.06	8.33
6 mo. money market	Treasury Bill discount rate; not compounded daily			
30 mo. Treasury note	The average rate on 30-month Treasury notes sold the previous month. The rate on this CD is compounded daily.			
Jumbo	——	——	——	——

4. Treasury notes are securities that the U.S. Treasury uses when it borrows on an intermediate and long-term basis.

rate on regular accounts. Moreover, to pay that high a rate a credit union would have to prove to the regulatory authorities that earnings are high enough to justify it.

On their CDs credit unions pay up to 8 percent on those pledged six years or more. And they pay the same as other institutions on the money market and on the Treasury note CDs. However, as noted above, a credit union Treasury note CD need only be pledged 18 months rather than 30 as in the case of the other institutions discussed so far.

Industrial banks offer both passbook savings and CDs, and often at higher rates than other institutions. Since deposits are not insured and since industrial banks are regulated only by the states, there is no federally imposed ceiling on the interest rates they may pay on deposits. Generally, these banks pay about ½ of 1 percent more than the rate on insured deposits in competing institutions. This is in excess of 6 percent on passbook accounts. They also offer certificates of deposit, and the rate on these is scaled upward from 6 percent to about 12 percent or even more depending upon the amount of the CD and the length of time for which it is pledged. One reason industrial banks are able to pay a higher yield is because they invest some of their funds in second mortgages, which typically yield more.

On March 31, 1980, President Carter signed a law that will phase out regulation Q, the federal regulation which sets the maximum interest rates thrift institutions may pay on deposits of all kinds. The phase-out will work as follows: The institutions will be permitted to raise all rates by ¼ of 1 percent during the next 18 months, another ¼ of 1 percent over the 18 months after that, and then another ½ of 1 percent per year for each of the three years after that. Over six years, then, interest rate ceilings will be permitted to drift up by 2 percent and then the ceiling will be completely abolished.

When regulation Q is finally abolished (in six years), all institutions will be free to set their own rates. Competition in the market will then determine what rates will be, but there will in all likelihood be a family of rates. That is to say, rates will probably vary with the length of time the deposit is pledged and possibly with its dollar size. The interest rate differential between commercial banks and other thrift institutions will tend to disappear.

Penalties on Early Withdrawals

While passbook savings deposits and NOW accounts may be withdrawn without penalty at any time, this is not true of a CD. There are really two different penalties for early withdrawals of CDs; one on CDs issued prior to July, 1979, and another one on CDs issued after that date. If a CD issued prior to July, 1979, is withdrawn early, the interest rate earned to date is reduced to the passbook rate and, in addition, three months of interest, also at the passbook rate, is assessed. For example, if you had a $1,000 four-year, 7.5 percent CD issued by a savings and loan in June, 1979, but then in June, 1981, you withdrew it, the interest for those two years would be calculated at 5.5 percent, not 7.5 percent. This would make the interest (compounded daily) about $113.00 instead of about $155.80. From that $113.00 would be subtracted three months' interest at 5½ percent or $13.75; you would get back your $1,000 plus $99.25 of interest.

The penalty on CDs issued since July, 1979, is the loss of three months' interest (at the CD's rate) if the deposit has a maturity of one year or less. If the CD has a maturity of more than a year, there is a loss of six months' interest. In neither case is the interest rate reduced to the passbook rate. On a $1,000 8 percent, 8-year CD withdrawn after one year, the penalty would be $40.

These penalties were imposed to discourage early withdrawals of CDs. It should be noted that the penalty is not assessed if a survivor withdraws the CD of a deceased person, or if the depositor is found to be mentally incompetent.

Liquidity has to do with how quickly you can convert your assets (deposits) into cash without making a price concession. Passbook deposits and NOW accounts are very liquid; CDs are less so because of the penalties described above.

The risk of loss on deposits is small. In reality it is virtually nil insofar as most deposits are concerned. This is because most deposits are now insured by an agency of the federal government. Therefore, if the financial institution were to go under, the federal government would make the deposits good.

Deposits at commercial banks and mutual savings banks are insured by the Federal Deposit Insurance Corporation (FDIC). To finance this insurance, the banks pay an annual premium of $1/12$ of 1 percent of their deposits into a fund which is used to pay depositors of banks that fail.

Each deposit (this covers demand deposits, savings deposits, NOW accounts and CDs) is insured up to $100,000. Remember, though, if you have several accounts, they are commingled and all of them together come under the $100,000 rule if they are in the name of the same person. However, you may have a total of $300,000 in insured deposits in a single bank; a $100,000 deposit in your name, $100,000 in your spouse's name, and $100,000 held jointly. If you have deposits in excess of this, you can obtain additional insurance in an amount up to $300,000 at another bank. Since there are about 14,000 banks in the U.S., and since most of them are insured, there is no problem here. To be sure, a few banks are not insured, and you might wish to avoid them. Those banks that are insured will display a metal sign indicating this in a prominent place, usually near the teller's window.

Deposits in savings and loan associations are also insured by an agency of the federal government; it is the Federal Savings and Loans Insurance Corporation (FSLIC). Everything I have said above about the FDIC and commercial bank deposits applies to the FSLIC and savings and loan association deposits. A few S and Ls are not insured, but they are few in number and are usually small associations in small towns.

The greatest weakness of the credit union is that all of its eggs are in one basket. In more technical terms, there is a lack of diversification of risk. The credit union is generally centered around one organization or business firm. Thus, if that particular firm is hard hit by a business recession, the credit union is likely to suffer financial reverses, because many of its members will probably lose their jobs. But now credit union deposits are also insured. In 1971, Congress authorized Federal Credit Union Share Insurance. It insures credit union shares up to $100,000 much as FDIC insures bank deposits. This insurance is mandatory for all federal credit unions; state credit unions may join on a voluntary basis. Consequently, the risk of holding credit union shares has been reduced substantially.

The risk involved in credit unions has been extremely small for a number of other reasons. Loans in excess of $400 are usually secured. Also, the management of credit unions has been excellent and somewhat conservative. Finally, there is a strong bond of loyalty and sense of responsibility among credit union members.

Industrial banks are the only thrift institutions whose deposits are not insured. Consequently, a depositor in an industrial bank assumes somewhat more risk. However, he or she would also enjoy a greater return, generally speaking. If you choose your industrial bank with care and select a financially strong one, your risk is not really great, however. Indeed, all of the thrift institutions have excellent records, and not many of them have failed in recent years.

United States government bonds can be classified into marketable and nonmarketable but redeemable. The marketable bonds are sold by brokers and appeal primarily to larger investors and institutions. They will be discussed in greater detail in Chapter 13. The nonmarketable bonds will be discussed here because they are designed for the small investor and because they are classified as thrift institutions. These bonds are issued in two different series; they were formerly called series E and series H, but in January, 1980, the Treasury made a few minor changes and the bonds are now called series EE and HH. The older series E and H bonds sold prior to 1980 are, of course, still outstanding.

Series EE and HH bonds being nonnegotiable are also nonmarketable. They cannot be used as collateral for a loan nor can they be sold to a third party. However, they are redeemable, which means that they can be returned to the U.S. Treasury at the option of the bondholder. Because of this redeemability feature, their price is stabilized and they do not fluctuate inversely with changes in the interest rate.[5]

Series EE bonds are discounted, whereas Series HH bonds are not. This merely means that Series EE bonds are sold below their face value and then, as time passes, their value rises to reflect accrued interest in accordance with a predetermined schedule. These bonds come in denominations with a face value of $50, $75, $100, $200, $500, and $1,000, $5,000, and $10,000. Since they are discounted, they are sold at a price below these figures. These bonds may be purchased only by individuals. Series EE bonds are sold at one-half of their face value and at maturity are worth 6.65 percent above their face value. That is, a $100 bond will sell for $50 and at maturity (currently in 11 years), will be worth $106.65. Consequently, their yield is determined by the length of time to maturity. Indeed, varying the length of time to maturity is how the Treasury changes the yield, if it wishes to do so.

TABLE 7–4. *U.S. savings bonds, series E, redemption values by denomination, December 1980.*

ISSUE YEAR	ISSUE MONTHS	$10	$25	$50	$75	$100	$200	$500	$1,000	$10,000
1980	June		19.13	38.26	57.39	76.52	153.04	382.60	765.20	7,652.00
	May		19.20	38.40	57.60	76.80	153.60	384.00	768.00	7,680.00
	Apr.		19.28	38.56	57.84	77.12	154.24	385.60	771.20	7,712.00
	Mar.		19.36	38.72	58.08	77.44	154.88	387.20	774.40	7,744.00
	Feb.		19.45	38.90	58.35	77.80	155.60	389.00	778.00	7,780.00
	Jan.		19.53	39.06	58.59	78.12	156.24	390.60	781.20	7,812.00
1979	Dec.		19.61	39.22	58.83	78.44	156.88	392.20	784.40	7,844.00
	Nov.		19.69	39.38	59.07	78.76	157.52	393.80	787.60	7,876.00
	Oct.		19.77	39.54	59.31	79.08	158.16	395.40	790.80	7,908.00
	Sep.		19.85	39.70	59.55	79.40	158.80	397.00	794.00	7,940.00

5. The reason Congress made these bonds nonnegotiable and redeemable was to protect the small investor from the unpleasant experience that took place regarding bonds sold during World War I. Those bonds were negotiable (and hence marketable). Many people bought bonds during the war but after the war their price fell drastically as interest rates rose. If people had to liquidate them due to an emergency, they suffered a substantial capital loss. Why the price of marketable bonds fluctuates inversely with changes in the interest rate is explained in Chapter 12.

TABLE 7–4. (cont.)

ISSUE YEAR	ISSUE MONTHS	$10	$25	$50	$75	$100	$200	$500	$1,000	$10,000
	Aug.		19.94	39.88	59.82	79.76	159.52	398.80	797.60	7,976.00
	July		20.02	40.04	60.06	80.08	160.16	400.40	800.80	8,008.00
	June		20.10	40.20	60.30	80.40	160.80	402.00	804.00	8,040.00
	May		20.18	40.36	60.54	80.72	161.44	403.60	807.20	8,072.00
	Apr.		20.27	40.54	60.81	81.08	162.16	405.40	810.80	8,108.00
	Mar.		20.35	40.70	61.05	81.40	162.80	407.00	814.00	8,140.00
	Feb.		20.43	40.86	61.29	81.72	163.44	408.60	817.20	8,172.00
	Jan.		20.52	41.04	61.56	82.08	164.16	410.40	820.80	8,208.00
1978	Dec.		20.60	41.20	61.80	82.40	164.80	412.00	824.00	8,240.00
	Nov.		20.69	41.38	62.07	82.76	165.52	413.80	827.60	8,276.00
	Oct.		20.78	41.56	62.34	83.12	166.24	415.60	831.20	8,312.00
	Sep.		20.87	41.74	62.61	83.48	166.96	417.40	834.80	8,348.00
	Aug.		20.96	41.92	62.88	83.84	167.68	419.20	838.40	8,384.00
	July		21.05	42.10	63.15	84.20	168.40	421.00	842.00	8,420.00
	Jan. thru June		21.14	42.28	63.42	84.56	169.12	422.80	845.60	8,456.00
1977	July thru Dec.		21.71	43.42	65.13	86.84	173.68	434.20	868.40	8,684.00
	Jan. thru June		22.31	44.62	66.93	89.24	178.48	446.20	892.40	8,924.00
1976	July thru Dec.		22.97	45.94	68.91	91.88	183.76	459.40	918.80	9,188.00
	Jan. thru June		23.67	47.34	71.01	94.68	189.36	473.40	946.80	9,468.00
1975	Dec.		25.38	50.76	76.14	101.52	203.04	507.60	1,015.20	10,152.00
	July thru Nov.		25.32	50.64	75.96	101.28	202.56	506.40	1,012.80	10,128.00
	June		26.14	52.28	78.42	104.56	209.12	522.80	1,045.60	10,456.00
	Jan. thru May		26.08	52.16	78.24	104.32	208.64	521.60	1,043.20	10,432.00
1974	Dec.		26.93	53.86	80.79	107.72	215.44	538.60	1,077.20	10,772.00
	July thru Nov.		26.86	53.72	80.58	107.44	214.88	537.20	1,074.40	10,744.00
	June		27.74	55.48	83.22	110.96	221.92	554.80	1,109.60	11,096.00
	Jan. thru May		27.67	55.34	83.01	110.68	221.36	553.40	1,106.80	11,068.00
1973	Dec.		28.57	57.14	85.71	114.28	228.56	571.40	1,142.80	11,428.00
	Sep. thru Nov.		28.14	56.28	84.42	112.56	225.12	562.80	1,125.60	11,256.00
	Aug.		29.06	58.12	87.18	116.24	232.48	581.20	1,162.40	11,624.00
	June thru July		28.99	57.98	86.97	115.96	231.92	579.80	1,159.60	11,596.00
	Mar. thru May		28.92	57.84	86.76	115.68	231.36	578.40	1,156.80	11,568.00
	Feb.		29.86	59.72	89.58	119.44	238.88	597.20	1,194.40	11,944.00
	Jan.		29.79	59.58	89.37	119.16	238.32	595.80	1,191.60	11,916.00
1972	Dec.		29.79	59.58	89.37	119.16	238.32	595.80	1,191.60	11,916.00
	Sep. thru Nov.		29.72	59.44	89.16	118.88	237.76	594.40	1,188.80	11,888.00
	Aug.		30.69	61.38	92.07	122.76	245.52	613.80	1,227.60	12,276.00
	June thru July		30.62	61.24	91.86	122.48	244.96	612.40	1,224.80	12,248.00
	Mar. thru May		30.53	61.06	91.59	122.12	244.24	610.60	1,221.20	12,212.00
	Feb.		31.52	63.04	94.56	126.08	252.16	630.40	1,260.80	12,608.00
	Jan.		31.45	62.90	94.35	125.80	251.60	629.00	1,258.00	12,580.00

Note: The sale of Series E Savings Bonds was terminated at the close of business June 30, 1980.
Source: U.S. Department of the Treasury.

Currently, if held to maturity, the Series EE bonds yield 6.5 percent per year on the average, but if redeemed prior to maturity, the yield is lower. The low yield during the early years of the bond is intended to discourage people from cashing them in. Tables 7–4 and 7–5 show how series E and EE bonds appreciate in value as the months pass. The tables are for December 1980 and show the value, as of that date, of bonds purchased at various earlier dates given on the vertical axis to the left. For example, a series E bond of $50 face value sold for $37.50 in December 1976 has a redemption value of $45.94 in December 1980. Each month the Treasury publishes a new table such as this. The table showing the value of series EE bonds is much smaller than the series E table because EE bonds have only been sold since January 1980. However, a series EE bond of $50 face value sold for $25 in January 1980 has a redemption value of $26.04 in December 1980. It should be noted that in the case of both series E and series EE bonds, the yield is less than 6.5 percent during the early years and more than 6.5 during the later years of maturity; the average over the entire period is 6.5 percent. Note, too, that these bonds can be held beyond their maturity date, and they will continue to earn interest (currently at 6.5 percent). This is why their redemption value can rise substantially above their face value. It should also be noted that the 6.5 percent average yield (the appreciation in the price of the bonds) is not taxed until the bond is redeemed. Then the interest is taxed all at once. This tax deferral makes the true yield a little more attractive than the 6.5 percent suggests.

The interest on Series H and HH bonds, which are sold in units of $500, $1,000, $5,000, and $10,000, is payable semiannually beginning six months after issue date; it is paid on each interest date by check and mailed to the addressee of record. These bonds are always sold at their face value. They are not coupon bonds, however. They are registered bonds and the interest is automatically sent to the bondholder. Series HH (and the old H) bonds also yield 6.5 percent per year.

Most Series EE and HH bonds are purchased through a payroll withholding plan. Large employers are set up to offer this service to their employees. These bonds are also sold by most commercial banks. There is also a $20,000 face value limit on the amount of Series HH bonds a person may purchase each year. The limit on series EE is $30,000 face value so one may purchase a total of $50,000 face value per year.

TABLE 7–5. *U.S. savings bonds, series EE, redemption values by denomination, December 1980.*

YEAR	ISSUE MONTH	$50	$75	$100	$200	$500	$1,000	$5,000	$10,000
1980	July-Dec				Not Eligible for Payment				
	June	25.50	38.25	51.00	102.00	255.00	510.00	2,550.00	5,100.00
	May	25.60	38.40	51.20	102.40	256.00	512.00	2,560.00	5,120.00
	Apr	25.70	38.55	51.40	102.80	257.00	514.00	2,570.00	5,140.00
	Mar	25.82	38.73	51.64	103.28	258.20	516.40	2,582.00	5,164.00
	Feb	25.94	38.91	51.88	103.76	259.40	518.80	2,594.00	5,188.00
	Jan	26.04	39.06	52.08	104.16	260.40	520.80	2,604.00	5,208.00

Source: U.S. Department of the Treasury.

Liquidity and Risk

All types of United States government securities are highly liquid. The marketable bonds (all but Series EE and HH) can be sold by telephoning a broker.[6] A highly organized market exists for these bonds. The nonmarketable Series EE and HH bonds are redeemable at the option of the bondholder. Hence they, too, are very liquid. They can be redeemed at almost any commercial bank.

While there is absolutely no risk of default involved in holding any government bonds, there is a risk of possible capital loss involved in holding all government bonds except Series EE and HH. Since their market price is permitted to fluctuate freely with the forces of supply and demand, it is possible that, if a person wishes to sell bonds before they mature, he or she will have to accept a lower price than that paid. However, since Series EE and HH are redeemable by the Treasury, their price is in effect stabilized; there is no risk whatsoever attached to these bonds.

Rate of Return

The yield on Series EE and HH is almost as high as the return a person could obtain from certificates of deposit in a savings and loan association or a bank. The yield on the marketable government bonds varies, but generally it is higher than on Series EE and HH and compares favorably with the return paid by any thrift institution. The major virtue of Series EE and HH bonds, in addition to their high degree of safety and liquidity, is that they provide an easy way of saving through a payroll withholding plan. Persons who lack the discipline to save on their own can usually arrange for their employer to withhold part of their weekly earnings to buy bonds.

SOME NOTES ON INTEREST

Interest seems to be a mysterious thing for some people; it shouldn't be. Interest income is also sometimes looked upon as somehow being less virtuous than other income. This is an erroneous view. There is nothing mysterious about interest and there should be no stigma attached to receiving it. Therefore, we shall next explore the theory of interest, simple interest, compound interest, the rule of 72, and how most thrift institutions calculate interest.

The Theory of Interest

Interest is the payment for the use of capital just as rent is the payment for the use of real property. Interest can be justified in several ways. Capital is productive and hence, like labor, it receives a return. Labor receives a wage; capital receives an interest payment. Liquid capital (money), however, must first be turned into real capital (plant and equipment) before it is productive.

A second reason for the payment of interest is because the supplier of capital (lender) assumes a risk (this risk may be large or it may be small) that the loan will not be repaid. This is the risk of default and lenders must be paid a fee (interest) to entice them to assume it. Moreover, the higher the risk of default, the higher the interest payment must be. Indeed, if the risk is high enough, no one will advance the capital, and there is a fringe of unsatisfied

---

6. The discussion in this paragraph applies both to the older series E and H bonds and the newer series EE and HH bonds.

would-be borrowers. In this sense, risk plays Hamlet in determining the level of interest among competing borrowers.

A third reason for the payment of interest is that most people prefer present dollars (or consumption) to future dollars. A lender gives up (it is hoped temporarily) present dollars, and hence present consumption, for future dollars, and hence future consumption. This is a personal sacrifice. For postponing consumption, the person must be given the reward of greater consumption in the future. Interest, then, is a payment for abstinence. This is also sometimes called time preference. People prefer present consumption to future consumption; they have a positive time preference, and interest must be paid as a bribe to entice them to postpone consumption. Or putting it another way, money or goods today is more valuable than the same money or goods in the future. We are impatient creatures. The old saw perhaps explains interest best: "A bird in the hand is worth two in the bush."

Simple Interest

When a contract is made between a borrower and a lender, the borrower agrees to pay the lender a fixed percentage sum of the amount borrowed (called the principal) periodically. Usually the amount of interest to be paid is stated as so much per year. If the agreement calls for an 8 percent interest rate, then on a $1,000 loan the borrower must pay $80 per year. The contract could call for an $80 payment to be made every year or it could stipulate a $40 payment every six months or $20 every three months. In each case, it would be 8 percent per year. If the interest payment is made each time it is due, then the amount borrowed remains a constant ($1,000 in the case above) and the interest becomes a constant percentage of a constant principal sum. This is called simple interest. However, this is not always the way it is done; consequently, we also have compound interest.

Compound Interest

If the contract calls for the interest to be retained by the borrower, then the principal sum grows as time passes. If a lender makes available to a borrower $1,000 to be compounded at 8 percent for a number of years, then at the end of one year the $80 interest is added to the original loan of $1,000, which now becomes $1,080. The next year the interest is 8 percent of $1,080, or $86.40. The $86.40 instead of being paid to the lender is again added to the principal sum of $1,080, now making it $1,166.40. Now interest will be calculated on $1,166.40, and so it goes year after year. This has been called paying interest on interest, but that may not be the best term.

In the above case interest was compounded annually. Interest can also be compounded semiannually, quarterly, monthly, weekly, or even daily. Compounding semiannually would call for adding $40 to the principal sum at the end of six months and then figuring interest on $1,040 for the second six months and so on. Compounding then results in a fixed percentage rate being calculated on an ever-increasing principal sum, and hence becoming proportionately greater with each passing period.

The Rule of 72

If a dollar is earning compound interest, it will eventually double in value; that is to say, a dollar will grow to become two dollars and so on. How quickly a dollar will double in value is determined by the interest rate and by how frequently it is compounded (annually, semiannually, quarterly, monthly, or even daily). You may see how long it takes for a dollar to double in value if compounded annually by looking at Table 1 in the appendix. But if tables are not available you can approximate the time needed to double by applying the rule of 72. This rule tells us that if you divide the interest rate into 72 you will get the approximate time needed for money to double, if earnings are compounded annually; for example, at 6 percent a dollar would double in 12 years ($72 \div 6 = 12$).

How Interest Is Calculated by Most Thrift Institutions

Not all thrift institutions calculate the interest that they pay precisely the same way. But there is enough similarity among them to present some general guidelines. Some institutions have a rule that any deposits must be made by a certain date (most often the tenth of the month) to draw interest for that entire month. A few institutions still calculate interest on a quarterly basis. The funds must be on deposit by the tenth of the quarter and remain there the entire quarter before interest is paid. But this method is being used by fewer and fewer institutions.

More and more institutions are now compounding interest on a daily basis. Interest is paid from the day the deposit is made until the day it is withdrawn. With modern computers, this is possible. Daily calculation of interest is a device that, in effect, permits banks to increase the real rate of return on deposits, and in recent years the growing competition for funds on the part of institutions has resulted in more and more daily interest computations. If, for example, interest is compounded daily at 5 percent, this makes the true yearly rate about 5.13 percent.

There are four general methods of calculating interest rates. The four methods are really means of establishing the balance upon which interest is to be computed.

First In First Out (FIFO)

This method deducts all withdrawals from the interest period's beginning balance. For example, if the interest period is quarterly and you have $1,000 in your account at the beginning of the quarter but sometime during the quarter you add another $1,000 (but too late to earn interest on it) and still later withdraw $100, the interest is calculated on $900. This is the least favorable method from the depositor's point of view.

Low Balance

This method calculates interest on your minimum balance during the interest period. In the example immediately above, the interest would have been calculated on $1,000.00. This second method is not much better than the first one and in the example above, if the $100 withdrawal had taken place before the $1,000 deposit, the two methods would have worked out to be the same.

Last In First Out (LIFO)

This method deducts withdrawals from the most recent deposits made during the period. Again in the example above, the $100 withdrawal would have been subtracted from the $1,000 deposit during the interest period. If the $1,000 deposit had come in early enough (generally before the 12th day of the interest period), the interest would be calculated on $1,900. If the deposit had not come in early enough, interest would be calculated on $1,000.

Day-In Day-Out (DIDO)

This method is also called the day of deposit to day of withdrawal and is the most favorable from the point of view of the depositor. In this case the interest period is one day and a computer calculates and compounds interest daily. In the above example, with a beginning balance of $1,000, another deposit of $1,000, and a withdrawal of $100, interest would have been calculated on $1,000 for some days, $2,000 for some days, and on $1,900 for some days. The day-in day-out method of calculating interest is now the most common, especially in metropolitan areas. But before you open a savings account you should check out which method is used by the various institutions, and then choose the most favorable one. The difference in the interest that you will earn under the FIFO method on the one hand, and the day-in day-out method on the other can be substantial.

Note, however, that there is a difference between daily compounding and the daily interest period. Only if the interest period is one day do you truly have a day-in day-out method. The interest period refers to the method of obtaining the balance on which interest is calculated. It is possible that under the first method described above (FIFO) the interest could be compounded daily; but it is on the beginning balance less withdrawal or $900 in our example, and not on each and every dollar for each day it was in the account.

In those cases where a method other than the day-in day-out method is used, the passbook holder should be careful not to withdraw funds a few days before the interest period ends. This could lose interest for a full quarter. It might be better to borrow money for a few days or weeks at, say, 9 or 10 percent until the interest payment is past in order to get 5 percent for a full three months. In some cases a depositor can do this from the same institution that has the deposit. (This explanation applies only to passbook savings; the interest on CDs was discussed under each of the institutions issuing them.) Table 7–6 illustrates the true yearly rate achieved because of daily compounding for a number of stated rates.

TABLE 7–6 *Stated and true or effective interest dated due to daily compounding*

STATED RATE %	TRUE ANNUAL YIELD %
5.00	5.13
5.25	5.39
5.50	5.65
5.75	5.92
6.00	6.18
6.25	6.45
6.50	6.72
6.75	6.98
7.00	7.25
7.25	7.52
7.50	7.79
7.75	8.06
8.00	8.33

QUESTIONS FOR REVIEW

1. What are thrift institutions?

2. How do thrift institutions assist individuals in a savings program?

3. Assuming inflation, what is the position of savers holding money? Assuming deflation, what is their position?

4. Distinguish between time deposits and demand deposits.

5. Differentiate between the mutual savings bank and the savings and loan association.

6. What is the basic difference between the Federal Deposit Insurance Corporation and the Federal Savings and Loan Insurance Corporation?

7. Can a person cash in a CD prior to its maturity?

8. What is the greatest risk of the credit union?

9. Compare the rates of return of the various thrift institutions.

10. What are the main advantages and disadvantages of holding government bonds over a commercial bank time deposit?

11. What is the difference between Series EE and HH government bonds?

12. What are marketable bonds?

13. Why did Congress make Series EE and HH bonds nonnegotiable but redeemable?

CASES

1. Lyndia Christensen, aged twenty-four, is a secretary in a large city and earns $250 per week. She would like to save as much as possible for her vacation, which she hopes to spend in Miami. She would also like to earn as much interest on her savings as possible but yet keep her principal liquid. By living on a tight budget, Lyndia is able to save $20 per week. Her vacation is still almost a year off, and she requests your advice as to where to invest her savings so as to achieve her objectives. Explain why you have selected certain institutions.

2. Keith Lawson works at the local foundry where he earns $400 per week. For the past several years, he has saved $25 per week, and he expects to continue saving this amount in the future. In the past, he has invested his savings in U.S. Government Series E or EE bonds. Recently, however, the company where he works has started a credit union, and also the branch office of a big savings and loan association has moved into town. Some of Keith's friends have suggested he should put his savings in these institutions. Keith is interested in yield and safety. Should Keith follow his friends' advice? Why?

3. Over the years Arthur Pedit has kept his savings in a savings deposit at the First National Bank in his hometown. He has accumulated almost $10,000 in his savings account, which is insured by the FDIC and on which he has been earning 5¼ percent interest. Can he earn more on his money by putting it in a mutual savings bank or a savings and loan association? Will his savings be as safe in these latter institutions? How would all of the above three compare with a credit union insofar as yield and safety are concerned?

4. Bernice Wilson has saved regularly and now has $2,000 in a Los Angeles savings and loan association. Recently she received notice from the institution that they are going to raise the rate they pay from 5¼ to 5½ percent which they said was the highest the law allowed. However, her good friend Dorothy Jenkins told Bernice that she is receiving 6 percent on her savings in a branch of the same savings and loan association in Santa Ana where she lives. Can you explain the apparent discrepancy to Dorothy and Bernice?

5. Find out the logic behind regulation *Q*.

6. Bob and Virginia Waring have a $1,000, two-year, 8 percent certificate of deposit in the Essex County Savings and Loan Association, which is only one month old. Now, because of an automobile accident, they need the money. Can they get it? What interest in dollar amounts will they get? What interest would they have gotten if the CD had been one year old?

SUGGESTED READINGS

The Bankers Magazine. A banking quarterly review, published by Warren, Gorham, and Larmont, Inc., 89 Beach St., Boston, MA.

Directors Digest. Published monthly by the United States League of Savings Associations, 111 E. Wacker Drive, Chicago, Ill.

Federal Home Loan Bank Board Journal. Published monthly by the Federal Home Loan Bank Board, 320 First Street, N.W., Washington, D.C. 20552.

Gup, Benton E. *Financial Intermediaries,* 2nd ed. Boston: Houghton Mifflin Company, 1980.

Mutual Savings Banks National Fact Book. Published annually by the National Association of Mutual Savings Banks, 200 Park Avenue, New York, NY.

Mutual Savings Banks Annual Report. Published by the National Association of Mutual Savings Banks.

1981 Credit Union National Association Yearbook. CUNA, P.O. Box 431, Madison, WI 53701.

1981 Finance Facts Yearbook. Washington, D.C.: National Consumer Finance Association.

1981 International Credit Union Yearbook. Washington, D.C.: CUNA International, Inc.

1981 Savings and Loan Fact Book. Published annually by the United States Savings and Loan League, 221 North La Salle Street, Chicago, Ill.

Savings and Loan Bulletin. Published monthly by the United States League of Savings Associations, 111 E. Wacker Drive, Chicago, Ill.

Savings and Residential Financing: 1970 Conference Proceedings. Chicago: United States Savings and Loan League.

The Wall Street Journal. Published daily by Dow Jones & Company.

APPENDIX A7

PRESENT AND FUTURE VALUES

We discussed interest rates above; what they are, how they are calculated, and why they are paid. However, you do not have to laboriously calculate interest, because you can read what the interest is from tables. This appendix contains some such tables. The first table, *"The Future Worth of a Dollar,"* is ordinary compound interest. The second table, *"The Present Worth of a Future Dollar,"* is a sort of negative interest which is called discounting. Then comes *"The Future Worth of an Annuity"* which shows how your savings deposits would grow if you deposited a uniform amount each year and it grew by compound interest. Finally, the fourth table, *"The Present Worth of Future Annuity,"* is the reverse of the third. It too involves interest calculations. It shows the sum of money needed today to be equal in value to a given number of future payments.

Future Worth of a Present Dollar

The present worth of $1 is, of course, $1. At 6 percent, however, $1 will grow to $1.06 in one year. Consequently, the future worth of a dollar in one year is $1.06 and in two years it is $1.124. This is how a dollar will grow if compounded at 6 percent. This is shown by the formula:

$$(1 + i)^N$$

where N is the number of years involved, and i is the going interest rate. This is the formula for calculating compound interest discussed above. However, one need not calculate this because tables have been constructed taking the formula into account. One dollar compounded at 6 percent for ten years will be worth $1.791. Table A7-1 shows these values.

TABLE A7-1. *Future worth of a present dollar* $(1 + i)^N$

YEARS HENCE	1%	2%	3%	4%	5%	6%	7%	8%	9%	10%
1	1.010	1.020	1.030	1.040	1.050	1.060	1.070	1.080	1.090	1.100
2	1.020	1.040	1.061	1.082	1.102	1.124	1.145	1.166	1.186	1.210
3	1.030	1.061	1.093	1.125	1.158	1.191	1.225	1.260	1.295	1.331
4	1.041	1.082	1.126	1.170	1.216	1.262	1.311	1.360	1.412	1.464
5	1.051	1.104	1.159	1.217	1.276	1.338	1.403	1.469	1.539	1.611
6	1.062	1.126	1.194	1.265	1.340	1.419	1.501	1.587	1.677	1.772
7	1.072	1.149	1.230	1.316	1.407	1.504	1.606	1.714	1.828	1.949
8	1.083	1.172	1.267	1.369	1.477	1.594	1.718	1.851	1.993	2.144
9	1.094	1.195	1.305	1.423	1.551	1.689	1.838	1.999	2.172	2.358
10	1.105	1.219	1.344	1.480	1.629	1.791	1.967	2.159	2.367	2.594
11	1.116	1.243	1.384	1.539	1.710	1.898	2.105	2.332	2.580	2.853
12	1.127	1.268	1.426	1.601	1.796	2.012	2.252	2.518	2.813	3.138
13	1.138	1.294	1.469	1.665	1.886	2.133	2.410	2.720	3.066	3.452
14	1.149	1.319	1.513	1.732	1.980	2.261	2.579	2.937	3.342	3.797
15	1.161	1.346	1.558	1.801	2.079	2.397	2.759	3.172	3.642	4.177
16	1.173	1.373	1.605	1.873	2.183	2.540	2.952	3.426	3.970	4.595
17	1.184	1.400	1.653	1.948	2.292	2.693	3.159	3.700	4.328	5.054
18	1.196	1.428	1.702	2.026	2.407	2.854	3.380	3.996	4.717	5.560
19	1.208	1.457	1.754	2.107	2.527	3.026	3.617	4.316	5.142	6.116
20	1.220	1.486	1.806	2.191	2.653	3.207	3.870	4.661	5.604	6.728
25	1.282	1.641	2.094	2.666	3.386	4.292	5.427	6.848	8.623	10.835
30	1.348	1.811	2.427	3.243	4.322	5.743	7.612	10.063	13.268	17.449

TABLE A7-1. *(cont.)*

YEARS HENCE	12%	14%	15%	16%	18%	20%	24%	28%	32%	36%
1	1.120	1.140	1.150	1.160	1.180	1.200	1.240	1.280	1.320	1.360
2	1.254	1.300	1.322	1.346	1.392	1.440	1.538	1.638	1.742	1.850
3	1.405	1.482	1.521	1.561	1.643	1.728	1.907	2.067	2.300	2.515
4	1.574	1.689	1.749	1.811	1.939	2.074	2.364	2.684	3.036	3.421
5	1.762	1.925	2.011	2.100	2.288	2.488	2.932	3.436	4.007	4.653
6	1.974	2.195	2.313	2.436	2.700	2.986	3.635	4.398	5.290	6.328
7	2.211	2.502	2.660	2.826	3.185	3.583	4.508	5.629	6.983	8.605
8	2.476	2.853	3.059	3.278	3.759	4.300	5.590	7.206	9.217	11.703
9	2.773	3.252	3.518	3.803	4.435	5.160	6.931	9.223	12.166	15.917
10	3.106	3.707	4.046	4.411	5.234	6.192	8.594	11.806	16.060	21.647
11	3.479	4.226	4.652	5.117	6.176	7.430	10.657	15.112	21.199	29.439
12	3.896	4.818	5.350	5.926	7.288	8.916	13.215	19.343	27.983	40.037
13	4.363	5.492	6.153	6.886	8.599	10.699	16.386	24.759	36.937	54.451
14	4.887	6.261	7.076	7.988	10.147	12.839	20.319	31.961	48.757	74.053
15	5.474	7.138	8.137	9.266	11.974	15.407	25.196	40.565	64.359	100.712
16	6.130	8.137	9.358	10.748	14.129	18.488	31.243	51.923	84.954	136.97
17	6.866	9.276	10.761	12.468	16.672	22.186	38.741	66.461	112.14	186.28
18	7.690	10.575	12.375	14.463	19.673	26.623	48.039	86.071	148.02	253.34
19	8.613	12.056	14.232	16.777	23.214	31.948	59.568	108.89	195.39	344.54
20	9.646	13.743	16.367	19.461	27.393	38.338	73.864	139.38	257.92	468.57
25	17.000	26.462	32.919	40.874	62.669	95.396	216.542	478.90	1033.6	2180.1
30	29.960	50.950	66.212	85.850	143.371	237.376	634.820	1645.5	4142.1	10143.

Present Worth of a Future Dollar

There is also the opposite of the future worth of a present dollar. It is the present worth of a future dollar. The present worth of a future dollar is less than a dollar by whatever the going interest rate is. This is called discounting, and it is taking interest away rather than adding it. This is shown by the following formula:

$$(1 + i)^{-N}$$

Table A7–2 shows these values.

TABLE A7–2. *Present value of a future $1* $(1+i)^{-N}$

YEARS HENCE	1%	2%	4%	6%	8%	10%	12%	14%	15%	16%	18%
1	0.990	0.980	0.962	0.943	0.926	0.909	0.893	0.877	0.870	0.862	0.847
2	0.980	0.961	0.925	0.890	0.857	0.826	0.797	0.769	0.756	0.743	0.718
3	0.971	0.942	0.889	0.840	0.794	0.751	0.712	0.675	0.658	0.641	0.609
4	0.961	0.924	0.855	0.792	0.735	0.683	0.636	0.592	0.572	0.552	0.516
5	0.951	0.906	0.822	0.747	0.681	0.621	0.567	0.519	0.497	0.476	0.437
6	0.942	0.888	0.790	0.705	0.630	0.564	0.507	0.456	0.432	0.410	0.370
7	0.933	0.871	0.760	0.665	0.583	0.513	0.452	0.400	0.376	0.354	0.314
8	0.923	0.853	0.731	0.627	0.540	0.467	0.404	0.351	0.327	0.305	0.266
9	0.914	0.837	0.703	0.592	0.500	0.424	0.361	0.308	0.284	0.263	0.225
10	0.905	0.820	0.676	0.558	0.463	0.386	0.322	0.270	0.247	0.227	0.191
11	0.896	0.804	0.650	0.527	0.429	0.350	0.287	0.237	0.215	0.195	0.162
12	0.887	0.788	0.625	0.497	0.397	0.319	0.257	0.208	0.187	0.168	0.137
13	0.879	0.773	0.601	0.469	0.368	0.290	0.229	0.182	0.163	0.145	0.116
14	0.870	0.758	0.577	0.442	0.340	0.263	0.205	0.160	0.141	0.125	0.099
15	0.861	0.743	0.555	0.417	0.315	0.239	0.183	0.140	0.123	0.108	0.084
16	0.853	0.728	0.534	0.394	0.292	0.218	0.163	0.123	0.107	0.093	0.071
17	0.844	0.714	0.513	0.371	0.270	0.198	0.146	0.108	0.093	0.080	0.060
18	0.836	0.700	0.494	0.350	0.250	0.180	0.130	0.095	0.081	0.069	0.051
19	0.828	0.686	0.475	0.331	0.232	0.164	0.116	0.083	0.070	0.060	0.043
20	0.820	0.673	0.456	0.312	0.215	0.149	0.104	0.073	0.061	0.051	0.037
21	0.811	0.660	0.439	0.294	0.199	0.135	0.093	0.064	0.053	0.044	0.031
22	0.803	0.647	0.422	0.278	0.184	0.123	0.083	0.056	0.046	0.038	0.026
23	0.795	0.634	0.406	0.262	0.170	0.112	0.074	0.049	0.040	0.033	0.022
24	0.788	0.622	0.390	0.247	0.158	0.102	0.066	0.043	0.035	0.028	0.019
25	0.780	0.610	0.375	0.233	0.146	0.092	0.059	0.038	0.030	0.024	0.016
26	0.772	0.598	0.361	0.220	0.135	0.084	0.053	0.033	0.026	0.021	0.014
27	0.764	0.586	0.347	0.207	0.125	0.076	0.047	0.029	0.023	0.018	0.011
28	0.757	0.574	0.333	0.196	0.116	0.069	0.042	0.026	0.020	0.016	0.010
29	0.749	0.563	0.321	0.185	0.107	0.063	0.037	0.022	0.017	0.014	0.008
30	0.742	0.552	0.308	0.174	0.099	0.057	0.033	0.020	0.015	0.012	0.007
40	0.672	0.453	0.208	0.097	0.046	0.022	0.011	0.005	0.004	0.003	0.001
50	0.608	0.372	0.141	0.054	0.021	0.009	0.003	0.001	0.001	0.001	

TABLE A7–2. *(cont.)*

YEARS HENCE	20%	22%	24%	25%	26%	28%	30%	35%	40%	45%	50%
1	0.833	0.820	0.806	0.800	0.794	0.781	0.769	0.741	0.714	0.690	0.667
2	0.694	0.672	0.650	0.640	0.630	0.610	0.592	0.549	0.510	0.476	0.444
3	0.579	0.551	0.524	0.512	0.500	0.477	0.455	0.406	0.364	0.328	0.296
4	0.482	0.451	0.423	0.410	0.397	0.373	0.350	0.301	0.260	0.226	0.198
5	0.402	0.370	0.341	0.328	0.315	0.291	0.269	0.223	0.186	0.156	0.132
6	0.335	0.303	0.275	0.262	0.250	0.227	0.207	0.165	0.133	0.108	0.088
7	0.279	0.249	0.222	0.210	0.198	0.178	0.159	0.122	0.095	0.074	0.059
8	0.233	0.204	0.179	0.168	0.157	0.139	0.123	0.091	0.068	0.051	0.039
9	0.194	0.167	0.144	0.134	0.125	0.108	0.094	0.067	0.048	0.035	0.026
10	0.162	0.137	0.116	0.107	0.099	0.085	0.073	0.050	0.035	0.024	0.017
11	0.135	0.112	0.094	0.086	0.079	0.066	0.056	0.037	0.025	0.017	0.012
12	0.112	0.092	0.076	0.069	0.062	0.052	0.043	0.027	0.018	0.012	0.008
13	0.093	0.075	0.061	0.055	0.050	0.040	0.033	0.020	0.013	0.008	0.005
14	0.078	0.062	0.049	0.044	0.039	0.032	0.025	0.015	0.009	0.006	0.003
15	0.065	0.051	0.040	0.035	0.031	0.025	0.020	0.011	0.006	0.004	0.002
16	0.054	0.042	0.032	0.028	0.025	0.019	0.015	0.008	0.005	0.003	0.002
17	0.045	0.034	0.026	0.023	0.020	0.015	0.012	0.006	0.003	0.002	0.001
18	0.038	0.028	0.021	0.018	0.016	0.012	0.009	0.005	0.002	0.001	0.001
19	0.031	0.023	0.017	0.014	0.012	0.009	0.007	0.003	0.002	0.001	
20	0.026	0.019	0.014	0.012	0.010	0.007	0.005	0.002	0.001	0.001	
21	0.022	0.015	0.011	0.009	0.008	0.006	0.004	0.002	0.001		
22	0.018	0.013	0.009	0.007	0.006	0.004	0.003	0.001	0.001		
23	0.015	0.010	0.007	0.006	0.005	0.003	0.002	0.001			
24	0.013	0.008	0.006	0.005	0.004	0.003	0.002	0.001			
25	0.010	0.007	0.005	0.004	0.003	0.002	0.001	0.001			
26	0.009	0.006	0.004	0.003	0.002	0.002	0.001				
27	0.007	0.005	0.003	0.002	0.002	0.001	0.001				
28	0.006	0.004	0.002	0.002	0.002	0.001	0.001				
29	0.005	0.003	0.002	0.002	0.001	0.001	0.001				
30	0.004	0.003	0.002	0.001	0.001	0.001					
40	0.001										
50											

Future Worth of an Annuity

There is also the concept of the future worth of an annuity. This is the amount of money that would exist at some future time if one added $1 per year and it was growing at an interest rate of 6 percent. If one added $1 per year for twenty-five years and it was earning 6 percent, it would have grown to $54.865; $25 of this would have been the contribution and $29.865 would have been interest. This is shown by the formula:

$$\frac{(1 + i)^{N-1}}{i}$$

Table A7–3 shows the various figures.

TABLE A7–3. *Future worth of an annuity* $\frac{(1 + i)^{N-1}}{i}$

YEARS HENCE	1%	2%	3%	4%	5%	6%	7%	8%	9%	10%	12%
1	1.000	1.000	1.000	1.000	1.000	1.000	1.000	1.000	1.000	1.000	1.000
2	2.010	2.020	2.030	2.040	2.050	2.060	2.070	2.080	2.090	2.100	2.120
3	3.030	3.060	3.091	3.122	3.152	3.184	3.215	3.246	3.278	3.310	3.374
4	4.060	4.122	4.184	4.246	4.310	4.375	4.440	4.506	4.573	4.641	4.770
5	5.101	5.204	5.309	5.416	5.526	5.637	5.751	5.867	5.985	6.105	6.353
6	6.152	6.308	6.468	6.633	6.802	6.975	7.153	7.336	7.523	7.716	8.115
7	7.214	7.434	7.662	7.898	8.142	8.394	8.654	8.923	9.200	9.487	10.089
8	8.286	8.583	8.892	9.214	9.549	9.897	10.260	10.637	11.028	11.436	12.300
9	9.369	9.755	10.159	10.583	11.027	11.491	11.978	12.488	13.021	13.579	14.776
10	10.462	10.950	11.464	12.006	12.578	13.181	13.816	14.487	15.193	15.937	17.549
11	11.567	12.169	12.808	13.486	14.207	14.972	15.784	16.645	17.560	18.531	20.655
12	12.683	13.412	14.192	15.026	15.917	16.870	17.888	18.977	20.141	21.384	24.133
13	13.809	14.680	15.618	16.627	17.713	18.882	20.141	21.495	22.953	24.523	28.029
14	14.947	15.974	17.086	18.292	19.599	21.051	22.550	24.215	26.019	27.975	32.393
15	16.097	17.293	18.599	20.024	21.579	23.276	25.129	27.152	29.361	31.772	37.280
16	17.258	18.639	20.157	21.825	23.657	25.673	27.888	30.324	33.003	35.950	42.753
17	18.430	20.012	21.762	23.698	25.840	28.213	30.840	33.750	36.974	40.545	48.884
18	19.615	21.412	23.414	25.645	28.132	30.906	33.999	37.450	41.301	45.599	55.750
19	20.811	22.841	25.117	27.671	30.539	33.760	37.379	41.446	46.018	51.159	63.440
20	22.019	24.297	26.870	29.778	33.066	36.786	40.995	45.762	51.160	57.275	72.052
25	28.243	32.030	36.459	41.646	47.727	54.865	63.249	73.106	84.701	98.347	133.334
30	34.785	40.568	47.575	56.805	66.439	79.058	94.461	113.283	136.308	164.494	241.333

TABLE A7-3. *(cont.)*

YEARS HENCE	14%	16%	18%	20%	24%	28%	32%	36%	40%	50%
1	1.000	1.000	1.000	1.000	1.000	1.000	1.000	1.000	1.000	1.000
2	2.140	2.160	2.180	2.200	2.240	2.280	2.320	2.360	2.400	2.500
3	3.440	3.506	3.572	3.640	3.778	3.918	4.062	4.210	4.360	4.750
4	4.921	5.066	5.215	5.368	5.684	6.016	6.362	6.725	7.104	8.125
5	6.610	6.877	7.154	7.442	8.048	8.700	9.398	10.146	10.846	13.188
6	8.536	8.977	9.442	9.930	10.980	12.136	13.406	14.799	16.324	20.781
7	10.730	11.414	12.142	12.916	14.615	16.534	18.696	21.126	23.853	32.172
8	13.233	14.240	15.327	16.499	19.123	22.163	25.678	29.732	34.395	49.258
9	16.085	17.518	19.086	20.799	24.712	29.369	34.895	41.435	49.153	74.887
10	19.337	21.321	23.521	25.959	31.643	38.592	47.062	57.352	69.814	113.330
11	23.044	25.733	28.755	32.150	40.238	50.399	63.122	78.998	98.739	170.995
12	27.271	30.850	34.931	39.580	50.985	65.510	84.320	108.437	139.235	257.493
13	32.089	36.786	42.219	48.497	64.110	84.853	112.303	148.475	195.929	387.239
14	37.581	43.672	50.818	59.196	80.495	109.612	149.240	202.926	275.300	581.859
15	43.842	51.660	60.965	72.035	100.815	141.303	197.997	276.979	386.420	873.788
16	50.980	60.925	72.939	87.442	126.011	181.87	262.36	377.69	541.99	1311.7
17	59.118	71.673	87.068	105.931	157.253	233.79	347.31	514.66	759.78	1968.5
18	68.394	84.141	103.740	128.117	195.994	300.25	459.45	700.94	1064.7	2953.8
19	78.969	98.603	123.414	154.740	244.033	385.32	607.47	954.28	1491.6	4431.7
20	91.025	115.380	146.628	186.688	303.601	494.21	802.86	1298.8	2089.2	6648.5
25	181.871	249.214	342.603	471.981	898.092	1706.8	3226.8	6053.0	11247.0	50500.0
30	356.787	530.312	790.948	1181.882	2640.916	5873.2	12941.0	28172.0	60501.0	383500.0

Present Worth of a Future Annuity

Finally, there is the present worth of a future annuity; that is, the lump sum of money that today has the same value as periodic future payments, the total of which would be larger than the lump sum. For example, at 6 percent, $12.783 in the hand is worth twenty-five annual payments of $1 each. This is shown by the formula:

$$\frac{1 - (1 + i)^{-N}}{i}$$

Table A7–4 can be used in lieu of the formula immediately above.

TABLE A7–4. *Present worth of a future $1 received annually for N years*

$$\frac{1 - (1 + i)^{-N}}{i}$$

YEARS (N)	1%	2%	4%	6%	8%	10%	12%	14%	15%	16%	18%
1	0.990	0.980	0.962	0.943	0.926	0.909	0.893	0.877	0.870	0.862	0.847
2	1.970	1.942	1.886	1.833	1.783	1.736	1.690	1.647	1.626	1.605	1.566
3	2.941	2.884	2.775	2.673	2.577	2.487	2.402	2.322	2.283	2.246	2.174
4	3.902	3.808	3.630	3.465	3.312	3.170	3.037	2.914	2.855	2.798	2.690
5	4.853	4.713	4.452	4.212	3.993	3.791	3.605	3.433	3.352	3.274	3.127
6	5.795	5.601	5.242	4.917	4.623	4.355	4.111	3.889	3.784	3.685	3.498
7	6.728	6.472	6.002	5.582	5.206	4.868	4.564	4.288	4.160	4.039	3.812
8	7.652	7.325	6.733	6.210	5.747	5.335	4.968	4.639	4.487	4.344	4.078
9	8.566	8.162	7.435	6.802	6.247	5.759	5.328	4.946	4.772	4.607	4.303
10	9.471	8.983	8.111	7.360	6.710	6.145	5.650	5.216	5.019	4.833	4.494
11	10.368	9.787	8.760	7.887	7.139	6.495	5.988	5.453	5.234	5.029	4.656
12	11.255	10.575	9.385	8.384	7.536	6.814	6.194	5.660	5.421	5.197	4.793
13	12.134	11.343	9.986	8.853	7.904	7.103	6.424	5.842	5.583	5.342	4.910
14	13.004	12.106	10.563	9.295	8.244	7.367	6.628	6.002	5.724	5.468	5.008
15	13.865	12.849	11.118	9.712	8.559	7.606	6.811	6.142	5.847	5.575	5.092
16	14.718	13.578	11.652	10.106	8.851	7.824	6.974	6.265	5.954	5.669	5.162
17	15.562	14.292	12.166	10.477	9.122	8.022	7.120	6.373	6.047	5.749	5.222
18	16.398	14.992	12.659	10.828	9.372	8.201	7.250	6.467	6.128	5.818	5.273
19	17.226	15.678	13.134	11.158	9.604	8.365	7.366	6.550	6.198	5.877	5.316
20	18.046	16.351	13.590	11.470	9.818	8.514	7.469	6.623	6.259	5.929	5.353
21	18.857	17.001	14.029	11.764	10.017	8.649	7.562	6.687	6.312	5.973	5.384
22	19.660	17.658	14.451	12.042	10.201	8.772	7.645	6.743	6.359	6.011	5.410
23	20.456	18.292	14.857	12.303	10.371	8.883	7.718	6.792	6.399	6.044	5.432
24	21.243	18.914	15.247	12.550	10.529	8.985	7.784	6.835	6.434	6.073	5.451
25	22.023	19.523	15.622	12.783	10.675	9.077	7.843	6.873	6.464	6.097	5.467
26	22.795	20.121	15.983	13.003	10.810	9.161	7.896	6.906	6.491	6.118	5.480
27	23.560	20.707	16.330	13.211	10.935	9.237	7.943	6.935	6.514	6.136	5.492
28	24.316	21.281	16.663	13.406	11.051	9.307	7.984	6.961	6.534	6.152	5.502
29	25.066	21.844	16.984	13.591	11.158	9.370	8.022	6.983	6.551	6.166	5.510
30	25.808	22.396	17.292	13.765	11.258	9.427	8.055	7.003	6.566	6.177	5.517
40	32.835	27.355	19.793	15.046	11.925	9.779	8.244	7.105	6.642	6.234	5.548
50	39.196	31.424	21.482	15.762	12.234	9.915	8.304	7.133	6.661	6.246	5.554

20%	22%	24%	25%	26%	28%	30%	35%	40%	45%	50%
0.833	0.820	0.806	0.800	0.794	0.781	0.769	0.741	0.714	0.690	0.667
1.528	1.492	1.457	1.440	1.424	1.392	1.361	1.289	1.224	1.165	1.111
2.106	2.042	1.981	1.952	1.923	1.868	1.816	1.696	1.589	1.493	1.407
2.589	2.494	2.404	2.362	2.320	2.241	2.166	1.997	1.849	1.720	1.605
2.991	2.864	2.745	2.689	2.635	2.532	2.436	2.220	2.035	1.876	1.737
3.326	3.167	3.020	2.951	2.885	2.759	2.643	2.385	2.168	1.983	1.824
3.605	3.416	3.242	3.161	3.083	2.937	2.802	2.508	2.263	2.057	1.883
3.837	3.619	3.421	3.329	3.241	3.076	2.925	2.598	2.331	2.108	1.922
4.031	3.786	3.566	3.463	3.366	3.184	3.019	2.665	2.379	2.144	1.948
4.192	3.923	3.682	3.571	3.465	3.269	3.092	2.715	2.414	2.168	1.965
4.327	4.035	3.776	3.656	3.544	3.335	3.147	2.752	2.438	2.185	1.977
4.439	4.127	3.851	3.725	3.606	3.387	3.190	2.779	2.456	2.196	1.985
4.533	4.203	3.912	3.780	3.656	3.427	3.223	2.799	2.468	2.204	1.990
4.611	4.265	3.962	3.824	3.695	3.459	3.249	2.814	2.477	2.210	1.993
4.675	4.315	4.001	3.859	3.726	3.483	3.268	2.825	2.484	2.214	1.995
4.730	4.357	4.033	3.887	3.751	3.503	3.283	2.834	2.489	2.216	1.997
4.775	4.391	4.059	3.910	3.771	3.518	3.295	2.840	2.492	2.218	1.998
4.812	4.419	4.080	3.928	3.786	3.529	3.304	2.844	2.494	2.219	1.999
4.844	4.442	4.097	3.942	3.799	3.539	3.311	2.848	2.496	2.220	1.999
4.870	4.460	4.110	3.954	3.808	3.546	3.316	2.850	2.497	2.221	1.999
4.891	4.476	4.121	3.963	3.816	3.551	3.320	2.852	2.498	2.221	2.000
4.909	4.488	4.130	3.970	3.822	3.556	3.323	2.853	2.498	2.222	2.000
4.925	4.499	4.137	3.976	3.827	3.559	3.325	2.854	2.499	2.222	2.000
4.937	4.507	4.143	3.981	3.831	3.562	3.327	2.855	2.499	2.222	2.000
4.948	4.514	4.147	3.985	3.834	3.564	3.329	2.856	2.499	2.222	2.000
4.956	4.520	4.151	3.988	3.837	3.566	3.330	2.856	2.500	2.222	2.000
4.964	4.524	4.154	3.990	3.839	3.567	3.331	2.856	2.500	2.222	2.000
4.970	4.528	4.157	3.992	3.840	3.568	3.331	2.857	2.500	2.222	2.000
4.975	4.531	4.159	3.994	3.841	3.569	3.332	2.857	2.500	2.222	2.000
4.979	4.534	4.160	3.995	3.842	3.569	3.332	2.857	2.500	2.222	2.000
4.997	4.544	4.166	3.999	3.846	3.571	3.333	2.857	2.500	2.222	2.000
4.999	4.545	4.167	4.000	3.846	3.571	3.333	2.857	2.500	2.222	2.000

PART TWO

Your Insurance and Annuity Program

In Part II we shall examine all types of insurance as well as annuities from a personal point of view.

Chapter 8 covers all forms of life insurance, and how the various policies differ. The chapter explains how the various policies work and what benefits they provide. We shall note that many life insurance contracts have a savings feature as well as a protection feature. Premiums and how they are determined will be analyzed, as will the major differences between stock and mutual companies. We shall also find out what life insurance companies do with the money they receive in the form of premiums over the years, and we shall examine the cost of insurance and why this varies from company to company. The questions that invariably arise are: what kind of insurance should I buy, how much should I buy, and when should I buy it? The chapter presents some guidelines which should help you in answering these questions.

Chapter 9 deals with health insurance. The various things covered by health insurance are examined. Both group and individual health policies are presented. It should be noted that health insurance, and especially group health insurance, is the modern way of financing medical care.

Chapter 10 introduces property and liability insurance. Insofar as property insurance is concerned, you need to protect your home and your auto against physical destruction. The homeowner's policy is the means whereby a home is protected against all hazards by means of one policy. Insofar as liability insurance is concerned, you need this for protection in case someone is injured on your property or in the event that you kill or injure someone with your car. Some guidelines are presented to enable you to decide how much property and liability insurance you need.

Chapter 11 does essentially four things. First, it introduces social security which is the base upon which to build your retirement income. Second, life insurance annuities are presented because they can be used to supplement social security. Third, we discuss pension plans which more and more people now have, and which also are a supplement to social security. Then, the chapter ends with a discussion of individual pension plans and notes the tax savings of the different pension plans.

Chapter Eight

Life Insurance

I don't know why I was ever started, since I was so soonly departed.

EPITAPH ON A CHILD'S TOMBSTONE IN A BOSTON CEMETERY

The objectives of this chapter are to

1 Explain generally how life insurance is financially possible and how actuaries can calculate the cost

2 Present the various types of ordinary life insurance

3 Make some suggestions that will help you choose a life insurance company

4 Present some guidelines to help you decide what kind and how much life insurance to buy

5 Present some other things that everyone should know about life insurance.

In this chapter we will examine life insurance in some detail. In chapter 1 it was pointed out that the earnings of the individual constitute the foundation of the family budget. The first reason for both life insurance and health insurance is to protect the income side of the budget.

Individuals face three risks to their income-earning ability: (1) They may die prematurely. (2) They may become disabled and thus have their earnings cut off. (3) If they are ill or disabled, their expenses will be increased due to the need for medical care. For purposes of income and budget protection, individuals should protect themselves against these three risks.

If individuals live until retirement age, a substantial part of their earning ability may then be cut off; consequently certain types of life insurance policies have "savings" features that will be pointed out later in this chapter. To accumulate savings through life insurance, then, is a second reason for buying insurance.

SOME GENERAL INSURANCE CONCEPTS AND PRINCIPLES

Insurance is a device by means of which one party through a contract, called the policy, for a consideration, called the premium, undertakes to assume for another party certain types of risk of loss. Insurance is basically social in nature since it represents cooperation for mutual protection. Through the payment of premiums by many insureds, the risk is spread over large numbers, and the few who suffer losses are reimbursed.

Gambling versus Insurance

To understand the bare fundamentals of insurance, it is necessary to distinguish between gambling and insurance. A horse player visits Tropical Park race track in Miami, Florida, for the purpose of betting on horses. Although the gambler is becoming involved with the risk of loss, this risk is quite different from the risk borne by the person driving an automobile down an icy street or the risk assumed by everyone that he or she will die tomorrow. In the first instance, the individual has created his or her own hazard, namely, that of attempting to pick a winner, and in the latter case the individual has not created the hazard being faced. The driver is faced with a hazard inherent in the nature of things and so is every individual because no one knows when he or she is going to die. Here we have one important distinction between gambling and insurance. Gamblers create their risks while those who face risks inherent in everyday living can make few choices about their fates.

The other difference between insurance and gambling is that the risk involved in insurance is predictable. Insurance actuaries can, if there are large numbers of drivers, predict to a high degree of accuracy how many of them will have accidents. They cannot predict which ones, but they can predict how many. They can also predict how many people will die each year, although they cannot tell which ones. The risk involved in gambling is not only self-created, but the possibility of winning is often sheer luck. How many times a person will win and lose, even over a long time, cannot be figured out mathematically with any precision.

Indeed, the authorities will not permit one to engage in gambling or semigambling activities by means of insurance. In the early 1600s, individuals did make insurance a form of gambling, mainly in the realm of maritime insurance policies. For example, a ship ready to set to sea and loaded with a valuable cargo would be inspected by various individuals hoping to make their fortunes. They would take out an insurance policy on a ship and a cargo in which they had no interest whatsoever. Then they would return home and hope, and probably sometimes pray, that the ship would sink. If they heard that the ship had sunk, they would immediately report to the insurance company, where they were paid the value of their policies. They had won their bet. This practice not only disturbed the insurance companies; it disturbed the members of the British Parliament even more. To prevent this sort of insured gambling, Parliament in the middle 1600s passed an act that prohibited individuals from obtaining insurance policies on *anything* unless they had in that thing what is today known as an "insurable interest." This "insurable interest" concept spread to other countries as well, including the United States.

Insurable Interest

For there to be an insurable interest, a relationship must exist between the insured and the event insured against, so that the happening of the event will cause the insured some injury or loss. A person insured must in some way be actually interested in the subject matter of the insurance at the time of loss. For example, let us consider a young lady who is a professional ice skater. Her professional life depends on the soundness of her limbs (oddly enough, the same is true for a race horse). If she falls and breaks a leg, she will be unable to earn any money for a long time. Therefore, she has an interest in insuring her legs; that is, an insurable interest. For someone else to insure the skater's legs would be in the nature of a gambling contract; such an individual ordinarily would not have an insurable interest in her legs. However, an impresario who is managing the ice show and who stands a risk of loss in the event the star's legs are broken also may be said to have an insurable interest. The individual who can suffer no direct loss has no insurable interest whatever. For there to be insurance, therefore, one must have an interest in the thing or in the event being insured against.

The same is true of life insurance. One cannot, generally speaking, buy a policy on a stranger. (The exception is if one lends him money. Then one has an insurable interest up to the extent of the loan. This is discussed under credit life insurance.) One can, however, buy a policy on a direct member of one's family. Most life insurance is purchased by and on the breadwinner of a family.

Mortality Tables and Life Expectancy

The underlying principle of any type of insurance is the law of averages. Highly trained and specialized mathematicians called actuaries can, with an amazing degree of accuracy, determine how many young men thirty years of age, out of a large number of young men thirty years of age, will die within the coming year. Note that emphasis has been placed upon *large* numbers. No actuary or any other mortal can predict when any one individual thirty years of age is going to die. But an actuary working with large numbers can predict within limitations how many young men out of that large number will die within the year. In short, what cannot be predicted for the individual can be predicted in the mass. This can be done because we know a good deal about deaths at every age level from past experience.

Using past experience, insurance companies construct and use mortality tables to spread the risk of loss over large numbers. In this way they are able to absorb risk. Taking our thirty-year-old men again as an example, the actuaries who have for a great many years compiled life insurance statistics will predict that out of 100,000 thirty-year-old men in good health alive at the beginning of the year, 213 will die during the forthcoming year. Life expectancy is calculated the same way. The table below shows part of a mortality table and illustrates deaths per 100,000 as well as life expectancy in years.

In the most simple case (without attempting to figure in anything for the company's operating costs, profit, and the like), the premium[1] for a thirty-year-old man under these circumstances would be $2.13 for every $1,000 of life insurance. The way this is calculated is simply that if 100,000 thirty-year-old men buy $1,000 life insurance policies, they would pay in a total of $213,000. In this simple case, then, the amount going into the company would be equal to the amount paid out to the beneficiaries of the 213 who died, and, at the end of the year, the company would have a total of zero remaining.

In real life things are not so simple. Just as in any other business, there must be additional sums included in the premium. In this case, the premiums include an amount to cover profits and operating costs.

It should be noted that some companies do not consider insurance age to be the same as actual age. Insurance age is one's nearest birthday. That is, the moment one is six months, one day old, one is one year old insurancewise. Persons remain one year old insurancewise

---

1. Premium is the amount paid for an insurance contract.

TABLE 8–1. *Mortality tables*

AGE	AMERICAN EXPERIENCE (1843–1858) DEATHS PER 1,000	AMERICAN EXPERIENCE (1843–1858) EXPECTATION OF LIFE (YEARS)	COMMISSIONERS 1958 STANDARD ORDINARY (1950–1954) DEATHS PER 1,000	COMMISSIONERS 1958 STANDARD ORDINARY (1950–1954) EXPECTATION OF LIFE (YEARS)	INDIVIDUAL ANNUITY TABLE FOR 1971 MALE (1960–1967) DEATHS PER 1,000	INDIVIDUAL ANNUITY TABLE FOR 1971 MALE (1960–1967) EXPECTATION OF LIFE (YEARS)	INDIVIDUAL ANNUITY TABLE FOR 1971 FEMALE (1960–1967) DEATHS PER 1,000	INDIVIDUAL ANNUITY TABLE FOR 1971 FEMALE (1960–1967) EXPECTATION OF LIFE (YEARS)	UNITED STATES TOTAL POPULATION (1969–1971) DEATHS PER 1,000	UNITED STATES TOTAL POPULATION (1969–1971) EXPECTATION OF LIFE (YEARS)
0	154.70	41.45	7.08	68.30	—	—	—	—	20.02	70.75
1	63.49	47.94	1.76	67.78	—	—	—	—	1.25	71.19
2	35.50	50.16	1.52	66.90	—	—	—	—	.86	70.28
3	23.91	50.98	1.46	66.00	—	—	—	—	.69	69.34
4	17.70	51.22	1.40	65.10	—	—	—	—	.57	68.39
5	13.60	51.13	1.35	64.19	.46	71.69	.23	76.99	.51	67.43
6	11.37	50.83	1.30	63.27	.42	70.73	.19	76.01	.46	66.46
7	9.75	50.41	1.26	62.35	.40	69.75	.16	75.02	.43	65.49
8	8.63	49.90	1.23	61.43	.39	68.78	.14	74.03	.39	64.52
9	7.90	49.33	1.21	60.51	.39	67.81	.13	73.04	.34	63.54
10	7.49	48.72	1.21	59.58	.39	66.84	.13	72.05	.31	62.57
11	7.52	48.08	1.23	58.65	.40	65.86	.13	71.06	.30	61.58
12	7.54	47.45	1.26	57.72	.41	64.89	.14	70.07	.35	60.60
13	7.57	46.80	1.32	56.80	.41	63.91	.16	69.08	.46	59.62
14	7.60	46.16	1.39	55.87	.42	62.94	.17	68.10	.63	58.65
15	7.63	45.50	1.46	54.95	.43	61.97	.18	67.11	.82	57.69
16	7.66	44.85	1.54	54.03	.44	60.99	.19	66.12	1.01	56.73
17	7.69	44.19	1.62	53.11	.46	60.02	.21	65.13	1.17	55.79
18	7.73	43.53	1.69	52.19	.47	59.05	.22	64.15	1.28	54.86
19	7.77	42.87	1.74	51.28	.49	58.07	.23	63.16	1.34	53.93
20	7.80	42.20	1.79	50.37	.50	57.10	.25	62.18	1.40	53.00
21	7.86	41.53	1.83	49.46	.52	56.13	.26	61.19	1.47	52.07
22	7.91	40.85	1.86	48.55	.54	55.16	.28	60.21	1.52	51.15
23	7.96	40.17	1.89	47.64	.57	54.19	.29	59.23	1.53	50.22
24	8.01	39.49	1.91	46.73	.59	53.22	.31	58.25	1.51	49.30
25	8.06	38.81	1.93	45.82	.62	52.25	.33	57.27	1.47	48.37
26	8.13	38.12	1.96	44.90	.65	51.28	.35	56.29	1.43	47.44
27	8.20	37.43	1.99	43.99	.68	50.32	.37	55.31	1.42	46.51
28	8.26	36.73	2.03	43.08	.72	49.35	.39	54.33	1.44	45.58
29	8.34	36.03	2.08	42.16	.76	48.39	.41	53.35	1.49	44.64
30	8.43	35.33	2.13	41.25	.81	47.42	.44	52.37	1.55	43.71

TABLE 8-1. *Mortality tables (continued)*

AGE	AMERICAN EXPERIENCE (1843–1858)		COMMISSIONERS 1958 STANDARD ORDINARY (1950–1954)		INDIVIDUAL ANNUITY TABLE FOR 1971 MALE (1960–1967)		INDIVIDUAL ANNUITY TABLE FOR 1971 FEMALE (1960–1967)		UNITED STATES TOTAL POPULATION (1969–1971)	
	DEATHS PER 1,000	EXPEC-TATION OF LIFE (YEARS)	DEATHS PER 1,000	EXPEC-TATION OF LIFE (YEARS)	DEATHS PER 1,000	EXPEC-TATION OF LIFE (YEARS)	DEATHS PER 1,000	EXPEC-TATION OF LIFE (YEARS)	DEATHS PER 1,000	EXPEC-TATION OF LIFE (YEARS)
31	8.51	34.63	2.19	40.34	.86	46.46	.50	51.40	1.63	42.77
32	8.61	33.92	2.25	39.43	.92	45.50	.53	50.42	1.72	41.84
33	8.72	33.21	2.32	38.51	.98	44.54	.57	49.45	1.83	40.92
34	8.83	32.50	2.40	37.60	1.05	43.58	.61	48.48	1.95	39.99
35	8.95	31.78	2.51	36.69	1.12	42.63	.65	47.51	2.09	39.07
36	9.09	31.07	2.64	35.78	1.20	41.68	.70	46.54	2.25	38.15
37	9.23	30.35	2.80	34.88	1.30	40.73	.75	45.57	2.44	37.23
38	9.41	29.62	3.01	33.97	1.40	39.78	.81	44.60	2.66	36.32
39	9.59	28.90	3.25	33.07	1.51	38.83	.87	43.64	2.90	35.42
40	9.79	28.18	3.53	32.18	1.63	37.89	.94	42.68	3.14	34.52
41	10.01	27.45	3.84	31.29	1.79	36.95	1.01	41.72	3.41	33.63
42	10.25	26.72	4.17	30.41	2.00	36.02	1.09	40.76	3.70	32.74
43	10.52	26.00	4.53	29.54	2.26	35.09	1.19	39.80	4.04	31.86
44	10.83	25.27	4.92	28.67	2.57	34.17	1.29	38.85	4.43	30.99
45	11.16	24.54	5.35	27.81	2.92	33.25	1.40	37.90	4.84	30.12
46	11.56	23.81	5.83	26.95	3.32	32.35	1.52	36.95	5.28	29.27
47	12.00	23.08	6.36	26.11	3.75	31.46	1.65	36.01	5.74	28.42
48	12.51	22.36	6.95	25.27	4.23	30.57	1.80	35.06	6.24	27.58
49	13.11	21.63	7.60	24.45	4.74	29.70	1.97	34.13	6.78	26.75
50	13.78	20.91	8.32	23.63	5.29	28.84	2.15	33.19	7.38	25.93
51	14.54	20.20	9.11	22.82	5.86	27.99	2.37	32.26	8.04	25.12
52	15.39	19.49	9.96	22.03	6.46	27.15	2.64	31.34	8.76	24.32
53	16.33	18.79	10.89	21.25	7.09	26.33	2.97	30.42	9.57	23.53
54	17.40	18.09	11.90	20.47	7.74	25.51	3.35	29.51	10.43	22.75
55	18.57	17.40	13.00	19.71	8.42	24.71	3.79	28.61	11.36	21.99
56	19.89	16.72	14.21	18.97	9.12	23.91	4.28	27.71	12.36	21.23
57	21.34	16.05	15.54	18.23	9.85	23.13	4.83	26.83	13.41	20.49
58	22.94	15.39	17.00	17.51	10.61	22.35	5.41	25.96	14.52	19.76
59	24.72	14.74	18.59	16.81	11.41	21.59	6.02	25.10	15.70	19.05
60	26.69	14.10	20.34	16.12	12.25	20.83	6.63	24.25	16.95	18.34
61	28.88	13.47	22.24	15.44	13.13	20.08	7.22	23.41	18.29	17.65

62	31.29	12.86	24.31	14.78	14.07	19.34	7.77	22.57	19.74	16.97
63	33.94	12.26	26.57	14.14	15.08	18.61	8.29	21.74	21.33	16.30
64	36.87	11.67	29.04	13.51	16.19	17.89	8.78	20.92	23.06	15.65
65	40.13	11.10	31.75	12.90	17.41	17.17	9.29	20.10	24.95	15.00
66	43.71	10.54	34.74	12.31	18.77	16.47	9.89	19.29	26.99	14.38
67	47.65	10.00	38.04	11.73	20.29	15.77	10.62	18.47	29.18	13.76
68	52.00	9.47	41.68	11.17	21.99	15.09	11.54	17.67	31.52	13.16
69	56.76	8.97	45.61	10.64	23.89	14.42	12.66	16.87	34.00	12.57
70	61.99	8.48	49.79	10.12	26.00	13.76	14.03	16.08	36.61	12.00
71	67.67	8.00	54.15	9.63	28.34	13.11	15.65	15.30	39.43	11.43
72	73.73	7.55	58.65	9.15	30.93	12.48	17.55	14.53	42.66	10.88
73	80.18	7.11	63.26	8.69	33.80	11.86	19.74	13.79	46.44	10.34
74	87.03	6.68	68.12	8.24	36.98	11.26	22.26	13.05	50.75	9.82
75	94.37	6.27	73.37	7.81	40.49	10.67	25.12	12.34	55.52	9.32
76	102.31	5.88	79.18	7.39	44.39	10.10	28.37	11.64	60.60	8.84
77	111.06	5.49	85.70	6.98	48.72	9.55	32.05	10.97	65.96	8.38
78	120.83	5.11	93.06	6.59	53.50	9.01	36.23	10.32	71.53	7.93
79	131.73	4.74	101.19	6.21	58.79	8.50	40.98	9.68	77.41	7.51
80	144.47	4.39	109.98	5.85	64.60	7.99	46.39	9.08	83.94	7.10
81	158.60	4.05	119.35	5.51	70.90	7.51	52.51	8.49	91.22	6.70
82	174.30	3.71	129.17	5.19	77.67	7.05	59.41	7.94	98.92	6.32
83	191.56	3.39	139.38	4.89	84.94	6.60	67.16	7.41	106.95	5.96
84	211.36	3.08	150.01	4.60	92.87	6.16	75.90	6.90	115.48	5.62
85	235.55	2.77	161.14	4.32	101.69	5.74	85.77	6.43	125.61	5.28
86	265.68	2.47	172.82	4.06	111.65	5.34	96.90	5.99	137.48	4.97
87	303.02	2.18	185.13	3.80	123.05	4.95	109.34	5.57	149.79	4.68
88	346.69	1.91	198.25	3.55	136.12	4.57	122.98	5.20	161.58	4.42
89	395.86	1.66	212.46	3.31	151.07	4.21	137.51	4.86	172.92	4.18
90	454.55	1.42	228.14	3.06	168.04	3.87	152.47	4.55	185.02	3.94
91	532.47	1.19	245.77	2.82	187.15	3.55	167.37	4.28	198.88	3.73
92	634.26	.98	265.93	2.58	208.46	3.26	181.78	4.04	213.63	3.53
93	734.18	.80	289.30	2.33	231.89	2.98	195.39	3.83	228.70	3.35
94	857.14	.64	316.66	2.07	257.15	2.73	208.07	3.63	243.36	3.19
95	1,000.00	.50	351.24	1.80	283.84	2.50	219.90	3.46	257.45	3.06
96			400.56	1.51	311.57	2.30	231.10	3.29	269.59	2.95
97			488.42	1.18	340.21	2.11	242.21	3.13	280.24	2.85
98			668.15	.83	369.77	1.94	253.82	2.97	289.77	2.76
99			1,000.00	.50	400.19	1.79	266.45	2.81	298.69	2.69
100					431.41	1.65	280.54	2.65	306.96	2.62
101					463.31	1.53	296.45	2.49	314.61	2.56
102					495.76	1.41	314.54	2.33	321.67	2.51
103					528.60	1.31	335.12	2.17	328.17	2.46
104					561.69	1.21	358.54	2.01	334.14	2.41

Table 8-1. Mortality tables (continued)

AGE	AMERICAN EXPERIENCE (1843–1858)		COMMISSIONERS 1958 STANDARD ORDINARY (1950–1954)		INDIVIDUAL ANNUITY TABLE FOR 1971 MALE (1960–1967)		INDIVIDUAL ANNUITY TABLE FOR 1971 FEMALE (1960–1967)		UNITED STATES TOTAL POPULATION (1969–1971)	
	DEATHS PER 1,000	EXPECTATION OF LIFE (YEARS)	DEATHS PER 1,000	EXPECTATION OF LIFE (YEARS)	DEATHS PER 1,000	EXPECTATION OF LIFE (YEARS)	DEATHS PER 1,000	EXPECTATION OF LIFE (YEARS)	DEATHS PER 1,000	EXPECTATION OF LIFE (YEARS)
105					594.88	1.13	385.12	1.85	339.60	2.37
106					628.02	1.05	415.24	1.70	344.60	2.34
107					660.95	.98	449.27	1.55	349.17	2.30
108					693.50	.92	487.65	1.41	353.33	2.27
109					725.52	.86	530.79	1.27	357.12	2.24

Notes: Mortality rates contained in the 1958 Commissioners Standard Ordinary table were obtained from experience of 1950–1954, but contain an added element designed to generate life insurance reserves of a conservative nature in keeping with the long-term guarantees inherent in life insurance contracts. Premiums for life insurance policies, on the other hand, are based on assumptions that include expected mortality experience. Mortality rates for the 1971 Annuity Tables are, again, conservative as related to the actual experience on which they are based.

Source: 1979 Life Insurance Fact Book, American Council of Life Insurance, pp. 108–9.

until they are 1½ years old chronologically, when they become two for insurance purposes. Other companies stick with the chronological age.

The 100,000 thirty-year-old men referred to above must be in good physical condition. Statistics upon which the actuaries determine the probability of the number of deaths in any age group are based on the assumption that those persons insured are in good physical condition and good mental health to begin with. If it were not for the requirement of good physical and mental health, obviously anyone with a disease would immediately rush out to the company and buy insurance, in which case the predictions of the actuaries would fall short of their mark and the companies would rapidly go out of business.

Loading Charges

In the hypothetical example given above, the rate or premium cost was $2.13 per $1,000 of insurance for a thirty-year-old male. It was also pointed out that nothing was added for costs or other expenses to the rate of $2.13 per $1,000 of insurance. This is called *pure insurance* or the pure rate. The premium cost to the individual is the pure rate plus other costs, and these other costs are called loading charges; in short, something is "loaded" onto the pure rate to make up the final premium cost. These other costs consist of commissions paid to the insurance agent and other operating costs of the insurance company. The greater percentage of the loading costs come from commissions paid. Generally speaking, life insurance agents receive two forms of commissions: first, the first-year sales commissions and, second, renewal service commissions. On the average, the life insurance agent's first-year sales commissions vary from 30 percent to about 55 percent of the premium, depending upon the company. In addition, the agent is paid a "renewal service commission" during the next nine years that the policy is in force. This rate varies, but generally amounts to 5 percent or less of the premiums during this time.

The mortality tables (or insurance premiums) are also loaded for fractional payments. Insurance premiums can be paid annually, semiannually, quarterly, or monthly. However, insurance companies make certain assumptions regarding the interest income they can earn and hence guarantee for their policyholders, and these assumptions call for annual payment of premiums. If one pays premiums on an other than annual basis, the insurance company has them for a shorter period of time and earns less interest. Therefore the tables are loaded for semiannual, quarterly, and monthly payments of premiums to make up for the loss of interest. In general, it can be shown that the total loading charges increase the cost of insurance between 20 and 25 percent over and above the pure or net insurance rate.

Level Premium Life Insurance

Notice in Table 8–1 that the number of people dying per year per 100,000 people rises with age. At age thirty, it is 213 deaths per 100,000; but at age forty-one it is 384; and at age fifty-one it is 911. This mortality experience rises and at advanced ages, it is quite high. Eventually, it reaches 100 percent; this happens at age ninety-nine. At age ninety-nine, all 100,000 people out of any 100,000 people are expected to die during the next year. Occasionally people do outlive the mortality tables and reach their one-hundredth birthday. Nevertheless, at age one-hundred one is actuarially dead and insurance companies publish one's picture in the local paper and pay off the policies even though one is still alive.

Since the mortality experience rises with age, logic would suggest that so, too, should premiums. Indeed, if one were to buy insurance on a year-to-year basis, this would be the case. Later, when one is quite old, premiums are almost prohibitive. However, insurance premiums are fixed. One buys insurance at age thirty and then pays those same premiums even when one reaches age fifty. This again is because of the marvelous law of averages that actuaries use in calculating premiums. These premiums are then used to build up reserves in the early years to be used in the later years. For example, the insurance company knows that eventually everybody dies. Therefore, for any large number of people (be it 10,000 or 100,000) the company can calculate its eventual total death claims. The company must collect, over the lifetime of this group, enough premiums to meet the total death claims, plus an allowance for expenses and a second allowance for a margin of safety. Since the company knows the schedule of deaths, it also knows the total number of monthly premiums it will receive. It now becomes a matter of arithmetic. The company knows total death claims and the total number of monthly premiums. It divides the former by the latter and it gets the monthly dollar premium required. This really amounts to averaging the premiums for individuals over their insurance contracts. This means that they pay higher premiums than they should during the early years and lower premiums than they should during the later years. For example, if at age twenty the mortality tables indicate that one's insurance premium should be $1.79 per month per $1,000 of insurance, one might nevertheless be charged a premium of $3.37. This is because later when one reaches age forty-five, one's premium should be $5.35, but one will still be charged $3.37. The excessive premiums of the early years go into a reserve and earn interest and are used to make up deficiencies in premiums in later years. Over the entire contract the deficiencies and excess offset each other. This level premium policy is illustrated in Figure 8–1.

Who Are the Policyholders?

According to a study made a few years ago by the Life Insurance Agency Management Association, about 86 percent of all American families have some life insurance. While more and more women are being insured, men still own most of the insurance in the United States.[2] While the study that made the figures available is a few years old, insurance companies believe that on a percentage basis, the statistics have not changed much. These figures include both individual and group plans. Individual plans, however, are in first place both in the number of people covered and by dollar amounts. This is because limits often are imposed by state law on how much group insurance can be purchased.

FIGURE 8–1. *Sample of a level premium policy, and what the premiums would be if they were recalculated on an annual basis.*

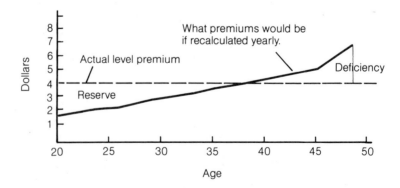

2. *1979 Life Insurance Fact Book*, American Council of Life Insurance, p. 16.

Part 2 / Your Insurance and Annuity Program

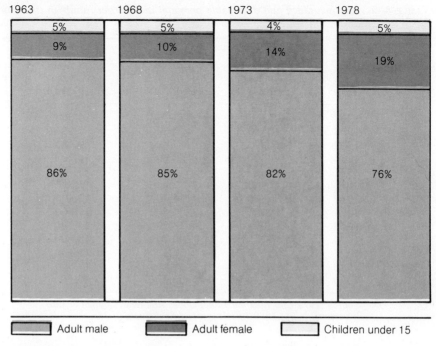

The average size policy purchased on women's lives has been increasing at a faster rate than that of men. According to the survey results, the average size ordinary policy for women increased by 287% between 1968 and 1978, and increased by 204% for men.

FIGURE 8–2. *Distribution of amount of ordinary life policies purchased, by sex of insured, in the United States. (Source: 1979 Life Insurance Fact Book, American Council of Life Insurance, p. 15.)*

The American people own about $3 trillion worth of life insurance, which they have purchased from more than 1,700 different life insurance companies in the United States. This figure averages about $35,100 per family. There is a positive correlation between income and amount of insurance owned. Generally, the higher the person's income, the more insurance he or she will have. However, there are some exceptions; such things as number of dependents and personal value judgments also will influence a person's decisions regarding the life insurance purchased. Table 8–2 shows the relationship between life insurance and personal income.

CLASSIFICATION OF LIFE INSURANCE POLICIES

The various types of life insurance policies sold in the United States can be classified and subclassified as follows:

1. Ordinary life insurance
    Term
    Whole life
        Straight life

TABLE 8–2. *Life insurance and disposable personal income per family in the United States*

YEAR	LIFE INSURANCE PER INSURED FAMILY	LIFE INSURANCE PER FAMILY	DISPOSABLE PERSONAL INCOME PER FAMILY
1967	$20,300	$17,100	$ 8,600
1968	21,500	18,300	9,100
1969	22,800	19,400	9,500
1970	24,400	20,700	10,100
1971	25,500	21,700	10,700
1972	26,900	22,900	11,300
1973	28,800	24,400	12,400
1974	31,200	26,500	13,100
1975	33,000	28,100	14,200
1976	35,000	30,100	15,200
1977	37,700	32,400	16,400
1978	40,800	35,100	17,800
1979	44,800	38,500	19,400

Source: *1979 Life Insurance Fact Book,* American Council of Life Insurance, p. 24; *1980 Life Insurance Fact Book,* p. 24.

Limited pay life
Endowment
Combination of two or more of the above
2. Group life
3. Credit life
4. Industrial
5. G.I. life insurance
6. Mutual savings bank and fraternal society life insurance

Ordinary life insurance accounts for the bulk of the insurance in force today. It is sold to individuals in multiples of $1,000 and it will be discussed next.

ORDINARY LIFE INSURANCE

The terminology covering ordinary life insurance policies is a bit confusing because not all companies use the same designations. There are just four kinds of ordinary policies. As noted above they are: term, whole life, endowment, and combinations of two or more of the above policies. However, there are two different kinds of whole life policies; they are the straight life and the limited pay life policies, which are not the same. Table 8–3 shows ordinary life insurance in force in the United States.

Term Insurance

Term life insurance is the simplest type of ordinary life insurance. Strictly speaking, term insurance consists of a contract given, usually for a short period of time, where most of

TABLE 8–3. *Ordinary life insurance in force in the United States, by plan*

PLAN OF INSURANCE	1974			1977		
	NUMBER OF POLICIES (000 OMITTED)	AMOUNT (000,000 OMITTED)	% OF AMOUNT	NUMBER OF POLICIES (000 OMITTED)	AMOUNT (000,000 OMITTED)	% OF AMOUNT
Ordinary						
Whole Life						
Straight life, premium paying	54,500	$ 496,600	49.2	60,300	$ 616,900	47.8
Limited payment life, premium payment	28,700	100,200	9.9	28,300	123,500	9.6
Paid-up	19,500	39,700	3.9	20,200	45,200	3.5
Endowment	11,900	43,000	4.3	11,900	52,200	4.1
Retirement income with insurance	2,400	17,500	1.7	2,400	21,700	1.7
Term						
Extended	5,000	16,700	1.6	5,600	20,700	1.6
Regular						
Decreasing	5,400	89,400	8.9	6,100	114,800	8.9
Other	3,800	83,300	8.3	4,700	147,400	11.4
Other						
Decreasing	——	68,200	6.8	——	79,600	6.2
Other	——	54,400	5.4	——	67,300	5.2
Total Ordinary	131,200	$1,009,000	100.0	139,500	$1,289,300	100.0

Source: 1979 Life Insurance Fact Book, American Council of Life Insurance, p. 22.

the monies paid into the company are also paid out. Although the policy may be for a one-year period, in practice there are relatively few one-year term policies issued. Most term policies are for either five years or ten years, the five-year term policy being the most popular type, although some companies sell twenty-year term, and even term until the person reaches age sixty-five. Generally this five- and ten-year term is renewable, and without a medical examination. This is one reason the five-year term is so popular; it can be continued if needed after the first five years are over or it can be dropped, if not needed. As one grows older, the chances of dying increase; therefore, although premiums are constant for the life of the policy, they increase if the policy is renewed as the individual grows older. In extreme old age the rate for term insurance becomes fairly prohibitive.

Most term policies are either renewable or convertible or both. This means that the company, in its contract with the insured, agrees either to renew the policy for the similar time period at a higher rate or to permit the contract to be converted or exchanged for another type of insurance contract (say permanent insurance) without medical examination. The renewable and convertible features are extremely important to the individual. For example, a person taking out a term policy might be in excellent health as of the date of the initial contract, and yet during the five-year period in which the contract is in force may experience failing health. Without the renewable or convertible feature, the person would be unable to obtain further life insurance.

In the one-year term policy, where it is renewable, the rates change from year to year. For example, an individual may pay $8.50 for $1,000 of one-year term. One year later the person is a year older and the risk of dying is greater; therefore, when the policy is renewed, a higher premium, say $9.50, is charged, and with each subsequent year the rate increases further. Typically in the five-year renewable term the companies prefer to establish a "level premium rate." What they do, in effect, is to average the rate over the five-year term, in accordance with the discussion above. If the policy is renewable, the rate for the second five years increases and becomes the average over the second five-year period.

If one buys twenty- or thirty-year term insurance, the premiums are also averaged out over the entire period. But, as noted above, term insurance is almost prohibitive in price if the applicant is old; because of this, twenty- or thirty-year term with premiums averaged out would also be fairly expensive.

Term insurance provides only protection and has no savings feature or so-called living benefits. In general, all premiums not needed to meet the expense of the insurance company are paid out as death claims and no cash surrender value is built up. Cash surrender value is explained in greater detail below.

Decreasing Term Rider

At the outset, it was stated that there are four basic types of ordinary insurance. This is true, though the statement may be startling to people who have heard of many different insurance policies. It is due to the fact that one can in effect play variations on a theme. For instance, one of the many types of term insurance is called the decreasing term policy, and it might be desirable in a certain situation. Suppose one has a $50,000 mortgage on a home and desires to protect the family or to keep them from the necessity of paying that mortgage in the event of one's death. Under some circumstances it might be desirable for the individual to turn to the decreasing term policy for this purpose. In the amortizing type of mortgage, where part of the principal and interest is paid each month, the amount paid on the principal increases with each monthly payment. Hypothetically, let us assume that when individuals take out the $50,000 mortgage, they make a payment of $450 a month. Assume further that out of the $450 monthly payment, in the first month, $400 is paid in interest and $50 to reduce the principal. This leaves a balance due of $49,950. It is obvious that for purposes of protection, by the end of the first month a $50,000 policy is no longer necessary. The mortgage could be paid off at the end of that first month if the individual or the estate had $49,950. The decreasing term policy can take care of this type of situation.

For this purpose, the companies will typically write or issue a level premium policy on a decreasing term contract for as long as the mortgage runs, and the policy will decline with the mortgage. Any payoff turned over to the beneficiary will be sufficient to pay off the mortgage. In short, the contract states in effect that as each month passes, the amount the company will pay on the policy decreases. If the insured dies when only $1,000 is due on the mortgage, this balance will be paid off; or if the insured dies at the end of the first month with a balance due of $49,950, this amount will be paid to the beneficiary. The net result is to cause the average monthly premiums to be considerably lower than they would be if a policy with a fixed amount due is purchased because, as each month passes, the amount the beneficiary will receive is reduced roughly in the same amount that the balance due on the mortgage is reduced.

Straight Life Policy

One type of whole life policy is the straight life policy. It builds up a cash surrender value and pays dividends. If the dividends are left with the insurance company, a straight life policy may eventually become a paid-up policy. Otherwise premiums are paid for as long as the policy is in force.[3]

As was pointed out in the discussion of the term policy, the premium rates should rise each year as the insured grows older. However, to avoid changing the rates each year, insurance companies developed the idea of averaging out the first five years' cost, the second five years' cost, and so forth. Thus in the five-year renewable policy, a constant level premium is paid during the first five years the policy is in force and a new and higher rate is paid during the second five years. The rate thus changes every five years. From this idea of averaging the rates every five years there grew the concept of averaging over an entire lifetime. For example, since it is possible to determine, on the average, the remaining life of a man aged thirty, it is possible to average out what the cost of protection would be over the balance of his life. This is exactly what is done. When the thirty-year-old man buys a whole life policy, his annual premium is greater than it would be if he were to purchase the same amount of term insurance. This is, in part, because the policy never expires. All term policies eventually expire. Hence, in the averaging process a straight life policy has to take into account some very high premiums because of advanced age.

As a result of averaging premiums over a lifetime on a policy that never expires, a higher reserve is built up than in the case of a term policy that eventually does expire. In a sense, some premiums are paid in advance and are called a reserve. These reserves are invested by the insurance company to earn interest income. This is the savings feature of a straight life policy and, because of it, the policy builds up a cash surrender value as the years pass. Cash surrender value is the amount available in cash if the owner voluntarily terminates the policy. The policy itself never expires, and premiums continue to be paid until the policyholder dies, at which time the beneficiaries are paid the face value of the policy. However, policyholders may choose to take the cash value (take their living benefits) and surrender their policy. Many people do this at an advanced age because they have no one financially dependent upon them. In effect, they have had insurance protection when they needed it and they have used insurance as a vehicle to generate savings for their old age.

The savings feature built into a straight life policy can be described as modest, not heavy, but it is precisely this modest savings feature, together with insurance protection, that has made it appealing to some people. As noted above, a straight life policy may become paid up if dividends are left with the company. A dividend is a return of part of the premium on participating insurance to reflect the difference between the premium charged and the combination of actual mortality, expense, and investment experience. It should also be noted that if a person lives long enough and the straight life policy remains in force long enough, it will eventually become an endowment policy. Endowment policies will be explained below.

Limited Payment Life Policy

The limited payment life insurance policy is the second type of whole life policy. It carries the idea of the straight life policy a step further. In short, if it can be determined what the annual rates or premiums should be for the straight life policy and also if it can be

---

3. A straight life policy pays dividends only if it is a participating policy. All policies purchased from mutual companies and some purchased from stock companies are participating policies. This is discussed in greater detail below.

determined what the average lifetime premiums will be, why not divide the lifetime premiums by twenty or thirty and get paid-up insurance?

This really amounts to a limited number of installment payments of the premium on such a policy for ten, twenty, thirty years, or to age sixty-five.

This policy provides for permanent protection, but the premiums are paid only for a certain number of years though the protection afforded is for the *whole life* of the individual. The most popular forms are the twenty-pay life and the thirty-pay life policies. The premium calculation is basically the same as that for the straight life policy, but, because the payments are made over a shorter period, the yearly or monthly premiums have to be greater. In practice, the insured pays much less than the face value of the policy during the limited payment period. The reason is that the company is able to invest the funds at compound interest from the time the initial payment is made until the time, on the average, when those insured will die. For example, an individual at the age of twenty might be said to have a life expectancy of an additional 51.20 years. Thus, on the average, the company will have the use of the money for a good many years before it has to pay it out. This also means that the cash value of the policy will continue to rise even after the period for payment of premiums has expired, until eventually, if the insured does not die first, the cash value will equal the face value.

The main reason for purchasing this type of policy is that some people want to pay for their insurance during the time when their earnings are the highest.

Another reason for buying a limited payment life policy is that it has a heavier savings feature built into it than does straight life. If a person wants to save systematically through life insurance, this type of policy provides a means of doing so. The reason the savings feature is greater is that the premiums are paid sooner than in straight life, hence more interest can be earned and also more premiums per year are paid.

The Endowment Policy

The endowment policy provides protection for a specified number of years, at the end of which period the insured will receive the face amount of the policy. This means that if an individual purchases a $10,000 endowment policy and then dies before the end of the specified number of years, his or her beneficiaries will receive the face amount of the policy. If this person lives for the number of years specified in the policy, the policy has matured and he or she will be paid the face value of the policy. At maturity, the face value and the cash surrender value are the same.

An endowment policy has a limited number of payments. The most popular are the twenty-year and thirty-year endowment plans. In an endowment policy, premiums are set at a level so that after the period is over, the cash surrender value is equal to the face value of the policy.

People who buy endowments usually do so because they want a specific number of dollars for a specific purpose sometime in the future. Funds to send a child to college or to provide for retirement income or a trip around the world might be financed through an endowment policy.

When the endowment plan is paid up, it is like money in the bank rather than like insurance. Beneficiaries are paid with the insured's own money after the endowment plan is paid up. When endowments become paid up, they are usually surrendered and the money used for some specific purpose such as those noted above. However, the policy could be left with the insurance company, where the cash surrender value would build up above the face value at some specified interest rate.

The stress in an endowment policy is obviously on savings. Premiums on endowment policies are even higher than on the limited payment life policy. Because these premium funds are then invested and earn interest, the amount paid by the company when the policy matures—or to the beneficiaries if the policyholder dies—is greater than the amount paid in as premiums by the individual.

In summary, one can state that in progression from term, to straight life, to limited payment life, to endowments, the premiums rise with any given age because the savings feature rises greatly also. A second reason why the limited payment life and limited payment endowment policies have higher premiums than equal amounts of a straight life policy is because premiums are, in part, paid in advance. It should be noted that endowment plans are not very popular anymore. This is because of their high savings feature. Because savings in the form of life insurance are eroded away by inflation, people do not save as much through this medium as they once did. Rather, they have chosen other media more immune to inflation, such as common stocks and real estate.

Other Types of Policies; Combinations

There are a number of other policies but they are variations or combinations of the above.

Modified Plans

Some insurance companies also sell what they call "Mod. Three" and "Mod. Five" life insurance. These modified plans are very simple and were designed for special groups. For example, suppose one feels the need for $40,000 of life insurance to protect one's family, but the premiums are a bit more than can be afforded now because one is just out of college and hence just starting out. In three or four years this insurance will be affordable. One could wait, but one may not have to.

The Mod. Three and Mod. Five plans have reduced rates the first three and five years respectively, after which time they rise. Since the first few years' premiums are substantially below those indicated by the mortality tables, the later years' premiums must be above the mortality figures. This is exactly the case. This type of policy appeals to people whose income is low now but promises to be high in the future—for example, someone starting out in a career in medicine or a promising young lawyer.

Family Plan

Another type of insurance plan is the family life insurance plan. This consists of a package of some term insurance and usually some whole life. Under the family plan, every member of the family has some insurance, and newborn babies automatically become covered so many days after birth. This is a family life insurance plan and should not be confused with the family income plan, which will be discussed below.

The head of the household has the most insurance under the family plan. The family can buy one or more units. Typically one unit is $5,000 (usually of whole life) on the main wage earner, $1,000 of term on the other spouse, and from $500 to $1,000, also of term, on each child. The package is simple, and as new children arrive they too are covered, usually with no increase in premiums.

It is also possible for an individual, rather than a family as a group, to buy some insurance package that includes a combination of two or more plans. The usual package consists of some term insurance and some form of whole life.

Family Income Plan

This is a package which usually consists of some term and some straight life. A twenty-year family income plan, for example, may provide that if the insured dies before the twenty years are up, the beneficiaries will receive so much per month for the balance of the twenty years. Then after twenty years the beneficiaries also receive the face value of the policy. If the insured does not die during the term of the policy, the term part of the policy expires, but the insured may continue the whole (straight) life portion of the policy at the rate that was in effect when the policy was purchased.

Cash Value Buildup
and Net Risk to the Insurance Company

We have seen why and how insurance policies, with the exception of term, build up cash surrender values. The cash surrender value should be looked upon as savings by the policyholder; it is like money in the bank because the policyholder may surrender his or her policy, take the cash surrender value (the living benefits), and call it quits at any time. If the policyholder dies before surrendering the policy, the amount of funds the beneficiary receives, which come from the insurance company's pocket, is the difference between face value and cash surrender value. This difference is also the amount of risk the insurance company assumes, a risk that declines dollarwise as the years pass. This cash surrender value and the risk the insurance company assumes is illustrated in the graph below. The two bottom curves are for a straight life policy, the two middle are for a twenty-pay life, and the two top are for a twenty-year endowment. The cash surrender value was calculated for a $25,000 face value policy on a twenty-year-old person in each case. The annual premiums are $322.25; $539.75; and $1,047.25, respectively. Each policy has two possible build ups: one (the lower curve) if you take the annual dividends in cash, and one (the upper curve) if you leave them to accumulate more interest. The cash surrender value builds up over the years, as depicted by the curves, and the savings are represented by the surface under the curve. The risk assumed by the insurance company is depicted by the surface or area above the curve, and, as is evident, this risk declines as the years pass. In the case of the twenty-year endowment policy, for example, if the person were to die at the end of the twentieth year, the company would simply give the beneficiary $25,000 of the policyholder's own money.

If the dividends are left with the company, the cash surrender value will build up more quickly and, in the case of an endowment policy, will equal the face value in a little over sixteen years, and if the policyholder dies about then, his or her beneficiaries are paid off with his own money. (In all cases, if there is a death claim the companies pay the face value or the cash value, whichever is the larger.) The amount of insurance a person has then declines as the years pass and the cash surrender value builds up.

At the end of twenty years the Limited Pay Life (LPL) and the endowment policy are paid up and premiums are no longer paid. The cash surrender value if not taken by the policyholder will now build up more slowly because only interest return adds to cash value. This is depicted by the dotted line. In the case of a whole life policy, the cash surrender value continues at a more uniform rate because in theory this type of policy is never paid up. There are two exceptions to this statement, however. First, if the policyholder outlives the mortality tables—which happens when one reaches the age of one hundred—the policy is paid up. At age one hundred one is actuarially dead, and insurance companies will pay off the policy. One has not won without dying, however, because cash surrender value is equal to face value. The other exception is when dividends are left with the company. In such a case, a straight life policy may become paid up before a person dies even though the person is not one hundred years of age. Whether it does depends upon the age of the person when the policy was bought and upon the interest rate the insurance company is able to earn. Any policy will build up more quickly if dividends are left with the company.

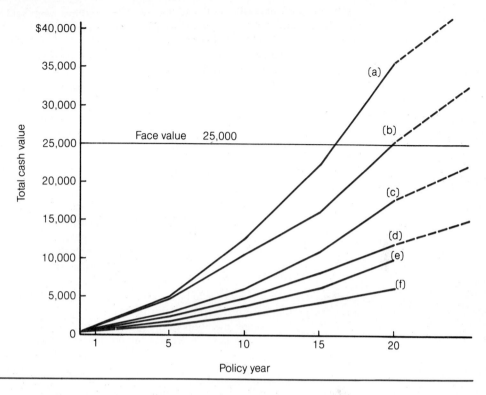

FIGURE 8–3. *The relationships between cash surrender value and face value for each of three insurance policies for a female aged 20. (a) Twenty-year endowment, dividends accumulated; (b) twenty-year endowment, dividends withdrawn; (c) twenty-pay life, dividends accumulated; (d) twenty-pay life, dividends withdrawn; (e) straight life, dividends accumulated; (f) straight life, dividends withdrawn. Dividends accumulated at interest are based on the 1979 dividend scale and are not guaranteed; dividends are withdrawn at guaranteed cash value. These graphs were furnished by a large eastern mutual life insurance company.*

OTHER TYPES OF LIFE INSURANCE

There are a number of other types of life insurance with which you should be familiar. One of the more important of these is that which is sold to an entire group rather than to an individual.

Group Life Insurance

The major difference between life insurance sold to an individual and that purchased by a group is one of administration. Insurance is often sold by the life insurance company to a business firm, and the business firm provides each insured employee with an insurance certificate. The premiums may be withheld from the employees' salary, or they may be paid entirely by the employer, or they may be shared.

A second difference between group life insurance and insurance sold to an individual is that group life involves neither an individual medical examination nor an individual application for insurance.

The group insurance package commonly consists of some term, which provides for benefits upon the death of the policyholder, and some medical insurance (which is health, not life insurance and is discussed in the next chapter) to pay for all or part of the medical bills of the employees covered. Usually employees automatically lose this group insurance when they leave the company, even by retirement. However, employees have the right to convert their group insurance to an individual policy within thirty days after leaving the employer, without a medical exam. If they do convert, they pay the higher premiums individual policies require.

Group insurance is nearly always cheaper than individual insurance, for several reasons. First, the employer may pay all or part of the premiums. Even if this is not the case, the administrative cost to the insurance company is less, and part of these savings are passed on to the policyholder. Since only one policy is written for many individuals, underwriting costs are reduced. Clerical and accounting costs are less for the same reasons, and the costs of premium collection also are less because the company involved remits one check per month for all the employees. In addition, commissions to insurance salespeople are eliminated or greatly reduced, the contract being often negotiated directly by the insurance company and the business whose employees are to be covered. Finally, in some cases a person would save because the premiums are determined by the average age of the employees covered. Because of this the younger members of the group subsidize the older a bit in some cases. Group life insurance is the modern way of buying life insurance because it is cheaper. However, there are limits, imposed by state law, on the maximum amount of group life insurance a person may buy. This is usually some multiple of the person's annual income. Because of this limit, group insurance cannot be looked upon as a complete insurance plan.

Credit Life Insurance

Another type of life insurance policy is the so-called credit life policy. Many financial institutions require that anyone borrowing money on a personal note be insured for the amount of the note. Thus a bank or other lending institution will automatically sell a creditor enough insurance to cover the amount of the loan in the event the borrower dies before the debt is paid. The lender merely sells the borrower the credit insurance; the institution has an arrangement with an insurance company that actually carries the policy.

It should be noted that credit life insurance is a specialized type of term policy. It is also most often sold on a group basis; the lender has an arrangement with an insurance company whereby all of its borrowing customers are covered by one plan.

There has been a very rapid increase in credit life insurance over the past few years. At year end 1979 a total of $179.3 billion of credit life was outstanding.

Industrial Life Insurance

Industrial life insurance is commonly referred to as the "nickel and dime" life insurance business. Most of the policies are sold to people in low-income groups and have an average death benefit of about $600. Approximately 66 million of these policies are in force, with a total coverage of about $40 billion.

Collections of premiums are made weekly by agents who in some cases literally go from door to door. As a result, the insurance is exceedingly costly and should be avoided wherever possible. The amount of industrial insurance in force is not growing to any significant extent, and in some recent years it has actually declined.

G. I. Life Insurance
(Government Insurance)

The United States government made insurance available to members of the armed forces for the first time during World War I. Term insurance, whole life, and endowment policies were offered. The limit was $10,000 face value.

During World War II the federal government once again provided insurance in the form of the National Service Life Insurance. This was the famous G.I. life insurance. It was issued as term insurance but the serviceman could convert it to permanent insurance within one year. When the serviceman was discharged, he could keep this insurance, and many did. The maximum amount of G.I. insurance that could be purchased was $10,000 and it was much cheaper than any insurance that any civilian company could provide. This is because the government paid for the administrative cost of the program, and, of course, there were no commissions.

The reason the government embarked upon these two insurance schemes was to provide protection against the risk of death due to war action. During both world wars private insurance companies inserted "war" clauses into all of their insurance contracts. If a person were killed in a war, the insurance would not pay off. During the Korean War, the "war clause" was again widely used and the federal government again provided government insurance. Today the "war clause" is not in general use, although some companies do use it. During the Vietnam War servicemen's group life insurance replaced the National Service Life Insurance and it is in effect today.

Today military persons are eligible to buy up to $20,000 of term life insurance from the government. They may buy $10,000, $15,000, or $20,000. The premium is $.75 per month per $5,000 of coverage. It is a group policy and is officially called Servicemen's Group Life Insurance. It is administered by the Veteran's Administration, but the insurance is provided by private insurance companies. The government acts just like an employer and buys a group plan for all service personnel. When people leave the service, they have one hundred and twenty days in which to convert their insurance with a civilian insurance company without taking a medical exam. If they do not convert, the insurance lapses.

Mutual Savings Bank
and Fraternal Society Life Insurance

In Connecticut, Massachusetts, and New York it is also possible to buy life insurance from mutual savings banks. The amount of mutual savings bank life insurance in force at year end 1979 was only $12 billion. Life insurance in force with regular commercial life insurance companies was $3.5 trillion at that time.

Fraternal societies also sell some life insurance to their members. But as in the case of mutual savings banks, the amount they sell is small. They had $54 billion of insurance in force at year end 1979.

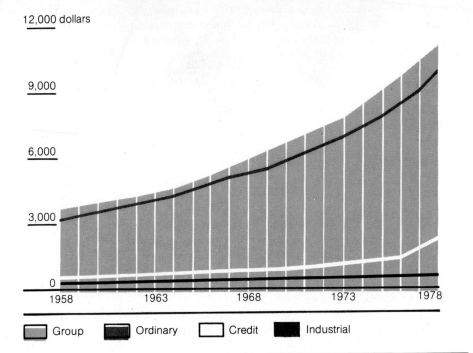

12,000 dollars

9,000

6,000

3,000

0

1958   1963   1968   1973   1978

Group   Ordinary   Credit   Industrial

FIGURE 8–4. *Average size life insurance policy in force in the United States.*
(Source: 1979 Life Insurance Fact Book, American Council of Life
Insurance, p. 24.)

WHAT YOU SHOULD KNOW ABOUT BUYING LIFE INSURANCE[4]

There are a number of things you need to know about buying life insurance. First, you have
to select an insurance company. Then you must decide when to buy life insurance, what
kind to buy, and how much. Finally, you will want to know something about insurance on
children and a non-working spouse. These are the things we will examine next.

Selecting a Company

There are over 1,700 life insurance companies in the United States and they are not all
the same. There are big and small companies; there are stock and mutual companies (this
will be discussed below); and the cost of life insurance will vary somewhat from company to
company. Therefore, when buying something as important as life insurance, you should
shop around.

Why Premiums Vary from Company to Company

Premiums of course vary with the type of policy and the age of the insured. The table
below shows this variation; the premiums shown are annual premiums per $1,000 of insur-

4. This material is drawn from Wolf and Associates, "Financial Seminars." Copyright 1976 by
Harold A. Wolf. Used by permission.

ance. Premiums, of course, must be set high enough to meet the expenses of running the company. These other expenses are largely wages and salaries of the insurance company employees. There is no figure for twenty-year term at age fifty because this company does not sell twenty-year term to a person fifty or older.

Premiums also vary from company to company for like policies on individuals of the same age. The following factors help explain this variation.

1. Some companies have a more favorable mortality experience. That is, their death claims are fewer (or come later) per ten thousand policyholders, and hence their mortality tables are more favorable than those of other companies.

2. Not all companies are equally efficient. Some have higher administrative and clerical costs than others.

3. Some companies earn a higher rate of return on their investments than others.

All these factors can affect the cost of life insurance policies. As in anything, you can often save money by shopping around before buying life insurance.

While there is an official mortality table (the 1958 Commissioners Standard Ordinary [CSO]), insurance companies are permitted to use their own mortality experience with only the proviso that it cannot be less favorable to the policyholder than the 1958 CSO. Consequently, with different mortality tables, premiums can vary somewhat from company to company.

Furthermore, not all companies are equally well managed and hence their costs are not the same. Even with companies that are equally well managed, the expense of running the insurance company, per $1,000 of life insurance in force, may vary with the size of the company and how fast it is growing. Generally speaking, newer and smaller companies have

TABLE 8–4. *Annual premiums per $1000 insurance*

	TERM			STRAIGHT LIFE	LPL	LPE
AGE	1 yr	5 yr	10 yr	0L	20L	20E
Male						
18	$1.85	$1.94	$2.01	$11.87	$20.46	$41.04
19	1.90	1.98	2.05	12.19	20.87	41.07
20	1.95	2.02	2.08	12.52	21.29	41.10
30	2.30	2.43	2.69	16.86	26.31	41.78
40	3.74	4.39	5.41	24.10	33.56	44.19
50	8.66	10.35	12.90	36.28	44.38	50.31
Female						
18	$1.82	$1.90	$1.95	$11.28	$19.79	$40.83
19	1.87	1.93	1.97	11.58	20.19	40.86
20	1.91	1.97	2.00	11.89	20.59	40.89
30	2.15	2.23	2.37	15.81	25.24	41.39
40	3.08	3.51	4.53	21.87	31.57	43.24
50	6.64	8.01	10.14	32.01	41.10	48.33

Figures furnished by a large eastern mutual life insurance company.

higher costs than older and larger companies. However, there are exceptions to this generalization.

The percentage yield on its investments that a company earns will vary from company to company. A company that consistently earns more can either pay a higher dividend or charge a lower premium.

A final reason why insurance premiums vary is that two different policies from two different companies while they appear about the same may not be. Only one of them may have a dismemberment clause, which provides so much for the loss of an arm or a leg. You may or may not want this coverage, but if your policy has it you will pay more. Also the guaranteed cash surrender value buildup over the years may differ on two otherwise like policies. In such a case, different amounts of savings are built into otherwise similar policies. This can, of course, be done by varying premiums or dividends.

Comparing Different Company's Policies

Comparing term policies is usually simple enough. Since usually no dividend is involved and there is no cash surrender value, a simple comparison of premiums per $1,000 of face value is all that is required.

In the case of permanent insurance, the analysis is more complex, but two or more similar policies can be analyzed to see which appears to be the better buy. This cannot be done with precision, but it can be approximated. First you must subtract the likely dividends from the gross annual premiums. Since future dividends are unknown, they must be estimated based upon past experience. This calculation will give you the approximate net annual premiums. You must now multiply this by say 5, and 10, and 20, to get your total premiums over the years. Then compare that to what the cash surrender value (which can be predicted with accuracy and which is stated in the policy) of the policy will be in 5, and 10, and 20 years. If you do this with several policies you will be able to spot the better buy. However, while this can give you a comparison among several policies, it ignores the interest you could have been earning with your premium dollars if you had invested them elsewhere. It also ignores the present value of dollars payable in the future, and future dollars are of course worth less than present dollars.

The recently developed interest-adjusted indexes attempt to take these factors into account and in so doing compare the cost of different policies. In the interest-adjusted method of calculating costs, each year's premium is assumed to earn interest (at say 5 percent). In calculating the index we first obtain the total (say 20 years) accumulation of premiums plus interest. From this we subtract, first, all dividends plus interest on them, and, second, the cash value of the policy at the end of twenty years. The result is the total (20-year) cost of the policy. It is then divided by the number of $1,000 units of coverage to get the 20-year cost per $1,000 of insurance. This cost per $1,000 is then divided again by a factor (34.57 in our case).[5] The final result is a dollar figure that if set aside each year at 5 percent would equal the net dollar cost of your policy. This will vary from company to company, but a recent random sample of nine different companies indicated that this interest-adjusted cost figure on a straight life policy on a thirty-five-year-old man varied from a low of $4.33 to a high of $6.68. While this interest-adjusted index is only an approximation and has little meaning by itself, it is a useful measure of the difference in the cost of a policy among the various companies.

5. This ($34.57) is the amount of money you would have if you added one dollar per year for twenty years and these dollars were earning interest at 5 percent. In many tables this figure is 33.066, but this is because most tables accrue no interest until the end of the year, whereas in our case we earn interest continuously over the entire year.

When is the Best Time to Buy Life Insurance?

The best time to buy life insurance is the day before you die, if you know when that is and if you are still healthy enough to buy it then.

More realistically, you buy life insurance when you need it and can afford it. This is in part a personal value judgment based upon your own set of priorities. But most people cannot afford all the insurance they need or want at the same time and consequently build up their insurance portfolio over a number of years starting out when they reach young adulthood. Don't wait until you have children, although the arrival of children increases the need for life insurance further. Also review your insurance program periodically. Your insurance needs will often change as you grow older. Sometimes you will need to buy more. At other times you may wish to let some term insurance expire, or surrender permanent insurance for cash.

The argument that you should buy insurance as early as possible because premiums rise with age is only of limited value. Premiums do not rise all that fast until about the middle or late thirties. Moreover, it makes little sense to pay premiums, even if low, if you do not need the insurance.

What Kind of Insurance—Permanent or Term?

What type of life insurance should be bought depends upon the individual. Is it being bought primarily for protection or for a savings program? Persons who need protection primarily should weight their insurance program toward term. Term insurance gives the maximum amount of insurance for the money. It often appeals to young people who have small children and need a good deal of insurance but have a limited income. Remember, however, that term insurance eventually expires.

If, on the other hand, you lack the discipline to save part of your income, you might want to enter into an agreement with an insurance company whereby they will save part of your income for you. In such a case, you should buy some insurance policy other than term.

It has been stated that one who can save on one's own should buy term insurance and then bank the differential in premiums between term and straight life. Would a person who did this be better off in twenty years? Whether this is true or not would depend upon how much interest one could earn. Probably in most cases one could earn a little more in a savings and loan association than an insurance company could earn for one. But this is not always true. Also, it must be remembered that in some cases there is a tax advantage in saving through life insurance. This is because any interest earned in a savings and loan association is fully taxable as income, whereas if one buys additional insurance with the interest the insurance company earns, it is not taxable. In conclusion, there is no hard and fast rule regarding what type of insurance one should buy. But if one needs mostly protection and has the discipline to save, one should lean toward term insurance. A person who lacks the discipline to save should lean toward permanent insurance. In many cases one might want some of each.

Some people, however, feel they should save via several media, if for no other reason than that one is never sure what the return on a future investment will be. Therefore, they would diversify their saving and investment portfolio and buy some permanent insurance for savings purposes.

There are essentially four ways to answer this question. They are: the needs concept which depletes capital, the capital needs analysis which maintains capital, the present value of future income concept, and the multiple income concept. We shall examine all four beginning with the needs concept.

Family Needs Concept—Depleting Capital

It might be useful to list all of the possible family financial needs, to arrive at the total amount of insurance needed to produce enough capital to meet these needs, should the insured die:

1. *Funeral and other final expenses* In addition to funeral expenses, there may be final medical and hospital bills to pay. There may also be administrative expenses and attorney's fees associated with probating a will and settling an estate. These expenses at a minimum will probably be $2,000 to $3,000 and may be much larger, especially if the estate is fairly large.

2. *Paying off the Mortgage and Other Debts* If there is a mortgage on your house, you may wish to pay it off as well as liquidate any other installment debt outstanding. You may have special mortgage and credit life insurance for this or it may be included in your regular insurance policy. There is no real way of estimating the dollar amount of this item; it will vary greatly from person to person. An alternative way of handling the home mortgage is not to pay it off but rather to include the mortgage payments in the regular family living expense needs. (See point 5 below.)

3. *Emergency Fund* You will no doubt want an emergency fund. You should already have this in a savings account, but if not it could be looked upon as part of your insurance needs. Many experts suggest this fund should be about twice your monthly take-home pay.

4. *College Fund* If there are college-bound children, college expenses become part of the insurance needs. You need not necessarily provide for full four-year college expenses because the students can earn income to help defray the cost, especially during the summer. On the other hand, it is difficult to calculate future college costs because of rapidly rising inflation. College costs vary a great deal even among state schools, but total costs (tuition, room and board, etc.) can easily reach $5,000 per year. At private schools this figure can go as high as $10,000 per year.

5. *Annual Family Living Needs* This consists of the day-to-day living expenses and is related to the personal or family budget discussed in Chapter 2. The amount will vary depending upon the size of the family, its age makeup, and accustomed standard of living, or the level of livelihood that you would like to provide. Remember, however, this item will go on for a number of years. Moreover, as the years pass this need will change; children will grow up and go on their own; this will be partly (or perhaps entirely) offset by inflation. The amount of insurance needed for family living would also need to be adjusted (presumably downward) to take into account other earning assets, social security benefits, and any private corporate pension payments to be received. You must remember that social security benefits for children continue until the children reach age eighteen (twenty-one in the case of students, including college students). The social security benefits paid on behalf of a surviving spouse do not begin until she or he reaches age sixty. (The time between

when the benefits for the children end and they begin again for the surviving spouse is known as the blackout years.)

Insurance to meet family living needs may also be reduced somewhat if it is reasonably certain that the survivor is willing and able to get a part-time (or even a full-time) job. You should also note that upon the death of the breadwinner, family living needs decline somewhat. This is because the income earner is also an income spender.

As noted above, a dollar figure cannot be suggested for family living needs; you must come up with a figure from your personal budget. However, there are some bench marks. Studies have indicated that a certain percentage of the breadwinner's gross income will typically suffice upon the breadwinner's death. This is shown in the table below.

6. *Retirement Living* Your insurance needs also include an amount for your own retirement. That is in case you do not die prematurely. To be sure, your retirement needs can be met by means other than insurance; we mentioned social security, private pensions, and other earning assets earlier. All of these factors reduce your insurance needs. Also it should be noted that the retirement living really includes family living needs and a bit more. It is only the added amount required if the insured is in retirement with the family.

7. *Totaling Your Insurance Needs; Points 1 through 6* Adding up all of the above 6 points will provide you with an answer regarding your insurance needs. Table 8–6 summarizes this. We left points 1 through 4 blank; fill in whatever amount is appropriate in your case and add it to the amount shown in point 7 to get your total insurance needs. We have also calculated a hypothetical figure for point 5 and 6. Remember not all of the entries will necessarily have a dollar figure. You may or may not have debts to pay off; you may or may not already have an emergency fund, and you may or may not need a college fund, and you may have other assets.

Remember also, however, that the last two items, the $10,000 for family living and/or retirement living, are annual and reoccurring expenses. You will have to multiply them by some figure, which will vary from person to person. It should be the life expectancy of the individual. If we multiply one of those two figures by say twenty years, or whatever is appropriate, we would get the lifetime needs. As noted

TABLE 8–5. *Approximate income needed upon the breadwinner's death*

ANNUAL GROSS INCOME	INCOME NEEDED UPON BREADWINNER'S DEATH (PERCENT)
$20,000 or less	70
$20,000–24,000	65
$24,000–28,000	60
$28,000–32,000	55
$32,000 & over	50

Source: Capital Needs Analysis, Thomas J. Wolff, Certified Life Underwriter. Vernon Publishing Services, Inc., Vernon, CT. Used with permission.

TABLE 8–6. *Worksheet*

1. Final expenses		$_____
2. Payment of debts		_____
3. Emergency fund		_____
4. College fund		_____
5. Family living		
Current budget	_____	
Less reduction in expenses after death of insured	_____	
6. Less new income from other sources	_____	
Equals insurance for family living (annually)	$ 10,000	
times 20 years	$200,000	
7. Retirement living (annually)	$ 10,000	
times 20 years	$200,000	
8. Point 6 or 7 times 20 years and then adjusted to take into account 6 percent interest and 5 percent inflation		$180,460
9. Total insurance needs (Points 1 through 4 plus 8)	Total	$_____

Source: Capital Needs Analysis, Thomas J. Wolff, Certified Life Underwriter. Vernon Publishing Services, Inc., Vernon, CT. Used with permission.

above, we don't add family living needs and retirement needs together; presumably it will be one or the other but not both. If we multiply the $10,000 annual needs by 20 we get $200,000, but if you had that much money now it would also grow by whatever interest rate it could earn. Consequently, less than that amount would be needed. But the $10,000 per year income would also be eroded by inflation. Therefore, if we wanted to provide $10,000 adjusted for inflation, we would have two variables in the calculation. We will assume an inflation rate of 5 percent and an interest rate of 6 percent. Now the problem becomes one of calculating how large a lump sum of money (insurance) is needed to provide for twenty annual payments of $10,000, adjusted for an inflation rate of 5 percent, if the remaining lump sum is also growing at 6 percent while being depleted by the annual payments. Any good insurance agent can give you the answer. The computation is quite complex but the agent can get the answer through the home office's computer. In our case above, it is about $180,000; that is to say, $180,000 dollars (insurance) invested at 6 percent, would provide twenty annual payments of $10,000, in real terms, if inflation is 5 percent per year, taking into account both interest income and principal withdrawals. The first year the recipient would get $10,000; the second year $10,500; the third year about $11,025, and so on. At the end of twenty years the $180,000 would be gone.

As an exercise, the reader may fill in the appropriate amounts for insurance needed because of items 1 through 4.

The above analysis of insurance needs has several shortcomings. First, it depletes capital. Also, in planning you cannot be certain of the future rate of inflation or the interest rate. Finally, twenty years might be too short a period of time and you could outlive your capital. Nevertheless, it is a place to begin in planning your insurance based upon family needs.

Capital Needs Analysis; Maintaining Capital

An alternative method of calculating the total amount of insurance you need is by means of "capital needs analysis."[6] This is similar to what we discussed immediately above, but it does not deplete the insured's capital. It utilizes the individual's balance sheet, capital analysis, and income analysis (Tables 8–7 and 8–8) to calculate the amount of insurance needed. This is shown in the tables below for a hypothetical person A. (Blank capital needs analysis tables which you may use to calculate your personal insurance needs follow Tables 8–7 and 8–8.) A's total assets as shown by the balance sheet are $218,000, with liabilities of $6,000. While this makes A's net worth $212,000, that is not the amount of capital available to A or to dependents in the event of A's death.

The capital analysis indicates that A's estate would have only $82,000 capital available for income-producing purposes. Taxes, the cost of administering the estate, and the paying off of a mortgage would reduce A's capital. A would also no doubt want to set aside something for a college fund, which would reduce further the capital available for investments. Finally, A's non-income-producing property (such as house, car, household furnishings, and other personal property) has to be netted out to obtain the $82,000.

The income analysis makes an assumption regarding social security income and the return on the $82,000. A relatively low 5 percent return is chosen because a long-run view is taken. There is no assurance that today's somewhat higher interest rates will prevail. In addition, if more than 5 percent is earned in some years, it should be retained (added to capital rather than used) to offset any future inflation. In any event, the total income provided falls $4,400 short of the goal. The goal in this case is 50 percent of present income. This 50 percent was chosen because economic and financial statistics indicate that upon the death of a breadwinner, if the mortgage payment and future college expenses are taken care of, about 50 percent of the income of a person at A's level is required to maintain the standard of living to which the family has become accustomed. The income analysis also shows that $88,000 of additional capital is needed to provide earnings equal to 50 percent of present income in the event of A's death. That capital can, of course, be provided by life insurance.

Present Value of Future Income Stream To Determine Insurance Needs

Using the present value of your future income stream is another method of determining your insurance needs. It is, after all, your income stream that you are protecting because that is what would be cut off in the event of death. This necessitates an estimate of your future lifetime income, which cannot be made precisely but probably can be done accurately enough.

Let us assume a thirty-five-year-old individual making $20,000 per year after taxes. (You need not fence in with insurance Caesar's annual tribute since insurance benefit payments are not subject to the income tax.) If the person continues at this level until age 65, she will earn $600,000 after taxes until she retires. However, the income will almost certainly rise above $20,000 per year, even if she receives no promotions—for two reasons. First, she will receive periodic productivity raises. Productivity increases are based on increased out-

---

6. This technique was developed by Thomas J. Wolff, Certified Life Underwriter, whose permission to use the material is gratefully acknowledged.

TABLE 8–7.

Balance sheet of _____ A. _____ **Date** _____

Assets		Liabilities	
Net equity in home Market value: 60,000 Mortgage: 40,000	$ 20,000*	Current bills	$ 1,500
Other real estate	————	Notes	2,500
Personal property	30,000*	Other debts	2,000
Death benefits under retire- ment plans	————		
Listed securities	12,000		
Stock options	————		
Life insurance	150,000		
Business interest	————		
Checking and savings accounts	6,000		
Other	════		════
Total	$218,000	Total	$ 6,000

Satisfied with amount saved Yes ☐ No ☐
Monthly amount that can be saved $_____

Capital analysis

Total assets	$ 218,000
Liabilities	$ 6,000
Taxes and costs of administration	16,000
Payment of mortgage	40,000
Cost of education	24,000
Non-income producing property	50,000
Total deductions	136,000

Capital available for income	$ 82,000
Income-producing assets not owned by you (including non-owned personal life insurance on your life).	═══════
Total capital available for income	$ 82,000
Expected earnings to age 65 ($ _____ × _____ years)	$_____

Source: *Capital Needs Analysis,* Thomas J. Wolff, Certified Life Underwriter. Vernon Publishing Services, Inc., Vernon, CT. Used with permission.

put per man-hour worked and are due to better tools, management techniques, and other innovations. The national average long-run productivity increase has been 2.5 to 3 percent per year. We will assume that level for our hypothetical person. In addition, most people will receive salary increases to offset inflation. Assuming inflation returns to its more reasonable and traditional level of 3 to 4 percent, the $20,000 will also grow by that amount. This gives us a growth rate of about 6 or 7 percent per year. Compounding the $20,000 by 7 percent over the thirty-year period gives us a lifetime income stream of about $1,889,220. However, future dollars must be discounted because they are worth less than present dollars. What we need is a figure which, if invested now and earning interest, and at the same time funds are being withdrawn periodically, would provide a total income stream over the next thirty years of $1,889,220. If we assume that the funds are earning 8 percent interest while the amount being withdrawn annually is originally $20,000 but is growing at 7 percent, then we can calculate an answer. (This is the same problem we faced above when we calculated the sum needed to provide $10,000 in real terms [or growing at 5 percent] for twenty years under family living needs in the discussion of insurance based upon need). Here the figure is $487,019. That is the present value of the future lifetime income stream of our hypothetical person aged thirty-five whose present $20,000 per year after-tax income is growing at a compound rate of 7 percent per year. That, in theory, is the amount of insurance the individual in question should have to fully protect her income stream. Moreover, with each passing year, her insurance needs decline because there is less and less future income to earn. When the person is sixty-four years old, the insurance needed to protect future income is exactly the same as the final year's earnings.

If the thirty-five-year-old individual described above purchased all this insurance, the annual premiums would be about $4,062 if it were 20-year term; $6,204 if it were 30-year term; and $12,414 if it were the cheapest form of whole life. Consequently, we can conclude that virtually no one can afford to pay the premium necessary to purchase all the insurance needed in accordance with the future income criteria. However, it is an important bench mark; we can use it and modify it in accordance with the "family need" criteria and personal value judgments. The amount of insurance needed under the future income stream criteria is the theoretical upper limit of a person's insurance needs. It is higher than the amount calculated under the needs criteria because the latter assumes that when the breadwinner dies, the family needs decline.

TABLE 8–8.

Income analysis

Present income (all income of both husband and wife)	$ 35,000
Income objective (50 % of above) (See below)	$ 17,500

Income presently provided

Capital available for income
$ 82,000 @ 5 % $ 4,100 (A)

Social security and other govern-
ment programs $ 9,000 (B)

Other income (if any) $_____ (C)

Total income provided now $ 13,100

Income shortage $ 4,400 (D)

New capital required (divide income shortage (D)
by assumed interest rate) $ 88,000 (E)

If there is an income surplus, reduce the "Capital Available for Income" by the amount necessary to eliminate the surplus. Enter the capital surplus on line E with a minus sign and continue on to the "Total Income Analysis".

Income objective

Based on a study by a group of economists, the following are typical income objectives in order to permit a family to "remain in their own world" after the death of the breadwinner. Assumption is that the mortgage on residence is paid and that educational expenses are provided for separately.

Annual gross income	*Percentage of gross income required*
Up to $20,000	70%
$20,001 to $24,000	65%
$24,001 to $28,000	60%
$28,001 to $32,000	55%
Over $32,000	50%

Source: *Capital Needs Analysis,* Thomas J. Wolff, Certified Life Underwriter. Vernon Publishing Services, Inc., Vernon, CT. Used with permission.

Balance sheet of _____ Date _____

Assets   Liabilities

Net equity in home
  Market value: _____   Current
  Mortgage: _____ $_____   bills $_____

Other real estate   _____   Notes   _____

Personal property   _____   Other
                                        debts   _____

Death benefits under retirement plans   _____

Listed securities   _____

Stock options   _____

Life insurance   _____

Business interest   _____

Checking and savings accounts _____

Other   ========   ========

Total $_____   Total $_____

Satisfied with amount saved Yes ☐ No ☐
Monthly amount that can be saved $_____

Capital analysis

Total assets $_____

  Liabilities $_____

  Taxes and costs of administration   _____

  Payment of mortgage   _____

  Cost of education   _____

  Non-income-producing property   ========

  Total deductions   ========

Capital available for income	$_____
Income-producing assets not owned by you (including non-owned personal life insurance on your life)	_____
Total capital available for income	$_____
Expected earnings to age 65 ($ _____ × _____ years)	$_____

Source: Capital Needs Analysis, Thomas J. Wolff, Certified Life Underwriter. Vernon Publishing Services, Inc., Vernon, CT. Used with permission.

Multiple Income Approach

The final approach to calculating the amount of insurance you should buy is simply to take your after-tax income and multiply it by some factor. The most common factors used are 3, 5, 7, and 10. The multiple selected will be determined by your age, the number of dependents, their ages, your total assets and liabilities, and income from property. Although this is still a somewhat arbitrary way of doing it, it can also be looked upon as a rule of thumb based upon experience.

The Final Decision

When all is said and done, the methods we have discussed of determining your insurance needs are only bench marks. When you have examined them, you still have to make a decision based upon what you can afford, and your personal value judgments and priorities.

Insurance for Children

Insurance for children should be a low-priority item. Children are not breadwinners as a general rule. Some people buy some form of insurance on their children which builds up a cash value in order to give them a nest egg to start out when they reach young adulthood. If the budget can afford this, such a plan is fine. But saving via insurance should be compared with the yield on alternative investment outlets.

The only other valid reason for buying insurance on a child is that it protects his or her insurability. Some people are uninsurable because of ill health. While it is possible that a person is insurable as a child, but will be in ill health and uninsurable as a young adult, this is remote.

The argument for buying insurance on a child because premiums are lower than they will be when the person reaches adulthood is not valid. Premiums are not that much higher until about the mid-thirties. Moreover, you should not buy something you do not need merely because it is cheap.

Insurance on a Non-Working Spouse

Although a spouse may not contribute money income to the family, the time and skills he or she provides for the family are very valuable and would be costly to replace in the case

Income analysis

Present income (all income of both
husband and wife) $_____

Income objective (_____ % of
above) (see below) $_____

Income presently provided

    Capital available for income
    $_____ @ _____ % $_____ (A)

    Social security and other govern- $_____ (B)
    ment programs

    Other income (if any) $_____ (C)

Total income provided now $_____

Income shortage $_____ (D)

New capital required (divide income shortage (D)
by assumed interest rate) $_____ (E)

If there is an income surplus, reduce the "Capital Available for Income" by the amount necessary to eliminate the surplus. Enter the capital surplus on line E with a minus sign and continue on to the "Total Income Analysis".

Income objective

Based on a study by a group of economists, the following are typical income objectives in order to permit a family to "remain in their own world" after the death of the breadwinner. Assumption is that the mortgage on residence is paid and that educational expenses are provided for separately.

Annual gross income	*Percentage of gross income required*
Up to $20,000	70%
$20,001 to $24,000	65%
$24,001 to $28,000	60%
$28,001 to $32,000	55%
Over $32,000	50%

Source: Capital Needs Analysis, Thomas J. Wolff, Certified Life Underwriter. Vernon Publishing Services, Inc., Vernon, CT. Used with permission.

of death or disability. The cost of child care alone would justify some insurance for income protection.

For example, while the death of one parent may not decrease family dollar income, it may necessitate a tremendous increase of family expenditures if the household is to be properly operated and the children are to receive adequate care. Although as a practical matter most families are unable to afford the premium payments to provide adequately for this type of life insurance, some protection is definitely needed where children are involved.

If there are two breadwinners in the family, then there is a reason for life insurance on both. Since there is a second income to protect, the analysis above regarding how much a person is worth applies to both the husband and wife. The future income of both partners can be calculated as the beginning or "scaling down" point in determining how much insurance is needed.

OTHER THINGS YOU SHOULD KNOW ABOUT LIFE INSURANCE

There are a number of other things about life insurance with which you should be familiar because they are often valuable provisions and are of benefit to you. We will discuss each of them briefly below.

Grace Period

After a premium is due but not paid, there is generally a grace period of twenty-eight to thirty-one days during which the premium may be paid without penalty. In the event that a policyholder dies during the grace period, the unpaid premium is collected from the amount paid to the beneficiary.

Reinstatement

Most policies contain a provision for reinstatement. If your policy has lapsed, you may, within a stated period, put it into effect again provided that you are insurable, and of course this implies another physical examination. If you pass the physical, you must then pay the overdue premiums together with interest.

Incontestability

After two years, your policy will ordinarily be incontestable. This means, in effect, that the company is given two years in which to check certain information given by you when you made your original application for the policy. In the event the company discovers that you made a materially false statement, it may seek to have itself released from the policy. After the incontestable period has passed, however, the company can no longer seek such release.

Nonforfeiture Value

What happens if one can no longer pay the premiums for some reason? If it is term insurance and has no cash surrender value, it will lapse after the grace period. If it is permanent life insurance and has built up a cash surrender value, one has four options in the case described above. (Recall from the discussion above that generally all policies except term build up a cash value after they have been in force for a few years and that this cash value increases as the years pass.) One's options are assured by the nonforfeiture values that in a sense guarantee the cash surrender value of your policy. These four options under the nonforfeiture value are as follows:

1. *Cash value.* A policy can be surrendered for its cash value. This cash surrender value can be taken in one lump sum or in a number of regular payments if it is large enough (usually $1,000 or more). This cash surrender value is like money in the bank and builds up because many policies have a savings feature built into them.

2. *Extended term insurance.* Often a policy includes a provision to the effect that if the holder fails to pay the premiums during the grace period, the policy automatically will remain in force as a term policy for as long as the cash surrender value of the policy will permit. For example, suppose you have a $4,000 cash surrender value in a $20,000 ordinary life insurance policy and you have failed to pay your premium during the grace period. Under the terms of the policy, it may be that the amount of cash surrender value ($4,000) would be enough to keep that policy in force as term insurance for nine or ten years. Your $4,000 equity in the policy actually is used to pay the premium on what will now be an *extended term policy*.

3. *Reduced paid-up insurance.* This is the third option under the nonforfeiture value, if one no longer wishes to pay premiums. One can reduce the face value of life insurance but keep it in force as paid-up permanent insurance. In the above case, your $4,000 cash surrender value on your $20,000 policy might provide a paid-up policy with a face value of say $10,000. This is now paid up in force and the death payment would become $10,000 but you no longer need to pay premiums.

4. *Automatic premium loan* (APL). Some insurance policies have a provision that grants the insured an automatic loan that is used to pay the premiums after the grace period has expired if the policy has a cash value. This is designed to prevent the policy from lapsing due to the insured accidentally forgetting to pay the premiums, which might happen if he or she is out of town on an extended trip. Then upon the policyholder's return the loan could be repaid and the insurance continue in its original form.

Borrowing on Your Life Insurance Policy

You may borrow the cash surrender value of your life insurance policy from the company and often you can use the policy as security for a loan from a commercial bank. Most states have laws requiring these loans to be made by insurance companies. However, insurance companies may wait as much as several months before making the loan. In practice, however, they make the money available almost immediately.

Insurance companies charge about 8 percent (annual percentage rate) interest on these loans which is as low as you can get anywhere. The theory behind these loans and low interest rates is that the policyholder is merely using his or her own money. The insurance companies must obtain the small interest which they charge because were it not for the policy loan they would invest the money elsewhere and their investment income would be greater. Since the insurance contract is made with an assumption of certain interest income, they have to charge a rate on policy loans.

There can be a danger in borrowing from your insurance company. First of all, these loans are single repayment rather than installment loans. Therefore, you must do some budgeting and set aside a sum every week or month so that you will be able to liquidate the loan eventually. Moreover, there is no obligation ever to repay the loan. Some people just continue to pay the interest. If there is a death claim on a policy with a loan outstanding, it is, of course, deducted before the face value is paid. In some states the borrower is not even required to pay interest. In such a case, if the amount borrowed plus the accumulating interest grow to equal the cash surrender value of the policy, it is cancelled. You end up with no insurance. Therefore, unless you are absolutely sure you will repay the loan, it is recommended that you think twice before borrowing from your insurance company. It might be better to use your policy as collateral for a bank loan. Such a secured loan will permit you to borrow at a favorable interest rate, and the bank will make you repay the loan.

Assignment

It is frequently possible to use one's life insurance policy as collateral (and hence reduce the interest rate) when borrowing money from banks and others. Lenders may feel it desirable for them to be assigned the policy, so that if the borrower dies before repaying the obligation, the debt will be paid from the proceeds of the policy. In order to assign a policy, however, one must have the right to change the beneficiary; otherwise, it will be necessary to obtain the beneficiary's consent. Furthermore, the policy specifically states that no assignment will be binding on the company until the company has been notified.

Ownership of the Policy

In a life insurance contract, there are the insured, the beneficiaries, and the owner of the policy. The meaning of *insured* and *beneficiary* is clear and needs no further elaboration, but the term *owner* requires a word of explanation.

Usually, but not always, the insured is also the owner. The insured can turn ownership over to the beneficiary. The owner of the policy, while living, has the right to modify the policy, change the beneficiary (if he or she has reserved that right in the policy), select the settlement options, surrender or cancel the policy, receive any insurance dividends, and any other rights which may exist. Upon the death of the insured (who may or may not be the owner) ownership of the policy is immediately and automatically transferred to the beneficiary.

There is one reason why a person may want to transfer ownership to the beneficiary prior to death—to avoid estate taxes. (Estate taxes are discussed in the last chapter.) If the beneficiary is not the owner prior to the death of the insured, then although the beneficiary receives the insurance claim upon the death of the insured, due to a quirk in the tax law one-half of it is subject to the deceased's estate tax (not income tax, but estate tax). If the beneficiary is the owner, this tax is avoided. To make certain that this tax savings is realized, however, the beneficiary-owner should have his or her own checking account and pay the insured's premiums with his or her own personal checks.

Change of Beneficiary; Third Party Rights

There may be many reasons why one might want the beneficiary in a policy changed, such as marriage, divorce, or newborn children. In order to effect such a change at any time, one must have reserved the right to change the beneficiary when originally taking out the policy; most policies contain a clause giving this right. The company will furnish the proper forms in order to effect the change. In some cases, where the insured has failed to reserve the right to change the beneficiary when taking out the policy, he or she must first obtain the consent of the present beneficiary in writing before the company will permit the change to be made.

One question that arises with regard to beneficiaries is what happens if a named beneficiary dies before the policyholder. Normally the company pays the money directly to one's estate. However, one or more persons can be, and usually are, named in the policy as contingent beneficiaries. In this case, the contingent beneficiary or beneficiaries receive the proceeds of the policy should the first-named beneficiary die before the insured.

Settlement Options

Several different settlement options may be chosen which will determine how insurance benefits are to be paid. These options may be selected by the owner of the policy or the beneficiary, depending upon the circumstances. The owner has first shot at selecting the options; if he or she does not do so, the beneficiary may. The owner of the policy is also usually the insured, but this need not be the case. If the payments are living benefits, the owner is also usually the beneficiary and he or she will choose the options. If the owner has selected a certain option and then dies, the beneficiary must live with that decision. If, as often is the case, the owner has not selected any option, then upon his or her death the beneficiary may do so. If the beneficiaries are of sound mind and able to handle money, it is probably best not to select settlement options until the benefits are to be paid. If the beneficiary is a minor or has shown that he or she cannot handle money, then the owner might want to provide for certain specific installment payments rather than one lump sum settlement. Anyone who has the right to select an option has the right to change it during his or her lifetime. If an installment option rather than a lump sum is selected, arrangements can be made for the payments to be made on an annual, semiannual, quarterly, or monthly basis.

There are five general options from which to choose:

1. *Lump Sum.* In this case the entire sum is paid at once and the beneficiary has the money management problem. However, when interest rates are high, this person might be able to earn more on his or her lump sum settlement than the insurance company can.

2. *Interest payment only.* The company holds the principal sum due under the terms of the policy. Arrangements are made with the company to pay interest at a guaranteed rate, the payments to be received for a stated number of years or for life. Upon the death of the beneficiary the principal could be paid to a secondary beneficiary. Or this option could have a proviso that at some predetermined future date the principal would go to the primary beneficiary if still alive. The point is, if only interest is paid, the principal would never be exhausted, and some provision must be made to pay it to someone eventually. Sometimes arrangements are made whereby the beneficiary can dip into the principal within limits. This, of course, would reduce future interest payments, but would provide flexibility and an additional source of money for the beneficiary in the event of an emergency.

3. *Installment payments.* The company makes regular payments in equal amounts until the fund is exhausted. During the time that such regular payments are being made, the company will add interest to the part of the money not paid out. If each payment is for a specific amount—for example, $50 per month—then the length of time during which the payments will be made depends upon the amount of the policy, the amount of the periodic income payment, and the rate of interest guaranteed in the policy.

   If the payments are to be spread out over a given time period—say ten or fifteen years—then the amount of each payment depends on the amount of the policy, the number of years the income is to be paid, and the rate of interest guaranteed in the policy.

Thus one can decide that the payments are to be made as a stated sum per month or can elect to have the money paid for a stated time period. One may, furthermore, when electing installment payments for the beneficiary, permit the beneficiary to "commute" the remaining payments. In other words, the beneficiary can stop the income payments and choose to take all the money that remains in one final payment. The policyholder may also arrange that any money left when the first beneficiary dies shall be paid in one sum or continued as income to one or more secondary beneficiaries.

4. *Life annuity income.* One may elect to receive as a settlement a life annuity income. Briefly, a life annuity gives the beneficiary, or annuitant, a stated income for as long as he or she lives. Annuities are explained in detail in Chapter 11.

In some annuity plans, if the annuitant dies before the payments reach a stated total amount or before the payments have been made for a stated period of time, arrangements can be made to have the payments made to a secondary beneficiary. The amount of each payment depends upon several factors, including the age of the annuitant when payment begins, the specified mortality table, the rate of interest guaranteed in the policy, the form of life annuity settlement used, and the amount of the policy.

Another variation of this option is sometimes chosen if there are two or more primary beneficiaries. It is the joint survivorship life income annuity. It is the same as life annuity income just described, except that payments are made until both beneficiaries are gone.

Disability Premium Waiver

The waiver of premium, or what is more commonly referred to as a "disability clause" in a life insurance policy, means that any premiums that fall due after the beginning of a total and permanent disability will be waived. Thus if one is disabled, the life insurance policy will continue in force because the company will make the premium payments. Disability must occur before one has reached a certain age, generally age sixty, and before the policy is paid up. In some cases, the disability must last for at least six months before premiums will be waived.

In order to have such a disability clause written into the policy, the insured must request it and must pay a small additional premium. In the final analysis, the disability clause written into a policy amounts to taking out additional insurance to insure that the premiums will continue to be paid if the policyholder is disabled. The addition to the premium is so small that its inclusion is highly recommended.

Accidental Death Benefits

The clause relating to accidental death benefits is sometimes also called "double indemnity." Under the provisions of this clause, the company promises to pay twice the face value of the policy if death occurs by accidental means. If the death is to be construed as "accidental," it must occur within a certain time after one is injured. Suppose, for example, that an injury occurs that causes hospitalization for, say, one year, and after a year death can be directly attributed to the accident. In such a case, the accidental death benefit clause of the policy will probably not apply. Most policies state that death must occur within ninety days after the accident to be construed as accidental death. Furthermore, there is commonly a second limitation to the accidental death clause; the accidental death must have occurred before age sixty or sixty-five, depending upon the policy.

The double indemnity clause further excludes from the meaning of "accidental" death death arising from certain kinds of accidents. The reason is either that these deaths result from risks that cannot be calculated or the cause of death is not accidental in the legal sense of the word. For instance, if a person jumps from a moving car, his or her death is suicide, not an accident, and the double indemnity will not hold. Or if a person has a heart attack while driving a car and is killed in an accident caused by the attack, that person is not covered even though the death is caused by the accident, not the heart attack.

It is even possible to obtain a triple indemnity clause in an insurance policy. In such a case, the company pays three times the face value in the event of accidental death as defined above. An added premium must be paid in order to obtain either a double or a triple indemnity clause. However, these added premiums are not high. A traveling salesperson or other frequent traveler might want to consider either a double or a triple indemnity clause.

Stock Insurance Companies Versus Mutual Companies

There has been much discussion over the respective merits of these companies. The *stock company* is a corporation, the ownership of which is in the hands of stockholders and, as in any other corporation, the business affairs of the corporation are run by a board of directors. The profit, if any, is distributed to the stockholders much in the same manner as that of any corporation.

A *mutual life insurance company,* on the other hand, is owned by the policyholders. No stock is issued. Basically the idea is that each policyholder is entitled to share in the profits of the company. The other side of the coin is that policyholders can be assessed—in theory at least—in the event of losses in excess of their reserves. The assessment is usually limited to 100 percent of the annual premium. However, there has been a tendency on the part of the mutual companies to issue a nonassessable insurance contract, and in this case the policyholder is virtually exempted from liability.

The management of the mutual company is entrusted to experts in the insurance business just as the management of the stock company is placed in the hands of experts.

Insurance Dividends

The distinction between stock and mutual companies is important because of dividends. Historically, insurance dividends have been paid by mutual companies to their policyholders. These should not be confused with the stock dividends given as a share of the profits to the stockholders of the stock companies. In the mutual company, if the income exceeds the amount needed to pay beneficiaries and expenses, part of it is returned to the policyholders in the form of dividends. The policyholder is generally given a choice of receiving the cash, applying the amount to subsequent premiums, buying paid-up additional insurance, or leaving it with the company at interest.

To compete with dividends paid to mutual policyholders, some stock companies issue a participating type of policy. This type of policy provides that the policyholder will share in the profits of the corporation along with the shareholders. Generally speaking, the premium rates of the participating policies are higher than those of the nonparticipating policies.

Frequently, the premiums on policies issued by stock companies are lower than those issued by mutual companies. These are the nonparticipating policies. Some stock companies, then, issue both participating and nonparticipating policies. Both of these are a competitive device to offset wholly or partially the dividends paid by the mutual companies to their policyholders. It might be added also that some stock companies argue that the dividends paid by the mutual companies are not all earnings being paid to the policyholders; these critics say that mutual companies charge too much in premiums in the first place and are thus merely returning the excess premiums. Mutual companies are of course quick to deny this charge.

Just under one-half of all life insurance policies are issued by stock companies and the balance by mutual companies. When buying life insurance and trying to choose between mutual and stock companies, keep in mind both the premiums and the dividends of mutual companies. The problem is often a difficult one because dividends are not guaranteed; however, a record of past dividends is usually available.

Another point to keep in mind when deciding between buying a policy from a mutual or stock company is the guaranteed buildup of cash surrender value. While the guaranteed cash buildup of stock companies is often somewhat higher than that guaranteed by mutual companies, the actual achieved cash buildup of the mutuals is usually better, especially in the long run. This is because if mutual companies earn more than they guarantee, they add it to the cash value, and in recent years this has happened. In the case of stock companies, any earnings in excess of that guaranteed may go to the stockholders, not the policyholders. Hence, the actual and the guaranteed cash buildups of a policy from a stock company are more likely to be the same.

Regardless of whether insurance dividends are a return of premiums or shared interest which the company earned with the policyholders' premiums, a policyholder receiving them must decide what to do with them.[7] There are several alternatives from which to choose.

1. The dividends may be taken in cash and disposed of as any other income.
2. You may apply the dividend toward the payment of future premiums. Your dividend will usually grow larger as the years pass because your cash surrender value grows larger, and after a time your dividends alone may pay your entire premium.
3. You may elect to leave the dividend with the company to be compounded at the going interest rate and continue to pay your regular premiums. If you do this, the cash surrender value of your policy will build up more rapidly than if you select option 1 or 2. Also it will become paid up more rapidly. However, under option 3 you will have to declare on your federal income tax the *added* interest that the company earns with your money. The dividend itself, however, is not taxable; but the interest earned with it is, and the company will send you a statement indicating what this interest is.
4. You may use the dividends to buy paid up additional insurance. If you do this, the face value of your policy goes up some every year and this incremental amount is paid up. A person who needs more life insurance may want to select this fourth option because it will save commissions. However, buying paid-up additions is like buying a single-premium-payment life insurance policy. One is really paying all future premiums in advance, and while the companies make an allowance for this, it is not very high. Consequently, a single-premium paid-up policy is more expensive than buying insurance the regular way. However, one's dividends might very well add several hundred dollars of paid-up additions each year. This fourth option also

---

7. The Internal Revenue Service has ruled that the entire dividend is a return of premiums for tax purposes. Hence insurance policy dividends are not taxable.

results in your cash surrender value rising more rapidly than if you select option 1 or 2 but less rapidly than if you select option 3. Selecting option 4 also relieves you of having to pay federal income taxes on the interest that your dividend earns as in the case of option 3. This is because your dividend earns no interest. You spent it on more insurance. Your dividend also earns no interest if you select option 1 or 2. Only under option 3 does your dividend earn interest. As noted above, your dividend is not taxable regardless of what you do with it. If you select option 4, however, you will earn dividends on the insurance you bought with previous dividends.

5. You may use your annual dividend to buy one year term. This will increase the face value of your policy by more than will option 4 for a number of years. After a time, however, option 5 may no longer be a means of providing the maximum amount of insurance because under option 4 the added insurance is permanent and the cumulative amount of it may surpass the amount of annual term you may purchase. If you select this option, your cash surrender value will build up at the same rate as under options 1 and 2.

THE SEVEN DONT'S OF LIFE INSURANCE

After taking out insurance policies many people handle them badly. The following suggests that there are proper ways of handling policies.

1. *Don't let insurance go to the wrong people*. Many things can happen here. A family may take out a policy and name a specific child as the beneficiary. If a second child is born, they take it for granted that the second child will share in the benefits of the policy, but this is not so. It is necessary for a rider to be attached to the policy specifically naming the second child as one of the beneficiaries, if that is desired. In the event of a divorce, it is necessary that the beneficiary be changed. If a man remarries and forgets to change the beneficiary, then the first wife will receive the proceeds of the policy in the event of his death. These two examples suggest that everyone's insurance program should be periodically reviewed. Every time a situation arises that changes the insurance needs, an individual should review his or her insurance program in order to make it conform with the changed circumstances.

2. *Don't let insurance dollars be foolishly dissipated*. The problem raised here is whether or not the beneficiaries should be given lump-sum payments or monthly payments. Some people just cannot handle large sums properly.

3. *Don't forget to pay the premiums when they come due*. Most policies carry a thirty-one-day grace period, which means that even if one fails to pay on time, the policy will stay in force during that period. After that period, however, in order to reinstate the contract it may be necessary to take a new physical examination. In the event that an unsuspected change in one's health crops up, it may be impossible to reinstate the policy.

4. *Don't give up policies thoughtlessly*. Changing the kind of insurance one has by taking advantage of conversion privileges in one's policy is often a wise move; not so dropping one policy and buying another. A change in policies is very likely to turn out disadvantageously. Irreplaceable guarantees may be lost. Moreover, the cost of setting up policies is substantial, and since the insurance company applies this to the policyholder in the early years, no cash surrender value is built up on a new policy for a while.

5. Don't hide policies in out-of-the-way places. A mislaid policy delays prompt settlement of a death claim. Make sure the family knows where policies are kept.

6. Don't ever throw away a policy, even if the premiums become unaffordable. Many a supposedly worthless policy has been discovered to contain valuable benefits available to an individual or his or her heirs.

7. Don't overlook the borrowing power of policies. Insurance companies will lend money against the cash value of a policy at relatively low rates of interest, as was pointed out above.

QUESTIONS FOR REVIEW

1. What is the difference between gambling and insurance?

2. What are the three risks individuals face to their income-earning ability?

3. Explain the concept of pure insurance.

4. Justify loading charges in life insurance.

5. If insurance premiums rise with age, how can life insurance companies sell level premium insurance?

6. How is term insurance different from (1) straight life, (2) limited payment life, (3) an endowment policy?

7. What is meant by guaranteed cash buildup? How do life insurance companies guarantee this?

8. Why is group insurance cheaper than ordinary life and industrial life insurance more expensive than ordinary life?

9. What is industrial life insurance and why is it so costly?

10. What type of insurance would appeal to a young person with a very young family? Why?

11. What are the reasons for buying life insurance, and who should buy it?

12. What are the two main factors to consider in determining how much life insurance to buy?

13. Why should a family's principal wage earner think of insuring his or her partner's life?

14. How does the grace period in a life insurance policy relate to a policy lapse?

15. Explain the nonforfeiture value and how it works.

16. How does a person change the beneficiary of his or her life insurance policy?

17. Discuss the method and possible reason for an assignment of a life insurance policy.

18. What is a waiver of premium in a life insurance policy?

19. Discuss the "age-old" arguments between the stock companies and the mutual companies.

20. Discuss life insurance policy dividends. What alternatives does a person have with respect to how he or she disposes of dividends? Are they taxable?

21. What are the "seven don'ts" of insurance?

CASES

1. Myrtle and Alfred Newman are in their early thirties and have two children—a boy of six and a girl of four. Myrtle has not worked outside the home since their son was born. Alfred, who works for a large retail store, earns $20,000 per year take-home pay. They are buying their home and have a monthly pay- ment of $350. Alfred has converted his $10,000 G.I. life insurance policy and is paying premiums on it. Also he has a $30,000 group life insurance policy on which his employer pays all the premiums. Recently an insurance agent suggested that Alfred buy some more insurance and recommended term insur-

ance. Should they take the agent's advice and buy more insurance? If so, should they buy term? If more insurance is required, how much more would you recommend?

2. Ellen Packer has a total of $50,000 of life insurance, which she purchased at various periods over the past twenty years. Ellen is now forty-five years old and her youngest child will be graduating from college next year. Of the $50,000 of insurance, $20,000 is term insurance that will expire in one more year. Should she renew it? Why or why not?

3. Sara and Kenneth Jones are in their middle sixties and have no dependents. Kenneth will retire in another year and will receive social security of $500 per month plus a pension from the company where he works of $300 per month. Sara has no retirement plan of her own. They own their home free and clear but have no other savings except a life insurance policy, which has a face value of $20,000 and a cash surrender value of $12,000. Should they surrender their life insurance policy in order to supplement their retirement income? Are there any other alternatives?

4. Donald and Sally McLaughlen are aged forty and thirty-five, respectively, and they have two children, ten and eight. Donald has an annual income after taxes of $25,000 per year and feels that his $35,000 of life insurance is adequate. However, Sally, who earns $14,000 a year, and the children have no life insurance. Do you recommend life insurance for them? Why or why not? If insurance should be purchased, how much?

5. Archebald and Henrietta Brown are a newly married couple in their late twenties. Archebald has $20,000 of life insurance and plans to buy more later if and when he can afford it. However, Henrietta has a $10,000 policy on her life which she purchased some time ago when she was single. Archebald believes they should surrender this policy, which has a cash surrender value of $1,200, but Henrietta is not sure. They request your advice.

6. Barbara Kidd is a 21-year-old senior in college. She is single and has no immediate plans to marry. She has accepted a job at $15,000 a year as an accountant with a large CPA firm when she graduates in June. She has no life

insurance at present, but will have a health insurance plan and $30,000 of group term life with her employer. Barbara is uncertain whether or not she should buy an individual plan either for savings or protection. Work out an insurance plan for Barbara and advise her as to how much and what kind of insurance she should buy.

7. Mary Rupp has decided she should buy an additional $10,000 of life insurance. The insurance agent has told her she could have term, straight life, limited pay life, or a limited pay endowment plan. Mary has noticed quite a difference in the premiums and requests your clarification.

8. Peter Calcins has a $20,000 straight life policy which has been paying dividends of about $100 per year recently. Peter has been taking the dividend in cash rather than leaving it to accumulate with the company because of tax reasons. What is this tax reason? What else could Peter do with his dividends? What else could he do and still not pay taxes on them?

9. Gordon Wetherly works as a chemist for Du Pont and earns $40,000 per year. He is forty-five years old and expects to retire at sixty-five on a company pension plan plus social security. Although he does not expect to advance much more with Du Pont, he can look forward to a good steady job at his present income until he is sixty-five. He is not sure he should buy very much insurance for savings purposes, but he does feel he should have some protection for his family. How much insurance should he have for protection purposes? What would the theoretical limit be? What kind of insurance would you recommend?

10. Wesley and Mary Roberts are a young couple in their early twenties. They have two children, a girl aged four and a boy aged six. Wesley earns $18,000 at his job with a local manufacturing plant. Mary is a former schoolteacher and will probably go back to work when their daughter starts school. Wesley has a good group medical plan where he works but no life insurance; however, he is a veteran of the armed forces and has $10,000 of government life insurance. He is wondering whether he should buy more life insurance, and if so, what kind and how much. Can you help him?

11. Alfred and Ruth McLain are a young couple in their early twenties who have just graduated from college. They have no children yet but hope to in the future. Alfred has just taken a job as a traveling representative with a large book publisher. Alfred and Ruth would like to begin planning their insurance program now, even though they do not feel they can at this time afford all the insurance they would like. Alfred makes $16,000 per year. Although Alfred's salary is modest at present, he feels he will double it over the next ten years, after which time it will probably level off. Can you plan an insurance program for them?

Note the kind and amount of insurance they should have today and ten years from today.

12. Barry Cohen is a millionaire in his thirties. He has inherited a vast sum of money, and since it is wisely invested in securities, Barry is able to live very comfortably on his investment income. He has never worked and he plans never to do so. He does not think he needs any life insurance. Do you agree? Why or why not? Does he need medical insurance? Is there any other kind of insurance that you can think of that Barry might need?

SUGGESTED READINGS

American Society of Certified Life Underwriters (CLU) Journal. Published quarterly by the American Society of CLU, 270 Bryn Mawr Avenue, Bryn Mawr, PA 19010.

Athearn, James L. *Risk and Insurance.* Englewood Cliffs, N.J.: Prentice-Hall, 1977.

Best's Review, Life-Health Edition. Published monthly by A. M. Best Company, Inc., Oldwick, N.J. 08858.

Casey, William J. *Life Insurance Desk Book.* Englewood Cliffs, N.J.: Prentice-Hall, 1976.

Cohen, Jerome. *Decade of Decision.* New York: Educational Division, Institute of Life Insurance, 1975.

Elliot, Curtis M., and Vaughan, Emmett J. *Fundamentals of Risk and Insurance.* New York: John Wiley & Sons, 1978.

Finance Facts Yearbook. Published annually by the National Consumer Finance Association, Washington, D.C.

Greene, Mark R. "Risk and Insurance." Cincinnati: South Western, 1977.

Huebner, Solomon S., and Black, Kenneth, Jr. *Life Insurance,* 8th ed. Englewood Cliffs, N.J.: Prentice-Hall, 1976.

The Journal of Insurance. Published bi-monthly by the Insurance Information Institute, 110 William Street, New York, N.Y. 10038.

Life Insurance Fact Book. Published annually by the Institute of Life Insurance, New York.

Mehr, Robert I. *Life Insurance.* Dallas: Business Publications, Inc., 1977.

Mehr, Robert I., and Cammack, Emerson. *Principles of Insurance.* Homewood, Ill.: Richard D. Irwin, 1980.

A Shopper's Guide to Life Insurance; A Shopper's Guide to Term Life Insurance. Write to Pennsylvania Insurance Dept., Harrisburg, Pennsylvania, for a copy.

Understanding Life Insurance, A Basic Guidebook. Milwaukee: Northwestern Mutual Life Insurance Co.

Chapter Nine

Health Care and Health Insurance

It is better to be rich and healthy than sick and poor.
ANONYMOUS

The objectives of this chapter are to

1   Present the various types of health insurance, both medical insurance and disability insurance, and explain what they are intended to do

2   Explore certain other things about health insurance

3   Introduce some nonprofit health plans

4   Suggest some guidelines to help determine your health insurance needs.

Among the hazards of life is the possible loss of earnings and income because of accident and sickness. In addition, there may be heavy medical expenses resulting from doctors' and hospital bills. Physicians' fees and hospital costs have been rising rapidly in recent years and will no doubt continue to do so. It is very possible, in the absence of insurance, for a major illness quickly to exhaust the savings of even the upper-middle income groups and force them deeply into debt.

The cost of a hospital room can easily run in excess of $100 per day. Expensive laboratory tests and the use of other expensive equipment is extra. Doctors' and surgeons' fees can in some cases run into the thousands of dollars. The American public spent $139.3 billion on health care in 1976. In recent years the cost of health care has been rising more rapidly than the overall price level. There are a number of reasons for this, including new and sophisticated equipment—which is very expensive—more skilled personal and better care, and an enormous increase in the demand for medical services generated by government programs. A chart, Figure 9–1, showing national health expenditures as a percent of gross national product over the last few years is below.

Some critics have suggested that a national health plan would reduce the cost of medical care. Whether this is true is highly controversial, as is the entire national health insurance proposal. However, national health insurance will be discussed later in this chapter.

Some maintain that health care costs will continue to rise unless the medical profession

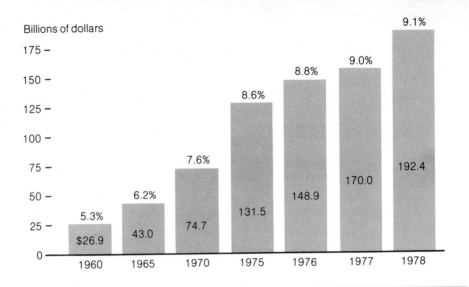

FIGURE 9–1. *National health expenditures and percent of gross national product. (Source: Source Book of Health Insurance Data 1979–1980,* Health Insurance Institute, p. 56.)

develops more paramedical services. Many of the routine things like giving shots, administering aid for minor ailments, and the like could be performed by medical personnel lower-paid than doctors. To some extent this has been done, but the medical profession is behind the dental profession in this regard. For example, there is no medical equivalent to the dental technicians. The critics, however, maintain that this would lower the quality of medical care, with possible disastrous results at times.

Health insurance has been developed in order to protect the individual from such high medical costs, as well as against the loss of income. Health insurance is a broad term that covers all insurance in this general area. It can be broken down into two subclassifications. They are medical insurance and disability insurance. Medical insurance covers medical expenses including doctors' fees, the cost of drugs, and hospital bills. Disability insurance protects against loss of income while sick or disabled. A number of different health insurance packages can be obtained under the two broad general classifications, just as a number of different life insurance packages are available under the four main classifications described in the previous chapter. In this chapter, we shall examine this available health insurance coverage.

Health insurance can be purchased on a group basis or on an individual basis. In order to buy group insurance, however, one must be eligible to do so, and usually group insurance is available to the employees of a firm. The premiums on group insurance are lower than on individual policies, for reasons explained below, and for this reason people who are able to take advantage of a group plan should do so.

In addition, health insurance provides coverage for the family of the insured. There are generally three different premiums quoted for any given policy. One is for a single person, another one for a couple with no children, and a third for a couple with children.

TYPES OF HEALTH INSURANCE COVERAGE

When discussing the type of coverage that can be obtained, we can classify health insurance into seven categories:

1. Hospital expense
2. Surgical expense
3. Regular medical expense
4. Major medical expense
5. Comprehensive coverage, which is a combination of all or some of the above
6. Dental insurance.
7. Disability or loss of income.

Table 9–1 shows the numbers in the United States who are covered under some form of health insurance. Many companies have developed two or three different health insurance packages and the individual may choose the one which best fits his or her budget. For

TABLE 9–1. *Number of persons with health insurance protection, by type of coverage, in the United States (000 omitted)*

END OF YEAR	HOSPITAL EXPENSE	SURGICAL EXPENSE	PHYSICIAN'S EXPENSE	MAJOR MEDICAL EXPENSE	DISABILITY INCOME SHORT-TERM	DISABILITY INCOME LONG-TERM	DENTAL EXPENSE
1970	158,847	151,440	138,658	103,544	58,089	10,966	11,972
1971	161,849	153,093	139,399	108,813	59,280	12,284	15,263
1972	164,098	154,687	140,873	113,837	61,548	14,538	16,853
1973	168,455	162,644	151,680	124,627	64,168	17,011	20,418
1974	173,140	166,434	158,170	131,438	65,282	17,799	27,855
1975	177,980	168,895	161,854	134,092	62,971	18,396	30,246
1976	176,581	167,432	163,094	134,992	62,250	17,779	41,559
1977	178,968	167,220	160,429	139,362	64,627	19,364	50,301
1978:							
Under 65	166,819	162,239	154,621	N.A.	N.A.	19,100	N.A.
65 and over	14,645	10,260	9,524	N.A.	N.A.	–	N.A.
Total	181,464	172,499	164,145	141,538	70,378	19,100	60,227†

N.A.—Not available.

†Preliminary estimate.

Note: For 1975 and later, data include the number of persons covered in Puerto Rico and other U.S. territories and possessions. The data refer to the net total of people protected, i.e., duplication among persons protected by more than one kind of insuring organization or more than one insurance company policy providing the same type of coverage has been eliminated.

Source: Source Book of Health Insurance Date 1979–1980, Health Insurance Institute, p. 12.

example, there could be a plan 1, 2, or 3 (or A, B, or C) with benefits (and premiums) declining as you move from plan 1 to 2 to 3, as will be noted below.

Hospital Expenses

This type of health insurance policy will pay all or part of a person's hospital bills. These policies can be purchased by an individual from a private insurance company or a group plan may be developed by the employer and a private insurance company. In addition to the insurance sold by private insurance companies, there are the various Blue Cross plans. These are nonprofit organizations persons can join on an individual basis if they are not eligible under a group plan. The Blue Cross plans are discussed in greater detail on pages 239–241.

As shown in Table 9–1 hospital insurance is the most widely held of all health insurance. In 1978 about 185 million people had this coverage. Most of these plans have a per day limit (usually applying only to the hospital room), but with this reservation will pay bills in connection with hospital rooms, board, laboratory fees, X-rays, and most other services furnished by hospitals. Usually the insurance company will make available several alternative hsopitalization plans. For example, the person could choose a $80, $90, or $100 per day hospital room allowance with premiums varying accordingly. A few plans provide for full payment of a semiprivate room. Generally, most other hospital fees such as laboratory work are covered in full.

There is also generally a limit to the number of days of hospital confinement this insurance will cover. This figure varies but generally the plans cover from 30 to 365 days of hospital care per illness. A certain period of time (usually ninety days) is required between hospital stays for the insurance to be effective again.

Surgical Expenses

Payment of surgical fees is not included in policies that cover hospital fees, and separate insurance plans have been developed to take care of them. Usually the company pays a given amount of dollars for certain types of operations. If the fee is above this figure, the person must pay the residual amount. The amount the policy will pay varies in accordance with the contract. Some policies pay a larger percent, but they have higher premiums. These plans are also sold on an individual as well as a group basis by the private insurance companies.

Blue Shield is the nonprofit equivalent to Blue Cross; it provides benefits for surgical fees on both an individual and a group basis. In the case of both hospital and surgical insurance, most of the policies are either group plans with private insurance companies or some kind of Blue Cross-Blue Shield coverage. The following list shows the schedule of fees paid for eight operations by a typical surgical plan.

1. Appendectomy — $600
2. Hernia inguinal, unilateral — 450
3. Hernia inguinal, bilateral — 600
4. Amputation, toe — 200
5. Cataract, removal — 800
6. Corneal transplant — 1,900
7. Tonsillectomy — 250
8. Brain tumor surgery — 3,100

Regular Medical Expenses

This type of insurance policy, which is meant to provide for general medical expenses not covered by surgical and hospital plans, takes care of such items as drugs and visits to a doctor's office. There may be provision for a maximum number of visits to a doctor per year, and there are also statements of maximum dollar amounts—if not per illness or accident, then per year. Many companies sell this type of coverage only on a group basis or as part of the package when selling comprehensive insurance, which will be described below. This type of policy has grown rapidly with the growth of group insurance in recent years. At the end of 1978 over 160 million people were covered.

This insurance will not usually cover such things as visits to the doctor for regular checkups. There must be an actual illness or accident involved.

Major Medical Insurance

The policy written for major medical insurance is really in the nature of catastrophe insurance. Most people feel that they could somehow pay medical bills up to $300, $400, or even $500, but after that the payments would be a financial catastrophe. Consequently, the major medical insurance policy was developed. The coverage may be for an individual only or it may be designed for the individual and his or her family. If a person has very high medical bills because of serious illness, the major medical coverage comes into play. Also, that portion of hospital, surgical, and regular medical expenses not paid by those policies can be submitted under the major medical plan. Major medical insurance can be purchased on a group or on an individual basis. Major medical insurance can be obtained from private insurance companies or from the nonprofit Blue Cross and Blue Shield organizations.

Deductible Feature

Generally, the major medical policy contains a deductible feature. The policyholder must pay the amount of the deductible. The insurance will pay for expenses beyond it. The deductible sum may range anywhere from $50 to $300. The higher the deductible, the lower the premium. If a policy has a $300 deductibility clause, this means that the policyholder pays the first $300 of a medical bill. In most major medical policies, the deductible feature applies on a yearly basis rather than on an illness basis. Therefore, once the person has paid a $300 deductible medical bill, all future medical expenses for the remainder of the year are submitted to the insurance company. This includes all the various bills that are not covered by the regular medical or surgical insurance.

Coinsurance Feature

Most of the major medical policies contain a coinsurance feature as well as the deductible feature, in accordance with which the company agrees to pay only a part of the total expense. Most companies agree to pay up to 80 or 90 percent of the cost, with the insured paying the remaining 10 or 20 percent. For example, assume a bill of $2,500 with a $300 deductible clause and an agreement on the part of the company to pay 80 percent of the total cost above the deductible; this would mean that the company would pay $1,760, with the remainder to be paid by the insured ($2,500 total bill, minus $300, or $2,200 × .80 or $1,760, which is to be paid by the company).

Benefits paid include virtually all kinds of health care prescribed by physicians. These include treatment given in and out of hospitals, special nursing care, X-rays, drugs, medical appliances, surgeons' fees, and many others. Major medical then covers many of the same things as does hospital insurance, surgical insurance, and regular medical insurance. However, major medical covers the big expenses that are above the maximums for the policies just noted. It is truly catastrophe insurance that acts as a supplement to basic hospital, surgical, or regular medical insurance.

Limitations

Most of the major medical polices contain a maximum amount that the company will pay. Generally, this figure ranges from $10,000 to $25,000, but it may go as high as $200,000, or even more in a few cases. These are usually lifetime limits. The limitation may also be written to cover any single illness or it may be written as a limitation for a year. The policy may read, for instance, that it will cover only $5,000 for any one illness, meaning that no matter how long the individual is hospitalized, the company will cease paying after the $5,000 has been used up. If the limitation applies to a policy year, then the company would make payments the following year in the event the policyholder was so unfortunate as to be hospitalized for that long. As an example, suppose the yearly limit of the policy was $10,000 and the total bill during one year was $12,000. The company would cease paying as soon as the $10,000 was used up; but as the next policy year started, the company would begin paying again if the illness continued. Generally, the policies are written so that as the second policy year starts, the insured must first pay the deductible amount before the company becomes liable. In addition, as noted above, most policies have a lifetime limit. This lifetime limit is usually several times the single illness or yearly limit. Generally, the lifetime limit is around $20,000, but it may vary a good deal and some go up as high as $40,000 and $50,000. There is even the so-called jumbo major medical policy with a lifetime limit of $200,000. Figure 9–2 shows the growth of major medical insurance over the past few years.

Comprehensive Medical Insurance

An inclusive medical plan called comprehensive medical insurance is an attempt to meet all health insurance needs with one package. Comprehensive insurance usually covers hospital expenses, surgical expenses, regular medical expenses, and major medical

FIGURE 9–2. *Major medical expense protection with insurance companies in the United States. (Source: Source Book of Health Insurance Data 1977–1978, 1979–1980, Health Insurance Institute, p. 24.)*

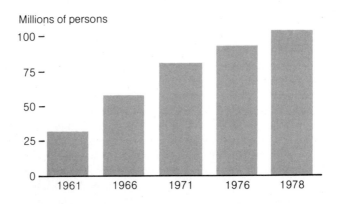

Part 2 / Your Insurance and Annuity Program

expenses. Some plans even include loss of income or disability insurance. The comprehensive medical plan is designed to meet short-term as well as long-term illnesses; thus it is a combination policy. In essence what happens is that major medical and the other type of insurance described above are put in one package. These policies are issued with the same sort of coinsurance feature. The deductible is usually somewhat lower under the comprehensive plan, and some plans do not have a deductibility feature. More and more of the health insurance sold today is put into one comprehensive plan. This reduces administrative and clerical costs and usually provides the policyholder a better return on his or her premium dollar.

Dental Insurance

A number of insurance companies are presently experimenting with dental insurance. Dental insurance covers, usually on some coinsurance basis, the cost of fillings, extractions, dentures, oral surgery, and most other dental expenses, including orthodontic work. The typical dental insurance plans have a deductibility feature. Dental expenses above the deductible feature are then coinsured with the insurance generally paying 80 percent. The plans also state the maximum amount the company will pay. Dental insurance is relatively new, and consequently many companies are not anxious to write it. One of the main problems is how to set premiums, since not enough actuarial experience exists.

Nevertheless, there has been substantial growth in dental insurance coverage in recent years. According to the Health Insurance Council and the Health Insurance Association of America, over 60 million people had some dental insurance coverage at year end 1978. Figure 9–3 shows this growth in recent years.

FIGURE 9–3. *Dental expense protection in the United States. (Source: Source Book of Health Insurance Data, 1977–1978,* Health Insurance Institute, p. 31.)

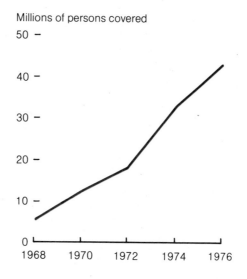

One of the hazards faced by everyone is that they will lose their ability to earn a livelihood temporarily or permanently due to a serious accident or illness. Some jobs in and of themselves are dangerous and on-the-job accidents could cripple a person for life. Some illnesses can render a person incapable of working even after recovery. Even people in relatively safe occupations can suffer from accidents. For example, through no fault of one's own, a person might be crippled for life instead of killed in an automobile accident. Indeed, some insurance executives believe that disability insurance is needed even more than life insurance. The probability of partial or total disability is greater than the probability of loss of life for relatively young people. Because of this likelihood, disability (often called loss of income) insurance was developed.

The first policy of this type was sold in 1847, although the modern policies began in 1898. However, very few people were covered prior to World War II. In general, the policies are designed to cover loss of income either as the result of a partial disability or as the result of permanent disability; but in no case may the coverage be more than the actual earnings of the individual. In short, if a person earns $250 per week, he or she cannot purchase a policy that would cover a loss of earnings of more than $250 per week.

The policies generally have two features: (1) payment as the result of loss of earnings from an accident and (2) payment as the result of loss of earnings from sickness that prevents one from earning a living.

These policies are written in a number of different ways. Most have a waiting period before benefit payments begin, and this waiting period varies. They pay a certain percentage (which varies) of earnings for various periods. Generally they can be grouped into those which provide short-term protection or long-term protection. The short-term policies provide benefits for various time periods up to two years, the long-term policies provide for protection for more than two years; some provide benefits for up to ten years, and more. A few even provide benefits until the insured is age 65.

Premium rates vary in accordance with the above conditions; the longer the waiting period before payments begin, the lower the premiums. And, of course, the longer the period over which the payments are made, the higher the premiums.

The rates also vary with the occupation of the individual. Professional and certain types of businesspeople find the premiums lower and the benefits more liberal than those for persons in more hazardous occupations. In the latter cases, the rates may be higher and the benefits lower.

This type of policy also often contains a provision stating that for dismemberment the insured is to receive a lump sum equivalent to a stated number of weeks' indemnity in the case of being disabled permanently. For example, if an individual has a policy that provides for payment of $100 a week in the event of total disablement and then loses a leg in an accident, the policy may provide that the policyholder is to receive a lump-sum payment of two hundred weeks times $100, or $20,000. Where such a lump sum is received, the individual does not receive the weekly benefits provided for in the policy.

More than a dozen varieties of limited disability insurance can be purchased to cover almost every situation imaginable. For example, an individual paying off a mortgage on a residence may purchase disability insurance to cover the mortgage payments. For a $3 to $4 a month premium, depending on age, the company will agree to pay up to five years of the monthly mortgage payments after a waiting period of fifteen days.

OTHER IMPORTANT THINGS ABOUT HEALTH INSURANCE

There are a number of other important things about health insurance with which one should be familiar. These will now be examined.

Items Not Covered

Certain expenses of a medical nature are usually not covered by health insurance, although sometimes some of them are. Some policies cover psychiatric care, some do not. Those that do often set a special limit on this item. Such things as abortions are generally not covered by most plans. Dental insurance, as noted above, can be obtained, but most health insurance plans do not cover these costs automatically. The cost of regular checkups is usually not covered. The cost of eyeglasses and eye examinations is generally not covered, but treatment of eye disease or eye surgery is. Vasectomies and circumcisions may or may not be covered; the same is true of surgery to correct natural deformities, such as a club foot. The general trend, however, is toward broader coverage in these areas.

100 Percent Coverage

Since health insurance policies have a coinsurance clause that pays usually only 80 or 90 percent of the medical bills, can a person buy two policies and then receive benefits in excess of expenses? The answer is no, but one may collect more than if one had only one policy. There are, however, only a few cases where a person could get two group policies, although one could buy two individual policies; but individual policies have substantially

"Don't worry, we'll have you on your feet and out of here in no time. Your hospital insurance doesn't cover much." (Source: Permission Cartoon Features Syndicate; from The Wall Street Journal.*)*

Chapter 9 / Health Care and Health Insurance

higher premiums. In the case where both husband and wife work and both are eligible for group insurance, they could have two policies. Or in rare cases persons could have two group plans if they had one with their employer and another one with a professional association such as, say, the American Accounting Association.

How would two such policies pay off if there were a claim? One policy would be classified as the primary policy; it would pay first in accordance with its terms and the other policy would then pay part or all of the rest. In nearly all cases the primary policy is the one obtained with the employer. In the case of a husband-wife team, the primary policy would be the one from the employer of the person in the family making the claim.

This coverage can best be illustrated with an example. Suppose a person has two policies, both with a $50 deductibility and an 80 percent coinsurance clause; assume a claim is filed for $1,050. The primary carrier would pay 80 percent of $1,000 or $800. The secondary carrier would then pay all or part of the remaining $250, depending upon what the contract said regarding secondary claims. It could be 80 percent of the $250; 80 percent of $200 ($250 less the deductibility), or 80 percent of $1,000, just as the primary carrier, with a limit of $250. In no case could a person get more than 100 percent coverage and in many cases one gets less. For this reason, it almost never pays to have two policies; a person pays double premiums and gets only marginal added protection.

Of course, if one doesn't tell the insurance companies one has two policies one might get a double payoff; but if the companies find this out, they will cancel. In the early days of health insurance, there was no question regarding whether a person had a second policy on the claim form, and some people did get double coverage. But now there is such a question on all forms for reimbursement.

Group Plans: The Modern Way to Buy Health Insurance

As noted above, any of the plans discussed above can be obtained on a group or individual basis. A group plan actually amounts to wholesaling insurance, and the features are the same as if an individual were to purchase his or her own policy. As a group member, however, one generally has the benefit of lower rates than if one were to purchase the policy on one's own.

There are a number of reasons why the rates are more favorable to the group, one being that there is a more favorable selection of risks. When it insures the group, the company usually insists that at least 75 percent of those eligible must join. Moreover, those who do join do not come with the idea that they will receive immediate benefits; and there are few cancellations. In some cases, the employee has no choice but to take the group insurance, that is, it is a condition of employment. In other cases, it is voluntary, and it is in these cases that the insurance companies insist that the policy is not effective until 75 percent of the eligible employees have joined. Another reason for more favorable rates is that the administrative costs are lower. As far as collections are concerned, the employer customarily withholds the amount of the premiums from the employee's paycheck. The commission paid to the agent who sells the group policy is lower than if he or she were to sell the same number of policies to many individuals.

It should perhaps be added here that frequently group health policies are a part of the so-called fringe benefits in labor-management contracts. Often the employer pays all or a part of the premiums and agrees to handle much of the paper work through the personnel office.

There is a growing trend toward the group method of meeting insurance needs. This is true not only of health insurance, but also of life insurance. The general pattern today is to have one package negotiated on a group basis. This would then include some sort of a comprehensive health plan as was described above together with some term insurance, all under one plan.

Guaranteed Renewable and Noncancellable Policies

In some cases, the insurance company retains the right to refuse to renew the policy when it expires. Indeed, sometimes the company has the right to cancel at any time during the term of the policy.

It is, however, possible to buy guaranteed renewable and noncancellable policies. A guaranteed renewable policy can be renewed until some predetermined age is reached. This is most generally age sixty-five. However, each time it is renewed, premiums can be increased if warranted.

A noncancellable policy is one that cannot be cancelled during the period of time it was originally stated to run. During this time, premiums also cannot be raised. Therefore, if a person bought a policy that is both noncancellable and renewable, the premiums cannot be raised during the period over which the policy runs. Then, when the period is over, the policy must be renewed if the policyholder chooses this, but now premiums can be raised.

How to Apply for Benefits

It is easy to apply for benefits under most health insurance plans. Every person with a health insurance plan receives a wallet-sized card from the insurance company. A person in a group plan has a group number and a certificate number on the wallet card. In the case of a hospital bill often the hospital staff will fill out the form and send it in. In the case of a doctor's bill or reimbursement for drugs, often the insured must fill out the form, but it is self-explanatory. Since in many cases the insurance company only pays part of the bill, instructions are sent indicating how much the patient is to pay over and above the insurance claim. Up until a few years ago, the companies often paid the doctor directly. Now more and more companies are paying the patient who in turn pays the doctor.

NONPROFIT HEALTH INSURANCE PLANS

In addition to being able to buy health insurance policies from profit-making life insurance companies, one can purchase them from nonprofit organizations. The most widely known such nonprofit organization is Blue Cross and Blue Shield. Blue Cross and Blue Shield plans are set up to cover a certain geographical area; sometimes this is an entire state and sometimes only a part of a state. Everyone in that area is theoretically eligible to join either through a group plan at the person's place of employment or as an individual.

Blue Cross is a cooperative nonprofit organization designed to pay hospital and other medical bills of its members, while Blue Shield is a similar nonprofit organization designed to pay surgical expenses. The latter is sponsored by groups of physicians, and for the most part Blue Cross handles the details of selling, billing, and collecting for Blue Shield. In year end 1979 over 85 million Americans were members of Blue Cross-Blue Shield plans of various types.

While there are a number of other independent private nonprofit organizations that provide health insurance for their members, they are relatively unimportant. Blue Cross-

Blue Shield is the only other major source (other than life insurance companies)[1] of health insurance protection. If one is eligible to participate on a group basis, rates are lower than for the individual plan. Blue Cross-Blue Shield plans do not provide for loss of income, but they do provide for major medical coverages as well as hospitalization, regular medical expenses, and surgical coverage. They have a comprehensive plan as described above under the insurance company plans, in which a number of items including major medical are sold in one package. Some Blue Cross plans also provide dental insurance.

Blue Cross

The payments for a Blue Cross policy depend on area; in some states, the cost of hospitalization is more expensive than in others. More important, the rates depend on the type of contract one purchases, for some contracts provide more benefits than others. In addition, rates vary depending on whether one purchases the insurance as a member of a group or singly.

The period of hospitalization covered varies from 30 to 365 days. For example, when a contract is purchased with a 365-day hospitalization period, it will usually state that if a period of more than 90 days separates the discharge and a new admission date, a new 365 days becomes available. There is usually a limit to how much Blue Cross will pay per day for a hospital room.

In addition, most of the plans pay all charges for operating room, recovery room, cast room, and cystoscopic room, plus all drugs in general use—with the exception of blood and blood plasma—as well as oxygen inhalations and physical therapy, all laboratory services, basal metabolism tests, electrocardiograms, and X-ray charges. If both husband and wife are covered, after nine months of membership maternity care is also included. If the entire family is covered, there is no extra cost for a newborn child; and when the mother is entitled to maternity benefits, the child is entitled to hospital nursery benefits. After the discharge of the mother and the child, the child thereafter is entitled to full benefits when he or she becomes a patient.

Under both the Blue Cross and the Blue Shield plans anyone under the age of sixty-five may enroll on an individual basis, and no physical examination is required. The policies are noncancellable except for nonpayment of dues or the fraudulent use of the membership. Furthermore, the benefits are not reduced if the individual changes residence. If there is a change of residence, there may, however, be a change in rates.

When persons retire and draw social security, they may keep or lose their Blue Cross-Blue Shield depending upon the local plan. However, more and more plans are adopting the modified Blue Cross-Blue Shield plan for retired people who wish to retain it. This policy consists of reduced coverage (and reduced premiums), which is intended to complement Medicare.

Blue Shield

While Blue Cross is designed to cover hospitalization, Blue Shield is designed to cover physicians' fees, whether surgical, surgical-medical, or general medical. Like Blue Cross, the basic rates of Blue Shield vary from state to state and from plan to plan. Most plans agree to pay the physician according to a basic schedule. For example, the physician might

1. It should be noted that the government's Medicare plan is a second alternative source for citizens over sixty-five. Group prepaid medical plans are also becoming popular. They are discussed below.

charge $400 for services and the Blue Shield payment schedule might call for a payment of $275. In such a case the subscriber would pay the balance of $125.

How much will be paid for a given operation varies from one section of the country to another. Also there are usually two or three different packages to choose from. A purchaser who is willing to pay a higher premium can obtain a higher surgical fee schedule. Some plans have even been sold that do not list the dollar amounts they will pay for a given operation but they state they will pay "reasonable and customary" surgical fees. That is, in effect they pay the entire bill the surgeon submits.

Most Blue Cross-Blue Shield plans have a deductibility clause as well as a coinsurance clause on the major medical part of their plan, just like the private insurance company plans. They also have a family rate and a lower rate for only a husband and wife, and a still lower rate for a single person.

Health Maintenance Organizations (HMOs)

In recent years another type of medical expense protection has developed through what are called health maintenance organizations. This method provides many of the same benefits as health insurance. It consists of group prepayment medical plans, often organized as nonprofit co-ops. These provide medical care for their members for a fixed fee per month. These groups own and operate clinics and hospitals and hire doctors, nurses, and other technicians. The professional medical personnel, including doctors, are paid an annual salary; consequently there is no set fee for such and such service. Membership is on a volunteer basis; but in order to join a person obviously must live in a geographical area where there is an HMO. Some of the more well known plans are the Health Insurance Plan of Greater New York, Kaiser Foundation Health Plan, Ross-Loos Medical Group of Los Angeles, Community Health Association of Detroit, and the Group Health Cooperative of Puget Sound.

These group plans can provide most of the benefits that their members need from their own resources. If the services of a specialist are needed and none of the group's doctors qualifies, the group hires an outside specialist on a fee basis. The group cannot provide disability insurance internally, but most HMOs buy that for their members from an insurance company.

These organizations also practice preventive medicine, and have been established recently as a hopeful alternative to costly medical care. The theory behind this preventive medicine is that it is cheaper, both moneywise and in human suffering, to prevent illnesses than to cure them after they are well established. This process involves periodic medical checkups and screening programs to detect early warning signs of health breakdowns. Most of the HMOs offer more comprehensive coverage than most regular group insurance plans. Not only do they provide for regular medical checkups, but many of them have neither a deductibility feature or a coinsurance clause. That is, 100 percent of all medical expenses are taken care of. The west coast Kaiser Foundation Health Plan was an early pioneer in this field.

Before an HMO can be set up, the states must pass enabling legislation; but now twenty-six states have done so. There are currently about 200 HMOs in the United States and their number is growing. Insurance companies are working with existing HMOs and have developed additional ones. HMOs are also sponsored by various governments, Blue Cross, hospitals, medical schools, consumer groups, employers unions, and a number of other organizations. Since 1972 the federal government has provided grants and loans for the planning, development, and initial operating costs of HMOs.

The evidence does suggest that HMOs reduce medical costs. Sources say that is because the medical dollar goes directly to the doctor; there is no (or at least there is less) expensive bureaucracy siphoning off dollars. While the salaried doctors working for an HMO generally make less money than doctors in private practice, they seem happy because they work fewer hours and their schedule is more regular.

National Health Insurance

A number of proposals have been made that the federal government become more involved in health care. These range all the way from a complete government takeover to plans designed to supplement the present insurance plans. For example, some plans would provide complete cradle-to-grave coverage for everybody. They would replace all private health insurance plans. Life insurance companies would be out of the health insurance business. Blue Cross-Blue Shield too would go out of business. The more limited plans would merely offer additional benefits over and above what present health insurance now provides. Some of the supplemental plans would give mainly catastrophe coverage over and above what private major medical now provides. Others would pay some of the expenses now paid by the public due to the deductibility and coinsurance clauses.

Those in favor of national health insurance maintain that the protection against catastrophic illnesses provided by most private major medical plans is inadequate. For example, upper limits exist per illness or per year, and for really serious and prolonged illnesses a person could exhaust the coverage. Also it is claimed the deductibility and coinsurance clauses are too high and hence medical care is still too expensive for many people. Then, too, some groups find it difficult to buy health care coverage. These are primarily people not covered by a group plan and whose health is too poor for them to buy an individual policy.

Those who are opposed to national health insurance maintain it is not needed or at most a supplemental plan is all that is needed. It is argued that not many will exhaust the benefits of a good major medical plan. If deductibility features or coinsurance is too high, the private companies can develop plans that have lower such features. The critics maintain that the old are covered by Medicare, the poor by Medicaid, and most others by plans where they work. (Medicare and Medicaid are discussed in the appendix to this chapter.) The cost of medical care, they argue, will not be reduced by a national health plan; it will merely be financed differently. It will have to be paid by higher taxes rather than through insurance premiums. Indeed, the critics maintain that national health insurance will cause the cost of health care to rise further because of an enlarged bureaucracy needed to administer it. They point to the experience with Medicare and Medicaid to substantiate their claim.

A number of proposals have been made to finance national health insurance. Some would use the regular funds from the general revenues of the Treasury. Others would finance it through the social security tax and raise rates to do so. Others would add a special health insurance tax to be paid in part by the employee and in part by the employer. One plan would even be financed in part with a tax credit. It would rely on private health insurance as now, but there would be a tax credit for health insurance premiums. (A dollar of a tax credit reduces taxes by one dollar and hence is more generous than merely being deductible from income before calculating taxes.) People owing no income taxes would get a free certificate from the government with which to pay their health insurance premiums. The estimated costs of the various national health plans range from about $10 billion to upwards of $100 billion per year.

HOW MUCH HEALTH INSURANCE TO BUY

While much life insurance is designed to protect the family economically in the event of the premature death of the breadwinner, much the same sort of economic catastrophe can result from a serious illness or accident. Indeed, a permanent disability may be more of a disaster than a death; not only is the income stream cut off, but expenses may rise. Consequently, along with life insurance, the individual needs protection against such contingencies as these.

Medical Insurance Needs

It is strongly recommended that no breadwinner be without at least a major medical insurance policy. If one is able to obtain group insurance where one works, there is not really much choice over what kind of health insurance to buy. There is a package (sometimes two or three different packages with varying benefits) available and one can accept or reject it. The reader should seriously consider accepting it. Group health insurance is usually the cheapest available.

Persons who are not members of a group and hence not eligible for a group policy should consider individual policies. At the very least, everyone should have a major medical policy. The cost can be kept within reason if the person puts the deductible feature between $200 and $400. Shop around and compare the local Blue Cross-Blue Shield plan with what a private life insurance company can offer. Persons who live in an area with a health maintenance organization are indeed fortunate. This is often the cheapest type of health insurance protection and it offers a means whereby an unattached individual can obtain group coverage.

Whether or not to buy hospital, surgical, and regular medical expense insurance, if one has the choice, is a matter of personal priorities. Certainly this should have a lower priority than major medical, and probably a lower priority than disability insurance. If the budget can afford it, fine; if not, a young and healthy individual might want to economize and take a modest risk here.

Disability Insurance Needs

Disability insurance should also be high on the list of priorities. Persons who have access to a good group plan should seriously consider it. Even if it must be bought on an individual basis, it should still be high on the list of priorities, in order to assure a monthly income in the event that regular income is cut off due to a lengthy illness or serious accident. Often professional and other groups are able to obtain this sort of insurance at relatively low rates. Consequently, this is one of the most rapidly growing areas in the insurance industry. Figure 9–4 shows the growth of private health insurance in the United States.

In order to calculate the actual dollar amount of your disability insurance needs you follow the same logic you did when you calculated your life insurance needs. You might want to review that portion of the life insurance chapter. We will only briefly summarize at this point. Since disability terminates the income stream (just as does death), the maximum amount of disability insurance would be the amount equal to your income stream. In theory as your income rises, your disability insurance needs also rise. Almost no one could afford this much disability insurance, but it is a bench mark where you can begin and then scale the amount down in accordance with your priorities and value judgments. In reality, most people buy a policy that provides for the payment of a certain percentage of their income.

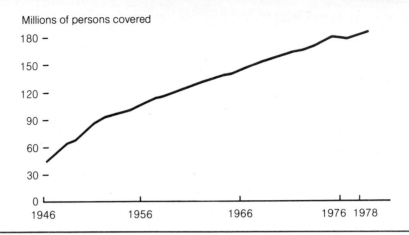

Millions of persons covered

180 –			
150 –			
120 –			
90 –			
60 –			
30 –			
0			
1946	1956	1966	1976 1978

FIGURE 9–4. *Growth of private health insurance in the United States. (Source: Source Book of Health Insurance Data 1977–1978, 1979–1980, Health Insurance Institute, p. 8.)*

Or you could use the needs criteria in determining your disability needs. This method is similar, but not identical to estimating your life insurance needs according to the needs principle. (See the chapter on life insurance.) We will summarize the points you should consider.

1. Gross annual living expense requirements.
2. Net annual living expense requirements. This is gross requirements less reduced expenses stemming from disability such as:
   a) Income taxes because disability insurance payments are nontaxable; neither are social security benefits.
   b) Transportation costs and other costs associated with holding a job which are reduced.
   c) Life insurance premiums which would be reduced by any disability premium waiver clause you may have.

This net annual living expense figure could be reduced further by the following items:

3. Sick pay if any should also be taken into account.
4. Spouse's income; current or expected future income if spouse were expected to go back to work in the event of a disability.
5. Social security disability payments.
6. Other disability benefit payments (such as corporate pension plan benefits where you work).
7. Investment income.
8. Actual net annual disability income needed which would have to be provided by disability insurance. Item 8 is item number 2 above less items 3; 4; 5; 6; and 7.

You will note that, unlike the estimate of life insurance needs, we have made no allowance for:

a) paying off the mortgage and other debts,

b) a college fund, and

c) an emergency fund.

This is because these items could be taken care of under item 2, net annual living expenses, in which case they would remain part of the personal family budget, although conceivably they could be taken into account by insurance; then your disability insurance needs would be greater. Table 9–2 shows the disability insurance requirements of a hypothetical Mr. and Mrs. X.

It is also possible to calculate your disability insurance needs by using a rule of thumb and taking a certain percentage of your income, say, 60 or 70 percent. But going through the eight steps above will provide you with a more precise figure.

You may also wish to adjust your disability insurance needs to take into account future inflation. This is done in the table below. Actual net annual disability income requirements (current disability insurance needs) come to $4,000. If we assume a long-run inflation rate of 5 percent and a 20-year disability requirement, we can get the inflationary factor. It is 33.066 and is obtained from table 3 (future worth of an annuity) in the appendix to chapter 7, "Savings Through Thrift Institutions." It indicates that if you start with one dollar, and you add one additional dollar each year, and the entire sum is growing by 5 percent per year, it will amount to $33.066 at the end of twenty years. Multiplying that by $4,000, we find that the total disability payout over twenty years will amount to $132,264. Dividing this last figure by twenty years, we obtain $6,613, which is the average disability insurance payout per year over the entire period—that is, the disability insurance needs of Mr. and Mrs. X adjusted for inflation. Currently their needs are $4,000, but this will rise to $10,612 in the twentieth year, if inflation continues at 5 percent. If they make arrangements for

TABLE 9–2

Disability insurance needs of Mr. and Mrs. X

1. Gross Annual Living Expense Requirements		$ 16,000
Income tax on $16,000 *estimated	$2,000	
Transportation and other cost reductions	500	
Life insurance premium reductions	500	
2. Net Annual Living Expense Requirements		$ 13,000
3. Sick pay (short term)		
4. Spouse's income		
5. Social security	$8,400	
6. Other disability benefits		
7. Investment Income	600	
8. Net Annual Disability Income Requirements		$ 4,000
9. Inflation factor 33.066 (20 years at 5%)		
10. Twenty-year income stream of $4,000 per year adjusted for 5 percent inflation ($4,000 × 33.066)		$132,264
11. Average yearly income ($132,264.00 ÷ 20)		$ 6,613

$6,613.00 per year, they will have a surplus during the early years ($2,613 the first year). They should put this surplus in an interest-bearing account, and then it becomes in a sense a reserve that can be used in later years when their needs rise above $6,613. Actually, providing for disability income of $6,613 yields slightly more than $4,000 in real terms over the years, assuming 5 percent inflation, because they will be earning interest on the surplus during the early years. However, this provides them with a hedge in the event that inflation rises above 5 percent.

QUESTIONS FOR REVIEW

1. How are accident and health policies classified?

2. Explain three types of coverage available in health policies.

3. What is disability insurance?

4. What is major medical coverage?

5. What is meant by coinsurance and the deductibility clause in health insurance?

6. Why is it more difficult to obtain dental insurance than other health insurance?

7. Does it pay to have two health insurance policies both of which provide the same benefits? Why or why not?

8. What are some of the things that most health insurance policies will not cover?

9. Is it best to buy health insurance on a group or on an individual basis, assuming the person has a choice? Why?

10. What is the difference between Blue Cross and Blue Shield?

11. Discuss health maintenance organizations.

12. What is the difference between hospital insurance and medical insurance under the Medicare program?

CASES

1. William and Wanda Brown have a health insurance coverage under the Blue Cross-Blue Shield plan. Now, however, William has an opportunity to join a group plan at his place of employment that is a somewhat better plan. Should he join and keep both policies or should he drop his Blue Cross-Blue Shield?

2. Bill and Jeanette Jones had the following medical bills last year:

   a. $160 for Mark, their six-year-old son;
   b. $190 for Suellen, their five-year-old daughter;
   c. $220 for Jeanette; and
   d. $195 for Bill.

   They have coverage for all medical and drug bills up to $100,000 with a $100 deductibility feature and an 80 percent coinsurance clause. How much will their policy reimburse them?

3. John Brown, aged sixty-six, recently retired and is drawing social security. When he left his employer, he was told his group life and health insurance would lapse. He has since tried to buy individual Blue Cross and Blue Shield coverage but has found out he cannot do so. Can you explain why not? If John cannot buy insurance, will he have to finance his medical bills on his own? What should John have done immediately upon retirement?

4. Ann and Jim Clark both work for the same employer, and both are enrolled in a group plan there. Their plan is a comprehensive plan that covers everything up to $10,000 per illness with a $50 deductibility and a 90 percent coinsurance clause. Recently Jim had major surgery. The hospital bill was $120 per day for ten days. The surgical fee was $1,250, and all other expenses such as drugs and the like came to $250. How much of the total bill will his insurance pay, and how much will he

pay? Will he benefit from the fact that he and his wife both have a policy? Are a primary and a secondary carrier involved? Would you recommend that the Clark family keep both of the policies they have?

5. Joan and Bill Rider both work for the same employer. They have a choice regarding their group health insurance. They can each buy a group policy for a single person or one of them can buy a policy for a husband and wife. Their benefits would be the same. What should they do?

6. While sliding down a water slide at a neighbor's swimming pool, Sara Scott hit her head at the bottom and knocked out one of her front teeth. Will Sara's parents' Blue Cross or Blue Shield pay for her dental surgery? Will the neighbor's homeowner's policy pay Sara's medical bills?

7. John and Alice Brown are a retired couple drawing social security benefits. Last winter John fell and broke his leg while shoveling snow; the fall also broke several teeth and he had to have oral surgery. While performing this surgery the dentist decided to remove two other teeth. John had the following bills:

Doctor's fees	$215
Hospital (emergency room; X-ray, and supplies)	$75
Rental of crutches	$25
Dental bill	$165

What proportion of this bill will Medicare pay and how much will John have to pay?

SUGGESTED READINGS

Avedis, Donebedian. *Benefits in Medical Care Programs.* Cambridge, Mass: Harvard University Press, 1976.

Best's Review, Life-Health Edition. Published monthly by A. M. Best Company, Inc., Oldwick, N. J. 08858.

Blue Cross-Blue Shield Fact Book, 1981. Published annually by the National Association of Blue Shield Plans, Blue Cross Association, 840 North Lake Shore Drive, Chicago, Ill.

Blue Cross Reports. Published quarterly by the Blue Cross Association, 840 North Lake Shore Drive, Chicago, Ill.

The Blue Cross Story, 1973. Published by the Blue Cross Association, 840 North Lake Shore Drive, Chicago, Ill.

A Brief Explanation of Medicare. Department of Health, Education and Welfare Publication No. (SSA) 73–10043.

Davis, Karen. *National Health Insurance: Benefits, Costs, and Consequences.* Washington, D.C.: The Brookings Institute, 1975.

"Duplicate Coverage." Pamphlet published by Blue Cross-Blue Shield. No date.

Follmann, J. F., Jr. "Dental Care Coverage." *Best's Insurance News* reprint.

Galton, Lawrence. *The Patient's Guide to Surgery.* New York: Avon Books, 1977.

Health Insurance for People 65 or Older. Washington: U.S. Department of Health, Education and Welfare. (You may obtain a free copy from a social security field office, which is found in any large city.)

"How to Shop for Health Insurance." HEW Publication, 1979. Consumer Information Center, Pueblo, CO 81009.

Inquiry, A Journal of Medical Care Organization, Provision and Financing. Published by the Blue Cross Association, 840 North Lake Shore Drive, Chicago, Ill.

The Journal of Insurance. A bi-monthly publication of the Insurance Information Institute, 110 William Street, New York, N.Y. 10038.

Mehr, Robert I., and Cammack, Emerson. *Principles of Insurance.* Homewood, Ill.: Richard D. Irwin, 1980.

Rosett, Richard N. (ed.). *The Role of Health Insurance in the Health Services Sector.* Washington, D.C.: National Bureau of Economic Research, 1976.

Somers, Anne, and Somers, Herman. *Medicare and the Hospitals: Issues and Prospects.* Washington, D.C.: The Brookings Institute, 1975.

Source Book of Health Insurance. Published annually by the Health Insurance Institute, 277 Park Ave., New York, N.Y.

Your Medicare Handbook. Department of Health, Education and Welfare, Baltimore, Maryland, 1979. Publication Number (SSA) 79–10050.

APPENDIX A9

MEDICARE

Probably the most far-reaching of the 1965 amendments to the Social Security Law was the Medicare provision. It provided for two kinds of health insurance for those over age sixty-five: hospital insurance and medical insurance. The hospital insurance has come to be known as Part A of Medicare and the medical insurance as Part B. Practically everyone sixty-five or older is eligible for the entire Medicare program.

Certain individuals get Part A (hospital insurance) automatically and need not pay for it. Moreover, these people get this insurance even if they are still working and hence not drawing social security; the test is to be over sixty-five and eligible for social security. The following people are all eligible for Part A of Medicare.

1. Everyone over sixty-five and eligible for social security or railroad retirement benefits.
2. Disabled people under sixty-five who have been getting social security disability benefits for two years or more.
3. People insured under social security (but not yet getting benefits because they are under sixty-five) who need dialysis treatment or a kidney transplant. Wives, husbands, and children of insured people under sixty-five may also be eligible if they need kidney dialysis or transplants. Moreover, these people receive all the benefits of Part A until one year after they no longer have the above-described kidney problems, e.g., a successful kidney transplant.

Everyone who is covered automatically has hospital bills paid by social security as outlined below, and it also includes posthospital care.

People who are not covered automatically but who are over sixty-five may join Medicare on a voluntary basis and receive the same benefits, but they must pay a monthly premium. This premium (for Part A) is $78.00 per month, and those who buy this insurance must also buy the medical insurance (Part B) for which the premium is an additional $9.60 per month. However, while they may not buy Part A without Part B, they may buy Part B without A. Indeed, this is what most of those over sixty-five and not eligible for Part A automatically have done. The high cost of hospital insurance has discouraged its use on a voluntary basis.

Those who are drawing social security and hence are automatically covered for Part A (hospital insurance) are not covered automatically with respect to Part B. However, they, too, may buy this coverage on a voluntary basis by paying the $9.60 monthly premium. The premiums are withheld from the retirement check of those drawing social security, whereas the others must send them to their social security field office.

Hospital Insurance (Part A)

The hospital insurance provides for the following three broad classes of benefits:

1. All but the first $180 of all covered hospital costs are paid for the first sixty days of what are called "benefit periods." Medicare will also pay all but $45 per day of all covered costs during the sixty-first through ninetieth day of each benefit period. A benefit period

begins when a person enters a hospital and ends when the person has not been a bed patient in any hospital (or any facility that provides mainly skilled nursing care) for sixty days in a row. After this period, if a person is hospitalized again, he or she has a new "benefit period" and is entitled to coverage again. There is no limit to how many benefit periods a person may have.

On January 1, 1968, a "lifetime reserve" was included in the law. This provides that sixty additional days are added to the hospital insurance. Unlike the ninety days, which are renewed at the end of each illness, the "lifetime reserve" is not renewed after it is used. It means that if the ninety days have been used in a benefit period, the patient can be covered for an additional sixty days or part thereof. During the additional days the hospital insurance pays all but $90 per day of covered hospital expenses. One exception to this is mental patients. There is a lifetime limit of 190 days on payments for treatment in mental hospitals.

2. In addition, Medicare will pay up to one hundred days in an extended care facility such as a nursing home. It will pay for all covered services for the first twenty days and all but $22.50 a day for up to eighty more days. Patients become eligible for the extended care payments, however, only if

- They need daily skilled nursing or rehabilitation care.
- A doctor determines they need this care and so orders it.
- They have been in a hospital for at least three days in a row before entering the nursing home.
- They are admitted to the nursing home within fourteen days after leaving the hospital.
- They were admitted for further treatment of a condition for which they were in the hospital.

3. Medicare also will pay for up to one hundred home visits by nurses or other health workers from a home-health agency for each benefit period.

Hospital insurance covers the cost of room and meals (including special diets) in semi-private accommodations (two to four bed), regular nursing services, and services in an intensive care unit of a hospital. It also covers the cost of drugs, supplies, appliances, equipment, and any other services ordinarily furnished to hospital or nursing home patients.

Hospital insurance does not cover doctors' bills, private duty nurses, the cost of the first three pints of blood needed, and convenience items such as a telephone or television set.

Medical Insurance (Part B)

The medical part of Medicare also has a deductible feature as well as a coinsurance feature. Basically, the medical insurance pays 80 percent of the reasonable charges after the first $60 in each calendar year. There are four exceptions to this general rule:

1. Laboratory and radiology services by doctors while one is a bed patient in a hospital are paid—without meeting the $60 deductible—at 100 percent of the "reasonable charges."
2. Home health services are covered at 100 percent after the $60 annual deductible.
3. Payment for services of independent physical therapists is limited to a maximum of $80 a year.

4. Payment for physicians' psychiatric services outside a hospital cannot exceed $250 a year.

With the exceptions noted above, medical insurance will cover the following:

1. Physicians' and surgeons' services at home, in the doctor's office, in a clinic, or in a hospital.
2. Outpatient hospital service in an emergency room or an outpatient clinic.
3. Health-home services up to one hundred visits. These visits are in addition to the posthospital visits one gets with hospital insurance.
4. Outpatient physical therapy and speech pathology services.
5. A number of other medical and health services prescribed by the doctor such as diagnostic services; X-ray or other radiation treatments; surgical dressings, splints, casts, braces; artificial limbs and eyes; certain colostomy care supplies; and rental or purchase of durable medical equipment such as a wheelchair or oxygen equipment for use in the home.
6. Certain ambulance services, certain services by chiropractors, and home and office services by independent physical therapists.

In some cases, Medicare covers medical costs incurred outside the United States, but generally this is not the case. If help is needed regarding Medicare, contact the nearest social security field office.

APPENDIX B9

MEDICAID

Since 1966 there has also been a Medicaid program. Medicaid was authorized under a Title 19 of the Social Security Act amendment of that year. It provides for the medical expenses of the indigent regardless of age. It is administered by the states and state funds are involved, although federal matching funds are also available on a 75 percent federal and 25 percent state basis. However, Medicaid is not mandatory; the states must pass enabling legislation. Also, the benefits vary from one state to another, although there are some minimum federal guidelines that the states must adhere to. The Medicaid program is administered by the various state departments of welfare or their equivalent.

Chapter Ten

Property and Liability Insurance

Who and where is the Forgotten Man in this case, who will have to pay for it all?

WILLIAM GRAHAM SUMNER, *THE FORGOTTEN MAN*

The objectives of this chapter are to:

1   Introduce the general concepts of insurance on the home and show how it works through the homeowner's policy

2   Present and explain other types of property and liability insurance on the home

3   Introduce certain other aspects of home insurance

4   Introduce a suggested home insurance program

5   Explore automobile insurance and examine how it works

6   Introduce a possible auto insurance program

7   Briefly outline specialty insurance

Property is subject to physical destruction from a number of hazards. There is the possibility of loss due to fire, flood, theft, and a number of other hazards. Or equally likely is the possibility that a person will destroy or damage somebody else's property. A good example is an automobile accident. Once again we turn to insurance for protection. Property insurance reimburses for the value of destroyed property. A policyholder should have property insurance for both personal and real property. Personal property includes such things as furniture, automobiles, and clothing. Real property includes any buildings attached to land, such as a house or garage.

Liability insurance protects the insured against claims for death or injury suffered by other people. People can be killed or injured on the insured's property and the policyholder is liable for these claims. Liability insurance is also necessary for those who drive automobiles. Automobile accidents too often result in bodily injury as well as property damage.

This chapter covers the following insurance protection:

Home Protection   (Protected by a Homeowner
  a. To protect property   Policy)

b. To protect against liability

Automobile Protection	(Protected by Automobile
a. To protect property	Insurance Policy)
b. To protect against liability	
Miscellaneous	(Protected by Various
	Types of Policies)

Property and liability insurance premium payments should be regarded as payment for the protection of family material assets. For example, the premiums paid on an insurance policy on a home are, in reality, protection in the event of the destruction of the home by fire or some other disaster.

A person who runs over someone with an auto exposes the family assets to loss by lawsuit. Because family assets are exposed to risk of loss, it is the purpose of this chapter to discuss some of these risks and point out how they may be shifted from the individual to an insurance company.

The principle of property and liability insurance is very much like the principle behind term life insurance. The risk of loss is spread over many units, and those few who actually suffer a loss are reimbursed by the insurance company—but indirectly by those policyholders who do not suffer a loss. In the case of fire insurance, the companies know how many homes will burn down each year but, of course, cannot predict which ones. The insurance companies also know how many people will run over somebody, but they do not know who they are.

INSURANCE ON THE HOME

If a home burns down, it could be a financial disaster for the owner. Consequently, a homeowner should have fire insurance. In addition, there are other hazards the homeowner faces that should also be insured against. For example, there could be damages due to wind, flood, smoke, theft, or people running over lawns and shrubs with their cars. Up until a few years ago, the homeowner had to buy a separate policy for protection against each of these hazards. Today, however, most insurance companies sell what they call the homeowner's policy. These policies have become very popular in recent years because they put all the homeowner's insurance needs into one package. Selling just one policy instead of several separate ones reduces the cost to the insurance companies by as much as 20 to 25 percent. These reduced costs are passed on to the homeowner in the form of lower premiums.

Homeowner's Policy

The homeowner's policy provides for four kinds of insurance. They are (1) property insurance on the home, (2) personal property insurance, (3) liability insurance, and (4) medical payment insurance. Generally speaking, the homeowner's policy includes the following protection for property damage:

1. Fire insurance on the house.
2. Extended coverage for such things as damage from wind, hail, falling objects, smoke, motor vehicles, and a number of others. This includes an allowance for additional living expense in the event the homeowner has to live in a motel for a few days.

3. Personal property insurance for loss of personal property due to fire, theft, or mysterious disappearances.

The homeowner's policy also provides the following liability insurance for the homeowner:

1. Personal liability insurance to cover injuries occurring on the homeowner's property.
2. Medical payment insurance to cover medical bills of persons injured on the homeowner's premises.

Most insurance companies have several different types of homeowner's policy packages to choose from. These have been given various names such as limited, basic, broad, all-inclusive, or all-risk. They are referred to as policies HO-1, HO-2, HO-3, and HO-5. The breadth of the extended coverage increases as one moves from policy 1 to policy 5; the premiums, of course, also increase.[1]

Property Insurance

Homeowner's policy HO-1 (basic) covers the fewest items. But it covers a good many more things than just fire. It usually includes damages due to wind, hail, falling objects, and a number of others. In the case of damage to a roof due to hail, however, the basic policy will not pay for the cost of a new roof. Rather, the damaged roof will first be depreciated and then the policy will pay for a lesser amount of damages. For example, if the roof was 10 years old when it was destroyed, and it is assumed it had a useful life of twenty years, the policy will pay for one-half of the cost of a new roof. Generally, under the broad and all-risks (HO-2 and HO-5) policies, the destroyed roof is not first depreciated and the policy pays for the entire cost of a new roof.

While nearly all homeowner's policies cover losses due to theft, in the case of the *broad* and *all-risk* policies, the coverage is more generous. For example, they would pay for what is called mysterious disappearance, whereas the HO-1 would not; that is to say, the HO-1 policy requires proof of theft such as a break-in or the like, whereas the broad or all-risk policy does not.

Some homeowner's policies also provide for living expenses if the homeowner has to move into a hotel because the home has been so severely damaged that it is unlivable. Or if it is a rental home, the fair rental value will be paid while the tenant vacates the home during repairs.

Generally speaking, in most states the HO-2 (broad) policy is the best buy. It costs only slightly more than the HO-1 and provides a good deal more protection. On the other hand, when moving from the HO-2 (broad) to the HO-5 (all-risks) plan, premiums rise substantially while the protection rises only modestly. However, check this out very carefully; what we have said is a generalization that may not be true in your state.

These all-risk plans cover everything except that which is specifically excluded, and that varies from company to company. Generally speaking, however, the all-risk plans do not cover much more than the broad HO-2 form. A typical HO-5 would cover all perils except war, nuclear radiation, earthquake, and flood. Table 10–1 summarizes the perils against which property is insured under the various homeowner's policies.

---

1. There are also homeowner's policies for renters and for condominium owners. They are classified as HO-4 and HO-6, respectively. The HO-1, etc. classification is generally used; however, in Texas and a few other southern states, the HO-A, HO-B, etc. classification is used.

There is also an HO-3 policy which some companies sell. It has some of the features of the HO-1 and the HO-2. It emphasizes personal property protection less than protection on the house. In that sense it is more like basic coverage (HO-1) insofar as personal property is concerned and more like broad coverage (HO-2) insofar as the house is concerned.

TABLE 10–1. PERILS
AGAINST WHICH
PROPERTIES ARE INSURED
(HOMEOWNER'S POLICY)

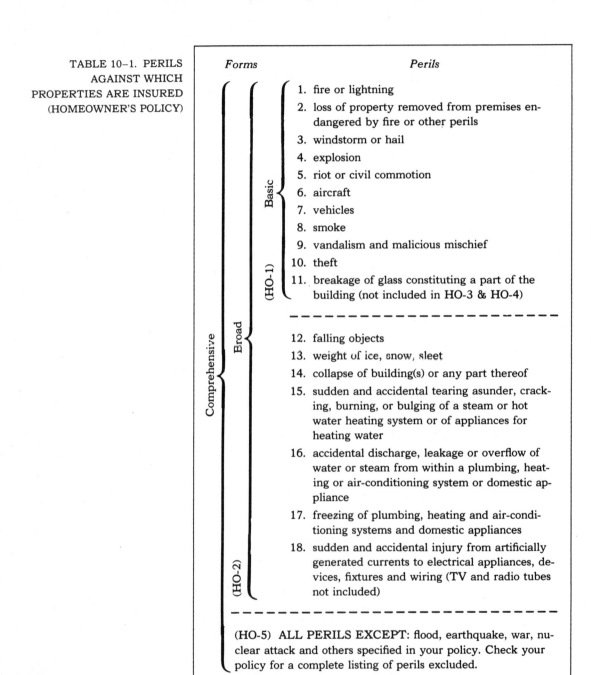

Forms

Perils

Comprehensive

Broad

Basic

(HO-1)

1. fire or lightning
2. loss of property removed from premises endangered by fire or other perils
3. windstorm or hail
4. explosion
5. riot or civil commotion
6. aircraft
7. vehicles
8. smoke
9. vandalism and malicious mischief
10. theft
11. breakage of glass constituting a part of the building (not included in HO-3 & HO-4)

(HO-2)

12. falling objects
13. weight of ice, snow, sleet
14. collapse of building(s) or any part thereof
15. sudden and accidental tearing asunder, cracking, burning, or bulging of a steam or hot water heating system or of appliances for heating water
16. accidental discharge, leakage or overflow of water or steam from within a plumbing, heating or air-conditioning system or domestic appliance
17. freezing of plumbing, heating and air-conditioning systems and domestic appliances
18. sudden and accidental injury from artificially generated currents to electrical appliances, devices, fixtures and wiring (TV and radio tubes not included)

(HO-5) ALL PERILS EXCEPT: flood, earthquake, war, nuclear attack and others specified in your policy. Check your policy for a complete listing of perils excluded.

Personal Property Coverage

Personal property is covered under a homeowner's policy along with real property. This covers such things as loss of furniture, clothing, cameras, rugs, drapes, furs, books, paintings, jewelry, and the like. It provides this protection not only against fire but also against loss due to theft, flood, vandalism, and in some cases mysterious disappearance. This type of policy also insures for loss of items away from the home. For example, a camera stolen from an automobile is covered by the personal property clause. This personal property coverage is written in a number of different ways, but most generally it will reimburse for losses up to 40 percent of insurance coverage carried on the home. If you have a $40,000 homeowner's policy, your personal property maximum protection would be $16,000. Most also have a deductibility clause, which amounts to 1 percent of the insurance carried on the house. That is to say, if the insured suffered a loss of $1,000 to personal property and has a $40,000 homeowner's policy, the insurance company would pay $600.

It is wise to have a written inventory listing all of your personal property and its value. For expensive items such as furs, jewelry, and the like the bills of sale should be kept so that you can prove their value. Photographs are also a good idea. If the value of your personal property exceeds 40 per cent of the value of your house, you may buy separate policy floaters on very valuable items such as furs, jewelry, and works of art. Insuring these items separately will probably reduce the value of your other personal property by about 40 per cent of the value of the house and hence it will be covered by the regular homeowner's policy.

Personal Liability Coverage

The homeowner's policy also provides personal and liability coverage.

The personal liability coverage protects the insured against claims from bodily injury to other people. It also protects against claims for damage to the property of others. The insured is protected against lawsuits because of injuries to others caused by pets, boats, and bicycles. The policy even covers a situation where the insured accidentally strikes another with a golf ball. It will cover any type of accident except automobile accidents and accidents related to business pursuits. For example, if a guest slips on the sidewalk and breaks his or her leg, the homeowner is covered. In the case of property damage, if you are burning leaves in your backyard and the fire spreads and damages your neighbor's house, you are covered. It even covers accidents away from home for which the insured or any member of the household is held responsible. The basic amount of personal liability insurance coverage is $25,000 in most states. However, larger amounts can be purchased. The personal liability policy does not cover employees who are injured while working in the home. If a gardener, maid, or a TV repairperson is injured, they are generally covered by workmen's compensation, not the homeowner's policy.

Medical Payments Insurance

The medical expense coverage generally applies only to accidents that occur in the residence of the homeowner. Medical payments provide reasonable medical expense payments for injuries to people who are injured on the premises of the insured. For example, the medical bills of a person who slips and breaks a leg on the homeowner's sidewalk are paid. The coverage also applies to injuries occurring off the premises of the insured, but only if they were caused by the insured, a member of the insured's family, or their pets. The basic coverage is $500 for each person injured, but larger amounts may be purchased. The coverage is extended only to injuries of others and does not cover the homeowner or members of the family.

Just as in the case of the personal liability clause in a homeowner's policy, the medical payment part of it does not cover employees injured while working in or around the home. In such a case, workmen's compensation also takes over.

Renter's Insurance

Many people who rent rather than own their home feel that they do not need property insurance (other than on their car). This is not true. First of all, they need a personal property floater policy. In addition, renters need a personal liability policy. Even if you are renting a house and the owner has such a personal liability policy, it generally applies only if the landlord is living in the house and it does not always protect the renter. If someone were to trip on the sidewalk and break his or her leg, the renter could be held liable. Most insurance companies sell what they call renter's insurance in one package to cover the above-mentioned items. This is the homeowner's policy for tenants, referred to as HO-4. Many insurance companies have more than one renter's package. That is, renters can choose between basic coverage or for a somewhat higher premium a more generous package similar to the broad coverage discussed above for owner-occupied homes.

Insurance on Condominiums

Some companies have developed a special homeowner's policy (HO-6) that applies to condominiums. Others use the HO-2 (broad) coverage to provide condominium protection. If the HO-6 policy is used, it provides essentially the same protection as the HO-2 plan.

Plain English Policies

In recent years there has been a move to sell policies that are written in language the layman can understand. The legal terminology has been removed and simple phraseology has been developed. These are similar to the various homeowner's policies in the protection they provide, and a person can buy basic, broad, or all-risks type of coverage. Only about twenty states currently have authorized plain-English policies, but they are becoming more popular. These policies are sometimes referred to as HO-76 because they were first introduced in 1976, but this is not an official designation.

Those who favor plain-English policies claim they are clearer and spell out more specifically what they cover; that is, the nonlegal language cannot be interpreted in several different ways. The opponents of plain-English policies maintain that legal language, although more difficult, is also more precise and therefore the traditional policies are less subject to several interpretations.

Separate Individual Policies

As noted above, at one time a separate policy had to be purchased for each hazard: one for fire, one for hail, wind, personal property, liability, etc. That made the total insurance cost more expensive. Today relatively few such policies are sold, but if you want only some of the hazard protection you can buy just that. But check that out very carefully. If you want only fire protection, that alone may cost you less than a homeowner's policy, but if you want coverage for two or three different hazards, you might save by buying a homeowner's policy. You should compare the costs and coverages carefully. Most people need the entire homeowner's package and this should be seriously considered.

Costs (Premiums) of Homeowner's Insurance

Premiums vary with the location of the property and type of construction. Certain areas are more susceptible to damage due to certain natural phenomena. Some areas are wind areas; others are in a hail belt; others, such as Florida and the Gulf Coast, are in the hurricane belt. Consequently, little can be said regarding costs regionally. However, Table 10–2 shows some data for a homeowner's coverage in four different areas.

Within a smaller area classified as having common hazards, rates vary primarily with the type of construction. There are generally three or four classifications and three or four different rates per $1,000 of insurance. However, there is also variation with what is built into the house. If it has central air conditioning and a fireplace, there is more value to be destroyed by fire. If there is a swimming pool, there is a greater hazard to small children. Rates will reflect these factors.

OTHER ASPECTS OF HOME INSURANCE

A number of other important provisions in home insurance policies are discussed below.

Actual Cash Value

One of the important clauses in some of the policies from the homeowner's viewpoint deals with actual cash value. The clause states that the company "does insure to the extent of the actual cash value at the time of the loss." This may mean that although there is a complete destruction of the building, the owner may not necessarily be paid the face value of the policy. It should be noted again that the face value defines the maximum liability of the company. Thus the actual cash value clause means that the company will pay the actual cash value of the building provided, of course, that it does not exceed the face value of the policy. Actual cash value is regarded as the reproduction cost of the building less depreciation.

TABLE 10–2. *Regional premium variation on a homeowner's policy*

CITY	PREMIUMS (ANNUAL RATES)
Boston	$497
Austin, Texas	425
San Francisco	122
Small town in Arizona	182

Note: In all cases the house is a $50,000 home exclusive of the lot. This means, of course, that the house is much more house in Arizona and Texas than it is in Boston or San Francisco. The premiums also include $25,000 coverage on personal property, $25,000 liability coverage, and $10,000 of medical payments coverage. In all cases there is an 80 percent coinsurance clause, and the deductibility is the same in all cases. The construction in all cases is the same: brick veneer. The houses are then the same in all respects except for size. Rates furnished by a large, well-known national company. Rates are as quoted in September 1979 and subject to change due to rising construction costs and other factors over which the insurance industry has no control.

Often, if a market value can be established, it is taken as actual cash value. It should also be noted that some states have laws requiring that in a case where a house is totally destroyed, the face value of the policy must be paid, not the actual cash value, if they are not the same.

Apportionment Clause

The standard policy has an additional clause that is important to the homeowner. It states, "This company shall not be liable for a greater portion of any loss, than the amount hereby insured against shall bear to the entire insurance covering the property against the peril involved, whether collectible or not."

The reason for this clause is that an individual may take out several policies with different companies. For example, a person who has a home valued at $50,000 could conceivably take out a policy with company A in the amount of $30,000 and another with company B in the amount of $20,000. In the light of the pro rata clause, however, company A would be liable only to the extent of three-fifths of any loss and company B to the extent of two-fifths of any loss. This clause also is effective in preventing a homeowner from getting more than the house is worth. If the person had two $30,000 policies on a $50,000 house and it was totally destroyed, each of the companies would pay $25,000.

Coinsurance

Most policies also have a coinsurance clause; it is to discourage the homeowner from having too little insurance on the home. This is a statement that the company shall be liable, in the event of loss, only in the proportion that the actual amount of insurance bears to the insurance theoretically required. The required or "proper" amount of insurance is not 100 percent of the value of the house but usually about 80 percent, although some companies may require 90 percent. This 80 or 90 percent figure, which has been set after years of experience, reflects the fact that relatively few houses are completely destroyed by fire. The purpose of the coinsurance clause is to adjust rates equitably among the various policyholders. Most fires do not result in total loss. Thus in the absence of a coinsurance clause, it might happen that an individual would be able to collect the full amount of the loss without paying much in the way of a premium. For example, suppose a house is valued at $50,000 and a fire policy is placed on it in the amount of only $10,000. A loss occurs in the amount of $5,000, and in the absence of the coinsurance clause, the full $5,000 would be collectible. This award would be unfair to other people who had insured their property for the proper amount and who had therefore been paying higher premiums.

In an 80 percent coinsurance clause, it states, "This company shall not be liable for a greater proportion of any loss or damage to the property described herein than the sum hereby bears to 80 percent of the actual cash value of said property at the time the loss shall happen, nor for more than the proportion which this policy bears to the total insurance thereon." In other words, if you do not carry insurance amounting to 80 percent of the cash value of the property and if a partial loss occurs, you must share that loss with the company. That is to say, you may recover only that proportion of the loss that the amount of insurance you actually have bears to the amount of insurance you should have under the coinsurance clause. This principle has long since been converted into the following formula:

$$\frac{\text{Amount carried}}{\text{Amount should carry}} \times \text{Actual loss} = \text{Recovery}$$

Suppose that the actual cash value of a home is $50,000 and that there is an 80 percent coinsurance clause in the policy. You have insured in the amount of only $33,200, and there is a loss amounting to $5,000. How much of the $5,000 loss can you collect? Substituting in the formula above:

$$\frac{\text{Amount carried (\$33,200)}}{\text{Amount should carry (\$50,000} \times \text{.80 or \$40,000)}} \times \begin{array}{l}\text{Actual loss (\$5,000) =} \\ \text{Recovery of (\$4,150.00)}\end{array}$$

On the other hand, assuming the same set of facts and assuming further that the proper amount of $40,000 of insurance was carried, then:

$$\frac{\$40,000}{\$40,000} \times \$5,000 = \$5,000 = \text{(Recovery)}$$

It should again be emphasized that if a house is totally destroyed by fire, the insurance company will not necessarily pay for the entire value of the house. In most states the company will pay a sum equal to the face value of the policy or the actual cash value of the home, whichever is less. Therefore, if a homeowner has a house with an actual cash value of $50,000 and because of an 80 percent coinsurance clause only carries $40,000 of insurance, that is the maximum the company will pay. If the house is totaled by a fire, the homeowner loses $10,000. The coinsurance clause, then, protects the company against people who buy far less fire insurance than they need but who still are fully protected against a fire that does not totally or nearly totally destroy the house. In order for the homeowner to be fully covered in case a fire totally destroys the house, he or she needs 100 percent coverage. Indeed, many mortgage lenders require the homeowner to buy 100 percent coverage as a condition of making the loan.

It is also wise for the homeowner to reappraise the value of the house occasionally and change the insurance accordingly. The value of houses has risen substantially because of inflation. Many policies provide for an automatic increase yearly.

A HOME INSURANCE PROGRAM

Families who own their own homes should undoubtedly have one of the several available homeowner's policies. This puts all the insurance needs in one package and saves on premiums. Most insurance companies have three different homeowner's policies to choose from. These are usually referred to as basic (HO-1), broad (HO-2), and all-inclusive (HO-5).

If a family does not have much personal property, it might want to consider fire insurance only. It can be purchased as a separate policy rather than with the homeowner's package. However, this would be a rather rare case, and furthermore such a family would still need extended coverage to protect itself from flood, wind, hail, and the like. Also some liability insurance would be needed. For most people, then, the homeowner's policy would be the best. Fire protection is the most important single item and the additional protection obtained under the homeowner's policy is obtained with only a slightly larger premium than what a straight fire insurance policy would cost. Whether the homeowner's policy should be basic, broad, or all-inclusive would be a matter of personal choice. However, probably for most families, the basic plan (HO-1) or the broad coverage (HO-2) would be adequate. Which of the two you select would be determined by your budget and your value judgments. It is true, however, that in many states the HO-2 policy is not much more expensive than the

HO-1 and it provides for quite a bit more protection. If you buy an HO-5 policy, you are paying quite a bit more in premiums for only marginal additional protection.

Renters should consider the homeowner's policy for renters. The alternative would be to buy a straight personal property floater, but this would not provide liability protection for injuries to others on the premises. A renter's policy would provide this protection.

Landlords who own a rental house might want an old-fashioned fire insurance policy with an extended coverage endorsement. Personal property coverage would not be needed if it is an unfurnished house, nor would medical payments coverage be needed. But a landlord would need liability coverage for the rental house. Both the tenant and the landlord need this since most policies cover only one or the other and the provisions are not transferable. Someone who slipped and broke his or her neck on the sidewalk in front of the rental house could sue both the tenant and the owner. Each would need a separate policy; the policy of one would not cover the other. The landlord can buy this as a supplement to this same personal liability protection already owned on the house in which he or she resides. It is usually a little cheaper this way.

There remains the question of how much insurance to buy. This is largely determined by the value of the house. Since most companies have an 80 or 90 percent coinsurance clause, this sets the floor on the amount of insurance. For full protection, however, a person would need to buy a policy with a face value equal to 100 percent of the value of the house. One's own priorities will dictate whether to select 80, 90, or 100 percent coverage.

Remember, too, that as time passes, most homes become more valuable due to inflation. Consequently, in many cases, the insurance on the home needs to be increased.

The amount of liability insurance you need to incorporate into your homeowner's policy will vary, too. The basic amount ($25,000 in most states) is what you will get in most homeowner's policies. You can obtain more than this, but in most cases this is enough. You need less liability insurance for your home than you do for your automobile. This is because there is less danger to guests and passersby. Also few of the injuries are as serious as some injuries caused by autos.

AUTOMOBILE INSURANCE

In recent years there have been many press reports concerning "excessive" awards granted by juries to victims of automobile accidents. Some critics have placed the blame for rising automobile insurance rates directly on plaintiffs' attorneys and easily influenced juries. On the other hand, many individuals have been victimized by insurance company adjusters and insurance company attorneys. It is just as easy to generalize from these injustices as it is from the excessive awards. Then, too, some state laws set an upper limit on the amount a jury may award for an accidental death. Oddly enough, since in most cases no limit is set for injuries, a person can collect more for a broken leg in these states than for a death.

In any event, automobile insurance is important. If an accident is due to the negligent operation of an automobile, the individual can be sued and without insurance a resulting award might prove to be financially disastrous. Automobile insurance can be broken down into four types:

1. Liability insurance, which protects you from lawsuits if you kill or injure someone or damage their property
2. Collision insurance, which reimburses you if your car is damaged
3. Comprehensive insurance, which protects against loss due to fire, theft, wind, hail, and falling objects

4. Medical payment insurance, which will pay the medical expenses of all passengers injured while in your car. Your policy also covers all members of your family while riding in any car.

Liability Insurance: Bodily Injury and Property Damage

This type of policy protects the owner of the car from claims resulting from the negligent operation of an automobile. It covers the owner both from claims resulting from killing or injuring another person or from damaging property. These policies are generally referred to as "five/ten" and "five" policies, "ten/twenty" and "five" policies, "twenty/forty" and "five," and so forth. The first two figures (five/ten or ten/twenty) refer to the bodily liability protection and the last figure to the property damage protection. Both the bodily liability protection and the property protection limits can go way above the limits described above. For example, one can buy $100,000/$300,000—$25,000 coverage.

The figures in a ten/twenty-five policy mean that the policy covers bodily injuries up to $10,000 to any one person and covers bodily injuries up to $20,000 for any one accident injuring two or more persons. For example, if one individual is run over because of the negligent operation of an automobile, then that person can collect a maximum of $10,000 under the terms of the policy. If two or more persons are struck by the auto, the maximum coverage—or to put it another way, the most that the victims can collect—on the policy is $20,000. In those states with financial responsibility laws (see below) the ten/twenty-five policy is the minimum a car owner must have to prove financial responsibility. Regardless of legislative action, a ten/twenty-five policy should be regarded by the individual as a bare minimum. Persons who have acquired wealth should certainly increase their coverage, and indeed many persons today carry $100,000/$300,000–$25,000 policies. The reasoning is clear. Just because you carry insurance in the amount of $5,000 does not mean that this is all that you will be liable for; an individual may obtain a judgment against you for $10,000 or more. In this case, if your coverage is only five/ten, the company will pay $5,000 to the plaintiff and you will be personally liable for the balance.

It should also be noted that the additional premiums required to finance a larger liability policy are not great. Therefore, it is recommended that you place a high priority on liability coverage. Coming up with a dollar figure is difficult, but some experts feel you should have, at least in the case of bodily damage, protection of an amount equal to your net worth. Others would add somewhat more than this to take into account future earnings. The net worth approach is often used because that is what is in danger if a law suit is filed and you don't have insurance protection.

Others feel that the proper amount of liability insurance should be geared to the current pattern of jury award in the geographical area where the insured lives. According to this, you would need more insurance in New York or California, where awards are typically higher than elsewhere. On the other hand, in Mississippi, Arkansas, or North Dakota, you would need less than in most other places. It is also true that sometimes there is no logical pattern to court award and hence it is somewhat arbitrary to determine your liability insurance this way. Nevertheless, a judgment could be based on both patterns of court awards and your net worth.

Collision Insurance

This type of insurance covers damage to the owner's car by reason of collision with another car or with any other object, fixed or movable, and by upset. The policy usually has a deductibility feature and the insurance covers the cost of repairs less the deductibility or the actual car value less the deductibility if the car is totaled. Thus if your car is completely demolished by a collision or by skidding off the road in a snowstorm, the company is liable— but only for an amount equal to the actual value of the automobile less the deductibility.

On some occasions, a car can be repaired after a collision, but the cost of repairing it is greater than the value of the car before the loss. In such a case, the cost of repairs has no bearing on the matter. If the car was valued at $500 before a loss and has a junk value of $100 after the loss, the company is liable only in the amount of $400, although it might cost $1,000 to restore the car to its original condition.

The greatest number of collision policies are issued on new automobiles, since most of the automobile purchases in the nation are made on the installment plan with a finance company or other institution financing the transaction. It is the financial institution that demands that the purchaser be insured. For example, when a bank finances the purchase of a new car, the car itself is used as the collateral for the loan. Then, if the driver runs the car into a telephone pole and wrecks it, the collateral is thereby reduced by an amount equal to the amount of the damages. Consequently, the bank is without collateral and, if the purchaser refused to pay the bank, it would have no other recourse than to sue on a promissory note that it holds; the purchaser might then have insufficient assets with which to pay off the judgment. To protect themselves, the financial institutions demand that the auto be covered by collision insurance.

The deductible feature of a collision policy is written as $50 deductible, $100, $200, $250, $300 and even $1,000 deductible. This means, in the first instance, that the insured will bear the first $50 of loss and the company agrees to pay the balance. Consequently, if there is a loss of $300, under the terms of a $50 deductible policy the insured pays the first $50 of damages and the company is liable in the amount of $250. Naturally, as the amount deductible increases, the premium rates decrease, because the risk of loss to the company is less.

One of the concepts that should be understood in connection with collision insurance is subrogation. Under the terms of the collision policy, the insured agrees that the company shall have the legal right to proceed against a negligent third party causing the loss and to prove damages in the name of the insured. The company has the right to step into the shoes of the insured, as it were, to proceed against a person causing the loss, and the insured agrees to cooperate fully with the company. For example, suppose a person is parked in a legal manner and another person driving negligently hits the parked car, causing damages in the amount of $500; assume that the insured has a $50 deductible collision policy. The company will pay the insured $450 and, under the terms of the policy, may commence a lawsuit against the negligent party to cover the $450 plus the $50 deductible. The insured person may in this manner recover his or her $50 out-of-pocket costs because the total amount of the suit will be $500.

Comprehensive Insurance

The comprehensive automobile insurance policy covers nearly all perils, with the exception of collision or upset and liability. Protection is given for any direct and accidental loss or damage to the automobile covered, as well as damage to the equipment usually attached to the vehicle. In addition, of course, the automobile is covered for fire and theft. The important clause from the point of view of the insured states that the company shall be liable for "breakage of glass, and other loss caused by missiles, falling objects, fire, theft, explosion, earthquake, windstorm, hail, water, flood, malicious mischief or vandalism, riot, or civil commotion." In short, the insurance policy governs nearly all sorts of damage, including malicious mischief, smoke, sprays, acids, abnormal tides, damage from rain, snow, and the like.

The company limits its maximum liability to the actual cash value at the time of the loss. Although it has the option of repairing or replacing the damaged property, its maximum obligation is still limited to the actual cash value.

Most of the comprehensive policies are written with a deductible provision. Generally, this amounts to a $25 or $100 deductible, meaning that the company will pay the amount over whatever the deductible may be.

One of the interesting coverages often put into some comprehensive policies is a clause providing for rental reimbursement for loss of use by theft. In this case, insured persons are paid, within limitations, for a vehicle that they may rent if their car is stolen. In fact, there is no liability on the part of the company until seventy-two hours after the theft has been reported *both* to the company and to the police. Then the company becomes liable only for amounts actually disbursed by the insured, usually up to a limit of so much per day, with an overall aggregate liability. Of course, as soon as the car has been located, regardless of its condition, the liability on the part of the company terminates.

Rates on a comprehensive policy vary with the region where one lives, and they are based on the past experience of loss. Rates in big cities tend to be higher than in smaller towns or in rural areas because of the greater likelihood of vandals slashing tires, etc. In certain rural areas of Colorado and Kansas, however, the lack of vandals is more than offset by the existence of hail or a combination of wind and dust, both of which will take the paint off a car. Indeed, rates on all automobile insurance vary regionally. Rates are generally higher in big cities than in small towns because the accident rate is higher.

Medical Payments Insurance

The basic endorsement calling for medical payments states that a company will pay within specified monetary limits, generally from $500 to $3,000, "all reasonable expenses incurred within one year from the date of the accident for necessary medical, surgical and dental services, including prosthetic devices, and necessary ambulance, hospital, professional nursing and funeral services" to persons injured "while in or upon, or entering into or alighting from the automobile . . . of the insured."

In recent years an extended medical payments insurance has appeared that in addition covers injuries as a result of "being struck, knocked down or run over by an automobile," or injured in a collision. If persons have this insurance, then they and their family are covered while riding in someone else's auto, or as a pedestrian, on a bicycle, or in any other way. People riding in the policyholder's car are also covered.

The rates for this endorsement are quite low but vary with location and amount of coverage.

No-Fault Insurance

Recently a great deal of interest has been generated in no-fault auto insurance for bodily injuries. Under no-fault insurance, the victim's insurance company will pay regardless of who is at fault. The insurance company can then sue the other driver or his or her insurance company. The idea is that often much time and money is saved by avoiding going to court. This is particularly true if it is not clear who is at fault.

At the present time about twenty-four states have some variation of no-fault laws on their books. However, there is no general agreement regarding what is meant by no-fault insurance. The purists would insist that true no-fault would bar tort lawsuits for minor injuries. The injured party would be required to accept payment for injuries and not be permitted to sue.

The injured party would receive payments from his or her insurance company to compensate for these three types of losses:

1. Income lost while injured
2. Medical and hospital bills
3. Expenses incurred in hiring maids and others to perform services formerly performed by the victim.

There is, however, an upper limit on the amount of lost income which could be recovered, and this varies from state to state, but often is about $5,000. Most states also set an upper limit on the amount of medical and hospital expenses that could be recovered (and this varies), but some states do not have a limit on this item. Finally, the limit that all states have on the recovery of expenses incurred in hiring help to perform certain tasks for the victim varies by states. For loss of life, loss of limb, or for losses exceeding the maximums, lawsuits would be permitted and no-fault would not apply. About sixteen states have such no-fault legislation on the books.

There are about eight states that have variations of no-fault laws. These states would permit no-fault settlements on a voluntary basis. The injured parties could sue for damages in any and all cases, even for minor injuries; but if they waived this right, the law would require that damages be paid regardless of who was at fault.

No-fault insurance does not apply to commercial vehicles, nor, generally speaking, does it apply to property damages.

Since only about one half of the states have no-fault insurance, there are numerous cases in which a driver from a non-no-fault (tort) state has an accident in a no-fault state with a driver covered by no-fault insurance, and vice versa. In such a case the no-fault driver is paid by his or her insurance company. Then that company and the other driver's insurance company settle the other driver's claim in the usual way. For example, if a Massachusetts driver (no-fault) has an accident in Texas (non-no-fault), the Massachusetts driver's claims are paid by his or her insurance company. This is because most no-fault policies are valid in all states. Then the Texas driver and his or her insurance company and the Massachusetts company settle the claim in the usual way, either amicably out of court or in court if necessary. If a Texas driver has an accident in Massachusetts, exactly the same procedure is followed.

The advocates of no-fault insurance maintain that under it not only are settlements for injuries made more quickly, but they are more certain. Indeed, they are almost automatic. Under a tort (or fault) system usually lengthy legal battles must be fought. Also if the victim was partly at fault, the doctrine of contributory negligence prevents a settlement. Proponents also argue average no-fault settlements would often result in the victim's getting more because there would be no court costs or attorney's fees to dilute the settlement. Under the tort system, less than one half of the liability insurance premium dollar is returned to the accident victim, according to a U.S. Department of Transportation study. Finally, proponents believe that no-fault saves a lot of time and money for the insurance companies, not only in the form of court costs and attorney's fees, but in administrative expenses as well. This in turn could reduce insurance premiums.

The opponents of no-fault say it is unfair in that it allows no settlement for pain and suffering or mental anguish. They also argue that by allowing damages automatically, many people who don't deserve them get them. (Presumably there are people who were at fault and have themselves caused, or at least contributed to, their injuries.) This, opponents say, increases insurance company costs and results in higher premiums.[2]

OTHER ASPECTS OF AUTOMOBILE INSURANCE

Here is some additional material on automobile insurance with which you should be familiar.

Financial Responsibility Laws

A few states have compulsory insurance laws and many others have laws concerning financial responsibility even though they have no compulsory insurance laws. Financial responsibility means simply that when an accident occurs, the state requires the individual to post a bond or its equivalent. The term "bond" is usually taken to mean cash or high-grade securities in the amount of the estimated damages. As a substitute for the bond, individuals may prove that they are "financially responsible" by proving that they are adequately insured. There is here no question of who was right or wrong in the accident; individuals must prove financial responsibility whether they were right or wrong.

The purpose of financial responsibility laws is to protect the victims of automobile accidents. The law attempts to do this by encouraging people to have at least the minimum amount of insurance and in this way increase the probability of the victim being able to collect to compensate for the damages.

While the purpose of financial responsibility laws is admirable, in some states these laws are ineffective either because of court ruling or poor enforcement. In others they work fairly well. For example, in some states, the car registration of motorists who fail to prove financial responsibility is withdrawn. In some states, it is common practice for the state police merely to remove the license plates from the vehicle, and the motorist is prohibited from driving it until they are returned.

The Uninsured Motorist Endorsement

Most states now require companies to offer policyholders the uninsured motorist endorsement for a slight extra premium. The uninsured motorist endorsement is quite simple and relatively inexpensive. It states that if you are injured as the result of an accident with an uninsured and negligent motorist or by a hit-and-run driver, your company will in effect insure that uninsured motorist for the "basic sum" in accordance with the laws of the state. The term "basic sum" is the minimum amount of bodily liability insurance sold. In most states this is ten/twenty, but in some it is five/ten. If your policy has this endorsement, your own insurance company pays you. But generally only for bodily injuries and no more than the basic sum. A few companies, however, will also pay a collision claim under the uninsured motorist endorsement if you have a collision policy with them.

It should be pointed out that your insurance company, after it pays you, has the right to sue the other motorist to recover what they paid. But in practice this is often difficult

2. Both sides maintain that their system would result in lower premiums. Neither side's case can be proven. The coming of no-fault insurance has not reduced premiums; indeed they have soared in recent years. However, much of this is attributable to inflation. A comparison of premiums in no-fault and tort states shows no discernible pattern.

because the uninsured motorist probably has no assets either. Or if the driver injures someone without stopping, there is little the company can do unless he or she is subsequently apprehended.

Assigned Risk Plans

With the development of financial responsibility requirements assigned risk plans were also developed to make financial responsibility possible. Liability insurance is one way of showing financial responsibility, but some drivers find it difficult to obtain insurance because of their driving record. Consequently, assigned risk plans were developed to take care of these people. A number of years ago when these plans were first set up, the companies got together and set up a pool. Then the companies all issued some policies to these higher risk drivers. The idea was that if the assigned risks were spread over all of the companies, none of them would have an excessive amount. In some states it is still done this way, in others more informal methods are used to spread these risks over all companies. The amount of insurance the assigned risks may buy is limited to the basic sum which varies from state to state but in most often ten/twenty bodily liability and five for property liability. In virtually all cases, the drivers who are assigned risks have to pay a much higher premium for their insurance than other drivers.

Preferred Risks

In a real sense, the preferred risk is the opposite of the assigned risk and came about as the result of competition among companies. In spite of the financial responsibility laws, many buyers, particularly in those parts of the country where rates are exceedingly high, began doing without insurance or purchasing only the minimum policies, such as a ten and twenty policy or even a five and ten policy in some states. Consequently, in order to increase their share of the market, some companies began issuing preferred risk policies at a lower rate, and other companies soon followed. In short, as a reward for safe driving the rate is lowered. As far as the company is concerned, the lowered rates are given only to selected risks, those who have had a safe record for a number of years.

In addition, some companies emphasize that they specifically will sell insurance only to nondrinking drivers, and that because of this they can charge lower premiums.

Insurance Rates and Costs

Rates vary from one section of the country to another. This is, in part, because juries typically grant larger awards in some areas. The price level (inflation) is also higher in some sections of the country than in others. Rates may also vary within any geographic region; generally they are higher in big cities than in small towns. The table below shows some of this regional variation in terms of one national company.

Rates also vary somewhat with the age and sex of the driver. Male drivers under age 25 pay a higher premium because they have a higher accident rate. In some states if you are under 25 and married, you get somewhat of a reduction from the general under-25 rate. Your driving record may also affect your rate. In some states if you have had several (the number varies from state to state but two to four is most common) moving traffic violations, your rates may be pushed above the regular rate. This is true even if you have had no accidents. If you have had an accident, and you got a ticket because of it, your rate could be adjusted upwards even more. On the other hand, some companies reduce rates below regular rates for those drivers between age 30 and 60 who have good driving records. The age

TABLE 10–3. *Regional auto insurance premium variations (semiannual premiums)*

	100/300/25	COLL. $200 DED.	COMP. $100 DED.	MEDS $2,000
Boston	129.00	224.00	158.00	3.75
Austin, Tx.	66.00	58.00	43.00	7.00
San Francisco	199.50	180.30	38.20	11.90
Mesa, Arizona	70.00	51.40	19.00	8.60

Notes: In all cases the cars are used only for pleasure and no driver is under twenty-five. The rates are for September 1979 and subject to change at any time due to inflation, larger court awards, rising auto repair prices, and other factors beyond the control of the insurance industry. Rates furnished by a large, well-known national company. The rates apply to 1979 Chevrolet purchased in October 1979 for $7,500 and are semi-annual rates.

range 30 to 60 is dependent on the theory that drivers under 30 are less cautious than those over 30, and that the reflexes of drivers over 60 have slowed down. Finally, rates on collision and comprehensive coverage vary with the type of auto as well as the factors noted above. The more expensive the auto, the more expensive the insurance.

While rates vary from place to place, and with differences among drivers, they are rising rapidly all over. Some attribute this to general inflation; others to more generous jury awards; still others to more costly cars that are more difficult (and hence costly) to repair. Rates vary from company to company even within a region and therefore you should shop around when buying insurance. However, it is also true that not all companies are equally prompt and fair in making settlement. Consequently you should give this factor some weight when choosing a company.

In some states auto insurance pays dividends just like life insurance, and these dividends vary. In some states rates are tightly controlled by state regulatory commissions; in others there is more competition. In many states the companies set rates which are then subject to approval by the state regulatory agencies. Some critics maintain that the regulatory agencies contribute to higher rates by protecting the weaker companies.

Lately critics have suggested certain reforms they feel will reduce rates or at least halt the upward trend. The following reforms have been suggested:

1. Mass marketing through group plans.
2. Better no-fault auto insurance laws.
3. Open rating (a system in which insurance companies would set their own rates rather than rely on the regulatory agencies).

This it is hoped would result in more competition and generate downward price pressure.

How Much Liability Insurance?

A person should certainly have liability insurance; this is almost a must. The question is how much to have? There is no hard and fast answer to this question; it must, in part, be a personal value judgment. However, as we noted above, your net worth is what you are protecting. Hence this is the place to begin. You might also give some weight to your future earnings and future increase in net worth. If there is a pattern of court settlements in your area for seriously injured or killed automobile victims, give that some weight. It should be noted that rates do not rise rapidly as the amount of liability insurance purchased increases over the basic five/ten-five unit.

How Much Collision Insurance?

Should you have collision insurance, and if so how large a deductible feature should you have? The answers depend upon the value of your car, how much you drive, where you drive, and the kind of driver you are. These factors cannot all be measured mathematically.

Once a car depreciates below a given figure, collision insurance should be dropped. The more you drive the more likely you are to have an accident; hence give this some weight. If you drive mostly in the country or small towns, the likelihood of an accident is less than if you live in a city and drive there, especially on the freeway. Only you know what kind of driver you are, hence only you can judge this point. But if you drive defensively, you do not need insurance as much (or can live with a higher deductibility) as would be the case if you drove offensively. Premiums on collision insurance vary regionally as well as with the value of the car. You should calculate the annual premium plus the deductibility as a percent of your car's value. We will have more to say about this later. Remember this percent will go up as you increase the deductibility, and this is a good way to save money. This ratio may also go up as your car becomes older and loses its value. Check with your agent to see what your saving would be if you increased your deductibility.

If you can reduce your premiums by $75 or $80 per year by increasing your deductibility from say $100 to $300, you will save money by doing so if you have an accident less frequently than about every three years. Also if you are an average driver and have a wreck, there is about a fifty-fifty chance it will be the other person's fault and his or her insurance company will pay. This improves the odds; now the $75 you save per year will finance the $200 additional deductibility about every year and a half. If you are quite sure you won't have an accident very often, you might want to consider a $500 or even a $1000 deductibility. Depending upon where you live and how expensive a car you have, you can save from $100 to $200 per year in premiums by choosing a $500 deductibility.

When to drop your collision insurance completely is a more difficult question. But once the annual premiums plus the deductibility together amount to a substantial percentage of the value of the car, you should consider dropping it. For example, suppose your car is worth $1000 and you have a $100 deductibility policy with an annual premium of $100. If the car were totaled, your out-of-pocket cost would be $200 (the premium plus the deductibility). You in a sense are paying $200 to protect $800 of property (the car's value of $1000 less $200 out-of-pocket cost). This ratio is 25 percent and you should consider dropping your collision insurance. Your car will continue to decline in value as the years pass (your premiums may too but probably by less). With the above ratio of 25 percent, if you totaled your car less than every four years, you would be better off to drop the collision insurance. This is especially true because, as noted above, the odds are improved by the fact that there is the possibility that the other driver's insurance will pay off.

How Much Comprehensive Insurance?

You should decide your comprehensive needs in the same way you decide your collision needs. See how much money you can save by raising your deductibility to say $100. On a new car you will want some comprehensive. As the car gets older, you will have to decide when the cost of protecting your property is costing more than its worth, giving some weight to how often you are likely to have a claim.

Medical Insurance and Uninsured Motorist Endorsement

Medical insurance is not expensive and you should seriously consider it. The same is true of the uninsured motorist endorsement. This also reimburses you for injuries suffered at the hands of a hit-and-run motorist even if he or she is not apprehended.

MISCELLANEOUS AND SPECIALTY INSURANCE

There are a number of other types of insurance with which one should be familiar. Some of these fall in the category of property insurance, some into liability, and some into specialty. Some of it is a bit unusual. A number of companies sell unusual insurance. We have all heard of Lloyd's of London, who will insure prospective parents against having twins or triplets. Less unusual is insurance on the hands of a pianist or a professional football quarterback. A singer, or for that matter a college professor, can get insurance on his or her voice. Lloyd's also sells what they call livestock mortality insurance. This is really term insurance on farm animals. Indeed, Lloyd's will sell insurance on almost anything. The bulk of Lloyd's insurance in the United States, however, is the extrahazardous insurance that most American companies do not solicit. Examples are fire insurance on expensive buildings and equipment located outside of any town and far away from any fire-fighting equipment.

Boat Insurance

One can hardly venture out on the open highway nowadays without seeing someone whiz past towing a boat. Consequently, there is both a growing need for and a concomitant growth in the number of insurance policies issued against a boating loss. These policies are designed first to protect against loss of boating equipment and second to protect against possible personal liability. The first category protects against such hazards as fire, theft, sinking, collision, capsizing, explosion, windstorm, hail, submerged objects, vandalism, and lightning. The policies, written in much the same manner as the automobile collision policy, are generally written as either $50, $100, $200, or $500 deductible policies.

In addition to the loss of equipment, the policies are also written to cover personal liability such as ramming a swimmer, injuring passengers as the result of a fire aboard your own boat, and ramming another boat with resulting personal injury to the persons aboard that vessel. The policies are generally written with a limit of $10,000 to $25,000, but go higher at an extra cost.

Trip Insurance

Most of these policies are a package that includes some term life insurance and some medical insurance. The life insurance could cover a person for all accidental deaths while on the trip or (at a reduced premium) just accidental deaths occurring while on the airplane, in or around the airport, or in a limousine going to or coming from the airport. Some are written so that if the insured is killed while in a common carrier he or she gets a certain amount, and somewhat less if killed while on the trip but not in a common carrier.

Most of these policies also have a medical insurance feature that pays up to 5 percent of the principal sum for medical bills due to an accident (but not due to an illness). There are a few exclusions regarding the medical insurance; for example, medical bills due to a skiing or hunting accident are not covered.

Generally these trip policies can be purchased in values from $5,000 to $300,000. The person who travels a lot may want to purchase continuous trip protection, which is available and which provides the same protection described above for any trips during the year, rather than purchasing it separately for each trip.

Crop Insurance

In the western states, specialized insurance companies sell crop insurance. Rates vary regionally and are so much per acre, based on past hail damage experience. But crop insurance can be obtained only if sufficient historical weather information exists to establish premium rates with actuarial accuracy.

Malpractice Insurance

Malpractice insurance primarily protects doctors and nurses against personal liability damage suits arising out of actual or alleged professional carelessness, but in recent years lawyers and accountants have been buying it in increasing numbers. This type of insurance is sold by some fire and casualty companies.

Malpractice insurance used to be quite cheap but this has changed in some states recently. Because of a changing legal philosophy, not only are larger awards now being made in malpractice suits, but in addition the courts have been more liberal in making awards. In some states even hospitals have lost their immunity from lawsuit. Consequently, in malpractice suits in those states both the doctor and the hospital are sued. California and New York are two states in which more and larger awards have been granted recently. As a result, malpractice insurance rates are very high in those states. Nevertheless, most doctors and nurses feel they have to have this kind of protection. However, due to its high costs some doctors have dropped it in recent years. This is called going naked. In other cases, medical societies or groups of doctors have formed their own insurance pool. Each of them puts so much into a kitty each month, which is then used to aid those doctors who are sued. This is really self-insurance.

Group Legal Insurance

Some experts believe that before too long insurance to pay for legal fees will be available on a group basis. Even today a few people have such protection but generally it is financed through a labor union, credit union, or other organization; insurance companies are not yet involved.

Generally, a contract is negotiated between a group and a law firm, which provides certain legal services free to the individual members of the group. The group pays the fees, and the individuals pay them indirectly through higher dues or some other such method. But it is using the insurance principle by spreading the legal fees of the few unfortunate enough to get into trouble actuarially over large numbers.

Major lawsuits are not covered, but such things as divorce, drafting of wills, minor disputes with landlords or finance companies, disagreements with retail merchants, and minor traffic violations are handled. In many cases relatively small sums of money are involved, and most persons are reluctant to spend money on attorney's fees (and possible court costs). The result is they often pay any claim made or represent themselves in court and invariably lose.

QUESTIONS FOR REVIEW

1. What coverage can be had from the personal liability policy?

2. What is the homeowner's policy?

3. What is the nature of the coverage one receives from a personal property coverage under the homeowner's policy?

4. What is the purpose of the apportionment clause in a fire insurance policy?

5. What is meant by coinsurance? Is a 90 percent coinsurance clause superior to an 80 percent clause? Explain why or why not.

6. If someone were to say that he or she had a "ten/twenty" automobile policy, what would he or she mean?

7. Explain the difference between liability insurance, collision insurance, and comprehensive insurance as it applies to a car.

8. What is no-fault auto insurance? What benefits are claimed for it? Is there general agreement regarding what is meant by no-fault insurance?

9. In general, explain the financial responsibility laws as they appear on the statute books of those states having such laws.

10. Discuss the uninsured motorist endorsement, bringing out how it works.

11. What is meant by "basic sum" of insurance?

12. What is an assigned risk pool?

13. What are preferred risks?

14. How are automobile insurance rates determined?

15. Discuss the reforms that have been suggested for the fire and casualty insurance companies.

16. Discuss property insurance programming.

CASES

1. Peter Green has a home valued at $40,000, and a few years ago he bought a homeowner's policy on it with an 80 percent coinsurance clause. Many of his friends have told him 80 percent is not enough and that he should have at least 90 percent. Do you agree? Explain why or why not.

2. Tom Singer is a traveling salesman who rents an apartment that, because of the nature of his work, is often unoccupied. Tom keeps a good many valuable personal items in it, and he is afraid of fire and theft. Can you give him advice with respect to insurance coverage?

3. Jim and Jean Sargeant have two cars—a brand-new Ford and a ten-year-old Plymouth. Jean does not think they should spend money on insurance for their old car but is willing to pay for complete coverage of the new. Jim is not so sure. Can you explain Jim's reasoning? Jean's?

4. Carolyn Roundtree has a year-old car and carries $10,000/$20,000 liability insurance, $5,000 property damage, some comprehensive, and collision with $100 deductible. Is this a wise policy? Carolyn thinks her rates are high. Can you show her how to reduce them? Carolyn's sister believes she should carry more liability insurance. Do you agree?

5. Joan Rider has just purchased a $4,000 Ford Maverick sedan. She will use it to drive to and from her job and also for pleasure. She expects to drive about twelve thousand miles per year, and she has financed the car at the local bank where she keeps her checking account. Help her work out an insurance program on her car; advise her what kind of coverage she should get and how much.

6. Wanda Williams of western Walla Walla, Washington, worked as a willing worker at the Workington Western Westport Welding Works while working her way through Witman Col-

lege in western Walla Walla, Washington. She will need to buy a car but will use it only to drive to and from work. She also will need to finance it. Advise her about what kind of car to buy and what financing arrangements are available. Also, decide if she should buy insurance on her car.

SUGGESTED READINGS

Analysis of Automobile No-Fault Statutes. General Adjustment Bureau, Inc., 123 William Street, New York, N.Y. 10038.

Athearn, James L. *Risk and Insurance,* 2nd ed. Englewood Cliffs, N.J.: Prentice-Hall, 1977.

Best's Review, Property-Liability Edition. Published monthly by A. M. Best Company, Inc., Oldwick, N.J. 08858.

Casualty Insurance Handbook. New York: Insurance Information Institute.

CPCU Journal. Published quarterly by the Society of Chartered Property and Casualty Underwriters (CPCU), Kahler Hall, Providence Road, Malvern, PA 19355.

Family Guide to Property and Liability Insurance. Published by the Insurance Information Institute, 110 Williams Street, New York, N.Y. 10038.

Gillespie, Paul, and Klipper, Miriam. *No-Fault; What You Save, Gain, and Lose With the New Auto Insurance.* New York: Praeger, 1972.

Greene, Mark. *Risk and Insurance.* Cincinnati: Southwestern, 1977.

Magee, J. H. *Property and Liability Insurance.* Homewood, Ill.: R. D. Irwin, Inc. 1974.

Mehr, Robert I., and Cammack, Emerson. *Principles of Insurance.* Homewood, Ill.: Richard D. Irwin, 1980.

Riegel, Robert; Miller, Jerome S.; and Williams, C. Arthur, Jr. *Insurance Prnciples and Practices: Property and Liabilities,* 6th ed. Englewood Cliffs, N.J.: Prentice-Hall, 1976.

Risk Management. Published monthly by the Risk and Insurance Management Society, Inc., 205 East 42nd Street, New York, N.Y. 10017.

"Speed Kills." *1973 Book of Street and Highway Accident Data.* Hartford, CT: The Travelers Insurance Company.

Statutes Affecting Liability Insurance; a Digest of State Statutes Relating to Negligence Actions and Liability Insurance Coverage, 15th ed. New York: American Insurance Association, 1974.

"Voice Behind the Wheel." *1971 Book of Street and Highway Accident Data.* Hartford, CT: The Travelers Insurance Company.

Chapter Eleven

Social Security, Annuities, and Other Pension Plans

The law locks up the common thief who steals the common's goose, but lets the greater felon loose who steals the commons from the goose.

The objectives of this chapter are to

1. Introduce social security and explain who is covered by it

2. Examine the social security tax structure, which finances social security benefits

3. Note how a person builds up social security protection

4. Help you estimate what your social security benefits will be

5. Introduce life insurance annuities and explain how they work

6. Examine a number of different annuities

7. Present pension plans and outline how they work

8. Discuss certain other individual retirement programs available to those who do not have a regular pension plan.

INTRODUCTION

This chapter deals with retirement income. Social security, private insurance annuities, and certain pension plans are the trinity of retirement programming. Virtually everyone has social security. It must be supplemented in order to provide a decent retirement income. Some people have various assets such as securities, real estate, and the like which provide some income. Others have life insurance annuities, corporate pension plans, or one of the various individual retirement plans. It is these that will be discussed in this chapter.

SOCIAL SECURITY

Social Security was established in the 1930s, and over the years the Social Security Act has been amended to cover more and more people, and to provide for more benefits. However, some of its provisions are administered by the state and local governments. At the present time the act provides for the following programs:

Administered by the federal government:

1. Old-age retirement
2. Survivors' benefits
3. Disability insurance
4. Medicare

Administered by the state and local governments:

1. Unemployment insurance
2. Public welfare

We shall not discuss unemployment insurance or public welfare because these vary a great deal from state to state. The federal program, however, will be discussed.

Who is Covered?

Almost everyone in the labor force, including the self-employed, is included under social security; this also includes members of the armed forces. Today the only exceptions are federal employees, some state and local employees, and ministers and other members of religious orders who file a form stating they are conscientiously opposed to receiving social security benefits because of religious convictions. Federal employees have their own separate retirement system. State and local employees may join social security, but it is voluntary. They may also drop out of social security. The group as a whole must vote and if the group is in favor of joining, all members of that group must join. A single individual cannot opt out. Most state and local employees have joined, but some are having second thoughts. Indeed, a few groups have dropped out. The question immediately arises, what happens to the benefits built up by state and local employees, if they decide to drop out of the program? If they are fully covered (generally 40 quarters or 10 years are needed to be fully covered, as is explained in greater detail below), they return their vested interest and will receive benefits when they reach retirement age. If they are not fully covered they lose whatever has been built up on their behalf. However, all members that drop out will lose their disability benefits 5 years after they drop out, because the law requires that to receive disability benefits the person must have been paying social security tax in 5 of the last 10 years prior to the disability.

Social Security Taxes

Everyone under social security must pay social security taxes (also called payroll taxes). In 1981 this was 6.65 percent on the first $29,700 of earnings. This is matched by the employer, and the sum is paid to the Social Security Administration.

The self-employed pay a higher tax because there is no matching contribution. Currently the self-employment tax is 9.30 percent on the first $29,700 of income. Part of the social security tax is earmarked to finance Medicare, and the remainder finances retirement benefits, disability benefits, and survivors' benefits.

Both the social security tax and the base income to which it is applied are scheduled to rise in future years in accordance with a law already passed by Congress. The income base (taxable wage) will be adjusted upwards to take into account average wage level increases throughout the U.S. The table below shows the increase in the tax rate. Since social security taxes are withheld through payroll deductions, they are automatically stopped when the maximum base income is reached. However, if you have two or more employers, you may have a tax withheld in excess of the maximum because each employer is required to withhold the maximum amount. If so, you can get it back by taking it as a credit against your personal income tax when you file your annual return.

Building Protection; Quarters of Coverage

In order to build up social security benefits you must earn what are called quarters of coverage. Formerly, a person received a quarter of coverage for every three months during which he or she paid social security taxes. That has been changed. Today a person receives one quarter of coverage for every $290.00 of earned income on which he or she pays social security taxes. Therefore, four quarters of coverage, the maximum which may be earned for the year, are obtained in any year during which you pay social security taxes on $1,160.00 of earned income. (Income from dividends, interest, rent, or capital gains are not subject to social security taxes and hence do not count.) It does not matter when during the year you earn this $1,160.00; even if you earn it all in one day you will receive four quarters of coverage. After 1980 this base will be adjusted upwards to take into account average wage level increases as well as increases in the cost of living.

Quarters of coverage are important because this is what determines whether you are eligible to receive benefits. The amount of benefits is determined by your income while employed, as will be shown below. That is, there is a loose and indirect connection between what a person earns (and pays in the form of social security taxes) and benefits received.

TABLE 11–1. *Social security taxes*

YEAR	TAXABLE WAGE	EMPLOYED		SELF-EMPLOYED	
		Tax rate	Maximum tax	Tax rate	Maximum tax
1978	$17,700	6.05%	$1,070.85	8.10%	$1,433.70
1979	$22,900	6.13%	$1,403.77	8.10%	$1,854.90
1980	$25,900	6.13%	$1,587,67	8.10%	$2,097.90
1981	$29,700	6.65%	$1,975.05	9.30%	$2,762.10
1982	$32,700	6.70%	———	9.35%	———
1983	$35,700	6.70%	———	9.35%	———
1984	$39,600	6.70%	———	9.35%	———
1985	$43,500	7.05%	———	9.90%	———
1986	———	7.15%	———	10.00%	———
1987	———	7.15%	———	10.00%	———
1988	———	7.15%	———	10.00%	———
1989	———	7.15%	———	10.00%	———
1990	———	7.65%	———	10.75%	———

Source: U.S. Department of Health, Education & Welfare, Social Security Administration

Note: By law, the social security tax base will rise to $29,700 in 1981. After that, unless Congress changes the law, the taxable wage will be increased automatically every year to take into account average wage-rate increases in the U.S. The figures shown for 1982–1985 are official HEW projections of expected increases.

The number of quarters of coverage needed to qualify for social security benefits varies with the year in which you become 62, in the case of retirement benefits, and with the age when you die or become disabled in the case of those benefits. These variations range from a minimum of 30 quarters to a maximum of 40 for retirement benefits, and 6 to 40 quarters in case of survivors' or disability benefits.

To calculate the quarters of coverage you need to qualify permanently for social security retirement benefits, work through the following three steps.

1. Take the year in which you were born
2. Add 62 to it
3. Subtract 1951 from the result

For example

$$
\begin{array}{r}
1923 \\
+62 \\
\hline
1985 \\
-1951 \\
\hline
34 \\
\end{array} = \text{quarters of coverage needed.}
$$

Social Security Trust Funds; What Happens to Money Collected?

Social security taxes go into a special social security trust fund. The monies are then invested in a special issue of U.S. government securities. In this way the money earns interest. Since social security taxes flow into the fund and social security benefits flow out of the trust fund, in any one year the fund may be built up or depleted. In recent years the fund has been depleted to the extent that Congress raised taxes drastically in 1977.

A few years ago Congress created several new trust funds; there is now a separate one for disability payments, hospital benefits, and medical benefits. The figure below illustrates these trust funds which had total assets of $45.13 billion as of January, 1980,[1] the latest figures available. It should be noted that the social security taxes that you pay are not earmarked to pay your benefits when you retire. Rather they are commingled and are used to pay benefits to those presently retired. Later when you are retired, the members of the labor force at that time will be paying social security taxes which will be used to provide for your benefits. In this way an inter-generation transfer takes place.

The Wage Statement Request

Once a year anyone may check his or her records by filling out a wage statement request, as illustrated in Figure 11-2, and sending it to the social security office in Baltimore, Maryland. The complete address is Social Security Administration, P.O. Box 57, Baltimore, Maryland 21203. This should be done at least every three years because that is the limit for correcting errors. A wage statement request card can be obtained from any social security district office and there is one in all large cities. Look in the telephone directory under United States government for the address and phone number of the field office nearest you.

When you hear from the social security headquarters, you can check their figures with

1. *Social Security Bulletin*, June, 1980.

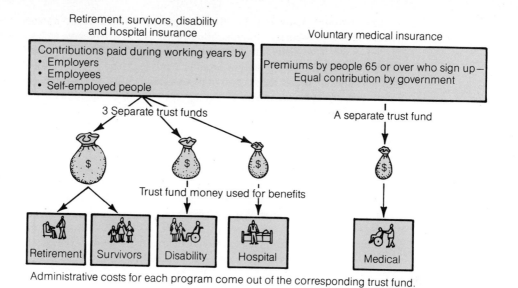

Retirement, survivors, disability and hospital insurance

Contributions paid during working years by
• Employers
• Employees
• Self-employed people

Voluntary medical insurance

Premiums by people 65 or over who sign up — Equal contribution by government

3 Separate trust funds

A separate trust fund

Trust fund money used for benefits

Retirement Survivors Disability Hospital

Medical

Administrative costs for each program come out of the corresponding trust fund.

FIGURE 11–1. Trust fund money can be used only for benefits and for the costs of administering the corresponding programs. (Source: U.S. Department of Health, Education and Welfare, SSI-35b, July, 1968, p. 4)

FIGURE 11–2. *Request for statement of earnings* (*Source:* U.S. Department of Health, Education, and Welfare.)

REQUEST FOR STATEMENT OF EARNINGS

SOCIAL SECURITY → NUMBER

DATE OF BIRTH → MONTH DAY YEAR

Please send a statement of my social security earnings to:

NAME _____

STREET & NUMBER _____

CITY & STATE _____ ZIP CODE _____

Print Name and Address In Ink Or Use Typewriter

SIGN YOUR NAME HERE
(DO NOT PRINT) _____

Sign your own name only. Under the law, information in your social security record is confidential and anyone who signs another person's name can be prosecuted. If you have changed your name from that shown on your social security card, please copy your name below exactly as it appears on your card.

the amount your employer claims to have reported, which is shown on your W2 income tax forms. The Social Security Administration's records you will receive will not show what your tax deductions have been, but rather whether your income has been reported and its dollar amount. That is the only important item to verify because your future social security payments will not be based directly on your taxes but rather on your income reported to the Social Security Administration. If the figures are not in agreement, contact your social security field office right away.

Retirement Benefits

When you reach age 65 you may receive full benefits (and remember full benefits is a range that varies with your earned income) if you have the proper quarters of coverage. If you retire around 1981, your benefits will be based on your average indexed earnings over about the past twenty years. We say "about twenty years" because it could vary a year or two depending upon if you retired in 1980, 81, 82, or 83. The actual number of years is determined by a rather complex formula. But your earnings over the past twenty years or so would first be indexed (adjusted upward) to take into account the amount of the average increase in overall U.S. wages over that same period of time. This is the same type of adjustment that is to be applied to the social security income tax base described above.

After your past twenty years, earnings have been indexed to today's average wages, another formula is used to determine your benefits. These benefits are then adjusted upwards every June to offset cost-of-living increases. The table below shows the approximate retirement benefits based upon various average yearly earnings.

Married couples both of whom work are discriminated against by the social security law. Both pay taxes, but when they retire they get only one benefit. If the husband's and wife's benefits are not the same, they get the larger of the two, but they can in no circumstances get both. The same is true of a widow or widower; they can choose their own benefits, or their spouse's, whichever is the higher.

The law also discriminates against some two-income married couples in another way. In some cases there is a social security benefit payment reduction for any public pension (federal, state, or local) received. This is a dollar-for-dollar reduction. Affected are benefits based on a spouse's social security. Moreover, for the reduction to be made, you must have a non-social security type public pension in your own right. In effect this point discriminates against couples both of whom work but where only one has social security, and the one that does not has a public pension plan other than social security. An example will clarify this. A and B are a married couple both of whom work. A has social security and B has a pension plan under a state or local government. When they retire, the social security benefits to be paid because B is a dependent of A will be reduced because B has a pension from a state or local government. While this provision of the law was passed in 1977, it will not apply to spouses who become eligible for public pensions before 1983.

Early or Late Retirement

You may retire as early as age 62, but if you do benefits are reduced. If you retire early, benefits are calculated in the regular way and are then reduced by $5/9$ths of 1 percent for each month you are under 65 at the time you retire. If you retire at 62, you are 36 months under 65 and hence your retirement benefits are 80 percent of what they would be at age 65 $(36 \times 5/9 = 180/9 = 20)$.

Delaying retirement beyond age 65 will increase your regular benefits by 1 percent for each year you delay retirement up to age 72; hence the maximum increase is 7 percent.

TABLE 11-2. *Monthly retirement benefits for workers who reached 62 before 1979 (effective June 1979)*

Average yearly earnings	FOR WORKERS Retirement at 65	at 64	at 63	FOR DEPENDENTS* Spouse at 65 or child	at 64	at 63	at 62	Family† benefits
$923 or less	133.90	125.00	116.10	67.00	61.50	55.90		200.90
1,200	172.30	160.90	149.40	86.20	79.10	71.90	50.30	216.30
3,000	276.80	258.40	239.90	138.40	126.90	115.40	64.70	397.50
4,000	325.60	303.90	282.20	162.80	149.30	135.70	103.80	556.40
4,400	348.80	325.60	302.30	174.40	159.90	145.40	122.10	618.20
4,800	369.30	344.70	320.10	184.70	169.40	154.00	130.80	673.40
5,200	388.20	362.40	336.50	194.10	178.00	161.80	138.60	728.40
5,600	407.30	380.20	353.00	203.70	186.80	169.80	145.60	755.20
6,000	426.70	398.30	369.90	213.40	195.70	177.90	152.80	782.60
6,400	445.80	416.10	386.40	222.90	204.40	185.80	160.10	810.10
6,800	466.10	435.10	404.00	233.10	213.70	194.30	167.20	837.80
7,200	490.20	457.60	424.90	245.10	224.70	204.30	174.90	867.10
7,600	511.70	477.60	443.50	255.90	234.60	213.30	183.90	895.40
8,000	530.40	495.10	459.70	265.20	243.10	221.00	192.00	928.20
8,400	541.70	505.60	469.50	270.90	248.40	225.80	198.90	948.00
8,800	555.20	518.20	481.20	277.60	254.50	231.40	203.20	971.30
9,200	567.10	529.30	491.50	283.60	260.00	236.40	212.70	992.40
9,600	576.60	538.20	499.80	288.30	264.30	240.30	216.30	1,008.90
10,000	587.70	548.60	509.40	293.90	269.50	245.00	220.50	1,028.40

Note: Every July, all social security recipients are given an annual cost of living increase. In July, 1980, this amounted to 14.3 percent. Therefore, if you increase every figure in the above table by 14.3 percent, it will be valid until July, 1981. Every July thereafter, you must increase it again by however much the cost of living has risen since the previous July.

*If a person is eligible for both a worker's benefit and a spouse's benefit, the check actually payable is limited to the larger of the two.

†The maximum amount payable to a family is generally reached when a worker and two family members are eligible.

Source: U.S. Department of Health, Education, and Welfare Social Security Administration HEW Publication No. (SSA) 79-10047 June 1979.

However, in 1982 this 1 percent increase becomes 3 percent and after that the maximum benefit for delayed retirement becomes 21 percent.

Limits to Earnings

The new law requires that one dollar of social security benefit payments be withheld for every two dollars of earned income above a certain amount (income from investments are excluded when making this calculation). In 1981 the maximum amount you may earn and not lose any benefits is $5,500. After 1982 the exempt amount shown will increase further automatically to offset increases in the cost of living. This provision of the law no longer applies when the social security recipient reaches age 72; then he or she can earn as much as desired and still receive full social security benefits.

Disability Payments

Disability payments dollarwise are calculated exactly the same way as retirement benefits, and dollarwise they are the same amount as retirement at age 65 benefits. To qualify you must be unable to engage in any substantial gainful activity. Merely being unable to perform your regular work is not enough to qualify you, if you can do other work. Moreover, your disability must be expected to last at least 22 months. Disability payments start after a five-month waiting period.

To be eligible for disability payments individuals must have credit for five years (twenty quarters) of work in the ten-year period ending when the disability occurred. There are two exceptions to this rule. Individuals disabled between the ages of twenty-four and thirty-one will need credits for only half the time between twenty-one and the age when they become disabled. Second, a person who becomes disabled before age twenty-four needs only one and one-half years of work credit out of the three-year period just prior to the disability. This amounts to only six quarters of coverage.

Survivors' Benefits; Family Benefits

In the case of death, the survivors receive a lump-sum settlement as well as a monthly payment. The lump-sum settlement is $255.00. The monthly benefit varies with the income of the deceased as well as with the number of dependents.

Normally these dependents are unmarried children under the age of eighteen and a spouse. Recent amendments provide that credit may also be given for children over eighteen and under twenty-two provided they are full-time students. Furthermore, the social security recipient may also count as a dependent child one over eighteen who becomes severely disabled before reaching eighteen and who continues to be disabled. A surviving spouse under 60 without dependent children does not qualify as a dependent; but after reaching age 60, he or she does. The period between when the youngest child is no longer a dependent and when the widow or widower reaches age 60 are called the blackout years. The surviving spouse receives no social security payments, but at age 60, they start again. Regardless of a widower or widow's age, he or she is considered a dependent while caring for a child under eighteen, and receives payments for herself or himself and the child based on the worker's social security account.

Student's Benefits

More than five hundred thousand students between the ages of eighteen and twenty-two receive monthly social security checks because of the death, disability, or retirement of a parent who worked long enough under social security. The student must be unmarried and attending an educational institution full-time to qualify to receive social security checks until the age of twenty-two based on his or her parent's eligibility. Under the social security law, a full-time student is one who attends a university, college, or junior college in the United States and whom the college considers to be in full-time attendance according to its standards for day students. A full-time student in high school or a trade or vocational school is one who is considered in full-time attendance by the school, is enrolled in a course of study lasting at least thirteen weeks, and is enrolled for at least twenty hours a week.

The Future of Social Security

During any given year the social security trust fund may be reduced. In the past, there were other years during which the trust funds would be built up again. In recent years, however, there have been more and more deficit years, which has caused some concern. The major reason for the decline of the fund is that, over the years, Congress has raised the benefits without a commensurate increase in social security taxes. Then, as noted above, a few years ago Congress added an escalator clause to the social security law. This provides for an automatic cost-of-living adjustment for all social security recipients. Every June all social security benefits are adjusted upward automatically to offset inflation. Some critics maintain that because of the escalator clause and other provisions added by Congress, the trust funds have been declining in recent years and will continue to do so in the future. There is currently less than one year's benefit pay month in the trust fund even though Congress raised taxes greatly in late 1977.

Because of this latest increase in social security taxes, they are now higher than personal income taxes for many American families. While the new social security tax structure has increased the flow of dollars into the trust fund, whether they will be adequate remains to be seen. This is especially true since social security benefits will be adjusted upward to offset inflation every year. Some critics are also concerned because a larger proportion of the population will be drawing benefits in the future as the population ages. On the other hand, some workers are now delaying retirement. No one, of course, knows what the future holds in store for social security, but the country seems deeply committed to it and almost certainly Congress will provide whatever resources are required to keep it going.

PRIVATE (LIFE INSURANCE) ANNUITIES[2]

An annuity is a contract with a life insurance company in which the company agrees to pay the annuitant an income stream for a specific period of time. The income stream may be fixed in dollar amounts per month or per year, or it may be variable. The specific period of time for which the payment is to be made may be for a given number of years, or it may be for life. If it is for life, the annuitant cannot outlive his or her income. An annuity then is a device to enable a person to retire. Annuities are sold by life insurance companies because life contingencies are involved. Life insurance protects you (rather, your beneficiaries) from having the income stream cut off due to a premature death. An annuity can protect you from outliving your accumulated assets due to a lengthy retirement period.

The Annuity Principle

To be sure, if your assets are large enough, and you can live on your investment income and never dip into the principal, you cannot outlive your income. But an annuity will enable you to dip into your principal and still not outlive it. This is because, as with life insurance, the insurance company applies the law of averages to large numbers of individuals. If each individual from among a large group of people of the same age were to rely on his or her individual accumulated assets, some would outlive their principal; others would not. Insurance companies, however, can guarantee that none will outlive their principal. While the company does not know which individuals in a large group will die at what age, the company does know how many will die at each age. The insurance company can scientifically liquidate the principal sum of all the individuals. Those who live to a ripe age will be drawing on the funds of those who die earlier.

2. The material on annuities and private pension funds is drawn from "Personal Financial Seminars." Copyright Harold Wolf and Associates. Used by permission.

While the company is liquidating their funds, it is also earning interest on that portion yet to be paid out.

Uses of Annuities

Generally speaking, annuities are used to provide retirement income. However, they can also be used to free capital and hence increase your retirement income and sometimes to save taxes.

For example, if you had accumulated assets of $200,000 over the years, you could invest this conservatively at, say, 8 percent and have an annual income of $16,000 to supplement other retirement income you might have. An annuity could increase this. A man age 65 can buy a single-premium straight-life annuity paying $10,741 per year for about $100,000. The other $100,000 could be invested to yield $8,000 or $9,000. The total income on your $200,000 is enlarged because you are scientifically liquidating part of the principal. To be sure, there would be less left for your heirs, and hence it might not appeal to you. However, for people without heirs it is a possibility. Also, in the above case, 64.7 percent of the $10,741 would not be taxable because it is a return of premiums rather than interest income.

Annuities may also reduce capital gains taxes in some cases. Suppose you have an apartment house valued at $100,000, of which the rental income is earmarked for your retirement. Now that you retire, however, you no longer want to be bothered managing the apartment. You would like to sell the building and invest the funds in good quality securities. However, you purchased the building some years ago, at $50,000, and if you sell it you will have a capital gains tax which could run as much as $14,000.[3] An annuity might help you in such a case. The prospective new owner might be willing to buy whatever annuity $50,000 would provide as partial payment for the apartment. If the annuity were a private annuity, capital gains taxes would not apply on the $50,000 capital gain. To be sure, income taxes would apply to the annual income from the annuity as it was received, but they might be lower since they are spread out over more years. It must be emphasized that in order to obtain this tax benefit it must be a private annuity, that is, not with an insurance company, and be an unsecured (no specific assets pledged) annuity. This does not mean it cannot be in writing and legally binding. Indeed, in the above case the annuity could be underwritten by a trust company, if the buyer of the apartment transferred property to the trust company. Moreover, such a private annuity could be a temporary annuity, technically called an annuity certain (5 or 10 years). This would then be a means of converting a large capital gain into an income stream over a period of years in order to minimize taxes.[4]

Annuity Premiums

Annuity premiums can be paid monthly, quarterly, semiannually or annually, just like life insurance. Premiums are paid over the years and a principal sum is accumulated on behalf of the individual. These premiums are, of course, invested by the company and earn interest on behalf of the individual.

These are the deferred annuities; that is, the payments to the individual are deferred until a later date. Over the years the annuity builds up a cash surrender value just like

---

3. A capital gains tax is a special tax on assets (wealth such as stocks, bonds, or real estate) which have risen in value over the years. This tax is too complex to explain at this point, but see chapter 17 for a complete treatment of it.

4. Using a private annuity this way to avoid taxes is a complex and intricate maneuver, and you should seek competent tax counsel beforehand.

"I provided for every retirement contingency except this one." (Source: Permission Cartoon Features Syndicate; from The Wall Street Journal.)

permanent life insurance. In the case of annuities this is called account value. Again as in the case of life insurance, a person can turn in an annuity at any time and take the account value. If the individual dies prior to when the payments are to begin, the beneficiaries generally receive the principal sum built up on his or her behalf. However, some insurance companies pay either the account value or the sum of all premiums paid in, whichever is the greater. This method of buying an annuity is a planned savings program.

It is also possible to buy an annuity in one lump-sum payment. People of some means may do this. Also people may use the cash surrender value of their paid-up life insurance policy to buy a single premium annuity when they wish to retire. This is generally one of the settlement options of life insurance policies.

Annuity Payments

The annuitant, of course, selects when he or she wants the annuity payments to begin. You can receive them monthly, quarterly, semiannually, or annually.

The dollar amount of the payment an annuitant will receive is determined by several factors: first, the principal sum built up on his or her behalf. This sum is dependent upon the total dollars in premiums paid, plus the interest they earned over the years. Then an allowance must be made for expenses by the insurance company. Finally, the amount of the annuity is determined by the age and sex of the annuitant, and the type of annuity selected.

The older you are when you start receiving payments, the higher the payment for any given principal sum. Women, since they live longer than men, on the average, receive a slightly lower payment than men of the same age, and with the same principal sum. This is because a woman will receive the payment for a longer period of time.

Classification of Annuities by Benefit Payments

Some insurance executives classify annuities into immediate and deferred. This has to do with when the annuitant is to begin receiving benefits, immediately or at some time in the future. An immediate annuity can be obtained only if you give a life insurance company one large lump sum as a premium.

Annuities can also be classified as to how long the payments are to be made and whether they are to be paid in fixed dollar amounts or in varying dollar amounts.

Straight Life Annuity

A straight life annuity provides for a periodic payment until the annuitant dies. This could be for one month or for thirty years or more, depending upon how long the individual lives. If the annuitant dies after even only one monthly payment has been made, the insurance company keeps the remainder of the principal sum built up on the annuitant's behalf. There is nothing left for his or her heirs. For this reason such an annuity guarantees the annuitant the largest possible payment. For this same reason this type of annuity is not very popular.

Life Annuity With Guaranteed Minimum Installments

This annuity pays an income to the annuitant for life, with a minimum number of payments guaranteed. If the annuitant dies before the guaranteed payments have been made, they continue to be made to the beneficiary until the guaranteed minimum has been made. Quite often a 10- to 20-year (120-240 months) period is selected. The insurance company must make payments until the annuitant dies or until ten (or twenty) years have passed, whichever occurs last.

Such an annuity is more expensive than the straight-life annuity, or putting it another way, an individual of a given age with a given principal sum built up, will receive a smaller yearly payment with this guarantee than without it.

A variation of this guaranteed minimum installment annuity is the guaranteed lump-sum annuity. In such a case, if the annuitant dies prior to the guaranteed number of payments the difference is paid to his or her beneficiary in one lump sum.

Guaranteed Premium Refund Annuity

This annuity is also called the installment refund annuity. It will pay an income for life with a guarantee that the total amount to be paid will be at least equal to the total premiums paid. If the person dies before collecting all the premiums he or she has paid over the years, the beneficiaries receive the difference. This difference can be taken in installments or in one lump sum.

Annuity Certain; or Temporary Annuity

The annuity certain is not really an annuity because life contingencies are not involved. In this case the insurance company will pay an income for a specific period of time, say ten years, and that is all. The payments continue for ten years—to the annuitant if he or she is alive and otherwise to the beneficiaries. At the end of ten years the payments stop even if the annuitant is still alive. This is the only so-called annuity that may expire even though the annuitant may still be alive. A variation of this annuity provides for payments for a specific number of years or until the annuitant dies, whichever occurs first. Needless to say, such annuities are not too popular, and not many are sold.

The Joint and Survivorship Annuity

The joint or survivorship annuity guarantees a payment for the entire life of two individuals. Since two individuals are involved, the risk to the insurance company is greater, and hence a given principal sum will provide a smaller benefit payment than will an annuity on one individual. Or, what is the same, the premiums needed to guarantee a given income are higher on a joint and survivorship annuity than on a single annuity. Often, but not always, the joint annuity is written so that when one member dies the payments, while they continue, decrease in amount. Most generally this reduction is to 75 percent, 66.6 percent, or even to 50 percent of what the two individuals were receiving. This lowers somewhat the cost of a joint annuity.

Joint annuities are always more expensive than an annuity on a single life, all other factors being equal. However, the dollar amount of an annuity that may be obtained with a given sum of money on a joint basis declines even more as the age gap between the husband and wife increases. This assumes, of course, that the wife is younger than the husband. For instance, if the husband were ten years older than his wife, the joint annuity would provide less than if he were only two years older—if in both cases it is to start when he reaches sixty-five and if the annuity were purchased at the same time and costs the same dollar amount. This is obvious because if an old man has a young wife, on the average she will be alive a long time after he is dead. If, on the other hand, the wife is sufficiently older than the husband, then it would appear that a joint annuity should be the same as a single annuity dollarwise. It does not work out that way, however, because on a joint annuity the life insurance company takes a risk on two lives, which is always greater than a risk on one life only. But if the wife is six or seven or more years older than her husband, the benefits are not greatly reduced by getting a joint annuity. An actuarially sound marriage, then, is one in which the wife is older than the husband.

Most annuity contracts (as well as life insurance contracts with a cash surrender value) permit the option of converting to a joint annuity at the time payments are to begin.

Cash Value of Annuities; Death Benefits

A true or straight-life deferred annuity has no life insurance and no cash surrender value. If you had such a plan and died prior to the annuity maturing, your dependents would get nothing; all your premiums would have been lost. Consequently, such plans are not very popular and very few are sold. Instead, insurance companies have developed what they call the retirement income deferred annuity.

This annuity is specifically for people who wish to save via an annuity and do not need or want much life insurance. This type of annuity generates a principal sum which consists of premiums paid plus interest earned less expense incurred by the life insurance company. This is its cash value. During the early years this cash value may be less than the total premiums paid because the company's expenses are higher during the first year. The clerical and administrative costs of setting up the annuity and the agent's commission are concentrated during the first few years. Consequently, a small amount of life insurance is often added to the package to offset this difference. Within a few years, however, the principal sum will exceed total premiums paid and, when that happens, the life insurance part of the package drops away. This growing principal sum, or accumulated savings, now becomes the death benefit while the deferred annuity is being purchased on the installment plan. This accumulated savings is also called the account value of the annuity and you can take it at any time by surrendering your annuity. This is just like in the case of your life insurance policy as you will recall from an earlier chapter.

The Fixed Annuity

Traditionally, annuities were nearly always fixed annuities; that is, they were contracts in which everything was determined and agreed to in advance. The only thing the insurance company did not know was the dollar amount of interest the annuity would earn over the years on future premiums, but a conservative assumption was made regarding this. The premiums were invested in bonds or mortgages that yielded a known return for a known period of time. The insurance company then could calculate very accurately how large a principal sum would be generated for any annuitant. Then when the annuitant retired, the insurance company would be able to guarantee a fixed dollar payment per month or per year for life. Actuaries have constructed tables that deplete the principal sum actuarily but also make an allowance for interest to be earned on the declining principal.

The major problem with fixed annuities is that inflation erodes the principal sum both while it is being built up and also while it is being paid out. Consequently, fixed annuities have become somewhat less popular in recent years and interest has been stimulated in the variable annuity.

The Variable Annuity

The variable annuity was developed in an attempt to protect the annuitant against inflation both during the premium-paying years and during retirement. Premiums on variable annuities are invested in common stock. Historically the price of common stock has more than kept pace with inflation, and consequently premiums invested in common stock would protect the principal sum against erosion. When the annuitant retired, enough additional dollars would have been generated to pay increased benefits taking inflation into account. Unfortunately, in recent years common stocks have not been a good inflationary hedge, but they have been over the long run, and one day they may again serve this purpose.

Under a variable annuity contract the premiums you pay are used to buy a block of stock called an accumulation unit. For example, if your premiums are $600 per year, this $600 may buy ten units in one month and fifteen units in another as the price of the stock fluctuates. Your principal sum being built up would accumulate more and more units as time passed. These units, and hence your principal sum, would fluctuate in value. Hopefully, however, each unit would rise in the long run and this, together with the new units you purchase, would provide protection against inflation.

When you retire, your accumulation units are converted into annuity units. You are then guaranteed a retirement income equal to the value of a fixed number of annuity units. This works as follows: First, all the value of your accumulation units is calculated at their market value to obtain your principal sum. Your first annual payment is then calculated in the same way as a fixed annuity would be. If, for example, your principal sum is $200,000, and the actuarial tables indicate that for a person of your age and sex a $10,000 annual payment could be made on a fixed annuity of the type you had chosen, then the first payment on your variable annuity would also be $10,000. The initial payment ($10,000) is then divided by the present market value of one accumulation unit. This indicates how many accumulation units are currently required to meet the $10,000. Suppose the market value of one accumulation unit is $50; then two hundred units are needed to make the first payment, and future payments will always be equal to the fluctuating value of two hundred units. It is expected that the value of the units will rise in the long run, increasing your $10,000 annual retirement income.

Most variable annuity contracts will give you the option to convert your variable annuity into a fixed annuity when you retire. In such a case the $10,000 initial payment described above would become fixed and guaranteed. The insurance company would simply convert the $200,000 principal sum in the accumulation units into fixed obligations in order to finance this. In such a case you would have hedged inflation during the accumulation period but not after retirement.

Combination Fixed Variable Annuity

It is, of course, possible to hedge your bets by buying both a fixed and a variable annuity in one package. The most popular combination is a 50-50 split between a fixed and variable; half of your premiums would be invested in common stock and half in fixed obligations. However, 25-75 fixed variable or 75-25 are also quite popular and a number of other combinations are also available.

The Variable Annuity, Common Stock, or Mutual Funds

Why buy a variable annuity? Why not buy mutual funds or common stock directly? Insofar as common stock is concerned, if a person's portfolio is big enough so that he or she can live on the dividend income alone, it would be all right. But if one has to draw on principal, one might outlive it. Only insurance companies can successfully assume the mortality risk by spreading it on an actuarial basis over large numbers of people and in this way make sure one does not outlive one's income.

For the small investor, variable annuities also provide a way of diversifying holdings of common stock more effectively. To be sure, mutual funds will do this as well, but the investor cannot get both diversification and assurance of not outliving the principal with mutual funds.

The Cost of Annuities

Several factors determine the cost of an annuity:

1. The age of the person receiving the annuity figured at the time the annuity is to begin
2. The age of the person when he or she begins paying premiums
3. The type of annuity selected
4. The monthly annuity payment you want
5. Your sex

Since annuities are the opposite of life insurance, the older you are when your payments are to begin, the lower the cost of a given payment. This is obvious, for the older a person is, the fewer the payments will be, on the average.

Insofar as annuity premium payments are concerned, they also vary with the age of the person when he or she buys the annuity, if it is a deferred annuity. A younger person will pay premiums for more years than an older person, and hence the yearly premium would be lower.

The cost also varies with the type of annuity. The straight life annuity, where the payments continue until the death of the annuitant with no guaranteed number of payments, is the least costly of all annuities.

Obviously, the larger the monthly payments you want, the higher the cost of an annuity.

Since women live longer than men, a fixed monthly payment for a woman will be larger than it will for a man of the same age. Or a fixed sum of money will buy a smaller annuity income for a woman. Insurance companies do not have separate annuity tables for women but charge women the same rate as for a man five years younger.

PRIVATE (AND GOVERNMENT) PENSION PLANS

The purpose of pension plans is to provide a retirement income to employees when they retire from the labor force, usually at age sixty-five. Such plans are designed to supplement social security retirement benefits. Regular money contributions are paid into the fund and are invested to earn interest. The fund then is available upon retirement. In some cases, deductions are withheld from the employee's wages, matched by the employer, and paid into the fund. In other cases, the employer makes the entire contribution. More and more of the plans are of the noncontributory type wherein the employer makes the entire contribution. As we shall see below, there are more tax benefits available if it is a noncontributory plan. In such a case, neither the interest earned by the fund nor the capital gain accruing to it on behalf of the employee is taxable until it is received upon retirement.

Management of the Fund; Insured and Non-insured Plans

Most pension funds are managed either by a life insurance company or the trust department of a bank. In reality, the insured plans are group annuities or life insurance and are financed very much like the annuities discussed above. Life insurance companies have a number of different financing and funding arrangements from which to choose. Upon retirement, however, generally retirees are given an annuity; at that time they select the various options (type of annuity) they want. In a sense, then, it is a group annuity while the fund is being built up. But upon retirement each individual retiree receives an individual annuity.

If the pension fund is managed by a trust department of a commercial bank, the pension fund contributions are invested in various securities much as in the case of life insurance managed funds. In both cases, the funds can be invested in fixed obligations like bonds, variable like common stock, or in a combination of the two in accordance with the wishes of the beneficiaries.

Vesting of Interests

Vesting of interest has to do with whether or not individuals get the dollars paid into a pension fund on their behalf if they should leave the company prior to retirement. If a pension plan is fully vested, the funds paid in on a person's behalf are legally hers or his and must be so earmarked; an employee who leaves the company prior to retirement would usually be given the dollars they represent in cash.[5] Prior to the imposition of federal government regulations on private pension plans in 1974, most pension plans were not fully vested, at least not immediately. Of course, the contribution made by the employee was, but the contribution of the employer was often lost if the worker left before retirement.

In some cases vesting takes place after a number of years; after that period of time, one takes one's pension rights with one. Since there is bound to be some turnover, lack of immediate vesting permits higher benefits to those who do retire, with a given cost, or reduces the cost of a pension plan with a given retirement program. Some employers also feel that lack of vesting reduces labor turnover. It is debatable whether this in itself is desirable, because it reduces the mobility of labor; mobility of both labor and resources is required, many argue, to keep our economy dynamic. In any event, if there is no vesting, those workers who leave the firm subsidize, so to speak, those who stay and finally retire. Federal regulations that now require certain vesting provisions as well as other matters are spelled out below.

Funding

Funding is another technical term with which you should be familiar. A pension plan can be 100 percent funded, partially funded, or zero percent funded. If a plan is not at all funded (zero percent), it is referred to as a pay-as-you-go plan. In such a case, an employer would take whatever money is needed out of operating revenue and pay retired employees a pension; the employee contributes nothing. This would, of course, reduce profits. A pay-as-you-go plan is considered actuarially unsound and there are very few of them.

At the other extreme are the fully funded plans (100 percent funded). A fully funded pension plan is one where assets are accumulated each year in an amount equal to the future pension benefits earned that year. Actuarially the future cost of a pension plan can be predicted with great accuracy. If the pension plan is then designed so that the annual buildup of future benefits (discounted to present value) is always equal to the annual buildup of assets, there is 100 percent funding. In such a case, every employee could be paid his pension at any and all times. One hundred percent funding can, of course, be achieved by keeping the benefits lower than in a partially funded plan, or the contributions (cost of the pension fund) higher.

Funding and vesting are somewhat related. If a plan is not vested, then many of the contributions made for personnel who leave the company will be left in the fund. They can be used to pay benefits to employees who actually do retire, hence full funding is unnecessary. The same can be said in reverse. If a plan is fully funded, it might just as well be fully and immediately vested because the monies are available.

Employee Retirement Income Security Act (ERISA)

Prior to the passage of the Employee Retirement Income Security Act (ERISA) of 1974, there were no federal controls over private pension funds and only loose, haphazard regulations at the state level. The act was passed in response to complaints that many workers were not obtaining their benefits upon retirement. Generally this was because

---

5. Sometimes persons get the retirement benefits when they reach sixty-five instead of the cash when they leave the company. For example, if a man leaves a company at age forty and has vested interests in a pension fund, he may not get a thing at that time, but the funds in the pension fund on his behalf will continue to draw interest until he is sixty-five, at which time he will get an annuity or whatever other benefit the plan calls for.

either their pension funds were not adequately funded and monies for retirement payments were not available or the plan was not *vested* and the employee left prior to retirement.

The federal act's main purpose was to establish minimum requirements regarding vesting and funding, but it contained some other provisions as well. For example, federal regulations are now imposed upon management of the fund. Fund managers may not buy for the fund property they own personally. Other possible conflicts of interest on the part of fund managers will be examined by the government. Pension funds cannot hold more than 10 percent of their assets in the form of stock or other property of the employing firm. (Established funds in violation of this law at the time of its enactment have ten years to comply.) The act also provides that each fund make an annual report to the Secretary of Labor and provide all employees covered with full information regarding their benefits, including access to financial records.

The act also established the Public Pension Benefit Guarantee Corporation (PPBGC). This is a government corporation and operates much like the FDIC. It guarantees pension rights, and if a pension fund collapses and cannot pay pension benefits the PPBGC could pay eligible retirees up to $750 per month. The PPBGC is to be financed with premiums collected from the employer amounting to $1 per worker per year ($.50 per worker in the case of multiemployer plans).

The act established minimum vesting procedures. Employers may choose one of three alternative methods of allowing workers to obtain vesting. First, they may decide to grant full vesting after ten years and provide nothing until then. Second, the employer may grant 25 percent vesting after five years, 50 percent after ten years, and full (100 percent) after fifteen years.

The third method of providing for vesting is to grant 50 percent vesting when the worker's age and years on the job total forty-five, providing the worker has been employed at least five years. This rule would then provide gradual increases until full vesting was achieved at the end of fifteen years.

If pension plans are vested, the matter of funding becomes very important. The 1974 act requires certain minimum funding provisions for all future pension fund obligations. The law also requires the employers to build up a fund over a period of thirty to forty years to make possible some funding of past nonfunded pension obligations.

These new regulations at the federal level will affect all the approximately thirty-five million people presently covered by private pension plans. Many thousands of different plans are involved. Public pension plans such as those developed by state and local governments are not covered by the federal act.

Pension Benefits

When you retire you will receive pension benefit payments in accordance with the provisions of your plan. These vary. In some cases, your fund will simply buy you an annuity from a life insurance company. In such a case, you will have to consider all of the various types of annuities discussed above.

Your pension plan will also build up a cash value, but you cannot generally get this prior to retirement. It is, however, paid to your beneficiaries if you die prior to retirement. In such a case, they might have to choose one of the annuities noted above, or the options discussed below. Some pension funds will allow you to withdraw your benefits upon retirement in one lump sum rather than in installments. Others do not give you this option. If you withdraw in one lump sum there could be a complex tax problem. The same is true if you withdraw this entire sum over say ten years, rather than over a longer period. Generally, a lump-sum withdrawal can be averaged and taxed over a ten-year period, but you should seek competent tax counsel on this problem for your specific case.

Some pension plans provide that the contributions made on your behalf are earmarked for you, are invested on your behalf, and then when you retire, the money built up is yours. This is sometimes called a money purchase plan. The amount of your benefit is, of course, determined by how much was paid in and how successful the fund managers were in investing the funds. Nothing is guaranteed while the fund is being built up. When you retire, you can usually take your benefits in one lump sum or in installments. But everything in your kitty is yours. A money purchase plan is really a fully funded plan because everyone in the plan has his or her own kitty and could be paid off at any time.

There are other so called "fixed benefit" plans. Under these plans, the funds contributed on your behalf are commingled with those of your fellow employees. While you have a claim, there are no specific dollars you can call your own. Instead of an individual kitty for each employee, there is a collectively owned group kitty.

When you retire, your benefits are calculated by a formula that usually takes into account your salary and the length of time you have been with the company. For example, you might receive 1 percent of your average salary over your last five years for every year with the company. If your average salary over the last five years was $20,000 and you were with the company thirty years, your pension would be $6,000 per year.

Under the fixed benefit plan your benefits then are not as directly tied to your contributions as is the case in the money purchase plans. Under this fixed plan, the group kitty could be used to provide you with your monthly payment or the fund could buy you an annuity with a life insurance company; the practice varies.

Most fixed benefit plans are not fully (100 percent) funded. The law requires some funding, enough to make it actuarily sound. Also the fixed benefit plan must belong to the Public Pension Benefit Guarantee Corporation (PPBGC) discussed above; the money purchase plan does not.

Savings Through Pension Plans

The funds that build up in a pension fund can be looked upon as savings insofar as society as a whole is concerned. Therefore the question arises, do pension plans reduce or increase overall savings? To answer this question we have to break savings down into three parts: (1) the individual voluntary saving made outside of pension funds, (2) the employees' contribution to the pension fund, and (3) the employer's matching contribution to the fund.

Individual voluntary savings seem to be reduced to offset the growth in savings generated by deducting pension fund contributions from employees' salaries. That is, many people apparently adjust their individual saving to take into account their equity buildup in a pension plan. However, what about the employer's contribution? That, too, is a savings but employees do not usually look upon it as theirs. This is particularly true if it is nonvested. People generally do not adjust savings number 1 above to take into account savings number 3. Therefore it is probably true that the development of pension funds has increased the overall savings of society, but this cannot be proven.

Tax Benefits of Private Pension Plans

There are some tax benefits that can be obtained with private pension plans. To obtain these benefits the plan must be what is called a qualified plan. That is, it must be approved by the Internal Revenue Service. If the plan is nondiscriminatory in that all employees participate in it on the same basis and is in compliance with the Employee Retirement Income Security Act discussed above, it will be approved.

In order to obtain the maximum preferential tax treatment, however, the employees of a firm would often have to take a voluntary cut in their salaries by an amount equal to the employer's added contribution. This is because the plan must be a noncontributory plan to obtain the maximum tax benefits. If, for example, $10 per week is deducted from each employee's salary and is matched by the company, the individual would be better off tax-wise to take a $10-per-week cut in wages, stop contributing to the fund, and have the employer contribute $20. (This is referred to as a salary reduction rather than a salary deduction plan.) The employee is now taxed on $10 per week less income; none of the $20-per week going into the fund on his or her behalf is taxed. Before, the $10 employee contribution was taxed; to be sure, the employee will pay a tax on the benefits later when he or she retires, but presumably at that time income will be lower and so, too, will his or her tax rate.

If you have a salary deduction plan, you will still enjoy some tax benefits, but they are now smaller. While the $10 deducted from your salary is taxed, the interest and capital gains that accrue to it are not taxed until retirement. It should also be noted that any contributions made by employers are fully deductible to them on their tax returns.

Government Pension Plans

All government-sponsored (administered) pension plans are exempt from the 1974 Federal Employee Retirement Income Security Act.

This includes all local government plans as well as state plans. There are literally hundreds of government pension plans, some of which are very good and some of which are rather poor. Consequently, only certain generalizations can be made.

Even though government plans are exempt from the 1974 act, they can be approved by the IRS, and if they are, the tax benefits discussed above apply.

Some government plans are managed by life insurance companies. Those are actuarily and financially very sound. Other government funds are managed by trust departments of commercial banks. They too are generally fairly high quality plans.

Still other government plans are managed by the governing unit itself or an agency established by the government for that purpose. In such a case, funding varies from plan to plan; it ranges from fairly high to virtually zero. Vesting provisions too vary from relatively early and complete vesting to no vesting whatsoever until the employee retires. If you are a government employee and have a pension plan with your employer, it is suggested that you investigate your plan very closely to determine just what benefits you have.

INDIVIDUAL TAX-SHELTERED RETIREMENT (PENSION) PLANS

If you are self-employed, you have to make your own plans for your retirement. You have to accumulate assets on your own. This has always been the case, but there are now five different vehicles for building a retirement fund that utilizes tax shelters. Some of these are only for the self-employed and some are for salaried individuals who qualify. These plans are:

1. The Keogh plan
2. The professional corporation

3. The Individual Retirement Account (IRA)
4. Individual tax-sheltered annuities
5. Deferred compensation plans

The Keogh Plan

In 1962 Congress provided a tax concession for the self-employed who save for their retirement by passing the Self-Employed Individual's Tax Retirement Act, generally called the Smathers-Keogh Act. Under this bill, an individual may, in certain cases, earmark savings for retirement and receive certain tax benefits. However, the individual cannot touch either the savings or the investment income earned until he or she is fifty-nine and a half years old to receive the tax benefits.

Prior to 1974, a person could earmark up to 10 percent of his or her earned income or $2,500 per year, whichever was smaller, for retirement and deduct it from his or her taxable income. In 1974, the Employee Retirement Security Act (ERSA) discussed above raised these figures to 15 percent and $7,500.

These savings are then invested in a personal retirement fund. Neither the income earned by the fund nor the capital gains accruing to it are taxed during the time the fund is being built up. Upon taking retirement benefits, the untaxed contribution into the fund as well as earnings and capital gains are taxed. However, in all likelihood, the individual's income is now lower, and hence taxes are less.

As noted above, the individual cannot use any of these funds, nor the interest they earn, until at least the age of fifty-nine and a half. There are two exceptions to this policy, however. Persons who become totally disabled can use their funds earlier, or if they die, their dependents may withdraw from the fund.[6]

Generally, in order to be eligible under the Keogh bill the individual must be self-employed and have income not subject to the withholding tax. The plan was designed to help such self-employed persons as doctors, lawyers, dentists, and accountants, as well as farmers and businesspersons operating as sole proprietors or partnerships. It does not apply, however, to accountants, lawyers, and other professional people who work for some business they do not own and who are on salary, except, as noted above, if they are not covered by a pension plan.

In order to enjoy these tax benefits, the applicant's position and plan must be approved by the Internal Revenue Service. Most people who have a Keogh plan have a financial institution administer the plan for them. These institutions have plans that have been approved. Any individual qualifying may plug into one of them. The individual may set up a self-administered plan, but this is more difficult because now the plan itself will need to be approved, and the process usually requires legal and financial advice. The applicant who qualifies under the Keogh plan should work through a financial institution.

After-Tax Contributions and the Defined Benefit Keogh Plan

There are now two ways in which you may increase your Keogh contribution in excess of 15 percent or $7,500 and receive tax benefits. First, you may add an additional amount

---

6. If persons take out any part of the funds in their Keogh plan prior to age fifty-nine and a half and they do not qualify for the two exceptions noted above, their entire plan is nullified and they pay the regular income tax on it in addition to a penalty tax. They will not be eligible to start another Keogh plan for five years. The penalty tax is imposed by counting every dollar in the plan as the equivalent of $1.10 for tax purposes.

over and above the 15 percent (but not to exceed 10 percent or $2,000 of your net income), but this would consist of after-tax dollars. However, the investment income and the capital gains accruing to these after-tax contributions are not taxable until the person retires and receives his or her benefits.

Second, you may establish a *defined benefit Keogh plan* (or modify an existing one) and then make tax-free contributions substantially in excess of $7,500. Under a defined plan you must define specifically what you want your future retirement benefit payments from your Keogh plan to be. There is a limit to how large a sum you may designate, and the limit is determined by your age and your net self-employed income. The limit is reduced somewhat the older you are when you make the designation because there are fewer years to accumulate the needed funds. However, at any age, the limit rises with the level of net self-employed income.

The overall limit (or maximum) on the retirement benefits you may select was set several years ago at $75,000 per year. This sum, however, is subject to cost-of-living adjustments annually and by early 1980, it had grown to $110,600. There is also a second limit to the benefit you may define; it may be no larger than the average of your last three years of self-employed income. This upper limit of $110,000 then would apply only to a relatively young person with a very large self-employed income. There are other guidelines for establishing your defined benefits, and they, of course, must be approved by the Internal Revenue Service. Once your defined benefits have been established, (and they may vary some from year to year as your income varies), you may make tax-free Keogh contributions of whatever is necessary to fund your Keogh plan to the extent needed to provide for the benefits you have chosen. This involves making some complex actuarial calculations. If you wish to establish a defined benefit plan, you will need to see the experts in the trust department of a commercial bank or a qualified estate or financial planner.

The Professional Corporation

The professional corporation provides many of the same benefits as the Keogh plan, except it is even more flexible and there is a higher limit than the 15 percent that applies to Keogh plans. The professional corporation can be used to defer taxes, but only by physicians, attorneys, dentists, CPAs, architects, engineers, and others who are required to obtain a license before performing their services. In that sense, the corporation's benefits are narrower than those of the Keogh plan; not all self-employed persons are eligible.

The professional corporation is the outgrowth of a series of court cases that finally resulted in the Internal Revenue Service ruling in August, 1967 that "organizations of doctors, lawyers, and other professional people organized under state professional association acts will, generally, be treated as corporations for tax purposes." Generally speaking, the professional corporation provides tax benefits by making certain benefits tax deductible that otherwise would not be deductible. These deductible items include the following:

1. A qualified retirement plan. This was available to these people before through the Keogh plan, but with the 15 percent limitation. The limit is 25 percent but no more than $25,000 under the professional corporation. In order to obtain the full 25 percent, however, there must be two parts to your plan: a profit-sharing plan and a qualified pension plan. Under the pension part, you must contribute 10 percent of the annual compensation each year. Under the profit-sharing part, up to 15 percent more may be contributed, but this part is voluntary. It need not be contributed; moreover, it can be contributed in some years but not in others. The professional

corporation plan must be set up so that it is nondiscriminatory; that is, all qualified employees must be covered.

2. Medical expense insurance. No limit as is the case for an individual.

3. Disability income insurance.

4. Group life insurance.

5. Deferred income plan. The corporation can withhold funds, invest them in securities or buy more life insurance with them, and then later pay them to the employees when they retire. This is actually similar to point number 1 above except that retirement plans must apply to all employees of the corporation whereas deferred income plans may be selective. Moreover, the 25 percent and $25,000 limitation does not apply to the deferred income agreement of a professional corporation.

Table 11-3 shows the tax savings gained by incorporation by a hypothetical doctor. Putting together a professional corporation is a job for an expert, and the self-employed professional who seems to qualify for incorporation should obtain professional tax guidance.

The Individual Retirement Account (IRA)

In 1974 Congress authorized salaried individuals who do not have a private corporate pension plan to establish their own Individual Retirement Account (IRA). Most people who work for corporations have a pension plan; the self-employed have their Keogh plan or the professional corporation. But there was a large minority of people who worked for corporations that didn't have pension plans. To eliminate this discrimination, the IRA was autho-

TABLE 11–3. *A graphic illustration of the benefits of incorporation*

BEFORE INCORPORATION	DR. JONES AGE 40	AFTER INCORPORATION
$60,000	Net income from practice	NONE
None	Salary	$48,000
$10,000 NOT Deductible*	Cost of retirement investments and $200,000 life insurance	$10,000 DEDUCTIBLE
$2,000 NOT Deductible	Health costs and health insurance premiums	$2,000 DEDUCTIBLE
$22,060	Income taxes (Federal Tax based on 1978 rates, assumed outside income equals exemptions and deductions)	$16,060
$25,940	SPENDABLE INCOME A NET GAIN OF $6,000.00	$31,940

*If this $10,000 earns a net of 6% until Dr. Jones is age 65 it will be worth $581,560. This will provide a GUARANTEED income for life in excess of $4,000 per month.

The $200,000 of insurance will be estate tax free if he dies and can also be made estate tax free when his wife dies, even though she gets all the income from it during her lifetime.

rized. The IRA logically works like the Keogh plan, but the limits are not the same. If you qualify, you may put 15 percent of your earnings, tax free, into a special account. However, this sum may not exceed $1,500 per year. The entire sum plus all investment income and capital gains accruing to it are not taxable until you retire and start drawing it.

Just as in the case of the Koegh plan discussed above, you cannot withdraw any funds from your IRA without a penalty until you are fifty-nine and a half years of age unless you become disabled; upon your death, your beneficiaries may withdraw from the account. Moreover, you must begin withdrawing funds at the end of the year in which you reach the age of seventy and a half.

If a husband and wife are both working, they may both set up their own separate accounts if they both qualify. In 1976, this provision was sweetened a bit. Now if only one member of a married couple is working and he or she qualifies for an IRA, the maximum contribution is $1,750, not $1,500. This was the so-called housewives pension clause inserted into the 1976 tax reform act.

There is also an IRA rollover provision which in some cases permits you to put funds into or take them out of an IRA without a tax payment. If, for example, you retire and receive a lump sum retirement benefit from your corporate pension plan, you may, if you are not yet ready to retire, place the entire sum into an IRA with no tax liability due. This permits a further postponement of taxes until you retire and actually draw benefits out. If later you go to work again, you can roll your IRA account back into a corporate pension plan if that is more advantageous.

Most IRAs are invested in deposits in commercial banks, savings and loan associations, mutual savings banks, or credit unions, and earn about 8 percent.

Individual Tax-Sheltered Annuities

Some people also qualify under section 403.B of the Internal Revenue Code for tax-sheltered annuities. These tax-sheltered annuities are the same as the individual annuities described earlier (and they can be straight life, refund guaranteed, joint survivorship, etc.), except that they receive the same tax treatment as do pension plans also described above. The tax is deferred until retirement.

The premium used to buy this tax-sheltered annuity is not taxed, nor is the income the annuity earns, until you retire and receive the benefits. For the tax benefits to apply, however, the entire premium must be paid by the employer. If you and your employer share the premium, only that portion paid by the employer is tax exempt. This must be the same salary reduction type of plan as in the case of private pension funds noted above.

Individuals who work for tax-exempt organizations and schools (including colleges) are the only groups eligible for tax-sheltered annuities; people working for profit-making corporations are not eligible. Congress authorized the tax-sheltered annuity because tax-exempt institutions have less of an incentive to establish a pension plan for their employees since there are no tax benefits available to institutions that are already tax-exempt. However, even if these institutions have established pension plans for their employees, they may still purchase tax-sheltered annuities over and above the pension plan in most cases.

The amount of salary reduction you may take to buy such a tax-sheltered annuity is limited. The limit varies depending upon what other types of tax-sheltered fringe benefits (such as a pension plan) you may have. Generally, the premium paid into a tax-sheltered annuity together with other tax-exempt retirement plans cannot exceed 20 percent of your salary.

The annuities described immediately above are completely tax-sheltered; both the premiums used to buy them and the interest they earn are not taxed. However, anyone may buy an annuity, as described earlier in the chapter, with after-tax dollars, and then defer the interest it earns, or the capital gain which may accrue to it, until he or she starts receiving the benefits upon retirement.

Deferred Compensation Plans

There are two general types of deferred compensation plans. For example, there are the so-called mass plans which apply to employees of non-profit institutions. Under these plans a person may defer up to 25 percent of his or her salary or $7,500, whichever is less. He or she would pay no tax on it nor on the interest or capital gained on it until retirement. Instead of paying the person this portion of his or her salary, the employer would withhold it, and invest it on the employee's behalf. Currently these funds may be invested in life insurance policies, annuities, mutual funds, or deposits in savings and loan associations, or credit unions.

There are also individual deferred compensation plans. These are negotiated between the employee and a profit-making employer. These make the most sense for high-income groups. High-paid executives only a few years away from retirement would be one example. Another would be the case of a professional athlete who signs a million dollar contract, with the sum being paid later over a number of years. In theory there is no limit to how much may be deferred under these individual plans, but each one must be approved by the IRS. Consequently, each plan is scrutinized by the IRS and must be considered reasonable. Hence informal limits may be imposed in this way.

Where to Invest Your Retirement Account

If you have an individual retirement program (either a Keogh plan, professional corporation, or an IRA), you may choose from a number of different investment outlets. You may put your funds in any of the following:

1. A savings deposit at a thrift institution
2. Annuities from a life insurance company (note you cannot buy life insurance, only annuities)
3. Mutual funds (discussed below in chapter 15)
4. The trust department of a commercial bank
5. Special issue of U.S. government retirement bonds.

Remember once you commit your funds to any of these outlets you cannot touch them until you are 59.5 years old, unless you become disabled or die.

If your account is relatively small and you wish to eliminate investment fees, you should consider a savings deposit in a thrift institution. However, then your return is fixed at a maximum of about 8 percent and you forego the possibility of any capital gains.[7]

If you choose annuities, you will have to pay regular insurance commissions, but you might earn more than 8 percent in some years. You should check this out very carefully. If you buy mutual funds, you will also have to commissions to pay, but now there is the possibility of a higher return including capital gains. This too should be checked carefully before you go ahead. If you select a trust department of a commercial bank, you will have to pay a

---

7. When short term interest notes are very high you can put your funds into a money market certificate and earn more than 8 percent.

management fee. This will generally be about ½ or ¾ of 1 percent of the first $50,000 of your account. It is then scaled down on larger accounts. However, trust departments also have a minimum management fee (generally about $150). For small accounts a trust department may not be the best but for a larger account you may want to investigate it because it provides for greater flexibility.

Finally, if you choose the special issue U.S. government bonds, you will have no investment fees, but your return is also lower than any of the others; currently it is 7 percent. It should be noted, few banks sell these special bonds. If you wish to purchase them, you may do so from any Federal Reserve Bank or branch or directly from the Treasury, Bureau of Public Debt, Securities Branch, Washington, D.C., 20226.

Whatever vehicle you choose, the benefits are substantial. The table below shows the differences over the years between the account of a person in the 33.5 percent tax bracket who saves $1,500, pays a tax on it, and puts it into a regular savings account and another person who puts $1,500 per year in an IRA or Keogh account. In both cases they are earning 5 percent.

SUMMARY OF YOUR RETIREMENT PROGRAM

Your retirement program will generally consist of some or all of the following:

1. Social security
2. Life insurance and annuities
3. Private corporate (or government) pension plans
4. Individual tax-sheltered pension plans
5. Any other income-producing assets you may acquire

Obviously all of these should be tied together in planning your retirement. Nearly everyone will have some social security. That is the beginning point. You should also take into account the cash value of any life insurance as well as any other income earnings assets which you may have. Most people will begin with these three items. Then you can take into account the other retirement plans discussed in this chapter. However, first you should estimate your retirement needs. This can be done by taking a percentage of your current income as a proxy for your retirement needs. See Tables 8–5 and 8–6. Indeed, you may wish to review the section in chapter 8 on insurance needs for retirement purposes or to take care of survivors: the principle is the same. Insurance is only one way of providing for retirement

TABLE 11–4. *Buildup of assets with and without IRA*

AT 5% INTEREST RATE	WITHOUT IRA	WITH IRA
6 years	$ 6,755	$ 10,748
12 years	$15,008	$ 25,229
18 years	$25,094	$ 44,741
24 years	$37,417	$ 71,030
30 years	$52,474	$106,451

Part 2 / Your Insurance and Annuity Program

needs. In this chapter we discussed meeting retirement needs via other methods. After determining your retirement needs, net that against what you have so far from social security, life insurance, and other income-producing assets to obtain your retirement need shortfall. You should then take into account what your corporate (or government) pension plan, if any, will provide. If there is still a shortfall, you might want to consider acquiring annuities or individual tax-sheltered programs, if you are eligible.

QUESTIONS FOR REVIEW

1. Social security is now said to be a matter of right. How is this different from a "needs" test, which is often a necessary prerequisite for welfare payments?

2. What are the different kinds of benefits that the federal government administers under the Social Security Act?

3. What is meant by quarters of coverage?

4. How are social security funds invested and how may these funds have an impact upon the economy?

5. How are ministers and the clergy covered by social security?

6. At present retired persons drawing social security cannot earn more than $5500 per year. Suppose they earn $5800 per year. How does this affect the total payment paid to them?

7. How may it be said that the annuity is, in the final analysis, an insurance problem?

8. Explain the three major purposes for which annuities are used.

9. Distinguish between the single-premium annuity and the annual-premium annuity.

10. Why are straight-life annuities often difficult to sell?

11. What is an annuity certain?

12. Under what circumstances may it be desirable to purchase a joint survivorship annuity?

13. Why is a straight-life annuity cheaper than a joint and survivorship annuity?

14. Explain briefly any three of the general types of annuity that life insurance companies sell.

15. What are the similarities and differences between the conventional or fixed annuity and the variable annuity?

16. What is the difference between "vesting" and "funding"?

17. Did the development of the private pension fund increase or decrease the overall savings of society?

18. Discuss the tax benefits Congress has provided for the self-employed if they establish a retirement program.

19. What is the individual retirement account?

20. How can it be stated that your insurance program and your retirement program are tied together?

CASES

1. John Fisher, aged sixty-five with no dependents, has been working off and on as a farm laborer all his life. Although he has never worked the year around, he has worked some each year. During the last five years, which were the best years of his life incomewise, John has never earned less than $3,000 nor more than $8,000. John is not certain whether he is eligible for retirement under social security. Is he eligible?

2. Ralph Butterwood died. He was covered under social security and had been making $18,000 per year or more for the last six years. He was fifty-four and his wife, Helen, is fifty. They had two children, nineteen and fourteen. What benefits will his family receive and for how long?

3. George Adams and Pete Gerrard are two elderly widowers drawing social security bene-

fits. George is seventy-three years of age and Pete is sixty-six. Both have part-time jobs checking out groceries at a large supermarket, and last year both made about $7,000. Pete lost some of his social security benefits, but George did not. Why? Can you calculate how much Pete lost? Pete found out that his twin brother earned $10,000 last year on some investments he had as well as $5,000 because of a part-time job. Pete wonders how much social security benefits his brother lost. Can you explain it to him?

4. Jane Stodard, thirty-two, has worked for a large manufacturing firm in Detroit for the last ten years and is currently earning $300 per week. Five years ago the union and the company agreed on a pension plan. The plan is partially funded and fully vested but only after ten years. Each week $20 is deducted from Jane's check and is matched by the company, hence $40 per week goes into the fund on Jane's behalf. Explain funding and vesting to Jane.

Recently Jane was offered another job, which pays $350 per week. Should she take it? How much of her pension will she lose if she does take the new job? How much cash will she take with her if she makes the move?

5. George and Esther Gant are both fifty-five and are looking forward to retiring when they reach sixty-five. They would like to begin planning now so that they will have about $1500 per month at that time. They know that social security will provide them with about $900 per month and that George will get a pension from his employer of about

$450 per month. They own their own home and a $25,000 whole life, life insurance policy. Can you help them with their retirement plan?

6. Tom and Mary Brown are reaching retirement age and seek your help in converting life insurance to annuities. The only other retirement income they will have is $950 from social security. They are both the same age and are unclear whether they should convert their life insurance to a single or a joint and survivorship annuity. What is your advice?

7. John Green is a man of substantial means with all of his funds invested either in securities or in property. He feels he can retire on his investment income, but recently he has heard he might want to consider annuities for other reasons. What would you advise?

8. Bob Price is self-employed. He earns $28,000 as an insurance agent. He is thirty-four years old, has a wife, Evelyn, and two children ages six and eight. He has $30,000 of life insurance. Bob saves regularly for the children's college education by putting $25 per month into a savings and loan association on their behalf. He now wants to start accumulating assets for his own retirement. He doesn't want to buy an annuity from an insurance company, but he is in a position where he can put aside about $3,000 per year. How should he invest it? Bob has heard that in some cases he receives tax benefits if he sets aside savings for his retirement. Can you explain how this works?

SUGGESTED READINGS

Cohen, Jerome. *Decade of Decision*. New York: Educational Division, Institute of Life Insurance, 1975.

"Financing Your Social Security Benefits; If You Become Disabled." U.S. Department of Health, Education and Welfare. (SSA)-79-10029, 1979. This is an annual publication.

"If You Work While You Get Social Security Payments." U.S. Department of Health, Education and Welfare, Social Security Administration. This is an annual publication.

Life Insurance Fact Book 1981. The Institute of

Life Insurance, 277 Park Avenue, New York, N.Y.

Melone, Joseph J., and Allen, Everett T., Jr. *Pensions, Profit Sharing, and Other Deferred Compensation Plans*, rev. ed. Homewood, Ill.: R. D. Irwin, 1976.

Meyers, Robert J. *Social Security*. Homewood, Ill.: Richard D. Irwin, 1975.

Nader, Ralph, and Blackwell, Kate. *You and Your Pension*. New York: Grossman Publishers, 1976.

Questions and Answers on Retirement Plans for the Self-Employed; Retirement Plans for Self-Employed Individuals. Washington, D.C.: Internal Revenue Service. No date.

Rejda, George E. *Social Insurance and Economic Security.* Englewood Cliffs, N.J.: Prentice-Hall, Inc., 1976.

"Social Security," and *Supplement to Social Security Handbook.* U.S. Department of Health, Education and Welfare. Washington, D.C.: Government Printing Office. This is an annual publication. You can get it free by writing or calling your local social security field office. Offices are located in all big cities.

"Social Security in Your Financial Planning." U.S. Department of Health, Education and Welfare. This is an annual publication.

"Social Security Information for Young Families." (SSA 10033) U.S. Department of Health, Education and Welfare, 1980.

"A Woman's Guide to Social Security." U.S. Department of Health, Education, and Welfare. Publication No. (SSA) 79-10127, 1979.

"Your Medicare Handbook." Washington, D.C.: U.S. Government Printing Office, 1981.

"Your Social Security." U.S. Department of Health, Education, and Welfare. Publication No. (SSA) 05-10035, 1980.

"Your Social Security Earnings Record." U.S. Department of Health, Education and Welfare. This is an annual publication.

"Your Social Security Rights and Responsibilities." U.S. Department of Health, Education and Welfare. Publication No. 05-10077, 1980.

PART THREE

Investments

In part three we shall analyze the problems of investing directly in the securities of American corporations, discuss ownership of mutual funds, analyze real estate ownership, and close with a few notes on exotic investments such as precious metals.

Chapter 12 presents the fundamentals of direct investments. First, the forms of business organization are presented, and then the various alternative investment objectives are outlined. Making direct investments entails some risks, and these risks are examined as well as methods of reducing them. The chapter closes by explaining where you can find investment information.

In Chapter 13 you will be introduced to the various securities from which you may choose. These are primarily bonds and stock, but there are numerous classifications of bonds and stock.

Chapter 14 discusses the securities exchanges, the brokers and dealers in securities, the quoting of securities, and how to go about buying and selling them. It also has some information on investment strategies, or when to buy what.

Chapter 15 first deals with investment companies (mutual funds) which are another means of investing indirectly. Then it discusses commodity and real estate investments. The chapter concludes with some comments on unusual (exotic) investment outlets.

Chapter Twelve

Some Fundamentals of Direct Investments

Investigate, then invest.
MOTTO OF MERRILL LYNCH, PIERCE, FENNER AND SMITH

The objectives of this chapter are to

1   Present the various forms of business organization; the investor should know about the organizational structure of the business firm in which he or she invests

2   Outline alternative investment objectives a person may attempt to achieve

3   Present the risks inherent in any business venture

4   Present techniques used in an attempt to reduce risk

5   Introduce the sources of investment data needed to make intelligent investment decisions

In this chapter we will examine direct investments. That is, we may invest directly in a business organization rather than in a financial institution, which would invest our dollars for us. A person can invest directly by becoming part-owner of a business or by directly lending it money. There are three general forms of business organization in which a person may invest, and we will briefly examine each. Before you invest in any of them you should determine your investment objectives because that will influence the investment vehicle you choose. For example, you must decide whether you wish to emphasize capital gains, or income, or both. There is also the question of whether to be a short-run or a long-run investor or perhaps both. Then you must further decide how much risk you are willing to take. Remember when you invest directly, you are assuming more risk than when you invest indirectly via a financial institution. Once having determined all these objectives, you are ready to attempt to find ways of investing so as to carry them out with the least amount of risk.

FORMS OF BUSINESS ORGANIZATION

Everyone should be familiar with how the businesses in which they may invest are organized. In our society we rely primarily on private individuals to own and utilize the means of production. Individuals do this through the ownership and operation of business firms. Generally, business firms are organized into single proprietorships, partnerships, and corporations. While partnerships and single proprietorships by far outnumber corporations in the United States, they are far less important by every other test. The noncorporate businesses have fewer employees, own fewer assets, and produce and sell far less. They are primarily small businesses owned by a few people. Often they are family affairs. There also are, of course, some small family-owned corporations. While some corporations are small, nearly all partnerships and single proprietorships are; and all large business entities are corporations.

The Noncorporate Forms of Business Organization

One noncorporate form is the *single proprietorship*. This is a business owned by one person, the simplest form of organization, and the easiest and quickest to enter. There need be no charter application or other papers to fill out to enter business. The business assets are commingled with the personal assets of the owner. Business debt and personal debt, too, are commingled. While there can be numerous employees, there can be only one owner. This form of business is fine for some small firms; but it cannot grow very large, as we shall see below.

The other noncorporate form of business organization is the *partnership,* which can be two or more partners. It has some advantages over the single proprietorship. For example, with several partners, usually more capital can be raised. Also a number of varying talents might be brought together.

In order to form a partnership, a partnership agreement must be drawn up. All states have laws governing partnerships and the agreement spells out the duties, rights, and liabilities of each partner.

While a partnership has some advantages over the single proprietorship, it has some disadvantages as well. It is less flexible if several partners have to be consulted before a decision can be made. It is not permanent; the death of one partner dissolves the partnership. Perhaps the greatest single drawback of a partnership is that all partners are liable without limits for the debts of the business.[1] One partner can commit the others by the decisions he or she makes. Nevertheless, the partnership form of organization works well in many cases. If confidence exists between partners, it may be fine for a small business. But like the single proprietorship, it is virtually impossible for a partnership to grow into a truly big business firm.

The Corporate Form of Business Organization

A corporation is a legal entity. It has been defined by Chief Justice Marshall as "an artificial being, invisible, intangible, and a device only in contemplation of law." It has many of the rights, duties, and powers of an individual. It can sue and be sued; it can sign contracts, borrow money, own property, and carry out regular business affairs. A corporation raises money by selling shares in itself called stock. Because a corporation is artificial it cannot do any of these things itself, but they are done in its name by the corporation's board of directors which are elected by its owners.

The various states grant corporation charters, and a corporation comes into existence when the certificate of incorporation is accepted by the proper state agency, usually the

---

1. To be sure, there are limited partnerships, but generally speaking it is true that all partners are liable for all business debts.

secretary of state of the state in which incorporation takes place. The people who do the incorporating are the owners and are called the stockholders. They invest money by buying the corporation's stock which is then used to acquire business assets (capital) to carry out the business activity for which the corporation was organized.

Corporate Bonds and Stock

As noted above, corporations issue and sell shares in themselves called stock. They also issue bonds. If you buy either, you are investing in a business directly.

Bonds are certificates of indebtedness, and if you buy bonds you are lending the business money. You are a creditor. All of the terms of the loan are fixed; you will get a certain percentage interest rate on your money for a certain period of time after which the corporation must also repay the loan.

Corporate stocks are certificates of ownership (also called shares) and if you buy stock you become a part owner of the business (you in a sense join the club). However, you are promised no return on your money. If the corporation is successful, it will earn a profit and, as an owner, part of that will be yours. You will not necessarily receive it in the form of cash, because the corporation may retain it. Only if the board of directors decided to pay out all or part of earnings in the form of dividends will stockholders receive cash. On the other hand, if the corporation is unsuccessful and suffers losses, you will also share in those. There is no promise made that your stock will ever be redeemed. Indeed as a stockholder, the only thing you are promised is that you will be permitted to vote for the board of directors who will manage the corporation.

Stockholders then assume more risk than bondholders. Bondholders must receive their interest before stockholders may get anything. Stockholders get only the residual share, or what is left over after all other claims have been paid. Because of this, stockholders are described as providing risk or venture capital.

There is also a special type of stock that is called preferred stock. It stands between bonds and common stock and bonds. That is, preferred stockholders' claims are satisfied after bondholders' but before common stockholders'. We will discuss bonds and stock in greater detail in chapter 13.

Advantages of the Corporate Form of Business Organization

The advantages of the corporate form of organization include:

1. An individual's liability is limited to his or her actual investment in the corporation. That individual's personal assets cannot be used to pay the debts of the corporation. In a single proprietorship or partnership, personal assets are available to pay business debts. But since the corporation is a legal entity, only corporate assets may be used to satisfy claims against the corporation. The individual stockholders can lose only what they paid for their own stock. This feature makes many people willing to invest in a corporation, which in turn permits the raising of large aggregates of capital.

2. Shares of stock (or ownership) in a corporation are easily transferred to another person. Corporate stock is negotiable, and can be sold to any other individual, or can be inherited by survivors. This gives a corporation an indefinite life and also contributes to raising large aggregates of capital. A partnership, in contrast, is dissolved upon the death of a partner, and if a partner wishes to sell his or her share to another person, the other partners must agree to this.

3. The small as well as the large investor may easily invest in corporations. To be sure, most investors in partnerships are small, but the capital requirements of even part-

nerships are too large for many investors. Extremely small amounts of capital (as little as a few dollars) can be committed to the corporation by buying a single share.

4. Many thousands of individuals can collectively be the owners of a single business via the corporation. This is not the case with other forms of organization.

5. The above advantages all contribute to the ability of the corporation to amass high sums of capital, to grow large, and to enjoy the benefits of greater efficiencies that often accompany greater size.

There may be other benefits that arise from the giant corporation. For example, if a firm is big it can hire better managerial and other specialized talent than can a small firm. On the other hand, some observers have expressed concern over the separation of ownership and control that a giant corporation makes inevitable. They state that the millions of stockholders who own (but are far removed from) the corporation cannot possibly influence the managers who do control the corporation. The managers may or may not be stockholders, but in any event, they are not responsible to their constituents and this, it is alleged, is unhealthy in a democracy.

INVESTMENT OBJECTIVES

There are many different stocks which you may buy. Therefore, you must decide upon your investment objectives before you can select one. A wit once remarked that the objective of any investor is to make money, and the more the better. This generalization, however, does not tell us very much. The easiest way to make money is, of course, to inherit it. If you have to make it yourself, it is more difficult. Historically, one of the best ways to make money has been to invest in securities, especially common stock. But during the last decade this has become more difficult. The market did not rise a great deal during the 1970s as it did during

"Gracious, I don't want to bring him back. I'd just like his advice on some investments." (Permission Cartoon Features Syndicate; from The Wall Street Journal.)

Chapter 12 / Some Fundamentals of Direct Investments

the 1960s. Some feel this is merely a trend; stocks are no longer as popular as they once were. Others feel corporate stocks are today very good buys because they are unduly depressed. Indeed, some say in light of earnings, corporate stocks are among the better investments available today, and as soon as the general public discovers this, their prices will rise. Nevertheless, you must still select which stock to buy.

With 20-20 hindsight vision we can see what we would have if we had done this or that twenty or thirty years ago. For example, if you had purchased one-hundred shares of General Motors stock in 1946 when it was selling at $47 per share, your one-hundred shares would have grown to six-hundred due to stock splits and your $4,700 investment would be worth about $40,000 today. This does not include the many thousands of dollars of dividends you would have received over the years.

Or to take another case, if you had purchased one hundred shares of IBM at $195 per share in 1946, your investment today would amount to about 25,558 shares due to stock splits and stock dividends over the years. Moreover, with IBM's recent market price of $69 per share, your original $19,500 investment would be worth approximately $1,765,572. Once more I have ignored the dividend income you would have received over the years.

But then perhaps you would have purchased LTV Corp. at its high price of $169 just over a decade ago in 1967. Its recent price was $14. In any event, any investor must come to grips with at least the following possible investment objectives:

1. Liquidity
2. Good and stable income
3. Capital gains
4. Security of principal
5. Hedging inflation
6. Short-term versus long term investments

Liquidity

Liquidity has to do with how quickly and easily an asset can be turned into cash without a price concession. Money is 100 percent liquid, while other assets vary depending upon their relative "moneyness." Cash, the most liquid of all assets, is in general followed by certain U.S. government securities, high-grade corporate bonds, preferred and common stock traded on organized exchanges, over-the-counter securities, first mortgages on real estate, and real estate holdings. Generally, securities listed on organized exchanges are very liquid because they can be sold at the market price by making a telephone call. Selling real estate, on the other hand, takes time.

Income

One investment objective might be to achieve a good income. Certain stocks pay a higher dividend than others. Then, too, today bonds yield a relatively high-interest income. An investor with income as an objective would choose from among these higher yielding securities.

Capital Gains

Capital gains, or capital appreciation as it is sometimes called, is an important modern investment objective. This attitude toward capital gains as an objective is something that has developed within the past thirty years. Before that, the ideas of income, liquidity, and safety were the objectives that were stressed. All this has been changed, however, by higher individual income taxes. This is because long-term capital gains (assets held more than twelve months) are taxed more favorably than income. This is explained in chapter 17. But because of taxes many people invest in securities they believe will result in capital growth rather than income. This may involve investment in the type of firm that has growth possibilities or the purchase of a security the investor has reason to believe is depressed in value. Aside from the tax angle, capital gains—if one is successful in obtaining them—often give a greater return on one's investment. This fact, together with the tax consideration, has made capital gains very attractive to some investors.

Security of Principal

Security of principal means the preservation of capital values through a conservative investment policy. It is a truism of course that this is the prime objective of any investor. Everyone desires to preserve the original principal. This can be done by good judgment, avoidance of highly speculative risks, and attempting to preserve capital from market fluctuations. Unhappily, all this is easier said than done. Moreover, security of principal and liquidity are somewhat inconsistent with high yield. A person who wants high yield or rapid appreciation must assume more risk and accept a greater likelihood of no return or sometimes of actual loss.

Hedging Inflation

Some investors may feel that prices will continue to rise. When prices rise, the real value of certain assets declines, whereas others tend to rise with inflation. As a rule, common stock and real estate are considered the best hedges against inflation. Bonds on the other hand, since they are fixed investments, are generally eroded by inflation. If the price level doubles, the value of the dollar falls by half. If prices rise, the person with fixed dollar assets suffers a loss in value of his or her assets. If one is dependent upon fixed dollars for income—as, for example, are the retired—one's standard of living will necessarily decline. Historically speaking, however, the price of common stock has at least kept up and in many periods surpassed the rate of inflation. However, in recent years this has not been the case. We noted above one reason for this may be because investors' attitudes and psychology have changed; they no longer have as much confidence in the future.

There are two reasons why the prices of common stock should be a good hedge against inflation. First, they represent real assets—physical things like plant, equipment, and inventory—and when prices rise, the prices of all things including the real assets rise. Second, corporations often plow earnings back into the business. This means that new machinery, plants, etc., are purchased on behalf of the stockholder. As a result, the value of one's stock will rise. Figure 12–1 illustrates how the cost of living has risen since 1900 and also how common stock prices have reacted. As you can see, they have more than held their own in the long run.

Short-Run Versus Long-Run Investments

How short is the short run? Any definition is, of course, arbitrary but certainly holding a security for less than a year or two is short run. Holding a security for twenty years or even five or ten is a long-run investment. You may draw your own chronological line. It is generally conceded that the small investor should play largely in the long-run end of the field. If you are a large investor, it might be worthwhile to devote the energy, time, and perhaps money needed to make a short-term gain. However, the small investor may not have the

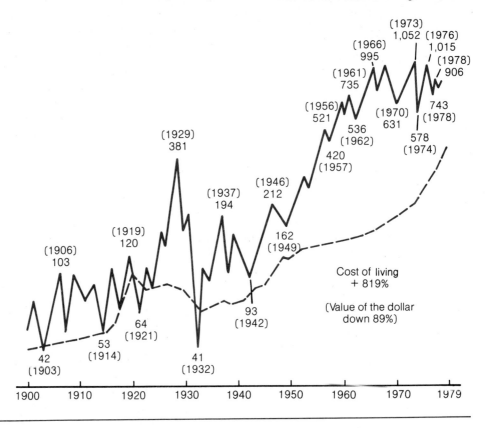

Dow-Jones industrial average + 1,946%

(1973) 1,052 (1976)
(1966) 1,015
995 (1978)
(1961) 906
735
(1956) (1970) 743
521 536 631 (1978)
(1962)
(1929) 420 578
381 (1957) (1974)

(1946)
(1937) 212
194

(1919)
120 162
(1949)

(1906)
103
Cost of living
+ 819%

64
(1921) 93 (Value of the dollar
(1942) down 89%)

53
(1914)

42 41
(1903) (1932)

1900 1910 1920 1930 1940 1950 1960 1970 1979

FIGURE 12–1. *Common stocks and the cost of living 1897–1979.* (*Source:* Johnson's Charts, Inc.)

time to watch an investment constantly. Also he or she cannot hire expensive professional advice. Moreover, even if he or she does make a nice short-term gain, in absolute dollars, it is likely to be small. Therefore, a small investor who gets in and out of the market frequently on a short-term basis will pay commissions that may eat heavily into any profits earned.

Therefore, most small investors probably should buy securities with an eye toward holding them for the long run. This does not mean that the investor can salt them away and forget about them. Any long-term investment can also turn sour and investors should review their portfolios periodically. Nevertheless, for most small investors the goal should be long-run investments—that is, held for at least a few years—not short-run speculation.

INVESTMENT RISKS

Our system is not a profit system as so many people like to claim. Rather it is a profit-and-loss system. Some firms prosper and show a profit while others lag behind and have losses. No firm can have losses in the long run and survive. And indeed, some firms go out of business from time to time. When they do, the stockholder absorbs the loss. Being an investor, then, is risky business. However, the reward for successfully assuming risk is financial gain, generally in the form of profits in one form or another.

Risk refers to the probability of future loss. Since there are a number of different risks involved in any investment, it is important that investors recognize those to which they may be exposed. Risks can be classified into six major types.

Risk of Business Failure

While some businesses prosper, others fail. In the event of business failure, a stockholder, having invested "equity" capital, may be entirely wiped out. Bondholders who have loaned money to the company may also find themselves wiped out, but not as frequently as the stockholders. If the bonds are secured by certain specific corporate assets, the bondholders may sell these assets and sometimes recover all of the loan, though more often than not they recover less. If the bonds are unsecured, the holder often collects much less than the loan.

Even investors in state or municipal bonds could find themselves in a precarious position in the event of a severe depression, but this has not happened on a widespread scale since the Great Depression of the 1930s.[2] It is generally conceded that one way to lessen the likelihood of being wiped out is to diversify one's investments by types of securities and issuers.

Market Risk

This is the particular risk resulting from fluctuations in market prices of securities over time, which may or may not have anything to do with how well the business firm is doing. Stock prices may decline due to a lowering of earnings in a particular firm, such a decline stemming from poor management or even a change in the public's tastes. Or earnings may fluctuate due to the business cycle, which will cause the market price of securities to fluctuate.

Price fluctuations in securities may also arise as a result of investor psychology. Many persons may decide simply to stay out of the market, thus reducing demand for securities and consequently lowering prices, even though firms' profits have not declined and may even have risen.

Price Level Risk

Another type of risk is that of changes in purchasing power of money. This risk is particularly applicable to those assets whose value is stated in terms of a fixed number of dollars. People who hold bonds and savings accounts are assuming this risk, as are people who hold idle cash. Indeed, those who hold idle cash are the most vulnerable to this risk.

For example, if a person holds money and the value of the dollar falls—which is another way of saying that prices rise—then in terms of real purchasing power the person who holds the money has lost. If the value of the dollar rises—which is another way of saying prices have declined—the real purchasing power of the dollar has risen and the person who holds the money gains. In a period of rising prices, the astute investor will try to move away from fixed assets into items such as common stock and real estate, which tend to appreciate with rising prices. In a period of falling prices (which we hardly see any more), the investor

2. To be sure, New York City came close to default a few years ago, and Cleveland defaulted on some of its bonds in 1979. It remains to be seen whether this default will be made good later.

should move from real estate and common stock into fixed assets yielding a fixed return, such as bonds.

While this person who holds idle cash is hurt the most by rising prices (inflation), the bondholders also suffer, and we can roughly calculate their losses. This brings us to the *nominal* rate of return and the *real* rate of return. The nominal rate of return is the money rate without an adjustment for inflation, and the real rate is after the inflationary adjustment. If you hold $1,000 in idle cash for one year during which the price level rises by 8 percent, your nominal rate of return is zero percent and your real rate is minus 8 percent. The value of your $1,000 has eroded to $920. If you hold a $1,000 bond paying 10 percent for one year during which prices rise by 8 percent, your nominal (money) rate of return is 10 percent and your real return is 2 percent. To convert the nominal rate to the real rate, subtract the rate of inflation from the nominal interest rate. In the above case, the real value of your $1,000 bond investment has grown only to $1,020.

Interest Rate Risk

This is the risk of loss that results from the changes in the monetary price of bonds due to fluctuations in the prevailing rates of interest. It is a risk important only with regard to investments in fixed obligations such as bonds and preferred stock. Even some U.S. government bond prices are affected by changes in the interest rates. When interest rates rise, bond prices fall; conversely, when interest rates go down, bond prices rise. There is nothing mystical about this process; actually it makes a great deal of common sense. We will illustrate this with an example which, while using an unrealistic low interest rate, illustrates the principle beautifully because the interest rate doubles. Suppose a corporation issues a $1,000 bond at 5 percent. This is a contractual obligation and the corporation must pay the holder $50 per year. Later, if interest rates double to 10 percent, in theory—depending upon the date of maturity—the old bond would drop in price to about $500. The reason is that with rates at 10 percent, any new bond issues would have to be offered with this same 10 percent yield; investors with $1,000 can now expect to get a return of $100 on their investments. Therefore, the holders of the old bonds will attempt to sell them and get in on the new rate, thus forcing the price down, until its market price is such that the fixed payment of $50 becomes closer to 10 percent of the bond's market price.

Actually the price of the old bond will not go down to $500, due to the fact that the company still has an obligation to repay the original $1,000 loan on the due date. If the bond becomes due the year after the new interest rate, then obviously it would be foolish for the holders of the bonds to sell at $500 when all they have to do is to wait a year and then demand $1,000 from the corporation. The bonds will nevertheless decline somewhat, and if they have twenty or more years to run, they will decline considerably.

If the interest rate declines, bond prices rise. Again suppose one holds a $1,000 bond paying 10 percent or $100 per year. If the interest rate declines to 5 percent, all a new investor can now expect as a yield on an investment of $1,000 is $50. Consequently, the demand for existing bonds paying $100 will increase and *theoretically* the older bond will rise to $2,000, again depending on maturity. Competition to obtain the older bond will theoretically bid its price up to the point where the $100 interest becomes 5 percent of the price of the bond, that is, $2,000. Again for practical reasons, however, it never goes that high in the real world of business.[3]

---

3. The longer the time to maturity, the greater the change in the price of a bond due to a given change in the interest rate. A bond would have to run to perpetuity (never become due) for a doubling of the interest rate to cut its market price in half. For example, if the interest rate rose from 5 to 7.5

What causes changes in the interest rate? Changes in interest rates are caused by changes in the demand for and in the supply of money. If money is thought of as any other commodity and interest as the price of the commodity, then when the demand is high and the supply constant, the price or interest rate will rise. When the demand is low, the price goes down, provided of course that the supply remains constant. Although this is not the place for a complete discussion, it should be mentioned here that the supply of money is to a degree regulated by the Federal Reserve System, and in this way so too is the interest rate. The basic reasons for this regulation of the interest rate are twofold. If the Federal Reserve had reason to fear deflation and recession, they would attempt to lower the interest rates in order to make borrowing by businesspersons more attractive, the idea being that if interest rates are lowered and businesspersons borrow, new capital will be created with a resulting upswing in the economy. On the other hand, if the Federal Reserve Board feared inflation, it would raise the interest rate. The underlying philosophy here is that if the rates are high, businesspersons will be deterred from new capital formation to a certain degree and the forces of inflation will be lessened.

Financial Risk

Financial risk is related to the debt (bond) equity (common stock) ratio. A high debt-to-equity ratio means that the corporation has a large fixed obligation (interest) to pay each year. If sales and profits decline severely in any one year, this could cause a burden. It is even possible that the heavy interest payment could not be met, and the firm be forced into bankruptcy. The higher the debt-to-equity ratio then, the higher the financial risk. However, the business firm often has some control over this risk.

Political Risk

Political risk has to do with changes in the legal environment in which the business must operate. If the government changes taxes, tariffs, subsidies, or imposes wage or price controls, the effect of this could have a bearing on political risk and could affect profits.

---

percent, then a $1,000 bond maturing in twenty years would decline to $800, because in twenty years the bond would be redeemed at its face value of $1,000. Hence the $200 capital appreciation over this period must be prorated over twenty years and included in the $50 per year the bond pays. The bond would appreciate $10 per year and hence the total yield would be $60 which is 7.5 percent of $800.

The formula for determining the market price (P) of a bond is

$$P = I \left| \sum_{n=1}^{M} \frac{1}{\left(1 + \frac{i}{2}\right)^n} \right| + F \left| \frac{1}{\left(1 + \frac{i}{2}\right)^M} \right|$$

where
$\quad P$ = current market price
$\quad I$ = coupon interest payment in dollars
$\quad n$ = payment period (six months in the case of most bonds)
$\quad M$ = total number of payments
$\quad i$ = market rate of interest
$\quad F$ = face value of the bond

In the case of a bond maturing in ten years paying $80 per year ($40 every six months) at a time when the market rate of interest is 4 percent we would have

$$P = \$40 \times 16.351 + 1000 \times 0.6729,$$

and the market value of the bond is $1,327.

Inherent in any investment are the risks already mentioned. While there are several ways in which some of these risks may be reduced, it should be noted that nothing much can be done about political risk. You must operate within the existing political environment.

In the case of interest rate risk, it too is difficult to diffuse. If you can forecast changes in interest rates you can really take advantage of this, but such forecasts are extremely difficult. When buying long-term bonds, one rule might be to buy them only if the yield is attractive enough to hold them to maturity, and then do so. Then any future paper losses will not be achieved. To be sure, you may possibly be prevented from taking advantage of future higher yields. Or if you are concerned about future interest rates changing, buy only short-term fixed obligations.

You can lessen financial risk (excess leverage in the firm's capital structure) by not buying the securities of highly leveraged firms.[4] Study their balance sheets; also examine the stability of earnings. A firm that has good and stable earnings is able to service a higher debt-to-equity ratio than a firm whose earnings fluctuate.

In reducing the price level risk you should strive to invest in firms whose sales and prices of the products which they sell are likely to keep up with inflation. This is likely to result in their profits keeping up with inflation; if their profits keep up, the prices of their securities are more likely to rise with inflation.

The risk of business failure can be reduced by selecting financially strong companies, innovative companies, and companies whose products are presently in great demand and are likely to remain so.

In the case of market risk, some companies are less vulnerable than others; for example, those companies selling a product for which the demand is more stable, such as food. You may wish to buy their securities.

Reducing risk then becomes a matter of selecting the right companies at the right time. This necessitates getting up-to-date information concerning general business conditions as well as specific industries and individual firms.

Reducing Risk by Business Trend Analysis

The trend of business conditions is indicated weekly and monthly by: figures on inventories, durable goods sales, price movements, employment, unemployment, industrial output, and GNP. These figures can give a clue as to whether the economy is moving up or down. There are cyclical movements up and down, but also broad overall long-run trends of economic expansion. By identifying broad upward or downward swings, and acting accordingly, risk can be reduced. If, for example, business conditions seem to be improving, one can buy securities with more confidence. If business conditions in general seem to be deteriorating, investors can reduce their risk by taking a more conservative stand insofar as securities are concerned. We will note below where some of these economic indicators are published.

Specific Industries and Firms

Industries are classified into groups for investment analysis—banks, food production, rails, and the like—and a movement either upward or downward of the business cycle may

4. See p. 340–41.

affect them in varying degrees. Although, generally speaking, if there is a general upward movement in business conditions, all groups move upward, and if there is a general downward movement, all groups have a tendency to move downward; some groups move to a lesser degree in either direction. For example, utility company earnings and sales are relatively stable, although there has been a secular trend upward. Auto stock tends to be more volatile, moving more rapidly upward during periods of expansion and just as rapidly downward during periods of contraction. Within each group, there are individual firms whose performance may be quite different from that of the group as a whole. Even during periods of contraction some firms earn more than others. Generally this can be attributed to good management. Within any group, one can find firms that have consistently paid good dividends to investors even during periods of severe recession, while others dealing with the same products are able to pay earnings only during relatively good times.

One can reduce risk by investing for the most part in those industries that typically have done well and whose future looks more promising than that of the economy as a whole. Such investment can be correlated with one's stand with respect to the economy in general. And finally, if investors select not only industries that have done well but firms that have the best records within good industries, they can generally reduce the risk even more.

Reducing Risk by Diversification

Risk can be reduced by diversification. Diversification means not putting all one's eggs in one basket. This is more difficult for a small investor to do than a large one. But diversification is a relative term and even a small investor should be able to obtain some diversification. Diversification can be achieved by firm, by industry, by type of security, and by investment objectives. For example, if you decide to buy oil company stock, pick two or three or even four different companies; pick the ones you feel are the best in light of the history of the industry and firm analyses. Also, diversify by buying stock of firms in different industries. You might also diversify by different types of securities; say, bonds and stock. Finally, give some thought to diversifying by investment objective; that is, some investments for growth, some for income, some for stability, etc.[5] Diversification reduces risk by broadening your investment base. If you broaden your base and are careful, your securities will include some that will fare better than average.

SOURCES OF INVESTMENT INFORMATION

Financial information can be obtained from newspapers, magazines, books, investment services, banks, brokers, investment counsels, and from a variety of other sources.

Newspapers

Greater amounts of information about business conditions are now in the financial pages of any large city newspaper. For more complete business and financial coverage, however, certain newspapers are superior to others.

Any serious investor should probably subscribe to *The Wall Street Journal*. This financial paper is published daily in six regional editions and is a morning paper. This journal

---

5. From a functional point of view, common stock can be classified into income stock, growth stock, cyclical stock, speculative stock, and defensive stock. These classifications will be discussed in detail in chapter 13.

publishes articles on general business and economic conditions both in the United States and abroad. It also has stories and articles on specific industries and corporations and news on labor and government relations. It is a treasure house of business and financial statistics, of past, present, and future trends. It also, of course, has complete stock market quotations, including the Dow-Jones Averages, as well as bond quotations.

Magazines and Other Publications

The better business and financial magazines are *Barron's Weekly*, the *Commercial and Financial Chronicle, Forbes, Business Week, U.S. News and World Report, Money, Fortune Magazine,* and the *New York Stock Exchange Magazine*, published by the New York Stock Exchange. These publications have articles on business and finance. They analyze general economic conditions, industries, and specific firms. The *Federal Reserve Bulletin* and the monthly *News Letters* published by the various district Federal Reserve Banks contain scholarly articles on business and finance and many useful financial statistics. The President's Council of Economic Advisors publishes its monthly *Economics Indicators,* which contains a wealth of statistical information. All of these, and, in addition, many books and pamphlets are available in any good library.

Brokerage Firms

Many of the large brokerage houses have libraries available to the public that contain many of the above publications. They also publish special studies and analyses made by their own research departments and provide their customers, free of charge, studies made by independent financial research services. One such study on Standard Oil of Indiana is shown in Figure 12–2. Many brokerage firms have their own weekly or monthly newsletter that they will send free upon request.

Additional information may be obtained from stockbrokers regarding both industries as a whole and individual corporations. For example, Merrill Lynch, Pierce, Fenner & Smith distributes a free publication entitled *Security & Industry Survey* approximately every three months. This is an analytical guide covering about thirty major industries and more than four-hundred individual companies. Each industry is classified in relation to the general market as "relatively favorable," "average," or "relatively unfavorable." Individual securities are listed as "long-term investment," "liberal income," "good quality-wider price movement," or "speculative." Such listings are quite in accord with the various investment objectives.

Investment Services

Although there are a number of services from which one may obtain research and advisory services with regard to whole industries and individual companies, the most popular are Standard and Poor's, Moody's Investors Service, Fitch Investors Service, the Value Line Investment Survey, and Argus Research Corporation. These services specialize in furnishing the public with the basic facts and figures on all securities publicly marketed and on the companies issuing them. From these services one may obtain information covering a period of many years on the assets, income, earnings, dividends, and stock prices of various corporations. The cost of these services is in many hundreds of dollars, but an individual interested may examine them free in a broker's office or at most large public and university libraries. These investment services make industry studies in which they appraise the future outlook at the various firms within each industry and their common stock. Standard and

INVESTMENT ANALYSIS

ARGUS RESEARCH CORPORATION ● NEW YORK, N.Y.

ARGUS

STANDARD OIL OF INDIANA

Copyright 1980, Argus Research Corporation
Not to be reprinted without express permission

May 27, 1980
Vol. 5, No. 33

HIGHLIGHTS

Well-managed Standard Oil of Indiana, the nation's largest domestic integrated oil company, ranks as the leading domestic driller and holder of the largest domestic acreage, whose onshore properties are twice as extensive as those of any other company. Crude oil decontrol, deep gas decontrol, and generous gas incentive prices give Standard Oil the economic incentive to step-up its drilling operations.

● Increased U.S. natural gas production in 1979 indicates that a reversal of the continuing output declines dating back to 1973 may be at hand. Crude oil production, after the moderate decline expected for 1980, should remain fairly stable for the next several years.

● Chemical activities, likely to recede in this recession year, should rebound significantly beyond 1980. Meanwhile, the recent acquisition of Cyprus Mines should augment the profitability of Standard's mineral sector.

Price (NYSE):103	**12-Mo. Rge: 121-60**
Symbol: SN	**Options Exch: C**
DJIA: 854.10	**S&P 500: 110.58**

Earnings:
1978: $7.36 1979: $10.23 1980E: $14.00
P/E Ratio (1980E): 7.4
P/E vs. S&P 500 P/E:
    (1980E): 0.96
    1974-1979 Range: 1.0-0.6
Earnings Growth Rates:
(SN) 1975-80: 20   1980-85E: 17%
(S&P 500)1975-80: 11% 1980-85E: 10%

Dividend: $3.60   **Yield 3.5%**
Financial Strength: Medium-High

Expected 6-12 Month Price Behavior
    Relative to S&P 500: Superior
Portfolio Selector Status:
    Category II - Capital Gains & Income

Standard of Indiana seems well-positioned to participate fully in any prospective major domestic exploration plays, thanks to its huge land holdings. In addition, rising production in non-Opec producing countries add stability to the company's supply position. Meanwhile, chemical earnings appear likely to achieve stable and up-trending growth rates beyond 1980. Standard of Indiana reported earnings of $3.91 per share for the first quarter of 1980 versus $2.39 last year. Although we do not expect quarterly results of this magnitude for the remainder of the year, we believe that the company will achieve a satisfactory profits showing this year. Given the likelihood of strong earnings growth in future years, the P/E ratio discount from the S&P 500 seems unwarranted, and should not long endure. Hence, we believe that SN will out-perform the market over the next six-to-12 months. We are adding SN to Category II -- Capital Gains & Income -- of the *Portfolio Selector*.

FIGURE 12–2. *A sample brokerage analysis.* (*Source:* Argus Research Corporation.)

Poor's, for example, publishes, among other things, their listed stocks report. This is a one- or two-page summary of every company listed on the New York Stock Exchange. It summarizes some vital statistics and analyzes recent developments and future prospects of the firm. It comes out periodically and is a separate sheet for each listed firm. This is called the "yellow sheet" in brokerage offices because it is printed on yellow paper. A reproduction of Standard and Poor's "Yellow Sheet" on General Electric is shown in Figure 12–3.

In addition, Standard and Poor's has their "Blue Sheet," which is an identical analysis for companies listed on the American Stock Exchange, and a "Green Sheet" for a good many over-the-counter securities. A Green Sheet is only published for the more well known over-the-counter firms.

FIGURE 12–3. *Standard and Poor's "Yellow Sheet." (Source: Standard and Poor's Corporation. This report was up-to-date at time of publication; subsequent changes are reflected in current Standard and Poor's reports.)*

General Electric 966

NYSE Symbol GE

Price	Range	P-E Ratio	Dividend	Yield	S&P Ranking
Jun. 3'80 48¾	1980 57½–44	8	3.00	6.2%	A+

Summary

General Electric is the largest manufacturer of electrical equipment, and holds leading positions in the electronics, nuclear power, consumer goods, and aerospace markets. Its important international business was expanded through the 1976 acquisition of Utah International, which derives most of its earnings from the sale of coal. Moderate earnings progress is expected for 1980.

Current Outlook

Earnings for 1980 are estimated at about $6.50 a share, up from 1979's $6.20.

Dividends have been raised 7.1%, to $0.75 quarterly from $0.70, with the July, 1980 payment.

The Technical Systems and Materials group should show further earnings progress in 1980, aided by gains in engineered materials and aerospace products. Higher capital spending should lead to progress for Industrial Products and Components. Helped by higher coking coal shipments, Utah International's earnings should also increase. Weakness in major appliance and color TV markets combined with rising costs will penalize the Consumer Products group. The Power systems business should be restricted by weakness in transmission and distribution equipment.

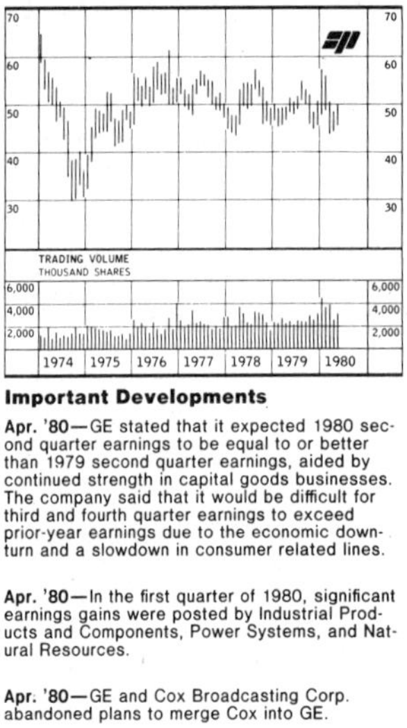

Sales (Billion $)

Quarter:	1980	1979	1978	1977
Mar.	5.88	5.08	4.44	4.06
Jun.		5.64	4.96	4.38
Sep.		5.61	4.84	4.35
Dec.		6.13	5.40	4.72
		22.46	19.64	17.51

First quarter 1980 sales rose 15.7%, year to year. Net income was up 12.6%.

Common Share Earnings ($)

Quarter:	1980	1979	1978	1977
Mar.	1.50	1.33	1.09	0.95
Jun.		1.69	1.40	1.20
Sep.		1.50	1.31	1.18
Dec.		1.68	1.59	1.46
		6.20	5.39	4.79

Important Developments

Apr. '80—GE stated that it expected 1980 second quarter earnings to be equal to or better than 1979 second quarter earnings, aided by continued strength in capital goods businesses. The company said that it would be difficult for third and fourth quarter earnings to exceed prior-year earnings due to the economic downturn and a slowdown in consumer related lines.

Apr. '80—In the first quarter of 1980, significant earnings gains were posted by Industrial Products and Components, Power Systems, and Natural Resources.

Apr. '80—GE and Cox Broadcasting Corp. abandoned plans to merge Cox into GE.

Next earnings report due in early July.

Per Share Data ($)

Yr. End Dec. 31	1979	1978	1977	[1]1976	1975	1974	1973	1972	1971	1970
Book Value	**32.08**	28.71	25.90	23.05	21.92	20.11	18.35	16.75	15.38	14.06
Earnings	**6.20**	5.39	[2]4.79	[2]4.12	[2]3.17	[2]3.34	[2]3.21	[2]2.91	[2]2.60	1.81
Dividends	**2.75**	2.50	2.10	1.70	1.60	1.60	1.50	1.40	1.37½	1.30
Payout Ratio	**44%**	46%	44%	41%	51%	48%	47%	48%	53%	72%
Prices—High	**55⅛**	57⅝	57¼	59¼	52⅞	65	75⅞	73	66½	47¼
Low	**45**	43⅝	47⅜	46	32⅜	30	55	58¼	46½	30⅛
P/E Ratio—	**9–7**	11-8	12-10	14-11	17-10	19-9	24-17	25-20	26-18	26-17

Data as orig. reptd. Adj. for stk. div(s). of 100% Jun. 1971. **1.** Reflects merger or acquisition. **2.** Ful. dil.: 5.35 in 1978, 4.75 in 1977, 4.09 in 1976, 3.12 in 1975, 3.31 in 1974, 3.18 in 1973, 2.87 in 1972, 2.57 in 1971.

Standard NYSE Stock Reports
Vol. 47/No. 112/Sec. 8

June 10, 1980

Copyright © 1980 Standard & Poor's Corp. All Rights Reserved

Standard & Poor's Corp.
25 Broadway, NY, NY 10004

966 General Electric Company

Income Data (Million $)

Year Ended Dec. 31	Revs.	Oper. Inc.	% Oper. Inc. of Revs.	Cap. Exp.	Depr.	Int. Exp.	Net Bef. Taxes	Eff. Tax Rate	Net Inc.	% Net Inc. of Revs.
1979	**22,461**	**2,754**	**12.3%**	**1,262**	**624**	**259**	**[2]2,391**	**39.9%**	**1,409**	**6.3%**
1978	19,654	2,534	12.9%	1,055	576	224	[2]2,153	41.5%	1,230	6.3%
1977	17,519	2,220	12.7%	823	522	200	[2]1,889	40.9%	1,088	6.2%
[1]1976	15,697	2,014	12.8%	740	486	175	[2]1,628	41.1%	[3] 931	5.9%
1975	13,399	1,340	10.0%	448	419	169	[2] 950	37.7%	581	4.3%
1974	13,413	1,371	10.2%	672	376	180	[2]1,001	38.2%	608	4.5%
1973	11,575	1,289	11.1%	599	334	127	[2]1,012	41.4%	585	5.1%
1972	10,240	1,129	11.0%	436	314	107	[2] 897	40.6%	530	5.2%
1971	9,425	1,011	10.7%	553	274	97	[2] 792	40.0%	472	5.0%
1970	8,727	884	10.1%	581	335	101	[2] 554	39.8%	328	3.8%

Balance Sheet Data (Million $)

Dec. 31	Cash	——Current—— Assets	Liab.	Ratio	Total Assets	Ret. on Assets	Long Term Debt	Common Equity	Total Cap.	% LT Debt of Cap.	Ret. on Equity
1979	**2,577**	**9,385**	**6,872**	**1.4**	**16,645**	**8.9%**	**947**	**7,362**	**8,461**	**11.2%**	**20.2%**
1978	2,463	8,755	6,175	1.4	15,006	8.6%	994	6,587	7,731	12.9%	19.6%
1977	2,278	7,865	5,417	1.5	13,697	8.4%	1,284	5,943	7,359	17.5%	19.4%
1976	1,613	6,685	4,605	1.5	12,050	7.7%	1,322	5,253	6,694	19.8%	18.1%
1975	853	5,566	3,963	1.4	9,764	6.0%	1,038	4,069	5,191	20.0%	14.9%
1974	372	5,223	3,880	1.3	9,369	6.9%	1,195	3,704	4,971	24.0%	17.2%
1973	322	4,485	3,492	1.3	8,324	7.4%	917	3,372	4,340	21.1%	18.1%
1972	294	3,979	2,870	1.4	7,402	7.4%	947	3,085	4,075	23.2%	18.0%
1971	286	3,639	2,840	1.3	6,888	7.2%	787	2,802	3,632	21.7%	17.6%
1970	206	3,335	2,650	1.3	6,199	5.4%	573	2,554	3,168	18.1%	13.2%

Data as orig. reptd. **1.** Reflects merger or acquisition. **2.** Incl. equity in earns. of nonconsol. subs. **3.** Reflects accounting change.

Business Summary

General Electric is the largest U.S. manufacturer of electrical equipment.

1979	Sales	Profits
Consumer products	23%	28%
Industrial products/comp.	20%	19%
Technical systems/materials	25%	25%
Power systems	15%	8%
Utah international	5%	15%
Foreign multi-industry	12%	5%

Sales to the U.S. Government were about 13% of total sales. Foreign customers accounted for about 21% of GE's net earnings.

Consumer products include major appliances, lighting products, housewares and audio products, and televisions, and television services. GE Credit Corp. accounts for 6% of GE's earnings.

Industrial Products include appliance controls, motors, electrical components for the construction industry, electronic components, and rail transportation equipment.

Technical Systems and Materials category includes military and commercial jet engines, defense electronics, engineering plastics, industrial cutting materials, medical and communications equipment, and data processing services.

Power Systems products are fossil-fuel turbines, nuclear power reactors, and transmission and distribution equipment.

Utah International's main businesses are Australian coking coal and steam coal operations. Utah also mines uranium, iron ore and copper, and has oil and gas units.

Dividend Data

Dividends have been paid since 1899. A dividend reinvestment plan is available.

Amt. of Divd. $	Date Decl.	Ex-divd. Date	Stock of Record	Payment Date
0.70	Sep. 14	Sep. 18	Sep. 24	Oct. 25'79
0.70	Nov. 16	Nov. 30	Dec. 6	Jan. 25'80
0.70	Feb. 15	Feb. 29	Mar. 6	Apr. 25'80
0.75	May 23	May 30	Jun. 5	Jul. 25'80

Next dividend meeting: mid-Sep. '80.

Capitalization

Long Term Debt: $938,100,000.

Common Stock: 227,838,531 shs. ($2.50 par). Institutions hold some 33%. Shareholders: 540,000.

Office—3135 Easton Tpke., Fairfield, Conn. 06431. **Tel**—(203) 373-2431. **Chrmn & CEO**—R. H. Jones. **VP-Secy**—W. A. Schlotterbeck. **VP-Treas**—R. E. Whitmyer. **Investor Contact**—C. D. Collison. **Dirs**—J. P. Austin, R. T. Baker, J. G. Boswell II, J. F. Burlingame, S. S. Cathcart, C. D. Dickey, Jr., H. H. Henley, Jr., H. L. Hillman, E. E. Hood, Jr., R. H. Jones, J. E. Lawrence, R. Lazarus, E. W. Littlefield, G. M. Low, G. G. Michelson, S. R. Pierce, Jr., L. T. Preston, G. H. Scribner, Jr., J. F. Welch, Jr., W. B. Wriston. **Transfer Agents**—General Electric Co., 570 Lexington Ave., NYC; First National Bank of Boston. **Registrars**—Morgan Guaranty Trust Co., NYC; First National Bank of Boston. **Incorporated** in New York in 1892.

Information has been obtained from sources believed to be reliable, but its accuracy and completeness are not guaranteed.

The Stock Exchanges

The New York Stock Exchange has its own research department and makes available a number of publications free of charge. Among these are *The New York Stock Exchange Market* and the *New York Stock Exchange Fact Book*. The American Stock Exchange makes available similar booklets called *Understanding the American Stock Exchange,* and *Amex Databook.*

Some of the smaller regional securities exchanges also have publications that are free to the public. In addition, some of the exchanges have libraries that contain extensive information and that are open to the public. While many of the publications of the organized exchanges will not provide specific investment information, they do provide good background information in the areas of business, finance, and economics.

Investment Counselors

Investment counselors will tailor an investment program for the individual investor according to the person's investment objectives. Investment counselors are professional investors and have their own skilled research departments. They, too, publish many studies, but these are available only to their customers. Investment counselors are expensive and hence not available to the small investor. The investor who has assets in excess of $100,000, however, and who wants investment advice might consider an investment counselor. Generally, large investment counselors will not accept clients with assets of less than $50,000 and some will require over $200,000. Their fees start at about .5 or 1 percent of the funds they manage and are scaled down from this level for their really large accounts.

Investment counselors will first determine the investment objectives of their clients. If they are older retired persons, they may need income. If they are younger persons, the objective may be growth. Once the objectives have been determined, different portfolio questions are indicated.

The counselors give their clients constant surveillance of their securities. The clients may give their counselors authority to buy or sell on their behalf and instruct their brokers to execute their counselor's orders. Or they may wish to retain veto power over their counselor's advice and execute their orders themselves.

While the investment counselor is a valuable source of investment information for some, as noted above, small investors cannot avail themselves of it.

Corporation Reports

Before an investor buys any given security, he or she may want to examine that corporation's financial reports—its balance sheet and income statement. Such reports give assets, liabilities, sales, expenses, earnings, dividends, and many more statistics, as well as top management's view concerning the future outlook of the business. Most corporations will send their balance sheet and income statement upon request; brokerage houses also have many of them on file in their offices.

Many laypersons are overwhelmed by these reports and feel that since they cannot understand them, there is no need to read them. This defeatist attitude is sheer nonsense. There is nothing difficult about either the balance sheet or the income statement. You learned about your personal balance sheet and income statement in Chapter 2. The corporate balance sheet and income statement are similar, except that different items and larger dollar amounts are involved. We shall work through both statements below. First, the balance sheet will be discussed.

```
I. Assets

Current Assets
  Cash                                          $    200,000
  Accounts receivable                             14,600,000
  Inventory                                       10,200,000
    Raw materials
    Goods in process
    Finished goods
Fixed Assets
  Land                                          $  5,000,000
  Building and equipment                          20,000,000
    Total assets                                 $50,000,000


II. Liabilities

Current Liabilities
  Accounts payable                               $13,500,000
  Short-term bank loan                            15,500,000
Fixed Liabilities
  Bonds outstanding (9%)                         $10,000,000
    Total Liabilities                            $39,000,000


III. Net Worth or Capital

Preferred Stock: 200,000 shares @ $10 per share $  2,000,000
Common Stock Outstanding: 1,000,000 of
  par value $1                                     1,000,000
Amounts in Excess of Par Value Received for Stock
  (paid in surplus)                                7,000,000
Retained Earnings (Earned Surplus)                 1,000,000
  Total Net Worth                                $11,000,000
  Total Liabilities and Net Worth               $50,000,000
```

FIGURE 12–4. *XYZ Corporation—Year End Balance Sheet, December 31, 198X.*

A balance sheet is broken into three major parts: assets, liabilities, and net worth. Total assets are always equal to total liabilities plus net worth. Net worth, the difference between assets and liabilities, is the stockholder's equity.

Let us examine assets first. They are split into short-term assets (current assets) and long-term assets. Short-term assets include cash, which is self-explanatory; since it is a nonearning asset, firms try to keep it low. Accounts receivable is the money owed the corporation because of sales that have been made and presumably will be collected within thirty days. Inventories, too, are self-explanatory. The fixed assets are valued at their cost less depreciation—the degree to which they are worn out. The company has total assets, with which it earns income. Assets permit the company to conduct its business.

To acquire these assets, however, the corporation had to assume some liabilities. Current liabilities are those due to be paid within a short time. Accounts payable come about because the firm buys, say, raw materials, which it will pay for within thirty days. They also include such things as accrued wages and taxes due but not yet paid. The short-term bank loans are money the company borrowed from a bank on a short-term basis. Fixed liabilities came about because when the present plant was built, the corporation sold $10,000,000 of bonds to finance it. Total liabilities represent the total amount the corporation owes, but some of these debts need not be paid for many years, although the interest on them must be paid annually.

The final item is net worth, and it belongs to the stockholders. It is the residual amount: the assets with which the company operates less the liabilities the company eventually will have to pay. Net worth is split into preferred stock, common stock at par on face value, amount of capital paid in which was in excess of par value, and retained earnings. Preferred stock is generally listed first because it is closer to bonds. It must be first netted out before getting the book value of the common stock. The par or face value of the common stock is shown and, immediately below it, the amount in excess of par received for it. This third item is often referred to as paid-in surplus. The final item under net worth is retained earnings. It is also referred to as earned surplus and it is profits the company earned in previous years but retained rather than paid out in dividends. Everything under net worth except the preferred stock belongs to the common stockholders. If that is divided by the number of shares of common stock outstanding, we obtain the book value per share of common stock (to be explained fully in chapter 13).

The balance sheet shows how much capital the company has to work with as well as how much of it is represented by bonded indebtedness and how much by stock. By comparing assets and earnings, the reader can ascertain the return to invested capital; also the percentage return on stockholder's equity and the earning per share of common stock can be calculated. These are all important factors if one is considering buying the company's stock.

We shall now briefly work through an income statement. While the balance sheet is a presentation of the company's affairs as of a given moment in time, like a photograph, the income statement is a presentation of what happened to the company over a period of time, usually a year, like the flow of water during a year. A hypothetical income statement is shown below.

FIGURE 12–5. *XYZ Corporation—Year End Income Statement, December 31, 198X.*

Sales	$11,700,000
Selling costs (advertising, etc.)	350,000
Cost of raw materials	3,300,000
Labor costs	3,750,000
Interest cost (on bonds)	900,000
Other costs (utilities, telephone, etc.)	100,000
Depreciation	1,000,000
Total Cost	9,400,000
Income (before taxes)	2,300,000
Taxes	1,104,000
After-tax profits	1,196,000

The income statement, also called a profit and loss statement or an operating statement, shows the cash flows through the company during the year and also the company's earnings or profits. Cash inflows or sales increase the company's (and the stockholder's) well-being; cash outflows decrease their well-being. Cash inflows or gross receipts are the same as sales, which were $11,700,000 for our company last year. Total costs are shown at $9,400,000 and are broken down into the various components. For most manufacturing firms, labor costs are by far the largest item. The other costs are self-explanatory, with the exception of depreciation, which needs a word of explanation. Depreciation charges are made because fixed assets such as plant and equipment eventually wear out. When they do, the company must have the money on hand to replace them. In our case, the building and equipment is valued at $20,000,000. If we assume it has a useful life of twenty years with no scrap or salvage value, we must set aside one-twentieth of its value or $1,000,000 every year so that when it wears out we will be able to replace it. Depreciation is an expense and reduces profits by $1,000,000 per year. However, it is a unique kind of cost, one that does not cause a cash outflow from the company. While the $1,000,000 depreciation expense reduces profits by that amount, the company still has the money and will keep it invested somewhere and add to it every year until the time comes to replace the building and equipment.

After taxes, profits are $1.196 million, which is just over 10.8 percent return on total net worth. This sum of $1.196 million can be paid to the stockholders in the form of a cash dividend or it can be retained by the company, in which case it will go into the earned surplus account in the balance sheet for next year. Most companies split their after-tax profits, paying some to the stockholder and retaining some. However, in the above case there are 200,000 shares of preferred stock outstanding and they must be paid a dividend before the common may receive anything. If we assume that they receive a 10 percent dividend on their par value of $2,000,000, this reduces profits by $200,000, which leaves a profit for the common stockholders of $996,000. This is a return of 11.07 percent on the common stockholders equity of $9,000,000.

When analyzing balance sheets and income statements, it is often wise to go over the past reports to discover trends. Are sales rising and if so, how much? How have profits behaved over a number of years? Are the ratios of costs to sales rising or declining? These and many other important questions should be kept in mind when analyzing corporation reports. For example, when analyzing the balance sheet, we should also examine earnings per share. This is obtained by dividing earnings, after taxes and after making an allowance for a payment to the preferred stockholders, by the total number of shares of common stock outstanding. In our case above we had after-tax earnings of $1.196 million. After the allowance shown above for preferred stockholders of 10 percent, there remains $996,000 which accrues to the common stockholder and amounts to 99.6 cents per share ($996,000 ÷ 1,000,000 shares).

Our company may or may not declare a dividend. If it does, we have a concept called dividends per share. By examining this over the years, we can determine if dividends per share are rising, falling, or remaining relatively constant. This may influence whether or not we wish to buy the stock.

We may also wish to compare earnings per share (99.6 cents in our case above) with the market price of the common stock. If we divide the market price of the common stock by the earnings, $.99½, we get a concept called the price earnings ratio. This ratio may be ten or twenty; it varies from stock to stock. But it is an indicator of whether the stock might be priced too high or whether it is a genuine bargain.

Finally, we may want to determine the yield of the common stock. This is simply the annual dividends per share divided by the market price of the stock and expressed in percentage terms. Once more, comparisons over time can be examined in order to help shed light on whether or not a given stock is a good buy.

Security analysts do not agree whether earnings per share or dividends (yield) per share is the best indicator of a stock's value. But all of these should be taken into account in making investment decisions. These and many other important questions should be kept in mind when analyzing corporation reports.

QUESTIONS FOR REVIEW

1. How does the corporate form of business organization differ from that of a partnership or single proprietorship?

2. One of the advantages of a corporation is said to be its limited liability. Explain.

3. What are the main objectives of most investors?

4. How do common stock investments help to hedge inflation?

5. What is the difference between a short-run and a long-run investor? Should the small investor be a short-run or a long-run investor?

6. Why are utility stocks considered a good hedge against recession?

7. Explain how holding your assets in the form of money or in an insured financial institution can possibly involve any risk of loss.

8. Why does the price of a bond move down when the market rate of interest rises? What determines how much it comes down?

9. What is "market risk"?

10. Purchasing a number of issues of oil stock is a good example of reducing risk by diversification. Do you agree or disagree? Substantiate your position.

11. Outline the major sources of investment information.

12. How does an investment counselor operate?

13. The "net worth" figure on a balance sheet is said to belong to the stockholders. Explain in detail.

14. In examining corporate balance sheets and income statements, why is it important to examine both for several years past?

CASES

1. Jim and Mary McGovern are a young couple in their early thirties. Jim, a partner in a CPA firm, earns about $24,000 per year; Mary, a graphic artist, earns about $15,000. They believe they should start an investment program, and they have decided to save $100 per month for the purpose of purchasing securities. What do you feel their investment objectives should be? Why? Should Jim and Mary be long-run or short-run investors and why?

2. Bob and Virginia Carels have inherited $10,000, which they would like to invest. They know that they can earn about 5½ percent on their money if they put it in a savings and loan association. However, they feel that prices will rise by about 7 to 10 percent per year on the average over the next few years

and would like an investment that either yields substantially more or will provide them with a hedge against inflation. What are the better methods of hedging inflation? Why is this the case?

3. Bertha Underwood is a widow whose husband left her a nice nest egg. She has a $500 per month annuity and an additional $50,000 that she would like to invest. She is considering two alternatives: she could buy corporate securities or she could go into partnership with her brother, who is in the trucking business. She believes the return would be about the same in either case, but one of her friends has told her that it is riskier to invest in partnerships than in corporations. Bertha cannot understand this. Can you explain?

4. Kermit and Rita Jones recently purchased $5,000 worth of high-grade corporate bonds yielding 9 percent with a maturity of twenty years. They fully expected to leave their funds invested for twenty years and then use the proceeds to help pay for their children's college education. How much interest would they earn over the twenty years if they kept their investment?

   However, two years after the purchase Rita became sick and they were forced to sell the bonds to obtain emergency funds. They were surprised to find that their bonds were now worth $6,000. Can you explain this?

5. Edward and Marcella have over the past twenty years built up a portfolio of $50,000 in common stock. They were fortunate at first in that they made good capital gains on their stock without a careful analysis; that is, almost everything they have bought appreciated in price during the decade of the 1960s. Now, however, they feel that the market is more risky and they would like to minimize that risk. Can you show them how? Why did they have such good fortune in the 1960s?

6. George Buck is a young Methodist minister who teaches philosophy of religion at the Southwest Theological Seminary in Dallas, Texas, and earns $20,000 per year. His wife, Marilyn, has her Ph.D. in social work from NYU and works as a consultant at the Texas School for the Blind and last year earned $41,600. Their combined salary provides a handsome surplus, and they would like your advice on how to invest it. They believe they have all the insurance they need; they already have $10,000 in a savings and loan association; and they own their own home. They are currently able to set aside about $1,200 per month. What advice would you give them?

SUGGESTED READINGS

American Stock Exchange Annual Report. New York.

Barron's Weekly. A weekly finance magazine.

Engle, Louis. *How to Buy Stocks,* 5th ed. New York: Bantam Books, 1976.

The Exchange. Magazine published monthly by the New York Stock Exchange.

Financial Analysts Journal. New York: Published bimonthly by The Financial Analyst Federation.

Fisher, Lawrence, and Lorie, James H. *Rates of Return on Investments in Common Stocks*. New York: Merrill Lynch, Pierce, Fenner, and Smith, Inc.

Fortune. A monthly magazine containing a great deal of information on business, economics, and finance.

Freund, William C., and Lee, Murray G. *Investment Fundamentals*. New York: American Bankers Association, no date.

How Over-the-Counter Securities are Traded. New York: Merrill Lynch, Pierce, Fenner, and Smith, Inc. Request copies from this firm.

How to Invest in Stocks and Bonds, New York: Merrill Lynch, Pierce, Fenner, and Smith.

How to Read a Financial Report. Merrill, Lynch, Pierce, Fenner, and Smith, Inc., 165 Broadway, New York, N.Y. 10006.

How to Understand Financial Statements. New York: New York Stock Exchange. Your broker can get this for you.

How You Get More Out of Financial News. Princeton, N.J.: Dow Jones & Company, Inc., The Educational Services Bureau.

Inflation and/or Unemployment. Philadelphia: Federal Reserve Bank of Philadelphia.

Levine, Sumner N. *The Dow Jones Irwin Business Almanac*. Homewood, Ill.: Dow Jones Irwin Publishing Co., 1979.

The Market Place. Chicago: Chicago Board of Trade.

Nelson, Paula. *The Joy of Money*. New York: Bantam Books, 1977.

Spiro, Herbert T. *Finance for the Non-financial Manager*. New York: John Wiley and Sons, 1978.

Time. A weekly magazine that contains a good deal of information on business and finance.

Tobias, Andrew. *The Only Investment Guide You'll Ever Need*. New York: Harcourt Brace Jovanovich, 1978.

Understanding the New York Stock Exchange. New York: New York Stock Exchange.

U.S. News & World Report. A weekly magazine that contains a good deal of information on business and finance.

The Wall Street Journal. Published daily by Dow Jones & Company.

What Everybody Ought to Know about this Stock and Bond Business. New York: Merrill Lynch, Pierce, Fenner, and Smith, Inc.

Zahorchak, Michael G. *The Art of Low Risk Investing.* New York: Van Nostrand Reinhold, 1977.

Chapter Thirteen

The Array Of Securities

October. This is one of the peculiarly dangerous months to specu-late in stocks. The others are July, August, September, October, November, December, January, February, March, April, May, and June.

MARK TWAIN

The objectives of this chapter are to

1   Introduce common stock and some of its value concepts

2   Classify stock in accordance with various investment objectives.

3   Introduce the various types of preferred stock

4   Present the array of different corporate bonds

5   Introduce U.S. government as well as state and local securities

6   Examine bond ratings and bond yields

In this chapter we will examine the various securities (obligations of issuers) available to the investor. The issuers of securities are, generally speaking, business firms and government, and they represent the demand for savings or, what is the same thing, the supply of securities. However, there is a wide variety in the type of securities and this is the primary concern of this chapter.

The buyers of securities represent the supply of savings, or the demand for securities. The demand for securities can be further broken down into the institutional demand and the demand on the part of individuals. The institutional demands stem from life insurance companies, corporate pension funds, mutual funds, and commercial banks. We will present the array of securities that are pertinent to the individual investor.

THE ARRAY OF STOCK AND GENERAL COMMENTS

Securities can be broken down into two broad general classifications: stocks and bonds. Each of these in turn can be broken down into a number of subdivisions. We shall begin with stock, which represents the ultimate of risk capital. This statement applies only to common stock, however; preferred stock is less risky. We shall examine common stock first and then preferred. Figure 13-1 is a picture of a common stock certificate.

Common Stock in General

For all practical purposes, there is only one kind of common stock. Common stockholders are the residual recipients of a corporation's income. Because they receive what is left after all others get their prior claim, the common stockholders' futures are closely tied to that of the corporation. If the corporation does well, the common stockholders will do well. If the corporation does poorly, the common stockholders will suffer. Common stockholders are also the last to be paid off in the event the corporation must be liquidated and sell off its assets. Owning common stock then is riskier than owning other securities. For these reasons the market value of common stock fluctuates more than that of other securities.

Common stock ownership conveys no rights except the right to vote at stockholders meetings, where the corporation's board of directors is elected and certain other corporate decisions are made. The common stockholder is never promised dividends. It is illegal for a corporation to pay dividends unless it earns them, and even then it is under no obligation to pay them.

While there is nonvoting as well as voting common stock, the former is rare, and it may not be listed on the New York Stock Exchange.

FIGURE 13-1. *Common stock certificate.* (Courtesy General Motors Corporation.)

Some Value Concepts of Common Stock

There are four general methods of valuing common stock: (1) par value, (2) book value, (3) market value, and (4) liquidation value. In most states it is now possible to issue a no-par-value common stock, and often this is done, although historically stock always had a par value. These terms can sometimes be confusing and need to be explained.

1. *Par value* is the face value of the stock printed on the certificate. A fixed and arbitrary value is assigned when the stock is issued; it has little financial significance. Even when the stock is issued, it may be at or above par. Today stock is usually sold substantially above par. Historically, par value was higher and a more meaningful indicator of what the stock was worth. If a stock was sold at below par, the stockholder was often held liable for the difference between the price paid for it and par value. Today this is no longer true because stock cannot legally be sold below par when it is first issued. Stock which has no printed face value is called no-par stock.

The major significance of par value is for tax purposes. In some states, where corporate franchise taxes are based on par value, it is to the interest of the corporation to keep par value low. Also, par value has some meaning insofar as preferred stock is concerned because the dividend is often based upon par value. Preferred stock is explained in greater detail below, where the importance of par value on preferred stock will become clear.

2. *The book value* of common stock is an accounting concept. It is what the stock is worth today from an accounting point of view. When you examined the corporate balance sheet you were introduced to the concept of net worth (assets minus liabilities). The net worth, less a possible allowance for preferred stock, belongs to the common stockholder. It is also called the stockholder's equity. Net worth (minus preferred stock outstanding, if any) divided by the total number of shares of common stock outstanding is the book value per share.

3. *Market value* is what you have to pay for the stock if you wish to buy it—or what you will get if you sell it. It is often above book value, and, if so, it is because the expected future income has been taken into account by investors and their demand has bid up the market price. This process is sometimes referred to as discounting the future. During the 1960s some stocks had a market value so far above the book value that they seem to have discounted not only the future but the hereafter as well. This is, generally speaking, no longer true.

4. *Liquidation value* is a meaningful term only if the life of the corporation is likely to be terminated. This is generally only the case with unsuccessful corporations. If a corporation is to be liquidated, its assets will be sold and if there is anything left after all its legal bills have been paid, the remainder will be divided up among the stockholders. This part left for the stockholder divided by the number of shares outstanding is the liquidation value. It would at first glance appear that liquidation value would be the same as book value (these could, of course, both be zero or negative). However, this is not necessarily so because the assets might be so highly specialized that no ready market for them exists.

Earnings, Yield, and Capital Gain on Common Stock[1]

The earnings and yield on common stock vary greatly from firm to firm and from time to time. Earnings are simply the total earnings after taxes per share. The yield is less than

---

1. This material is drawn from Wolf and Associates, "Personal Financial Seminars." Used by permission.

earnings because an adjustment must be made to net out the corporation's retained earnings. Yield then is the actual dividends paid as a percentage of the price of the stock. An example of earning and yield will clarify this.

$$\frac{\text{total after tax earnings}}{\text{total number of shares outstanding}} = \frac{\$7,500,000}{1,000,000 \text{ shares}} = \$7.50/\text{share}$$

In most cases part of this $7.50 is paid out in the form of dividends and part is retained and plowed back into the corporation for expansion. However, the entire $7.50 belongs to the stockholder, and that portion retained will increase the book value and hopefully the market value of the stock. Earnings per share is an important criterion in determining whether you might want to buy a given stock. A comparison of earnings with the market price of a given share gives us its price earnings ratio which is an important analytical tool. Let's assume our stock above, earning $7.50 per share, is selling at $75. We now may calculate its price earnings ratio (PER). It is

$$\frac{\text{market price}}{\text{earnings per share}} = \frac{\$75}{\$7.50} = 10$$

Other stock will have different price earnings ratios. To determine whether a given stock is a candidate for purchase, examine its P/E ratio and also how its earnings per share have grown over the years. If its earnings per share have grown at the rate of 10 percent per year and if you believe that rate of growth will continue into the future you can project its earnings into the future. If $7.50 is compounded at 10 percent for five years, earnings per share in five years should be about $12.08. If a PER of 10 seems valid, then in five years a PER of 10 would put the market price of the stock at $120. This would provide a nice capital gain. This is one way of seeking out good common stock investments. Compare various price earnings ratios (PER), project future earnings, and locate stocks that are underpriced in today's market and whose prospects for growth are good.

Yield as noted above is simply the annual dividend payment per share divided by the market price. In our example above, assume that there is a 50 percent dividend payout rate. Then

$$\frac{\text{dividends per share}}{\text{market price per share}} = \frac{\$3.75}{\$75.00} = 5\% \text{ yield.}$$

The next question is how much should the yield be; also how does the 5 percent yield compare with other stock in companies that provide the same or similar business risk and market risk. The investor must make a personal decision regarding how much of a yield he thinks he should have in light of alternative investment opportunities open to him that have comparable risk. Moreover, if a capital gain is also expected, a lower dividend yield is usually acceptable.

In the above case where, in addition to a $3.75 dividend, $3.75 is retained by the corporation, the market price (as well as the book value) of the stock will tend to rise. I say tend to rise, but this is true only if the retained profits are successfully reinvested in expanding the business and its profits. In such a case the stockholders get part of their reward in the form of capital appreciation rather than in cash dividends. As will be explained below, this may very well be to the investor's advantage taxwise because capital gains are taxed at a more favorable rate than are dividends.

Traditionally it has been felt by most investors that the dividend yield on a common stock should be higher than the yield on bonds—to compensate the investor for the greater risk associated with common stock. And traditionally the yield on common stock has been higher. But in recent years, due to high interest rates, sometimes bond yields have been higher. Even if stock yields were below bond yields, certainly earnings (dividends plus retained earnings) on common stock should be superior to bond yield. In many cases they are, but the retained earnings are not always reflected in common stock price appreciation, and in such a case, the yields and capital appreciation on stock combined might be below the yield on bonds. This has sometimes been the case in recent years.

However, investing in common stock has traditionally been one of the better ways to participate in the future economic growth of the country because profits rise with growth, and this often shows up in the form of capital gains on stock. Economic growth is a function of population growth and of technological change. Technological change will enhance profits either by reducing costs or by bringing forth new or improved products, or by some combination of the two. New and improved products enhance profits by increasing sales.

Figure 13-2 illustrates how dividends have risen over the past forty years in relation to the cost of living. If we considered the total earnings on common stock (dividends plus retained earnings), the record of common stock would look even better.

Perhaps the best measure of how good an investment a common stock has been is to take into account the total economic increment it has provided its owner. This includes cash dividends as well as capital gains, which are influenced by retained earnings but may very well be higher or lower than retained earnings indicate they should be. Suppose you had

FIGURE 13-2. *Industrial stock dividends vs. cost of living. (Source: Investment Companies, Mutual Funds and Other Types, 1980, Wiesenberger Financial Services, a division of Warren, Gorham & Lamont, Inc., p. 57.)*

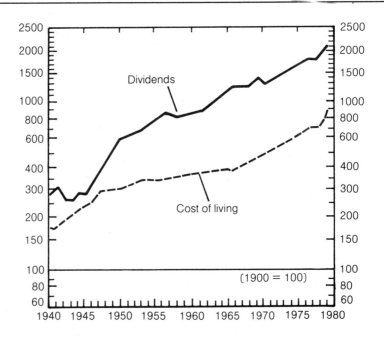

Part 3 / Investments

purchased a common stock for $50 per share. Suppose too that its after-tax earnings were $5 per share and that it retained $2.50 and paid a cash dividend of $2.50. Clearly its dividend yield would be 5 percent but its total earnings 10 percent. But if the market price of the stock had increased over the year to $60 per share, the total economic increment it has provided is $12.50 (the $2.50 of retained earnings is included in the $10 capital gain, but the $2.50 dividend is not). A return of $12.50 on a $50 investment is 25 percent. To be sure, in order to realize this capital gain in the form of cash, the stockholder would have to sell the stock. Nevertheless, the capital gain cannot be ignored. The next year it may be more or less. Table 13-1 illustrates these ratios; Figure 13-3 shows how corporate dividends, profits, and taxes have fluctuated in recent years.

Rankings or Ratings of Common Stock

Bonds have long been rated as to their credit worthiness, with AAA being the highest quality. This will be explained below under "The Array of Bonds." In recent years, there have developed stock ratings, or rankings as they are called. The best known of these is Standard and Poor's rankings. Stocks are ranked somewhat differently than bonds, however. Stocks are not ranked in terms of degree of protection for principal and interest. However, the ranking services take into account such things as the product produced, managerial capabilities, financial structure, and past earnings and dividends. In addition, growth and stability of earnings are assessed and the long-run record of performance. In light of all that, a ranking is assigned with A + being the highest. The following eight rankings are currently used:

- A+ Highest
- A High
- A− Good
- B+ Median
- B Speculative
- B− Highly speculative
- C Marginal
- D In reorganization

TABLE 13–1. *Possible returns on stock*

ABC STOCK		PERCENT RETURN ON INVESTMENT	
Purchase price		$50.00	
Earnings (per year)		5.00	10%
Dividend	$2.50		5%
Retained Earnings	2.50		
Capital Gains		10.00	20%
Due to Retained Earnings	2.50		
Due to Other Factors	7.50		
Economic Increment		12.50	25%

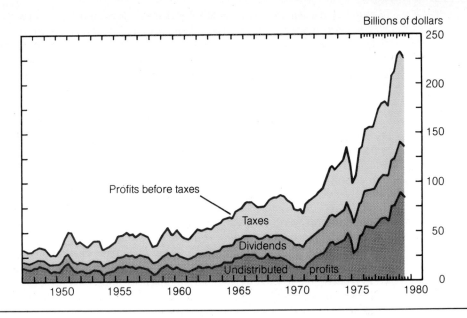

Billions of dollars

Profits before taxes

Taxes

Dividends

Undistributed profits

FIGURE 13-3. *Corporate profits, taxes, and dividends. (Source: 1979 Historical Chart Book,* Board of Governors of the Federal Reserve System, p. 60.)

Classification of Common Stock

Common stock can be classified into a number of different categories. It is possible to identify growth stock, income stock, cyclical stock, defensive stock, blue-chip stock, speculative stock, and others. Investment opportunities change as do people; so a stock that at one time may be considered a growth stock may at another time be regarded as an income stock. Also, some stock may have the characteristics of several classifications; defensive and income stocks, for instance, may in some cases be the same. Obviously some stock may have some of the attributes of all four. Income and growth stocks—indeed all stocks—have some cyclical aspects. Nevertheless, many stocks fall by and large into patterns. You should select stock in accordance with your investment objectives which were discussed in the previous chapter.

When stocks are classified as speculative or blue-chip, they are in reality classified according to risk. These are relative terms, as there is an element of speculation in all stock and an element of investment in all. The least speculative (most blue-chip) stock over the years has probably been American Telephone and Telegraph. The most speculative (least blue-chip) stock is probably Dry Gulch Gold and Uranium, or some other stock like it. We shall examine all of these classifications.

1. Growth Stock

Growth stocks are generally considered to be those that have good earnings but a very low dividend yield because the company is reinvesting the bulk of its earnings in expansion. This investment increases both the book value and the market value of the stock, and the stockholder's goal in such a case presumably is to achieve capital gains through the appreciation of the stock. A growth company, then, is one that has a good record of high and growing earnings per dollar invested, one that is doing better each year than the year before. Moreover, the company is using these earnings to expand its capacity. It is producing a product for which the demand is expected to increase greatly in the future.

Growth stocks were the glamour issues of securities just a few short years ago. Electronics, drugs, and space stock were among them. The stock market decline in 1969 and 1970 tarnished some of these stocks. But that has happened before and no doubt will happen again.

To buy a growth stock, one may have to pay a high price, as many of them have excessively high price/earnings ratios. This is because the stock market is said to discount the future. If the company is earning a high rate of return per dollar invested and the rate is expected to increase further because the demand for the product is going to increase in the future, the market price of the stock will be bid up. Since the future profits of the company look good, up goes the market price of its stock. This process is called discounting future profits. In some cases it may be too late to buy such a stock; but, on the other hand, if the company continues expansion at its present rate, the stock will often continue to climb.

Let us assume that a given growth stock has discounted profits five years into the future and is selling for $100 per share. Its price earnings ratio is out of line from an investment point of view; but if it is really a growth company, then five years from now it will still have discounted profits five years into the future (or perhaps seven) and may be selling for $200 per share. The opposite possibility is that its growth may be over or slowing down and that it may not rise much above $100. The secret to success in growth stocks is to find them first. This often means buying a speculative security. The investor wants the stock of a firm that will become the General Motors of the space industry. If a person buys a proven growth stock, he or she pays for it, since it has already discounted the future. (Indeed, a few years ago some of these stocks were at a level that suggested they might have discounted the hereafter as well.) Some stocks that are typically looked upon as being growth stock include those of IBM, Coca Cola, and some of the newer, smaller, minicomputer companies. Growth stocks generally appeal to younger people who do not need income at the present time but who want capital gains they will take later.

2. Income Stock

Income stocks are those in companies whose earnings are good but that either are not growing much or are growing with external funds.[2] They may be mature companies producing a product for which the demand has stabilized. They are companies, moreover, that pay out a large proportion of their earnings each year in the form of dividends. Utilities, tobacco, and food are considered such income areas. Not only are dividends fairly high but they are steady because the earnings of the companies are steady. AT&T for many years has been considered an imcome stock par excellence; it had for a long time yielded a steady return. Its current yield is about 9.5 percent. Income stocks in general appeal to older people who may need the income for retirement and who would benefit less from long-term growth. However, a good yield is one criterion that should be used by everyone in selecting stock for a well-balanced portfolio.

3. Cyclical Stock

Cyclical stock fluctuates widely over swings in the business cycle. It is the stock of those companies whose sales and earnings vary greatly. The steel, nonferrous metals, and the machine tool industry are examples. Because earnings fluctuate, so too do dividends and the

---

2. External funds are funds obtained by selling new issues of bonds or common stock.

market price of the stock. Nearly all stock fluctuates somewhat with swings in the business cycle, but cyclical stocks do so more than others.

Investors who buy a cyclical stock are betting that economic and business conditions will improve. In this connection, a word of warning is in order. The buyer should beware of selecting a cyclical stock after there has been an unusual jump in either sales or earnings unless the outlook is relatively certain that the up-trend will continue. Once sales and/or earnings have risen substantially, it is often already too late to buy cyclicals; now is the time to sell.

The Wall Street maxim in relation to cyclical stock is "Buy on bad news, sell on good." Investors in cyclical stock should buy when sales and earnings are down, sell when these figures are favorable. To do so one must, of course, be flexible and in a position to hold onto the stock for a considerable period of time, frequently for several years. However, this is true for any stock. No one but a professional speculator, and certainly no small investor, should go into the stock market on a short-term basis.

4. Defensive Stock

Defensive stock is often income stock. It would probably be more accurate to say that most defensive stock is income stock but not as many income stocks could be classified as defensive. A defensive stock is one that declines less than most on a general downturn. By the same token, it may not rise as much in a general upturn. The reason is that the company's sales and hence its income are more stable over the business cycle because the demand for its product is more stable. Such companies include some of the food and cigarette makers, but usually utilities are considered the best defensive stocks. Some utilities have been considered growth stock recently, especially if they are in an area that is growing rapidly, such as Florida or Arizona. Most utilities, however, pay out a considerable portion of their earnings as dividends and hence are more income and defensive than growth and defensive. Some analysts look upon defensive stock as the opposite of cyclical stock. If you expected the economy in general to be heading into a recession, you might well sell any cyclical stocks you had and buy either bonds or defensive stock. This is known as taking a defensive position.

5. Blue-chip Stock

When classifying stock according to risk, blue-chip stock is the least risky—least risky both as to missing a dividend and declining in price, although the price does decline when the market in general declines. Generally, however, the price of blue-chip stocks will decline less in a general downturn than the average. They are the stocks of the old well-established companies that have proved they can earn profits. They cannot be classified by industries at all, because some industries have both blue-chip companies and firms that either are not tested or that for other reasons are considered highly speculative.

A list of blue-chip stock would include General Motors, General Electric, American Telephone and Telegraph, Exxon, Standard Oil of California, and other firms of similar financial strength.

6. Speculative Stock

These stocks are untried securities, often stocks of new, small firms whose chances for success are not great or firms that at least are untested. Some of the small mining and uranium stocks are examples, as are the small electronics. Investors should not put any money in these stocks unless they can afford to lose it if the worst comes. The probability of gain is small, but the amount of gain would be great if it should come. One assumes a great risk in buying them. A small investor with few funds should probably never buy highly speculative securities. A person of means may want to take a flyer on them occasionally.

Speculation is a relative term, as pointed out before, and some people take a chance on a mildly speculative stock. Of course, all stock has at least a slight element of speculation attached to it.

Incidentally, the investor can speculate with bonds as well as stock. One can buy bonds that are in default at a tremendous discount and hope for a substantial return when the firm is liquidated.

Preferred Stock

Preferred stock is a special kind of stock issued by a corporation that gives some kind of preference to the purchasers. Generally the preference takes the form of a fixed return or dividend and a preference as to assets. For example, a preferred stockholder may be given a 9 percent return. This 9 percent is figured on the face or par value of the stock. Thus if a stock share were issued at $100 par and it were a 9 percent preferred, the stockholder would be entitled to $9.00 per annum on each share of stock he or she holds, provided there are enough profits to pay the $9. This $9 per share, moreover, is due and payable before any distribution can be made to the common stockholders.

In addition to the preference in the form of earnings, the preferred stockholders are generally entitled to share in the assets of the corporation at dissolution before the common stockholders may receive any of the money. That is, if the corporation decides to go out of business either voluntarily or involuntarily, the preferred stockholders will divide the assets and pay themselves off at par value before the common stockholders may receive any part of the assets. Some variations of preferred stock are examined below. Figure 13-4 shows a preferred stock certificate.

Cumulative and Noncumulative Preferred Stock

A corporation issuing 9 percent cumulative preferred stock is liable to the preferred stockholders for past dividends that have not been paid. Suppose a company fails to pay dividends for three years, and the stock (with a $100 par value) calls for a payment of 9 percent and is cumulative; then the company must pay the cumulative preferred stockholders $27 at the end of the three years before any money is payable to the common stockholders.

Notice that corporations do not have to pay dividends to preferred stockholders even if they have the profits. They must merely pay the preferred before they may pay the common; and if the preferred is cumulative, they must pay all back dividends before common can be paid. Sometimes there are limits to how far back dividends have to be paid, such as three-year or five-year cumulative. Other preferred cumulative stocks have no limits, and all back dividends have to be paid before common stockholders can receive anything.

On noncumulative preferred stock the corporation need only pay the current year's dividends before it may pay dividends on the common stock.

Participating Preferred

With this type of preferred stock, if the earnings are sufficient, the preferred stockholders not only are given their agreed dividends but are entitled to share equally in the dividends paid to the common stockholders. Generally where there is a participating preferred stock, the preferred stockholders are paid their agreed-upon rate, say $9 per share, then the common stockholders are paid an equal dividend, or $9 per share, and after that the

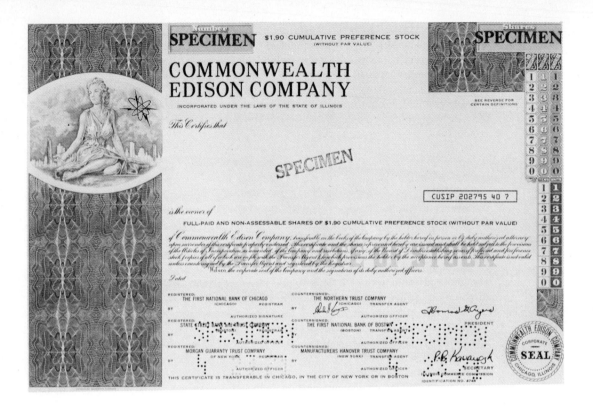

FIGURE 13-4. *A preferred stock certificate.* (Courtesy Commonwealth Edison Company and the First National Bank of Boston.)

remainder of the money is distributed equally among the preferred stockholders and the common stockholders.[3]

Cumulative Participating Preferred

Obviously these two features can be combined, and we have then a preferred stock that must be paid past dividends before common is paid any dividends, and then will share equally with the common anything that remains.

Callable or Redeemable Preferred

Callable preferred stock is preferred stock issued by a corporation with a provision that the corporation has an option to buy the stock back from the preferred stockholders on terms

---

3. The figure of $9 is not quite accurate because the price of the common and preferred stock is not usually the same. The common stock may be selling for $50 per share, whereas the preferred in this example has a face value of $100. Moreover, the price of the common stock often fluctuates widely over a period of time. Therefore a participating agreement must be spelled out at the time the preferred stock is issued; generally it will give the common the same percentage return that the preferred has received, after which they share equally. But this means that the common must be evaluated at the time the preferred is issued, because its price fluctuates in the market. Usually the market price (or some price near it) of the common at the time the preferred is issued is taken; the common would get 9 percent of that, and then sharing would begin.

specified at the time the stock is issued. For example, callable preferred stock may be issued at $100 per share and may be callable at $110. That is, if the corporation desires to exercise its option, it may buy back the stock at the call price of $110.

Corporations issue stock of this nature so that if the market is such that they could issue a new preferred at, say, 7 or 8 percent rather than at the old rate of 9, they can convert. Or they may wish to clean up their capital structure and eliminate the preferred. As far as the market is concerned, very seldom will the market price exceed the call price because of the possibility of redemption by the issuer.

Convertible Preferred

This is preferred stock that can be exchanged for common stock by the stockholders at their option. The exchange ratio is determined at the time the stock is issued. Therefore, if the common stock of the corporation appreciates in the market, it will pull the preferred up with it. Convertible preferred stock has all the advantages of preferred, as well as of the common, just as in the case of convertible bonds which are discussed below.

A Footnote on Preferred Stock

Preferred stock may have the features of a bond or the features of common stock, or some of each. If it is participating preferred, it is a bit closer to common because it shares the good fortune of the common. However, it may not share as much of the bad. If it is non-callable and nonparticipating, it is closer to a bond. Its rate of return is fixed, and it will fluctuate in the market like a bond with variations in the interest rate. If it is convertible into common, it again shares in the good fortune of common but not necessarily in the bad because it will rise in price with the common but will not necessarily fall if the market price of the common declines.

THE ARRAY OF BONDS AND GENERAL COMMENTS

Corporate bonds are certificates of indebtedness. They are legal liabilities of the corporation. Bonds are long-term obligations and the corporation is obligated to pay a fixed interest rate for so many years, and then to redeem the bond at face value. This interest must be paid even if it is not earned. The interest on bonds must be paid first before a payment can be made even to preferred stockholders. In the event the corporation is liquidated, bondholders are repaid their capital even before preferred stockholders. This is why bonds are considered senior securities: their needs must be taken care of first.

Corporate Bonds in General

Corporate bonds are nearly always issued in denominations of $1,000 face value which is also referred to as par value. When the word *bond* is used, it is assumed to be of that denomination. The interest rate and maturity date are shown on the face of the bond. The interest rate shown thereon is called the coupon rate which, if 9 percent, obligates the corporation to pay $90 per year until the bond matures. Often, this would be paid at the rate of $45 every six months.

Bonds may be sold at their face value, above it, or below it. If a bond is sold below par, it is said to be at a discount; if above par, it is at a premium. If a bond sells at a premium and has a coupon rate of 10 percent, the yield is less than 10 percent. A bond sold at a discount has a yield greater than its coupon rate. Yields and the coupon rate, then, are not the same.

Bond prices fluctuate in the market inversely with changes in the going market interest rate, as we noted in the previous chapter. Generally, when corporations offer new issues of bonds, they are issued at par or close to it.

Most corporation bonds are coupon bonds; that is, they have interest coupons attached, and generally a coupon is due and payable every six months. The bondholder clips the coupon and mails it to the trustee for the interest. Often the coupons can be redeemed at banks. These bondholders are the people Thorstein Veblen had in mind when he referred to the coupon clippers. Noncoupon bonds do exist, the interest on which is automatically mailed to the bondholder by the trustee.

Most bonds in the United States are registered. They have the name of the owner on the face of the instrument, and they cannot be transferred without endorsement. The corporation issuing the bond must have a trustee (usually a bank) who keeps the records and mails interest payments.

Some bonds, however, are bearer bonds, which means that they are not registered, but they are rare in the United States. Bearer bonds are always coupon bonds, whereas registered bonds can be either coupon or noncoupon bonds.

In addition to corporate bonds, there are also United States government bonds and state and local bonds, called municipal bonds. Each of these can be classified into subgroups, which we shall now cover beginning with the corporate subgroup. Figure 13-5 is a picture of a corporate bond.

Mortgage Bonds

These bonds are secured by a mortgage on all or part of the corporate property. A trustee, frequently a bank, is appointed to act for the bondholders. Title to the property is transferred to the trustee for the benefit of the bondholders. In the event that the corporation fails to pay either the interest or the principal when due, the trustee forecloses on the assets it holds and distributes the proceeds pro rata to the bondholders.

There are first-mortgage, second-mortgage, and sometimes even third-mortgage bonds. In these cases, first-mortgage bonds are the senior security and have a first claim to the assets if the company is to be liquidated.

Collateral Trust Bonds

These are corporate bonds secured by collateral other than real estate. The collateral may be stock in other corporations or other security owned by the corporations, such as promissory notes and accounts receivable. Often these bonds are issued by investment companies or other financial institutions that have securities of other companies but usually not much real estate.

Equipment Trust Obligations

These are securities issued by corporations with specific equipment of the corporation used as security of the loan. Title to the equipment vests in a trustee, who holds it for the benefit of the owners of the bonds. This sort of security had its inception with the railroads, which pledged their rolling stock, but it has been extended to other types of corporate equipment as well. In the case of the railroads, an equipment trust bond is issued with rolling stock for security. In the event of default, the trustee sells the engines and box cars and pays the proceeds to the bondholders.

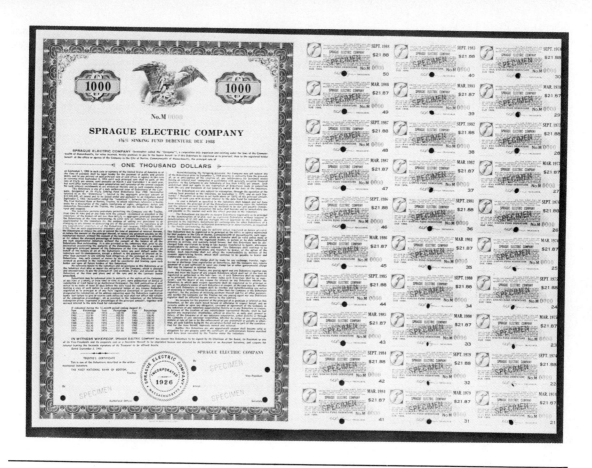

FIGURE 13-5. *A corporate bond.* (Courtesy Sprague Electric Company and the First National Bank of Boston.)

Debentures

A debenture bond is a bond issued by a corporation for which no specific assets are pledged. The general credit rating of the corporation is at stake, and any and all assets can be seized if these bonds are in default. However, if first-mortgage bonds, collateral trust bonds, or equipment trust obligations are also outstanding for which specific assets have been pledged, these specific assets cannot be used to satisfy the claims of debenture bondholders until the other bondholders' claims have been met. In the case where the debentures were issued first, then they usually have a clause in them that requires they have equal rights with any future mortgage bonds.

Convertible Bonds

Convertible bonds can be exchanged for a predetermined number of common stocks at the option of the bondholder. Convertible bonds are also usually debentures, but they need not be. The principle of convertible bonds is similar to that of convertible preferred stock. If the corporation does well, the convertibles take on the features of common stock, whereas if the corporation does poorly, the convertibles have the features of bonds. Convertible bonds pay a fixed interest rate like any bond and must be redeemed at maturity. However, they include a clause that permits the bondholder to convert them to common stock in the future at a rate determined when the bond is issued. If, for example, the common stock of the corporation were selling at $100 per share when the convertibles came out, the convertibility feature would permit one $1,000 bond to be converted to approximately ten shares of common stock at the option of the bondholder. If two or three years later the common stock were selling at $150 per share, the $1,000 bond could be converted into securities worth about $1,500. In reality, the market price of the bond would be bid up to about $1,500. Convertible securities, then, both preferred stock and bonds, may permit the holders to have their cake and eat it too. Corporations issue them for two reasons: (1) The corporation may be weak or it may be issuing bonds at a time when savings are in short supply, and hence it must add the convertibility feature as a sweetener to sell them. (2) It may issue convertible bonds because this reduces the interest rate, say, from 9 to 8 percent.

Income Bonds

Income bonds may be debentures or mortgage bonds or any other variety. Income bonds are unique because the interest on them does not have to be paid unless it is earned. Usually because of this qualification, they carry a higher rate of interest, but in spite of it are not very popular, and very few of them are issued.

Serial Bonds

Serial bonds, too, can be debentures or some other kind. Their unique feature is that an issue of serial bonds is numbered, and the different numbers mature at different times. This permits the corporation to redeem a few of these bonds each year according to a predetermined schedule.

Callable Bonds

Callable bonds might be debentures, mortgage bonds, or some other kind, but in addition they can be called in and the principal repaid at the option of the corporation. The corporation will insert the call feature if it believes it can refinance later at a lower rate of interest or if it believes that it will be able in the future to operate without bonded capital.

The Capital Structure of a Firm; One Reason Why Earnings Vary (Leverage)

Some firms have raised more capital via the sale of bonds both absolutely and relative to their total capital than other firms. This variation can be explained in part by management philosophy. However, it is also in part due to different kinds of business operations. Certain types of firms can safely raise a larger proportion of their capital by selling bonds than can others because their earnings are more stable from year to year. Such a firm may use more borrowed capital in the hope of increasing the earning (and yield) on their common stock. Raising capital via bonds imposes a fixed cost upon the corporation and introduces *leverage* into its earnings. Leverage can be positive or negative. Positive leverage comes about if a business can borrow capital at say 8 percent by selling bonds, and then earn 10 percent with it. The 2 percent differential accrues to the common stockholder. However, negative leverage will be generated if next year the firm only earns 6 or 7 percent on the capital it borrowed at 8. Firms that have high and stable earnings can safely build more leverage into their capital structure than can low- and fluctuating-income firms. An illustration will make leverage clear.

Take two hypothetical firms (see Tables 13-2 and 13-3); they are identical to begin with and each earns a 10 percent return. But then they both expand, firm A by selling another million dollars of common stock and firm B by selling a million dollars of bonds. Both firms doubled in size and in sales and in profits before any interest was paid. However, the earnings return to common stock rose to 12 percent for one firm and remained unchanged for the other. This is an illustration of positive leverage.

If, next year, both firms' incomes before interest were to fall to $120,000, then firm A would be earning 6 percent for its stockholders while firm B would earn only 4 percent. This is an illustration of negative leverage. Certain firms whose incomes are more stable, like utilities, often are able to take greater advantage of leverage. This also explains why their incomes are often higher.

While the amount of leverage a firm has built into its capital structure may influence earnings, it is by no means the only factor. The quality of management, the type of product it sells, how effectively it innovates and creates new and better products are equally important. Nevertheless, you should look at a firm's capital structure before you buy securities. This is especially true if you are concerned that business conditions may worsen in the future and with them corporate profits. It may be a method of rejecting certain stocks if you are taking a defensive position.

Money Market Instruments

Money market instruments have become popular among some individuals in recent years as an investment vehicle because of high short-term interest rates. Money market instruments consist of Treasury bills (discussed below), banker's acceptances, and commercial paper. The interest yield on commercial paper exceeded 16 percent for a time in 1980, and on Treasury bills 15 percent.

Commercial paper consists of short-term promissory notes issued by large, nationally known, financially strong corporations (such as GE, Ford, GM, Westinghouse) to meet their general short-term credit needs. Generally it has a maturity of from 30 days to as long as 240 days. It is discounted (sold below its face value) and, when it matures, the corporation redeems it at face value, the difference being the interest. It is a fixed obligation and logically could be looked upon as a short-term bond. Because it is short-term, its price does not fluctuate much with changes in the interest rates. Therefore, by investing in it, the investor not only receives a high return, but assumes virtually no risk of capital loss. It is also

TABLE 13–2.

	BEFORE EXPANSION		
Firm A		Firm B	
Capital stock (20,000 shares at $50 per share)	$1,000,000	Capital stock (20,000 shares at $50 per share)	$1,000,000
After tax earnings	100,000	After tax earnings	100,000
Percentage return	10%	Percentage net	10%

TABLE 13–3.

	AFTER EXPANSION		
Firm A		**Firm B**	
Capital stock	$2,000,000	Capital stock	$1,000,000
(40,000 shares at $50		Bonds at 8%	1,000,000
per share)		After tax but before	
After tax earnings	200,000	interest earnings	200,000
Percentage return	10%	Interest	80,000
		Earnings for shareholders	120,000
		Percentage return	12%

a good buy when rates are relatively low, but are expected to rise. By moving into it at such times, the investor protects his or her liquidity, assumes no risk of capital loss, and earns some interest. It is also a good way to invest money on a short-term basis while looking around for a good long-term investment.

Unfortunately, the minimum amount of commercial paper that may be purchased is $25,000. This eliminates many small investors. As noted above, the minimum maturity is thirty days. It should be noted, however, if you have $100,000 or more to commit, this thirty-day minimum does not apply. You can in such a case buy it with a maturity of only a few days. Commercial paper can be purchased through large commercial banks which charge a fee (generally $25 to $30) for this service.

Virtually everything we have said about commercial paper applies to banker's acceptances, except that they are issued by firms with slightly less strong credit ratings and are somewhat less well known nationally. However, these firms may have very good credit ratings and be well known on a regional basis. Consequently, their paper is issued through, and underwritten by a bank that is familiar with the issuer's credit rating; hence, the name "banker's acceptances." The bank stamps the paper accepted and in so doing the bank also becomes liable. In a sense the paper is now just like a cashier's check. As noted above, the interest rate, maturity, etc. is about the same as for commercial paper.

We also noted above that, generally speaking, many small investors cannot buy this paper directly. However, they can buy it indirectly and in small amounts. A number of brokerage houses have organized money market mutual funds (these are described in greater detail in the next chapter). You may buy this paper through them in multiples of as low as $500 and enjoy the same high yield when short-term interest rates are high.

U.S. Government Securities in General

Here I shall discuss United States government securities other than the Series EE and HH savings bonds, which were presented in chapter 7 on thrift institutions. There are three varieties of such marketable government securities:

1. U.S. Government bonds
2. Treasury notes, and
3. Treasury bills

1. *U.S. Government bonds.* Marketable U.S. Treasury bonds are long-term obligations of five years or more and often run over twenty years. Since they are marketable, they fluctuate in the market inversely with fluctuations in the interest rates. Some wealthy individuals buy them, but not many small investors do; the latter usually buy the safer (from the point of price stability) Series EE and HH bonds. Financial institutions, on the other hand, are important buyers of long-term government bonds. Insurance companies, investment companies, and private pension funds commit millions of long-term dollars in government bonds each year.

The bonds have a coupon and interest is paid every six months. To collect the interest, it is merely necessary to detach the coupon when the interest is due, take it to a bank, and deposit it. The bank will collect the interest.

2. *Treasury Notes.* Treasury notes are similar to Treasury bonds but generally have shorter maturities: they run from two to as high as ten years. They have a coupon (are not discounted), which provides for an interest payment every six months; they are negotiable and marketable, so they fluctuate in the market inversely with fluctuations in the interest rate. These securities are very much like government bonds, except their maturities are shorter. These are not securities a small investor would buy; institutions and wealthy individuals might.

3. *Treasury Bills.* These bills are short-term bearer obligations of the United States government. Because they are discounted when issued, the interest is the difference between the price at which the Treasury sells them and their face value. The minimum amount that may be purchased is $10,000, and they can be obtained in multiples of that amount. They have a maturity of ninety days, six months, and sometimes one year. Although a few wealthy individuals may buy them if they have funds temporarily idle while seeking long-term investments, Treasury bills are primarily purchased by financial institutions in order to put their funds to work immediately while they are seeking permanent long-term outlets for them. Sometimes, however, industrial corporations buy them with funds set aside for future tax or dividend payments.

There is one case when the relatively small investor might want to consider investing in Treasury bills: when savings are in very short supply and interest rates are very high. This happened in 1973 and 1974 when the rate on Treasury bills reached about 10 percent for a few months. However, it soon declined to the 5 to 6 percent range. Then in 1979 and 1980 the Treasury bill rate soared once more, and reached 15 percent early in 1980. During such periods, it might be worthwhile for the small investor to take money out of a savings account and invest it in Treasury bills (remember $10,000 is the minimum amount needed). The difference in yield makes the purchase of the Treasury bills worthwhile. Indeed this is precisely what happened.

Treasury bills can be purchased through a bank, which makes arrangements to buy them in a block and then parcel them out to customers. Banks used to provide this service free of charge, but in recent years they began to assess a fee. The cost varies from bank to bank, but generally it runs from $10 to $20 per transaction.

If you have a modest to fair-sized portfolio of stocks and bonds, you should consider having one or two Treasury bills in it when interest rates are high. It could be rolled over every ninety days or six months and would provide the short-term liquidity every portfolio should have.[4] You could also more easily take advantage of a very high rate of interest when it occurred. When interest rates are low, you should consider putting the proceeds from a

---

4. Rollover is a technical term that merely means that when a Treasury bill matures and is paid off, the money is reinvested in another one.

maturing Treasury bill in a savings and loan association. You would then move your liquid funds between a savings account and a Treasury bill, depending upon which paid the higher return.

State and Local Securities[5]

State and local government securities appeal to high-income investors because their interest income is exempt from federal taxation. Usually bonds of a state, or a political subdivision of a state, are exempt from state income taxes as well. Because of this exemption, municipalities often yield a lower return than United States government securities. Competition on the part of wealthy investors for these securities reduces the yield below that indicated by the risk and often below that of United States Treasury obligations. The justification given for tax exemption is that it reduces the cost of financing schools and other public institutions at the local level. The opponents of tax exemption argue that it is merely a loophole that enables high-income groups to avoid the payment of taxes. The average investor should probably never buy these securities. If you are in a high-income bracket, however, you should investigate them. Often one would have to get a 10 or 12 percent return on alternative investments to be as well off, after taxes, as one is with a 5 or 6 percent tax-exempt return. Table 13-4 below shows the tax equivalent yield you would have to obtain on, say, corporate securities to match various tax-free rates.

Not only do state and local governments issue these tax exempts, but so do their political subdivisions, such as schools, sewer and water districts, toll road commissions, and a number of others. In recent years pollution control bonds have also been developed. These are issued by private corporations, are backed by the credit of the corporation, and are used to finance air or water pollution control devices. However, if they are issued under the auspices of a state or local government, they are tax exempt. There are a number of different kinds of such tax-exempt securities, some of which are long-term securities (bonds) and some short-term notes. They may be classified as follows:

1. General Obligation Bonds
2. Special Tax Bonds
3. Revenue Bonds
4. New Housing Authority Bonds
5. Pollution Control Bonds (also called Industry Revenue Bonds)
6. Moral Obligation Bonds
7. Short-term Notes

1. *General Obligation Bonds.* Most municipal bonds are in this category. They are secured by the full faith and credit of the taxing entity issuing them. That is, the full and unlimited taxing powers of the issuing government are pledged to back them up. These presumably are the least risky municipal bonds (except for the new housing bonds which are guaranteed by the federal government) that can be issued by local governments. The risk, of course, varies from one government to another.

2. *Special Tax Bonds.* These bonds are secured not by the full faith and credit of the issuing government, but by only part of it. They are payable only from a specific and listed tax source. In some cases, a new and specific tax is imposed to support a new bond issue

5. This material is drawn from Harold Wolf and Associates, "Personal Financial Seminars." Used by permission.

TABLE 13–4. *The tax-free equivalent*

TAXABLE INCOME (THOUSANDS OF DOLLARS)	% TAX BRACKET	TAX-FREE YIELD										
		4.00%	4.50%	5.00%	5.50%	6.00%	6.50%	7.00%	7.50%	8.00%	8.50%	9.00%
$ 20–24	28%	5.56%	6.25%	6.94%	7.64%	8.33%	9.03%	9.72%	10.42%	11.11%	11.81%	12.50%
24–29	32	5.88	6.62	7.35	8.09	8.82	9.56	10.29	11.03	11.76	12.50	13.24
29–35	37	6.35	7.14	7.94	8.73	9.52	10.32	11.11	11.90	12.70	13.49	14.29
35–45	43	7.02	7.89	8.77	9.65	10.53	11.40	12.28	13.16	14.04	14.91	15.79
45–60	49	7.84	8.82	9.80	10.78	11.76	12.75	13.73	14.71	15.68	16.67	17.65
60–85	54	8.70	9.78	10.87	11.96	13.04	14.13	15.22	16.30	17.39	18.48	19.57
85–109	59	9.76	10.98	12.20	13.41	14.63	15.85	17.07	18.29	19.51	20.73	21.95
109–162	64	11.11	12.50	13.89	15.28	16.67	18.06	19.44	20.83	22.22	23.61	25.00
162–215	68	12.50	14.06	15.63	17.19	18.75	20.31	21.88	23.44	25.00	26.56	28.12
OVER 215	70	13.33	15.00	16.67	18.33	20.00	21.67	23.33	25.00	26.67	28.33	30.00

Note: Taxable income is given for a joint return, based on tax tables effective beginning January 1, 1979.

when it comes out. For example, a new sewer system may be financed by such bonds which are then to be repaid by a special tax levied on the citizens. These are riskier than full faith and credit bonds of the same entity, and hence their yield is higher.

3. *Revenue Bonds.* These are not faith and credit bonds. These are frequently issued by certain political subdivisions such as a toll road commission or a state university which have no taxing powers. However, the interest and principal is to be repaid by the revenue (tolls from turnpikes or rent from college dormitories) to be raised by whatever the bonds finance. Sometimes municipal water and electric departments sell such bonds, which are to be repaid solely from the water and electricity rates which are charged. Since no government's faith and credit are pledged, these revenue bonds are generally considered riskier, and because of this, their yield is higher than bonds of the same entity that have taxing power behind them.

4. *New Housing Authority Bonds.* Public housing authorities may issue bonds to finance the construction of low-income housing. The rental income from the housing is earmarked to meet the obligations of the bonds. But if the rental income is insufficient to do so, the Federal Housing Assistance Administration makes up the difference with federal funds. In effect then, these bonds are backed by the federal government and they are virtually riskless. Because of this their yield is also low. In recent years some state and local governments have established Home Finance Agencies which sell tax-exempt bonds. The monies are then channeled into mortgage loans, some of which finance housing which cannot be considered low-income. These bonds are under fire by the IRS and may very well lose their tax-exempt status.

5. *Pollution Control Bonds.* These are a special type of revenue bond. They are issued by a government entity or at least under its auspices. However, they are the liability of a private corporation. The bonds are used to finance air or water pollution control facilities of a corporation. The entire credit of the corporation, or in some cases only the revenue of the plant that receives the pollution control equipment, is pledged. Because of this, these bonds are considered riskier and their yield is generally among the highest of all tax exempts. You should appraise these as corporate bonds. In some cases these may be among the better buys of the tax exempts if they are issued by a financially strong corporation. If the corporation defaults, it can at least be forced into bankruptcy. The trustee of the bondholders can seize the assets of the corporation, sell them, and pay off the bondholders. The bondholders will seldom lose, although the common stockholders quite likely will. On the other hand, when a government defaults, it may be more difficult to sell its assets. The trustee for the bondholders cannot seize Central Park and sell it.

6. *Moral Obligation Bonds.* Some of the revenue bonds are also called moral obligation bonds. This merely means that, although the taxing powers of a government are not pledged to back the bonds, the state legislature has gone on record as having a moral obligation to repay the principal and interest if it cannot otherwise be repaid; that is, if the revenue is inadequate. This is supposed to make them less risky and hence enable the borrowing agency to obtain revenue at a lower rate than otherwise. How much weight you should give to a moral obligation commitment when making your appraisal on risk is a judgment that only you can make.

7. *Short-Term Tax Exempt Municipal Notes.* There are also short-term notes generally running from six months to two years. These would appeal to you if you were uncertain about long-term interest rates and did not want to become locked in at a fixed rate for a number of years. If you buy these, you will be able to reappraise the situation a year hence.

These notes may be full faith and credit or revenue obligations. The full faith and credit are sometimes tax anticipation notes; that is, taxes due in six months or a year are pledged to pay off these notes. The revenue notes are backed by revenue expected some time in the near future.

Some of these short-term notes are construction notes, sometimes called bond anticipation notes. They are used to finance the construction of something that will take a year or two. When the construction is complete, long-term bonds are sold to pay off the short-term notes.

There are also some short-term project notes (for example, to finance construction of low-income housing) that are guaranteed by the federal government. These provide temporary funds to finance low-income housing. When the construction is complete, long-term housing authority bonds are sold to repay the short-term notes. Rental income is now earmarked to pay the interest and principal of the long-term bonds. These federally guaranteed notes are riskless, and hence the yield is lower.

Some of the short-term construction notes and even the revenue note discussed above are also moral obligation. The moral obligation in such a case is the same as that which was discussed above under moral obligation bonds.

State and Local Bond Trusts

Recently, a number of closed-end investment trusts have been established through which tax-exempt bonds can be purchased indirectly. These work very much like mutual funds. They can be purchased in multiples as low as $1,000. Most of the bonds in these trusts are A-rated or better. However, some of the trusts are spiced with some lower-rated bonds in order to increase the yield. There is, of course, a secondary market for these trust certificates and hence they need not be held to maturity. These are discussed at greater length in chapter 15.

Bonds and Credit Ratings

The amount of interest paid on corporate bonds is determined by the credit rating of the company, length of maturity of bonds, and demand for and supply of money at the time of the issuance of the bond. With regard to United States government bonds, credit rating is not a factor; however, both length of maturity of bonds and demand and supply of money at the time of the issuance will determine the rate paid by the federal government. For example, if the supply of money is short, the rates of the "governments" will be forced up just as the interest rate is with any other borrower. However, because of the relatively riskless character of the government issues, the amount paid by the government in interest will be lower than that paid by corporations. The rate on state and local bonds, too, varies with the same factors, although, as noted above, the fact that the interest is tax-free keeps the rate on these securities low, generally speaking.

Interest rates on all fixed obligations vary with the length of time the securities run to maturity. Generally when rates are relatively low, long-term bonds yield more than short-term debt obligation. However, when interest rates in general are relatively high, often short-term obligations yield a higher return than long-term.

With respect to credit rating, the higher the rating, the lower the interest rate on corporation bonds as well as on state and local bonds. There are services that assign a credit rating to bonds, these ratings being an attempt to measure the quality of bonds or their degree of gilt-edgedness. Moody's, which is probably the most widely used bond rating service, has nine classifications of risk. Triple A bonds are the highest quality and C bonds the lowest. A triple A bond carries little risk of default, whereas a C bond is in default and has very little prospect of ever being paid off. If you buy a C bond, you are probably buying a lawsuit.

The accompanying list gives the nine ratings assigned by Moody's. Your broker can tell you which rating any corporate bond has. Remember any bond below Baa (which is medium grade) is a speculative bond investment.

Moody Bond Ratings

■ Aaa
■ Aa
■ A
■ Baa
■ Ba
■ B
■ Caa   } Speculative Bonds
■ Ca
■ C   In Default

Standard and Poor's is another bond rating service similar to Moody's. Its symbols, however, are slightly different and they have several more classifications. Standard and Poor's ratings are shown below.

Standard and Poor's Bond Ratings

■ AAA
■ AA
■ A
■ BBB
■ BB
■ B
■ CCC   } Speculative
■ CC
■ C
■ DDD)   In Default. The different D bonds indicate that the bondholders would get
■ DD }   different amounts back upon liquidation, with the D rating being the low-
■ D   )   est.

Bonds and the Small Investor

Many financial experts consider that a small investor should not invest in corporate bonds. In order to have a substantially safer investment than stock, one must select a triple or double A bond. The return on such high-grade bonds, however, is not much more than on other fixed assets such as savings and loan CDs. Why, then, go to the bother of buying bonds and paying brokerage fees, especially since corporation bonds come in denominations of $1,000? (State and local bonds normally come in minimum amounts of $5,000.00). While there is some merit to this view, there is also another side.

One should not buy a bond unless one has $1,000 to salt away as a long-term investment. If the investor can get an extra 1 or 2 percent yield on a high-grade bond and if it is to be invested to pay for a college education some years later, bonds are fine. However, the small saver should also have some fixed investments in safe and liquid assets such as deposits in a thrift institution or series EE or HH government bonds. That is, don't put your first saving in bonds.

Bond Yields

You have already learned that a bond has a coupon rate of interest and a market rate of interest. This latter is also called the yield. For example, if a $1,000 bond has a coupon rate of 9 percent, this indicates that the corporation will pay a fixed dollar amount ($90) per year. But if you purchased such a bond that matures in one year at a discount (you paid, say, $990.90) the actual yield is equal to the $90 interest you will get plus the $9.10 capital appreciation. Your actual percentage yield is $99.10 ÷ 990.90 or 10 percent.

We should also recognize the following yield concepts:

1. Nominal Yield and Real Yield
2. Average Yield to Maturity
3. Tax-equivalent Yield of a Municipal Security
4. Tax-free Equivalent Yield of a Taxable Yield
5. Annual Yield to Maturity

1. The nominal yield is stated in money terms and not adjusted for inflation. To convert the nominal rate to the real rate, we must subtract the rate of inflation from the money (nominal) yield. If, in the case discussed above, the price level had risen by 5 percent during the year, the real yield would, of course, be 5 percent.

2. In a few cases (primarily U.S. Series E bonds), the actual yield is not the same each year. U.S. Series E bonds, you will recall, are discounted. Then their redemption price is predetermined for each coming month and in each future month, the price rises somewhat. However, if you were to plot this price rise, you would not get a smooth line. Their yield is lower in the early years. We therefore talk in terms of average yield per year if held to maturity. For a Series E bond this is currently 6.5 percent, and for the newer series EE also 6.5 percent.

3. The tax equivalent yield is the term used when discussing municipal bonds. Since interest on municipal bonds is not taxed, a 5 percent return there is also the after-tax yield. The tax-equivalent yield is that yield you would have to get on a corporate bond so that, after personal income tax on it, you would have the same amount left that you could have earned on a municipal bond. Consequently, the tax-equivalent yield will vary from person to person depending upon their individual income tax bracket. For a person in the 50 percent tax bracket, the tax-equivalent yield to a 5 percent municipal bond is 10 percent; for a person in the 33 percent tax bracket, it is 7.5 percent. The tax-equivalent yield, then, is that level to which the yield must be adjusted up in order to give you a sufficiently higher return so as to enable you to pay taxes and still be as well off as with a tax-exempt yield.

To obtain the tax-equivalent yield, divide the tax-free yield by 1 minus your tax bracket; use the following formula:

$$\frac{\text{Tax-free Yield}}{1 - \text{your tax bracket}} \quad \frac{.05}{1 - .33} = \frac{.05}{.66} = .07575$$

The tax-equivalent yield of a 5 percent tax-free yield for a person in the 33 percent tax bracket is 7.58 percent.

A table showing the various tax-equivalent yields is shown above on p. 345.

4. We can also go in reverse and find the tax-free equivalent of a taxable yield. We multiply the taxable yield by 1 minus the tax bracket. Or use the formula (taxable yield) × (1 − tax bracket). In the above case: .07575 × 1 − .33 = .07575 × .66 = .05

5. There is also the concept of annual yield to maturity, which is important if the bond is sold at below (or above) par and has a number of years to run. This comes about because, in calculating yield to maturity, you must consider not only the dollar amount of interest you will receive each year but also the annual capital gain (or loss) as the bond matures and its market price moves toward its face value. The following formula approximates the yield to maturity:

$$\frac{\left(\begin{array}{c}\text{annual interest}\\\text{payment}\end{array}\right) + \dfrac{\text{maturity value less market price}}{\text{years to maturity}}}{\dfrac{\text{maturity value } + \text{ market price}}{2}}$$

For example, a bond with a face value of $1,000 paying a coupon interest rate of 8 percent running over 10 more years, and purchased at $800, will give us:

$$\frac{\$80 + \dfrac{(\$1,000-\$800)}{(\quad 10\quad)}}{\dfrac{\$1,000 + \$800}{2}} = \frac{\$80 + \dfrac{200}{10}}{\$900}$$

$$\frac{80+20}{900} = \frac{100}{900} = 11.1 \text{ percent}$$

QUESTIONS FOR REVIEW

1. What is meant by par value, book value, and market value?

2. What is the difference between earnings and yield, as most brokers define it, on common stock?

3. What is meant by total economic increment insofar as a common stockholder is concerned?

4. Explain what is meant by a growth stock, income stock, and cyclical stock.

5. What are the advantages and disadvantages of preferred stock?

6. Distinguish between cumulative, noncumulative, and cumulative participating preferred stock.

7. The market price of callable preferred stock is said to have a "lid" on it. In short, there seems to be a top market price. Why is this so?

8. How do bonds differ from common stock?

9. Explain the idea behind the equipment trust obligation.

10. What might lead a corporation to issue convertible bonds?

11. What is a debenture?

12. Why can some firms raise a larger percentage of their capital from the sale of bonds than can other firms?

13. What is meant by leverage?

14. What is the difference between a Treasury note and municipal bond.

15. In the rating of bonds, how many classifications are there?

16. Should a small investor buy bonds? Why? If yes, what kinds of bonds would you recommend?

CASES

1. Janice Spier recently inherited some common stock. The par or face value on the stock is $10 per share, which gives Janice a total investment value of $5,000. Recently, however, she received from the corporation a report that gave the book value of the stock as $25 per share, which would make her investment $12,500. Then last night at a dinner party someone mentioned the same corporation and said he had just bought 100 shares of it at $102 per share. At this point Janice is confused. Could you straighten her out? What makes the par value, the book value, and the market value differ?

2. About a year ago Dale and Genevieve Mac-Masters purchased one hundred shares of participating preferred common stock yielding 8 percent on their investment of $150 per share. It was a new issue at the time of purchase, and the common stock at that time was selling for $50 per share. In the first year the company involved had a very good year and has announced that the final dividend on the preferred stock will be paid soon. What is the dividend (for the year) on the preferred?

   The company also announced that there would be a participating dividend later after the common stockholders had received their share. What is the dividend that must be paid on the common before the common and preferred stocks share equally that which remains?

3. Thomas and Rita Andrews purchased $5,000 face value of callable convertible bonds a year ago at par, paying 9 percent coupon rate. How much money did they invest, not counting brokerage fees? What is their annual dollar income from the bonds?

   The call feature provided for a call at the option of the company at $1,025. The convertible feature permitted Thomas and Rita to convert each bond into ten shares of common stock. What was the approximate price of the common stock at the time the convertibles were issued?

   Over the past year the company has been extremely prosperous, and the price of the common stock has risen to $200. What is the price of the convertible bonds? Explain.

4. Some time ago Gordon and Lillian Rider purchased a $1,000 face value convertible bond having a coupon rate of 9 percent. They got the bond at a 5 percent discount. What is their total investment? What is their actual yield?

   The bond is convertible into twenty shares of common stock. What was the approximate price of the common stock when the bond was issued? The present market price of the common stock is $160 per share. Should Gordon and Lillian convert? If they do, what will be the value of their investment? What is the present value of their convertible bond?

5. John Farely can truly be considered a small investor. While he has $3,000 in a savings and loan association and some life insurance, he has no other investments. He feels he should now start acquiring some securities directly. He can set aside $100 per month for this purpose. He is undecided between common stock, preferred stock, and bonds. Can you advise him? In so doing, bring out the differences between the three above-mentioned securities. Also state why he should buy what you recommend.

6. Judy Brown is saving a few dollars a month and wants to invest them in common stock. She has heard that certain firms like utilities have more leverage built into their capital structure than some other firms. She is unclear about what leverage means. Can you explain it to her? Also Judy would like to know why utilities generally have more leverage in their capital structure than most other firms.

SUGGESTED READINGS

Barron's Weekly. A weekly finance magazine.

Building a Second Income. New York: Francis I. Dupont and Company.

The Exchange. Magazine published monthly by the New York Stock Exchange.

Financial Analysts Journal. New York: Published bimonthly by The Financial Analyst Federation.

Hedging Highlights. Chicago: Chicago Board of Trade.

How to Invest in Stocks and Bonds. New York: Merrill Lynch, Pierce, Fenner & Smith, Inc.

How You Get More Out of Financial News. Princeton, N.J.: Dow Jones & Company, Inc., The Educational Service Bureau.

Instruments of the Money Market. Richmond: Federal Reserve Bank of Richmond, 1977.

Jessup, Paul E. *Competing for Stock Market Profits*. New York: John Wiley and Sons, 1974.

The Kiplinger Washington Letter. A weekly newsletter with a good deal of material on business and finance.

New York Stock Exchange Fact Book. Published annually by the New York Stock Exchange.

A Perspective on Yields. Chicago: Chicago Board of Trade, 1977.

Questions and Answers About the Stock Market. New York: Merrill Lynch, Pierce, Fenner & Smith, Inc.

Smith, Keith V., and David K. Eiteman. *Essentials of Investing*. Homewood, Ill.: Richard D. Irwin, 1974.

Tax-Exempt Bonds and the Investor. Washington, D.C.: Investment Bankers Association of America.

U.S. News & World Report. A weekly magazine that contains a good deal of information on business and finance.

The Wall Street Journal. This is a daily financial newspaper, published by Dow Jones & Company, Inc.

Well Beyond the Average: The Story of Dow Jones. New Jersey: Dow Jones & Company, Inc., The Educational Service Bureau.

What Every Woman Investor Should Know. Washington, D.C.: Investment Bankers Association of America.

You and Your Money; A Financial Handbook for Women. New York: Merrill Lynch, Pierce, Fenner, & Smith, 165 Broadway, New York, N.Y., 1979.

Chapter Fourteen

The Investor and the Securities Market

Buy low, sell high.
OLD WALL STREET ADAGE

The objectives of this chapter are to:

1   Introduce securities exchanges, brokers, and dealers

2   Discuss the quoting of securities

3   Examine how securities may be bought and sold

4   Introduce dividends on common stock

5   Suggest some possible techniques for making investment decisions

6   Present some other things you should know about securities

INTRODUCTION

An investor who wishes to buy or sell securities does so in the open market. The open market for securities is "the works." It consists of all the organized exchanges on which securities are listed. It also includes the over-the-counter market. Broadly defined, it also includes the brokers and dealers who operate in the open market and make it go. In this chapter we shall examine the open market and the buying and selling of securities therein. We will also examine earning on stock and some supplemental material on securities which you might find useful.

In the last few years the stock market has lost some of its former glamour, and many small investors have left the market. This was because of the sharp decline the market suffered in 1969 and 1970, and again in 1973 and 1974. Many of these small investors have still not returned to the market and this, together with a more selective buying pattern of the institutional investors, has kept the market depressed although it has come back somewhat. Meanwhile, profits have improved and hence in view of earlier investor attitudes, there are some really good buys in the market. But attitudes have changed, some say permanently. If this change is indeed permanent, then this discussion of securities may not excite too many people. However, I don't believe this change in attitude is permanent: sooner or later the market will come back. Nevertheless, it is true that the price of securities is in large part determined by investors' attitudes and this attitude is different than it was a decade ago. For example, many investors do not feel as they once did that common stocks are a good inflationary hedge. All this does not mean that you shouldn't buy common stock; it merely means you should, as always, buy them carefully. Therefore we will also examine some investment strategies that will be useful in portfolio management.

SECURITIES EXCHANGES, BROKERS, AND DEALERS

In the United States there are two major organized exchanges (the New York Stock Exchange and the American Stock Exchange) whose major function is to facilitate the sale of securities. In addition, there are a number of smaller regional exchanges. While the greatest volume of business on the organized exchanges takes place in the area of common and preferred stock, they also handle the sale of some bonds and warrants. To deal directly on an exchange, one must be a member or own a seat. Many of the members are security dealers as well as brokers; they are broker-dealers. Brokers are individuals who execute orders for third parties for a commission. Dealers, on the other hand, act as principals and buy for their own account and also sell from them, hoping for a profit margin between the buy and sell price. In doing this they are said to make a market in the securities they buy and sell.

The New York Stock Exchange

In 1792 twenty-four broker-dealers met "under the shade of a buttonwood tree on Wall Street" where they agreed that "we will not buy or sell from this day for any person whatsoever, any kind of public stock at a less rate than ½ percent commission of the specific value and that we will give preference for each other in our negotiations."[1] This was the birth of the New York Stock Exchange.

Today about 1,550 corporations have their common stock listed on the New York Stock Exchange (NYSE). In addition, about 2,700 bonds, 500 preferred stock, and a few warrants[2] are listed on the exchange for a total listing of approximately 4,800 securities. There are 1,366 seats on the New York Stock Exchange, and a person may become a member only by buying a seat from a member who is willing to relinquish it. The price of a seat has ranged from a low of $17,000 in 1942 to a high of $625,000 in 1929. In the late 1960s this 1929 high was approximated on several seats which changed hands, but more recently the price has been around $200,000.[3]

The members of the exchange are classified into a number of categories. About half the members are commission brokers; the rest are divided among floor brokers, specialists, registered traders, bond dealers, or a combination of the above capacities at different times.

1. *Commission Brokers* Some members act solely as commission brokers. These are the ones who are partners or officers of firms doing business with the public. They have

---

1. Birl E. Schulty, *The Securities Market and How It Works,* 5th Ed., New York: Harper, 1946, pp. 2–3.
2. See below for a definition and discussion of warrants.
3. The New York Stock Exchange, *1980 Fact Book,* p. 54.

offices where they contact the public (in the case of a large firm like Merrill Lynch they have many members and many offices throughout the country). They buy and sell securities for their customers in return for which they are paid a commission.

2. *Floor Brokers* These are the members of the exchange who assist commission brokers who are unable to handle all of the volume when trade is heavy. They ensure that orders are executed more quickly. They used to be called contract brokers a few years ago, before that "two-dollar" brokers because that was the fee they charged historically. Their fee is now higher and comes out of the regular fee paid to the commission broker.

3. *Specialists* The physical area of the New York Stock Exchange being large, it is frequently impossible for a member to get around fast enough to execute customers' orders. Certain brokers therefore specialize in buying and selling certain stocks at certain posts on the exchange floor. Each security is sold at a given location, and the specialists stay at that post and execute orders for a few securities at the order of their fellow brokers. Also the specialists are responsible for the execution of conditional orders. Investors give an order to buy if the price drops to $34; this instruction goes into the specialists' books, and if and when the price reaches $34, they execute. The specialists also act as dealers and make a market in the stock in which they specialize. They are supposed to stabilize short-term movements in the market and in this way contribute to orderly conditions. However, specialists cannot buy or sell for their own accounts if there are unfilled orders from the public at the market price. If there are no unfilled orders or if the market is sluggish and buyers and sellers are having difficulty getting together on a price, the specialists are to enter the market on either the supply-sell or demand-buy side, whichever is necessary to help stabilize the market. Specialists are expected only to help stabilize short-term swings; they are not expected to take continued losses to stem long-term movements. Actually, the specialists will make rather than lose money by helping to stabilize short-term movements because they are in and out of the market frequently and if they make even a fraction of a point on many transactions, they soon add up.

Finally, some specialists will use their inventories to fill odd lot orders which are discussed below.

4. *Registered Traders or Floor Traders* These are members who buy and sell on their own accounts; in reality, they deal in stocks themselves with the idea of making a profit on their purchases. They are able to do so because as members of the stock exchange they do not pay a regular commission, but a greatly reduced member commission. In addition, they are also professional traders and they get in and out of the market on a short-run basis and take advantage of short-run price movements of common stock. Sometimes they also serve either as commission brokers for a few customers or as floor brokers for other commission brokers. They have been criticized because it is thought that they contribute to market instability in individual securities. For example, by becoming particularly active in an individual firm's stock, a floor trader might cause wide fluctuations in that particular issue.

Buying Odd Lots

On the organized exchange, transactions are usually carried out in round lots which consist of 100 shares. However, small investors would want lesser amounts. There used to be dealers who specialized in odd lots and who would maintain an inventory in stock and buy and sell in any amounts from 1 to 99. Dealers who specialize only in odd lots have passed from the scene. Odd-lots transactions are now carried out directly by some brokers who maintain an inventory of stock and stand willing to trade in any odd lot amounts. Those (usually smaller) brokers who do not themselves maintain an inventory will fill their customer's odd-lot orders by going to members of the New York Stock Exchange (usually specialists or registered traders) who do carry an inventory and who do deal in odd lots, although this is a minor part of their business. On odd-lot purchases there is still the one eighth of one dollar ($.125) per share odd lot fee, which is added to the price of stock (subtracted from it if you sell). This is over and above the regular commissions that are discussed below.

The Historical Record of the NYSE

People have been buying and selling securities for many years and, as noted above, the roots of the New York Stock Exchange can be traced back to 1792. Moreover, the market has had many ups and downs over the years. This is because the market is one of the most, if not the most, sensitive of all institutions in our society. It reacts to any and all news, good or bad. Bad news will nearly always send it down; what is considered good news may send it up or down. However, these are the short-run fluctuations. The long-run trend has been up more often than down.

While the deepest and most severe stock market decline took place with the crash in 1929, there have been other sharp declines as well. After the 1929 crash the market generally stayed depressed until the big bull market shortly after World War II.

At various times, different stocks have been popular. For a number of years after World War I, railroad stocks were the "in thing." While they made somewhat of a comeback after the Great Depression, they never regained their former popularity. More recently, electronics and computers have been the glamour items in the stock market. Much of the historical record of the stock market can be seen graphically in Standard and Poor's chart in Figure 14–1.

The American Stock Exchange (AMEX)

The second major stock exchange is the American Stock Exchange, called *Amex* for short. This market was originally outside in the street, but has been inside since 1921. There are fewer securities listed on the American Stock Exchange than on the New York Exchange and the requirements for listing are less rigorous. To be listed in either exchange a company must meet certain tests as to dollar amount of assets, earnings, market value of its stock, and number of publicly held shares outstanding. In addition, the corporation must publish certain financial information about itself.

Presently there are 284 regular members plus 121 associate members. The associates are permitted to trade through the regular members at reduced commissions. About 1,400 securities are listed on the American exchange.

As for commission brokers, specialists, and so forth, the operation of the American exchange is much like that of the New York Stock Exchange.

A seat on the American exchange went for less than $50,000 in 1976. This compares to a high of $350,000 some years ago and to an all-time low of $1,000 in 1941.

The Regional Exchanges

The New York and the American Stock Exchanges are national institutions. There are also a number of smaller stock exchanges that serve only the region in which they are located. The three major regional exchanges are the Midwest Stock Exchange, the Philadelphia-Baltimore-Washington Stock Exchange, and the Pacific Coast Stock Exchange. Many of the stocks listed for the regional exchanges are also listed on either the New York or the American Stock Exchange. The existence of the Pacific Coast Exchange permits trading in those dually listed stocks three additional hours after the close of the NYSE and AMEX. In addition, the regional exchanges list some securities of regional companies that are listed nowhere else.

Brokerage Commissions

There are brokerage commissions you must pay when buying or selling securities. At one time these commissions were set by the New York Stock Exchange (NYSE) and by the Security and Exchange Commission (SEC), but no more. In 1975, the SEC agreed to let the free market determine commissions; brokers are now free to set their own commissions, and on large orders the broker will negotiate commissions in advance with the buyer or seller. On most regular orders, however, brokers have a schedule they follow, and these schedules vary somewhat from broker to broker.

The calculation of the commissions by the regular brokerage houses is quite complex and hence a table showing them is not possible. However, three variables are taken into account in setting them.

1. The dollar amount of money committed. Commissions decline, as a percent of the money committed, as the latter rises.
2. The number of shares purchased. Commissions per share decline as the number of shares purchased increases.
3. The price of the shares. Commissions per share rise as the price of the shares selected declines. This one is the "kicker" which can offset the first two factors.

If, for example, you buy 100 shares priced at $50 (commit $5,000). One (typical) broker will charge you $83. If you purchase 200 shares priced at $25 per share (again commit $5,000), the same broker will charge you $105.67, and on 500 shares at $10 you would pay $131.17.

The above discussion applies to round lots of one hundred shares. If lesser amounts (odd lots) are traded, the commissions are calculated the same way, and then an additional odd-lot fee of one-eighth of one dollar ($.125) per share is added. Note that you pay these commissions when you buy as well as when you sell stock.

In recent years discount brokers (also called security discount houses) have sprung up. They charge commissions that are often substantially below those charged by regular brokerage houses. They can do this because they offer no investment advisory services and provide no research reports. They merely execute orders. You can find discount brokers by looking at the ads in the financial papers.

Securities Dealers

Securities dealers make a market in a security and buy and sell on their own account. They are not paid a commission but earn their living on the difference between what they pay for a security and what they sell it for. For example, a share of stock may be quoted as having an asked price of $11 and a bid price of $10. This means that the dealer will pay you $10 for the stock share if you wish to sell one; on the other hand, if you desire to purchase a share, you must pay $11. This leaves a spread of $1, out of which the dealers pay their expenses and receive their profits. Because dealers stand ready to buy and sell at all times, they are said to "make a market."

Stocks that are sold through dealers are usually "over-the-counter" securities. While many stock issues are listed on either the New York Exchange or the American Stock

FIGURE 14-1 *Stock market and business history since 1926 (Source: Courtesy of Standard and Poor's Corporation. This report was up to date at the time of publication; subsequent changes are reflected on current Standard and Poor's reports.)*

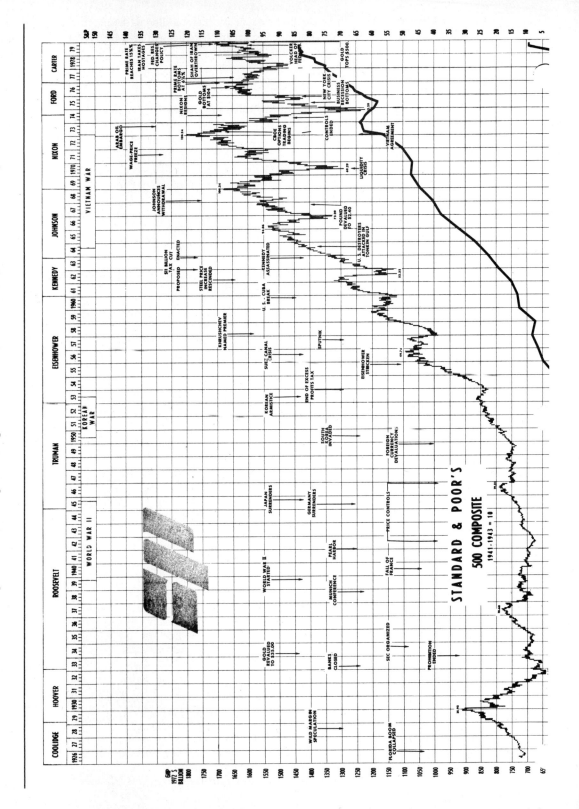

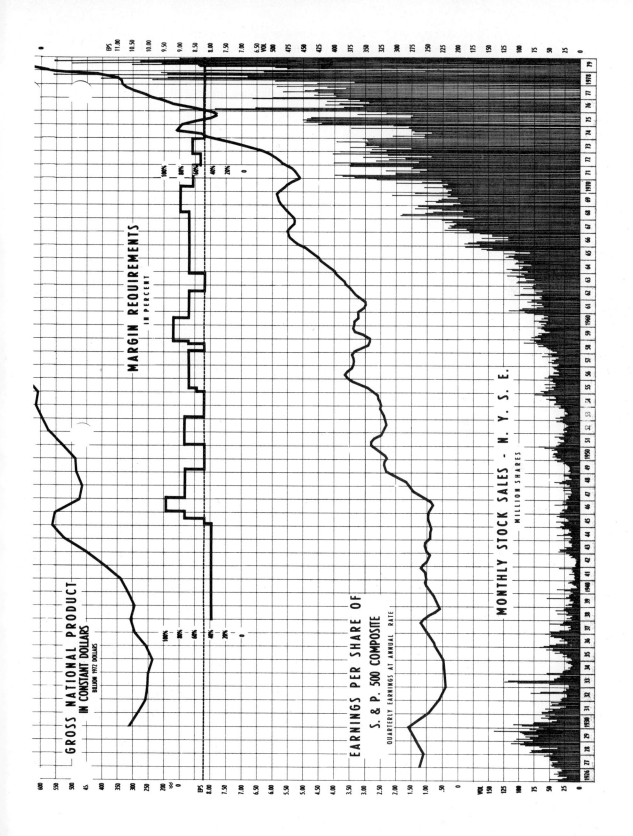

Exchange and are bought and sold by a broker acting as an agent, many other issues are not listed. The nonlisted stocks are the so-called over-the-counter stocks and are purchased and sold exclusively by dealers. In the final analysis, a securities dealer is a merchant whose stock in trade consists of stocks and bonds. In most instances, dealers specialize in a few lines of merchandise; that is, they handle only a relatively small number of unlisted stock.

When an individual desires to purchase some shares of an unlisted stock, he or she contacts a broker. The broker checks the market for the unlisted stock designated. Actually, the broker contacts dealers who are making a market for that particular issue. Then the broker gets in touch with the purchaser to inform him or her of the lowest asked price. If the purchaser still wants the issue, a sale is made.

QUOTING SECURITIES

Amost every daily metropolitan newspaper has a financial page where securities prices are quoted, some of which are more elaborate and complete than others. Most of the more complete financial pages quote the price and the activity of the stocks and bonds *traded* the previous day, but some late evening papers have current day quotations. The emphasis here is on the word *traded*. If a particular security has not been traded, it is not listed. If ABC, Inc. has not been traded, for instance, the price is not given, obviously because no price has been set.

In addition to the listed securities, the more complete financial pages carry the bid and asked prices of the over-the-counter securities. These will be discussed in detail later.

The Listed Stock

Those issues traded the previous day are arranged in alphabetical order on the financial page of the more complete metropolitan newspapers, and appear under this arrangement:

52 Weeks										
High	Low	Stock	Div.	% Yield	P/E Ratio	Sales in 100's	High	Low	Close	Net Change
65⅞	53⅛	Gen. Mot.	6.30e	11	4	2593	59⅝	58⅛	58¼	−1⅛

As shown in the third column, the stock here is General Motors. Immediately to the left of that are shown the high and low prices of that stock over the past 52 weeks. Moving now to the right, we will note all the other information the quotation conveys. Under Div. we see 6.30e indicating dividends of $6.30 were paid over the past year. The % yield shows 11 and that is the dividend yield as a percent of the market price of the stock. However, some earnings were retained by the company and hence the price earnings ratio of 4 is shown in the next column. There we see that sales for the day were 259,300 shares. During the day's trade, the stock of General Motors fluctuated and reached a high of $59⅝ per share, a low of $58⅛, and it closed at $58¼. On the basis of these figures, why was there a net change of −1⅛ of a point? The net change figure is the difference between the closing price for that day and the closing price of the previous day, not the difference between the high and the low on the day in question. Obviously, yesterday's closing price can be either higher or lower than today's opening price. The preceding day's closing price in our example was 59⅜. Note that stocks advance or decline in steps of one-eighth of one dollar.

Frequently there is a footnote in the quotations. For example, in the above example under Dividends, there is a lowercase "e" after 6.30. This and other footnotes that appear are explained at the bottom of the list of quotation under the heading of explanatory notes. In our case, the lowercase "e" means that General Motors has paid or declared dividends of 6.30 during the past twelve months. A footnote under the explanatory notes may point out that the corporation is in bankruptcy or in receivership or one of a number of other valuable bits of information.

A portion of the NYSE market quotes for 4/3/80 appears below.

The Dow-Jones Averages

In addition to prices of individual stocks, most financial pages also publish the Dow-Jones Averages, which are supposed to indicate which way the market is going in general. The Dow-Jones Average is really four different averages: one for industrials, one for transportation, one for utilities, and one a composite of the other three. These averages date back to 1896.

The industrial average, based on the stock of thirty industrial companies, is calculated by adding the prices of these thirty stocks and then dividing by thirty. The transportation average with twenty transportation company stocks in it (this formerly included just rails, but now it has some airlines and trucking lines as well) is calculated in the same way, as is also the utility average, which contains the stock of fifteen utilities.

There are a number of criticisms of the Dow-Jones Averages, especially of the industrial average. First, it is argued that thirty stocks are not a large enough sample. Second, all of the stocks in the Dow-Jones Averages are blue chips such as General Motors, General Electric, Exxon, Du Pont, and American Telephone; such stocks as these, it is argued, are not representative of the market as a whole. Finally, the Dow-Jones Averages are only crudely adjusted for splits. Over the years many of the stocks have been split a number of times; moreover, not all of the thirty have been split the same amounts. Those companies that have never split their stock or have split it less have a greater weight in the averages than the others. The statistical formula used by the Dow-Jones publishing company to correct this has only partially done so.

The Dow-Jones industrial stock price averages are shown in Figure 14-2. The bar graph going back several months shows the high, low, and close for the day. There is also a market diary that indicates the number of issues traded, the number that advanced, the number that declined, and the number that remained the same.

Other Stock Averages

There are a number of other stock averages, the best known of which are the Standard and Poor's and the New York Stock Exchange composite average of all common stocks that are traded on the New York Stock Exchange each day. About 1,550 stocks are listed, but a few are not traded each day. Therefore the number of stocks in the index varies from day to day but usually is close to 1,550. The New York Stock Exchange Average was started in 1966; the prices of all stocks traded on a given day are added up on a computer and then the figure is divided by the number involved. The New York Stock Exchange also has an average for industrials, consisting of 1,000 stocks; one for utilities, which includes 136 stocks; one for transportation made up of 76 stocks; and one for the stocks of 75 financial institutions of various kinds.

TABLE 14–1 A portion of the New York Stock Exchange market quotations for April 3, 1980 *Source:* Reprinted by permission of *The Wall Street Journal,* © Dow Jones & Company, Inc., 1980. All Rights Reserved.)

40 **THE WALL STREET JOURNAL,**
Thursday, April 3, 1980

Wednesday's Volume
39,987,310 Shares; 207,200 Warrants

TRADING BY MARKETS

	Shares	Warrants
New York Exchange	35,210,000	207,000
American Exchange	100	....
Midwest Exchange	1,637,800	....
Pacific Exchange	1,102,100	....
Nat'l Assoc. of Securities Dealers	903,510	200
Philadelphia Exchange	569,500	....
Boston Exchange	258,200	....
Cincinnati Exchange	306,100	....
Instinet System	20,600	....

NYSE – Composite

Volume since Jan. 1:	1980	1979	1978
Total shares	3,453,636,081	2,047,480,027	1,558,344,296
Total warrants ..	19,418,900	10,860,749	4,514,700

New York Stock Exchange

Volume since Jan. 1:	1980	1979	1978
Total shares	3,057,958,131	1,803,701,767	1,362,006,846
Total warrants ..	19,416,200	10,499,600	4,517,300

MOST ACTIVE STOCKS

	Open	High	Low	Close	Chg.	Volume
Howrd John.....	14¾	15¾	14¼	15⅝	+ ⅝	628,800
Aetnal fe s......	33⅛	35¼	33⅛	34¾	+1⅝	391,500
IBM ss...........	54¾	56	54⅝	55½	+ ⅝	373,500
Amer T&T	48⅞	49	48½	48⅝	− ⅛	363,700
Int T&T	24½	26	24⅜	25½	+1⅜	360,000
Am Cyan.........	26⅞	29	25⅞	29	+2¼	349,600
Texaco Inc......	33¼	33⅝	32¾	32⅞	+ ⅜	336,900
Mobil s...........	66⅛	68⅝	65⅞	67	+1⅛	330,900
EngMnCh s......	25⅞	26¼	25¼	25⅜	+ ⅞	325,000
GulfUtdCp	17	18⅛	16½	17½	+ ½	324,400
Tex Util..........	16⅝	17¼	16⅝	17	+ ¼	312,000
Penna PwLt......	14¾	15⅝	14⅝	15⅝	+ ⅞	301,700
SearsRoeb	16	16⅛	15⅞	16⅛	+ ⅛	298,000
Sony Corp........	6⅞	7	6⅞	7	+ ¼	295,900
Citicorp	18½	19¼	18½	19¼	+ ¾	289,700

52 Weeks High	Low	Stock	Div.	Yld %	P-E Ratio	Sales 100s	High	low	Close	Net Chg.
		— A-A-A —								
43¼	29½	ACF	2.24	7.1	6	30	31¾	31½	31⅝	.....
18⅜	11½	AMF	1.24	10.	5	2304	12⅜	12	12	− ⅜
20	12½	AM Intl	.28	1.9	..	1786	15⅛	14½	15⅛	+ ⅛
12¼	7⅞	APL	1	12.	29	26	8⅛	8	8⅛	+ ⅛
40⅛	24¾	ARA	1.82	6.7	5	309	27¼	26¾	27¼	+ ⅜
54⅞	23½	ASA	3.15e	8.4	..	677	38½	37⅛	37½	− ½
12¾	8⅛	ATO	.60	6.8	3	54	9	8⅞	8⅞	.....
31¾	17	AVX s	.32	1.4	11	69	23	22¾	22¾	.....
43⅜	30¾	AbbtLb	1.20	3.2	12	692	37⅛	36½	37	+ ¼
34¼	17½	AcmeC	1.40	5.9	5	3	23⅞	23⅞	23⅞	.....
4⅞	2¾	AdmDg	.04	1.3	5	8	3	2⅞	3	.....
14½	11	AdaEx	1.49e	12.	..	7	12	11⅞	12	+ ⅛
6⅛	3⅝	AdmMI	.20e	5.0	13	13	4	4	4	− ⅛
46⅜	26⅞	AMD n		..	12	236	32⅞	31⅜	31½	−1⅜
36⅞	28⅝	AetnLf	s2.12	6.1	5	3915	35¼	33⅛	34¾	+1⅝
28¼	15	Ahmans	1.20	7.2	3	1	16¾	16¾	16¾	.....
3¼	2⅛	Aileen		..	..	25	2¼	2⅛	2⅛	.....
43⅛	26½	AirPrd	.80	2.4	9	1162	34	33	33¾	− ½
28¼	16⅛	AirbFrt	1.20	6.7	8	52	18	17½	17⅞	+ ⅜
17½	7¾	Akzona	.80	7.4	5	46	11	10½	10⅞	.....
8¼	5½	AlaP	dpf.87	15.	..	38	5⅞	5¾	5¾	.....
84	58½	AlaP	pf 9	15.	..	z190	58¾	58½	58¾	+ ¼
01⅞	75½	AlaP	pf 11	15.	..	z90	75½	75½	75½	.....
89⅞	60½	AlaP	pf 9.44	16.	..	z1000	60	d59½	60	− ½
79½	53	AlaP	pf 8.28	15.	..	z170	54¼	54	54	−1
15¾	13⅛	Alagsco	1.48	11.	6	1	13⅛	13⅛	13⅛	.....
55⅛	16	AlaskIn	.80	2.1	15	225	38¾	36¼	38⅛	+2⅛
36	23¼	Albany	s 1	3.9	7	42	25½	24	25½	+1½

52 Weeks High	Low	Stock	Div.	Yld %	P-E Ratio	Sales 100s	High	low	Close	Net Chg
47¾	34¾	BigThr	.88	2.1	14	79	42½	42	42½	+ ⅛
33⅜	16½	Binney	.92	5.0	9	12	18¾	18½	18½	− ⅛
29¼	12	BisFSL	s.80	5.7	4	37	14⅛	13	14	+1¼
25¼	17⅝	BlackDr	.76	3.9	8	397	19½	18⅞	19⅜	+ ⅝
24½	13⅞	BlairJn	s 1	6.5	5	11	15½	15⅛	15⅜	+ ¼
25½	15	BlissL	1.10	6.6	5	11	16⅝	16⅜	16⅝	+ ½
27¼	21¼	BlckHR	1.60	7.0	9	39	23¼	22⅞	22⅞	+ ⅛
37⅞	23½	BlueB	1.80	5.7	6	317	31¾	31⅛	31⅜	− ⅝
5¾	2⅞	BobbieBr		..	150	36	3⅛	3	3	.....
68⅞	37¼	Boeing	1.80	3.3	7	2261	55½	53⅝	54⅝	+1⅛
39	32	Boeing	wi	..	..	80	37⅝	36½	37	+ ¾
42½	27	BoiseC	1.75	5.8	5	241	30⅜	29	30	+ ¾
27⅞	20	Borden	1.82	8.9	5	1242	20⅜	20	20⅜	− ⅛
42⅞	27⅜	BorgW	2.30	7.1	4	121	33	32½	32½	− ⅜
7¼	3⅛	Bormns	.20e	6.2	20	23	3¼	3⅛	3¼	+ ⅛
23½	18¾	BosEd	2.72	14.	6	193	19⅞	19⅜	19¾	+ ⅜
84¾	61	BosE	pf8.88	14.	..	z160	64½	64	64½	.....
11⅛	8⅜	BosE	pr1.17	14.	..	11	8⅜	d 8¼	8¼	− ⅛
13⅞	10	BosE	pr1.46	15.	..	11	10⅛	10	10	− ¼
13¾	6¾	Braniff	.20	2.5	..	1760	8⅛	7¾	8⅛	+ ⅜
29⅞	20¾	BrigSt	1.20a	4.9	7	88	25	24¼	24¼	− ½
39¼	30½	BristM	1.60	4.8	10	581	34	33⅛	33⅝	+ ⅛
44¼	32	BristM	pf 2	5.5	..	5	36¾	36¼	36¼	−1
38½	21⅞	BritPet	1.67e	5.4	6	59	31¼	31	31⅛	+ ⅝
18⅞	12½	BrkwGl	1.08	7.9	6	21	14¼	13¾	13¾	− ¾
25	18¾	BkyUG	2.22	11.	6	16	19¾	19	19⅝	+ ⅜
26½	18¼	BkUG	pf2.47	13.	..	4	18⅜	18⅜	18⅜	− ¼
30⅛	16¾	BwnSh	1.20	5.4	5	9	22¾	22⅜	22⅜	− ⅛
30	12⅝	Brown	.30	1.2	7	86	24½	24¼	24¼	− ⅝
28¾	21⅝	BwnGp	2	8.7	4	48	23¼	23	23	.....
17⅞	11⅝	BwnFer	.70	4.8	9	288	14⅝	14	14½	+ ⅝
15⅝	10⅜	Brnswk	.90	7.7	5	309	12⅛	11⅝	11⅝	− ½
30	22¾	Brnsk	pf2.40	10.	..	16	23	23	23	− ¼
33½	17½	BrushW	s 1	4.1	8	63	25¼	24½	24½	− ⅛
25	16⅛	BucyEr	.88	4.8	7	62	18½	18¼	18⅜	− ⅛
6⅛	4¼	BudgC	pf.60	13.	..	2	4½	4½	4½	− ¼
19½	12⅝	BufFor	s 1	7.4	7	10	13½	13½	13½	− ¼
16⅜	7¾	Bundy	1	11.	7	12	9	9	9	+ ¼
19⅛	14⅛	BunkrH	2.04	14.	..	11	15	14¾	14¾	.....
32⅜	17¼	BunkR	1.20	5.5	6	83	22½	21	22	+ ¾
20	15	BurlInd	1.40	9.2	6	89	15½	15⅛	15¼	− ¼
80¾	43¾	BurlNo	2.10	3.6	4	315	58⅛	57⅝	57¾	− ⅛
71½	42¾	BrlNo	pf2.85	5.6	..	6	52	51¼	51¼	− ¼
35¾	22¾	Burndy	1	3.6	8	19	27¾	27¼	27¾	+ ¼
8⅞	3	BrnsRL		..	35	193	5⅜	5¼	5¼	.....
87½	62	Burrgh	2.60	3.9	9	510	67½	66	67¼	+1
15	11	ButlrIn	s.52	4.5	6	45	11⅞	11¼	11⅝	+ ¼
18¼	9½	Buttes		..	13	44	13¼	12¾	13	+ ½
		— C-C-C —								
43⅞	27	CBI Ind	s1a	2.8	11	26	36¼	35¼	36	.....
56¾	44⅛	CBS	2.80	6.1	6	141	47¼	46¼	46¼	− ⅝
11¼	5½	CCI		..	4	202	6⅞	6½	6⅝	− ¼
12⅞	6⅞	CLC		..	10	6	7¾	7⅝	7¾	− ⅛
18¾	10⅛	CNA Fn		..	3	64	13½	12¾	13½	+ ½
22¾	15	CNA	pf 1.10	6.7	..	18	16½	16	16½	+ ¼
11⅞	8	CNAI	1.14a	14.	..	20	8⅜	8¼	8¼	.....
71	48⅛	CPC	3.40	5.8	8	293	58⅞	58¼	58⅞	+ ⅜
16¾	13¼	CP Nat	1.88	13.	6	6	14¼	14⅛	14¼	+ ¼
28½	13⅛	CTS	.80	5.5	6	38	15	14½	14½	− ¾
68⅝	34⅝	CabotC	2	3.5	7	238	56½	55¼	56½	+1½
21⅝	7⅝	Cadence		..	3	8	9¼	9⅛	9¼	+ ⅛
36⅛	10	Caesars	s	..	12	1166	13¼	12½	13	+ ⅝
54¾	16⅛	Callhn	2.75e	8.6	6	139	33⅛	31¾	32⅛	− ⅛
24	18¾	Callhn	wi	..	..	12	22¼	21½	22¼	+ ½
7¼	2¾	CamerB		..	5	9	3	2⅞	3	.....
39⅞	17	CmRL	g s.60a	2.1	..	53	29½	28⅜	28⅜	−1⅛
34⅞	25¼	CamSp	1.90	7.2	6	x158	26⅜	25¾	26⅜	+ ⅝
27⅞	19⅞	CampT	1.20	5.5	7	42	22	21⅝	21⅝	+ ⅛
43¾	23⅜	CdPac	g1.70e	..	..	708	32⅜	31¾	31¾	− ⅝
29¼	18¼	Cannon	1.20b	5.6	6	25	21⅝	21⅛	21½	− ⅛
49⅞	37	CapCits	.20	.4	10	28	45½	45	45	− ½
24⅞	16	CapHold	1.08	6.5	6	255	17⅜	16⅝	16⅝	− ⅝
9⅜	4	Carlng	g .10	..	10	186	6	5½	5⅞	+ ¼
29⅝	18¼	Carlisle	s.90	4.1	5	19	21¾	20⅞	21¾	+ ⅝
29½	21⅛	Carnat	1.66	7.6	6	32	22¼	21⅞	21⅞	− ⅛
10	6⅛	CaroFrg	.44	6.4	4	22	7	6⅞	6⅞	− ⅛
22	14⅞	CarPw	2.08	12.	6	159	17¼	16⅞	17	− ⅛
27⅜	18¼	CarP	pf2.67	14.	..	24	19¼	18⅞	18⅞	− ⅝
36	24¾	CarTec	1.90	6.1	7	141	31¾	29½	31¼	+1½
13⅛	10¾	CarrGn	.79e	6.9	..	3	11½	11½	11½	+ ¼
21⅞	12¾	CarsPir	1.10	7.9	4	5	14	13¾	14	+ ¼
20⅝	14⅞	CartHw	1.10	7.3	6	7	15¼	15⅛	15⅛	+ ⅛
8¾	6	CartWal	.40	5.9	7	4	6¾	6⅝	6¾	+ ⅛
13⅝	7⅝	CascNG	.92	10.	5	13	9⅛	9	9⅛	+ ⅜
19	10⅛	CastlCk	.80b	7.0	10	131	11½	10¾	11½	+ ⅝

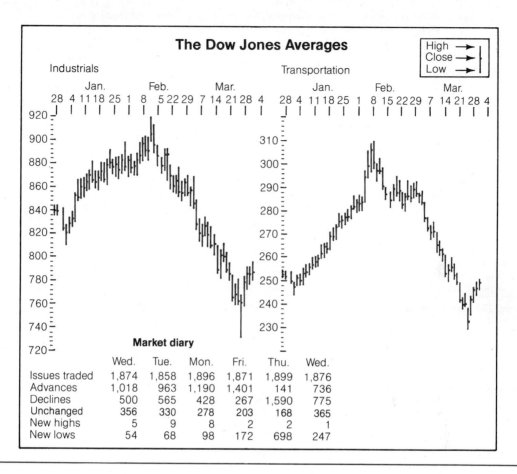

FIGURE 14–2. *The Dow-Jones averages—industrials and transportation. (Source: The Wall Street Journal,* April 3, 1980. Reprinted by permission of *The Wall Street Journal,* © Dow Jones & Company, Inc., 1980. All Rights Reserved.)

The Standard and Poor's averages include four hundred stocks in the industrial average, twenty stocks in the transportation industry, forty in the utility averages, forty in the financial averages, and a composite of all five hundred of these stocks. Both the Standard and Poor's and the New York Stock Exchange averages are considered more reliable indicators of which way the market in general is moving than the Dow-Jones Averages because they include more stocks. Table 14–2 shows the New York Stock Exchange and the Standard and Poor's averages for April 3, 1980, and the same averages for a year earlier. Figure 14–3 shows the movement of the Standard and Poor's average over the past few years.

Bull and Bear Markets

Bull and bear markets are technical terms to indicate which way the market in general is going. If the market rises far enough and long enough, it is referred to as a bull market. If it

TABLE 14–2. *Market indicators other than the Dow-Jones Averages, and trading activity April 3, 1980.*

	1980	—Change—		1979
N.Y.S.E. Composite	58.20	+ 0.37	+0.64%	57.71
Industrial	66.46	+ 0.32	+0.48%	63.82
Utility	33.93	+ 0.25	+0.74%	39.08
Transportation	49.76	+ 0.32	+0.65%	45.90
Financial	56.27	+ 1.18	+2.14%	59.21
Amer. Ex. Mkt Val Index	238.05	+ 3.73	+1.59%	180.65
American Stock Exchange revised Tuesday's index to 234.32.				
Nasdaq OTC Composite	135.80	+ 2.66	+2.00%	132.75
Industrial	160.66	+ 2.79	+1.77%	146.69
Insurance	140.70	+ 4.13	+3.02%	142.06
Banks	95.12	+ 0.99	+1.05%	107.95
Stand. & Poor's 500	102.68	+ 0.50	+0.49%	102.65
400 Industrial	115.49	+ 0.34	+0.30%	114.63

Volume of advancing stocks on N.Y.S.E., 22,330,000 shares; volume of declining stocks, 9,800,000. On American S.E., volume of advancing stocks, 2,210,000; volume of declining stocks, 820,000. Nasdaq volume of advancing stocks, 9,552,000; volume of declining stocks, 1,565,900.

Source: The Wall Street Journal, April 3, 1980. Reprinted by permission of *The Wall Street Journal,* © Dow Jones & Company, Inc., 1980. All Rights Reserved.

FIGURE 14–3. *Stock price indices. (Source: Federal Reserve Chart Book, May 1980,* Board of Governors of the Federal Reserve System, p. 70.)

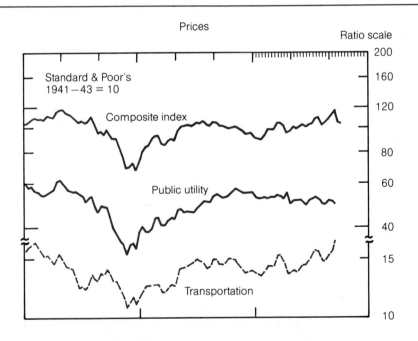

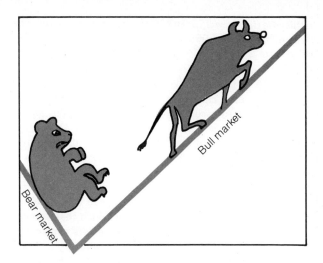

FIGURE 14–4. *Ups and downs of the market.*

falls far enough and long enough, it is referred to as a bear market. The stock averages discussed above are the tests used to determine whether the market is bullish or bearish. If the market just bounces around and moves up and down a bit from day to day, it is neither bearish nor bullish. For that to be the case, there must be a trend. The investors who buy heavily because they believe the market will rise in the future are called bulls. Those who are selling because they believe a decline is coming are called bears. And if the bulls outnumber the bears, the market will rise. If the reverse is the case, it will fall.

Quoting Over-the-Counter Stocks

Some people have the idea that because a stock is not listed and consequently is traded over the counter, there must be something wrong with it. This is just not true. Many over-the-counter stocks are as good as and frequently better than some of the securities listed on the organized exchanges. There are, however, some securities that do not qualify for listing, and these over-the-counter stocks are more risky.[4]

The over-the-counter prices are quoted by bid and asked prices. For example,

Stock & Div.	Sales in 100's	Bid	Asked	Net Chg.
Justin Ind. 60	118	$20\frac{3}{4}$	$21\frac{1}{4}$	$-\frac{1}{2}$

4. In order to be listed, the firm must be of a certain size as measured by assets. It must also have a minimum number of common stocks outstanding and a minimum number of stockholders. And it must be willing to publish certain basic financial facts about itself. Some firms that qualify for listing prefer to remain unlisted.

In this case the stock is Justin Industries, a manufacturer of building materials; it pays a yearly dividend of $.60; 18,000 shares changed hands on the day in question; the bid and asked prices were 20¾ and 21¼, respectively. The net change from the last quotation was −½.

This means in most cases that an individual who desires to sell a share of stock will receive $20.75 per share, less brokerage fees. An individual who desires to purchase the stock must in most cases pay $21.25 per share plus brokerage fees.

I say "in most cases," because these quotations are the current market quotations at which some dealer is willing to execute. But in the over-the-counter market your broker may wish to haggle and may make a counter-offer to buy at below the asked price, which may be accepted by one of several dealers who make a market in the stock in question. Moreover, the quoted bid and asked prices shown above are generally the lowest asked price and the highest bid price, and they may be that of two different dealers. In addition, the bid and asked prices are both subject to change without notice. However, all dealers have their own bid and asked prices at which they stand ready to either buy or sell. The difference between the two figures is the dealers' spread and represents their profit margins. Dealers, as noted, are individuals or firms who buy and sell on their own accounts and may actively make a market in a number of stocks. The "Net Chg." merely indicates in which direction the last bid has moved and by how much. Often there is no entry in this column, which merely means that the bid price has not changed since the previous day. Commissions on over-the-counter securities are, generally speaking, the same as those on the listed securities.

Corporate Bonds Quotations

Corporate bonds are frequently listed on both the New York and the American exchanges. Those that are not so listed are traded over the counter. Bond quotations are not printed on the financial pages of all daily newspapers but may be found in financial papers such as *The Wall Street Journal*.

The quotations for bonds traded on the exchange are listed in alphabetical order. After the name of the company there appears the nominal coupon rate of interest paid per $1,000, which is the face value of the corporate bonds, and the maturity date. We will use as an example ATT (American Telephone and Telegraph). They have a number of different issues outstanding but one reads as follows:

Bonds	Cur. Yield	Vol.	High	Low	Close	Net Change
Att 8⅝ 07	12	114	72½	71	71	−2

The coupon rate of 8⅝% ($86.25 per $1000-dollar bond) will be paid until the year 2007 when the bond matures. The current yield of 12 percent is shown next, then the sales volume, in thousands of dollars, followed by the high and low and closing price for the day, and finally the net change in the closing price from the previous day (note that the coupon rate of 8⅝ provides a yield of 12 percent because the bond is selling at $710).

Corporate bonds always have a face value of $1,000, but the newspaper quotations drop the last digit. A quotation of under 100 means that the bond is selling at a discount, while over 100 indicates it is at a premium.

The closing price of the bond quoted above was 71. This indicates that it was selling at $710 and since this is at a discount of $290, the actual yield is 12 as shown and is above the

8⅝ coupon rate. The easy way to get the market price of a bond is to convert the stock market page quote to decimals and then multiply by 10. For example, a quote of 84⅜ would become $84.375 × 10 = $843.75.

The person buying corporate bonds must also pay brokerage commissions. These commissions also vary from broker to broker, but generally they are a certain percentage of the money committed together with a fixed fee. This percentage declines as the amount of money involved rises. In addition to the percentage fee, there is a flat per-bond fee which varies from $5 to $10. Where the fee is fixed within the $5 to $10 range is determined by the number of bonds purchased and the length of time to maturity, declining with the number of bonds bought and rising with the length of time to maturity.

Treasury Bond Quotations

Marketable United States Treasury bonds are quoted somewhat differently from corporate bonds. To begin with, they are priced in thirty-seconds of a dollar. Secondly, there are bid and asked prices because they are all sold over the counter. Thus the following quotation means that this is a United States bond issue carrying a 9¼ percent coupon interest rate; it will mature in May, 1989. At the close of the trading day, the bid price was 91.12. Actually, 91.12 means 91 and $^{12}/_{32}$ or $91.37. Since Treasury bonds are sold in units of $1,000, $91.37 × 10 = $913.70, the bid price. The asked price of 91.16 means 91$^{16}/_{32}$ or $91.50 × 10 = $915.00. The bid change of −1.18 means that the price has gone down by 1 and $^{18}/_{32}$ or about $1.56 since the previous day. At the current price the yield or return is 10.69 percent interest.

Rate	Mat.	Date	Bid	Asked	Bid. Chg.	Yield
9¼	1989	May	91.12	91.16	−1.18	10.69

BUYING AND SELLING SECURITIES

Securities can be purchased for cash or they can be purchased with borrowed funds; that is, they can be purchased on margin.

Cash Sales

In a cash sale when the transaction is completed, a bill is sent to the purchaser, who has five business days in which to pay for the stock. When selling, the seller also has five days in which to deliver the securities. The purchaser may actually take physical possession of the stock or he or she may instruct the broker to hold the stock for him or her in the purchaser's account. This is referred to as keeping in the street name and is discussed below.

Margin Purchases

Margin purchases are made with funds that are partly borrowed. The word *margin* refers to the percentage of the buyer's own funds needed to buy stock; the remainder may be borrowed from a broker. For example, if a share of stock is priced at $100 and the margin requirement is 75 percent, the purchaser must have that in cash, and may borrow no more than $25. Currently margin requirements are 50 percent; consequently, one half of the money for stock purchases may be borrowed. The Federal Reserve System sets margin requirements and they have been as high as 100 percent in the past (no borrowed money may be used). The Federal Reserve raises margin requirements if it is believed there is excessive speculation in securities. If the market (and the economy in general) is in the doldrums, the Federal Reserve may lower margin requirements, thus making it easier for investors to enter the market with borrowed funds. This in turn, it is hoped, would increase the demand for stock and also create an environment more favorable to overall economic activity.

An investor has an incentive to buy on margin only if he or she feels the price of securities will rise by more than the interest cost of the loan. A problem could arise if the investor on margin is wrong and the market declines. Then the margin could be wiped out and the investor would have to cover. This works as follows: the rules require that the market price of the stock must be at least equal to the borrowed funds. In the case of a stock selling at $100 purchased with a 50 percent margin requirement, there would be no problem until and if the market price declined below $50. But if the price declined to $45, the borrowed funds ($50) would be $5 less than the market value of the stock. The investor would be called by the broker to "cover"; that is, come up with $5 more of his or her own funds (then the market price $45 is again equal to the loan). Today with relatively high margin, the market would have to come down a good deal before an investor would have to cover. However, in the olden days when margins were often much lower (sometimes only 10 percent) this was sometimes a problem. For example, a $100 stock would only have to decline below $90 before a 10 percent margin was wiped out and the broker would call for the investor to cover. If he or she could not, the stock would be sold. In the olden days during a declining market the inability of many margin investors to cover resulted in their stock being sold. This contributed further to the decline. This is another reason why relatively high margins are required today.

Short Sales

Short sales are the opposite of margin purchase. The investor has an incentive to do this only if he or she believes the price of a stock will decline. When selling short the investor sells stock he or she does not own. Rather the stock is borrowed from a broker (stock can be borrowed just like money) and sold at its current price in the market. For example, if a stock is selling at $100 per share, you can borrow it from your broker and sell it. Then if, sometime later, its price declines to $80, you can buy it in the open market (from the same broker you borrowed it from), repay it, and pocket a profit of $20 less brokerage fees. You are also required to make up any dividend which was missed while you held a short position in the broker's stock. Selling short, then, is a speculative technique that enables persons to make a profit if they correctly forecast that the price of the security they purchased will decline. If those who have taken a short position are wrong and the security rises in price, they, of course, lose money.

Since both buying on margin and selling short is engaging in speculation, it is not recommended for the small investor, especially one who is a relative newcomer to security investments.

Types of Orders

There are a number of types of orders either to buy or sell that an individual might place with a broker. These are the following:

1. Conditional buy order. An order to buy a certain number of shares under certain specific conditions. For example, you might order your broker to buy one hundred shares of ABC if the price declines from its present level of $50 to $45.

2. Conditional sell order. An order to sell a certain number of shares of a specific security under specific conditions; for example, if the stock rises to a certain level.

3. Market order. Either a buy or a sell order of a specific number of shares of a specific security at the current market price. It is left to the broker to obtain the best price possible for the client if it is an over-the-counter security and hence subject to haggling pricewise.

4. Good-till-cancelled order. A type of order continuing in force until it is either executed or cancelled. This applies to conditional orders. A new order at a different price cancels the former order if made by the same customer.

5. Stop order. An order to buy or sell conditioned upon a specific price. Frequently it is used as a selling device in order to prevent losses or as an attempt to ensure a profit. For example, an individual may have purchased at $10 a share of stock he believes will rise to about $15, and he puts in a stop order at $15. The stock will automatically be sold at $15. Or a person may have purchased a stock at $10 and it may have risen to $20. The purchaser may have reason to believe that it will advance even higher, but to protect herself in the event of a downward movement, she may place a stop order at $15. Thus if the stock does go down to $15 per share, the order will be executed immediately. This is sometimes called a stop loss order because it prevents the stock from falling below a certain price.

DISTRIBUTION OF EARNINGS FROM STOCKS

There are a number of reasons why people own common stock; capital gains, hedging inflation, and dividend income are among the more common. The graph below illustrates how dividends, earnings, and stock prices have risen over the years. Insofar as dividends are concerned, there are cash dividends and stock dividends.

Cash Dividends

Dividends must be paid out of corporate earnings. The percentage of earnings distributed varies from company to company, but, generally speaking, runs from 40 to 80 percent. However, in some cases cash dividends are zero; the corporation retains its entire earnings. Dividends do not have to be paid; rather they are declared at the discretion of the board of directors of the company. Most states have laws providing that dividends may be paid only out of current or past earnings. They may not be given out of paid-in capital.

1. *The Declaration Date and the Announcement Date.* The day the board of directors meets and declares a dividend is the declaration date. The day this declaration is announced to the press is the announcement date. Often these two dates may be the same, but sometimes the public announcement may be delayed a few days. Firms listed on the NYSE are required to send prompt notices of dividend declarations to the Exchange.

2. *The Record Date.* This is the date that the corporation counts heads to determine who owns how much stock. The NYSE rules require that the record date be at least ten days

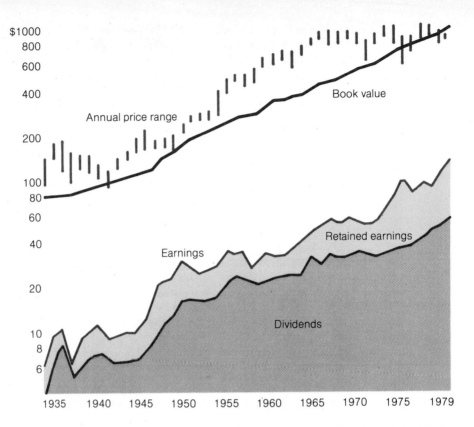

The accompanying chart and tables show that from 1935 to 1979, Dow-Jones Industrial Average:
• Earnings have increased +2,049%.
• Dividends have increased +1,020%.
• Book values have increased +1,131%
• Stock prices have increased 482% from the 1935 year-end to December 31, 1979.
• Price/earnings ratios declined to their lowest levels in 1974 and were close to these low levels on December 31, 1979

FIGURE 14–5. *Forty-five-year performance of the Dow-Jones Industrial Average, 1935–1979. (Source:* Johnson's Charts, Inc.)

later than the announcement date. Owners as of this date, according to the corporation's records, will receive the dividends.

3. *The Ex-Dividend Date.* The ex-dividend date is the first day that the purchaser of a stock does not receive the dividend that has been declared on it. Thus when it is said that a stock is ex-dividend, it is being sold without the dividend. This is four business days before the record date, because the rules of the New York Stock Exchange allow four days in which to deliver stock one has sold or four days to pay for stock one has bought. The price of a stock often drops by the amount of the dividend when it goes ex-dividends.

4. *The Payment Date.* This is the date the dividends are actually paid. Established corporations with a good record of earning and a pattern of dividend payments usually pay dividends quarterly. The dividend checks are mailed to the stockholders of record by the

trustee (usually a trust department of a bank) who keeps the stockholder records for the corporation. Figure 14–6 calendars these important dates.

Stock Dividends

Directors may avoid a cash distribution by using a stock dividend. For example, a 10 percent stock dividend would result in each stockholder receiving from the company one additional share for every ten shares currently held. If fractional shares are issued because the stockholder's holdings are not evenly divisible by ten, provisions are usually made for stockholders to buy (or sell) fractional shares from the corporation so they can come out even. While increasing the number of ownership shares, this policy leaves the owner with the same equity as formerly held in the corporation. Although theoretically such a device should cause a decline in the market because it has increased the supply of the stock, occasionally the reverse is true because it may cause more interest in that particular stock and thus create more demand for it in the market.

INVESTMENT STRATEGIES; TIMING OF INVESTMENT DECISIONS, OR WHEN TO BUY WHAT

When it comes to making investment decisions, you have to decide not only what to buy, but when to buy. The importance of timing and the selection of securities is illustrated by the following example of what "might have been." Say you had invested $1,000 in Crown Cork

FIGURE 14–6. *Dividend dates calendar.*

SUNDAY	MONDAY	TUESDAY	WEDNESDAY	THURSDAY	FRIDAY	SATURDAY
			1	2	3 ABC Corp. met and declared dividend	4
5	6	7 ABC Corp. announced a dividend to be paid Sept. 30 to stockholders of record Sept. 22	8	9	10	11
12	13	14	15	16 Ex-dividend Date	17	18
19	20	21	22 Record Date	23	24	25
26	27	28	29	30 Payment Date		

in January, 1949. You held it until January, 1957, then sold it and bought Boeing with the proceeds, held Boeing until January, 1961, and then converted to Brunswick, which in turn was liquidated in December, 1969. How much money would you have? Exactly $145; a big loss over the years. By late in 1973 this would have declined further to $104. Now assume you bought the same securities but in a different order. First, you invest $1,000 in Boeing in January, 1949. Second, sell Boeing in January, 1957, and use the proceeds to acquire Brunswick. Third, sell Brunswick in January, 1961, and acquire Crown Cork. By December, 1969, your investment would have reached $2,607,210. Then you should have switched to bonds and preserved your capital and you could have been earning about 8 percent or more on it. However, had you continued to hold Crown Cork, by mid 1977, your $2,607,210 would have declined to about $750,000. "What the Lord giveth the Lord taketh away." Moreover, if you switched to long-term bonds in 1969 or 1970, you should have unloaded them in about 1976 and moved into short-term debt obligations like Treasury bills or commercial paper. Then you could have ridden up the rise in interest rate to its current all-time high without a capital loss. If you had done that, you would have several million dollars of highly liquid funds. What to do today? Stay short until interest rates decline, and when you are sure the downswing is permanent, jump into long-term bonds to weather the storm and take the capital gain. When the economy hits bottom, convert your bonds into good quality stocks that are depressed, if you can find any. Easy to say, but hard to do.

So much for what might have been and what you should do now, but this bit of history does not help in deciding when (and what kind) of securities to buy. This brings us to an old Wall Street saying, "The public is always wrong." But this, too, is no answer when we are trying to decide when to buy securities and which ones. Obviously some times are better than others and some securities are better buys than others. Another view is that for the long-term investor, any time is a good time. This too does not help much. Merrill Lynch has a motto, "Investigate, then invest"; again this is of little help. But there are some techniques that will help you to decide when to buy what as well as what to buy. We will examine some of these below.

Selecting What Securities to Buy

First you must decide upon your investment objectives such as growth, income, or any of the others discussed in Chapter 13. After you have made a choice you must identify the growth (or income) industries. Any competent brokerage house can help you do this. All industries' past records and future prospects are studied and analyzed periodically. Your broker will have these industry studies. If an industry has a good growth record, its management has proven itself, and its product is such that the demand for it will likely remain high or even rise, you have a growth area. Next you must compare the various growth industries and appraise their relative prospects for future growth. Some may be closer to maturity (end of growth) than others. Finally, after you have selected the industry (or industries), you must pick the firms within that industry that offer the best buys. This again necessitates a comparative appraisal of future prospects based in part on past records. The studies made by the investment services will often indicate which firm within an industry is the better buy, according to their view. They also sometimes list stocks in various industries in accordance with which seem best for income, appreciation, good quality, and speculative features. Figure 14–7 shows price variations of 1,490 New York Stock Exchange–listed stocks in 1979 without identifying them. Figure 14–8 illustrates the past performance of the stock of 65 different industries during the past ten years. The variation is remarkable.

If your goal is income rather than growth, follow the same procedure: selection of income industries, then comparative appraisal within the industry to identify the better

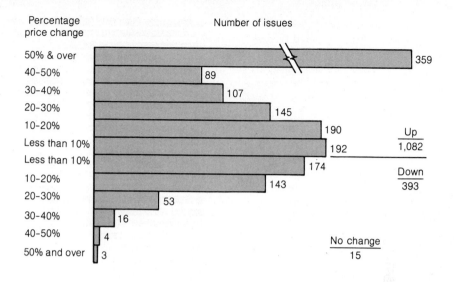

FIGURE 14–7. *Percentage price changes of 1,490 New York Stock Exchange common issues in year ended December 31, 1979. (Source: New York Stock Exchange Fact Book, 1980, New York Stock Exchange, Inc., p. 23.)*

buys, using industry studies and any other reliable information you or your broker can obtain. I cannot give you a sure formula. Moreover, you will not always be right; sometimes you will make mistakes. But if you do your research carefully and make your decision intelligently, you should be right more often than wrong.

If you wish to invest in stocks that swing more with the business cycle, your broker can help you select such stock. Steel and autos are good examples. Again you must make the industry and firm analysis. Remember all stocks swing with the business cycle, but some swing more than others.

Investing with Cyclical Swings

This involves an analysis of business conditions. You should buy when business conditions are improving and sell when the economy seems to be slipping into a recession. In this case you must decide what to buy and when to buy it. You can get a general feel for business conditions by following economic indicators and business statistics (these were discussed in Chapter 12), but making decisions on timing based on this involves economic forecasting and that is hard. Among the economic indicators to watch in order to get a clue on which way the economy is moving, is the stock market price level itself. Since the stock market is a lead indicator, when you decide the economy is finally moving strongly in one direction or the other, the stock market has already adjusted, at least in part, to take this into account. It is perhaps too late to benefit. On the other hand, while you may not get in on the ground floor, you may still benefit because the market will usually continue to move in its general direction. This is nebulous advice, but it is the best there is with regard to timing to benefit from cyclical swings.

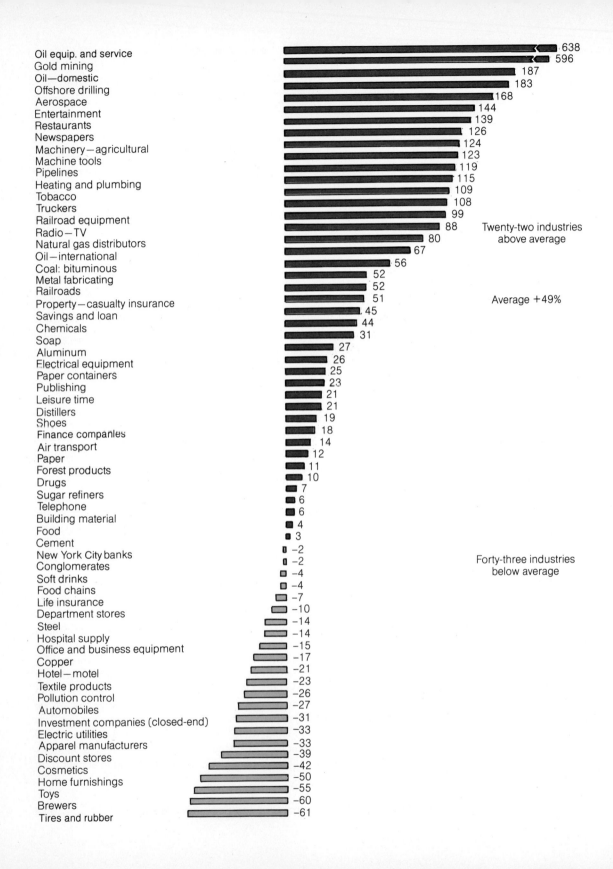

Industry	Value
Oil equip. and service	638
Gold mining	596
Oil—domestic	187
Offshore drilling	183
Aerospace	168
Entertainment	144
Restaurants	139
Newspapers	126
Machinery—agricultural	124
Machine tools	123
Pipelines	119
Heating and plumbing	115
Tobacco	109
Truckers	108
Railroad equipment	99
Radio—TV	88
Natural gas distributors	80
Oil—international	67
Coal: bituminous	56
Metal fabricating	52
Railroads	52
Property—casualty insurance	51
Savings and loan	45
Chemicals	44
Soap	31
Aluminum	27
Electrical equipment	26
Paper containers	25
Publishing	23
Leisure time	21
Distillers	21
Shoes	19
Finance companies	18
Air transport	14
Paper	12
Forest products	11
Drugs	10
Sugar refiners	7
Telephone	6
Building material	6
Food	4
Cement	3
New York City banks	-2
Conglomerates	-2
Soft drinks	-4
Food chains	-4
Life insurance	-7
Department stores	-10
Steel	-14
Hospital supply	-14
Office and business equipment	-15
Copper	-17
Hotel—motel	-21
Textile products	-23
Pollution control	-26
Automobiles	-27
Investment companies (closed-end)	-31
Electric utilities	-33
Apparel manufacturers	-33
Discount stores	-39
Cosmetics	-42
Home furnishings	-50
Toys	-55
Brewers	-60
Tires and rubber	-61

Twenty-two industries above average

Average +49%

Forty-three industries below average

Another view on this cyclical swing holds that it should be largely ignored. That is, be a long-run investor and ignore short and intermediate ups and downs. This too has merit, but obviously there are times when it seems prudent not to buy, generally speaking (for example, during the early stages of a recession when stocks are moving down rapidly).

Specific Security Analysis

Security analysis consists of examining yield and earnings, making an appraisal of expected future growth in these items, and then deciding whether the security is a candidate for acquisition.

1. *Yield Analysis.* Yield, you will recall, is the dividend divided by the market price of the stock. A person may operate under the rule of thumb that when the yield on a security reaches 8 or 9 percent it becomes a candidate for acquisition. Conversely, when the yield declines to less than say 6 percent it becomes a candidate for liquidation. This yield analysis has been given more weight recently because the American investor has become more yield-conscious in recent years. Examining yield also forces the investor to compare the yield on stock with that of alternative investments. You should remember that yield is more applicable if your objective is to acquire income stock.

2. *Price Earning's Ratio.* Earnings are total earnings (or profits) after taxes per year. Dividing through, we get earnings per share. For example,

$$\frac{\text{total after tax earnings}}{\text{total number of shares outstanding}} = \frac{\$7,500,000}{1,000,000 \text{ shares}} = \$7.50/\text{share}$$

In most cases, part of this $7.50 is paid out in the form of dividends and part is retained and plowed back into the corporation for expansion. However, the entire $7.50 belongs to the stockholder, and that portion retained will increase the book value and hopefully the market value of the stock. A comparison of earnings with the market price of a given share is an important analytical tool and might be a factor in determining whether or not you buy a given stock. Let's assume our stock above earning $7.50 per share is selling at $50. We now may calculate its price earnings ratio (PER).

$$\frac{\text{market price}}{\text{earnings per share}} = \frac{\$50}{\$7.50} = 6.66$$

Other stock will have different price earnings ratios. Generally growth stock will have a higher PER than income stock. To determine whether a given stock is a candidate for purchase, examine its P/E ratio and also how its earnings per share have grown over the years. If its earnings per share have grown at the rate of 10 percent per year and if you believe that rate of growth will continue into the future, you can project its earnings into the future. If $7.50 is compounded at 10 percent for 5 years, earnings per share in 5 years should be about $12.08. If a PER of 6.6 seems valid, then in 5 years a P/E ratio of 6.66 would put the market price of the stock at about $80. This would provide a nice capital gain. You must now also look at how large a dividend this stock is paying, and compare the expected future dividends as well as expected future price appreciation, with alternative stock. This is one way of seeking out good common stock investments. Compare various

FIGURE 14–8. *Stocks of sixty-five industries, January 1, 1970–December 31, 1979. (Source:* Johnson's Charts, Inc.)

price earnings ratios, project future earnings, look at dividends, and locate stocks that are underpriced in today's market and have good growth prospects.

Formula Timing

Formula timing is the use of some predetermined signal or combinations of signals to tell the buyer what to do. One of the more elementary methods of formula timing makes use of the price earnings ratio, or yield analysis. A given price earnings ratio is a buy signal and another is a sell signal. The investors may regard a selling price of ten to fifteen times earnings as the norm. If the stock is selling at less than ten times earnings, it is usually regarded as cheap and should be bought. If a stock is selling at more than fifteen times earnings, investors regard the price as inflated, and it should be sold. You would not buy indiscriminately within these P/E ratios, but rather selectively from certain stocks which become candidates when these ratios are achieved. The buy and sell limits would obviously be higher if you were buying growth rather than income securities. Nevertheless, this method will give you clues as to what to buy and when.

More elaborate formula timing plans have been developed for the investor with a large portfolio. Such a portfolio would be divided between stocks and bonds, and some ratio between the two would be selected to begin with, at whatever level stock prices were at that time. Let us assume we begin by having 50 percent of our assets in bonds and 50 percent in stocks, and our formula is tied to some average such as the Dow-Jones industrial stock average. When the price of stocks declines by a given amount—say 25 percent—the investor sells bonds and buys stocks to restore the 50/50 ratio. If stock prices rise by a predetermined amount, the investor sells stocks, takes the capital gain, and buys bonds to keep the market price ratio 50/50. Much more complicated formula timing plans have been developed, but the basic idea behind them is the same. Plans that are split between bonds and stock in the manner described above answer only the question of timing. They do not tell us what to buy, and judgment has to be used. Moreover, while they are workable for the large investor, they are not as feasible for the small investor.

Another variation of formula timing calls for a gradual liquidation or acquisition of a given security once the formula has given the signal. For example, a person who has decided to sell a stock because the price/earnings ratio is too high might decide to liquidate one-tenth of his or her holdings per month until they are gone. The same is true of acquisitions. The investor phases into the market cautiously to test the validity of the formula.

Dollar Averaging

Dollar averaging, or more strictly speaking "dollar cost averaging," consists of purchasing a particular stock with a constant number of dollars at uniform intervals. The result is that the stock is fluctuating and the investor is purchasing more shares when it is depressed than when it is inflated. For example, $500 will purchase twelve shares when the market is down and eight when it is up. The investor is purchasing more than half of the shares at a favorable price, and in the long run the law of averages will work for the investor. Table 14–3 is an example of dollar averaging. The average cost is $400 divided by 39 or about $10.25 per share.

The real difficulty with dollar cost averaging is that it assumes the investor will be able to have at hand a constant flow of dollars to invest over a given time period. In addition, there is the problem of bad timing or bad luck; the investor might happen to invest each time at the top of the market. In addition, it must be admitted that there is a certain psychological block in investing as the market is dropping.

TABLE 14–3. *Dollar averaging.*

PERIOD OF PURCHASE	AMOUNT	PRICE PER SHARE	NUMBER OF SHARES
1	$100	$10	10
2	$100	$ 5	20
3	$100	$20	5
4	$100	$25	4
	$400		39

Random Selection; The Random Walk

Recently, a school of thought has developed which suggests that a random selection of common stock may result in as fine a portfolio as will elaborate analysis. This view holds that a stock's future price movement cannot be predicted by an analysis of its past price movements. This is related to the efficient market hypothesis. In general, the efficient market hypothesis (EMH) states that the prices of securities traded in the market fully reflect all available information, and furthermore the market reacts instantaneously and in an unbiased manner to all new information. The EMH may be stated in its weak, semi-strong, or strong form.

The weak form of the EMH suggests that current market prices fully reflect all possible pertinent historical information. Because of this, future stock prices cannot be predicted on the basis of past movements, cyclical swings, or past price highs and lows of stock prices.

The semi-strong form of the EMH suggests that current market prices of securities fully reflect all *publicly* available information, such as annual reports and quarterly earnings announcements; that is, not just historical information but all pertinent information.

The strong EMH goes even further and gives the market even more credit. It states that current market prices reflect fully *all* information whether it is publicly available or not, such as insider's information.

The random walk hypothesis is a variation of the weak EMH, and states that at any time the next change (either up or down) in security prices and the magnitude of that change is random; that is, prices will move independently of past price movements.

If the random walk hypothesis is correct then one of its implications is to adopt a "buy and hold" strategy. This is because in the long run no historical analysis will permit the selection of a portfolio of stocks which will outperform a portfolio selected at random. A buy-and-hold strategy provides an added bonus; if adopted, investment and transaction costs of turning your portfolio over will be eliminated.

The semi-strong and strong forms of the EMH, if correct, also suggest you might just as well select your stock at random.[5] Even if you use more than public information you cannot outperform the market consistently. That is, fundamental and statistical analyses regarding sales, earnings, expected future growth, etc., is not helpful because the market knows more

---

5. Technically speaking, this is true only if your portfolio is large enough to enable you to obtain diversification by random selection. If you are a small investor, a random selection will not necessarily give you a well-diversified portfolio, and the strong and semi-strong EMH suggests that diversification is also important and indeed diversification should be given greater weight than random selection. So for the small investor the answer is random selection tempered by diversification.

about these things than you do, and it will adjust to this information before you can act. While knowledge of an industry and of a company, and general know-how about the economy and the market, may permit successful prediction of the future value of a given stock from time to time, sheer statistical analysis will not provide better results than a random buy-and-hold selection strategy in the long run. The random walk theory and the EMH do not suggest that stock prices do not respond to changes in pertinent information. Rather it states the market is so efficient that it quickly adjusts to all information on all stocks so that the individual cannot benefit by trying to outdo the market.

This theory is highly controversial. First of all, one could challenge the view that the securities market, if sufficiently efficient, will discount all stocks to the point where they are all approximately equally good (or bad) buys. If an analysis is made, some obviously good and some obviously poor buys can no doubt be discovered from time to time. If we eliminate these obvious extremes, perhaps a random selection will provide results that are as good as poor analysis will provide. But the analysis need not be poor; all investors can develop some degree of sophistication if they are willing to devote the time.

Selecting What Stocks to Sell

If you buy stocks, you should perhaps also sell them from time to time. Some investors hold the view that if they buy the right stock, they need never sell. This view may have some merit if you buy only the bluest of the blue chips like AT&T, G.E., or GM (it also has some merit if you subscribe to the random walk theory). However, most stockholders should review their portfolios and weed out the weaker stocks from time to time.

The decision to sell a stock is similar to the decision to buy. You must review the firm whose stock you own and also compare it with other firms. Would you, for example, buy more of a given stock that you now have and are reviewing? Or is some other stock a better buy? If the answer to the first question is no and the second yes, you should seriously consider selling the stock under review. If a stock has not done well or has had losses, the temptation might be to hold on to it in the hope that it will recover. This policy is not always sound; sometimes it is best to take your losses and admit your mistakes. Even if the stock does recover in the future, you would be better off to take your losses now if you can find a stock that will rise more.

Some people also feel that they should not sell a stock that has risen substantially since they purchased it. Why get off a winning horse? This is tempting reasoning, but again you should make the decision in light of your appraisal of what this stock will do in the future relative to others. Sometimes certain stocks are overpriced and if you own them you should sell and take your capital gain.

I said before that the small investor should be a long-run investor rather than a short-run investor, at least for the most part. This statement is still true, but it does not negate what was said above regarding portfolio review. By portfolio review I do not mean you should constantly get in and out of the market, always seeking better buys. What is meant is that even the long-run investor should not go to sleep at the switch. How often should you review your portfolio? Some people keep it under review all the time. But if you do not, you should probably take a good look at your securities at least every six months. Again, this does not mean you should sell something every six months; rather that you should look to see. Perhaps you should, perhaps not.

QUESTIONS FOR REVIEW

1. Discuss the various types of brokers on the New York Stock Exchange.

2. How do brokers and dealers in securities differ?

3. What is the Dow-Jones Average and what does it attempt to show?

4. What are some other stock averages besides the Dow-Jones? What are the weaknesses and strengths of the stock averages?

5. Explain briefly the differences between a bear market and a bull market.

6. On over-the-counter stock, what are meant by bid, asked, and net change?

7. Who controls margin requirements and what is the purpose of this control?

8. When a person buys stock on margin and it declines, he or she may be required to "cover." What does this mean?

9. Explain a short sale and how it differs from a conditional sale.

10. Explain what is meant by ex-dividend date and how it is determined.

11. Outline several techniques for reaching decisions with respect to timing of security purchases.

12. What is meant by portfolio review? Why should you review your portfolio periodically?

13. What is the "random walk" as applied to securities?

14. What risks do you face if you simply buy good stocks and then forget about them for twenty years?

15. What is meant by keeping securities in the street name? What are its advantages and disadvantages?

16. How does a stock split differ from a stock dividend?

17. What are preemptive rights? Discuss the differences between these rights and warrants.

18. What are puts and calls?

19. What do legal regulations as applied to securities attempt to accomplish?

CASES

1. Rodney and Melba Johnson are a young couple who have just inherited $20,000. They live comfortably on their modest salaries and since they do not need the money, they have decided to invest it in securities. Should they be long-run or short-run investors? Do you think now is a good time to buy common stock? If you advise buying, what kind of stock would you recommend?

2. Elmer and Susan Green are a couple in their middle thirties with twin boys aged six months. Elmer works in the local factory and makes just enough for the four of them to get along until Susan rejoins the work force. Last week Elmer heard that he will receive $5,000 from his father's estate. They have decided not to use the money to buy the house they have always wanted but rather to save it for their children's college fund. How should they invest it? Elmer and Susan know that govern-

ment bonds and banks are the safest but feel the return is too low. They are thinking about buying bonds and stocks. Should they? If so, what kind would you recommend?

3. Judy Smith is an elderly widow who has just received a check for $100,000 from a life insurance company in payment for her husband's death. Although she owns her own home, the $100,000 will be her sole support. She does not feel she should buy an annuity but rather that she should invest the $100,000 and live off the income. Do you think she is wise? If she invests the money, what kind of securities would you recommend? Why?

4. Alfred and Helen Walker own two different common stocks. They are one hundred shares of ABC corporation and one hundred shares of XYZ. Their ABC stock was recently split three for one, and before the split it was sell-

ing on the New York Stock Exchange for $120 per share. What, in theory, is the price now? Why may the price not fall that much? How many shares do they now own?

The Walkers' XYZ stock was selling for $140 per share on the American Stock Exchange when they received a 100 percent stock dividend. How many shares do they now own? What is the theoretical price of the XYZ stock? How big a stock dividend would they have had to receive to have the same number of shares of XYZ stock as they have of ABC? What is the difference between a stock split and a stock dividend?

5. George Kennedy owns fifty shares of common stock, and the corporation has informed him he has preemptive rights on a new issue coming out. At present there are one million shares outstanding, and the new issue will consist of one hundred thousand shares. How many new shares can George buy? Why? What is the idea behind preemptive rights? The market price of George's stock is $80 and the new issue is coming out at $75. If George decides to sell his preemptive rights rather than exercise them, what will he get for them?

6. Five years ago Bernice Edwards received 100 warrants attached to some convertible bonds she bought. These warrants entitled her to buy common stock on the same corporation at $15 per share. However, the common was selling in the market at the time for $5 per share. Yesterday, Bernice checked and found that the common is now selling at $35 per share. What are her warrants worth?

7. Sally Ann and Bill Herod purchased one hundred shares of ABC Corporation stock in 1946 for $195 per share. Since then the following stock splits and stock dividends have taken place:

1948 7 for 4 stock split
1949 5% stock dividend
1950 5% stock dividend

1951 5% stock dividend
1952 5% stock dividend
1953 5% stock dividend
1954 5 for 4 stock split
1956 2½% stock dividend
1957 2 for 1 stock split
1958 2½% stock dividend
1959 2½% stock dividend and
      3 for 2 stock split
1961 3 for 2 stock split
1964 5 for 4 stock split
1966 3 for 2 stock split
1967 2½% stock dividend
1968 2 for 1 stock split
1973 5 for 4 stock split
1978 4 for 1 stock split

Recently the market price of ABC was $70 per share. How many shares of ABC stock do Sally Ann and Bill own and what is their investment worth?

8. Betty and Harry Hoffman purchased one hundred shares of XYZ in 1946 and put it in a safety deposit box to take out upon retirement. They paid $47 per share at the time of purchase. Since they purchased the stock there has been a two-for-one split and also a second three-for-one split. Recently the stock was selling in the market for $60 per share. How many shares do they have and what is their investment worth?

9. Bill and Betty Pasmack recently moved across country to Seattle, Washington, where Bill took a new job. After moving into their new home and unpacking, they couldn't find their securities. Betty said that since they were registered they had nothing to worry about; they would simply report it to the company and have new ones issued. Bill, however, is not sure that it is all as simple as that. Can you explain what they must do to have new securities issued? What if they do not have the serial number of their securities? What can people do to prevent or minimize the likelihood of losing securities?

SUGGESTED READINGS

Amex Databook. Fact book published annually by the American Stock Exchange.

Christy, George A., and Roden, Foster P. *Finance:*

Environment and Decisions. New York: Canfield Press, Division of Harper & Row, 1976.

"The Dow Jones Averages." Education Service Bureau of Dow Jones & Company, P. O. Box 300, Princeton, N.J. 08540, 1977.

Engle, Louis. *How to Buy Stocks,* 5th Edition. New York: Bantam Books, 1976.

"The Exchange Market and the Public Interest." The New York Stock Exchange Annual Report.

Fogler, Russell H. *Analyzing the Stock Market,* 2nd ed. Columbus, Ohio: Grid Inc., Publishers, 1978.

Forbes Magazine. A weekly magazine with a great deal of material in it about business and finance.

Francis, Jack Clark. *Investments Analysis and Management.* New York: McGraw-Hill Book Company, 1980.

How Over-the-Counter Securities are Traded. New York: Merrill Lynch, Pierce, Fenner & Smith, Inc.

"How to Read a Financial Report." Merrill Lynch, Pierce, Fenner & Smith, Inc., N.Y.

Market for Millions. New York: American Stock Exchange.

"Market Statistics." Chicago: The Chicago Board of Options Exchange.

The Merrill Lynch Guide to Writing Options. Merrill Lynch, Pierce, Fenner, and Smith, Inc., 165 Broadway, New York, N.Y. 10006. You can get this from your local Merrill Lynch broker.

Nelson, Paula. *The Joy of Money.* New York: Bantam Books, 1977.

New York Stock Exchange Fact Book. Published annually by the New York Stock Exchange.

The New York Stock Exchange Market. Education Service Bureau, Dow Jones & Company, P. O. Box 300, Princeton, N.J., 08540

Rates of Return on Investments in Common Stock. New York: Merrill Lynch, Pierce, Fenner & Smith, Inc.

Smith, Keith V., and David K. Eiteman, *Essentials of Investing.* Homewood, Ill.: Richard D. Irwin, 1974.

Standard & Poor's Stock Guide. New York: Standard & Poor's Corporation, 1981.

Tax Considerations in Using CBOE Options. Chicago: The Chicago Board of Options Exchange, 1976.

Understanding the New York Stock Exchange. New York: New York Stock Exchange.

Understanding Options. Chicago: The Chicago Options Exchange, 1977.

The Versatile Option. New York: The American Stock Exchange, Inc., 86 Trinity Place, New York, N.Y. 10006.

Well Beyond the Average: The Story of Dow Jones. New Jersey: Dow Jones & Company, Inc., The Educational Service Bureau.

What Every Woman Investor Should Know. Washington, D.C.: Investment Bankers Association of America, undated.

APPENDIX 14A

SUPPLEMENTARY MATERIAL ON COMMON STOCK

There are a number of other points on common stock with which you should be familiar, among them what to do if you lose securities, keeping securities in the street name, stock splits, preemptive rights, stock warrants, and the options market for common stock.

WHAT TO DO IF YOU LOSE SECURITIES

Securities should be kept in a safe place like a safety deposit box at a bank. Since most securities are registered, they can be replaced, but this is neither easy nor cheap. If securities are lost, notify the transfer agent immediately. If you do not know the name of the agent, your broker may be able to tell you, although sometimes you may have to write to the company issuing the stock. The transfer agent will want the certificate numbers of the missing shares. Consequently, you should have a list of these numbers available.

Upon notification, the transfer agent puts a stop on the stock to prevent its sale. The next step is to get the company to issue new replacement shares. And this costs money. Nearly all companies require an indemnity bond as protection against any possible future loss. While the corporation would not suffer a loss if the old securities reappeared and were successfully sold, a brokerage house would, and the bond is used to indemnify them. Generally a bond of 100 percent of the value of the securities is required. You can put up the bond in cash or have a bonding company do so. If you use a bonding company, you have to pay premiums that generally amount to about 4 percent of the stock's value.

KEEPING SECURITIES IN THE STREET NAME

In order to eliminate the possibility of loss, some investors keep their securities in the street name. This merely means that the purchaser does not take physical possession, but rather leaves the securities with the broker, who stores them in a safe. This makes it easier to sell the securities. All that is required is a phone call; the owner need not sign them and deliver them to the broker. This also protects the individual from loss of the securities due to fire, theft, or misplacement. The reason securities held in the street name can be sold by making a phone call is that they are in the broker's name. The securities of hundreds of customers are all lumped together this way. While in theory there is some danger here, they are as safe as money in the bank. The brokers are subject to the regulations of the New York Stock Exchange and the Security and Exchange Commission. They cannot sell these securities without permission, nor may they borrow money on them. The brokers must carry a fidelity bond to cover losses due to fraud and insurance to cover theft.

There is some slight danger if the broker goes bankrupt, but there is protection even here. The New York Stock Exchange has a $25,000,000 fund into which all brokers pay, which would be used to reimburse stockholders' losses due to broker bankruptcies. Also, the federal government recently established a form of insurance for this purpose. It is similar to the insurance under the Federal Deposit Insurance Corporation (FDIC) to protect bank depositors. This insurance is more fully discussed at the end of this appendix.

STOCK GIFTS TO MINORS; UNIFORM GIFTS TO MINORS ACT

Most states have passed the Uniform Gifts to Minors Act. This makes it easier for a person to buy securities for his or her children. The security will be made out to "Jane Doe, Trustee for John Doe, Junior" under the Texas Uniform Gifts to Minors Act, or of whatever state you are a resident. This makes the income taxable only if the minor child has a high enough taxable income to pay taxes. That is to say, the gift is, and must be by law, irrevocable. However, the trustee can sell the security as long as he or she retains the principal on behalf of the child. The interest (or dividends) too must be retained for the child. The trustee may only manage the securities. No one, not even the child, can touch the fund until the child becomes twenty-one (now eighteen in many states), at which time he or she gains full control.

Many people buy small amounts of high-quality securities for their children and build a portfolio to be used later to finance specific projects such as a college education.

STOCK SPLITS

A stock split occurs when a corporation increases the number of shares of stock outstanding by sending additional shares of stock to existing stockholders without demanding additional payment. In so doing, the total net worth of the corporation is unaffected and yet the book value of each individual share is reduced. Theoretically, the existing stockholders have received nothing that increases their share of the corporate assets. For purposes of illustration, assume a corporation with a net worth of $15,000,000 and one million shares, which would make the book value $15 per share. If the stock is split two for one—meaning that each shareholder is to receive two shares in exchange for each share now held—a shareholder who had one hundred shares before would now have a total of two hundred.[6] But the company, since it received no additional capital, would still have a net worth of $15,000,000. Since now twice as many shares have a claim on it, the book value of each share would drop from $15 to $7.50. If the market value had been $30 per share before the split, theoretically it would fall to $15. Often, however, the market value does not fall this much. The point is that the shareholders' positions would not be changed. The question then is, why do corporations split the stock?

The main reason is that lower-priced stock sometimes has a psychological attraction to investors. Then, too, sometimes lower-priced stocks are more accessible to more people. When the stock is split, the initial reaction is that the price of the stock is lowered; at the lower price more investors are attracted to the stock, and consequently there may be a tendency for market prices to be forced upward more rapidly, once more from the lower price. Also many people, not knowing that theoretically they are no better off, think that somehow the stockholders have magically got something for nothing. Because this makes this corporation's stock more attractive to them, they buy it and bid up its price.

From a financial point of view, a stock split and a stock dividend are the same. A two-for-one split or a 100 percent stock dividend would double the number of shares a person had and would cut the book value in half. Theoretically, the market price would be cut in half, too. That is to say, the two-for-one split discussed above and a 100 percent stock dividend would accomplish the same dilution per share. Generally stock dividends are used when smaller dilution is desired. Many stock dividends are 10 to 20 percent. Sometimes, however, stock dividends are used when a corporation cannot or does not want to pay a cash dividend but feels it must declare something to satisfy the stockholders. A stock dividend is not taxable as income.

From a technical accounting point of view, there is a slight difference between a stock split and a stock dividend. A stock dividend does not change the par value of the stock; a stock split might. Generally, a dividend reduces earned surplus, although on rare occasions it might reduce paid-in surplus. Moreover, a stock dividend does not require an exchange of stock; the company simply mails the increased shares to the stockholder. (Of course the same is true of a stock split, if it is a no-par stock.) As noted above, a stock dividend will dilute both the book value and the market price of the stock in the same manner as a stock split.

PREEMPTIVE RIGHTS

The capital of a firm may be reduced or increased. A capital reduction is rare, and it would necessitate returning to the stockholder part of the stockholder's capital. This could happen in a government anti-monopoly action against a company which was then required to divest itself of certain assets.

It is quite common, however, for a corporation to increase its capital, and then the question is, what are the rights of the stockholders under such a situation? It can readily be

---

6. The stock must be exchanged because par value is cut in half. If the stock is no-par stock, a two-for-one split could be accomplished without an exchange. The company would simply mail the stockholder one additional share for each share owned.

seen that the relative strength of an individual stockholder could be affected if the capital of the corporation is increased. Suppose again that there are ten stockholders, each with one share, and the total assets of the corporation consist of $1,000. Thus each of the stockholders may be said to own 10 percent of the corporation and also 10 percent of the voting rights. Suppose further that the corporation desires to issue $1,000 in additional stock so that its asset cash will be $2,000. To accomplish this, it sells ten additional shares at $100 each. If an outsider buys all these shares, then his or her interest in the corporation will be 50 percent, and all old stockholders will have their interest reduced from 10 percent per share to 5 percent. Thus the old stockholders will be adversely affected by such a transaction.

To prevent this sort of imposition on the existing stockholders, the courts and the law have long since handled the situation by what are known as "preemptive rights." This is the right of the existing stockholders to purchase a proportionate share in the increase of the capital stock of the corporation. This right does not always exist, however. In some cases it exists because the corporate charter grants it and in some cases because the state law of the state of incorporation requires it. If neither state law nor corporate charter grants preemptive rights or if they are waived, then the corporation may go to the public or outside investors if it wants to expand its capital. A *right,* therefore, is defined as a privilege possessed by a stockholder to purchase *a pro rata share* of a new stock issue offered by the corporation at a specific price and for a specific time period.

Rights are issued by corporations that seek to raise additional capital. For example, suppose a corporation desires to raise about $7,500,000. It has outstanding one hundred thousand shares of common stock valued in the market at $100 per share. If it sells one hundred thousand new shares at $75 per share, it will have its $7,500,000. In accordance with preemptive rights it will give all existing stockholders the right to buy one new share for each share they already have. In this case, the company is increasing its capital by 75 percent. I have put the example this way to simplify calculations. Usually a firm will increase its capital by only 10 or 20 percent, and a person in such a case will have the right to buy a new issue for every ten or five shares he or she owns, respectively.

The firm usually sells the new stock at a price below the market price of the outstanding shares in order to expedite the sale. Since there cannot be two prices, when the new issue comes out, the market price of the old will fall and the new will rise; and the price, in the example above, will be approximately $87.50. Mr. *X,* who before had one share valued at $100, purchased a new one for $75. His total investment is $175 or $87.50 per share. If Mr. *X* had ignored his rights, he would now have only one share valued at $87.50. His equity would have been diluted by $12.50. The example also illustrates the value of rights; it is, in this case, $12.50.

If Mr. *X* could not afford to pay $75 for his new share, he could have sold his rights for $12.50 in cash and prevented a dilution of his equity in this way. That is to say, rights are valuable and if you do not have the money to exercise them, sell them. If you neither exercise nor sell them, they will expire after a time. Usually the company will offer to buy an investor's rights if he or she does not wish to exercise them. Sometimes if a large issue is coming out, an organized market develops in rights and one can both buy and sell them from a broker.

When rights are granted, the person who buys that stock in the market automatically gets the right, until the stock goes "ex-right." This is logically the same as a stock going "ex-dividends." For example, the company issuing the rights announces that stockholders of record on Friday, February 1, 1981, will receive the rights. The stock goes "ex-rights" in the market four days before this date because of the four-day delivery rule. When a stock goes "ex-rights" its price in the market generally declines by the amount of the value of the right.

Companies issue rights because it is an easy way to raise capital and it is also cheaper than to come out with a general public issue. It saves the corporation investment banker's fees; the stockholders also receive their stock more cheaply because they don't have to pay commissions.

Since persons usually get a right for every ten or twenty shares they already have, there arises the problem of fractional rights. Suppose you had fifteen shares of stock and were given rights to buy one share of new stock for every ten of the old. Obviously you cannot buy $1\frac{1}{2}$ new shares. Usually the company will either buy back fractional rights or offer to sell the investor enough fractions for an even number of shares.

There is a formula that can be used to calculate the value of a right, although ordinary logic and arithmetic are all that is needed in a simple case such as the one discussed above. However, if eight or ten shares of stock are required to obtain the right to buy one new share, the formula may be helpful. It is the market price less the subscription price divided by the number of old shares plus one, which are needed to get one of the new.

$$\text{Or,} \quad \frac{M - S}{N + 1} = V$$

Where M = market value of old
S = subscription price
N = number of shares needed to buy one of the new
V = value of the right

In the case above we had,

$M = \$100$
$S = \quad 75$ and hence our formula tells us

$$\frac{\$100 - \$75}{2} = \$12.50$$

A second reason for preemptive rights—not very important in most cases—is to prevent dilution of control. For example, if you owned 10 percent of the stock in a given corporation, you would have 10 percent of the votes at the stockholders' meetings. If you were not permitted to continue to buy the same 10 percent of any new issues, your relative voting strength would decline. This is not important at all for most stockholders because they have so few shares that they don't really have any influence at corporate elections. However, for a few large stockholders it might be a factor.

STOCK WARRANTS

A warrant is a certificate evidencing an option to purchase new securities, usually common stock, at a stated price for a stated time period. Sometimes, however, the time period is for perpetuity. The distinction between the right and the warrant is that the right is generally issued under the preemptive right privilege to existing stockholders, while a warrant may be issued aside from the preemptive rights to nonstockholders. Warrants are originally attached to other securities when they are issued and generally are attached to either bonds or preferred stock. Some warrants are not detachable, and hence they cannot be sold separately; but others are detachable, and a market exists for them.

When a corporation feels that it may have difficulty in selling a particular preferred stock or bond issue, it may offer warrants along with each security that will enable the purchaser to buy additional shares of common stock. These warrants, called "purchase warrants," are generally extended for relatively long periods of time or even perpetually.

Thus the preemptive stock rights are different from warrants. The rights have a relatively short life, which may be days or weeks. When a corporation attaches warrants to bonds or preferred stocks, it is more easily able to sell them. Since warrants permit the holder to purchase common stock at a predetermined price, they are a speculative device. They make the mother security more attractive, a fact best illustrated with an example.

Suppose the Adjax Corporation issues 9 percent bonds maturing in twenty years with detachable warrants on the bonds. Anyone who buys a bond also gets a warrant. The warrant permits the owner to purchase one share of common stock at, say, $30 per share at any time during the next three years. The common stock is presently selling for $20 per share, however, and hence the warrant has speculative value only. If it is detachable, it may sell for a dollar or $.50 or even less. But the $30 and the three-year period are fixed. If the common stock of the Adjax Corporation rises to, say, $40 before the three years have elapsed, the warrant will be worth $10; its price will have moved from $1 to $10. This is a tremendous percentage increase, but it is in the nature of warrants. They have tremendous leverage. Once the stock rises above the warrant price, warrants have positive value and will appreciate by some multiple of the further appreciation of the common stock. By the same token, warrants move downward with common stock but by greater magnitudes.

If you buy bonds with warrants attached, the warrant may have value in the future. If it does not, you simply remain a bond investor.

WHAT TO DO WITH RIGHTS AND WARRANTS

Oddly enough, many investors have no idea what to do with either rights or warrants, some of which are destroyed physically and many of which are permitted to lapse. Three choices are open to the investor. One is to permit them to lapse; as has already been indicated, many people do just this. Another alternative is to exercise the right, and the warrant if and when it has value; however, it may be that investors holding the warrants or rights are unable to do this because they lack available cash or are unwilling to because they lack any further interest in the particular stocks issued. The third alternative is to sell the rights, and the warrant if it is detachable, which can be done through any broker.

The Options Markets; Puts and Calls

Although there are a number of other stock options[7] the major ones are puts and calls, both of which are speculative devices.

A call option is a contractual and legal privilege of buying a given number (usually one hundred) of shares of a given common stock for a given period of time at a price determined at the time the call is purchased. For example, if you buy, say for $200, a thirty-day call on United States Steel at $25 this means that at any time during the next thirty days the seller is required to sell you one hundred shares of U.S. Steel for $25 per share if you request it. If U.S. Steel rises to $45 during this period, your $200 will have grown to $2,000. Your net return is $1,800 ($2,000 minus the $200 option price). This again is a tremendous percent-

---

7. The various stock options one can buy in the options market should not be confused with the stock option plans many corporations make available to their key employees. In the case of corporate stock option plans, certain key executives are granted the privilege (option) of buying a certain number of shares of common stock from the corporation, usually at the market price of the stock at the time the option is granted. The option price is then, however, frozen for the executives for a period of time, usually several years or more. Then if the market price rises substantially, the option holders can execute and make a nice gain. The main justification for providing key executives stock options is to give them a vested interest in the corporation and hence a greater incentive to perform well.

age return on your money. If U.S. Steel does not move, on the other hand, you have lost $200. Options permit one to speculate in one hundred-lot shares with only a relatively few dollars; they also hold out the possibility of a high rate of return on one's money; and the maximum amount that can be lost is the price of the option.

A put option is exactly the reverse of a call option. It is the privilege of selling one hundred shares of a given stock for a given period of time at a price determined at the time the put is purchased. A person buying a put is speculating that the market price of that stock is going down.

Options may run up to nine months before they expire. A market in options is now being made on the Chicago Board of Options Exchange, the American Stock Exchange, the Philadelphia Stock Exchange, the Midwest Exchange, and the Pacific Stock Exchange. The Chicago exchange is by far the largest. It is to the options market what the New York Stock Exchange is to the stock market.

If you wish to buy (or sell) an opinion, your broker can make the arrangement through one of the organized options markets mentioned above. There are brokerage commissions for this that are similar to (but generally a little lower than) the stock commissions discussed above.

Table A14–1 shows some options listed on the Chicago Board of Options Exchange. An entry might appear as follows:

Option	Price	Jan Vol.	Jan Last	April Vol.	April Last	July Vol.	July Last	N.Y. Close
Exxon	80	418	$2^5/_8$	124	$4^1/_4$	32	$5^7/_8$	$77^1/_4$

It identifies first of all the corporation (Exxon) on which there is an option. Then moving to the right, we see the option price at which shares may be purchased ($80 per share). That is, if you buy this option you may buy 100 shares of Exxon at $80 per share. Moving to the right, we see under "Vol." that 418 options were sold. "Last" means that the last option sold was priced at $2^5/_8$; that is, the premium which is $2^5/_8$ per share ($2.63) or $263.00 for the option on 100 shares, the smallest amount sold. This option expires on the third Saturday of January. (Options always expire on the third Saturday of the month shown.) If you want an option that runs to April, it will cost you $4^1/_4$ per share of $425.00 for an option on 100 shares. For a July option the sum is $587.50. The last column, "N.Y. Close," gives the price at which Exxon closed on the New York Stock Exchange that day. It was $77^1/_4$. This means, then, that if you choose the January option, you could, by paying a premium of $263.00, have the right to buy one hundred shares of Exxon at $80 per share until the third Saturday of January, even though it is worth only $77^1/_4$ today.[8] Obviously, the buyers of this option think the price of Exxon will rise. If you wish to hold that option until April of next year, the premium is $425.00 and to go out to July it is $507.50. If you examine option quotes in *The Wall Street Journal*, you will note that sometimes an "a" or "b" appears. An *a* means that no option for that stock was traded that day; a *b* means no option going out that far exists.

Writing Options

Instead of thinking about buying options, more and more sophisticated investors are thinking in terms of selling them (called writing options). There are two ways of writing call

---

8. Since the market is closed on Saturday, the options really expire on the third Friday of the month, but this is a technicality. The option will state that it will expire on the first Saturday after the third Friday of the month in question.

Chicago Board

Listed Options Quotations

Wednesday, April 2, 1980

Closing prices of all options. Sales unit usually is 100 shares. Security description includes exercise price. Stock close is New York or American exchange final price. p-Put option. o-Old shares.

			– Apr –		– Jul –		– Oct –		N.Y.
Option	&	price	Vol.	Last	Vol.	Last	Vol.	Last	Close
Alcoa		.. 50	10	10⅛	21	11¾	a	a	59⅜
Alcoa		.. 60	93	1¾	96	6⅛	a	a	59⅜
Alcoa		...70	27	1-16	119	2¼	49	3¾	59⅜
Am Exp		25	10	4¾	10	5½	a	a	29⅝
Am Exp		30	66	¾	35	1¾	28	2½	29⅝
Am Exp		35	a	a	a	a	15	1¼	29⅝
Am Tel		.45	b	b	140	5	270	6	48⅝
Am Tel		.50	281	¼	155	1 13-16	299	2 15-16	48⅝
Am Tel		.55	2	1-16	37	⅜	139	1	48⅝
Atl R		.. 60	3	27¼	b	b	b	b	87¼
Atl R		.. 70	6	18½	13	20	b	b	87¼
Atl R		...80	84	8⅜	90	11½	3	13½	87¼
Atl R		...90	94	1½	94	5¾	10	9	87¼
Atl R		..100	224	⅛	242	2¾	3	6¼	87¼
Atl R		..110	134	1-16	586	1⅜	9	3¼	87¼
Avon		30	b	b	43	5½	a	a	34⅛
Avon	p	... 30	b	b	125	13-16	43	1½	34⅛
Avon		... 35	324	¾	164	2¾	12	4	34⅛
Avon	p	.. 35	375	1⅝	201	2 11-16	21	3½	34⅛
Avon		... 40	105	1-16	87	1	28	1⅝	34⅛
Avon	p	... 40	a	a	15	6	a	a	34⅛
Avon		... 45	3	1-16	43	⅜	b	b	34⅛
Avon		... 50	1	1-16	6	⅛	b	b	34⅛
BankAm		20	67	3¾	b	b	b	b	23⅝
Bankam		20	b	b	31	4⅝	b	b	23⅝
BankAm		20	b	b	b	b	75	5⅝	23⅝
BankAm		25	366	¼	294	1⅜	110	2½	23⅝
BankAm		30	a	a	60	⅜	57	⅞	23⅝
Beth S		..20	55	15-16	10	2¼	a	a	20⅜
Beth S		. 25	25	1-16	63	½	49	1	20⅜
Beth S		..30	a	a	10	¼	127	9-16	20⅜
Burl N		. 50	37	7½	3	11½	8	14½	57¾
Burl N		. 60	117	1⅜	30	5¾	27	8⅛	57¾
Burl N		. 70	150	1-16	38	2 9-16	21	4¼	57¾
Burl N		. 80	a	a	21	1	3	2¼	57¾
Burrgh		..60	11	7½	a	a	a	a	67¼
Burrgh		..90	a	a	2	⅝	a	a	67¼
Citicp		...15	b	b	1	4½	13	5¼	19¼
Citicp		.. 20	483	⅜	141	1⅝	219	2½	19¼
Citicp		...25	a	a	137	¼	114	¾	19¼
Delta		.. 35	6	⅝	?	2½	5	3½	34⅜
Delta		... 40	a	a	a	a	5	2	34⅜
Dig Eq		. 60	5	5⅛	a	a	a	a	64½
Dig Eq		. 70	a	a	4	4½	a	a	64½
Disney		..45	10	1⅜	a	a	a	a	45
du Pnt		..30	b	b	a	a	2	8½	36⅛
du Pnt		. 35	142	1¾	23	3¾	2	5	36⅛
du Pnt		. 40	63	¼	26	1 5-16	16	2⅜	36⅛
du Pnt		. 45	24	1-16	4	½	55	1 1-16	36⅛
Eas Kd		.40	187	8	104	9⅞	22	10¾	47⅝
Eas Kd	p	40	216	1-16	213	⅝	80	1	47⅝
Eas Kd		.45	1002	3½	347	5¾	108	7⅝	47⅝
Eas Kd	p	45	2099	7-16	527	1 13-16	70	2¼	47⅝
Eas Kd		.50	1957	⅝	508	3⅛	85	4⅝	47⅝
Eas Kd	p	50	686	2½	477	3¾	56	4¼	47⅝
Eas Kd		.60	72	1-16	467	¾	b	b	47⅝
Eas Kd	p	.60	25	11⅜	4	12	b	b	47⅝
Exxon		..50	22	7	13	8¾	28	10¼	56½
Exxon		..55	149	2¾	35	4⅞	3	7⅝	56½
Exxon		..60	220	½	108	3	63	4⅝	56½
Exxon		..70	42	1-16	443	¾	49	1⅞	56½
F N M		10	a	a	15	4½	8	4½	14¼

			– May –		– Aug –		– Nov –		N.Y.
Option	&	price	Vol.	Last	Vol.	Last	Vol.	Last	Close
Mobil		.. 50	120	17¼	9	19¾	b	b	67
Mobil		...55	403	13⅜	94	17	4	17¼	67
Mobil		...60	1507	9½	169	13¼	47	16	67
Mobil		...65	1003	6½	55	11	85	13¼	67
Mobil		...70	2943	4¼	322	8⅛	115	10½	67
Mobil		...80	3083	1⅞	613	5	149	7¼	67
Mobil		...90	2147	⅝	659	2⅞	361	4⅞	67
N Semi		15	68	6⅝	a	a	7	8¾	21¼
N Semi		.20	415	2½	53	4	11	5	21¼
N Semi		.25	145	11-16	217	1⅞	68	2⅞	21¼
N Sem o		16⅝	40	5½	a	a	b	b	21¼
N Sem o		20	108	2½	2	4¼	b	b	21¼
N Sem o		23⅜	142	1 3-16	18	2½	10	3¾	21¼
N Sem o		26⅝	245	7-16	47	1¼	104	2 7-16	21¼
N Sem o		30	12	1-16	204	¾	15	1 9-16	21¼
Occi		... 20	248	4⅞	7	5¾	41	7⅛	23½
Occi		... 25	997	1 9-16	338	3¼	117	4¼	23½
Occi		... 30	1014	½	290	1½	164	2¼	23½
Occi		... 35	204	⅛	95	¾	68	1⅜	23½
Raythn		. 60	12	12¾	13	15	b	b	72
Raythn		. 70	18	5¼	58	7¼	a	a	72
Raythn		80	82	15-16	16	3⅛	2	6	72
Rynlds		. 30	128	2	101	3⅜	15	4⅛	31¼
Rynlds		. 35	35	⅜	20	1½	29	2⅛	31¼
Rynlds		.40	a	a	a	a	20	1	31¼
Slumb		.. 70	2	36¾	b	b	b	b	104
Slumb		.. 80	24	27	22	29⅞	b	b	104
Slumb		.. 90	34	16¾	a	a	b	b	104
Slumb		100	140	10	53	14½	8	17¾	104
Slumb		110	121	4¼	49	9¼	4	14¼	104
Slumb		120	402	1½	26	5⅜	4	9¼	104
Skylin		..10	17	1 1-16	18	1⅝	37	2⅛	10¾
Skylin		..15	255	1-16	21	⅜	2	13-16	10¾
Southn		..10	a	a	25	1⅝	61	2¼	11⅛
Southn		..15	20	1-16	7	⅛	411	5-16	11⅛
St Ind		.. 80	15	21	8	22	b	b	99⅝
St Ind		.. 90	87	11	11	16	a	a	99⅝
St Ind		100	324	4¾	55	9⅛	2	12	99⅝
St Ind		110	166	1¾	12	5	1	8½	99⅝
St Ind		120	54	⅝	6	2½	a	a	99⅝
Tx Glf		..30	70	5¾	5	8	a	a	34¾
Tx Glf		..35	108	3	20	5¼	3	6¼	34¾
Tx Glf		..40	40	1⅜	69	3⅜	8	5	34¾

TABLE A14–1. Portion of the options listed on the Chicago Board of Options Exchange, April 2, 1980. (Source: Reprinted by permission of *The Wall Street Journal*, © Dow Jones & Company, Inc., 1980. All Rights Reserved.)

options: covered and uncovered. If you write a covered call option, this means you already have the stock; an uncovered call is on a stock you do not own and is a little more risky. Many financial advisors feel that writing covered options is a good strategy for conservative investors because it can increase their yield, as we shall see below.

Many option writers adhere to the following two rules of thumb. Never write a call on a stock you do not already own (write only covered options). Write calls only on stock you are thinking about selling anyhow—or at least would not mind selling if the price went much higher, that is, on a stock that has risen about as much as you think it will and on which you are willing to take your capital gain or on a stock that has not done well and you are ready to sell for that reason. Some option writers, however, select what they think will be a good income stock and one that does not fluctuate much in price and then sell options on it. It is not unusual for option writers to double their yield on a stock by writing options. For example, if you own a stock providing you with a 9 percent dividend yield, writing several options per year on it could very well give you an additional 9 percent or even more. In reality there are three ways in which you can benefit from owning a stock and writing options on it. There is first of all dividends; second, possible capital appreciation (there is also the possibility of capital losses); and third, option income. All three of these should be netted to obtain your true economic improvement.

One final word on options, however. If you are a newcomer to security ownership and are just beginning to learn about them, or if you are a small investor, don't write options yet. Wait until you gain some experience and become more sophisticated. Then you might want to consider it.

The Government and Securities

There are some legal safeguards in the area of securities that provide the investor with some protection. They include the following:

1. *Federal Laws on Securities.* Federal legislation dates from the financial reforms in the 1930s. Prior to 1933, there were some state laws regulating the sale of securities, but most of them were not very effective. These were the so-called "blue sky laws." They varied from state to state and were designed primarily to avoid the worst abuses of some traveling securities salespersons.

In 1933 and 1934, the federal government passed legislation regulating the sale of securities. The Security Act of 1933 primarily regulated the sale of new securities issues; and as such it applies more to the investment bankers. The Security Act of 1934 was concerned primarily with the sale of outstanding securities; as such it applies to the operations of brokers and dealers. These acts as amended are the basis for our federal regulations today. The main protection provided by these acts is *full disclosure*. All pertinent financial information must be made public on all new securities sold to the public. This is generally done through the publication of a prospectus, which is a pamphlet available from any broker on any new issue.

The second main provision of these acts is to prevent stock market manipulation. Prior to the coming of federal regulations in the 1930s there were a good many manipulative operations carried out by insiders to the detriment of the public. Stock prices were artificially manipulated up to attract the public; then the insiders quietly unloaded at a large gain, and let the prices fall back down, imposing large losses on the public.

The law also established the Securities and Exchange Commission (SEC), which administers the law and serves as the watchdog for the public.

2. *Registration of Security Dealers.* The law also provides for the registration of securities, organized exchanges, and security dealers and brokers with the SEC. This consists of making available certain reports and more detailed information than might otherwise be available. Again the idea here is full public disclosure of all pertinent financial information.

Dealers and brokers must show, to the satisfaction of the SEC, that they are reputable people, and in some cases they must meet certain capital requirements.

In addition to the legislation discussed, there is some internal regulation. Members of the National Association of Security Dealers must adhere to a set of fair practices. The organized exchanges also have rules and regulations, designed to protect the public, that all members must observe.

3. *Securities Insurance.* In 1970, Congress passed and the President signed a bill establishing the Securities Investor Protection Corporation (SIPC). It is to security buyers what the Federal Deposit Insurance Corporation (FDIC) is to bank depositors. It protects investors up to $50,000 per account against the loss of securities due to failure of broker-dealers. This does not, of course, protect the investor from losses suffered due to misfortunes suffered by corporations that have issued the stock. Rather, it protects investors who keep their securities in the street name and have their broker keep physical possession of them. This protection was the outcome of the stock market crash in 1970 that caused some broker-dealers to go under.

All broker-dealers engaged in interstate security operations must join the SIPC. They are then assessed an annual fee, which varies with the size of their operations. These fees go into a fund used to reimburse security owners who suffer losses due to their broker going bankrupt. Some brokers have purchased additional insurance from private insurance companies to cover their customers' accounts in excess of $50,000. The amount of this private insurance varies, but generally it runs up to several hundred thousand dollars. Much of this private insurance provides protection not only against the broker going under, but also protection against loss of securities because of theft, fire, or natural disaster.

Chapter Fifteen

Investment Companies (Mutual Funds) and Other Outlets for Surplus Funds

The public is always wrong.
OLD WALL STREET ADAGE

The objectives of this chapter are to

1   Introduce the two major types of investment companies

2   Present the various objectives of investment companies

3   Discuss the advantages and disadvantages of investment companies

4   Indicate where you can obtain information on investment companies

5   Introduce the highly specialized and technical commodities market

6   Discuss a number of different possible real estate investments

7   Present a special investment company

8   Note a number of unusual investment outlets

An investment company is a financial intermediary (or financial institution) that collects, usually in small dollar amounts, the savings of many individuals. It then invests these funds in the securities of various other corporations. It is an arrangement whereby the savings of many small savers are pooled so as to become one large fund to be managed collectively for the benefit of all of the participants. An investment company, therefore, is a specialized one-layer financial holdings company. The persons who buy the securities of these investment companies are said to be investing indirectly. They own part of the investment company and the investment company owns the securities of other companies. The securities the investment company owns, on behalf of its owners, are referred to as the underlying securities, and it is the value of the underlyings that gives value to the shares of the investment companies. The relationship between the investment company, its owners, and the underlying securities is shown by the chart in Figure 15-1.

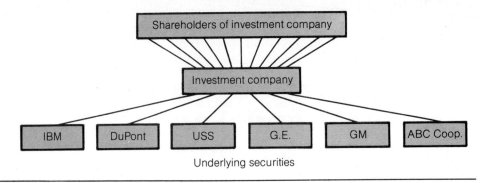

FIGURE 15–1. *Investment company relationships.*

THE CLASSIFICATION OF INVESTMENT COMPANIES

Certain types of investment companies are also called mutual funds. In fact, the terms "mutual funds," "investment company," and "investment trust" are used interchangeably to designate a variety of financial institutions that provide investors with the opportunity of investing indirectly in various corporations. In reality, however, only the open-end investment company (the open-end as opposed to the closed-end company will be explained below) is referred to as a mutual fund by the financial community. For the most part, investment companies invest most of the funds they receive in common stock. However, some companies buy substantial amounts of bonds and preferred stock. Any profits are shared among the shareholders of the mutual fund.

For all practical purposes, investment companies can be classified as open-end and closed-end. But each of these can be further analyzed according to their investment policies and objectives.

Closed-End Investment Companies

Closed-end investment companies have a relatively fixed amount of capital. To issue securities they need permission from the Securities and Exchange Commission (SEC), just like any corporation. They then have an authorized common stock issue, and when that is sold, they can sell no more unless another issue is approved. Once that issue is sold, therefore, you can no longer purchase it directly from the company but only from a broker in the open market. Moreover, closed-end investment companies do not stand ready to redeem their securities as do open-end companies. Shares in closed-end companies are frequently listed on the stock exchanges, although some are sold over the counter; and when buying and selling them, one pays the regular brokerage fees described in chapter 14. The price of closed-end shares is, therefore, determined not only by the price of the underlying securities, but by all the psychological factors that affect the supply and demand of closed-end shares in the market. There have been times when the market price of closed-end shares was below the market price of the underlying securities. This is referred to as selling at a discount. In recent years some closed-end shares have been at a premium or above the value of their underlying securities, but generally speaking most of them have been at a discount since 1970.

Closed-end investment companies sometimes also acquire capital by selling bonds to the public, a practice that introduces the element of leverage into their capital structure. Leverage was discussed in chapter 13 in greater detail. Building a lot of leverage into a firm's capital structure can in some cases result in a sudden and rapid increase in earnings and hence in the price of the common stock of a firm. Obviously, the reverse can happen as well. Closed-end investment companies have various amounts of leverage built into their capital structure, and this amount varies from time to time. Consult with your broker if you wish to find a company with some leverage in its capital structure.

Open-End Investment Companies (Mutual Funds)

There is no legally set limit to the number of shares an open-end investment company (mutual fund) may sell. The number of shares it may sell is limited only by what investors will buy. Such a company issues its shares continuously as it sells them; indeed, it is called open-end because its capitalization is not fixed.

Open-end funds also stand ready to buy back their shares from investors at any time at a price determined by the price of the underlying securities. Their price is calculated twice daily by dividing the total number of shares outstanding into the market value of the portfolio of the underlying securities.

Since open-end funds raise no capital by selling bonds, their entire capital is equity capital. No leverage is built into capital structure, although it might be in their underlying securities. Many open-end companies charge what is known as a loading fee when they sell their shares. Their fee varies from company to company, but generally it is 7 to 9 percent. The fee is only paid when the shares are purchased and not again when they are redeemed.

Open-end companies are much more popular than closed-end companies.

OBJECTIVES OF INVESTMENT COMPANIES

The buyer of investment company shares faces the same problem as does the direct buyer of common stock: which one to buy? There are over seven hundred investment companies and several hundred well-known companies. Moreover, not all of them are the same. Their records are not the same, and their objectives are not the same. Even among those with the same objectives, their records vary. When you buy investment company (mutual funds) shares, you must first of all examine the ones with the same objectives as you have, and then choose what appears to be the best fund within that group.

All mutual funds state their objectives. For example, growth, income, etc. Sometimes these objectives are broadly stated, and hence there is a good deal of overlap, and some funds frankly admit that they have several objectives. Consequently, classifying investment companies in accordance with their objectives cannot be done with complete precision, but it can be done well enough to consider the following types of funds:

1. Growth funds
2. Income funds
3. Partially income, partially growth funds
4. Balanced funds
5. Tax-exempt funds
6. Money market funds
7. Other funds

Growth Funds

The objective of a growth fund's managers is to achieve long-term growth (or price appreciation) in the value of the securities in their portfolio. Certain growth industries would be selected for their portfolio. Firms within those industries with a proven record of growth in sales and earnings and firms that typically plow a high percentage of their earnings back into the business are the target.

Income Funds

Funds with the objective of earning income would purchase more bonds and blue-chip stocks. They would select stocks in companies with a good record of earnings and a history of a high dividend payout. There are a good many income funds and they appeal to older investors needing income perhaps for retirement purposes.

You may wish to review growth stock and income stock which were discussed in detail in Chapter 13 because those are precisely the stock that these two types of funds would seek.

Partially Income, Partially Growth

Those funds striving for both income and growth could be the balanced funds mentioned below or widely diversified common stock funds with an emphasis on blue-chip stocks. These funds' portfolios would also probably include some utilities, which have a good record of earnings and some of them a good record of growth, especially if they are located in a geographic area with heavy population growth.

Balanced Funds

A fund that has balanced objectives is one that usually emphasizes growth, income, and stability or maintenance of principal. However, these three objectives are given various weights or priorities at different times. The fund has both bonds and common stock and often preferred stock in its portfolio. However, the relative amounts of bonds and stock vary from one time to another, depending upon the fund's managers' appraisal of future conditions. If the future looks gloomy, they may take a more defensive position by increasing the proportion of bonds that they hold. Generally, the amount of bonds in a balanced fund varies from 20 to 80 percent, depending upon the managers' outlook.

These balanced funds are also sometimes called diversified funds.

Tax-Exempt Funds

In recent years mutual funds have been established that buy only state and local bonds on which the interest is exempt from the personal income tax. These, of course, appeal to high tax bracket investors. In reality, many of these are more like a fixed investment trust. For example, one of them will buy, say, $10 million of various tax-exempt municipals on behalf of the fund shareholders. This $10 million package is then kept until maturity and there is no fund management fee because the fund need not be managed. Others buy and sell municipal bonds and turn their portfolio occasionally; they do charge a management fee.

In many cases, the minimum amount of state and local bonds that may be purchased directly is $5,000. Owning them indirectly through a fund makes it possible to own them in lesser amounts.

Money Market Funds

A few years ago a number of money market funds were developed. That was at a time when interest rates, and especially short-term notes, were very high. The money market funds specialize in buying very short-term securities in the money market. Such things as Treasury bills, commercial paper, and bankers' acceptances are selected. These are highly technical areas and few individuals are able to buy these securities directly; it takes literally thousands of dollars to buy commercial paper, for example. And the commercial paper interest rate went to almost 12 percent in 1974. In 1979 the commercial paper rate and the Treasury bill rate exceeded 15 percent and 12 percent respectively. Then in early 1980 rates went even higher. These funds always become more popular when short-term rates are high; later when rates come down, monies are withdrawn. Consequently, the dollar volume of these funds fluctuates greatly. When interest rates are low, these funds are invested mostly in bank certificates of deposit at perhaps 5 or 6 percent.

Money market funds were developed to enable the small investor to get into this high interest area. Most of them were established and are managed by the various brokerage houses. Generally, they do not charge a commission when the small investor buys or sells. Rather they take a fraction "off of the top," as it is said. For example, if they earn, say, 13.60 percent interest, they will keep about .4 or .5 percent, leaving 13.20 for the investor. The interest on these funds is very volatile, and fluctuates daily.

Other Funds

A number of other funds are less popular. One of these is the specialty fund, which invests only in, say, electronics; others specialize in some other industry. Some specialize in foreign securities. Needless to say, a specialty fund may also be a growth, income, or balanced fund.

At one time the so-called "hedge" funds were popular, but recently they have fallen from favor. They would take a very aggressive position because their goal was short-term capital gains. They were highly leveraged and often purchased securities on margin.

The real estate investment trust (REIT) is another special fund which was very popular a few years ago. Technically speaking, the real estate investment company is really called a trust. Nevertheless, the result is the same as that of an investment company; a number of individuals provide the capital, which is then invested in real estate. The real estate company is subjected to certain legal restrictions to prevent speculation in land. Real estate investments in general are discussed below and the real estate investment company will be analyzed in greater detail there.

Finally, there is the small business investment company (SBIC) very much like the investment companies described above except that, as the name implies, it invests solely in small business. These companies have received favorable tax treatment by Congress to encourage the flow of equity capital to small firms. These investment companies work closely with the Small Business Administration, which has some federal funds it can make available to small business.

Grouping of Funds

Many mutual funds, especially the larger and more well established ones, are set up in what are referred to as *groups*. One management team will handle a growth fund or income fund and perhaps several more. This amounts to several funds with different investment objectives being brought under the same roof with a common sales force and the like. This union broadens the appeal of the group and, as far as the individual investors are concerned, provides greater flexibility since they can switch from one fund to another within the group by paying only the small transfer fee, usually $5.

OTHER THINGS YOU SHOULD KNOW ABOUT INVESTMENT COMPANIES

There are a number of other things about investment companies with which you should be familiar.

You should know about the advantages and disadvantages of investing in investment companies. Then, too, you will need to learn about where you can find information on investment companies to help you select what hopefully will be the better ones. Finally, you should be aware of the cost of buying mutual shares. These are primarily commissions for the salespersons and are called loading fees. They are not uniform and there are even some "no load" fees.

Tailoring the Fund to the Investor

When buying mutual funds, then, individuals must decide what their investment objectives are and select a fund with the same objectives.

For example, a retired person will generally select an income fund, one that tries to select good income securities for the underlying securities in its portfolio. A younger person who has time to take advantage of growth and who perhaps does not need the income presently will be more attracted to a growth fund, which hopefully will be successful in selecting for its underlying securities the stock of corporations that will grow in the future. A person willing and able to take an aggressive stance might pick a hedge fund, a more conservative person perhaps a maintenance of principal and income fund or a balanced fund.

Advantages and Disadvantages of Mutual Funds

Three general advantages may accrue to the buyer of mutual funds, as opposed to buying common stock directly, especially a small investor. They are diversification, professional management, and constant surveillance. The major disadvantage is the high acquisition cost.

1. *Diversification.* The small investor, to be sure, finds it more difficult to diversify than the large investor. Diversification, as noted in chapter 12, consists of investing in a number of different industries. Small investors with only a few thousand dollars cannot buy common stock of very many different industries. They either have to assume the higher risk of "putting all of their eggs in one basket," or reduce the risk (and possibly the return) by investing conservatively. Mutual funds can make a real contribution in aiding the small investor to diversify.

2. *Professional Management.* Other management qualities of mutual funds vary greatly. If you select a good mutual fund, the added fees you pay for management are probably well worth it. On the other hand, you might get management that is professional only in the sense that they charge a fee.

3. *Constant Surveillance.* This is probably a plus factor. Many small investors make excellent choices regarding the common stock they buy, but then they forget about them. A

given stock that is a good buy today may not be six months or a year from now. Not only should you try to buy good stocks at the right time, but you should sell them at the right time, or at least before it is too late. Small investors may not have the time (even if they have the ability) constantly to watch and analyze their portfolio.

4. *High Cost.* The major disadvantage of investing in mutual funds is the high acquisition cost. These loading fees, as they are called, vary from fund to fund and there are some no-load funds, which also will be examined below. In addition to the loading fees that must be paid to acquire mutual funds, management charges fees to manage the funds. These fees generally are financed out of the dividends that the underlying securities provide. Nevertheless, it is another cost that in the final analysis comes out of income the mutual fundholder otherwise would get. Because of the relatively high acquisition cost, mutual funds are a poor vehicle for the short-term investor who wants to get in and out of this market periodically because his or her goal is a relatively short-term and possibly modest capital gain.

The management costs are a fraction of 1 percent of the total assets in the fund. Often this is .5 percent of the first $500,000 in the fund and is then scaled down in several steps as the size of the fund increases.

The acquisition costs of closed-end investment companies are the same as the regular brokerage commissions charged when you purchase stock directly. Open-end companies (mutual funds), however, charge a loading fee that varies from 2 or 3 percent to as high as about 8 or 9 percent (except for the no-load funds discussed below). This percent is calculated on the dollars you commit, and goes to the broker or other middle man from whom you buy the funds. To be sure, you only pay this loading fee once. Mutual fund shares are redeemable at the option of the holder and almost always without a redemption fee. Nevertheless, these high loading fees almost necessitate that you become a long-run investor.

Some mutual funds will scale the loading fees down in a series of steps on large purchases. However, the first reduction does not usually apply until the amount purchased is about $10,000 or $15,000, depending upon the fund.

Net Asset Value

The term *net asset value* is used to indicate the price of mutual funds. It is calculated by adding up the market value of all the underlying securities in the fund's portfolio and then dividing that by the number of mutual fund shares outstanding. This is done daily on a computer, and mutual fund shares fluctuate daily with fluctuations in the price of their underlyings.

Since the price of mutual fund shares is determined directly by the price of the underlying securities, they are never sold at a premium or discount as may be the case when closed-end company shares are involved. Moreover, the funds stand ready to buy back (redeem) their shares at the net asset value.

No-load Funds

A growing number of open-end investment companies (mutual funds) sell their shares directly to the public at the asset value and do not have a loading charge. These companies, however, do not solicit business as actively and if you want to buy their shares, you have to take the initiative. They do not have any brokers out actively selling their shares; hence there are no commissions and no loading fees. A few of the older and hence more well known no-load funds are the Price Row Fund, Scudder, Stevens and Clark Fund of Boston, and De Vegh Fund of New York. However, there are many others, and a number are currently being organized. A growing interest in these funds exists on the part of the investor. In 1980 there were about 186 no-load funds with assets of over $10 billion.

Because they have no sales staff, it is a little more difficult for the potential investor to obtain the pertinent information on no-load funds. However, you can write the company and get their literature and prospectuses. In addition, a No-Load Mutual Fund Association (NLMFA) was formed recently. This association, located in Valley Forge, Pennsylvania, 19481, is a new and additional source of information on no-load funds.

If you write the NLMFA, they will send you a list of their members. This will include the size of each of the no-load funds, when it was organized, its investment objectives, and its address. You can then select those that have the same investment objectives you are seeking and contact them. Since there are no salespersons, you will have to contact the company itself because brokers may not be willing to buy shares for you.

You can identify the no-load funds in the financial pages quite easily. There is a NL in the column, "offer price." Table 15–1 shows some mutual fund listings as they appear on the financial pages. "NAV" is the net asset value; the offer price is what you would have to pay. The difference between the two represents the loading fee, except where an NL appears under the offer price, which identifies a no-load fund. "NAV chg." indicates the change in the net asset value from the previous day.

Most of the early no-load funds developed out of the operations of the investment counselors discussed in chapter 12; they developed their mutual fund operations to service smaller clients. Recently some no-load funds have been developed by some of the investment services, the incentive being the management fees they would get. The no-load funds generally charge the same management fees as the other mutual funds.

Liquidation or Withdrawal of Mutual Funds

Some people invest in mutual funds for a specific purpose such as retirement income or to finance a child's college education. When you wish to withdraw you may do so at the net asset value and almost always no fees are charged. You may withdraw in a lump sum or in any one of a number of different installment plans; either monthly, quarterly, semiannually or annually. Further, you may withdraw only the income earned by the fund and leave the principal intact, or you may dip into the principal. If you withdraw from the fund for retirement purposes, you should consider converting the fund into an income fund if this has not already been done. Or you might want to withdraw in a lump sum and buy a like insurance annuity with the proceeds. If your fund is with a group system you may switch from, say, a growth fund to an income fund for only a very nominal transfer fee of $10 or $20. Most of the larger funds are grouped, and have an income fund, growth fund, balanced fund, etc., all under the same roof. This is another reason why the mutual fund you buy must be selected with care; selecting a good group provides greater flexibility.

If you do switch from one fund to another within a group, in setting up a withdrawal program (or at any time for that matter) you may be realizing a substantial capital gain and have a tax problem. Hence the tax factor must be given some consideration when deciding whether to switch or not.

Information on Investment Companies

General information on investment companies can be obtained from the same sources that are available for any other type of investment information. The financial pages of most metropolitan newspapers carry price information and sometimes articles on certain companies. Papers like *The Wall Street Journal* and magazines like *Forbes, Business Week,* and

TABLE 15–1.
SAMPLE
MUTUAL FUND
LISTINGS

Mutual Funds

Wednesday, April 2, 1980

Price ranges for investment companies, as quoted by the National Association of Securities Dealers. NAV stands for net asset value per share; the offering includes net asset value plus maximum sales charge, if any.

Fund	NAV	Offer Price	Chg.
Acorn Fnd	20.80	N.L.	+ .20
ADV Fund	11.60	N.L.	+ .12
Afuture Fd	12.22	N.L.	+ .08
AGE Fund	3.34	3.60	...
AIM Funds:			
Conv Yld	10.87	11.63	+ .10
Edsn Gld	10.14	10.84	+ .08
HiYld Sc	8.71	9.32	+ .01
Alpha Fnd	12.85	N.L.	+ .09
Am Birthrt	11.11	12.14	+ .07
American Funds Group:			
Am Bal	7.58	8.28	+ .02
Amcap F	9.94	10.86	+ .09
Am Mutl	10.14	11.08	+ .06
An Gwth	7.37	8.05	+ .05
Bnd FdA	11.64	12.72	...
Cash Mt	1.00	N.L.	...
Fund Inv	6.91	7.55	+ .03
Gth FdA	9.31	10.17	+ .07
Inc FdA	6.90	7.54	+ .05
I C A	7.74	8.46	+ .05
Nw Prsp	6.85	7.49	+ .03
Wash Mt	6.43	7.03	+ .03
American General Group:			
A GnCBd	6.39	6.98	...
AG Entp	8.15	8.91	+ .17
High Yld	9.25	9.92	+ .01
A G Mun	16.78	17.62	– .04
A G Res	1.00	N.L.	...
A GnVen	16.26	17.77	+ .32
Comstk	10.16	11.10	+ .20
Fd Amer	7.98	8.72	+ .02
Harbor	9.23	10.09	+ .03
Pace Fd	19.00	20.77	+ .57
Prov Inc	3.26	3.51	+ .02
Am Grwth	(z)	(z)	...
Am Heritg	2.38	N.L.	– .01
Am Ins Ind	4.77	5.21	+ .05
Am Invest	7.89	N.L.	+ .12
AmInv Inc	10.43	N.L.	– .02
AmNat Gw	3.46	3.78	+ .03
Amway Mt	7.03	7.52	+ .17
Am Opt Eq	(z)	(z)	...
Axe-Houghton:			
Fund B	7.12	7.74	+ .03
Income	3.88	4.22	+ .02
Stock Fd	6.84	7.48	+ .08
BLC Gwth	13.08	14.30	+ .19
Babsn Inc	1.40	N.L.	...
Babsn Inv	10.28	N.L.	+ .04
Beacon Gr	9.81	N.L.	– .01
Beacon Hll	9.50	N.L.	– .05
Berger Group Funds:			
100 Fund	9.80	N.L.	+ .10
101 Fund	8.63	N.L.	+ .01
Bos Found	8.84	9.66	...
Bull & Bear Group:			
Capam	8.91	N.L.	+ .03
Capitl Sh	8.95	N.L.	+ .10
Golcnd	10.69	N.L.	– .01

Fund	NAV	Offer Price	Chg.
Thrift Tr	9.38	N.L.	...
Trend	23.35	N.L.	+ .31
Financial Programs:			
Dynam	6.62	N.L.	+ .04
Industl	4.68	N.L.	+ .03
Income	7.68	N.L.	+ .05
First Investors Fund:			
Bond Ap	12.32	13.28	– .03
Cash Mg	1.00	(z)	...
Discovr	6.39	6.98	+ .10
Growth	8.46	9.25	+ .08
Income	6.33	6.92	...
Optn Fd	5.97	6.44	+ .03
Stock Fd	7.04	7.69	+ .04
Tx Exmt	8.47	9.13	– .02
Fst 'VRate	1.00	N.L.	...
44 Wall St	14.07	N.L.	+ .20
Fnd Grwth	4.24	4.63	+ .01
Founders Group Funds:			
Growth	6.05	N.L.	+ .06
Income	12.45	N.L.	+ .03
Mutual	7.65	8.36	+ .01
Special	14.27	N.L.	+ .19
Franklin Group:			
Brwn Fd	4.14	4.46	+ .04
D N T C	10.06	10.85	+ .19
Growth	5.98	6.45	+ .07
Income	1.80	1.94	+ .02
Mony Fd	1.00	N.L.	...
US GvSc	7.20	7.76	...
Utilities	3.92	4.23	+ .09
Res Capt	6.80	7.33	+ .15
Res Eqty	4.44	4.79	+ .03
Fundpack	(z)	(z)	...
Funds Incp Group:			
Cm IncS	8.05	N.L.	+ .09
Currt Int	1.00	N.L.	...
Indus Tr	10.03	10.29	+ .09
Pilot Tr	7.83	N.L.	+ .07
GT Pac Fd	9.91	N.L.	– .03
Gatewy Op	14.25	N.L.	+ .09
GE S&S Pr	26.83	N.L.	+ .14
Genl Secur	10.66	N.L.	+ .05
GovtInv Tr	1.00	N.L.	...
Grad CRsv	1.00	N.L.	...
Grth IndSh	24.88	N.L.	+ .18
Hamilton Group:			
Fund	4.10	4.48	+ .04
Growth	8.41	9.19	+ .03
Income	6.39	N.L.	+ .04
Hartwll Gt	21.24	N.L.	+ .37
Hartwll Lv	13.62	N.L.	+ .36
Holding Tr	1.00	N.L.	...
Horace Mn	16.25	17.57	+ .12
INA HiYld	9.05	9.71	+ .01
IndsFd Am	5.07	N.L.	+ .04
Investors Group Funds:			
IDS Bnd	4.38	4.54	...
IDS Cash	1.00	N.L.	...
IDS Gth	8.12	8.83	+ .11

Fund	NAV	Offer Price	Chg.
M I F Fd	7.26	7.85	+ .06
M I F Gro	4.50	4.86	+ .03
Mutual of Omaha Funds:			
Amer	9.77	(z)	...
Growth	4.02	4.37	+ .03
Income	7.88	8.57	+ .03
Mon Mkt	1.00	N.L.	...
Tax Free	10.27	11.16	– .03
Mutl Shars	36.60	N.L.	+ .24
NtlAvia Tc	31.37	N.L.	+ .37
Natl Indust	13.40	N.L.	+ .11
National Securities Funds:			
Balanc	8.61	9.28	+ .05
Bond	3.32	3.58	+ .01
Dividnd	4.28	4.61	+ .01
Preferd	5.54	5.97	+ .04
Income	5.21	5.62	+ .02
Liq Rsv	1.00	N.L.	...
Stock	8.68	9.36	+ .08
Tax ExB	8.54	9.09	– .02
Grwth	5.81	6.26	+ .07
New Eng Life Funds:			
Cash Mg	10.00	N.L.	...
Equity	16.88	18.35	+ .08
Grwth	11.29	12.27	+ .07
Income	10.03	10.90	– .05
Ret Eqty	16.57	18.01	+ .07
Neuberger Berman Mngt:			
Energy	18.52	N.L.	+ .14
Guardn	28.63	N.L.	+ .24
Liberty	3.72	N.L.	+ .01
Manhtn	3.17	N.L.	+ .03
Partner	15.13	N.L.	+ .16
Schus Fd	11.92	N.L.	+ .15
Newton Gr	14.06	N.L.	+ .09
Newtn Inc	7.10	N.L.	– .01
New World	(z)	(z)	...
NY Ventur	15.27	16.69	+ .17
Nichlas Fd	12.50	N.L.	+ .23
Nomura C	7.30	7.64	– .48
Noeast Inv	10.68	N.L.	+ .14
Nuveen BF	7.30	7.64	+ .04
Omega Fd	12.14	12.26	+ .23
One Wll St	15.42	N.L.	+ .17
Oppenheimer Funds:			
Aim Fnd	14.60	15.96	+ .20
Opp Fnd	7.51	8.21	+ .09
High Yld	17.91	19.21	+ .08
Income	6.84	7.48	+ .01
Mony Br	1.00	N.L.	...
Optn Inc	20.12	21.99	+ .14
Special	15.45	16.89	+ .16
Tax FrB	7.06	N.L.	+ .01
Time Fd	10.53	11.51	+ .10
OTC SecFd	23.11	25.12	+ .05
Paramnt	8.48	9.27	+ .16
Penn Mutl	4.76	N.L.	+ .05
Penn Squ	6.95	N.L.	+ .08
Phila Fund	8.96	9.79	+ .09
Phonx Cap	9.81	10.72	+ .08
Phoenx Fd	8.93	9.76	+ .03
Pilgrim Group:			
Mag Cap	3.81	4.11	+ .07
Mag Inc	7.05	7.60	+ .04

Fund	NAV	Offer Price	Chg.
Selected Funds:			
Selct Am	6.32	N.L.	+ .04
Mon Mkt	1.00	N.L.	...
Selct Spl	13.72	N.L.	+ .15
Sentinel Group Funds:			
Apex Fd	3.33	3.64	+ .02
Bal Fund	6.79	7.42	+ .04
Com Stk	11.44	12.50	+ .09
Growth	9.65	10.55	+ .07
Sentry Fd	(z)	(z)	...
Sequoia	20.53	N.L.	+ .21
Shearson Funds:			
Apprec	28.77	31.44	+ .04
Daily Dv	1.00	N.L.	...
Income	16.05	17.54	– .03
Invest	12.46	13.62	+ .03
Shrm Dean	6.02	N.L.	– .17
Sierra Gro	11.92	N.L.	+ .11
Sigma Funds:			
Capitl Sh	11.23	12.27	+ .16
Invest Sh	9.96	10.89	+ .07
Trust Sh	8.18	8.94	+ .05
Venture	9.46	10.34	+ .13
Sm Barney	11.88	12.51	+ .05
Sm BrIncG	13.17	13.86	+ .07
So GenFnd	13.44	14.07	+ .08
Sowest Inv	7.86	8.50	+ .10
SowInv Inc	4.41	4.77	+ .02
Sovern Inv	12.30	12.95	+ .10
State Bond Group:			
CmSt Fd	4.63	5.06	+ .04
Diversf	4.62	5.05	+ .02
Progrss	5.20	5.68	+ .06
StateF Bal	(z)	(z)	...
State FrGr	(z)	(z)	...
StateSt (a)	52.59	N.L.	+ .39
Steadman Funds:			
Am Ind	2.65	N.L.	+ .03
Assoc Fd	.84	N.L.	...
Inves Fd	1.25	N.L.	+ .01
Oceang	7.75	N.L.	+ .06
Stein Roe Funds:			
Balanc	17.83	N.L.	+ .13
Cash Res	1.00	N.L.	...
Capit Op	14.08	N.L.	+ .21
Stock Fd	14.72	N.L.	+ .14
Strattn Gth	17.13	N.L.	+ .16
Survey Fd	12.14	13.27	+ .12
Tax Mg Ut	15.89	N.L.	+ .09
Temp Grth	6.12	6.69	+ .06
Temp WF	13.78	15.06	+ .18
Tempor Iv	1.00	N.L.	...
Trans Cap	(z)	(z)	...
Trans Inv	(z)	(z)	...
Travl Equ	14.53	15.88	+ .20
Tudor Hdg	7.49	N.L.	+ .10
20thCen Gr	(z)	(z)	...
20th Cen Sl	(z)	(z)	...
Unifd Accu	4.62	N.L.	+ .03
Un Mutual	8.88	N.L.	+ .07
Union Service Group:			
Brd St Iv	10.41	11.22	+ .10
Natl Invs	7.04	7.59	+ .07
Un Capit	16.26	17.53	+ .07
Un Cash	1.00	N.L.	...
Un Income	9.86	10.63	+ .05

(*Source: The Wall Street Journal*, April 3, 1980. Reprinted by permission of *The Wall Street Journal*, © Dow Jones & Company, Inc., 1980. All Rights Reserved.)

Barron's are other good sources. *Forbes* and *Barron's* especially should be noted because they make special studies from time to time wherein they analyze and compare the past record of various investment companies. *Forbes* magazine has a special annual study of mutual funds that comes out every August. It publishes articles and analyses of mutual funds and statistical data on each of the major funds. There are statistics on assets, sales changes (loading fees), expenses per $100 of fund assets, dividend returns, and average annual growth rates over a number of years, as well as the performance over the most recent twelve months. Various investment services, such as Moody's, Value Line Investment Services, and Standard and Poor's, publish information on investment companies. In addition, your broker may have a wealth of useful information.

Three investment company services specialize in analyzing and publishing information on investment companies. Two of these services publish their reports annually; they are *Investment Companies, Mutual Funds, and other Types,* published by Wiesenberger Financial Services, Inc. of 870 7th Avenue, New York, and *Johnson's Investment Company Charts,* published by Hugh A. Johnson and Company, 545 Elmwood Ave., Buffalo, New York. These studies analyze most of the leading investment companies, appraise their various performances, and compare them with the performance of the stock market in general. The Wiesenberger study, for example, has an investment index that compares the performance of various types of funds. The Wiesenberger study and the Johnson study can be purchased or they can be perused at most brokerage houses. Finally, there is *Fundscope.* This is a monthly publication dealing with mutual funds published by Fundscope, Inc., 1900 Avenue of the Stars, Los Angeles, California, 90067. Like the other services mentioned, it has articles and analyses as well as statistics on the individual investment companies. It provides a growth or appreciation record, an income record, and a stability record of the individual funds.

Which Funds Have Done Well?

When choosing what fund to buy, do so in light of your investment objectives. Even after choosing a growth fund or a balanced fund or an income fund, many choices are available. Not all funds perform the same. And differences in performance can be attributed primarily to the differences in management.

If you are buying a growth fund (and even some others with different objectives), it should be doing somewhat better than the Dow-Jones Industrial Averages. Otherwise you can buy common stock directly (choosing from the blue chips that make up the Dow-Jones) and save the extra cost of buying mutual funds. However, only some of the mutual funds have done better than the Dow-Jones Averages over the years. Some have not done as well.

Just as stock price averages have been constructed to show how stock prices are moving, averages or indexes can also be constructed of the price of mutual funds to show how mutual funds in general are performing. Two of the better-known mutual fund averages are those published by Hugh A. Johnson and Company and by Wiesenberger Services, Inc. These two companies specialize in publishing data and analysis on investment companies. Figure 15–2 is from Wiesenberger. It shows several mutual fund indexes. One is for a number of growth funds, one for growth/income funds, one for income funds, and one for a number of balanced funds. The growth fund has increased by about 57 percent since 1970. The income fund has actually outperformed the growth fund, having risen 85 percent during the same period, while the growth-income fund and the balanced fund are up 70 and 54 percent respectively. These records can be compared with that of Standard and Poor's industrial average which rose about 35 percent during this time.

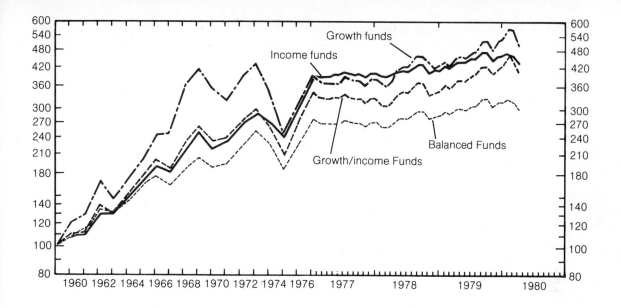

FIGURE 15–2. *Wiesenberger mutual fund indexes. (Source: Investment Companies 1980,* Wiesenberger Financial Services, a division of Warren, Gorham & Lamont, Inc.)

We can also analyze the performance of the mutual funds with Johnson's Charts. Johnson has four different mutual fund averages: (1) a growth fund average, (2) a growth and income fund average, (3) an income fund average, and (4) a balanced fund average. Table 15–2 shows these averages since 1960. The growth average rose 178 percent during this period; the growth-income averge 138 percent; the income average by 18 percent; and the balanced fund average by 46 percent. The Dow-Jones Industrial Average for this same period is also shown and it rose by 38 percent; more than the income fund and balanced fund average, but less than the other two. The table also presents a number of other financial and economic indicators. Also shown are two tables which illustrate how the Johnson mutual fund averages have performed relative to other investments you might make.

While mutual fund averages are useful, the prospective buyer of mutual funds must also look at the record of the individual companies. Some of them performed even better than the fund averages shown; some, of course, not so well. You can get literature from the fund that you are interested in buying and compare their past record with both the fund averages, the Standard and Poor's average, and the Dow-Jones Averages. This gives a clue to how well the fund is managed. A good past performance is no assurance of success in the future; however, it's probably better to bet (if bet you must) on a past winner.

You can also compare the growth of many individual funds with both the Standard and Poor's stock index and the Dow-Jones index by using Johnson's charts, which you can probably find at most brokerage houses. Johnson has plotted the performance of individual funds and has included a transparent overlay of both the Dow-Jones and the Standard and Poor industrial averages. By comparing the two you can see at a glance which funds have outdone the stock averages and which have not. Another source that will aid you in evaluating

TABLE 15-2. *Securities markets of the past 20 years, 1960–1979.*

	JAN. 1 1960	JAN. 1 1965	JAN. 1 1970	DEC. 31 1979	% CHANGE 10 YRS. 1970- 1979	% CHANGE 15 YRS. 1965- 1979	% CHANGE 20 YRS. 1960- 1979
Cost of living index	88.0	93.6	112.9	229.9	+104%	+146%	+161%
Value of the dollar	100.0	94.0	77.9	38.3	− 51	− 59	− 62
Dow-Jones industrial average	679.36	874.13	800.36	838.74	+ 5	− 4	+ 23
Standard & Poor's 500 stock index	59.89	84.75	92.06	107.94	+ 17	+ 27	+ 80
New York stock exchange index	32.15	45.65	51.53	61.95	+ 20	+ 36	+ 93
Value line composite average	—	113.55	130.49	121.91	−- 7	+ 7	—
American stock exchange index	—	—	120.01	247.07	+106	—	—
S. & P. utilities	44.74	74.52	56.09	50.24	− 10	− 33	+ 12
S. & P. high-grade corporate bonds	92.37	95.26	62.15	45.53	− 27	− 52	− 51
S. & P. municipal bonds	99.27	112.6	68.70	67.47	− 2	− 40	− 32
S. & P. long-term government bonds	84.60	87.14	63.84	45.40	− 29	− 48	− 46
S. & P. preferred stocks	144.3	165.6	97.7	69.03	− 29	− 58	− 52
Savings bank deposit	100.0	100.0	100.0	100.0	0	0	0
Johnson growth fund average	100.0	138.7	222.9	278.0	+ 25	+101	+178
Johnson growth & income fund average	100.0	134.3	174.4	238.1	+ 37	+ 77	+138
Johnson income fund average	100.0	123.5	128.1	118.2	− 8	− 4	+ 18
Johnson balanced fund average	100.0	131.1	135.7	145.5	+ 7	+ 11	+ 46

Source: Johnson's Charts, Inc.

mutual funds is *Forbes Magazine*'s annual August analysis of all the leading mutual funds. This analysis compares the funds' performance with the Standard and Poor's 500-stock average. You can tell at a glance which ones have outperformed the averages and which have not. Finally, you should look at *Fundscope,* a monthly publication that has articles and analysis on mutual funds as well as statistics on a company-by-company basis.

Earnings, Reinvestment, and Taxation of Investment Companies

Investment companies receive interest and dividend income from the securities they own. A good deal is distributed by the companies to their shareholders, a practice encouraged by the federal income tax law. The earnings of ordinary corporate income are subject to federal tax, but that portion the investment companies receive is exempt from being taxed again at the investment company level under certain circumstances; that is, if the investment company distributes 90 percent or more of the interest and dividends it receives, that 90 percent is exempt from federal corporate income taxes. The other 10 percent is taxed in accordance with the regular corporate income tax laws. If it were not for this tax provision, there would be triple taxation on the earnings distributed by investment companies. The

TABLE 15-3. *Performance statistics—35 years of ten-year periods, 1945–1979.*

PERIOD	DOW-JONES INDUSTRIALS	S. & P. 500 STOCKS	JOHNSON GROWTH FUNDS	JOHNSON STOCK FUNDS	JOHNSON BALANCED FUNDS	COST OF LIVING	SAVINGS BANK DEPOSIT	U.S. GOVT. BONDS	HIGH-GRADE CORPORATE BONDS	PREFERRED STOCKS
1970–79	+ 5%	+ 17%	+ 25%	+ 29%	+ 7%	+104%	0%	−29%	−27%	−29%
1969–78	− 15	− 7	− 17	− 12	− 16	+ 91	0	−29	−27	−34
1968–77	− 8	− 1	− 14	− 8	− 8	+ 83	0	−25	−23	−24
1967–76	+ 28	+ 34	+ 28	+ 32	+ 10	+ 77	0	− 9	−25	−32
1966–75	− 12	− 2	+ 7	+ 6	− 15	+ 75	0	−16	−38	−47
1965–74	− 30	− 19	+ 2	− 4	− 22	+ 66	0	−25	−41	−53
1964–73	+ 12	+ 30	+ 56	+ 45	+ 9	+ 50	0	−20	−34	−45
1963–72	+ 56	+ 87	+137	+113	+ 44	+ 40	0	−19	−32	−36
1962–71	+ 22	+ 43	+ 72	+ 59	+ 22	+ 37	0	−17	−29	−32
1961–70	+ 36	+ 59	+ 82	+ 69	+ 27	+ 33	0	−25	−32	−31
1960–69	+ 18	+ 54	+125	+ 92	+ 26	+ 28	0	−23	−33	−32
1959–68	+ 62	+ 88	+213	+154	+ 57	+ 23	0	−21	−27	−23
1958–67	+108	+143	+264	+202	+ 78	+ 19	0	−24	−28	−25
1957–66	+ 57	+ 72	+123	+ 93	+ 36	+ 19	0	−13	−19	−12
1956–65	+ 99	+103	+142	+113	+ 52	+ 19	0	−17	−19	− 9
1955–64	+116	+136	+127	+111	+ 56	+ 17	0	−17	−18	− 7
1954–63	+172	+202	+201	+167	+ 85	+ 15	0	−16	−16	− 3
1953–62	+123	+138	+154	+122	+ 61	+ 14	0	−12	−15	− 7
1952–61	+172	+201	—	+178	+ 89	+ 13	0	−15	−17	− 7
1951–60	+162	+185	—	+163	+ 73	+ 19	0	−16	−22	−19
1950–59	+239	+257	—	+213	+ 96	+ 24	0	−25	−25	−21
1949–58	+229	+263	—	+215	+102	+ 20	0	−16	−17	−11
1948–57	+141	+161	—	+112	+ 56	+ 21	0	− 7	−11	− 6
1947–56	+182	+205	—	+138	+ 66	+ 28	0	−13	−16	−23
1946–55	+153	+162	—	+142	+ 92	+ 47	0	− 6	− 8	−11
1945–54	+165	+171	—	+115	+ 63	+ 50	0	− 2	− 2	− 1
Average 26 Periods (1945–1979)	+ 89	+107	—	+103	+ 44	+ 40	0	−17	−23	−22
Average of 18 Periods (1953–1979)	+ 48	+ 65	+ 96	+ 77	+ 28	+ 45	0	−20	−27	−26

Source: Johnson's Charts, Inc.

TABLE 15-4. *Performance statistics—15-, 20-, 25-, 30-year periods ending December 31, 1979.*

PERIOD	DOW-JONES INDUSTRIALS	S. & P. 500 STOCKS	JOHNSON GROWTH FUNDS	JOHNSON STOCK FUNDS	JOHNSON BALANCED FUNDS	COST OF LIVING	SAVINGS BANK DEPOSIT	U.S. GOVT. BONDS	HIGH-GRADE CORPORATE BONDS	PREFERRED STOCKS
15 Years 1965–1979	− 4%	+ 27%	+101%	+ 93%	+ 11%	+146%	0%	−48%	−52%	−58%
20 Years 1960–1979	+ 23	+ 80	+178	+165	+ 46	+161	0	−46	−51	−52
25 Years 1955–1979	+107	+200	+379	+347	+100	+187	0	−57	−61	−61
30 Years 1950–1979	+319	+544	+864	+785	+232	+225	0	−59	−63	−62

Source: Johnson's Charts, Inc.

individual investment company shareholder must, of course, pay a tax on the dividends received in accordance with the regular personal income tax laws. (See chapter 17 for a discussion of this.)

Investment companies also often realize capital gains. This is treated the same way as the earnings described above; if they distribute at least 90 percent of their realized capital gains, only the investment company shareholder pays the capital gains tax on it. The investment company pays the capital gains tax on the gain they retain. Again the 90 percent provision is to avoid tax discrimination on capital gains earned by the investment companies.

You may choose to reinvest your earnings and capital gains described above in your mutual fund, and usually without a loading fee. Even if you reinvest, the tax treatment described above applies. In fact, you and the company do not even need to exchange checks if you agree to invest. For the beneficial tax treatment to hold, the company need only offer to pay 90 percent of its earnings and capital gains; if you sign an agreement for them to reinvest, they will do so automatically.

Who Should Buy Investment Company Shares?

To answer this question investors must analyze their personal affairs in light of what I have said above about the advantages and disadvantages of investment companies. It also depends upon how much time purchasers have to watch their investments (if they buy common stock directly) and how much skill they may have in selecting good securities. Some investment companies are better than others, and it may be almost as difficult to select a good investment company as it is to select a good common stock directly. A person who is building a portfolio of common stock must go through the analyzing and selecting process time and time again—a never-ending task. By choosing the investment company route, an investor only has to make the selection decision once.

The investment company route must be a long-run commitment so that the relatively high loading costs are spread over many years. Buyers must remember, too, to select a company whose investment goals are the same as their own. For example, is growth or income most important? Some of the no-load companies should be considered if they meet an individual's investment objectives.

Investment Company Legislation

With the stock market boom of the 1920s, investment companies became extremely popular and a large number of people invested in them. Unfortunately, many of the companies took unwarranted risks, and in the crash that followed large sums of money were lost by the shareholders. This situation led to an extensive study of investment companies by the Securities and Exchange Commission. Based on these studies, Congress passed the Investment Company Act of 1940 which requires that practically all investment companies register with the SEC, which to a certain extent regulates their activities. The act as amended sets up standards for such things as the statement of policies of the company, the number of shares authorized for closed-end companies, the sale of securities, and the advertising standards. Generally when new shares are issued, a prospectus explaining the details of the issue must be published. Those companies that refuse to register are limited in the scope of their activity; they may not use the mails for the purchase or sale of securities and may not engage in interstate commerce. The companies that do qualify are called "registered investment companies."

In 1970, Congress passed an amendment to the Investment Company Act. The two main provisions of the amendment were to eliminate the front-end load and to see that other loading fees are not excessive. The amendment has in effect virtually eliminated the front-end load, by providing for a partial or sometimes total refund of the loading fees if the shareholder withdraws from the fund contract within a specified period of time and if there is an excessive front-end load.

INTRODUCTION TO OTHER OUTLETS FOR SURPLUS FUNDS

In addition to mutual funds, a person may invest in commodities, real estate, and a number of unusual (sometimes called exotic) investments. Each of these will now be examined. We hasten to add, however, that, with the exception of real estate, these are not for the typical small investor because there is a larger element of speculation involved. Nevertheless, they may be right for some people and hence will be examined.

COMMODITY MARKETS[1]

Some people have made money in commodities, but this is more in the nature of speculation than investing. Consequently, the small investor should probably steer clear of commodities. Probably so too should all but the professional speculator who makes a living through buying and selling commodities. Nevertheless, a few words on the commodity markets are in order.

The price of certain commodities fluctuates widely over short periods of time for a variety of reasons. The supply can change sharply due to crop failure caused by adverse weather or loss of production due to a strike. Demand for certain commodities, too, can fluctuate due to changed public tastes or governmental policies. These sharp changes in supply and demand can create sharp price changes. Because of these fluctuations, speculators have entered the market. There are future prices and spot or cash prices. The spot price is the price paid for delivery today, but the future price is the price paid today for commodities to be delivered at a specified time in the future. There is a one-month, two-month, three-month future price, and so on.

Since there are future markets in commodities, and professional speculators that operate in them, business firms that use these commodities can hedge their operations and protect themselves from sharp price fluctuations. In the process, the speculator may make a lot of money. Hedging works as follows: Suppose a candy manufacturer has signed a contract to supply some candy. The price has been set and it will take a month or more to make and deliver the candy. In the meantime, the candy manufacturer does not want to carry a large inventory of sugar but does want to protect itself against sharp price increases. It will buy sugar futures. This will freeze the price of sugar for, say, thirty days. While the future price may be slightly higher than the present or spot prices, it is known, and presumably the candy manufacturer negotiates its contract with future prices in mind. For the small price differential, it can avoid carrying a large inventory in sugar and also protect itself (hedge) against sharp price increases in sugar, its major input cost.

For those lucky enough to have problems with high income taxes, commodities offer an opportunity to transfer short-term capital gains from one year to the next or to convert

---

1. I wish to acknowledge the help I have received in developing the section on commodities from Professor Edna Villar of Pan American University.

short-term capital gains into long-term capital gains. This involves a device known as a *tax straddle* or *spread*. A straddle is simply the purchase of a commodity against the sale of another. In a limited-risk spread, the spreader buys a commodity for a nearby month and sells for a more distant month. With this type of straddle, specific prices are immaterial. The direction of the market move is also unimportant, since one contract will result in a profit and the other in a loss regardless of a price rise or a price decline. To ensure further the objective of tax avoidance, the spread must be initiated in a commodity that has wide price fluctuations. When price changes have resulted in a short-term loss sufficient to offset the taxable short-term gains, the losing position is liquidated and simultaneously reinstated in another nearby month (to maintain the straddle position), thus effectively locking in the gains in the profitable position. *Voila!* Your tax liability has been postponed until the next year, when the straddle is liquidated.

To convert short-term gains into long-term gains requires that the profitable transaction occur in the option month that is purchased rather than sold and that it be held for more than one year. Before establishing a limited-risk tax straddle, however, it is strongly recommended that traders consult a tax expert to verify that this type of transaction will suit their needs and that they utilize the services of a commodity specialist familiar with the procedure.

There are speculators, hence a futures market, in certain foods, grains, fats and oils, textiles, and metals. Futures quotations may be found in the financial pages of the large metropolitan newspapers. The Chicago Board of Trade is the largest commodities market in the nation. However, there are a number of others, including the Kansas City Board of Trade, the Minneapolis Board of Trade, the Chicago Mercantile Exchange, the New York Coffee and Sugar Exchange, the New York Cocoa Exchange, the New York Cotton Exchange, and the New York Commodity Exchange. Again, I would like to emphasize that the commodities market is highly technical and is not a place where small investors should put their money. The table below shows the futures market prices for gold as reported in *The Wall Street Journal* on April 3, 1980.

FINANCIAL REAL ESTATE INVESTMENTS

There are two major ways of investing in real estate. First, investing in mortgages, and second, owning real property outright. If you invest in mortgages you are lending money to a homeowner to help her to finance her home; on this loan you receive interest.

Mortgages[2]

A mortgage is a legal document given by the prospective homeowner (borrower) to the lender. The borrower who gives the mortgage is called the mortgagor and the lender who receives the mortgage is called the mortgagee. The mortgage stipulates the terms of the loan such as: the interest rate, the monthly payments, and the length of time over which the loan is to be repaid. In addition, under it, the borrower agrees to pay all taxes, assessments, and

---

2. In early 1980 interest rates on mortgages (and other investments as well) went sky-high. Whether they will remain at their record levels, of course, no one knows. One reason mortgage interest rates rose to their current level is because in 1980 the federal government nullified all state mortgage usury laws. However, this nullification only applied to mortgage lending financial institutions. Individuals making mortgages loans *are still subject* to the state usury laws. State usury laws vary from a low of 9.5 percent to a high of 21 percent, although several states do not have a usury limit. If you as an individual decide to invest in mortgages, be sure to check the usury law in your state. *You are still subject to it.*

other charges levied against the property; also to keep it in good repair, and fully insured against fire and other hazards.

The mortgage also provides for foreclosure, and repossession of the home by the mortgage lender in the event that the homeowner defaults. In some states a deed of trust is used in place of a mortgage but it provides for the same arrangements.

Most mortgage loans are made by financial institutions such as savings and loan associations and mutual savings banks, but there is no reason why an individual with surplus funds cannot make such a loan to a homeowner. When a person makes a mortgage loan, he or she in effect pays off the seller of the home (sometimes the builder if it is a new home) and then the purchaser gives the lender a mortgage such as described above.

If you wish to make a mortgage loan, see a realtor or a builder; they can put you in contact with a prospective mortgagor. You should probably retain an attorney to draw up the mortgage, at least the first time you do this.

Mortgages are negotiable just like corporate bonds, and can be sold just like corporate bonds. The interest rate on a mortgage is fixed for the duration of the loan, and hence if

TABLE 15–5. FUTURES PRICES AS PUBLISHED IN *THE WALL STREET JOURNAL*, APRIL 3, 1980.

Futures Prices

Wednesday, April 2, 1980

Open Interest Reflects Previous Trading Day

GOLD (CMX) – 100 troy oz.; $ per troy oz.

	Open	High	Low	Settle	Change	Lifetime High	Lifetime Low	Open Interest
Apr	499.00	500.00	483.50	490.80	− 7.70	895.00	212.00	5,199
May	....	....	....	497.80	− 7.70	605.00	485.00	44
June	516.00	517.00	499.00	506.00	− 9.00	916.00	225.00	18,584
Aug	533.00	533.00	514.00	522.40	− 9.40	932.70	229.50	14,509
Oct	548.00	548.00	532.00	538.80	− 9.80	946.30	236.00	12,710
Dec	564.00	564.00	548.00	555.20	−10.20	959.90	270.30	20,332
Feb81	583.00	583.00	569.00	571.60	−10.60	973.20	282.80	21,187
Apr	596.00	596.00	582.00	588.00	−11.00	986.50	322.50	18,053
June	612.80	612.80	602.50	604.40	−11.40	999.80	332.00	10,457
Aug	614.00	619.00	614.00	620.80	−11.80	963.10	420.00	8,065
Oct	....	....	....	637.20	−12.20	1026.4	557.50	2,132
Dec	653.00	653.00	653.00	653.60	−12.60	981.00	637.00	532
Feb82	....	....	....	670.00	−13.00	676.00	676.00	4

Est vol 8,000; vol Tue 12,775; open int 131,808, +625.

GOLD (IMM) – 100 troy oz.; $ per troy oz.

	Open	High	Low	Settle	Change	Lifetime High	Lifetime Low	Open Interest
Apr	497.00	497.00	491.00	497.00	− 3.00	512.00	454.00	22
June	512.00	516.00	498.00	507.30	− 7.70	914.50	226.00	12,481
Sept	536.50	538.00	522.50	530.30	−12.70	938.00	200.80	8,542
Dec	560.00	562.00	550.00	553.50	−10.50	957.50	207.70	5,145
Mr81	585.00	585.00	572.50	576.50	−13.50	976.00	201.30	2,798
June	598.00	602.00	598.00	599.50	−15.00	993.90	351.70	2,153
Sept	621.50	627.00	621.50	622.30	−16.70	1011.0	455.90	797
Dec	....	....	....	644.90	−18.30	1031.9	618.00	239

Est vol 3,255; vol Tue 3,346; open int 27,015, −181

(*Source*: Reprinted by permission of *The Wall Street Journal*, © Dow Jones & Company, Inc., 1980. All Rights Reserved.)

interest rates rise after a given mortgage has been agreed upon, the market price of the mortgage declines. The market price of mortgages, then, fluctuates inversely with changes in the going interest rate, and consequently mortgages may be sold at a premium or at a discount from their face value; again this is just as in the case of corporate bonds. (See Chapter 12 for a discussion of this in the case of bonds.)

Determination of Mortgage Yields

Since the price of mortgages, purchased from another mortgagee, fluctuates, the yield is not necessarily the same as the fixed interest rate specified in the mortgage itself. It should also be noted that mortgages are not as liquid as corporate bonds; it takes time to sell them to someone else. For this reason, the yield on mortgages is generally higher than on corporate bonds. The true yield on a mortgage, of course, is determined by how much above or below face value it is sold. To determine the approximate yields, the following formula is used.[3]

$$Y = \frac{R(P) + \left(\dfrac{P - C}{N}\right)}{\left(\dfrac{P + C}{2}\right)} \times 100$$

Y = approximate yield
P = principal balance of the mortgage
C = the cost to the investor of the mortgage
N = number of years the mortgage runs until paid
R = coupon rate of interest the mortgage carries

Assume, for example, a mortgage with a face value of $20,000 running over ten years, bearing a fixed interest rate of 10 percent which you can purchase for $18,000.

$$(1) \quad \frac{.10(\$20,000) + \left(\dfrac{20,000 - \$18,000}{10}\right)}{\left(\dfrac{20,000 + 18,000}{2}\right)} \times 100$$

$$(2) \quad \frac{\$2000 + \left(\dfrac{2000}{10}\right)}{\dfrac{38,000}{2}}$$

3. Note the word "approximate." The reason for approximation is that the components of the problem are themselves only averages. The figures used are generally average interest earned per year. This is true where monthly payments are made (this is not the case, however, in this oversimplified problem). To be strictly accurate, yields must be figured using compound interest functions.

$$(3) \qquad \frac{\dfrac{2000 + 200}{38,000}}{2}$$

$$(4) \qquad \frac{2200}{19,000} \times 100 =$$

$$(5) \qquad y = 11.58 \text{ percent approximate}$$
$$\text{yield}$$

We noted above that a mortgage is less liquid than corporate bonds, and hence the yield is higher. Mortgages also generally are riskier than corporate bonds. This too will increase their yield above bonds. However, the degree of risk varies with the credit rating of the mortgagor. When making a mortgage loan, you must appraise the credibility of the mortgagor. You must also consider the age and the condition of the house, and what portion of its total value you are financing. The general rule is that the individual should not make a mortgage loan in excess of 75 percent of the value of the house. You should also remember that there are some costs involved if you have to foreclose and repossess the home. All these factors will have a bearing on the yield on mortgage loans. You must also decide whether the yield on a given mortgage is sufficiently higher than your alternative investment opportunities. If it is not, you can bargain to increase it by asking for a larger discount.

Second Mortgages

In the above discussion we have had in mind first mortgages. There are also second mortgages, which are riskier. In the event of a foreclosure and sale of a house on which the mortgagor has defaulted, the second mortgage is not paid off until after the first mortgagee has been completely repaid. An illustration will make the second mortgage clear. Assume that in the above case the investor purchased a $20,000 face value mortgage for $18,000 on a home with a value of $40,000. If the homeowner wants to sell it, the buyer would have to make a down payment of $20,000 to buy the seller's equity, and take over his mortgage. If, however, he has only $15,000, he might assume a second mortgage for $5,000 as well as the original first mortgage. Second mortgages are for smaller dollar amounts and run over fewer years than firsts. Generally they run for four or five years for several thousand dollars. The new homeowner now has two monthly payments to make. While somewhat riskier, second mortgages provide the investor with a higher yield, 15 or 16 percent and even 18 percent being quite common. However, if the person granting the second mortgage has a sufficiently high income and a good credit rating, many mortgage lenders will assume the higher risk in order to obtain the higher yield. The yield on discounted second mortgages is calculated by applying the formula shown above, just as in the case of first mortgages.

Other Real Estate Investment Vehicles

Several other methods of investing in real estate will be noted briefly.

1. *Mortgage Companies.* In some instances where several individuals have relatively small amounts of investment funds, it might be advisable for them to form a corporation, either for the purpose of purchasing mortgages or other real estate instruments or for the purpose of purchasing land or both. Five persons with $20,000 each might form a corporation with capital of $100,000 and engage in purchasing mortgages at a discount. Where the

mortgages are amortized monthly, it is advisable for the investors to keep the monthly payments in the corporation and to reinvest the payments and thus keep their funds invested at all times.

2. *Development Companies.* Investing in a development company is another outlet for funds of the individual. A development company is one organized for the purpose of buying and developing land. These are frequently rather large operations with either listed or unlisted stock available to the public. On the other hand, many of these corporations are local and their stock is sold only on the local (as opposed to the national) over-the-counter market. But because securities in these development companies may be purchased from nearly any local stock broker, individuals may make as modest or extensive investments as they please.

3. *Syndicate Investing.* It is frequently possible for several individuals with limited funds to form a syndicate for the purpose of purchasing and managing real estate. An agreement is drawn, generally calling for a statement as to the amount to be invested by individual members, together with the disposition of the proceeds and capital upon the premature death of an investor. In addition, the agreement includes a statement of the property purchased—or about to be purchased, if that is the case—and a statement concerning the appointment of a syndicate manager, who is usually given full control of all matters pertaining to the purchase, management, and selling of the property. Syndicate real estate investing should not be confused with the real estate investment trust described below or the development company noted above. Syndicate investing usually involves only a small number of people and stock is not sold to the public. The real estate investment trust and the development company sell stock and may become public corporations.

Real Estate Investment Trusts

Another possible outlet for surplus funds is the real estate investment trust, which generally resembles the mutual fund. It is a specialized holding company that sells stock in itself to the public. However, instead of investing in stocks as the mutual fund generally does, the investment is in real estate. The main inducement for the real estate investment is the fact that it is exempt from paying the corporate income tax provided it distributes at least 90 percent of its income to the holders of the trust certificate of ownership.

In order for the trust to be exempt from the corporate income tax, it must strictly follow the law, which requires:

1. That there be more than one hundred shareholders
2. That no five persons directly or indirectly own 50 percent or more of the shares
3. That 90 percent of its taxable income must be distributed to the shareholders
4. That it derive at least 75 percent of its gain from rents, capital gains, or mortgage income
5. That it derive no more than 25 percent of its income from dividends and interests in other concerns (provided that only 75 percent of its income results from investments outlined in point 4. For example, if 85 percent of the income were from rents, then only 15 percent would have to come from dividends and interests in other concerns.)
6. That it hold property for a minimum of four years
7. That it be separate from the management of the real estate it holds

The trust provides more liquidity than most real estate investments. For example, if you own a trust certificate, you may sell it. By the same token, if you wish to become part of a trust, you may purchase a certificate.

In reality, real estate investment trusts are specialized closed-end investment companies. In addition, some of them borrow money and have leverage built into their capital structure just as do some closed-end investment companies. In recent years, they have become an additional source of substantial mortgage capital, and this capital does not seem to dry up as much during periods of extremely tight credit as is the case with more traditional sources.

Real estate investment trusts (REIT) have also begun to specialize to some extent. There are now about five types: (1) equity, (2) short-term mortgage construction, (3) long-term mortgage, (4) hybrid, and (5) specialized. Generally, however, most of them can be classified as those that buy securities representing real estate investments (mortgages) and receive a fixed-interest income and those that buy the real estate directly and receive a rental (and perhaps a capital gain) income. In recent years, a good many REITs have been organized and are owned as subsidiaries of commercial banks and mortgage bankers.

Many individuals who invest in real estate shy away from the real estate investment trust because of the lack of individual control and the fact that the investment must be in income-producing property. For example, the trust cannot purchase a piece of raw land for development purposes or for capital gains. These two facts have prevented the trust from becoming as successful as it might have become.

In recent years many real estate investment trusts have had some additional difficulty. Not only were they subject to the same forces that caused the stock market to decline in 1973 and 1974, but they were also the victims of additional factors. Those owning apartments were caught by soaring utility bills. While now more apartments have individual meters, a few years ago there was only one meter per apartment house and the tenant rented on an all-bills-paid basis.

In some areas apartments were also overbuilt, and hence some REITs had excessive vacancies. Then, too, interest rates soared in 1973 and 1974. Since REITs continually borrow on a short-term basis, their interest costs rose. Also some builders went bankrupt due to rising interest rates and construction costs. Many of the builders had borrowed money from REITs and hence when they went under, REITs owned a lot of half-finished housing. Due to all of these factors, REIT's profits declined and in some cases disappeared. Consequently, their stock fell more than most. Some of them were in serious trouble and had to be liquidated or merged. Since interest rates are now lower and since the effects of higher utility rates have, to a greater extent, been shifted to tenants, the heat on REITs is now less intense. While many are still in a precarious position and some additional mergers and bankruptcies may be necessary, the better REITs should do better in the future than they have in the recent past.

DIRECT REAL ESTATE INVESTMENTS

So far I have discussed primarily buying securities that represent real estate investments. It is also possible to own and manage real estate directly, primarily for income purposes, but also for capital gains, as a hedge against inflation, or for tax reasons.

Income properties are generally divided into two categories: residential income properties, including individual homes, duplexes, and apartment houses, and nonresidential, which include commercial space, office space, and industrial or warehouse space.

Single Family, Duplexes, or Multifamily (Apartments) Residentials

When you buy rental property you must choose whether to buy a single family dwelling, a duplex, a triplex, or an apartment. How much money you are able to invest will be a constraint that may rule out everything but a single family unit. If on the other hand you are able to invest more, and have a choice, you must come to grips with the following questions:

1. What type of residential unit is in the greatest demand? Indeed, what is the demand for all of the various types of units?
2. What is the supply of currently available rental units of the various types which would compete with you in providing housing? It is possible that the demand for apartments is greater than for single family units, but nevertheless apartments may be overbuilt while single family rentals are very scarce.
3. What size of family unit (small or large house) is in greatest demand relative to the available supply?
4. What part of the community is the best location for various types of residential units?
5. What is the cost of acquiring a residential unit?
6. What are maintenance costs and rental incomes?

All this will require an analysis of population growth in the area, residential values, monthly rents, construction rates, rental unit vacancies rates, yield on capital invested, whether the population is in large part transient or permanent, and personal income.

Calculating Yield on Direct Real Estate Investments

In order to determine whether or not to buy a rental unit, you must calculate the expected yield and compare that with the yield you could get on an alternative investment. Yields are calculated as follows: Assume a person can purchase a single-family dwelling at $20,000 with $2,000 down. Monthly payments—including insurance and taxes—are $200. As a rule of thumb, investors in this type of property figure two months' rent for vacancy and repairs annually. Assume that the property can be rented for $250 per month. With two months' rent deducted for vacancy and repairs, the net rental will amount to $2,500 per year. Payments on the mortgage, including taxes and insurance, are $2,400 per year; hence, not including any gain in equity, the net is $100 per year. This is equal to a return of 5 percent on the $2,000 investment, which is not really very high considering the factor of relative nonliquidity of the asset. However, if you consider the equity buildup, about $200 more return per year would be added. The yield now becomes 15 percent. If the house is also expected to be a good inflationary hedge, it might be a desirable investment in the eyes of many investors.

Take another hypothetical case, where the facts are the following:

Cost of house		$25,000
Down payment	$11,000	
Mortgage at 6%	14,000	
Monthly payment	141 × 12	1,692
Rent	250 × 12	3,000

| Maintenance and vacancies (2 months' rent) | 500 |
| Net income | 808 |

Yield 808 ÷ 11,000 = 7.35%

In this case the investor obviously bought an older house because she took over a 6 percent mortgage on a house with a fairly large equity in it. Not including the equity build-up, it is yielding 7.35 percent, and this is more attractive than the other case above. If we include the equity buildup of about $25 per month that is included in the $141 monthly payment, we have a net income of $1,108 or 10.1 percent. The reason the yield, after allowing for the equity buildup, is lower than in the first case is because a larger investment (the down payment of $11,000) was required to buy this house. In this case the yield may still be high enough to entice the investor if it serves as an inflationary hedge. Also all rental property provides a tax shelter as the next example will show.

Consider the following:

Cost of home		27,400
Down payment		5,739
Mortgage at 7% VA		21,661
Rental income $270 × 11		
(assume vacancy rate of 1 month per year)		2,970
Expenses		
Taxes	$ 441	
Insurance	86	
Maintenance and Repairs	200	
Total before interest and depreciation	$ 727	
Mortgage payment (interest only at 7%—VA loan)	$ 1,600	
Cash flow (net interest)	$643	
$643 ÷ $5,739 = 11.2% return		
Equity buildup	$276	
Cash flow plus equity buildup	$919	
$919 ÷ $5,739 = 16% return		
Depreciation $23,000 over 20 years at 125%—$23,000 × .0625 = $1,437.50		

The above rental house is obviously about ten years old because it has a 7 percent VA mortgage on it. To buy it, a substantial down payment is required, but often five- to ten-year-old homes are the best buys. In this case, you are acquiring $21,661 of funds at 7 percent; a real bargain at today's interest rate.

If you can keep the house rented eleven months out of the year, the gross rental income is $2,970.

Notice that we selected eleven months rather than ten because we made a separate estimate for maintenance unlike in the first two examples. The taxes, insurance, maintenance, and repairs amount to $727 and if the interest on the mortgage (about $1600) is added in, there is $643 of rental income left for the first year. This $643 of cash flow, divided by the $5,739 down payment, yields a 11.2 percent return. If we add equity buildup of $276 to that, we obtain a total return of $919 which if divided by $5,739 provides a return of 16.0 percent on invested capital.

Since this is a rental house, we may depreciate it for tax purposes. Since it is an older house, depreciation is not as generous as the law allows on a new house. However, you may still depreciate the cost of the home, less the value of the lot. This figure would be about $23,000. It can be depreciated over twenty years since it is an older house, but only at 125 percent of the straight line method. The straight line method would be 5 percent of $23,000 each year for twenty years. One hundred twenty-five percent of this would be 6.25 percent of the undepreciated part each year. Consequently, for the first year, depreciation would be 6.25 percent of $23,000 or $1,437.50. This brings your $643 of rental income to zero for tax purposes. In addition, you have a second tax shelter of $794.50, which you can offset against ordinary earned income to reduce your taxable income by that amount. Your total tax shelter is equal to the depreciation ($1,437.50) but it will decline slightly in each passing year.

If a person owns nonresidential real estate, the net income and the percentage return are, of course, calculated in the same general manner.

Our final illustration is a more recent acquisition: a 10-unit apartment complex at a price of $200,000, 80 percent of which is financed at 10 percent.

Apartment		$200,000
Down payment		40,000
Mortgage at 10% interest		160,000
Rental income (10 unit at $250 per month)	$30,000	
Less 10% for vacancies and maintenance	3,000	
Net Rental Income		27,000
Taxes & Insurance		4,000
Mortgage payment $1,404 per month Equity buildup 1st year ($899)		16,848
Income (Cash Flow) $6,152 ÷ $40,000 = 15.38%		6,152
Income plus equity build up		7,051

$7,051 ÷ $40,000 = 17.63%

Depreciation over 20 years at 125% = $190,000 × .0625 = $11,875

The yield on the $40,000 invested is 15.38 percent without adding in the equity buildup. If it is added in, the return is 17.63. The depreciation again at 125 percent of the straight line method is .0625 × $190,000 (this assumes the lot is worth $10,000) and provides a tax shelter of $11,875 the first year. This will shelter all of the rental income plus an additional $5,723.

Reasons Other Than Yield for Investing in Real Estate Directly

We have already noted two reasons other than yield on invested capital for investing in real estate directly. They are to obtain an inflationary hedge and a tax shelter. Real estate recently has been appreciating in value much more rapidly than the general price level in most parts of the country. However, the investor must be certain to have good quality real estate; old, decaying buildings in poor locations may not appreciate with inflation.

Related to inflation, but somewhat different, is the real capital gain that may be obtained in owning a house or other real estate. A piece of property may become more valuable, even with stable prices, if its location improves as time passes; a house out too far when purchased may be located in just the right suburb in about five years.

Finally, owning rental property may provide a tax shelter. Not only are the interest and property taxes paid deductible on income taxes, but a depreciation allowance is permitted. On a relatively new home worth $50,000, this can easily be $2,000 to $2,500 the first few years. The depreciation allowance can nearly always exceed the net rental income, which then becomes tax-free. The amount by which the depreciation exceeds the net rental income can be used to reduce other income (including salary). Thus, depending on your tax bracket, the saving can be substantial.

Investing in Vacant Land

Over the long run, investment in large amounts of land offers an excellent opportunity for capital gains. The problem of most individuals in this regard is an inability to finance the purchase in the first place. Persons with large sums to invest attempt to pick land lying in the natural path of growth of a city and either hold it for resale at a higher price or divide it into lots for sale in the future or immediately.

For the small investor, small amounts of land can be purchased in almost any price range. In some parts of the country, it is easy enough to buy a lot for as little as a few dollars down and a few dollars per month. Sometimes opportunities are thus available to resell these lots at a profit. Initially the problem is that the investor is dependent upon the developer. Suppose, for example, that a lot is purchased on the basis of $100 down and $10 a month. It is entirely conceivable that the developer may have several thousand lots left in the development to sell, in which case the investor must wait until the developer has sold out the lots before realizing a profit. It is possible, however, for investors in a lot to make a small profit if they purchase the lot when the deveopment is just beginning, provided that they obtain a choice lot—waterfront property, for example—and provided that, as the development grows, the developer raises the initial prices as the demand increases.

The disadvantage of investing in raw land is that it may be a long time before its value rises greatly. In the meantime, the investor must pay taxes annually while receiving no income. Nevertheless, if a person has the staying power and can take a long-run approach, there are opportunities in this area. The advantages of investing in raw land are that there are no maintenance costs, no tenants to complain, and none of the other inconveniences of managing rental units.

Projecting City Growth

When investing in real estate, it may sometimes be necessary to project city growth. This is particularly true when investing in vacant land.

Someone once remarked, "Buy a lot on the edge of the city when you are young and it will support you in your old age." To a large degree this is still true, provided that the property purchased is at the proper edge of the proper city. In order to project city growth you should first examine the business climate and the economy in the area to ascertain if economic growth is likely to be rapid, slow, moderate, or even nonexistent. If it has growth potential, you must ascertain if space is available for growth. If there is, you must then analyze population growth and construction statistics to determine in which direction the city may be growing. If the city is growing in several directions, you must try to ascertain which area can sustain the growth most effectively. This requires knowledge of available space and ease of access to it.

A major question is, in which direction will the city grow, and how fast?

Without special study in this area, the best that can be hoped for are rules of thumb, such as the following:

1. Residential areas tend to move outward along main arteries of travel.
2. Residential areas tend to move toward high ground and away from rivers (where there are rivers).
3. Growth moves toward open country and away from geographical barriers.
4. High-grade stores follow high-grade residential districts.
5. High-grade residential districts develop along rapid transportation lines.

Nonresidential Real Estate

The nonresidential real estate market is divided into three broad categories: (1) commercial or business space, (2) office space, and (3) industrial and warehouse space. In all of these areas the supply of space is more often than not limited by municipal zoning regulations. A zoning regulation is a limitation placed on the use of land by a municipality. The supply of land outside the borders of urban areas, however, is generally not as limited.

1. *Commercial and business space.* Most of us cannot hope to acquire downtown business space unless it is in a decaying area, and that may not be desirable. Most downtown real estate is too valuable and not often for sale. Business property can be acquired, however, in outlying areas, in which businesses will move. In such a case you must investigate zoning ordinances and also patterns of population growth. You must also take into consideration the availability of parking and the accessibility of traffic and public transportation to your possible site.

2. *Office and professional building.* Many office and professional buildings are downtown and for the reasons noted above the acquisition of them is beyond the means of most of us. However, some space is again needed in the suburbs and outlying areas. Doctors sometimes cluster around hospitals that may be in the suburbs. Office space is also sometimes sought in or around shopping centers, or near other retail outlets. As in the case of commercial space, you will need to study zoning ordinances, traffic patterns, population growth, movements, parking facilities, and accessibility of the site before selecting one.

3. *Industrial and warehouse property.* Like commercial property, industrial and warehouse sites are often limited by municipal zoning regulations. With the growth of suburban rings around the standard metropolitan areas, the demand for industrial space has shifted somewhat from the central city to the areas outside. Important in the selection of an industrial site is handy transportation and easy accessibility for workers.

It should also be noted that many businesses needing such facilities prefer to buy and not lease. This definitely limits the opportunity for investments in this area. However, some small industrial and warehouse facilities might be available occasionally.

OTHER (UNUSUAL) INVESTMENT OPPORTUNITIES

I will close this chapter with a few notes about some rather unusual places to invest money. I hasten to add, however, that the typical small investor should probably not choose these as a primary (or even secondary) investment outlet. The idea that the average person can achieve a sizeable (or even a moderate) return by investing in these items is a myth. On the other hand, a few unique individuals may be qualified by training or experience to dabble in one or more of these areas. I am referring to investments in the following:

1. Stamps and coins
2. Precious stones
3. Yachts
4. Furs
5. Antique cars
6. Other antiques
7. Paintings and other works of art
8. Gold
9. Silver and platinum
10. Foreign currency
11. Scotch whiskey

1. While some coin and stamp collections are worth considerable money, most individuals who own them gathered them as a hobby and not as a conscious investment undertaking. While it may be possible for an expert to identify certain stamps and coins that can be purchased cheaply today and are likely to be very expensive a number of years from now, there must be an element of chance in this. My advice is: Do not purchase stamps or coins except insofar as your budget permits you to do this as a hobby.

2. Most people who invest in precious stones choose diamonds, but some select emeralds, or other rare gems. In the case of diamonds, only high quality ones are appropriate for investment purposes. The price of high quality diamonds has risen substantially during the past few years and many are never made into jewelry, but rather are held by investors.

Adam Smith said many years ago that diamonds have no use value but a very high market value; air, on the other hand, has a very high use value, but no market value. That is, air is a free good. This is no longer completely true because a good deal of money is spent keeping the air clean and industrial diamonds are used as cutting tools. Generally speaking, however, diamonds are of value because they are extremely rare and because people want them for, in part at least, psychological reasons.

Since diamonds have risen greatly in value in recent years, some investors have chosen them as an inflationary hedge. Up until recently I would have advised all but the most sophisticated of the very wealthiest investors to refrain from investing in diamonds. However, in recent years some changes have taken place in the diamond industry, and if these changes continue, diamonds may become an investment outlet possibility for a few more investors than formerly. They are still not, however, something the average small investor should buy.

If an investor buys a $5,000 diamond from a jeweler, it may be worth $10,000 or $15,000 five years from now, but only if you were to buy it, not if you want to sell it.

In diamonds there is the wholesale market and the retail market. The markup at the retail level is 50, 60, 70, and even as much as 100 percent. Therefore, unless you can buy in the wholesale market, don't buy because when you sell you will sell them at the wholesale price. Buying retail and selling wholesale will nearly always be a losing game. There is also the problem of finding a buyer if you wish to sell. Many wholesale dealers will sell, but will not buy. They can acquire their supply of new diamonds directly or indirectly through the DeBeers nework.[4] Those dealers that buy back diamonds from the public, buy them at the wholesale price less a discount.

Therefore, while diamond investments are not for everybody (indeed they are not for most people), there may be a few investors who have enough wealth to consider holding a small portion of their investment portfolio in the form of diamonds. As a rough rule of thumb suggests, unless you have a net worth of at least $200,000 and an after tax income of $50,000 or more, and have acquired your insurance portfolio and other high priority assets, you should not consider investing in diamonds. Even then, buy only a small amount for purposes of diversification and as a possible inflationary hedge. For potential diamond investors, there is an appendix at the end of the chapter to aid them in their diamond investments.

What I have said about diamonds is also true of emeralds. High quality emeralds have risen by over 30 percent during the past year. However, many low quality emeralds have been poor investments in recent years. Even if you are fortunate enough to obtain high-quality stones, at fair wholesale prices, you are speculating. Moreover, as in the case of diamonds, there is the problem of reselling them.

3. Some people even buy yachts (and other boats) believing they will appreciate in price just like a house. Not always so. Once more, if you are rich, you may try it. Some very expensive yachts are worth much more today than when they were built three or four years ago. But this is generally not true of cheaper boats. Also, in the case of yachts, there are high maintenance and insurance costs.

4. A fur coat priced at $5,000 a year ago might well be priced at $6,000 today. Don't buy a mink coat, however, unless you can afford it and unless you wish to wear it. While the price of mink coats in furriers' showrooms keeps going up, the resale value of mink coats in citizens' closets does not. You might have difficulty selling a used mink coat, even if it had never been worn and were in perfect condition. Buying used clothes is degrading, and the people who buy fur coats are usually able to afford a new one. You would be better off to buy and stockpile blue jeans. They have risen in price from about $5 to $15 over the last few years, and there are still some used clothing stores in the big cities where you can sell used clothes. However, I do not recommend buying blue jeans as an investment; you will probably not make much money. You may even lose.

5. Antique cars are like other antiques. Their supply is fixed and hence as the demand for them increases, their price will rise. However, unless you can afford this rather expensive hobby, don't invest the rent money in a 1929 Dusenberg or Auburn Roadster.

6. Investing in various other antiques might be a possible investment outlet for a few. However, the amateur should also not go in for a heavy investment in any antiques. Buying some antiques as a budgetary item is another matter. After a time, the collector might even develop enough expertise to become a dealer of antiques. Then he or she might earn a livelihood in this field and possibly even invest some money in an inventory of antiques and hope for a capital gain. There are also many part-time dealers in antiques who make some

---

4. The DeBeers Consolidated Mines Ltd. controls 85 percent of the new uncut diamonds released every year. Only about 220 people in the world are permitted to buy diamonds from DeBeers at their sights in London. These are the "sight holders" and they make up one of the most exclusive closed clubs in the world.

money in it. Unless you are a lover of antiques, do not invest in them and even then do so on a very small scale only, until you become an expert.

7. Everything I have said about antiques applies to paintings and other works of art. Investments should not be made in this area except by experts, and even then only sparingly. If you like art and if you are in a position to become a dealer in art, then some investments in it may be in order. We have all read about the few unusual cases where someone has purchased a work of art at a relatively low price and then found some years later it was worth a fortune. These cases are extremely rare and are fortuitous. There are also the few cases of a wealthy individual buying an expensive painting, not as an investment, but finding out that it has indeed been a good one. Again, this is not for the average person.

Occasionally, a small investor may buy an original by a young and unknown artist for a few hundred dollars to discover it worth substantially more as time passes and as the artist becomes more famous. It is fine to do this, if your budget permits it, but you should like the painting for its own sake and be prepared to consider it a consumer item in the event that it does not appreciate in value.

Everything I have said about art holds true for rare books.

8. From 1934 to 1975 it was illegal for Americans to own gold bullion, and some people invested in gold coins, or in the stock of gold mining companies. Gold stocks did rise during the first half of the 1970s as the world price of gold rose. (The organized world gold markets were in London and Zurich.)

During the first half of the decade of the 1970s the world price of gold rose from about $40 (the U.S. Mint price was $35) to almost $200 per ounce. In reality, most of this increase took place before 1975 when it became legal for Americans to hold gold bullion. Then, in 1975 and 1976 when Americans did not buy gold in large quantities, its price came down again to just over $100 per ounce in 1977. In 1978 and 1979, however, gold rose once more and in the last half of 1979 it briefly rose to almost $450 per ounce (its high was $447) but then fell back to just under $400. Then in January 1980 it rose to over $880 per ounce, but fell back quickly to the $650 level.

The moral of the story is that the price of gold fluctuates a great deal and it is risky. Buying it is highly speculative. However, some feel the long-run trend is up, and that gold is a good long-term investment because it is an inflationary hedge. For that to be true, it would have to increase in price in excess of inflation because it yields no interest or dividend return. An ounce of gold will still be only an ounce of gold in one or ten or twenty years. (To be sure, this is true of any of the unusual investments discussed in this selection.) Whether the price of gold will continue up, of course, no one knows, but some advisers are now telling their wealthy clients that some gold holdings (usually a relatively small amount) may be in order on the grounds of diversification. But what about the small investor?

Insofar as bullion is concerned the minimum amount that may be purchased is 100 troy ounces or 3 kilograms (a troy ounce is heavier than a regular ounce, there being about 12 troy ounces per pound). A kilogram is equal to 32.15 troy ounces or 2.7 pounds. In either case, then, these minimum purchases amount to a little over eight pounds and cost approximately $65,000. This disqualifies most small investors. In addition there are costs involved in holding gold bullion. First, the premiums or commissions paid to dealers are from 1 to 1.5 percent. Also, most states have sales taxes, and often these must be paid on gold purchases. (In this sense, it is considered a consumer item rather than an investment item.) There are also shipping charges, insurance charges, and storage charges. These can add another 1 to 1.5 percent of the cost of the bullion. Then when you wish to sell it, you need to have it assayed to determine its quality and fineness. All these costs, together with the fact that gold yields no interest return, suggest that the small investor should be very wary of gold.

If the small investor insists on buying gold, he or she should probably select one of four gold coins: the South African "Krugerrand," the Canadian "Mapleleaf," a special Mexican gold "peso," or the Austrian "Corona." Each of these coins contains about one ounce of gold; hence their price fluctuates with the daily market price of gold. You can buy these coins from various brokers, coin dealers, and a few banks, and the comissions are generally about the same as on gold bullion. Most brokers sell a minimum of 5 coins, but some banks and coin dealers will sell in smaller amounts, though often they charge higher commissions on sales of less than five coins. You should shop around when buying gold coins because commissions will vary. While you have to pay a sales tax on these coins, there are usually no shipping or insurance costs, and if you have a safe deposit box, no storage costs. Since they are stamped they do not have to be assayed when sold.

9. Silver and platinum too have risen substantially. In mid-1979 silver bullion was priced at over $15 per troy ounce up from just over $5 a year earlier; then, in early 1980, it rose to over $50 per ounce before declining to that $15 range once more. Platinum too rose from $280 per ounce a few years ago to $800 in early 1980, then fell to about $500 in late 1980. Silver, being a cheaper metal than gold, has often been called the poor man's gold. Silver and platinum both have industrial uses, and that, as well as speculator-investor demand, has helped drive up the price of these two metals. If you can buy a large amount, you may buy these two metals directly from the industrial suppliers and avoid dealer commissions, and you may also be able to get it at the wholesale price. If you are a small investor and wish to buy silver, you should investigate bags of silver coin that are sold on the New York Mercantile Exchange, and by some coin dealers.

The minimum silver bullion purchase set by most dealers is 5,000 troy ounces, which makes its price $75,000. The minimum platinum bullion purchase is 50 troy ounces at about $500 per ounce or $25,000. Commissions on silver and platinum purchases are similar to those discussed above under gold, as are the shipping, insurance, and storage charges, and sales taxes. Everything we have said about investing in gold applies to silver and platinum. It is highly speculative.

10. Foreign exchange can also be purchased and if the dollar continues to decline, a profit would be made. Probably the best currencies to hold would be Swiss francs or German marks. The value of the dollar relative to foreign currencies is determined, in large part, by the rate of inflation in the U.S. relative to inflation abroad. Switzerland and West Germany have had less inflation and hence their currencies have risen relative to the dollar.

Some experts feel investing in Swiss francs and West German marks is analogous to investing in gold. This is because when the dollar price of gold rises, the franc and mark price of gold do not necessarily rise also. Or if they do, they do so by less, and consequently, the dollar falls relative to these currencies. The historical record supports this. While the price of gold in dollars has risen greatly, the price of gold in francs and marks has risen by much less.

It also costs less to hold foreign currency than to hold gold bullion. Nevertheless, when you buy foreign currency you are speculating a bit.

11. Scotch whiskey is another item that became fairly popular a few years ago. The idea was that the investor would purchase raw whiskey, hold it until properly aged, and then sell it. Actually, only warehouse receipts for whiskey were delivered; later these were then sold. Just like in the case of commodities, actual delivery was almost never taken.

A few years ago, some distilleries in Scotland were actually pushing these sales via the mails. However, the Securities and Exchange Commission now exercises some control over offers to sell Scotch, primarily in that the seller or broker of Scotch must be registered with the SEC. This stopped most of the easy mail sales.

There are still a few legitimate brokers in New York who do buy and sell Scotch, however. Nevertheless, you should be careful about buying Scotch. Its price can fluctuate a good deal just like other commodities. The view held by some that a person can always buy raw whiskey, hold it until it ages, and then sell it at a good profit is a myth. If it were that easy, the distilleries would store it all themselves and keep the profit. The price of both raw and aged whiskey fluctuates. Sometimes aged whiskey is even cheaper than raw. Buying whiskey is a high-risk speculative undertaking and the small nonprofessional should refrain from doing so.

QUESTIONS FOR REVIEW

1. What are mutual funds and what is the underlying rationale for the existence of mutual funds?

2. Distinguish between a closed-end investment company and an open-end investment company.

3. Suppose a mutual fund salesperson were selling a balanced fund. What does this mean?

4. What is a hedge fund, an income fund?

5. How do the objectives of various mutual funds differ?

6. Why should a mutual fund do at least somewhat better than the Dow-Jones Averages before becoming a candidate for acquisition?

7. What are some of the advantages that one receives when one buys mutual funds? Are there any disadvantages?

8. How is the value of a share in an open-end company determined?

9. What are loading charges as related to mutual funds?

10. What is a no-load fund? How can no-load funds stay in business?

11. How are the earnings of investment companies taxed?

12. What factors should be considered before a person buys mutual funds?

13. Discuss the commodities markets. Would you recommend investing in commodities? Why or why not?

14. What is a discounted first mortgage?

15. What factors must be taken into account when calculating the yield on a mortgage?

16. What is a real estate investment trust?

17. Discuss art, painting, and the like, as investment outlets.

18. Why is it that dealers in art, etc., are in a better position than the rest of us to make investments in art?

CASES

1. Bill and Nancy Greenwood have over the years accumulated $10,000 of savings that are in a savings and loan association earning 5½ percent compounded semiannually. Bill and Nancy feel that now is a good time to take $5,000 of it and invest it in common stock. They think they should be getting more than 5½ percent. Recently somebody told them they should investigate mutual funds rather than invest in common stock directly. Is this a good time to buy stock? Can they expect to receive more than 5½ percent by going into equities? Would you recommend mutual funds or buying common stock directly? Explain your answer.

2. Rita Roundsetter has just inherited $25,000 and is undecided how to invest it. She has never owned common stock and is inexperienced with respect to securities. Nevertheless,

she thinks she should buy equities. Is she wise? Would you recommend buying common stock directly or mutual funds? Rita is thirty-four and has no dependents; what kind of stocks (or mutual funds) would you recommend?

3. Ruben Haywood has an income of $30,000 per year and has decided to set aside $100 per month to buy equities. However, since he has had very little experience with securities, and since he does not have the time to watch his portfolio carefully, he considers that he should own common stock indirectly through an investment company. Do you agree?

Ruben is also undecided between open-end and closed-end investment companies and owning stock directly. As far as investment companies are concerned, which stock do you think Ruben should buy?

4. Robert Shafer works in the trust department of the Bank of America and is earning $28,000 per year. He is twenty-eight, married, and has one child. He expects his income to be rising over the years and thinks it is time for him to acquire some equities. Since he is not going to be able to invest very much at first, he cannot get much diversification. Nevertheless, he still thinks it would be foolish for him to buy mutual shares and pay someone to handle his investments for him. Do you agree? What kind of stock (or mutual shares) would you recommend for Robert?

5. Joan Rider is a twenty-four-year-old school teacher who has her own car fully paid for and $1,000 in the bank. She wants to invest in equities but is undecided whether to buy common stock directly or indirectly through a mutual fund. One of the things she dislikes about mutual funds is the high acquisition costs. Would you advise her to invest directly or indirectly? Specifically what kind of direct or indirect investments would you advise?

6. Jim and Virginia Hansen are in their early thirties and have a combined income of $24,000 per year. They have two children— six and four years old—and want to start saving now for their college education. They are able to save $25 per month for each child and will earmark it for a college fund. How should they invest it? Can you make specific recommendations?

7. Clem Kensington has inherited $50,000 and has savings of $20,000 in a savings and loan association that is paying 5½ percent. It seems to him that he should be getting at least 8 percent, and therefore he is thinking about taking $20,000 out of the savings and loan association, putting it with the $50,000 he inherited, and buying a mortgage. The other alternative is to buy a duplex, live in one unit, and rent out the other.

Clem has found out that he can get a mortgage that will yield him a 12 percent return. He has also found a duplex he can buy for $70,000 that has a net rental income of $4,200 per year. Which is the better investment? Explain fully.

8. Billie Stewart is a young lawyer with $50,000 to invest. She has decided to invest it in some real estate venture, but is uncertain what type of venture she should choose. She has investigated first mortgages and has discovered she can obtain a 12 percent yield. Now she learns that second mortgages are available. Most of these are $3,000 to $5,000 and will yield her about 15 percent return on her money. Why is the yield difference so great on first and second mortgages? Would you recommend that she buy first or second mortgages? Why? Why are the second mortgages usually only for several thousand dollars while first mortgages run up to $50,000 and more?

9. Joe and Dorothy Jenkins have $500,000 that they wish to invest in various real estate ventures. They have considered buying both first and second mortgages, buying land on the edge of the city in which they live and holding it for capital gain, and buying shares in a real estate investment trust. What would you advise?

10. John and Mary Whippet decided to retire from their ranch near Aspen, Colorado, and move to Denver. Consequently, they sold their ranch for $250,000, which they hope to invest in the Denver area in order to live off the income. They have decided to invest in income-producing property rather than in securities, and they are thinking in terms of either an apartment building, which they could manage, or an office building. How much yield would they need on their investment to make it superior to corporate bonds? Advise

them regarding the merits of investing in an apartment versus an office building.

11. After living in Denver for several years, John and Mary Whippet found time on their hands; therefore, they decided to go into an additional part-time business for themselves. Mary has always liked antiques and has suggested they become antique dealers. John is not so sure. They seek your advice.

SUGGESTED READINGS

Anderson, Paul Edward. *Tax Factors in Real Estate Operations,* 3rd ed. Englewood Cliffs, N.J.: Prentice-Hall, 1976.

"Before You Speculate." The Chicago Mercantile Exchange, 444 West Jackson Boulevard, Chicago, Ill. 60606.

Financing Small Business: Report to the Committee on Banking and Currency and the Select Committee on Small Business of the U.S. Congress by the Federal Reserve System. Washington, D.C.: U.S. Government Printing Office. This is a basic source of information on small business.

"Forbes Mutual Fund Survey." *Forbes Magazine.* This is an annual survey that comes out every August.

Green, Fred T. *Thrift and Home Ownership.* Chicago: United States Savings and Loan League, no date.

Hedging Highlights. Chicago: Chicago Board of Trade.

Hoagland, Henry E., and Stone, Leo D. *Real Estate Finance,* 6th ed. Homewood, Ill. Richard D. Irwin, 1977.

How to Build Profits by Controlling Costs. New York: Dun & Bradstreet, Inc.

How to Buy and Sell Commodities. New York: Merrill Lynch, Pierce, Fenner, and Smith, Inc.

Investment Companies, Mutual Funds and Other Types. Latest edition of this annual publication. Wiesenberger Financial Services, Inc., 870 7th Avenue, New York, N. Y. 10019.

Johnson's Investment Company Charts. Latest edition of this annual publication. Hugh A. Johnson Investment Company, 545 Elmwood Avenue, Buffalo, New York 14222.

Kuehn, W. H. *Pitfalls in Managing a Small Business.* New York: Dun & Bradstreet, Inc.

Minority Enterprise: Small Business Investment Company. Washington, D.C.: Small Business Administration.

Mutual Fund Fact Book. Investment Company Institute, 1775 K St., N. W., Washington, D.C. This is an annual publication.

SBA, What It Is, What It Does; SBIC Financing for Small Business; SBIC Industry Review; SBIC Industry Trends. Washington, D.C.: Small Business Administration.

The Small Business Administration (SBA) is a government agency and it publishes numerous pamphlets on small business management. It also publishes a *Handbook of Small Business Finance.* Its address is 1441 L Street, N. W., Washington, D.C. 20416.

Speculating on Inflation: Future Trading in Interest Rates, Foreign Currencies, and Precious Metals. New York: Merrill Lynch, Pierce, Fenner, and Smith, Inc., 1979.

Springer, John L. *The Mutual Fund Trap.* Chicago, Illinois: Regnery, 1974.

U.S. News & World Report. A weekly magazine that contains a good deal of information on business and finance.

Well Beyond the Average: The Story of Dow Jones. New Jersey: Dow Jones & Company, Inc., The Educational Service Bureau.

Wendt, Paul, and Cerf, Alan R. *Real Estate Investment Analysis,* 2nd ed. New York: McGraw-Hill Book Company, 1979.

Wiedemer, John P. *Real Estate Investments.* Reston, VA; Reston Publishing Company, 1979.

APPENDIX 15A

BUILDING A PORTFOLIO; THE ORDER OF PRIORITIES IN ACQUIRING ASSETS

You have studied a number of different investment outlets. In building your portfolio, the watchword should be diversification. You might want to acquire stocks and bonds, life insurance, savings accounts, perhaps a home, rental real estate, and possibly a number of other assets. The portfolio will, of course, differ for different people. Some people will want to own a home of their own; others, because of temperament, will not. Nevertheless, there is the question of the order in which you should acquire the various assets. The first savings generated should be invested differently than certain later ones. Certain assets are high priority assets like, for example, life insurance and a highly liquid passbook savings deposit which is available in the case of an emergency. Assets which serve as tax shelters should also be given a high priority in some cases. Other assets have various degrees of lower priorities, and this will vary from individual to individual. Nevertheless, assets can be grouped into three general categories of priorities as shown below. Some investors may not acquire enough assets to consider the acquisition of the third category. Also there may be some overlap in that some investors will begin acquiring assets in the middle priority range before they completely satisfy their highest priority requirement.

1. Highest priority (to be acquired first)
   Passbook savings account
   Life insurance
   A home (if this fits your temperament)
   A Keogh plan or an individual retirement account (IRA) (if you qualify)
   College trust fund for children
2. Middle priority
   Stock
   Bonds
   Mutual funds
   Rental property
   Tax-exempt state and local bonds (only if you have a tax problem).
3. Lower priority
   Raw land
   Gold and diamonds (only small proportion of your total assets)
   Speculative stock
   Exotic tax shelters such as equipment leasing and cattle feedlot operations

APPENDIX 15B

DIAMOND INVESTMENTS*

Most investors are not and cannot become expert in grading and appraising diamonds. Therefore, until recently they were at the mercy of the diamond dealers, and as in everything there are some unscrupulous dealers. The situation was compounded by the fact that diamond appraising was subjective, and no uniform criteria existed for objectively grading them. Now, however, diamond grading has become more standardized, and the standards used were developed by the Gemological Institute of America (GIA). There are four prominent diamond grading labs in New York that will issue a grading certificate. These labs are: The American Gemological Laboratories (AGL), the Gemological Institute of America (GIA), the International Gemological Institute (IGI), and the European Gemological Laboratory (EGL). Most high-quality diamonds are now traded almost exclusively on the basis of what the certificate issued by one of these independent grading labs says.

The fee for grading a diamond varies with its size and generally runs from $50.00 to $100.00. It is usually paid by the seller. Moreover, a diamond need be graded only once, although some buyers request a grading verification. A verification is simpler and less time consuming than a grading. This is because during the grading process the lab makes a complete map of the diamond, and when verifying, the diamond is merely checked against the map.

It is important to emphasize that grading and appraising are not the same thing, although to be sure there is a relationship between the grade of a diamond and its value. The four grading labs do not appraise diamonds, they only grade them. But once a grading certificate has been issued for any given diamond, expert diamond dealers are able to appraise it. The best way to obtain a diamond's true wholesale value is to get its grading certificate and then find out at what price a diamond dealer will buy that stone from you.

The grade and hence the value of a diamond is determined by its carat weight, color, clarity, and cut quality. These are the four C's of diamond valuation. The test for weight is simple; the diamond is weighed.

COLOR

Color quality is designated by assigning a letter grade (D through Z) with D the highest quality and Z the lowest.[1] The test for color is really a test for the absence of color. The lower the level of color the higher the rating, and ideally a diamond should have no color. This is because it would then break up and reflect light without imparting any of its own color to that light. However, if a diamond has enough natural color in it, it may be considered a "fancy color diamond" and is rated beyond Z and actually is valued more highly because of its color. Although very rare, diamonds come in green, red, blue, yellow, and brown. Most

---

*This material is drawn from Wolf and Associates, "Personal Finance Seminars." Used by permission.

1. The reasons A, B, and C are not used to measure color is because many retail jewelers use these three letters to value their diamonds and they represent nonstandardized scales.

diamonds, however, contain faint tinges of yellow, and the less the yellowness, the higher the value and the rating. A "D" rating has virtually no yellow (is colorless).

CLARITY

Clarity has to do with the absence of impurities and imperfections, such as carbon spots, gas bubbles, hairline cracks, and natural blemishes. The size and location of these imperfections are considered when assigning a clarity grade.

The following grades are used:

FL Flawless.
IF Internally Flawless.
VVS Very Very Slightly imperfect.
   VVS_1 (There are two subclassifications in this grade.)
   VVS_2
VS Very Slightly imperfect.
   VS_1 (There are two subclassifications in this grade.)
   VS_2
SI Slightly Imperfect.
   SI_1 (There are two subclassifications in this grade.)
   SI_2
I Imperfect.
I_1 (There are three subclassifications in this grade.)
I_2
I_3

Good quality investment diamonds are considered to be VS or better; diamonds graded below I_3 are considered industrial diamonds.

THE CUT

The test for cut quality is subjective, but there are three major factors to consider; the shape, the style, and the quality of the cut. A round cut is generally superior to a pear, marquise, oval, or emerald-shaped cut, all else being the same.[2] This is because a round cut is best at reflecting light, and hence is more sought after in the marketplace.

The style of the cut is virtually always the "American Cut" (sometimes also called the "Brilliant Cut," because it reflects more light than any other style of cut). The American cut style was developed by a physicist after much study about 80 years ago. It has not and probably cannot be improved upon.

The round cut does not mean that the diamond is a sphere or ball. Rather, if a round diamond is viewed from the top it appears as a circle. Viewed from the side a diamond looks sort of like a kite with its top cut off. The area of maximum width of a diamond is called a girdle. It is analogous to the equator of a sphere. The upper half is called the crown (northern hemisphere), the lower half is referred to as the pavillion (southern hemisphere), and both of them have facets cut into them. The top of the diamond is flat and is called the table (or the arctic ocean). The bottom of the diamond comes to a tip and is called the culet (or south pole).

---

2. The reason all diamonds are not cut round is because sometimes its color, clarity, or net size can be improved by choosing a different cut.

The quality of the cut, while somewhat subjective, is determined by a number of measurements. These measurements include:

1. The table percentage.
2. The depth percentage.
3. The pavillion depth.
4. The crown angle.
5. The girdle.
6. The symmetry of the cut.
7. The finish.
8. The fluorescence.
9. The culet.

1. The table percentage refers to the ratio between the table diameter and the diamond's diameter at the girdle.
2. The depth percentage is the relationship between the total depth of the diamond and the diamond's diameter at the girdle.
3. The pavillion depth refers to the relationship between the pavillion depth and the total depth. The pavillion you will recall is the lower, faceted part of a diamond.
4. The crown angle refers to the angle of the upper (crown) facets away from the horizontal girdle.
5. The girdle refers to the line around the diamond. It can be looked upon as the equator. It can be thick or thin.
6. Symmetry has to do with the geometry of the cut. For example, if you look at the diamond from the top, how perfect is the circle in the girdle. The table top and the equator (girdle) should both be horizontal if viewed from the side, and a line drawn down from the middle of the table top should hit the culet. The rating for symmetry can be poor to excellent.
7. Finish refers to the quality of the diamond's polish. Ratings can be poor to excellent.
8. Fluorescence refers to the glow that some diamonds give off under fluorescent light. The less the glow, the higher the quality of the diamond.
9. The culet is the south pole of the diamond; the bottom tip of a diamond comes not to a tip, but rather to a tiny leveled off area.

HOW TO SELECT DIAMONDS

Investors buying diamonds, especially for the first time may wish to limit their purchases to what could be referred to as blue chip diamonds (the term is used by some just like in the case of common stock).

Blue chip diamonds are considered to have the following characteristics:

1. ½ carat to 3 carat.
2. top 5 color grades.
3. top 5 to 6 clarity grades.

4. round American (or Brilliant) cut.

5. certified by one of the four grading labs mentioned above.

6. meets the quality cut outlined in the following table.

Table percentage	53–65 percent
Depth percentage	57–63 percent
Pavillion depth	41–45 percent
Crown angle	30–35 degrees
Girdle	Avoid gems with an extremely thin or extremely thick girdle.
Symmetry	Any stone rated good or better.
Finish	Any gem rated good or better.
Fluorescence	If the rating states the diamond has strong fluorescence, it is of lower quality. Anything less than strong is satisfactory.
Culet	If the grading labs do not mention the culet in the certificate which they issue, it is acceptable. All comments about the culet such as "large culet" or "no culet" are negative comments.

Price-wise the blue chip diamonds would currently (1980) run from about $2,000 to $240,000 at the wholesale level. For example, a ½ carat diamond at the fifth color and fifth clarity grade and meeting the other specifications noted above would be valued at about $2,000. The upper level in the blue chip category would be a three carat top color and clarity grade with a price of about $240,000. For $20,000 you could probably get a one carat diamond in the third color and clarity grade. To these figures you would have to add about ten percent in commissions to the dealer (paid both when you buy and when you sell) and whatever the sales tax is in your state.

Insofar as diamonds are an inflationary hedge their prices should rise over the years. Since the supply of diamonds is controlled, and since the DeBeers Consolidated Mines Ltd. has a vested interest in a stable but rising price level for diamonds, some investors feel that diamonds are a good long-run inflationary hedge. It should be pointed out that the range in the quality of a diamond which is considered an investment grade diamond seems to be widening. For example, five years ago when someone said "investment quality" it often was taken to mean D flawless. If this widening trend continues, it could be a good strategy to buy diamonds just inside or just outside the lower end of the investment quality range.

Virtually all wholesale diamond dealers are in New York. Therefore, if you live in Ogallala, Nebraska, or Puyallup, Washington, this becomes a problem because you must buy your diamonds in New York to obtain a satisfactory price. There are several ways that you can make a New York contact. First, some diamond dealers advertise in the *New York Times, The Wall Street Journal,* and the *Financial Planner,* the journal of the International Association of Financial Planners. Second, your local jeweler in Puyallup or Ogallala may serve as a conduit through whom you can contact a reputable dealer. After all, he or she must buy diamonds somewhere.

One word of warning: When you buy a diamond, make sure it has been graded by one of the four grading labs noted above and that you have a certificate that states the diamond's characteristics. There are some unscrupulous diamond dealers. If they state (or give a certificate) that the diamond has been graded *in accordance with* the GIA standards, be leery. Accept only genuine grading certificates of one of the four labs. Only then can you be assured of attaining a diamond that is what it is reputed to be. One final warning, you should be prepared to hold diamonds over the long-run. There is no interest or dividend return and only capital appreciation provides a return. Diamonds are considered a high-risk investment and therefore only a small proportion of any portfolio should consist of diamonds. However, in recent years they have been a good inflationary hedge.

QUOTING DIAMONDS

One of the problems of investing in diamonds is the fact that they are not very liquid; some dealers will sell but will not buy back. This lack of liquidity too may be changing. Diamonds may soon be traded much like securities in the over-the-counter market with all diamond dealers tied together by a computer network. Diamonds that have been graded by one of the four diamond grading labs may even be quoted price- and quality-wise. A newly established firm, Polygon Corporation, in a joint venture with the Xerox Corporation, is developing a computer system to do this. If and when this network is completed, Polygon will play a role in diamond trading similar to the role played by NASDAQ (which is the National Association of Security Dealers Automated Quotation) in trading over-the-counter securities.

Once this system is in place it will be much easier to buy (and especially sell) investment quality diamonds. Consequently, diamonds will become much more liquid as investment, and the demand for them is then likely to increase. Security brokers (such as Merrill Lynch) may even enter the market as they have in the case of gold. What this broadening of the market will do is anybody's guess. Generally, broadening a market tends to stabilize prices, but on the other hand, making it possible for more individuals to get in and out of the market more quickly and easily may also introduce an element of instability.

PART FOUR

Home Ownership, Taxes, Estate Planning

In part four I shall present home ownership, taxes, and the tools of estate planning. A home is the biggest investment the average person will ever make; in fact, in many cases it represents one's life savings. It is important, therefore, to plan ahead in this area. Chapter 16 deals with the problems of home ownership. There are both advantages and disadvantages of home ownership. One of the advantages, as you shall see, is that a home provides the homeowner with certain tax benefits. Next the chapter considers the major factors you should consider when buying a house as well as how much a house is worth. The remainder of the chapter then deals with the complex area of home financing.

Chapter 17 examines taxes; some state and local taxes are examined, but most of the chapter is devoted to the federal personal income tax. How the law works, and what items are dropped in moving from gross income to adjusted gross income are examined early in the chapter. Then itemized deductions and tax credits are presented. The chapter ends on the special capital gains tax, and on some supplemental information on the tax law.

Chapter 18, the final chapter of the book, introduces the tools of estate planning. One of the goals of estate planning is to conserve the assets accumulated over a lifetime and to prevent the government from grabbing them upon death. The first step in estate planning consists of gathering the facts and drawing up a will. This will assure that your assets are disposed of in accordance with your desires. Then trusts are introduced. Trusts are an invaluable tool in estate planning and in minimizing taxes. Gifts, another tax-minimizing tool, are also introduced, and the very complex gift and estate tax law is examined.

Chapter Sixteen

Home Ownership

The rich worry about taxes, the poor worry about the rent.

MARK TWAIN

The objectives of this chapter are to

1   Present the advantages and disadvantages of home ownership

2   Introduce the factors that must be considered when buying a house

3   Discuss the factors determining the value of a house

4   Show how homes are financed, and the cost of financing them

5   Discuss large versus small down payments

6   Illustrate how home loans are paid off

7   Examine some of the hidden costs of buying a home

INTRODUCTION TO HOME OWNERSHIP

The subject of home ownership may be tied into the budget in many ways. Most of us who own our homes must meet a monthly mortgage payment that represents a substantial proportion of our budget. It is a fixed payment that must be met for many years. In addition, many people consider part of the monthly payment on the home to be a type of forced saving because with each monthly payment the individual's equity or ownership in the home increases. Others relate home ownership to the family budget because the interest paid on the mortgage as well as the real property taxes constitute large tax-deductible items.

The popularity of home ownership is attested to by the fact that in the late 1970s about 64 percent of the families in the United States owned their own homes. The rate of increase, however, has slowed down in the last few years. This is generally believed to be due to the greater availability of rental units, very high interest rates, and increases in construction costs in recent years.

There are a number of advantages to home ownership which should be examined. These are not equally important to all people but nevertheless factors to be considered.

Personal Factors

Some people attach great importance to the peace of mind, pride, security, greater privacy, and convenience that owning a home provides. Some also feel that homes are often in a less congested area than apartments, and for this and other reasons provide a better environment in which to raise children.

Tax Advantages

There is a considerable tax advantage to home ownership. A homeowner pays interest on the mortgage and local property taxes on the home, while a person who rents an apartment pays rent. The latter, however, includes a sum to enable the landlord to pay the interest and tax; hence the renter pays these costs indirectly. Because of this hidden cost for the renter, homeowners have a tax advantage over persons who rent. If their income, exemptions, and other deductions are the same as the renter's, they will pay fewer taxes. This is because homeowners may deduct from their incomes, when calculating their taxes, interest on their mortgage and property taxes. Rent, of course, cannot be deducted. This can best be illustrated by an example. Assume two childless couples whose circumstances are identical except that one rents and one is buying a house. Both have adjusted gross incomes of $15,500 and total deductions because of medical expenses, contributions to charity, their church, and so forth, amount to $2,000. The couple buying a home, however, has additional deductions of $2,160 due to interest and property taxes ($50 per month taxes and about $130 per month interest is not unreasonable for even a modest home). The couple buying a home will take a total deduction of $4,160 while the one renting can take only $3,200. This is the zero bracket amount that married couples may take if filing jointly. The homeowners' taxable income is $960 lower. Moreover, the higher the tax bracket, the greater the tax advantage from home ownership. The nature of our tax laws enables the homeowner to pass part of the interest and property taxes on to Uncle Sam.

Even the homeowner who no longer has mortgage payments to make and lives in a community that has no property taxes is receiving favorable tax treatment because of imputed rent income received on which he or she pays no taxes. Again an example will illustrate. Assume two individuals working side by side for the Ajax Corporation, each making a salary of $20,000 per year. Each owns a home that is fully paid for, but while Ms. A lives in hers, Mr. B rents his and lives with relatives. Both have a $40,000 home free and clear. Mr. B receives $1,000 of net cash rental income after all expenses including his property taxes and depreciation. He pays a tax on $21,000. Ms. A in reality should look upon her cost-free living as worth about $1,000, which she really receives as income in kind. For these two individuals to be treated equally they should both pay taxes on either $20,000 or $21,000. But Ms. A pays on $20,000 and Mr. B on $21,000.

The same logic would apply if, while Ms. A invested her savings in her home, Mr. B rented and invested his savings in high-grade corporate bonds. After a time Mr. B would have interest income that is taxable, while Ms. A's rent income received in kind is not.

Homestead

In some states, laws have been enacted making it possible for persons to declare their home to be their homestead. This prevents the home from being seized to satisfy certain private debts. In some states, there is a dollar limit to the amount of real estate protected against seizure. The homestead act does not, of course, prevent the mortgage lender from foreclosing if mortgage payments are not made. Also, the government is not prevented from seizing the property if it has a valid claim against the owner. But with these two exceptions, the property is protected. In some areas, property taxes are also reduced by a modest amount if a homestead claim is filed.

A Home as an Inflationary Hedge

A home is one of the best inflationary hedges available. A person who rents and invests savings in a savings account or even in securities is likely to see them eroded as time passes and prices rise. Not so with a home, at least not in most cases. Generally, a home will appreciate as much, and sometimes more, than overall prices during times of inflation. This is because when prices rise, so too do building materials and labor costs, and these two items make up the largest part of the cost of a house. Consequently, during inflation, the cost of building new houses rises; and this generally brings up the price of older houses as well. The following table shows how the price of houses sold by region has risen over the years, as well as an overall U.S. figure.

Disadvantages of Home Ownership

Some people consider maintenance and the bother of yard work as a disadvantage of home ownership. This includes such things as painting every few years. From time to time the roof will need repairs. Occasionally, a plumber will have to be called and certain built-in appliances like the hot water heater, furnace, and air conditioner do wear out and have to be repaired or replaced. All of these things can be avoided by the apartment dweller, as well as the yard work like raking leaves, cutting the lawn, and shoveling snow. Since most people do these chores themselves, little monetary cost is involved, but the homeowner's time is committed.

Insofar as costs are concerned, it has been estimated that maintenance will run about 1½ percent of the cost of the house per year. It should be remembered too that this is the average cost, and in some years the cost will be considerably higher than in other years. Then, too, as noted above, there may be the inconvenience and added work of maintenance.

TABLE 16–1. *Median sales price of new private one-family houses sold, from 1972 to 1978.*

YEAR	U.S.	NORTH-EAST	NORTH-CENTRAL	SOUTH	WEST
1972	27,600	31,400	29,300	25,800	27,500
1973	32,500	37,100	32,900	30,900	32,400
1974	35,900	40,100	36,100	34,500	35,800
1975	39,300	44,000	39,600	37,300	40,600
1976	44,200	47,300	44,800	40,500	47,200
1977	48,800	51,600	51,500	44,100	53,500
1978*	55,700	58,100	59,200	50,300	61,300

*1979, U.S. total: 1st qtr., $60,600, 2d qtr., $63,200.
Source: Statistical Abstract of the United States: 1979, U.S. Bureau of the Census.

Some people consider the big investment required to be a homeowner a disadvantage. The fact that a home is not very liquid and would require time to sell reinforces this disadvantage.

To Rent or Own a Home

When comparing renting and buying, many people compare renting an apartment as opposed to buying a house. This is not completely valid because you are comparing two different things. Usually (but not always), a house is larger than an apartment. In addition, the homeowner has more privacy than a tenant in an apartment and a backyard, which the tenant lacks. Also, homeowners are building up an equity in their houses. Consequently, you cannot compare the monthly mortgage payment on a house with the monthly rental payment and reach a decision. You must also give some weight to all the things discussed above under advantages and disadvantages of home ownership.

To be sure, houses can also be rented. If you were to compare the monthly rent on a house with the mortgage payment on a like (or similar) house, you would have a more meaningful comparison.

Then, too, you must look at the comparison with respect to the long run and the short run. A homeowner does not build up much equity during the first few years of home ownership. This is because most of the monthly payments go for interest. Also, the first year will necessitate additional closing costs and possibly expenditures for putting in a lawn and other landscaping.

When buying a house as opposed to renting one, you are almost certainly better off financially to buy, except possibly in the short run. That has been the case in the past and it is likely to be so in the future. However, if you are only going to be in the community a year

"We're at the home of Jim and Mindy Marks, who are about to discover that their utility bill has gone sky-high. Let's watch." (Source: Drawing by Maslin; © 1980 The New Yorker Magazine, Inc.)

or two, you might want to rent for the somewhat greater convenience and possibly less expense; for example, no maintenance cost, no landscaping (needed on new homes only), no closing costs, no possible realtor's fee when you sell, and the like. In the long run then, especially if your mortgage is lower than your monthly rent, probably you should buy.

If it is a matter of indifference to you whether you live in an apartment or buy a house and you want to make the decision between buying or renting strictly on a financial basis, then you have a more complex task. You will have to consider the following:

1. The monthly rent and the monthly mortgage payment
2. The dollar amount of property taxes and interest you will be paying and your tax bracket, since these two items are tax deductible
3. How much your house is likely to appreciate in price per year
4. How long you are likely to be living in the community before you move

Whether you should buy or rent, then, is a question that must be analyzed on an individual basis. It will vary from time to time and place to place and from person to person. You might be living in an area that is overbuilt with apartments. Hence, rents might be relatively low. If that is the case at a time when interest rates are very high and few homes are being built and hence they are very costly, you could be better off to rent at least for a time. If, later, apartments are no longer overbuilt and hence rents rise and at the same time interest rates decline, this might be the time to investigate home ownership.

When you decide whether to rent or buy you should go back to Chapter 2 and review the material on the personal budget and on housing expenditures. You should compare your housing expenses from renting and from buying in a carefully drawn-up budget.

Tenant's Rights

If you rent, you have certain rights; however, you also have certain responsibilities. Although there are some apartment owners and homeowners who will rent on a month-to-month basis, most require a lease. Leases generally run for six months or a year. This means you are committed for that period; you cannot ordinarily break a lease. However, there are exceptions. If you are transferred by your employer, most states have laws that will permit the lease to be broken by paying one month's rent. Indeed, you should put this into the lease; a statement in a lease indicating that if you are transferred or other mitigating circumstances occur, the lease shall become null and void is desirable. Read your lease carefully. It will spell out all of your rights and responsibilities. Moreover, don't hesitate to request that certain things be added to your lease if you think it necessary: such things as when the rent is due, who will pay the utilities, the fact that certain repairs are needed when you move in, the amount of the deposit, the condition of the rug, the broken patio door, and the like. Be a reasonable tenant, but know your rights. While there are unreasonable landlords, most of them will deal fairly with you if you do with them.

Most landlords will demand a deposit, which may vary from $100 to several hundred dollars or often the equivalent of one month's rent. Be sure the lease states you will get this back if you vacate the rental unit in as good and clean condition as you accepted it.

If you are a student, you may want your lease to run concurrently with the school year. Or, if you want it for a longer time, you may want a clause in it to permit you to sublease it, say during the summer.

A landlord who won't honor the terms of the lease can be held accountable. In most states, there are small claims courts or the equivalent where you can easily and inexpensively make the landlord fulfill the contract.

Many college students often complain they never get their deposit back; this is often their number one complaint. There is no need for this if you have not caused any damage. But treat the property as if it were your own. Many students are quite careful inside their unit, but very careless about running over lawns, flowers, shrubs, and the like.

FACTORS TO CONSIDER IN BUYING OR BUILDING A HOME

A number of factors must be considered before buying or building a home. First of all, the decision must be made between renting and owning your home. I noted above there are some advantages to apartment living, and the same applies to rented homes. This is a personal thing; some people are natural homeowners, some are not. For our purposes, we will assume that the decision has been made to be a homeowner. The thing you have to decide is what price range can you afford.

How Much House Can You Afford?

There used to be and to some extent still are, four rules of thumb that are used by mortgage lenders to indicate how much of a house a prospective homeowner could afford. They are

1. The price of the home (including the lot) should be no more than two and one-half times the purchaser's annual gross (before tax) income.
2. The amount borrowed to purchase a home should be no more than two times the purchaser's gross annual income.
3. The monthly mortgage payments of a homeowner (which includes reduction of principal, interest, taxes, and insurance—PITI) should be no more than 25 percent of the homeowner's gross income.
4. Total housing costs should not exceed one week's take-home pay (note this is net, not gross, income).

The first three rules are not all that different; they all work out about the same. Under the first rule a person making $18,000 per year could swing a house worth $45,000. He could also finance about $36,000 of it under the second rule and hence would need a down payment of about $9,000. This is the often standard 20 percent.

Under the third rule he could pay $375 per month (18,000 ÷ 12 = $1,500 × 25% = $375). Moreover, historically about 1 percent of the mortgage would cover the monthly payment needed to cover the reduction of principal, interest, taxes, and insurance. In the $36,000 mortgage noted above this amounts to $360. Since the person making $18,000 per year could pay $375, the rule agrees with the first two.

Rule four was more often applied to renters but sometimes to homeowners as well. Under it the person could not quite qualify under the case noted above. One week's gross pay is $346 (18,000 ÷ 52). The net (after taxes) would be even less depending upon a number of things.

In recent years all of the rules have been stretched a bit. Obviously the higher a down payment you are able to make, the more house you can afford. But the rules have been modified in other ways. The 2½ times rule is now sometimes the 3 times rule. The 2 times rule is now sometimes the 2½ times rule, and the 25 percent has been modified to 30 percent in some cases. This has been done because interest cost and construction costs, and hence housing costs, have risen faster than income. In addition, many people have been willing to make a greater sacrifice to acquire a home because home ownership has proven to be a good investment. If you do this, do so with care, and budget wisely. If you are a two-income family this is easier to do, and many homeowners have done so. Indeed, this also partly explains why there are more and more two-income families.

New House or Older House?

Since you have decided to become a homeowner, you must choose whether you want to buy a new house or an older one or to build one from the ground up. Also you must decide whether to deal with a real estate agent or the owner directly. When buying a new house, you are at least usually assured of getting one in which everything works. Or if the wiring is wrong or the roof leaks, the builder will usually repair it at no cost. A greater degree of expertise is needed to evaluate an older house to determine that everything in it is in working order. If something goes wrong after you have bought it, the previous owner will not usually make an adjustment. On the other hand, if the house is relatively new, say two or three years old, most of the bugs and defects that appear in new houses (e.g., wiring, etc.) will have been repaired.

If the house is quite old, it may be more difficult to finance than a new one. Lenders generally require higher down payments on really old houses. If the house is used but relatively new, there will be an existing mortgage on it. There may be a problem if the new buyer is unable to take it over. A second mortgage may be required. This is explained in greater detail below.

The Energy-Efficient Home

With today's high cost of energy you should give some weight to the degree to which the home you are considering buying is energy-efficient. In the case of new homes minimum amounts of insulation are now required in the walls and ceiling by various local building codes. However, weatherstripping around doors and windows is not always included. If you live in the north, you should also check the cost of storm windows if they are not included.

Homes built prior to the 1970s, when energy was cheap, often did not have adequate insulation. Hence, if you are considering an older home you should check this.

Remember too that if there are trees near your house that provide shade, they will reduce your air-conditioning bill if you live in a section of the country that has long hot summers.

Ceiling fans are coming back. A home with ceiling fans will lessen substantially the amount of time your air conditioning will need to run. And fans use much much less energy than an air conditioner. If the home has two separate heating and air conditioning units, it is a more energy-efficient home. This is because a section of the house can be isolated and not heated or cooled if it is not being used. Even if your house has only one unit, you can reduce energy consumption somewhat by turning off the ceiling or floor vent and not heating or cooling a specific room.

Remember too that a two-story house is more energy-efficient than a rambling one-story ranch style house with the same livable square footage. (It is also cheaper to build.) This is because there is less roof for heat or coolness to escape.

While a house that is highly energy-efficient will usually cost more than one that is less efficient, this is usually more than offset in lower household operation costs. See Chapter 2 on the budget for household operation costs. Remember too that a highly energy-efficient home will also have a higher resale value. Finally, keep in mind that you may make almost any home more energy-efficient by adding more insulation, weatherstripping around windows and doors (or storm doors), and by planting shade trees.

Building a House to Specifications

In building a house, the owner will have a lot of headaches, but this may be the only way to get what one really wants. The headaches come from disagreements and misunderstandings with the contractor and from the fact that the average person does not have construction expertise. Also, the average person may not be able to read blueprints well enough really to visualize what the completed structure will look like. As construction takes place, owners will discover things they will want changed and this is expensive. If an architect is hired to take care of some of these things and draw up plans, there is, of course, the added expense of those fees.

My advice is, do not make the first house you own one you build from the ground up. Buy an existing house first and learn something about houses. Then later if you have the time to devote to it, and the patience, you may want to build your dream home from the ground up. If you build, you will need a construction loan to build it and then a long-term mortgage after it is completed.

Using a Realtor

If you buy a house through a realtor, it may cost you more; on the other hand, it may be worth it. While the seller of a house pays the realtor's commissions, he or she will generally try to pass them on to the buyer in the form of a higher price. Sometimes sellers are successful and sometimes they are not.

Realtors' fees vary from state to state and even within towns in a given state but they generally run from 5 to 6 percent. Usually in the bigger cities they are 6 percent, while in some of the smaller towns they are closer to 5. Many people wishing to sell their home find the market value of it (sometimes they deliberately set a price way above the market value) and then add the realtor's fees to this figure.

Most listings are now on a cross-listing basis, which means that listing it with any realtor in town will automatically list it with all realtors. A listing is for at least ninety days and during that time sellers must pay the realtor fees even if they sell the house to someone on their own. After the listing has expired, then the homeowner may sell without paying the commissions if it is to a buyer who has not been shown the home by the realtor. If a prospective buyer has been shown the home by a realtor during the listed period, the commissions must be paid if it is bought within a given perod, usually six months, after the listing has expired.

Whether realtors' fees are shifted to the buyer in the form of a higher price depends upon the tightness of the housing market. But realtors are supposed to protect both the buyer and the seller. For example, a good realtor will discourage a homeowner from pricing the house unrealistically high. Also, a realtor will encourage a homeowner to make any necessary repairs to get the house in first-class condition.

The Neighborhood

In considering proposed construction or the purchase of an existing structure, the buyer must take the neighborhood into account. With the growth of a city or even a fairly small town, neighborhoods or districts are created. For the most part, they are the result of economic pressures, which cause them to be in a constant state of flux. As a result of changes in neighborhood—more often than not from a higher to a lower level of use—there develops what is known to the real estate appraiser as economic obsolescence. *Economic obsolescence* is defined as the impairment of desirability and usefulness of property brought about by economic and environmental changes of a neighborhood.

In general, older sections of a city begin their decline soon after newer sections begin to make a strong appeal to home buyers. The prospective purchaser of a home should look for a neighborhood containing a high percentage of owner-occupied homes as distinguished from tenant-occupied homes. Neighborhoods containing a high percentage of the former tend to be more stable with regard to value. Further, one should look for a neighborhood that contains well-planned and well-located homes of the same physical characteristics. It is also desirable if the residents of the neighborhood have good steady jobs with above-average income. Nearness to schools and good shopping centers is also a factor.

Contrary to what one would expect, in some older sections in some cities property values have held up very well; often values have even appreciated. This is because they are desirable places to live, for example, the Georgetown section of Washington, D.C., and Back Bay in Boston. In addition, urban renewal or restoration will usually enhance the value of older property.

The checklist below should be helpful in selecting the neighborhood. Consider each of the following items to determine whether the location of the property will satisfy your personal needs and preferences:

1. Convenience of public transportation
2. Stores conveniently located
3. School conveniently located
4. Absence of excessive traffic noise
5. Absence of smoke and unpleasant odors from factories
6. Play area available for children
7. Fire and police protection provided
8. Residential usage safeguarded by adequate zoning
9. Traffic patterns during the rush hours
10. Taxes and possible future assessments for sewers, water systems, etc.
11. General stability of the neighborhood

The Lot and the House

In selecting a building site, the buyer must notice such details as whether it is located in the prevailing wind, which may carry noxious odors from factories and railroads. The person considering the purchase of a lot must consider a number of questions. Will the lot be appropriate for the proposed structure? Is the drainage good enough to prevent standing water in the event of abnormal or even normal rainfall? Will the soil support the proposed structure? In the event septic tanks are necessary, have percolation tests been run to determine the ability of the soil to handle a septic tank? An important area of investigation is the availability of utilities, such as electricity, telephone, and water supply. In some parts of the country the need to drill for water would render many sites uneconomical. Probably one of the best ways to select a site after it has been determined that the neighborhood is satisfactory is to use such a checklist as the following, which can be expanded to meet local conditions.

Lot

Consider each of the following to determine whether the lot is sufficiently large and properly improved:

1. Size of front yard satisfactory
2. Size of rear and side yards satisfactory
3. Walks provide access to front and service entrances
4. Drive provides easy access to garage
5. Lot appears to drain satisfactorily
6. Lawn and planting satisfactory
7. Septic tank (if any) in good operating condition

House

Consider each of the following to determine whether the house is satisfactory:

EXTERIOR CONSTRUCTION

1. Wood porch floors and steps
2. Windows, doors, and screens
3. Gutters and wood cornice
4. Wood siding
5. Mortar joints
6. Roofing
7. Chimneys
8. Paint on exterior woodwork
9. Driveway and sidewalk

INTERIOR CONSTRUCTION

1. Walls free of excessive cracks
2. Walls and ceiling free of stains caused by leaking roof or sidewalls
3. Door locks in operating condition
4. Windows move freely
5. Fireplace works properly
6. Basement dry and will resist moisture penetration
7. Mechanical equipment and electrical wiring and switches adequate and in operating condition
8. Type of heating equipment suitable
9. Adequate insulation in walls, floor, ceiling, or roof
10. Wood floor finish
11. Linoleum floors
12. Condition of rugs

13. Sink top
14. Kitchen appliances
15. Bathroom fixtures
16. Painting and papering
17. Exposed joists and beams

Condominium or House?

Some people prefer a condominium to a house. A condominium provides some of the benefits of owning a house and some of the benefits of apartment living. Condominiums are apartment-like structures, but residents receive *title* to their units. They must make a down payment and arrange their mortgage, if financed, just as for a house. Moreover, they can sell at any time they wish.

The condominium owners have the same tax benefits as homeowners and they build up equity like a homeowner. They have all the building maintenance problems to take care of in their unit.

They are more like an apartment dweller in that they have no yard work to perform. There may be a common yard that they can enjoy with other condominium owners in the building. Sometimes this includes a common swimming pool, tennis court, and putting green. Instead of maintaining these facilities, the individual is assessed a fee each month and a maintenance crew is hired.

When buying a condominium, the owner joins the condominium association and all members have one vote in deciding matters in accordance with the provisions as set forth in the condominium agreement that all members must agree to abide by. Generally speaking, the condominium owners may sell their unit to anyone they choose. However, the condominium may contain a general statement requiring that new owners be acceptable to the members, and if they are not that the group will have the right to buy the unit back, if it chooses to do so.

Choosing between a house and a condominium is a personal matter. Those who want some of the benefits of home ownership but not all of the problems might choose this compromise, although they give up some backyard privacy.

Town House

This concept has several meanings. In the bigger Eastern cities it may merely be a house in the city rather than in the suburbs. In some cases, older decaying areas have been renovated and have become fashionable residential sections of the city. In many cases town houses are expensive. The Georgetown area in Washington, D.C., is an example of an area with expensive renovated town houses.

In other cases, the town house may be a multifamily unit, with each resident owning the unit he or she occupies. In this case, the town house is similar to the condominium, although there may not be a common yard, swimming pool, and the like. Of course, all the tax benefits of home ownership apply.

Co-ops

In some cities, there are co-op apartments and even co-op homes. These co-ops are nonprofit corporations, and the residents of a co-op housing unit, technically speaking, do not own their unit. The corporation does, and each resident owns some stock (certificates of ownership) of the corporation. Often the number of apartments in a co-op is quite large and home co-ops may cover an entire city block. Generally, the homes are connected and are built facing the street on all four sides of the block. The center then becomes a courtyard and serves as a common backyard.

Since the apartments (or homes) in a co-op are of varying sizes (and value), the amount of stock a co-oper has is prorated accordingly. The price residents have to pay for the stock is then similar to the down payment on a house. The co-oper than makes a monthly payment (which varies in accordance with the value of the individual unit) to the co-op; this includes interest, taxes, insurance and reduction of principal, and the co-op makes one mortgage payment to the mortgage holder. There is then one common mortgage on twenty or thirty different rental units rather than each being financed separately. As the years pass and the mortgage is reduced, the theoretical value of the co-op shares rises.

Since co-op housing is a relatively new development, few of them have been around long enough to have their mortgage paid off. However, when the common mortgage is paid off, there is usually some arrangement for the co-op to be dissolved and all co-opers to obtain title to their units. Each co-oper may be expected to help in doing yard work or there may be a monthly fee to have this done.

A co-op is similar to a condominium, but legally it is different. In a condominium, each unit has a separate mortgage and each resident has title to his or her property. In a co-op, there is one mortgage and the resident owns shares in the co-op. However, co-op owners may sell their shares to nearly anyone. Sometimes, however, the prospective owner must be acceptable to the group. If the person is not, the co-op corporation will buy the shares back, generally speaking.

That portion of the co-oper's monthly payment that goes for the payment of interest or property taxes is fully deductible for tax purposes, just as in the case of the home or condominium owner. The co-op may offer one advantage over the individual residential unit, since on a mortgage often for hundreds of thousands of dollars (or even millions) the interest rate may be a little lower.

One question may have occurred to you. Since a co-op is a nonprofit corporation, who would have an incentive to establish one? The answer is realtors, builders, and land developers, who would stand to make a profit due to realtors' fees or in the construction of the building. There is one possible disadvantage to owning a co-op. Since there is one mortgage and since the value of the co-op shares rises as equity is built up, the new prospective buyer would need a large down payment to buy a co-op unit. In the case of an individual mortgage, it can be refinanced, but with a common mortgage this is not possible. This problem can be solved in some states where banks and savings and loan associations can make long-term loans using co-op stock as security.

Mobile Homes

Recently more and more people have been buying mobile homes. At one time these units appealed primarily to people whose jobs required that they move a good deal, like construction workers. Today, however, primarily because they are so much cheaper than a regular home, many young couples as well as older retired people are buying them.

There are two varieties of mobile homes. There is the true mobile home, which is on wheels and is moved from place to place. Many retired people have these trailers and go south during the winter. Then there is the so-called "moble home," which is on blocks and may have elaborate extensions built onto it. It can never again be moved and will remain permanently in a trailer or mobile home park.

In the past a mobile home was always a trailer with or without wheels. Recently, *motor homes* have been developed; these are self-propelled units generally built on a truck frame. Many of these units have become the second homes discussed below.

Mobile homes were financed like cars until a few years ago. Loans for them were considered consumer loans, the interest rates were similar to rates on cars, and they had to be amortized over several years just like auto loans. Indeed, some lenders still feel this way; if they have wheels, they can be moved, and thus loans for them are similar to an auto loan. However, in the last few years, a number of changes have been made. Mobile home loans are now made for up to twelve years. One reason is that mobile homes may now run as high as $15,000 or $16,000. Interest rates on mobile home loans, on the other hand, are still in the same general range as on auto loans: around 14 percent or more. Generally speaking, at least a 10 percent down payment is required to obtain a mobile home loan.

Prefabricated Houses

Until recently, the use of prefabricated homes was greatly restricted by zoning laws. While still true in many areas this is slowly changing. Often prefabricated homes are found in the low-income areas of the community or are used as vacation homes. Until recently lenders did not finance them over more than ten years. This too is slowly changing. Prefabricated homes while still cheaper than others, now sell for up to $50,000 and are a much better product than a decade ago. Another advantage of buying a prefabricated home is that it takes much less time to assemble it than to construct a home from the ground up. The major disadvantage is that you will have less choice and flexibility as to style and design.

Second or Vacation Homes

Some of the more affluent members of society have summer or vacation homes. These are, if not mobile, usually located on a lake, at the beach, in the mountains, or at some other resort area. In some cases these homes are also an investment property. Arrangements can be made to rent them when they are not used by the owner. Most large resort areas have a service that makes the rental arrangements. People have purchased single-family units, condominiums, motor homes, prefabs, and trailers for their second homes. Of these single-family units, condominiums are the easiest to rent, since a service usually exists to do this for the property owner.

HOW MUCH IS A HOME WORTH?

When a person is purchasing a newly constructed home, there is little that one can do concerning the price; the builder sets the price and for all practical purposes it generally remains at that level. Seldom will the builder bargain. The price is usually the cost of the house plus the builder's profit margin. A prospective purchaser can estimate the value of an older home that he or she is interested in purchasing. In addition, individuals placing their homes on the market should be able to estimate the selling price. Between the owner and the buyer who deals directly with the owner there may then be genuine bargaining.

The total worth of a property is made up of three parts—the house itself, the land, and other improvements.

The first step in determining the value of the house is to measure it. Each of its rooms should be measured, including closet space, but not including the garage or other unfinished space such as a patio. Suppose it contains fifteen hundred square feet. Next, ask your bank, local contractor, or real estate dealer for the current building costs in your area. Let's say that they are $40 per square foot. Therefore, the house would cost about $60,000 to build today. In recent years construction costs have risen rapidly, as shown by Table 16–2. In this case $60,000 is the basic worth of the house—if it is in top condition. If it is not, the cost of the needed repairs such as new screens, painting, a new roof, etc., must be deducted. The basic cost, even if the house is in top condition, must be reduced somewhat on an older home to take into account an allowance for depreciation; the house is, after all, partly worn out. If the house is functionally obsolescent or in a rapidly changing neighborhood, its value may be further affected. For example, if it lacks central heat or air conditioning or has high ceilings and major remodeling is required, this detracts from the value. While this is related to repairs it is somewhat different.

The value of the house is further lowered if it is in a decaying neighborhood. This is really discounting, to the present, the future expected decline in the area. Conversely, if the neighborhood is being restored, its future value is likely to rise because of this. After you have valued a house in this manner, you must then add an additional sum for the lot.

Another method of evaluating an existing house is to study the prices at which similar houses have been sold recently. This method, however, provides only a bench mark. First of all, few houses are precisely alike. Also other similar houses may be in better or in worse condition, and the location may make a difference. In addition, some sellers are in a hurry to sell, others are not, and this can affect prices. Consequently, analyzing the market price of recently sold similar houses will result in a range of prices. You must then make an allowance for any needed repairs or remodeling as well as an allowance for differences in the size of the lot and the desirability of the location. Nevertheless, analyzing the market price range of recently sold houses is a beginning. Applying judgment to that plus keeping in mind construction costs will enable you to appraise fairly a house that is for sale.

TABLE 16–2. *Percentage change in cost of selected building materials.*

MATERIAL	1974	1975	1976	1977	1978	1979*
Concrete products	20.3%	7.0%	5.7%	6.9%	14.6%	12.2%
Douglas fir	—15.3	19.6	26.3	7.6	20.5	11.6
Southern pine	—18.5	10.1	27.8	24.7	8.1	11.6
Plumbing fixtures	24.0	1.3	9.6	7.1	6.0	10.4
Heating equipment	22.1	4.5	4.3	4.6	5.8	8.5
Hardwood lumber	—22.7	—12.9	36.4	14.0	30.2	8.2
Paint	25.8	5.2	4.2	4.9	6.9	7.3
Millwork	2.0	7.4	11.1	11.5	18.3	6.6
Plywood	—10.3	13.9	21.0	10.0	10.3	5.9
Asphalt roofing	47.7	5.0	2.5	20.8	11.1	4.5
Building board	1.0	8.6	9.5	18.4	9.3	—2.1
All materials	16.5%	6.0%	9.9%	8.7%	12.0%	10.2%

*12 months ending October.
Source: Savings and Loan Fact Book '80, United States League of Savings Associations, p. 22.

Land (Lot)

Using the market price as described above to evaluate real estate results in the house and the lot being appraised together. If you wish to evaluate a lot separately, you can do so by reading advertisements in the local newspaper and talking with real estate brokers. This will enable you to determine the current value of a lot with a high degree of accuracy. Other lots of equal size and desirability in the same area would be worth about the same amount. The market price of similar lots that were recently sold is a good indicator of the value of a lot. Land value may also be increased substantially by a change in character of an area from rural to urban.

Other Improvements

Improvements enhance the value of the property and sometimes they should be evaluated separately—for example, if you have added them yourself. These include such items as landscaping, a garage or an added carport, a swimming pool, a basement made into a cozy playroom, an open attic that has been transformed into bedrooms, a patio, or even a well-built barbecue pit. The value of these items should be estimated and added to the total cost of the house and the land. This is normally done by taking the original cost of the improvement adjusted by depreciation or some other factor to take into account the wear and tear on it. However, during periods of rapid inflation some people use replacement cost and then adjust that down by depreciation. The grand total of the house, the land, and the improvements, after adjustments have been made as suggested above, will give an estimate of value. Table 16–3 provides a format for estimating fairly closely the value of a home.

HOME FINANCING

About nine out of ten Americans who purchase or build a residence do so with the help of some sort of mortgage financing. The mortgage is the security for the debt. The borrower is called the mortgagor and the lender the mortgagee. The borrower gives the mortgage and the lender is said to take the mortgage. Most mortgage loans are made by financial institutions, but a few individuals make some. The institutions involved are savings and loan associations, mutual savings banks, life insurance companies, mortgage banks, and some commercial banks. In addition, the trust departments of some commercial banks may finance a few mortgages, and recently credit unions were authorized to do so. However, up to now very few credit unions are active in mortgage financing.

Basically there are three main types of mortgages which we will now examine: the conventional mortgage, the FHA insured mortgage, and the VA guaranteed mortgage. There are also a few unusual mortgages such as single payment, variable, and graduated; they too will be examined below.

The Conventional Mortgage

A conventional fixed-payment mortgage is an arrangement solely between the lending institution and the buyer of the home. The institution lends its money and, until a few years ago, it assumed the entire risk of loss, but now there is insurance which pays any losses suffered by the lender due to a default. Conventional mortgage loans may be made for as long as thirty years, but many of them run over far fewer years than this.

In most states, savings and loan associations are now able to make loans up to 95

TABLE 16–3. *How to find the value of any house*

Fill in the form below, one item at a time. As subtotals for such items as repairs are reached, add or subtract them as the case may be. The figures you will fill in at the end of the chart will be a realistic appraisal of what your house is worth at today's prices.

Room no. 1 Length _____ feet	Width _____ feet	Length × Width _____ feet
Room no. 2 Length _____ feet	Width _____ feet	Length × Width _____ feet
Room no. 3 Length _____ feet	Width _____ feet	Length × Width _____ feet
etc.		

Total Square Feet
Cost of construction today $ _____ per square foot.
Cost to build today: _____ sq. ft. × $_____ (cost per square foot) = house value $_____.

Cost of needed repairs:
    1. Screens   _____
    2. Outside paint   _____
    3. Kitchen wallpaper _____
    4. Gutters   _____
    5. Other   _____
                              Deduct $_____ for repairs needed.

Functional obsolescence:
    1. Bathroom fixtures _____
    2. Lighting   _____
    3. Lack of central heat
       or air conditioning _____
    4. Other   _____
                              Deduct $_____ for modernizing.

Changes in neighborhood affecting value:
    Add $_____ (if neighborhood has improved)
    or
    Deduct $_____ (if neighborhood has deteriorated)

Land Value:
    Value of land by comparison $_____ (add to total)

Improvements:
    1. Fireplace   _____
    2. Basement playroom _____
    3. Finished attic   _____
    4. Patio   _____
    5. Storage wall   _____
    6. Under-stairs closets _____
    7. Full bath added   _____
    8. Enclosed porch   _____
    9. Landscaping   _____
  10. Insulated attic   _____
  11. Attached garage   _____
  12. Swimming pool   _____
  13. Other   _____
        Add: $_____for improvements

                                  Total value of property $_____

percent of the value of the home. Up until recently, 80 percent was the maximum amount in most states because there was no mortgage insurance available on conventional mortgages. However, with the coming of private mortgage insurance (PMI), lenders are willing to make larger loans and the law allows it in most states. PMI works just like any insurance plan. A premium is assessed against the homeowner, and this goes into a kitty used to pay any losses the lender might suffer if there is a default. To be sure, the interest charged on a 95 percent mortgage loan is usually a little higher than on a 90 percent loan, which in turn is higher than on an 80 percenter. While lenders may lend up to 95 percent of the value of the home, how much they actually advance varies from time to time. When money is very scarce they require a larger down payment than when money is more plentiful.

The interest rate on mortgages varies from time to time and place to place. Usury laws vary by state and this sets the upper ceiling. When money is more plentiful and interest rates are below the usury ceiling, they still differ from state to state because the demand for loans relative to the supply of mortgage money varies geographically. Generally speaking, rates are lower in the Northeast and Middle Atlantic states than in the Sun Belt and in California. The Northeast and Middle Atlantic states during such times (plentiful money) are considered surplus states and often money from them moves to the mortgage deficit states in the Sun Belt. The real reason for this, of course, is that growth is faster in the Sun Belt.

The rate of interest also varies from time to time. Generally speaking, all geographical areas have relative shortages of money at times and relatively plentiful supplies at others (but as noted above the relative degree varies regionally). Occasionally mortgage money is so scarce that it is very difficult and sometimes even impossible to obtain at any interest rate. This was the case in the late summer of 1973 and through much of 1974.

In 1979 mortgage interest rates hit an all-time high, and even bumped into interest rate usury ceilings in some states. Lenders responded by requiring a larger down payment, and by tightening credit standards in other ways.

The FHA Mortgage

The FHA mortgage is a loan secured by a mortgage and given by an approved lending institution, but the loan is insured by the Federal Housing Administration. It is important to note that the government does not do the lending but merely acts in the nature of an insurance company. The borrower pays .5 percent (that is ½ of 1) annually of the unpaid loan balance as a premium for the "insurance policy." In the event of default in the payment of the loan by the buyer, the lending institution is paid for certain losses—not in cash but by long-term government bonds.

There is an upper limit to the insurance FHA provides. On a single-family dwelling, the insurance provided is equal to the loan but with a maximum of $60,000. Because of this, if you buy a home under FHA financing for more than $60,000, you have to have a down payment for the difference.

In order for a prospective home buyer to qualify for an FHA-insured loan, he or she must meet certain credit and income requirements. In addition, the home itself must meet minimum appraisal standards as established by the FHA. This latter fact provides the buyer with some protection. On the other hand, this necessitates FHA inspection of the home, which takes time. This and other FHA red tape result in more time being required for a FHA loan to be approved than in the case of a conventional loan. Although the maximum length of FHA loans changes from time to time, the current maximum maturity is thirty years. The minimum down payment required on an FHA mortgage varies from time to time as FHA regulations change; this down payment also varies with the value of the house. At the present time, an approved lending institution may lend up to 97 percent of the first $25,000 of the appraised value of the house, and 95 percent of that portion over $25,000. On a $50,000 house then, a down payment of $2,000 would be required. Because these loan-to-value ratios are frequently changed by the FHA commissioner, it is necessary to obtain the current figures by asking a local real estate broker or lending institution.

The maximum interest rate on an FHA-insured loan is set by the federal housing commissioner, subject to statutory limitations, and it too is changed from time to time. The current legal maximum rate is 11.5 percent—plus .5 percent for the insurance premium—making a total to be paid of 12 percent.

Sometimes FHA financing is more difficult to obtain than conventional and sometimes the reverse is the case. This is because the legal ceiling on interest rates on these two types of mortgage loans are not always the same. However, during the last decade all interest rates have risen.

The VA-guaranteed Mortgage

A VA-guaranteed mortgage is a loan on which the Veterans Administration guarantees payment to the lending institution or to an individual lender in the event of default by the veteran-buyer under the terms of the Servicemen's Readjustment Act of 1944 as amended. There are limits, however, and VA can guarantee only up to 60 percent of the sales price of the house (since a VA loan does not require a down payment, the sales price and the loan may be the same) with a maximum guarantee of $25,000.

To qualify for a loan of this type, the veteran must have served in World War II between September 16, 1940, and July 25, 1947, or in the Korean conflict between June 27, 1950, and January 31, 1955. Under the previous terms of the act, which was last amended in 1970, veterans of both World War II and the Korean conflict may apply any time. There is no longer an expiration date. Congress passed an act in 1966 which made veterans of Vietnam eligible for the VA mortgage, and in 1970 the amended act also extended indefinitely the period during which they may apply.

Also in 1970 Congress extended the benefits to all personnel who have served honorably in the armed forces. Hence, today all veterans are eligible. A few years ago Congress for the first time permitted veterans who have had one VA loan but sold the house which it financed, to obtain a second VA loan in certain cases.

The present legal ceiling on VA-guaranteed mortgages is 11.5 percent, but this changes periodically. While a VA mortgage can be financed with no down payment, the maximum maturity period is now thirty years. The maximum loan that a lender may make under a VA guaranteed loan is $100,000, but as noted above the maximum guarantee is only 60 percent of the sales price with a maximum guarantee of $25,000.

Billions of dollars of investors' money are tied up in various types of mortgages. Figure 16-1 and Table 16-4 illustrate total residential mortgages outstanding over the years, as well as mortgages outstanding by type of lender and type of property.

Single-Payment Straight Mortgages

Prior to the 1930s, financing the purchase of a home was quite different. Usually the mortgage was for about five years and no provisions were made for monthly amortization payments. Rather, only the interest was paid every year, and at the end of the period, when the mortgage became due, the entire sum was to be repaid. Under such a system, of course, home buyers had to do their own budgeting and lay aside a sum every month. Very few people, however, could save enough money to repay the entire mortgage in five years;

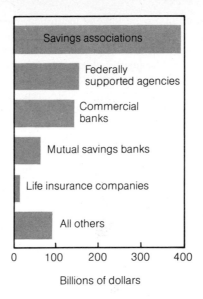

Savings associations

Federally
supported agencies

Commercial
banks

Mutual savings banks

Life insurance companies

All others

0   100   200   300   400

Billions of dollars

FIGURE 16–1. *Mortgage loans outstanding on one- to four-family homes, by type of lender, year-end 1979. (Source: Savings and Loan Fact Book '80, United States League of Savings Associations, p. 31.)*

consequently when the mortgage came due, at least part of it had to be refinanced. A mortgage usually had to be refinanced several times before it was finally liquidated.

One of the shortcomings of the single-payment mortgage arose over its refinancing. If it came due at a time when loans were hard to get, refinancing was often difficult. Also the process resulted in higher total interest costs than amortized mortgages. Interest had to be paid on the entire amount borrowed for the entire period, rather than monthly on the declining balance, as is now the case.

Second Mortgages

Second mortgages were discussed in the previous chapter. Here we will merely note that seconds come into existence when the purchaser does not have sufficient funds to make the necessary down payment to pay the owner his or her equity in an existing (not a new) home. The purchaser pays off what proportion of the equity he can and assumes a second mortgage for the remainder.

The Wrap-around Mortgage

Another way of financing a home if the buyer does not have enough funds to assume an existing mortgage, is to use the wrap around mortgage. This is often done if the seller is willing and able to finance the sale and assume the wrap around mortgage; the new mortgage literally wraps around the old mortgage. This technique works particularly well if the existing mortgage is quite small. An example will make this clear. Suppose a seller has an older home for sale for $50,000 with only a $10,000 mortgage left on it. If the buyer has

TABLE 16-4. *Mortgage loans outstanding, by type of lender and type of property, year-end 1979 (preliminary, in billions of dollars).*

| LENDER | RESIDENTIAL PROPERTIES | | | COMMERCIAL PROPERTIES | FARM PROPERTIES | TOTAL MORTGAGE LOANS |
	ONE- TO FOUR- FAMILY	MULTI- FAMILY	TOTAL			
Savings associations	$393.4	$ 38.5	$ 431.9	$ 43.8	*	$ 475.8
Commercial banks	146.1	12.6	158.7	77.7	$10.4	246.8
Mutual Savings banks	64.7	17.2	81.9	16.9	*	98.7
Life insurance companies ..	15.4	19.4	34.8	72.1	12.3	119.2
All others	248.7	44.3	293.0	29.5	70.7	393.2
Total	$868.3	$132.0	$1,000.3	$240.0	$93.4	$1,333.7

Note: Components may not add to totals due to rounding.
* Less than $50 million.
Source: Savings and Loan Fact Book '80, United States League of Savings Associations, p. 31.

$15,000, he could pay that down and the seller might take a $35,000 mortgage which includes (wraps around) the $10,000 due on the original. The seller would then continue to pay off the original $10,000 mortgage and the buyer would need worry only about the new $35,000 one.

In some cases, however, the wrap around mortgage may result in a violation of the usury laws. Consider the following situation. A house which has a $40,000 mortgage at 8 percent is sold for $100,000. The buyer pays $20,000 down and signs a mortgage of $80,000 with the seller at 12 percent and the seller continues paying off the old 8 percent $40,000 mortgage. This yields the seller about $9,600 the first year on the $80,000 mortgage but after paying 8 percent on the $40,000 (which amounts to about $3,200) the net return is $6,400. What percentage return is this to the seller? $6,400 is 8 percent of $80,000. But the seller only advanced $40,000 and $6,400 is 16 percent of $40,000, and some attorneys feel that is what the courts may hold to be the true interest rate in a case such as this. Moreover, as you will recall from Chapter 15, this 16 percent return may violate various state usury laws. Most importantly, individuals are still subject to all usury laws, even though the federal government nullified usury laws insofar as institutional lenders are concerned in 1980. Check this out very carefully before you finance any mortgage, wrap arounds or other types.

The Graduated Payment Mortgage (GPM)

Under this mortgage the monthly payments start out substantially below what they should be but then increase by $3 or $4 per month for a number of years. This increase usually levels off after 5 or 10, or sometimes even 15 years. Since some of the principle is repaid later than under a straight fixed mortgage, the homeowner pays more interest. However, such a mortgage permits more young and lower income people to qualify for home ownership, if their income is expected to rise in the near future. This mortgage may also have a variable interest built into it. If it does, then how much monthly payments increase per month in the future is also in part determined by how much interest rates rise in the future. It is conceivable that during the first few years there could be negative amortization (increase in the principal borrowed) if interest rates rise rapidly enough. The GPM is in the experimental stage and very few have been made.

Other (Unusual) Mortgages

There are three other unusual mortgages which are being experimented with. First, the flexible rate mortgage. It provides for the payment of interest only (nothing for principal) for 2 or 3 years. Then payment for principal is added. Second, there is the deferred interest mortgage which defers some of the interest. Under it less interest and principal than is needed to amortize a loan is collected the first 3 or 4 years, and after that time the deficiency is made up. This mortgage may be similar to the graduated payment mortgage discussed above, but the adjustment is made in one or two steps rather than continuously each month. Finally, there is the price level adjusted mortgage. Here the mortgage payments are simply adjusted upward from time to time to take into account inflation. These last 3 mortgages I have introduced are very much still in the experimental stage and very few of them have been made.

Variable Interest Rate Mortgages

Recently it has been proposed that the interest rate that lenders charge on mortgages be adjusted periodically to reflect more nearly the true market rate. The proponents of this view hold that it makes no sense to be locked in at 8 or 9 percent for twenty years when in five or ten years from now the market may dictate 6 percent. While a 6 percent interest rate on home mortgages may seem fantastic today and something we will never see, that is what the rate was not much more than ten years ago. On the other hand, rates may go up to 12 or 14 percent, or even higher.

Under variable interest mortgages, the rate is subject to being adjusted every six months but only if certain other rates such as marketable U.S. government (or corporate) bond rates change. Normally there is a limit (usually two or three percent) on the overall upward or downward movement during the life of the mortgage. There are three methods of adjusting the variable interest rate. First, changing the monthly payment with the maturity remaining constant. Second, changing the length of the maturity with the monthly payment remaining constant. And third, various combinations of the first two.

The difficulty in using a variable rate is that when rates are high the borrower may be willing to sign a variable contract and hope that rates come down. But the lending institution is more reluctant to do so. During times when rates are low, the reverse is the case: the lender favors variable rates, the borrower does not. Consequently, variable rates are not being used much but a few savings and loan associations are experimenting with them.

Renegotiable Mortgages

A modification of the variable interest rate mortgage is the re-negotiable mortgage, sometimes called the roll over mortgage. Under it, interest rates are re-negotiated every 3, 4, or 5 years as the case may be. There would be a negotiated rate change as the market changed, but it would not be an automatic adjustment tied to some money market indicator. Under this mortgage the lender is obliged to re-negotiate and renew the mortgage; he cannot cancel it. The borrower, on the other hand, may pull out at renewal time and get a new mortgage elsewhere. These new re-negotiable mortgages were approved by the federal regulatory agencies in April of 1980, and all federally chartered savings and loan associations are now permitted to make them. The maximum interest rate adjustment (either up or down) is ½ of 1 percent per year for a total of 2½ percent on a 5-year re-negotiable. There is also a 5 percent limit over the entire 20 or 30 year life of the mortgage.

In Canada these re-negotiable mortgages are much more common than in the U.S. They are not a new innovation, however. Prior to the 1930's this is how mortgages were typically financed, as noted above under the single payment straight mortgages.

Reverse Mortgages

Older people whose mortgage is paid off and wish to retire may sign a reverse mortgage whereby they sell their home back to a lending institution. Instead of making a monthly payment, they receive one. As time passes they own a smaller and smaller portion of their home; or, what is the same, a larger and larger mortgage debt is built up on it again, as their equity in it declines. Usually only a portion of the value of the house (about 50 to 75 percent) can be reverse-mortgaged this way. While this can provide retirement income for a time, it is risky business because after a number of years if the retirees are still living they will have to sell their home to pay off the debt. Or they can try to refinance it and pay off another regular mortgage once again. However, if they were in such financial difficulty they had to reverse-mortgage their home, they probably could not now pay off a regular mortgage. My advice would be, if you need to sell your home to obtain retirement income, sell it outright and move into a smaller one, or into an apartment, and invest the difference.

Assumptions and Refinancings

The prospective buyer who does have the necessary down payment to buy the equity in a house can take over an older existing mortgage. He or she then assumes all of the obligations of paying it off. This is often advantageous because by taking over an older existing mortgage the buyer may obtain funds at the interest rate prevailing several years ago, which might have been lower. On the other hand, if rates were higher several years ago, the buyer might want to consider refinancing.

Sometimes lending institutions will not let a buyer assume an existing mortgage at the old interest rate. They will insist on refinancing at today's presumably higher rate, or in some cases they will permit the assumption but will escalate the interest rate up to the current level. Whether or not lenders are able to force refinancing or escalate the interest rate is determined by the wording in the mortgage (deed of trust). Many (probably most) of the mortgages written during the last few years have a clause that permits the lender to require this. But some of the older ones do not.

If you have to refinance, not only must you pay today's (possibly high) interest rates, but also you must pay all the added *closing costs* which are considerable and which are avoided if you are able to obtain an assumption. Closing costs are discussed in detail below.

It should be noted that the escalation of interest rates and forced refinancing are not permitted on FHA and VA mortgages.

Penalties

Since, in giving a mortgage loan, the lender has made an investment of a substantial amount of money at, say, 10 percent for a long period of time, the lender wants to receive the interest income year by year. Over the years, interest on a mortgage may amount to thousands of dollars. Homeowners, on the other hand, might like to save this interest cost; if in the future their incomes should rise, they might want to make extra mortgage payments.

Or if they should inherit a large sum of money, they might want to pay off the mortgage—perhaps even before the ink is dry on it. Other extra or windfall income might be used to reduce greatly or pay off a mortgage early.

In order to prevent or discourage the buyer from repaying the mortgage more quickly than agreed, the lender often insists on a penalty clause. As far as lending institutions are concerned, these penalties are also defended on the basis that administrative and investment costs are involved in reinvesting early repayments, as well as on the basis that they partially compensate for lost income from interest.

In some cases, a penalty clause merely states that a fee, usually 1 or 2 percent, is charged for mortgage payments that are made in advance of the schedule. For example, if a person paid off in one payment a $5,000 mortgage, the penalty would be $50 or $100. Often, then, the penalty is small enough not to discourage greatly early repayment.

In other cases the penalty clause applies only to extra payments in excess of a given amount per year, say $1,000 or $2,000. In still other cases, penalties are calculated by applying the interest rate on the mortgage against the advance payment for so many months. There are three-month and six-month penalty clauses. For example, if a 9 percent $20,000 mortgage carried a six-month interest penalty and if you paid it off in advance, the penalty would be six months' interest on the amount paid off at 9 percent. If you paid off all $20,000, the penalty would be $900. And in some cases the penalty clause drops out completely and automatically after a given period of time, say five years. The homeowner should, however, try to get a mortgage that does not contain a penalty clause. Usually the conditions in the money market will determine whether penalties are inserted into the mortgage. If funds are hard to obtain, not only will interest rates be higher but penalty clauses will more likely be inserted into the terms. If funds are plentiful, the homeowner will receive a lower rate of interest and can more easily avoid a penalty clause. However, since a certain amount of bargaining is possible, one should always try to get a mortgage without a penalty clause or the least unfavorable penalty possible.

If one succeeds in avoiding a penalty clause, and in some cases even if one does not, it may sometimes pay to refinance. If, for example, you obtain a mortgage at a time when competitive conditions indicate a 10 or even 11 percent interest rate and then a few years later rates are only 7 or 8 percent, it may pay to refinance. Remember that in doing this you have most of the closing costs to meet again, as well as the penalty, but if interest rates have declined enough the saving may more than offset these two items.

Financing by Means of Trades

In recent years the amount of financing by means of trades has increased. For the most part, these trades have been arranged by builders and by real estate brokers. They have been encouraged by the Federal Housing Administration, which has made FHA-insured loans available for trades.

In most instances when one speaks of making a trade, one really means trading up, moving from a less expensive home to a more expensive home. In so doing, the equity of the purchaser in the cheaper (and possibly older) home is used as a down payment on the more expensive home.

Selling A House

Any time the original owner sells a house (without refinancing it), he or she is still liable to the lender if the new buyer defaults on the loan. This is true for FHA and VA mortgages as well as for the conventional mortgage. This is because the original contract between the lender and the buyer is binding insofar as the lender is concerned even though the house changes hands. It is possible for the original owner to be relieved of this obligation, but only by getting a written release from the lender. While the lender does not have to grant the release, most of them will do so. Most people selling a house, however, do not bother to get a release. Actually, there is very little possibility that they will ever suffer a financial loss because there is legal recourse against the new buyer. Also, if the new buyer takes over an existing mortgage, there is usually enough equity built up in the house so that the seller is safe. If the new owner cannot assume the mortgage and the down payment required, the house can be refinanced. In such a case, the original owner can never again be held liable. Refinancing, however, requires that all of the closing costs be paid again (see below). Only a seller who accepts a second mortgage assumes any substantial risk.

Large Down Payment vs. Small Down Payment

The size of the down payment individuals make is most often determined by the amount of cash available to them at the time they purchase the home. Assuming that one has a choice, however, the question is whether one should make a large or small down payment. Note that even when persons are seeking FHA-insured or VA-guaranteed mortgages, they can if they desire make a down payment that is larger than the minimum. In any event, they should consider the following factors:

1. *The cost*. With a large down payment an individual may be able to reduce the period of time the loan will run before maturity. This will result in considerable interest savings and is related to the amount of the monthly payments discussed below. In addition, even if an individual places a large down payment on a property and the time to maturity remains the same, he or she will still save money on interest. For instance, a home buyer who borrows $25,000 at 10 percent interest for a twenty-five-year period will pay $43,154 in interest during the life of the mortgage. On the other hand, if the same borrower needed only a $20,000 mortgage for the same number of years at the same interest rate, interest payments would drop to $29,525—the person would save $13,629. In other words, the $25,000 mortgage will cost the borrower about 46 percent more than the smaller $20,000 loan. In addition, if a larger down payment is made, often the interest rate is reduced somewhat.

2. *Possibility of moving*. Each year nearly one out of every five American families moves to a new location. If there is a possiblity that you are going to move, it is advisable to put as small a down payment on a home as possible when purchasing it. Many people consider that the competition between the sale of an older home and a newer home to a large degree rests with the size of the down payment, for it is easier to sell a home requiring a $1,500 down payment than it is to sell a home requiring a $5,000 down payment. Therefore, if one has a small equity in a home, it may be easier to sell if one has to move.

Interest on Mortgages

Both FHA-insured and the VA-guaranteed loans have maximum rates of interest set by law. Sometimes the rates you have to pay are at this maximum level and sometimes they are below it. Currently the FHA loan carries 11.5 percent interest—the legal maximum—plus .5 percent for the payment of the insurance premium on the unpaid part of the loan. The interest rate on conventional loans fluctuates from time to time and also varies from one part of the nation to another, depending on the supply of money available for mortgage loans. Many states have usury laws that set the upper ceiling on rates on conventional mortgages.

These vary, but typically they range from 10 to 12 or 13 percent. In all three cases, however, the interest rates reflect the supply of and demand for funds available for home mortgages. During periods of ample supply and moderate or even heavy demand for funds, the interest rates move downward. When money is tight or in short supply and demand remains relatively high, the interest rates rise. As noted above, the interest cost is an important component of total costs. Therefore, you may wish to give some weight to the level of interest rates in determining the amount of your down payment.

Interest rates may also vary slightly with the amount of the down payment. If there is a substantial down payment, interest rates may be reduced from one quarter to one-half of 1 percent from what the rate would have been with a lower down payment. Over the years, a quarter or a half of 1 percent difference can amount to a good deal of money, especially on a big mortgage. One half of 1 percent on $20,000, for example, is $100 per year.

For any given home, then, the size of the down payment will affect the size of the monthly payment as well as the total interest paid over the years. Table 16-5 illustrates this. A $40,000 home is financed over twenty-five years at 10 percent with a large, a medium, and a relatively small down payment.

Monthly Payments

The monthly payment varies not only with the amount of the mortgage but also with the length of the mortgage, the interest rate, and usually with the level of taxes and insurance premiums. A higher interest rate, all else being equal, tends to increase the monthly payments. The longer the number of years for which the mortgage runs, the lower the monthly payments with any given interest rate and dollar amount of the loan. However, if one reduces the monthly payments by increasing the length of the mortgage, one pays more total dollars in interest over the years.

When buying a house, the down payment is not always subject to variation; usually a person must have the $2,000 or $10,000 in cash, or whatever the figure is. The exception has been discussed previously. Buyers do have some control over the length of the mortgage and, to a slight extent, over the interest rate if they shop around. If the house buyer wishes to save total interest costs, the person should select the amortization time period that makes the monthly payments as large as he or she can easily bear. On a $20,000, twenty-year, 10 percent mortgage, monthly payment (not including insurance and property taxes) would be $193.01. Total payments over the twenty years would be $46,322.40 and interest over the years would amount to $26,322.40. The same mortgage financed over twenty-five years

TABLE 16–5. *Amortization of a $40,000 house with varying down payments over a twenty-five-year period at 10 percent interest*

	A	B	C
House	$40,000.00	$40,000.00	$40,000.00
Down payment	10,000.00	15,000.00	20,000.00
Mortgage	30,000.00	25,000.00	20,000.00
Monthly payment (interest & princ. only)	272.62	227.18	181.75
Total dollars paid	81,786.00	68,154.00	54,525.00
Total interest over the 25 years	51,786.00	43,154.00	34,525.00

would have monthly payments of $181.75 and total payments of $54,525, of which $34,525 would be for interest. By reducing monthly payments by $11.26 the buyer pays an additional $8,202.60 in interest over the years. This is not to say that mortgages should never be stretched out to reduce monthly payments. Sometimes such a step is necessary; and one of the benefits of a thirty-year mortgage is that it reduces monthly payments to the point where people can buy homes who otherwise could not do so. I am merely saying that one should make the decision with eyes open and not lengthen the mortgage just to reduce monthly payments. Table 16-6 shows the monthly payments necessary to amortize a given loan at 10 percent interest over a given number of years. It includes interest and reduction of principal only.

Monthly payments can include four items: interest, reduction of the principal, insurance premiums, and local property taxes. Interest and reduction of the principal are self-explanatory, but insurance premiums and property taxes are worth noting. Nearly all lenders will insist that insurance to protect the house against loss due to fire or other physical damage be obtained. Even if the lending institution did not demand it, it would still be a good idea, for no property owner should be without fire insurance. In addition to fire insurance, sometimes a life insurance policy is bought on the mortgage so that if the borrower dies before paying off the mortgage, the insurance company will pay it. This type of life insurance is similar to the decreasing term rider that was explained more fully in chapter 8. Here I will merely note that a decreasing term rider mortgage insurance is a policy the face value of which declines at the same rate as the principal on a mortgage that is being amortized.

Although property taxes vary from community to community, they must be paid annually or seminannually in most cases. Since they usually run to several hundred dollars or more, a person who does not budget for them will have difficulty paying them. Many lending institutions include one-twelfth of the annual tax liability and add it to the monthly payments. These funds then go into a special account called the escrow account, which is then used by the institution to pay the taxes when due. It may do the same with insurance premiums (both mortgage credit life insurance and hazard insurance premiums).

Some people object to these monthly payments for insurance and property taxes on the ground that under this method of payment they are paying in advance and the financial institution has the use of their money for a time before it pays the bills. This is the same as an interest-free loan to the bank. However, you should keep in mind that the lending institution is providing you with a real service. It is doing your budgeting for you and it also takes care of the paperwork involved in keeping the records and paying the taxes and insurance premiums. However, if you object to this advance payment, you should bargain with the lending institution and try to keep it out of your monthly payments. If the down payment is fairly large, you can probably keep the life insurance and the tax payments out, but it is more difficult to avoid including fire insurance premiums. These latter premiums, however, are relatively small.

If you succeed in keeping some of the above items out of the monthly payments, you should do your own budgeting and set aside one-twelfth of the sum each month. Then not only will you be sure of having the funds when they are due, but you can put them in a savings account and receive interest perhaps from the very bank that has your mortgage.

Since the interest cost is a major item when buying a home, you should bargain to reduce it if you can. A larger down payment may enable you to save a quarter or a half of 1 percent. You might also save a quarter of 1 percent by shopping around. One quarter of 1 percent interest on a $30,000 loan over twenty years will save approximately $800. Although this is not a lot of money, there is no reason to throw it away.

TABLE 16-6. *Monthly payment necessary to amortize a loan at 10%.*

TERM AMOUNT	15 YEARS	16 YEARS	17 YEARS	18 YEARS	19 YEARS	20 YEARS	21 YEARS	22 YEARS	23 YEARS
$ 22500	241.79	235.33	229.78	224.97	220.79	217.13	213.93	211.11	208.62
23000	247.16	240.56	234.88	229.97	225.69	221.96	218.68	215.80	213.26
23500	252.54	245.79	239.99	234.97	230.60	226.79	223.44	220.49	217.89
24000	257.91	251.02	245.10	239.97	235.51	231.61	228.19	225.18	222.53
24500	263.28	256.25	250.20	244.97	240.41	236.44	232.95	229.88	227.16
25000	268.66	261.48	255.31	249.97	245.32	241.26	237.70	234.57	231.80
25500	274.03	266.71	260.41	254.97	250.23	246.09	242.45	239.26	236.44
26000	279.40	271.94	265.52	259.96	255.13	250.91	247.21	243.95	241.07
26500	284.78	277.17	270.63	264.96	260.04	255.74	251.96	248.64	245.71
27000	290.15	282.40	275.73	269.96	264.94	260.56	256.72	253.33	250.34
27500	295.52	287.63	280.84	274.96	269.85	265.39	261.47	258.02	254.98
28000	300.89	292.86	285.94	279.96	274.76	270.21	266.22	262.71	259.62
28500	306.27	298.09	291.05	284.96	279.66	275.04	270.98	267.41	264.25
29000	311.64	303.32	296.16	289.96	284.57	279.86	275.73	272.10	268.89
29500	317.01	308.55	301.26	294.96	289.48	284.69	280.49	276.79	273.52
30000	322.39	313.78	306.37	299.96	294.38	289.51	285.24	281.48	278.16
30500	327.76	319.01	311.47	304.96	299.29	294.34	289.99	286.17	282.80
31000	333.13	324.23	316.58	309.96	304.20	299.16	294.75	290.86	287.43
31500	338.51	329.46	321.69	314.96	309.10	303.99	299.50	295.55	292.07
32000	343.88	334.69	326.79	319.95	314.01	308.81	304.25	300.24	296.70
32500	349.25	339.92	331.90	324.95	318.91	313.64	309.01	304.93	301.34
33000	354.62	345.15	337.00	329.95	323.82	318.46	313.76	309.63	305.97
33500	360.00	350.38	342.11	334.95	328.73	323.29	318.52	314.32	310.61
34000	365.37	355.61	347.22	339.95	333.63	328.11	323.27	319.01	315.25
34500	370.74	360.84	352.32	344.95	338.54	332.94	328.02	323.70	319.88
35000	376.12	366.07	357.43	349.95	343.45	337.76	332.78	328.39	324.52
36000	386.86	376.53	367.64	359.95	353.26	347.41	342.29	337.77	333.79
37000	397.61	386.99	377.85	369.95	363.07	357.06	351.79	347.16	343.06
38000	408.35	397.45	388.06	379.95	372.88	366.71	361.30	356.54	352.33
39000	419.10	407.91	398.28	389.94	382.70	376.36	370.81	365.92	361.61
40000	429.85	418.37	408.49	399.94	392.51	386.01	380.32	375.30	370.88
41000	440.59	428.82	418.70	409.94	402.32	395.66	389.82	384.69	380.15
42000	451.34	439.28	428.91	419.94	412.13	405.31	399.33	394.07	389.42
43000	462.09	449.74	439.13	429.94	421.95	414.96	408.84	403.45	398.69
44000	472.83	460.20	449.34	439.94	431.76	424.61	418.35	412.83	407.96
45000	483.58	470.66	459.55	449.93	441.57	434.26	427.86	422.22	417.24
46000	494.32	481.12	469.76	459.93	451.38	443.91	437.36	431.60	426.51
47000	505.07	491.58	479.97	469.93	461.20	453.57	446.87	440.98	435.78
48000	515.82	502.04	490.19	479.93	471.01	463.22	456.38	450.36	445.05
49000	526.56	512.50	500.40	489.93	480.82	472.87	465.89	459.75	454.32
50000	537.31	522.96	510.61	499.93	490.63	482.52	475.40	469.13	463.60
51000	548.05	533.41	520.82	509.93	500.45	492.17	484.90	478.51	472.87
52000	558.80	543.87	531.03	519.92	510.26	501.82	494.41	487.89	482.14
53000	569.55	554.33	541.25	529.92	520.07	511.47	503.92	497.28	491.41
54000	580.29	564.79	551.46	539.92	529.88	521.12	513.43	506.66	500.68
55000	591.04	575.25	561.67	549.92	539.70	530.77	522.93	516.04	509.95
56000	601.78	585.71	571.88	559.92	549.51	540.42	532.44	525.42	519.23
57000	612.53	596.17	582.09	569.92	559.32	550.07	541.95	534.81	528.50
58000	623.28	606.63	592.31	579.91	569.14	559.72	551.46	544.19	537.77
59000	634.02	617.09	602.52	589.91	578.95	569.37	560.97	553.57	547.04
60000	644.77	627.55	612.73	599.91	588.76	579.02	570.47	562.95	556.31
61000	655.51	638.01	622.94	609.91	598.57	588.67	579.98	572.34	565.59
62000	666.26	648.46	633.16	619.91	608.39	598.32	589.49	581.72	574.86
63000	677.01	658.92	643.37	629.91	618.20	607.97	599.00	591.10	584.13
64000	687.75	669.38	653.58	639.90	628.01	617.62	608.50	600.48	593.40
65000	698.50	679.84	663.79	649.90	637.82	627.27	618.01	609.86	602.67
67500	725.36	705.99	689.32	674.90	662.35	651.39	641.78	633.32	625.85
70000	752.23	732.14	714.85	699.90	686.89	675.52	665.55	656.78	649.03
72500	779.09	758.28	740.38	724.89	711.42	699.65	689.32	680.23	672.21
75000	805.96	784.43	765.91	749.89	735.95	723.77	713.09	703.69	695.39
80000	859.69	836.73	816.97	799.88	785.01	772.02	760.63	750.60	741.75
85000	913.42	889.02	868.03	849.87	834.08	820.27	808.17	797.51	788.11
90000	967.15	941.32	919.09	899.86	883.14	868.52	855.71	844.43	834.47
95000	1020.88	993.61	970.15	949.86	932.20	916.78	903.25	891.34	880.83
100000	1074.61	1045.91	1021.22	999.85	981.26	965.03	950.79	938.25	927.19

Source: *Eighth and Quarter Monthly Mortgage Calculator, Publication No. 67,* Financial Publishing Company, p. 149. Copyright © 1972 by Financial Publishing Company.

Part 4 / Home Ownership, Taxes, Estate Planning

Amortization of a Home Loan

Prior to the 1930s, homes were financed through a single-payment straight mortgage running about five years. Now, however, a monthly payment is made to pay off or amortize the loan in installments.

A fixed monthly payment includes interest, reduction of principal, and perhaps taxes and insurance. A $30,000, twenty-year mortgage at 10 percent would require a monthly payment of $289.51 to be amortized in twenty years, exclusive of taxes and insurance. Since the interest is calculated each month on the unpaid balance, that balance and the interest paid declines a little bit each month. Inasmuch as the $289.51 payment is constant, the savings in interest are applied to reduce the principal a little more each month. These calculations have been made and printed in table form, and you can get such an amortization table for the asking from most banks or savings and loan associations.

The $289.51 monthly payment mentioned above includes interest of $250.00 the first month and $39.51 for the reduction of the principal. If we add $75 for taxes and $25 for insurance, the total monthly payment becomes $389.51. The second monthly payment would include less interest and a little more reduction of principal; for example $249.67 and $39.84 respectively. The insurance and tax payments would presumably remain constant in the short run, although every few years they are adjusted upward. These four monthly payments and the way they appear over time can be depicted graphically, as is done in Figure 16-2. Time is measured on the horizontal axis and the monthly payments on the vertical axis. This same relationship can be shown in a different manner, as illustrated by Table 16-7.

FIGURE 16–2. *Relationships among the four payments included in single monthly loan payments. The graph is not geometrically accurate; it is only intended to illustrate the principle of the amortization of mortgages. The tax and insurance payments may be adjusted upward periodically as taxes and premiums are raised.*

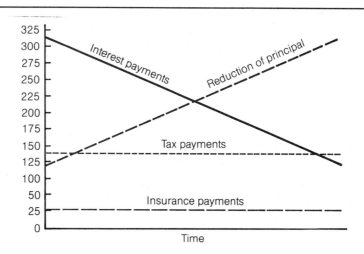

TABLE 16–7. *Relationship between payments and amount*

PAYMENT NO.	INTEREST	PRINCIPAL	BALANCE
1	$250.00	$ 39.51	$29,960.49
2	$249.67	$ 39.84	$29,920.65
3	$249.34	$ 40.17	$29,880.48
4	$249.00	$ 40.51	$29,839.97
5	$248.67	$ 40.84	$29,799.13
6	$248.33	$ 41.18	$29,757.95
7	$247.98	$ 41.53	$29,716.42
8	$247.64	$ 41.87	$29,674.55
9	$247.29	$ 42.22	$29,632.33
10	$246.94	$ 42.57	$29,589.76
231	$ 23.03	$266.48	$ 2,497.63
232	$ 20.81	$268.70	$ 2,228.93
233	$ 18.57	$270.94	$ 1,957.99
234	$ 16.32	$273.19	$ 1,684.80
235	$ 14.04	$275.47	$ 1,409.33
236	$ 11.74	$277.77	$ 1,131.56
237	$ 9.43	$280.08	$ 851.48
238	$ 7.10	$282.41	$ 569.07
239	$ 4.74	$284.77	$ 284.30
240	$ 2.37	$284.30	$ 0.00

Final Payment	$286.67	Total No. Payments	240
Total Payment	$69,482.40	Total Principal	$30,000.00
		Total Interest	$39,482.40

Points

Sometimes points are used when a loan is made. Generally, points are added during periods of tight money, and the tighter the money supply the greater the number of points added. A point is one percentage point of the mortgage loan and, technically speaking, is paid by the seller of the home. However, sometimes points are shifted to the buyer. On a $40,000 mortgage loan upon which 6 points are assessed this amounts to $2,400. In theory, this sum is withheld from the amount the lending institution gives the seller. However, being aware that this is going to happen, the seller will attempt to raise the price of the house, over and above its fair market value, by this amount. While this price escalation is not always successful, if market conditions are tight and upward price pressures on homes exist, the seller may be successful in shifting this "point cost" to the buyer, at least in part. The lending institution receives this "points" sum, and it is considered additional compensation to offset the fact that the regular interest rates are too low because of a usury law ceiling.

If an institution makes a $40,000 loan on a $50,000 house in which the seller has a $10,000 equity, and charges 10 percent interest and also assesses 6 points, then the institution advances the seller only $7,600. The buyer assumes a $40,000 mortgage at, say, 10 percent. In a sense the lender receives 16 percent return the first year.

If the interest rate is bumping up against the usury ceiling, adding points is the only possible way for the lender to increase his yield above what the usury law allows. If interest rates are substantially below the usury ceiling, points may not be assessed. The interest charge can be out in the open. If interest rates are only a bit below the usury ceiling, one or two points may be assessed. This may be done in an attempt to disguise the true interest and make it appear it is a bit lower than it really is.

Making an Offer on a House; Earnest Money

When a seller offers a house, he or she or the real estate agent draws up a sales contract. This piece of paper spells out the terms of the sale. It will describe the house, list the asking price, note the present mortgage, etc. By signing this contract a prospective purchaser agrees to buy the house. However, usually the prospective buyer will make a counter offer by changing the terms somewhat, perhaps lowering the price.

In order to ascertain whether or not the offering price is reasonably close to the true market value, ask your realtor. He or she can give you a fairly good answer. Also check the selling price (not the offered price) of other comparable homes that have been sold recently. Many sellers will price their house above the realistic market value in the hope that they will find a naive person (sucker) who will pay it. Often sellers will come way down from their offer price. You can negotiate with the seller but only indirectly through the realtor. Another thing you should find out from your realtor is whether selling prices generally have been close to asking prices. How to ascertain the realistic market value of a house is discussed in greater detail earlier in this chapter under the subheading, "How Much is a Home Worth."

When you finally decide what you are willing to pay, you should make a counter offer. This counter offer is signed by the prospective buyer and conveyed to the seller by the realtor with a down payment (usually $500 to $1000, depending upon the price of the house) called earnest money. There may be several counter offers between the buyer and seller; this is how you negotiate over the price. The buyer must sign any counter offer he or she makes and present earnest money with it. If the seller signs the buyer's counter offer, it is a binding deal.

In some states this earnest money goes to the seller immediately and in others it goes into an escrow account until the transaction is closed. In any event, when both buyer and seller have signed the contract, it is binding and either can force the other to comply. However, in practice the seller can nearly always back out by returning the earnest money, because it would require a lawsuit to force compliance. A buyer who wanted to back out, however, would generally lose the earnest money. That is why the offer (sales contract) must carefully spell out all the conditions desired by both parties. For example, the buy offer will always be a conditional offer and effective only if satisfactory financing can be arranged. An earnest money contract is shown in Figure 16-3. Note that under the heading "special conditions," a number of provisions have been written into the contract. This is more often done on older homes than on brand-new homes.

Closing Costs

When the buyer and seller of a house have reached an agreement, they and the realtors involved get together to close the deal and sign the necessary papers. A representative of the lending institution also attends the closing which indeed may be held at the office of the lending institution. It is often at the closing that the surprised buyer first becomes aware that closing costs are involved. On a $50,000 house, there may be additional hidden closing fees of from $500 to $1,500. The question is, what do these costs consist of? The totals generally vary with the section of the country in which the loan is being made. Generally, however, they include the following:

REALTOR®

EARNEST MONEY **CONTRACT**

RECEIVED OF_____William Jones_____in the form of___check____,
the sum of_____FIVE HUNDRED AND NO/100------------------------ $500.00_____,
being earnest money deposited with the undersigned to be held by the undersigned in escrow in accordance with the terms and conditions stipulated herein.

The depositor, hereinafter called PURCHASER, agrees to purchase the following described real estate from SELLER, together with all improvements thereon in present physical condition unless otherwise specified herein, in Travis County, Texas:

Locally known as No.____2705 Ashdale_____

Property description: Lot___17_____Block_____

Addition:____Allandale Place, Section 1_____

____Austin, Texas_____

Total Price $__40,000__to be paid by PURCHASER as follows: $__500.00___as earnest money which is hereby deposited with____Don's Realty_____then $_7,500____cash on delivery of deed as herein provided, and

contingent upon Purchaser obtaining a loan at a Financial Institution in the amount

of $32,000

THE SAID EXECUTED note or notes to be secured by Vender's Lien and Deed of Trust, with the usual covenants as to taxes, Insurance, and default.

PRORATIONS: SELLER shall furnish tax certificates showing all taxes paid through the year 19_78_; taxes for the current year, current rents if any, and interest if any to be prorated as of date of delivery of deed.

TITLE EVIDENCE: SELLER agrees, at his option and expense, to furnish to PURCHASER an owner's title policy; or a complete abstract of title and to place order for same within___10___days from date herein.

CONTRACT UNDER TITLE EVIDENCE: If abstract is furnished, PURCHASER agrees within_not/app. days from the receipt of said abstract either to accept the title as shown by said abstract or to return same to the SELLER with the written objections to the title. If the abstract is not returned to the SELLER with the written objections noted within the time specified, it shall be construed as an acceptance of said title. _as possible

SELLER AND PURCHASER agree to consummate this sale within _as soon/ days after title company, in event of title policy, or attorney, in event of abstract, approves the title, unless otherwise agreed herein. In the event abstract is furnished and valid objections to title are made, SELLER shall have _not/app_ days after written notice to remove such objections or furnish a policy of title insurance.

PURCHASER acknowledges that he has been advised that he should have the abstract examined by his attorney if furnished an abstract or in the alternative he should be furnished with or should obtain a policy of title insurance.

Any restrictions, zoning ordinances, or conditions imposed by any addition, or subdivision, of which this property is a part, shall not be recited as objections to this title.

WARRANTY DEED: SELLER agrees, when any title defects have been cured, to deliver a General Warranty Deed, properly executed, conveying said property free and clear of all liens whatsoever except as herein provided, to said PURCHASER, or assigns; PURCHASER shall then and there pay the balance, if any, of said cash payment, and shall execute the note or notes and deed of trust herein provided for.

POSSESSION: SELLER agrees to give possession at time sale is consummated unless otherwise specified herein.

BREACH OF CONDITIONS: IF SELLER FAILS to comply with any of the above requirements, within the time specified, the earnest money may, at option of PURCHASER, be returned to PURCHASER UPON RETURN AND CANCELLATION of this receipt or PURCHASER may enforce specific performance. IF PURCHASER FAILS to consummate this purchase as specified for any reason except title defects or other reasons as set forth herein, SELLER shall have the right to retain said cash deposit as liquidated damages for the breach of these conditions or SELLER may enforce specific performance.

AGENT'S COMMISSION: It is agreed that____Don's Realty_____of Austin, Texas, is the procuring cause of this sale and by acceptance of these conditions, SELLER promises to pay to said agent a commission of___6%___of the sale price above set out (on the consummation of the sale or upon breach thereof.) If the PURCHASER fails to consummate this purchase as specified for any reason except title defects or other reasons set forth herein, it is agreed that SELLER shall pay to agent one-half of the earnest money as his commission in such instance, provided, however, that agent's one-half shall never exceed___6___% of the total sale price above stated. By SELLER'S signature to this contract, SELLER affirms Agent's right to sell the above described property.

SPECIAL CONDITIONS: Purchaser to have access to property for cleaning purposes prior to closing, effective upon date of agreeable contract. All plumbing, electrical, heating and cooling systems, appliances to be in good working order at time of closing. Purchaser to have opportunity to inspect same at Purchaser's convenience prior to closing. Seller to provide termite-free inspection certificate dated no earlier than 10 days prior to closing. Existing drapes, curtains, rods, carpet, refrigerator to remain. Patio door to be repaired to close and lock property.

ENTIRE AGREEMENT: This Contract contains the entire agreement. There are no other agreements, oral or written, and the terms of this contract can be amended only by written agreement signed by all parties hereto, and by reference made a part hereof. The terms and conditions shall not be effective unless accepted by both PURCHASER and SELLER.

EXECUTED IN_quadruplicate____this_19_day of_August___, 19_78_, at Austin, Travis County, Texas.

_____   By_____
            Escrow agent

Accepted:_____   Accepted:_____
                        Seller   Purchaser

Accepted:_____   Accepted:_____
                        Seller   Purchaser

1. Title insurance
2. Credit reports
3. Attorney's fees
4. Origination fee

5. Fire and other hazard insurance reserve
6. Tax reserve
7. Survey
8. Recording fee

Title insurance costs vary depending on the amount of the loan and the company with which the policy is placed. Fire insurance rates, credit reports, and attorney's fees all vary somewhat regionally. Furthermore, the closing costs differ depending on whether the loan is a conventional mortgage, a VA-guaranteed mortgage, or an FHA-insured mortgage; but in general the same items are included.

A note on the attorney's fees is in order at this point. In purchasing as important and expensive an item as a home, it is well worthwhile to engage the services of an attorney. The $100 or $150 that it costs is usually well spent. When entering into a legal agreement, it is best to have an expert explain all the fine print. This is over and above the attorney's fees shown on the closing costs statement. The latter are for the fees of the lender's attorney who drew up the papers.

In past years it was also necessary to have a title search, to confirm the fact that the legal title of the property was vested in the seller and that he or she could legally transfer it to you. Presently most people buy title insurance rather than have their attorney conduct such a search. This insurance policy protects the buyer against any loss because of a defect in the title. While this is typically paid for by the seller, sometimes the buyer also has to buy title insurance. In this latter case it is to protect the lender; that purchased by the seller protects only the buyer.

Another item under closing costs consists of what is called the origination fee (sometimes called finder's fee) or lender's fee. This is generally 1 percent of the mortgage, and if one is buying from a builder or a real estate broker it is supposedly a fee they receive for making the arrangements for the loan. Even if one is dealing directly with a financial institution, the fee is often charged. It is essentially then a gimmick to increase the return of the broker, or the financial institution. Again conditions vary from one section of the country to another, but generally the only way to avoid paying the finder's fee is to make the arrangement for the loan yourself with a commercial bank. Commercial banks are not as liberal as other lenders with respect to whom they will make a loan, but they are less likely to charge a finder's fee.

Other typical costs are appraiser's fees, credit reports, the cost of hiring a surveyor to survey the property and ascertain its exact boundaries, and a fee for an amortization table. There may or may not be a charge for these. Sometimes hazard insurance is shown twice on a closing statement; once for the first year's premiums, which must be paid in advance, and again for a one or two month's premium, which goes into an escrow account for next year's premiums. Property taxes must also be provided for. If it is an existing house, there may be extra funds in a tax escrow account which you will have to buy. If it is a new house, a tax payment may or may not be required; sometimes a one or two month tax payment is required at closing, sometimes not.

We discussed points above. They are assessed at closing but are assessed to the seller. All other closing costs except the premium on the title insurance, as discussed above, are paid by the buyer. Figure 16–4 shows a disclosure settlement statement. These are not standard forms; each is a sample and many variations exist.

FIGURE 16–4. *Disclosure settlement statement.* (*Source:* Courtesy of Stewart Title.)

Form Approved
OMB No. 63-R1501

A. U.S. DEPARTMENT OF HOUSING AND URBAN DEVELOPMENT	B. TYPE OF LOAN:
	1. ☐ FHA 2. ☐ FMHA 3. ☒ CONV. UNINS.
	4. ☐ VA 5. ☐ CONV. INS.
	6. FILE NUMBER 7. LOAN NUMBER
	120179
SETTLEMENT STATEMENT	8. MORTG. INS. CASE NO.

C. NOTE: This form is furnished to give you a statement of actual settlement costs. Amounts paid to and by the settlement agent are shown. Items marked "(p.o.c.)" were paid outside the closing; they are shown here for informational purposes and are not included in the totals.

D. NAME OF BORROWER	E. NAME OF SELLER	F. NAME OF LENDER
JOHN DOE BUYER and wife, MARY JO BUYER	IMA GOODE SELLAR, a single person	NEW MORTGAGE COMPANY

G. PROPERTY LOCATION	H. SETTLEMENT AGENT	I. SETTLEMENT DATE:
29849 University Row Austin, Texas 78747	STEWART TITLE COMPANY	
	PLACE OF SETTLEMENT	
	812 San Antonio	12-10-79

J. SUMMARY OF BORROWER'S TRANSACTION		K. SUMMARY OF SELLER'S TRANSACTION	
100. GROSS AMOUNT DUE FROM BORROWER:		**400. GROSS AMOUNT DUE TO SELLER:**	
		401. Contract sales price	65,000.00
101. Contract sales price	65,000.00	402. Personal property	
102. Personal property		403.	
103. Settlement charges to borrower *(line 1400)*	1,627.34	404.	
104.		405.	
105.		Adjustments for items paid by seller in advance:	
Adjustments for items paid by seller in advance:		406. City/town taxes 12-10-79 to 1-1-80	18.92
106. City/town taxes 12-10-79 to 1-1-80	18.92	407. County taxes 12-10-79 to 1-1-80	9.93
107. County taxes 12-10-79 to 1-1-80	9.93	408. Assessments to	
108. Assessments to		409. Maintenance to	
109. Maintenance to		410. Commitment Fee to	
110. School/Taxes 12-10-79 to 1-1-80	29.57	411. School Tax 12-10-79 to 1-1-80	29.57
111. to		412. to	
112. to		**420. GROSS AMOUNT DUE TO SELLER:**	65,058.42
120. GROSS AMOUNT DUE FROM BORROWER:	66,685.76	**500. REDUCTIONS IN AMOUNT DUE TO SELLER:**	
200. AMOUNTS PAID BY OR IN BEHALF OF BORROWER:		501. Excess deposit (see instructions)	
201. Deposit or earnest money STC	1,000.00	502. Settlement charges to seller *(line 1400)*	6,461.50
202. Principal amount of new loan(s)	52,000.00	503. Existing loan(s) taken subject to	
203. Existing loan(s) taken subject to		504. Payoff of first mortgage loan 12-10-79	37,242.67
204. Commitment Fee		505. Payoff of second mortgage loan	
205.		506.	
206.		507.	
207.		508.	
208.		509.	
209.			
Adjustments for items unpaid by seller:		Adjustments for items unpaid by seller:	
210. City/town taxes to		510. City/town taxes 1-1-79 to 1-1-80	328.92
211. County taxes to		511. County Taxes 1-1-79 to 1-1-80	172.68
212. Assessments to		512. Assessments to	
213. School/Taxes to		513. Maintenance to	
214. to		514. School/Taxes 1-1-79 to 1-1-80	513.96
215. to		515. to	
216. to		516. to	
217. to		517. to	
218. to		518. to	
219. to		519. to	
220. TOTAL PAID BY/FOR BORROWER:	53,000.00	**520. TOTAL REDUCTION AMOUNT DUE SELLER:**	44,719.73
300. CASH AT SETTLEMENT FROM/TO BORROWER:		**600. CASH AT SETTLEMENT TO/FROM SELLER:**	
301. Gross amount due from borrower *(line 120)*	66,685.76	601. Gross amount due to seller *(line 420)*	65,000.00
302. Less amounts paid by/for borrower *(line 220)*	53,000.00	602. Less total reductions in amount due seller *(line 520)*	44,719.73
303. CASH (☐ FROM) (☐ TO) BORROWER:	13,685.76	603. CASH (☐ TO) (☐ FROM) SELLER	20,338.69

HUD-1 (Rev. 5-76)

L. SETTLEMENT CHARGES	PAID FROM BORROWER'S FUNDS AT SETTLEMENT	PAID FROM SELLER'S FUNDS AT SETTLEMENT
700. **TOTAL SALES/BROKER'S COMMISSION** Based on price $ 65,000.00 @ 6 % =		
Division of commission *(line 700)* as follows:		
701. $ 3,900.00 to Ben Hustlin Properties		
702. $ to		
703. Commission paid at settlement		3,900.00
704.		
800. **ITEMS PAYABLE IN CONNECTION WITH LOAN.**		
801. Loan Origination fee 1 %	520.00	
802. Loan Discount 4 %		2,080.00
803. Appraisal Fee to	POC (80.00)	
804. Credit Report to	20.00	
805. Lender's inspection fee		
806. Mortgage Insurance application fee to		
807. Assumption Fee		
808. Commitment Fee		
809. FNMA Processing Fee		
810. Pictures	15.00	
811. Tax Service Fee		18.50
900. **ITEMS REQUIRED BY LENDER TO BE PAID IN ADVANCE.**		
901. Interest from 12/10/79 to 1/1/80 @ $ 16.61 /day	365.42	
902. Mortgage insurance premium for mo. to		
903. Hazard insurance premium for yrs. to Homeowner's Insurance Group	254.00	
904. Flood Insurance yrs. to		
905.		
1000. **RESERVES DEPOSITED WITH LENDER**		
1001. Hazard insurance 1 mo. @ $ 21.16 per mo.	21.16	
1002. Mortgage insurance mo. @ $ per mo.		
1003. City property taxes 2 mo. @ $ 27.41 per mo.	54.82	
1004. County property taxes 2 mo. @ $ 14.39 per mo.	28.78	
1005. Annual assessments (Maint.) mo. @ $ per mo.		
1006. School Property Taxes 2 mo. @ $ 42.83 per mo.	85.66	
1007. Water Dist. Prop. Tax mo. @ $ per mo.		
1008. Flood Insurance mo. @ $ per mo.		
1100. **TITLE CHARGES:**		
1101. Settlement or closing fee to		
1102. Abstract or title search to		
1103. Title examination to		
1104. Title insurance binder to		
1105. Document preparation to Goodlaw & Willing	65.00	35.00
1106. Notary fees to		
1107. Attorney's fees to to		
(includes above items No.:		
1108. Title insurance to Stewart Title Company	30.00	382.00
(includes above items No.:		
1109. Lender's coverage $ 52,000.00 − 30.00		
1110. Owner's coverage $ 65,000.00 − 382.00		
1111. Escrow Fee	15.00	15.00
1112. Restrictions	2.00	
1113. Messenger Service		
1200. **GOVERNMENT RECORDING AND TRANSFER CHARGES**		
1201. Recording fees: Deed $ 9.00 Mortgage $ 9.00 Releases $ 5.00	18.00	5.00
1202. City/county tax/stamps: Deed $ Mortgage $		
1203. State tax/stamps: Deed $ Mortgage $		
1204. Tax Certificates		6.00
1205.		
1300. **ADDITIONAL SETTLEMENT CHARGES**		
1301. Survey to William I. Sketch	85.00	
1302. Pest inspection to Termite City		20.00
1303. Mechanical Inspection to Austin Inspection Service	47.50	
1304.		
1305.		
1400. **TOTAL SETTLEMENT CHARGES** *(entered on lines 103, Section J and 502, Section K)*	1,627.34	6,461.50

SELLER'S AND/OR PURCHASER'S STATEMENT

Seller's and Purchaser's signature hereon acknowledges his/their approval of tax prorations, and signifies their understanding that prorations were based on figures for preceding year, or estimates for current year, and in event of any change for current year, all necessary adjustments must be made between Seller and Purchaser direct; likewise any DEFICIT in delinquent taxes will be reimbursed to Title Company by the Seller.

We approve the foregoing settlement statement, in its entirety, authorize payments in accordance therewith and acknowledge receipt of a copy thereof.

Signature _____   _____

_____   _____

Seller   Purchaser

_____

Escrow Officer   HUD-1 (Rev. 5-76)

Chapter 16 / Home Ownership   467

QUESTIONS FOR REVIEW

1. Discuss the reasons for home ownership.

2. Explain in detail the current tax advantage of home ownership.

3. What is involved when persons declare their home a homestead?

4. Discuss the relative merits of buying a new and an older house.

5. What factors should be looked into prior to purchasing a home?

6. What problems are involved in building a house from the ground up?

7. Discuss the advantages and disadvantages of buying a condominium.

8. Discuss the three major types of mortgages available to the home buyer.

9. How can a home purchase be financed by means of a contract?

10. Why is the size of the down payment on a house important?

11. Explain the concept of amortization as it pertains to the purchase of a house.

12. How does the variable interest rate work?

13. What is a penalty clause in a mortgage?

14. Discuss, in the order of importance to the home mortgage field, the various financial lending institutions.

CASES

1. Ernie and Eloise Johansen are presently living in an unfurnished apartment renting for $230.00 per month. They have saved up $5,000, which they think is enough for a down payment on a $50,000 home. One lending agency has told them it will give them a twenty-year mortgage for $45,000 at 12 percent. Another financial institution has offered them a loan at 11 percent for twenty years if they can raise another $5,000. They can borrow $5,000 on their life insurance policy at 6 percent. Which offer should they take? What will be the total interest charges in both cases? They believe they can pay back the loan on their insurance over a two-year period.

2. Timothy and Martha Hennessey have found a home selling for $40,500 which they would like to buy. They have discovered they could finance it with a 10 percent down FHA loan for thirty years at 11.5 percent. Under these conditions what would be their monthly payments for interest and reduction of principal? They are now renting at $280 per month. Would you recommend that they buy? The Hennesseys could, however, easily make a down payment of 20 percent and if they did, the lending institution would charge them only 11 percent interest. Which should they do? How much interest would they save if they financed with the 20 percent down payment? What would the monthly payments be for in-

terest and reduction in principal if they bought the home with a 20 percent down payment?

3. Samuel and Lillian Jelesberg are presently renting an apartment for $330 per month. They have discovered that they can buy a $65,500 home with a $13,500 down payment and assume a twenty-five-year mortgage at 9 percent interest. What would the interest on this loan be? The property taxes on the home amount to $800 and insurance premiums are $144 per year. Sam and Lillian feel this is cheaper than renting. Are they right? Would you recommend that they buy or continue to rent? Why?

4. Howard and Patricia Jones would like to buy a new ranch-style house that is on the market for $75,000. The Joneses have two children, and Howard has an annual income after taxes of $20,000. They do have $5,000 which they could use as a down payment and then assume a mortgage of $70,000. Can they afford to buy this home? Why or why not?

5. Frank and Myrtle Brodowski are thinking about buying a home. They have found a split-level house that will suit their needs for $54,975. They can get it for no down payment on a 30-year VA loan at 11.5 percent interest. However, they could afford to make a

down payment of up to $5,000. Frank thinks they should do this and save interest charges. What would you recommend and why?

6. Carolyn and Bill Calkins have been renting a nice apartment for $250 per month. Most of their friends are homeowners and therefore

are enjoying certain tax benefits that Carolyn and Bill cannot obtain. What are these benefits and how do they work?

While Carolyn and Bill would like the above benefits of home ownership, neither of them enjoys yard work and the like. Is there a solution to their problem?

SUGGESTED READINGS

The Appraisal Journal. This is a quarterly publication of the American Institute of Real Estate Appraisers, 430 North Michigan Ave., Chicago, Ill.

Appraisal Review Journal. This journal is published three times per year by the National Association of Review Appraisers, Suite 410, Midwest Federal Building, St. Paul, Minn.

Arnold, Alvin L., Wurtzebach, Charles H., and Miles, Mike E. *Modern Real Estate.* Boston: Warren, Gorham and Lamont, 1980.

"Digest of Insurable Loans and Summaries of other Federal Housing Administration Programs." Washington, D.C.: U.S. Department of Housing and Urban Development, March 1977.

"Fair Housing U.S.A." Washington, D.C.: U.S. Department of Housing and Urban Development, 1976.

Federal National Mortgage Association 1981 Annual Report. Washington, D.C.

FHA Home Owner's Guide. Washington, D.C.: Federal Housing Administration.

Harwood, Bruce. *Real Estate Principles.* Reston, VA: Reston Publishing Company, 1977.

"Home Mortgage Insurance." U.S. Department of Housing and Urban Development, 1976.

"Homes: Construction, Maintenance, Community Development." Washington, D.C.: U.S. Government Printing Office, December 1976.

The Real Estate Appraiser and Analyst. This is a bimonthly publication of the Society of Real Estate Appraisers, 645 North Michigan Avenue, Chicago, Ill.

Real Estate Review. This journal is published quarterly by Warren, Gorham and Lamont, 210 South Street, Boston, Mass. 02111.

Savings and Loan Fact Book. Chicago: United States Savings and Loan League, latest edition.

Seller Services. This is a bimonthly publication on homeownership, published by the Federal National Mortgage Association, 3900 Wisconsin Avenue, N.W., Washington, D.C. 20016.

The Story of Modern Home Financing. Chicago: United States Savings and Loan League, latest edition.

Unger, Maurice A. *Real Estate Principles and Practices,* 4th ed. Cincinnati: South-Western, 1979.

Wendt, Paul, and Cerf, Alan R. *Real Estate Investment Analysis,* 2nd ed. New York: McGraw-Hill Book Company, 1979.

What You Should Know Before You Buy a Home. Chicago: United States Savings and Loan League, latest edition.

Wiedemer, John P. *Real Estate Investments.* Reston, VA: Reston Publishing Company, 1979.

Your Housing Dollar. Chicago: Money Management Institute, Household Finance Corp., 1979.

Chapter Seventeen

Taxes

The only thing certain in this world is death and taxes.
ANONYMOUS

The objectives of this chapter are to

1   Introduce briefly the principles of taxation, and note state and local taxes

2   Present federal taxes concentrating on the federal income tax

3   Analyze how the federal income tax works

4   Note what income is taxable

5   Introduce adjusted gross income and the Page 1 deductions

6   Discuss allowable itemized deductions

7   Examine certain tax credits which can reduce taxes

8   Define capital gains and show how they are taxed differently

9   Present a few tax savings tips

INTRODUCTION TO TAXES AND EXPENDITURES

The amount of all levels of government expenditures (state, local and federal) has risen sharply in recent years. Back in 1913, all levels of government spent approximately $3 billion. For the 1981 fiscal year, federal expenditures alone are expected to be about $616 billion. To be sure, today's dollars have been eroded by inflation to the point where today's $616 billion would only be about $245 billion in 1940 dollars.

Among the reasons for this growth are the great growth in population, the tremendous increase in the demand for more and better government services, and enlarged defense expenditures. Along with this growth in government expenditures came a great increase in taxes.

Taxes Expenditures and National Income

The big increase in government expenditures (and hence taxes) really started with World War II as far as the federal government is concerned, and shortly after the war for state and local governments.

The other side of the coin from expenditures is taxes. As noted before, these have grown with expenditures. Total federal taxes were $188.4 billion in 1971; this amounted to 24.6 percent of national income. In 1979 this tax figure had grown to $465.9 billion which amounted to 24.2 percent of national income. The table below shows total taxes and expenditures and their percent of national income over the years. The chart below plots these same figures as a percent of gross national product (GNP).

Comparing taxes and expenditures with national income and gross national product is one indicator of the cost (or burden) of government, since it is out of our income that we pay our taxes.

The above figures were aggregates; to get your personal share, you can compare your personal taxes with your personal income. The percentage of your income taxed away is called the effective tax rate. Note that the above included only federal taxes. If we add state and local taxes, the aggregate figure becomes $790.9 for 1979. This amounts to 33.4 percent of GNP and 41.1 percent of national income.

Principles of Taxation

There are five general principles of taxation and some of them are controversial.

1. *Ability to Pay.* For example, there is the ability-to-pay principle. This suggests that high-income groups should pay more than low-income groups. This has been used to justify the income tax and even the progressive income tax. Attempts have been made to link this principle with equity. A tax based on ability to pay is the most equitable tax, it is argued. While most would probably agree, at least to some extent, with the ability-to-pay principle, there is some disagreement as to who has the most ability. Not all agree that income is the sole test. Also, even if the ability principle (and hence the income tax) were accepted, there

TABLE 17–1. *U.S. taxes, expenditures, and national income*

YEAR	TAXES	EXPENDITURES	FISCAL YEAR NATIONAL INCOME	TAXES NATIONAL INCOME	EXPENDITURES NATIONAL INCOME
1971	$188.4	211.4	858.1	22.0%	24.6%
1972	208.6	232.0	951.9	21.9	24.4
1973	232.2	247.1	1,064.6	21.8	23.2
1974	264.9	269.6	1,136.0	23.3	23.7
1975	281.0	326.2	1,215.0	23.1	26.9
1976	300.0	366.4	1,359.8	22.1	27.0
1977	357.8	402.7	1,525.8	23.5	26.4
1978	402.0	450.8	1,724.3	23.3	26.1
1979	465.9	493.6	1,924.8	24.2	25.6
1980*	532.2	572.7	——	——	——
1981*	600.8	616.0	——	——	——

*Estimate.

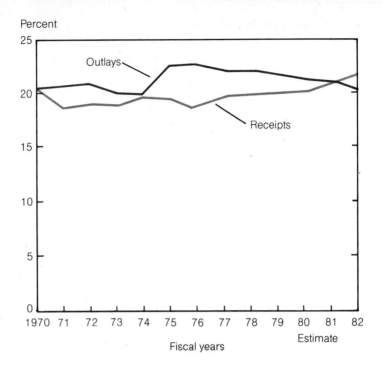

FIGURE 17–1. *Budget outlays and receipts as a percent of GNP. (Source: The United States Budget in Brief, Fiscal Year 1980,* Office of Management and Budget, p. 2.)

is disagreement as to how progressive the tax should be. And, of course, there can be no final answer here. Some groups even say any income tax should be proportional (everyone being taxed at the same percentage rate). People do not agree on what is equitable.

2. *The Benefit Principle.* This concept suggests that taxes should be levied so that their burden would be distributed in accordance with the distribution of the services that the taxes finance. This, too, has the ring of equity to it until it is examined critically. For example, this principle is sometimes used to defend the view that only people with school-aged children should be required to finance the schools as they are the beneficiaries of schools. This, of course, is not true because all of society, hence all citizens, benefit from schools. The benefit principle breaks down very quickly. How can the benefits of roads, schools, a system of courts, law enforcement, defense, or any other government service be allocated differently to different people? They cannot, hence almost no one defends the benefit principle.

3. *The Political Expediency Principle.* Some hold that if taxes have to be raised, then whichever taxes it is politically possible to raise should be selected. This view holds that all taxes are diffused throughout the system and all of them are paid out of current income. Since economically it doesn't matter, politicians should select any one they can. While this principle can neither be proved nor disproved, political leaders do seem to give it some weight.

4. *The Principle of Conveniency and Certainty.* Taxes should be as simple as possible in order to make them easy to pay. By this I mean the time needed to calculate the tax bill

should be minimized. Complexities in tax forms should be avoided. The most complex tax that the average taxpayer will face is the income tax. Its complexities are defended on the basis that equity requires some complexities.

Taxes should also be certain and the dollar amount not subject to various interpretations. This too is difficult to achieve.

5. *The Ease of Administration Principle.* This is similar to principle number 4 above, except that it applies to the collecting agencies. Taxes should be easily collectable, and the cost of collection as small a portion of the tax revenues as possible.

While some of these principles may be inconsistent, they must nevertheless be given some weight by the tax authorities. Probably the concept of equity is the most troublesome. People disagree as to what is most equitable, and attempts to achieve greater equity may also make the tax laws complex.

STATE AND LOCAL TAXES

While some states and even some cities impose income taxes, the bulk of state and local tax revenues are from sales and property taxes. The largest single portion of the property tax goes to support the schools, but the city and county governments also derive some revenue from it. And many cities today also have a sales tax.

The bulk of the sales tax receipts, however, flow into state treasuries. Other major sources of revenue for states in addition to income taxes are gasoline, liquor, and cigarette taxes. In this chapter, I will discuss primarily the sales and property taxes at the local level and the federal income tax because those are the major taxes for most people.

Sales Taxes

As noted above most of the revenue generated by the sales tax goes to the states, but some local governments receive some sales tax revenue. In some areas, there are exempted or nontaxed items and in other states there are none. The most commonly exempted items are food consumed in the home and services such as doctors' fees, haircuts, laundry bills, and the like. Generally, rates vary from 3 to 7 percent for the states' share, and some cities add a bit more to this, usually 1 or 2 percent. The retail merchant must collect this tax and usually can keep a small part of it (this varies from state to state but generally is 1 percent of the taxes due) to cover collection cost.

The sales tax is generally considered to be regressive. That is, it takes away a larger portion of a low income than a high one. This is simply because it is a tax on consumption, and low-income persons consume more (save less) of their income than do high-income persons. For example, let us assume that Mr. A has $10,000 after withholding tax take-home income per year, and let us say he saves $500 and consumes $9,500, and lives in an area that levies a 5 percent sales tax. Depending upon whether or not food and services are taxed, he will pay about $475.00 in sales taxes per year. This is, of course, 4.75 percent of his take-home pay. Let us assume Ms. B is earning $20,000 take-home pay per year and lives in the same town. But she saves $2,000 of it; hence, she pays about $900 in sales taxes, which is 4.5 percent of her income.[1] As incomes rise further, the percentage taken away

1. Actually a sales tax of 5 percent may result in taxes of more than 5 percent of total consumption. This is because most purchases are in small amounts and fractional dollars are taxed at a higher rate. There are breaking points on the tables that the merchants use to calculate the tax and often the five cent per dollar tax is reached at seventy cents.

under the sales tax generally declines further. In spite of the fact that sales taxes are taxes on consumption, most citizens seem to prefer this to a state or local income tax. In part this may be because it is paid in small amounts and therefore seems more painless. The sales tax has two other virtues. First, it is broad-based and raises a lot of revenue and the administrative and collection cost is very low relative to the revenue it raises.

Property Taxes

While some state and local governments impose a personal property tax—on automobiles, boats, and the like—and some even on intangible personal property—on bank accounts and securities—these taxes do not raise much revenue. The biggest single property tax for most individuals is the one on real estate, that is, on the person's home. Consequently, I will limit my discussion to it. The real property tax is a very ancient device. It is also not considered the best tax, but it will no doubt remain with us.

Criticisms of the Property Tax

The real property tax has been criticized on the following grounds:

1. It is costly to administer. A good deal of manpower is devoted by the taxing agency to keeping records, collecting the taxes, and appraising property for tax purposes.
2. It is inequitable. Not all property of equal value is on the tax rolls at equal assessments. Often older property of equal value, not having been reappraised for many years, is on the tax rolls at a lower value than newer property. Moreover, in many cases the assessors are poorly trained, which may result in unequal assessments.
3. It violates the ability-to-pay principle. This is often true because the size of one's income, not the value of one's property, is the best measure of ability to pay. While there may be a relationship between income and the value of a person's property, the relationship is not a good one.
4. It penalizes pride of home ownership. Persons who maintain their property well and maintain or improve its value often must pay a higher tax than the persons who allow their property to become run-down. Some critics even maintain that the property tax helps to create slums.
5. The tax base does not automatically expand to provide for added tax revenues as the local government's need for revenue grows.
6. It encourages flight from the central cities to the suburbs, where taxes usually are lower.
7. The tax is sometimes regressive. Larger and more valuable property is often assessed at a lower percentage of its market value than cheaper property.

The only good thing that the critics of the property tax have to say about it is that it does raise a good deal of revenue, and that since it is an old tax people do understand it and will put up with it. On the other hand, there is more and more grumbling about the property tax and many observers believe most cities have reached the limit to the amount of revenue their property tax can raise. Yet local governments often have their hands tied. Not being sovereign, they have to receive permission from their state government before they can impose a sales or an income tax. In some cases a constitutional amendment would even have to be passed before the local governments could impose an income tax.

Paying the Tax

The property tax is generally shared by the city government, the county government, the state government, and the school system, with the latter getting the largest share. Sometimes, however, a portion of the tax is also earmarked for specific items such as a sewer or water district. In some areas, the tax is paid to one of the above-mentioned governments (usually the city or the county) and is then disbursed to the other unit in accordance with the predetermined percentage share each is to get. In other areas, the various local governments cannot get together and the homeowner must write two (or more) checks and pay the county's share and the city's share separately.

Computation of the Property Tax

The computation of the property tax is about the same all over. The only variables are the appraised (or assessed) value and the tax rate or mileage rate. The assessed value generally varies from about 20 percent to 75 percent of the market value of the property.

The tax rate applied to assessed value to obtain the actual tax liability is stated either as a percentage (so much dollarwise per $100 of assessed valuation) or in mills (a mill is one-tenth of one cent). It varies from area to area. For example, a house with a $5,000 assessed value could be taxed at 12 percent of its assessed valuation or 120 mills per hundred dollars of assessed valuation. In both cases the tax on it is $600.

State and Local Income Taxes

A growing number of states and a few cities have an income tax (in some states, on the other hand, income taxes are unconstitutional). A few years ago most of the states having income taxes had laws on the books that did not take advantage of the federal income tax. Therefore, after filing federal taxes, one had to go through the ordeal again at the state level. Recently, more and more states have tied their income taxes into the federal government's in one way or another. Consequently, after filing the federal form, a copy of it could be sent to the state authorities as verification of earned income and only a relatively simple additional state form would be needed. The only shortcoming of this system is that many of the inequities in the federal income tax law are incorporated into the state income taxes.

Other State and Local Taxes

A number of other taxes are levied by state and local governments. The most important of these are gasoline and tobacco taxes, taxes on liquor and hotel rooms, the personal property tax, personal intangible property tax, license and fees such as on a car, estate and inheritance taxes, and corporate income taxes. This does not exhaust the list, but it includes the major ones in use today.

FEDERAL PERSONAL INCOME TAXES

Although there are other federal taxes (for example, on corporations), the federal income tax is the largest revenue producer and the tax that has the biggest impact on the average citizen. Consequently, I will limit my discussion to it. In fiscal 1980 the federal government collected about $234.2 billion through personal income taxes. In fiscal 1981, personal income taxes are expected to generate about $.45 out of each dollar that the government receives. (The second largest source of revenue was the social security tax which yielded about $160 billion in 1980; the third largest tax, corporate income tax, yielded approximately $70 billion.) Figure 17-2 illustrates where the federal dollar comes from and where it goes.

The federal income tax has been described as a house of horrors. It is that—not only because of its complexities but also because of some inequities in it. However, it should be noted that equity and inequities are often in the eye of the beholder. People do not agree on what is equitable.

Cash Versus Accrual Basis

All taxpayers are required to account to the federal government and to keep such records as will enable them to render a true account. In accordance with the tax regulations, individuals may keep their records on either a cash basis or an accrual basis.

Most taxpayers keep their accounts—or to be more precise, render their returns—on a cash basis. Under the cash basis any income received is taxable during the year in which it was received even though it may have been earned in the previous year. This is usually only a factor to be considered by some self-employed professionals who may render a service in, say, December and receive their fees in January. The same is true of legitimate deductible expenses; they must be deducted the year actually paid, even though they may have been incurred earlier.

Some businesses and self-employed individuals have chosen an accrual basis of accounting. Under it income is placed on the books when earned even though it is not received until later. The same is true of expenses; they count for tax purposes when incurred, not when paid.

FIGURE 17–2. *The budget dollar, fiscal year 1981 estimate. (Source: The United States Budget in Brief, Fiscal Year 1981, Office of Management and Budget.)*

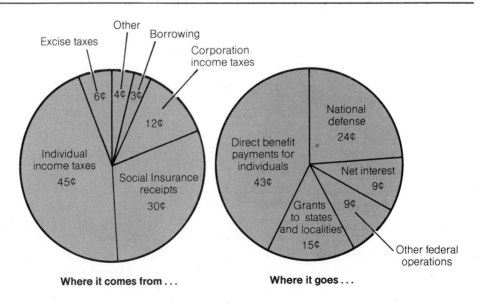

Where it comes from . . .   Where it goes . . .

Part 4 / Home Ownership, Taxes, Estate Planning

Who Must File a Return and Pay a Tax?

Generally speaking, any individual must file an income tax return for any year in which he or she had a gross income of $3,300 or more, if single. If married and filing jointly, the figure is $5,400. The first $2,300 a single taxpayer earns is not taxed; it is called the zero bracket amount. In addition, the taxpayer has a $1,000 exemption for him- or herself. For a married couple filing jointly the zero bracket amount is $3,400, and this together with the two $1,000 exemptions makes the first $5,400 tax free. There is a second $1,000 exemption for any person over sixty-five and another one if blind. An additional $1,000 exemption is allowed for each dependent you have. The zero bracket amount and exemptions you have for yourself, your spouse, for being over sixty-five, and for being blind determine whether or not you must file a return. The exemptions you have for other dependents do not count in determining whether you must file, but they do count in determining whether you pay taxes. In some cases, then, a person must file a return even if he or she owes no tax. Indeed, if a person has a refund coming he or she must file a return in order to get it. Table 17-2 illustrates the income levels at which a person must file a return regardless of whether or not a tax is due.

The zero bracket amount, the amount allowed as an exemption for dependents, and indeed many things discussed in this chapter will be changed somewhat almost yearly. Hence you should get the latest instructions for the form 1040. This is put out by the IRS in early January every year and can be picked up at any post office.

Earned Income Credit

In 1975, Congress began extending relief to low-income taxpayers by means of the earned income credit. This is a credit against taxes due amounting to 10 percent of a person's earned income up to a maximum credit of $500. Earned income includes such things as wages and salaries, but not such things as interest and dividends. For example, a taxpayer with an annual salary of $5,000 would be entitled to a credit of $500. The earned income credit is unique in that it is refundable. This means that if the above taxpayer with a credit of $500 had a "precredit" tax liability of $200 and had not had any taxes withheld, he or she

TABLE 17–2. *Who must pay a federal income tax*

CATEGORY	INCOME
Single	$3,300
Single, Over 65	4,300
Married, Joint Return	5,400
Married, Joint Return, One Spouse Over 65	6,400
Married, Joint Return, Both Spouses Over 65	7,400
(Add another $1000 for blindness).	
For Example:	
Married, Joint Return, Both Spouses Over 65	
and Both Blind	9,400
Married, Joint Return, Both Spouses	
Under 65 with 5 minor children*	5,400

*Minor children do not count in determining who must file a return; they do count in determining who must pay a tax.

would receive a payment of $300. However, the amount of the earned income credit is reduced by 12.5 percent of the earned income in excess of $6,000. Therefore, the credit is reduced to zero for earned incomes above $10,000. It should be noted that this earned income credit applies only to heads of households who also have dependent children. Some taxpayers therefore do not benefit from this. Also this credit is different from most tax credits which are taken on page 2 of form 1040. This one is calculated from special tables and is taken on line 57 of the 1040 form.

Income Subject to Tax (Gross Income)

All income unless specifically excluded by law is considered taxable income; that is, wages and salaries, bonuses, tips, commissions—everything. Insofar as these items are concerned, it is the gross amount, not the net amount after, say, withholdings.

The following items then are included:

1. All wages and salaries including tips and bonuses.

2. All interest and dividend income, except interest on bonds issued by state and local governments and their political subdivisions which is specifically exempt by law. Interest on savings deposits is taxable in the year it is credited to your account, not when it is entered into your passbook. Interest on corporate and U.S. government bonds which pay the coupon rate is taxable when it is paid. Interest on series E (and EE) bonds is obtained via an appreciation in their price over the years. If the taxpayer is on an accrual basis, their increase must be reported and a tax paid on it annually. A taxpayer on a cash basis may report and pay a tax on the annual increase or she may elect to report it only when it is realized upon the redemption of the bonds.

3. All cash dividends on corporate stock (both common and preferred) must be reported. However, the first $100 ($200 on a joint return) is not taxable. The tax law permits exclusion of the first $100 on a simple return and $200 on a joint return. Stock dividends also are not taxable nor are so called dividends on life insurance policies. For tax purposes, they are considered a return of premiums and not an earned dividend.

4. Alimony awarded by a court is taxable although one lump sum settlements are not.

5. All rent and royalty income is taxed. If you own an apartment house you must report and pay a tax on the rent you receive. If you receive royalties from an oil well, you must report it. The same is true of royalties received by an author of a book. However, in the case of rent and royalties only the net income is taxed. You may first deduct all the legitimate business expenses incurred (including depreciation where applicable) in generating the rent or royalty income.

6. Profit from a business or profession is taxable; again, you may first deduct expenses incurred in generating the income. If you are self-employed, this applies to you. If you own and run a corner grocery store, the rent, etc. is a legitimate business expense. The salary a physician in private practice pays a nurse and a receptionist as well as the rent on his or her office is deductible from the physician's gross to obtain net or taxable income.

7. Gains from the sale or exchange of property are considered capital gains and are taxable. Generally, this includes gains on the sale of stock or bonds and real estate. However, capital gains are taxed under a special section of the law and are usually taxed at a lower rate than regular income. The taxation of capital gains is quite complex and is explained in greater detail below under the section of this chapter entitled "*Capital Gains and Losses.*"

8. Payments received from pensions or annuities are often taxable at least in part. The taxation of pensions and annuities is very complex and is discussed in greater detail below.

9. Income from farms, estates, and trusts is taxed as ordinary income. This applies to farm income received by an absentee tenant who shares in the proceeds of the crop. As before, the expenses incurred in raising the crop (such as fertilizer, tractors, local taxes on the land, etc.) are deducted first. Income received from a trust is taxable, but it must actually be received. Income earned by a trust on behalf of a beneficiary, but retained by the trust, is not taxable insofar as the individual is concerned. However, the trust itself may be subject to a tax. This very complex issue of trust is explained in detail in the next chapter.

10. Generally speaking, sick pay is now included in gross income and is subject to taxation. There are two exceptions, however. First, if the sick pay is financed through an insurance company and the premiums are wholly paid by the employee (the insured) and not by the employer, then the sick pay is not taxable. The other exception is when the person is permanently and totally disabled. In such a case, the sick pay is excluded from taxation, but only up to a limit of $100 per week or $5,200 per year. This exclusion, however, is reduced dollar for dollar by adjusted gross income in excess of $15,000, and hence at an income of $20,200 it disappears. Sick pay is not listed separately, but is included with your regular wage or salary.

11. Unemployment compensation is included in gross income in some cases. If total adjusted gross income, together with unemployment compensation, is more than $20,000 ($25,000 if the taxpayer is married and filing jointly), it is subject to taxation. In such a case you must pay a tax on whichever of the following is the smaller: (1) total unemployment compensation, or (2) one half of that portion of other total adjusted gross income and unemployment compensation, which together exceeds $20,000 if the taxpayer is single and $25,000 if married and filing jointly.

12. Income from most other miscellaneous sources is also taxable. Normally, prize money or the fair market value of noncash prizes must be reported as income. Any money made from gambling in Las Vegas or any other place must be included as income; gambling losses, on the other hand, may not be deducted—except from the winnings themselves, to arrive at a net gain.

13. State and local income tax refunds must be reported as taxable income in the year it is received, if the refund is for a year in which the taxpayer itemized her deductions. This is because state and local income taxes are legitimate itemized deductions.

Nontaxable Income

There are some exceptions that need not be included as income. Among these, but not altogether inclusive, are scholarships and prizes for scholarly works. If you were to win the

TABLE 17–3.

Individual tax computation	
Gross income	xxxx
minus deductions and exemptions	xxxx
Taxable income	xxxx
Tax computed on taxable income at applicable rates	xxxx
minus credits	xxxx
Income tax payable	xxxx

Nobel prize, for example, you would not need to pay taxes on it. While scholarships and honorariums are not taxable, the stipend received by college students who hold teaching or research assistantships is. The logic behind not taxing gifts, honorariums, or scholarships is that the taxing authorities do not consider them income; they do consider the stipend from a teaching or a research assistantship as income. Most government payments made to veterans and their families, workman's compensation payments, interest from state and municipal bonds, as was previously explained, casualty insurance payments received, gifts, disability and death payments, damages awarded by the courts, and inheritances are not subject to the income tax. There are separate gift and inheritance taxes both at the state and federal levels, but at the federal level there are high exemptions. Moreover, legal loopholes exist by which inheritance and gift taxes can be avoided legally. Gift and inheritance taxes are explained in the next chapter. Table 17-4 illustrates the various sources of income and shows whether or not they are subject to the federal income tax.

TABLE 17–4. *Checklist of taxable and nontaxable income*

ITEM	TAXABLE	NONTAXABLE
Accident insurance proceeds		x
Alimony and separate maintenance payments periodically received	x	
Bad debt recovered, to extent of prior tax benefit	x	
Bequests		x
Board and lodging, unless furnished for convenience of employer	x	
Bonuses received as compensation for services rendered	x	
Capital gains	x	
Clergymen		
Rental value of parsonage furnished as part of compensation		x
Salaries, fees, contributions, etc., received for personal services	x	
Commissions received as compensation for services rendered	x	
Damages awarded by a court		x
Dismissal pay received	x	
Dividends		
In cash or property from corporate earnings accumulated after March 1, 1913 (there is a partial exclusion; see above)	x	
In stock of corporation where proportionate interest of stockholders is not affected		x
On life insurance policies		x
Executor's fees	x	
Farmers' income including government payments received under A.A.A. and other acts	x	
Gambling winnings	x	
Gifts		x
Inheritances		x
Interest on		
Bank savings accounts	x	
Bonds of a state, city, or other political subdivision		x
Building and loan accounts	x	
Federal obligations issued on or after March 1, 1941	x	

TABLE 17–4 *(continued)*

ITEM	TAXABLE	NONTAXABLE
Industrial bonds	x	
Notes	x	
Tax refunds	x	
Insurance benefit payments		x
Jury fees	x	
Legacies		x
Marriage settlement, lump-sum payment received		x
Moving expenses of family paid by employer (in some cases. See below.)		x
Notary public fees	x	
Old age benefits		
Under Railroad Retirement Act		x
Under Social Security Act		x
Partnership income, distributive share of partnership		
profits	x	
Political campaign contributions received by candidates		x
Prizes won in contests, exhibits, fairs, raffles, etc.	x	
Professional fees	x	
Rents	x	
Royalties received	x	
Salaries and wages	x	
Scholarships		x
Sick pay (Taxable in most cases)*	x	
Social security benefit payments		x
State and federal employees' salaries	x	
Strike benefits from labor unions	x	
Teachers' salaries	x	
Tips	x	
Tuition paid by employer	x	
Unemployment benefits under		
Railroad Unemployment Insurance Act		x
State Unemployment Compensation Laws		x
War veterans		
Bonuses		x
Pensions		x
Workmen's compensation benefits		x

*Sick pay is not taxable in the case where the person is totally disabled, or if it is financed through an insurance company and the premiums were paid by the individual rather than by the employer.

Gross Income

The above income items subject to taxation are together referred to as gross income. It is one of the first entries made on the personal income tax forms. It can be reduced somewhat before you calculate your tax, but before I discuss that I shall examine a few other things about the income tax law.

Joint Returns or Income Splitting

Historically, those married persons living in the community-property states (namely Arizona, California, Idaho, Nevada, New Mexico, Texas, and Washington) had a tax advantage over married persons living in the other states. In the community-property states, the legal concept is that one-half of the earnings of any spouse belong to the other spouse. If a married person earns $20,000 per year, $10,000 of this is the wage earner's and the other $10,000 is the spouse's. This made a substantial difference in the amount of tax paid by them, the reason being that the income tax is graduated, or progressive as some people call it. Thus the tax on a single return of $20,000 is greater than on two $10,000 returns.

In order to put all married couples on an equal footing taxwise, Congress in 1948 wrote into the Internal Revenue Code a statement that gives married taxpayers the option of income splitting by filing a joint return. Ordinarily when a married couple files a joint return, they save substantially in taxes. Whether a couple is married for tax purposes is determined by their status on December 31 of the year in question. There is one exception to this rule; if one of the members of a marriage dies, the survivor may elect to file a joint return that year.

The tax savings arising from income splitting can best be shown by an illustration (see Table 17–5). Let us assume two individuals, each with an income of $20,000 per year, two dependents, and each taking zero bracket amount. One splits income and one does not.

Different tables are available for those who file a joint return than for those filing a single return and the benefits described in the example just above and shown in Table 17–5 are built into them. Moreover, the higher a person's income, the greater the tax saving from income splitting; the joint return has in effect reduced the progressiveness of the tax structure.

The Discrimination against Married Couples

The above example suggests that the tax law discriminates against unmarried individuals by permitting income splitting because two individuals earning the same income, even if they have the same dependents, pay differing amounts of taxes if only one of them is married. However, recently many married couples have complained that they are discriminated against if both members hold jobs. This is because if each of them earns $15,000, their $30,000 total income is taxed more heavily than the $30,000 represented by two single individuals each earning $15,000; the married couple is taxed at the $30,000 tax bracket and the singles at the $15,000 one. Both of these charges are true because of the progressive nature of the tax structure. The purist would say that a single person earning

TABLE 17–5. *Tax savings from income splitting*

JOINT RETURN		SINGLE RETURN	
Income	$20,000	Income	$20,000
Dependents	2,000	Dependents	2,000
Taxable income	18,000	Taxable income	18,000
Tax	2,739	Tax	3,498
	Savings = $759		

Note: Zero bracket amount is not shown because it is built into both the tax tables and the tax rate schedule.

$30,000 per year should not have a heavier tax burden than a married person earning $30,000, as the joint return allows, and that a married couple each of whom earns $15,000 per year should not have a heavier tax burden than the combined burden of two singles each earning $15,000. In some cases singles have a heavier tax burden; in other cases married persons do. It is mathematically impossible to eliminate both of these types of discrimination under a progressive tax structure unless some formula is developed to give relief to a married couple both of whom work. As was pointed out before a congressional committee holding hearings on this subject, it is impossible for both ends of a see-saw to be up at the same time.

Head of a Household

Many persons who are unmarried are nevertheless the head of a household with many of the same expenses as a married person. Prior to October 31, 1951, individuals fitting into that category could file only individual returns and were thus placed in an unfair position compared with married persons who were able to file joint returns. After the 1951 date, the persons qualifying as heads of households were granted approximately 50 percent of the benefits given to married couples filing a joint return.

To qualify as the head of the household, an individual must be unmarried at the end of the tax year. He or she must further have maintained a household in which lives any person closely related for whom the taxpayer would ordinarily be entitled to a deduction. He or she must contribute over half the cost of maintaining the home, which has been interpreted to mean property taxes, maintenance costs, mortgage payments or rent, and the like plus the cost of food consumed on the premises.

Declaration of Estimated Tax for Individuals

If you have income not subject to withholding you may have to file a declaration of your estimated income and pay a tax on it quarterly. People who are self-employed and those with substantial interest, dividend, or other so-called nonearned income would have to do this. If you do not have very much income not subject to withholding, you may avoid filing this form by increasing the amount withheld from your salary over what it normally would be. The rule is that if your withholdings are 80 percent or more of your total tax liability, there is no penalty for not filing a declaration on your other income.

Tax Exemptions

All taxpayers have at least one $1,000 exemption, and that is for themselves. If they attain or are over the age of sixty-five before the end of the taxable year, they are entitled to a second exemption. In the event they are blind, they are entitled to a third exemption. Thus it is possible for the individual to have three exemptions totaling $3,000.

A married taxpayer is entitled to an exemption for his or her spouse if a joint return is filed. If a separate return is filed, each would probably take his or her own $1,000 exemption, although one could take it, and then the other would have zero exemptions. Further, if the spouse is over the age of sixty-five, an additional exemption may be claimed for him or her, and another possible exemption for the spouse if he or she is blind—unless of course these exemptions are claimed in his or her own behalf.

Further exemptions may be claimed in the amount of $1,000 for each dependent. However, a child or other dependent must have received more than half his or her support from the taxpayer (or from husband and wife if a joint return is filed). But if the child is married, then in order for the parent to claim him or her as an exemption, the child must not file a joint return with his or her spouse. A further qualification is that the child must have been either a resident of the United States, Canada, Mexico, the Republic of Panama, or the Canal Zone or an alien child adopted by and living with the United States citizen abroad.

In the case of a child or foster child under age nineteen or a student over nineteen (including college students), sometimes a double exemption is possible. If individuals under nineteen earn more than $3,300 (the zero bracket amount plus the $1,000 exemption), they must file a return and use themselves as an exemption. But if they are your children and you furnish more than one-half of their support, you can count them as dependents also, and deduct a full $1,000 for each. The same is true of full-time students, including college students, over nineteen, but not over twenty-two years of age. However, to obtain a double exemption for full-time students between age nineteen and twenty-two they must be unmarried.

Tax Withholding

Employers are required to withhold a portion of their employees' wages for income tax purposes. This scheme has been referred to as collection at the source, or the pay-as-you-go scheme. Its purpose is both to assure the government that the taxes will be paid and to make it easier for the taxpayer. Prior to the withholding tax, many taxpayers had to borrow from banks and other sources in order to pay their income taxes on time.

When persons first start work with an organization, they file with the employer a withholding tax exemption certificate (this is the W-4 form), which contains a statement of the number of exemptions to which they are entitled. Employees may if they desire claim fewer exemptions than they actually have to make sure they do not owe any taxes when the year is over. The employer will then withhold a percentage of wages based on the number of exemptions and the level of the wage or salary.

At the end of the year the employer gives the employee two or three copies of what is known as a W-2 form, showing the amount paid in wages, the amount withheld, and the amount of social security tax withheld, if any. (You will get three copies if you live in a state that has a state income tax and two if you live in a state that does not have a state income tax.) It is the W-2 form that forms the basis for the tax returns of those persons working for wages and salaries. The original copy of the W-2 form is submitted with the tax return and a duplicate is retained for the taxpayer's files.

The Taxation of Annuities and Pensions

Annuities

An annuity is ordinarily thought of as an insurance contract providing for regular payments to the insured at a fixed rate and continuing throughout the life of the insured or for a certain number of years. Thus a prize fighter who has a high income during the early years of his career might pay an insurance company a lump sum, the agreement being that at the age of forty the fighter is to receive $500 per week for the rest of his life. The problem from the tax point of view is

1. The lump sum given in exchange for the insurance annuity contract has already been taxed, and it would be manifestly unfair to tax it again as the fighter receives the $500 per week after reaching age forty.
2. However, if a prize fighter were to invest X dollars in corporate bonds, he would

receive interest, which is taxable. The same logic applies to annuities; part of the $500 per week that he receives each and every week after reaching forty until he dies is really in the nature of interest on the lump sum that he invested with the insurance company. In short, part of the $500 return is principal and part of the return is income; and the problem is to determine which part is income so that it may be taxed.

To determine the tax, the Internal Revenue Code has worked out a formula that provides for what is known as an exclusion ratio. This is determined by dividing the amount invested in the contract (and on which taxes have already been paid) by the expected return from the contract. For example, suppose $20,000 is the amount invested in the contract and, purely hypothetically, the annuitant is to receive $150 per month for life, and further that his age is such that his "expected" return will be $30,000. Then

$$\frac{\$20,000}{\$30,000} = 66\frac{2}{3} \text{ percent}$$

This means that the annuitant can exclude $66\frac{2}{3}$ percent from the gross income of each $150 monthly payment that he receives, or $100. Thus on an annual basis, of the $1,800 received, $1,200 is excluded from gross income and $600 is reportable as gross income subject to taxation. This is true even if the annuitant outlives the estimated life on which the exclusion ratio is based.

Pensions

A pension plan may also involve an annuity. This comes about in a number of ways. First, the entire cost of the annuity may be paid by your employer. In this case the entire amount received by you each year must be included in gross income, and this amount is fully taxable. However, generally the problem that arises is what happens if the employer contributed *part* of the payment of the annuity and the employee contributed the other part? The manner in which it is taxable depends upon how the payments are made.

1. If the plan provides that you will recover your total cost, or the amount you contributed over the years, within the first three years after the first payment to you starts, then the proceeds received by you are not taxable until after you have received your total cost. After that, the total pension payment is treated as income and must be reported on your return as gross income.
2. If you are not expected to recover your cost within three years, the pension is treated in the same manner as was outlined above under annuities. In short, your exclusion ratio must be established, this being your investment divided by the expected return.

In some cases, however, depending on the type of pension, you may be required to include the contribution of your employer in your gross income (and pay a tax on it) at the time the employer's contribution is made. This is the case where the pension plan is fully vested but is not what is considered "qualified" by the Internal Revenue Service. If this was the case, then, when determining the amount of the investment, your contribution plus the contribution of the employer are included in the investment, which has already been taxed. This is the figure that is employed to determine the exclusion ratio. Since this increases the investment figure and since the expected return figure remains the same, the percentage to be excluded rises and the net effect is that a lower amount of your pension is included in your gross income for tax purposes after the pension payments begin. For example, suppose the expected return is $10,000 and the investment is $5,000:

$$\frac{\$5,000}{\$10,000} = 50 \text{ percent}$$

Therefore 50 percent of the annuity payment can be excluded from gross income.

Now if the payments made on your behalf had been taxable at the time your employer made them and if over the years they totaled, say, $4,000, the total investment is $9,000.

$$\frac{\$9,000}{\$10,000} = 90 \text{ percent}$$

Ninety percent of the annuity may be excluded from gross income after the annual payments of the annuity begin.

If the pension plan is referred to as "qualified" by the Internal Revenue Service, the payment made by the employer into the pension fund on behalf of the employees while they are working is not taxable as income so far as the employees are concerned. Moreover, the employers can take the payment as an expense when calculating their tax. But when these employees retire, that portion of their pensions that comes from the employer's contribution is now fully taxable as income. Just how the plan must be set up to be considered qualified is too complex to examine here. If your firm has a pension plan, you can find out whether it is qualified or not and perhaps what is required for qualification from your personnel department.

This discussion of annuities and taxes has merely scratched the surface. There are many, many different types of annuities and pension plans, and the tax treatment depends upon the type of plan. But keep in mind that in the final analysis the whole purpose is to exclude from the tax any amount on which you have already paid a tax and to include in gross income any monies you will receive and on which you have paid no income tax.

Two types of pension payments paid to retired persons are not subject to any form of federal taxation. The first of these is social security payments; those persons who have income from this source need not report it. A second type of pension not subject to the federal income tax is the veteran's pension, paid because of a service-connected disability. Regular military retirement pay, however, is taxable.

Income Averaging and Maximum Tax Provision

In some cases you can save money by income averaging; this is true if your income fluctuates sharply or if your income rises rapidly from a relatively low level. A special schedule G is used for this. In effect, it puts the taxpayer in a lower tax bracket by allowing the high-income years to be averaged (and hence reduced) with low-income years. If after subtracting $3,000 from your taxable income the balance is significantly over 30 percent of the total of your taxable income for the last four years, it will probably pay you to average. If it is just over 30 percent, averaging may or may not be beneficial. In such a case, you should calculate your taxes both ways to ascertain which will minimize them.

There is also a maximum tax on earned income provision. This provides that no one need pay more than a 50 percent rate on earned taxable income. Other (so-called nonearned) income can be taxed as high as 70 percent.

486   *Part 4 / Home Ownership, Taxes, Estate Planning*

Earned income includes wages and salaries, tips, and all compensation for services rendered. Excluded from earned income is all return for the use of land or capital. Interest, dividends, and rent are therefore excluded.

ADJUSTED GROSS INCOME; PAGE 1 DEDUCTIONS

Certain deductions may be taken from gross income to arrive at adjusted gross income. Then certain other expense items may be taken to reduce adjusted gross income further to obtain taxable income. These latter items are called the itemized deduction. I will examine them below, but first I will note those items that may be taken in moving from gross to adjusted gross income. Generally, they include the following:

1. Deductions for expenses attributable to a trade or business.
2. Deductions for expenses that can be attributable to rent or royalty income.
3. Deductions consisting of expenses for meals, travel, and lodging incurred by the taxpayer while away from home in connection with the performance of services as an employee or owner of a business.
4. Deductions for depreciation and depletion allowed to a life tenant of property or to an income beneficiary of property held in trust.
5. Certain deductions allowed as losses from the sale or exchange of property.
6. Moving expenses can be deducted in many cases, though not always.
7. Sick pay, if it is included in your gross pay, may be deducted here before arriving at adjusted gross income, in those relatively few previously discussed cases where it is not taxable. Sick pay is now fully taxable with two exceptions. First, sick pay received by a person who is totally and permanently disabled is not taxable up to $5,200 per year. Second, sick pay financed by an insurance policy, the premiums of which were completely paid by the individual and not the employer, is also not taxable.
8. The law allows a capital gain adjustment between gross and adjusted gross income. Sixty percent of your net long-term capital gain (assets held more than one year) may be excluded from your adjusted gross income. The treatment of capital gains is now very complex and is treated more fully below.
9. Contributions to Keogh retirement plan by self-employed persons. The Keogh retirement plan was discussed in Chapter 11.
10. Contributions to an individual retirement account (IRA). This, too, was discussed in Chapter 11.
11. Interest penalty payments that are charged on early withdrawals of certificates of deposit (CD) may be deducted at this point when moving from gross to adjusted gross income.
12. Alimony payments are deductible in some cases.

ITEMIZED DEDUCTIONS

Up to this point, I have discussed the page 1 deductions that are taken in moving from gross income to adjusted gross income. Certain other deductions may be taken by the taxpayer who qualifies in moving from *adjusted gross income* to *net income,* also called taxable income. These are the itemized deductions examined below. First, however, I will examine the case of the person who does not wish to itemize or who is not permitted to itemize because his or her legitimate deductions do not exceed the zero bracket amount.

The Zero Bracket Amount

The zero bracket amount replaced what used to be called the standard deduction. The federal income tax is progressive and the rates technically start at zero; and a zero rate applies to the following income:

Taxpayer's status

1. Single taxpayer or unmarried head of household	$2,300
2. Married, filing jointly	3,400
3. Married, filing separately	1,700

In addition, there is a $1,000 exemption for the taxpayer and another $1,000 for each dependent. Both the exemptions and the zero bracket amount are built into the tax tables, but only the zero bracket amount is built into the tax schedule. The election to itemize deductions may be made only if these deductions exceed the zero bracket amount.

If you use the so-called short form (1040A) the IRS will calculate your taxes for you if you request it. You may use the short form only if your income is $20,000 or less ($40,000 if married and filing jointly) and your interest and dividend income do not exceed $400 apiece.

Itemized Deductions

The itemized deductions that can be taken only on Schedule A are of no value unless they exceed the zero bracket amount. If the taxpayer has a few large items, however, such as interest on a mortgage, and property taxes, these alone will often give a deduction in excess of the zero bracket amount. If this is the case, it is worthwhile to keep records so that all of the various smaller items can be added in as well. I will discuss each of the major itemized deductions.

1. *Taxes.* Most general state and local taxes paid by the taxpayer during the taxable year are deductible. The major taxes involved are state and local income taxes, retail sales taxes, real estate taxes, and personal property taxes such as on automobiles and boats. Tables are available that can be used to establish the sales tax deduction for every state (sales taxes vary by state). If you bought a big item during the year such as a boat, car, or airplane, you can deduct the sales tax on it in addition to what the tables allow.

Real estate taxes are probably the most important single tax insofar as the average person is concerned because it is usually the largest tax. If an individual has an adjusted gross income of $20,000 per year, and his or her real property tax is $1,200, that alone will reduce the taxable income to $18,800.

2. *Interest.* Interest is another big deduction for many taxpayers, especially if they are paying off a mortgage. All interest paid on personal debts—such as mortgages, notes, loans on life insurance policies, and personal loans from finance companies—is deductible. There are a few exceptions, for example, interest on money borrowed to purchase tax exempt securities is not deductible.

During the first few years when an individual is making payments on a mortgage, much of the money is for the payment of interest and consequently will constitute a major deduction on the part of the average taxpayer. Of a hypothetical $400 a month paid by a taxpayer during the first year of a mortgage, it may be that as much as $300 a month constitutes interest payment, and this amount is deductible. Over a full year, this can amount to $3,600 or more.

3. *Contributions.* Contributions to approved institutions operated for religious, charitable, literary, scientific, educational, or eleemosynary purposes may be deducted, although such deductions must not exceed 50 percent of the taxpayer's adjusted gross income (in some cases it cannot exceed 20 percent).

4. *Casualty, theft, and bad debt losses.* These items are deductible to some extent. Loss of value of property as the result of accident, fire, storm, theft, riot, rebellion, uprising, or other casualty loss not covered by insurance is deductible. The amount of the loss is computed by determining the value of the property just before the loss. From this figure, in order to determine the net loss for tax purposes, the taxpayer must deduct the salvage value plus any insurance received. In addition, he or she must bear the first $100 of the loss.

5. *Medical and Dental Expenses.* A taxpayer may deduct certain medical expenses on Schedule A of the tax form. The deduction is broken into two parts. First, one half of medical insurance premiums may be deducted but these items cannot exceed $150. The remainder of the insurance premiums are added to any other medical expenses and they are deductible but only to the extent that they exceed 3 percent of adjusted gross income.

Expenses for medicines and drugs are included in the other medical expenses to the extent that the total cost of medicines and drugs exceeds 1 percent of the adjusted gross income.

6. *Auto Expense.* If you use your car for business purposes or to generate other income, the expense of running it can be deducted. If, for example, you have some rental property, and you use your car to manage it, part of your auto expenses are a legal deduction. If your car is used for both business and pleasure, you must prorate the expense in accordance with the ratio of business to pleasure mileage per year. The cost (or mileage) of driving to and from work is not considered a business expense and hence is not deductible. If you prorate your expenses, be sure to keep good records, and include all of them. The cost of all oil and gas, repairs, taxes, insurance, parking fees, tolls, etc.—everything, including an allowance for depreciation. (Depreciation is explained in greater detail below.) Also keep accurate records of miles driven for both business and pleasure. If 60 percent of the mileage driven was for pleasure (which, remember, oddly enough includes to and from work), and 40 percent was for business, you may deduct 40 percent of your total auto expenses.

An alternative method of calculating your auto expenses is to take so much per mile of business or other legitimate driving. This includes business mileage as well as mileage incurred in charitable work and trips to and from hospitals and doctor's offices if they were medically necessary.

7. *Education Expenses.* With greater attention being paid to higher education, there is a greater need for the explanation of the deductible features of education expenses. They are deductible only for maintaining your skills or improving your skills in your employment or other trade or business or for meeting the express requirements of your employer or the requirement of applicable law or regulations imposed as a condition to the retention of your salary or employment. In short, education is only deductible if it is necessary in order to keep your job.

Remember, however, that expenses incurred for obtaining a new position, meeting minimum requirements, obtaining a substantial advancement in position, or for personal purposes are not deductible. For example, if a middle-aged woman decides to take a night course in American literature just for her own amusement, the expenses are not deductible. However, if a lawyer takes a refresher course to maintain her skills, this is deductible.

College tuition is not deductible, although Congress periodically discusses the possibility of allowing tuition as a deductible item.

8. *Depreciation.* Although most people have only one source of income, many people have income other than that from wages and salaries and consequently may become involved in problems of depreciation. For example, a person who owns rental property may depreciate the home and take the depreciation as a deduction. An accountant, lawyer, physician, or other professional person may recover the cost of books and certain other equipment through depreciation only.

Depreciation is defined as wear and tear on property used in a trade or business as well as obsolescence. In order to take depreciation as a deduction on the income tax you must have certain kinds of property; one cannot claim depreciation on land, stock, bonds, or securities. You must also know the date the property was acquired, because its life is figured from that date, and you must know the cost or other basis of the property.

The depreciation is computed on the fair market value of the property as of the date purchased. The useful life of the asset must be ascertained, for that may be the number of years over which depreciation may be charged. For tax purposes, however, the depreciation period may be less than the actual useful life, and this period varies from asset to asset. For a rental house it may be twenty years; for an auto used for business purposes, it is about five years. The value of the asset may then be written down (depreciated) so much per year over the period of years agreed upon, at which time the asset is carried on the books at its scrap value, if any. The dollar write-down is then a legitimate itemized deduction.

There are two main methods of computing depreciation: the so-called straight-line method and the accelerated method. The straight-line method works as follows: Assume that a typewriter used for profit has an original cost of $400, that the estimated life of the machine is ten years, and that it has no scrap value. In such a case the machine is depreciated at the rate of 10 percent or $40 per year, and its original cost will be recaptured at the end of the ten-year period. Hence, the taxpayer will be allowed to deduct $40 per year. If a given machine costs $1,000 and has a useful life of ten years, the taxpayer would be permitted to deduct 10 percent per year, or in this case $100 per year.

One way of calculating accelerated depreciation is called the sum of the digits method. It can be illustrated with an example. Suppose you have a machine costing $1,000 with a useful life of five years and no scrap value. The sum of the digits is $1 + 2 + 3 + 4 + 5 = 15$ and the first year's depreciation would be $5/15$ or $1/3$ of $1,000. Since there are five years to go, 5 divided by the sum of the digits gives us the allowance for the first year. The next year only four more years remain, and therefore 4 divided by the sum of the digits or $4/15$ is the depreciation allowance; $3/15$ for the third year, and so on.

Another common method of calculating the accelerated depreciation is the double declining balance. I can illustrate how it works with the following example: Suppose you have a $20,000 machine that has no scrap value and that you are going to depreciate over twenty years. Using the straight-line method would give you $1,000 the first (and each of the following) year. Under the double declining method, however, after calculating the first year's depreciation you simply double it; hence you get $2,000 the first year. The second year the machine is only worth $18,000, one-twentieth of that value is $900, which you double and get your depreciation of $1,800. The third year it is valued at $16,200 ($20,000 less $3,800) for purposes of depreciation, and one-twentieth of that number doubled is $1,620, which is your third year depreciation. So it continues through the life of the asset.

In the case of a rental house which you wish to depreciate, the sum of the digits or the double declining balance method may not be used. Often the straight-line method is used, but recently the IRS has allowed a slightly accelerated depreciation rate. On a new house, a

150 percent straight-line rate may be used and on an older house the figure is 125 percent. Once more an example will illustrate this. If you have a $20,000 rental house to be depreciated over twenty years, the straight-line method would give you $1,000 per year. If you use 150 percent, you simply jack up the depreciation charge by that amount and the first year's depreciation becomes $1,500. The second year the house is only worth $18,500. Hence the normal straight-line depreciation would give you $925, but 150 percent of that value is $1,387.50, and so on as the years go by. If it is a used house, the straight-line method can only be accelerated by 125 percent.

There are a few gray areas in the case of depreciation. For example, can a self-employed consultant deduct depreciation on his home, if he has an office in it? If the office is used primarily for consulting, he can deduct a prorated part of his house. If his house has nine rooms and he uses one for his office, and his house is valued at $50,000, he may depreciate his house as explained above in the case of a rental, but only take one ninth of the final figure (or he may make the proration on the basis of square feet).

If the consultant's office is not used primarily (and this has been interpreted as almost solely) for consulting, he may not charge a depreciation allowance on it. The same gray area exists for a musician who gives piano lessons in her home. If she gives enough lessons on her piano in her home, she may be able to depreciate part of her piano as well as part of her home. She has to prorate her piano in accordance with its use, and the room in which it sits as explained above.

TABLE 17–6. *Checklist of deductible and nondeductible items*

ITEMS	DEDUCTIBLE	NON-DEDUCTIBLE
Alimony and separate maintenance payments taxable to recipient	x	
Automobile expenses (car used exclusively for pleasure)		
Gasoline taxes imposed on consumer	x	
Interest on finance loans	x	
License fees (property tax portion only)	x	
Ordinary upkeep and operating expenses		x
Burglary losses, if not covered by insurance	x	
Casualty losses not covered by insurance (fire, flood, windstorm, lightning, earthquakes, etc.)	x	
Charitable contributions to approved institutions (limited to 50% of adjusted gross income; in some cases 20%)	x	
Domestic servants, wages paid		x
Dues, social clubs for personal use		x
Employment fees paid to agencies	x	
Expenses for care of children (in part)	x	
Federal income taxes		x
Fines for violation of laws and regulations		x
Funeral expenses		x
Gambling losses, to extent of gains only	x	
Gift taxes		x
Gifts to relatives and other individuals		x

TABLE 17–6. *(continued)*

ITEMS	DEDUCTIBLE	NON-DEDUCTIBLE
Income tax imposed by state	x	
Inheritance taxes		x
Interest paid on personal loans	x	
Life insurance premiums		x
Medical expenses in excess of 3% of adjusted gross income (including the cost of artificial limbs, artificial teeth, drugs and medical supplies prescribed by a physician, eye glasses, hearing aids, dental fees, hospital expenses, to extent not covered by insurance). One-half of medical insurance premiums (but not to exceed $150) may be deducted, and the premium in excess of $150 is subject to the 3% rule	x	
Old-age benefit tax withheld by employer		x
Political campaign contributions (Up to $50; $100 on a joint return)	x	
Property taxes, real and personal	x	
Residence for personal use		
Improvements		x
Insurance		x
Interest on mortgage loan	x	
Loss from sale of		x
Rent paid		x
Repairs		x
Taxes	x	
Termite damage		x
Sales tax, state and local	x	
State gasoline taxes		x
Teachers		
Fees paid to employment agencies	x	
Traveling expenses attending professional meetings	x	
Traveling expenses to and from place of business or employment		x
Unemployment taxes imposed on employees under state law	x	
Uniforms for personal use including cost and upkeep, if not adaptable for general use (nurses, policemen, jockeys, baseball players, firemen, trainmen, etc.)	x	
Union dues	x	
Use taxes imposed on consumers under state law	x	

TAX CREDITS

After you have itemized all of your deductions, you can use them to reduce your adjusted gross income, presumably by more than the zero bracket amount. Then you obtain your taxable income and calculate your tax liability. But then there are tax credits. A tax credit is better than a deduction because it reduces not your income subject to tax, but rather your actual tax itself. That is, after you have calculated the taxes due, every tax credit you have will reduce them dollar for dollar. There are a number of tax credits for which you may be eligible, and I will discuss the more common ones.

Political Contributions

You may take as a tax credit contributions to candidates for political office. One-half the contribution may be taken but this is limited to $50 for singles and $100 for marrieds filing jointly.

Tax Credit for the Elderly

The tax credit for the elderly (formerly called the retirement income credit) is a limited exemption in the form of a credit against the tax. It is designed to give the low-income elderly a modest tax break. Its determination is somewhat complicated, and you can qualify only if you are sixty-five or over or if you are under sixty-five but have retired under a public retirement plan. A public retirement plan is one set up for public servants, such as city officials and schoolteachers. In both cases, only the taxable portion of any pension is considered in computing the tax credit.

If you qualify, the credit for the elderly is calculated on all income received (including earned income) except social security and other tax-exempt pensions and annuities. The credit is 15 percent, but the maximum amount of income on which the credit may be calculated is $2,500 for singles and married persons filing jointly if only one spouse has reached age sixty-five. If both spouses are sixty-five or older, the 15 percent credit can be calculated on up to $3,750 of income. The income on which the tax credit is calculated (the $2,500 and $3,750) must be reduced by one-half of the taxpayer's adjusted gross income above $7,500 in the case of a single individual and $10,000 in the case of a married couple, and by the amount of social security or other pensions that are excluded from gross income received. Because the maximum income base is $3,750 or $2,500, the maximum credit comes to $375 for a single individual and $562.50 for a married couple both of whom are sixty-five or older. Table 17–7 illustrates the retirement income credit. In the example in the table, the individual would calculate his or her taxes in the regular way on the 1040 form and then reduce the tax due by $262.50 if married and if each person is over sixty-five.

TABLE 17–7. *Tax credit for the elderly*

SOURCE	INCOME	
Earnings	$3,000	
Rent	2,000	
Interest and dividends	100	
Taxable portion from annuity	1,500	
Social security	2,000	(must offset other credit base income)
Total taxable income	6,600	
Maximum credit base	3,750	
Less social security	2,000	
Credit base	1,750	
Income tax credit is $262.50, 15% × $1,750 =	$262.50	

If the taxpayer had other income of, say, $5,000, providing a total taxable income of $11,600, he or she would (if married) have to subtract half of that in excess of $10,000 from the $3,750 maximum tax credit base in addition to subtracting social security. In the above case, that would necessitate subtracting another $800 from $3,750, making the credit base $950 and 15 percent of that would make the actual tax credit $142.50. At an income level of $17,500, then, the income credit disappears.

A word of warning: This is a simplified example, and those eligible for the credit should consult someone in the Internal Revenue Service or their tax accountant if they have reason to believe that theirs might be a more complicated situation.

Child and Other Dependent Care

Child care expenses is another tax credit to which many taxpayers are entitled. The same is true of expenses for other dependents if they are disabled. The child care or care of other dependents, however, must be incurred in order to enable the taxpayer to be gainfully employed. The person being cared for must be under fifteen years old or disabled. The credit may be taken by a couple even if only one works full-time, if the other works part-time, or is a full-time student. The credit includes the cost of services received outside the taxpayer's home such as in a day care center. It is allowed even if the care is provided by a relative or member of the household if such person is not a dependent of the taxpayer.

There are, however, limits to how large a child care credit may be taken. First, the credit may not exceed 20 percent of the total cost of the care. Second, the credit may not exceed 20 percent of the lesser of the taxpayer's earned income, or the taxpayer's spouse's earned income. There is also an overall limit of $400 per child, and $800 for two or more.

Investment Tax Credit

The investment tax credit (ITC), generally speaking, applies only to those engaged in some business venture, but it may apply to some self-employed as well. This credit is 10 percent and applies to any business investment you make except most buildings. (The law now allows this credit for certain single-purpose agricultural structures.) If you invest $10,000 in expanding your business (say, you buy a couple of pickup delivery trucks), you may take a 10 percent credit and reduce your taxes by $1,000.

This credit, of course, applies to a self-employed person who has business assets. For example, if an author buys a new typewriter, she is eligible. Or a music teacher who buys a new piano on which he gives lessons may take the 10 percent credit on the new instrument.

Residential Energy Credit

Homeowners, and renters as well, may take a tax credit of 15 percent of expenditures on energy-saving devices up to $2,000.00. Covered are expenditures on insulation, storm windows and doors, weatherstripping and caulking, and automatic thermostat set-back devices. Fifteen percent of the above expenditures up to a maximum credit of $300.00 may be taken.

Solar heating and cooling equipment, wind energy devices, and geothermal energy installation expenses may be taken as a credit under a different provision of the law. In this case 20 percent of the expenditures, but not to exceed a credit of $2,000, may be taken. If these costs are in excess of $10,000, then a second credit of 10 percent of this excess, but not to exceed a credit of $200.00, may be taken. The total maximum credit here then is $2,200. In addition, the expenditures must have been made after April 19, 1977. The expenditure must also have been made on the taxpayer's principal residence to be available for the tax credit.

CAPITAL GAINS AND LOSSES

Capital gains and losses is another area about which a few words are in order. This is because under the income tax law taxpayers are frequently given special treatment if they have either a loss or a gain from the sale or exchange of a capital asset.

Capital Assets

Capital assets consist of certain property held by the taxpayer. It may be income-producing property such as rental houses, stocks, bonds, and the like, or it may be non-income producing such as the owner-occupied house of the taxpayer or his or her personal boat or auto. If you have a capital loss on a personal boat, car, or house (nonincome-producing assets), it does not provide you with a deduction; on the other hand, capital gains on such personal assets are taxed.

Most income-producing assets, on the other hand, may generate both capital gains and losses for tax purposes. However, certain income-producing assets do not. If the income-producing capital assets are used as stock in trade or business, any gain or loss they generate is treated as ordinary income. That is, stocks and bonds held by a security dealer do not qualify, but if held by an ordinary individual they do. The same is true of inventory held by a business, and houses held by a builder or realtor that are for sale. If these capital assets appreciate in price while being held by the dealer, realtor, builder, or other business person dealing in them, the resulting gain is considered income, when realized, and taxed as such. The words "when realized" are important. A capital gain (or loss) is not considered a gain until the capital asset is sold and the gain is realized.

Capital gains then come about when qualified capital assets are sold at a price in excess of what they were acquired for. Capital loss comes about if assets are sold at below their acquisition price. It should be noted that many capital gains are illusory because they are solely the result of inflation. Others are real, in the sense that they are, in part at least, not the result of inflation and their price appreciation has been in excess of inflation. The tax law does not differentiate between real and inflationary capital gains; they are all taxed the same way.

Short-term and Long-term Gains and Losses

Capital gains and losses may be broken down into short-term and long-term. Short-term are those on capital assets that were held one year or less before being sold. Long-term gains (and losses) are those realized on assets held more than one year before sold. It is important to note once more that the asset must actually have been sold and the gain or loss realized. Paper gains and losses do not count. Generally speaking, short-term gains or losses are treated like income whereas long-term gains and losses receive more favorable treatment. This is explained immediately below.

Merging of All Gains and Losses

A taxpayer may have some or all of the following:

1. Short-term capital gain
2. Short-term capital loss
3. Long-term capital gain
4. Long-term capital loss

You must merge the short-term gain and losses to get a net short-term position. You must also merge the long-term gains and losses to get a net long-term position. Next, the net short-term position is merged with the net long-term position to get a net capital gain (or loss) position. If this net capital gain position is short-term it is treated and taxed as ordinary income. If the total capital gain position is long-term it is treated differently, as explained below.

Tax Treatment of Capital Gains and Losses

If all of your merged short-term and long-term capital gains and losses results in a net short-term gain, it is taxed as ordinary income. If all of your merged short-term and long-term capital gains and losses results in a net short-term loss, it can be used to reduce your other (earned) income by a like amount before you calculate your taxes on it.

If your net position (as described above) is a long-term capital gain, 60 percent of it can be excluded; that is, you pay no tax on it. The other 40 percent is taxed as regular income. Since the tax rate on non-earned income, such as capital gains, goes as high as 70 percent, the maximum tax rate on long-term capital gains is 28 percent because only 40 percent of the gain is taxable (40% $\times$ 70% = 28%). You will recall, however, that earned income (that derived from wages and salaries) is subject to a maximum tax rate of 50 percent. Therefore, for a person to be subject to a 70 percent tax bracket (which is reached at $108,300 if single and $215,400 if married and filing jointly) that person would have to have a lot of non-earned income; that is, income in the form of rent interest and dividends.

If all of your merged long-term and short-term capital gains and losses results in a net long-term capital loss, it can be deducted from your other income, but $2 of net long-term loss is needed to offset one dollar of other income. The maximum income offset is $3,000 per year, but any loss in excess of that can be carried forward until it is exhausted. If, for example, you have a $10,000 long-term capital loss, $6,000 could be used to reduce your otherwise taxable income by $3,000. The other $4,000 of loss could be carried forward to next year and reduce your income for tax purposes by $2,000.

There are four possible gain or loss positions which I shall illustrate with an example. I shall assume in each case that the taxpayer has an income of $20,000 exclusive of the gain or loss.

First, there may be a gain because the net short-term gain is greater than the net long-term loss. If an individual has a net short-term gain of $5,000 and a net long-term loss of $4,000, he or she merges them and adds $1,000 to the $20,000 of other income and pays a tax on $21,000.

Second, the net long-term gain may be in excess of the net short-term loss. In this case only 40 percent of the merged long-term gain over the net short-term loss is included in income and is fully taxed as income. In the above case, if we reverse our figures, there is a net long-term gain of $5,000 and a net short-term loss of $4,000. Merging them provides a

$1,000 net long-term gain. But, because of the exclusion provision, only 40 percent of that gain, or $400, is added to the $20,000 and the tax is computed on $20,400.

Third, there may be a net short-term capital loss after merging net long-term and net short-term positions. The taxpayer may deduct the entire sum of such loss up to a limit of $3,000 from other income dollar for dollar. (Amounts in excess of $3,000 may be carried forward and deducted in future years until it is exhausted.) If, for example, the taxpayer has a net short-term loss of $5,000 and net long-term gain of $4,000, he or she may deduct $1,000 from other income. In our hypothetical case of a taxpayer with income of $20,000, it declines to $19,000 for tax purposes.

Fourth, there may be a net long-term capital loss in excess of the net short-term capital gain. Using the same figures in the case above there is a long-term loss of, say, $5,000, which after being merged with a $4,000 short-term gain results in a net long-term loss of $1,000. This $1,000 net loss may be deducted from ordinary income, but $2 of long-term loss are needed to offset $1 of income. Consequently, the hypothetical taxpayer who has $20,000 adjusted gross income will have his or her tax computed on $19,500.

Capital Gains on Owner-occupied Homes

A concluding footnote on capital gains is in order. It has to do with capital gains on the sale of owner-occupied houses. If the gain is reinvested in another house purchased by the taxpayer within eighteen months or in a new house she has built within twenty four months, she need pay no capital gains tax whatsoever on this transaction. However, if the former house sells for more than the cost of the new, then all or part of the gain is taxable.

In 1978 Congress also provided a once in a lifetime exclusion in some cases. Any taxpayer, age 55 or over, may take a once in a lifetime tax exclusion of $100,000 capital gain on the sale of a house which has been his or her principal residence for at least three years during the last five years ending on the date of sale of the house. This provision applies to homes sold after July 26, 1978.

OTHER THINGS YOU SHOULD KNOW ABOUT TAXES

There are a few other things about taxes with which you should be familiar—such as tax shelters and legal tax avoidance, some tax savings tips, and the tax forms themselves.

Legal Tax Avoidance

In 1979, national income was $1,924.8 billion and total personal income tax receipts were about $217.8 billion. This means that if the entire income had been subject to taxes, an average rate of only about 11 percent would have provided the same revenue. But of course the entire income is not subject to taxes. There are the normal deductions of $1,000 per person and all the other exemptions and deductions noted above. Over the years the tax base has eroded seriously because of legal loopholes discovered in the law by tax accountants or opened up by the courts or by Congress.

I noted above the loopholes that apply to many individuals, such as deductions for interest on mortgages, local property taxes, and income splitting. Congress has in addition provided special loopholes for the wealthy, and a battery of clever accountants and attorneys is constantly developing others. These are far too complex to describe in detail here, but I will note the more obvious and glaring ones.

Certain groups that have expense accounts have an obvious advantage over the rest of us. They can live lavishly and the company deducts their expenses for tax purposes. You and I, in effect, pay for their lavish living. Capital gains is another loophole. High-income groups devise ingenious schemes for converting ordinary income into capital gains, which are taxed at a lower rate.

There are other tax loopholes (or tax shelters as some prefer to call them) such as cattle-feeding operations, rental property, leasing of business assets, and tax-exempt interest-bearing bonds. If you have rental residential property, you can take accelerated depreciation on it. If you own your own business and you expand it, there is available to you the 10 percent investment tax credit. That is, you can take 10 percent of the dollar amount by which you expand your business and reduce your taxes by that. This, together with accelerated depreciation, may very well enable you to shelter a good deal of income. Corporate pension plans, the professional corporation, Keogh plans, and the IRA are other methods of sheltering income from taxes. These were discussed in a previous chapter. Many of these tax shelters that permit legal tax avoidance (as opposed to illegal evasion) are complex and if they apply to you, you should check with your tax accountant.

Tax Saving Tips

If you are a modest income person, you cannot hire a high-priced accountant to save taxes for you. There are, nevertheless, some things you may do that will save you money. In some cases where you never seem to have enough deductions to exceed the zero bracket amount, you might be able to do so every year by proper planning.

Consider the following suggestions:

1. Keep good records. Then you will not forget to take all the deductions that are legally yours.
2. Don't forget to include the sales taxes you pay on big items such as cars, boats, and airplanes.
3. Plan ahead especially when making certain big expenditures. If, for example, you have large non-insured dental (e.g., orthodontist) bills, which are often financed on the installment plan over several years by the dentist as the service is rendered, consider telescoping as many of them as possible into one year. This may be beneficial even if you have to borrow to do so.
4. Pay your auto and other personal property taxes every other year. These are usually due early in the year, but generally the bill comes in December of the previous year. In one year pay them at the normal time such as, say, January or February. Then pay next year's in December of the same year. This is referred to as bunching in alternative years when you itemize to exceed the zero bracket amount; the other year you use the zero bracket amount.
5. Do the same with other deductible items which are beginning-of-year or end-of-year expenses, if flexibility permits this. For example, such things as union and professional association dues.
6. Other year-end planning can also save you taxes. Any deductible items coming due in early January can be paid in late December, if you can get the bill a bit early.
7. If you are planning on taking some large long-term capital gain, consider taking part of it in December and part in January, if this is possible. That portion of your capital

gain that will be taxed is subject to a progressive rate up to 70 percent. By taking your gain piecemeal, you may be able to lower the tax rate which applies.

8. If you are eligible for a Keogh plan or an IRA, for heaven's sake establish one.

Using a Professional Tax Preparer

If your income consists solely, or even mostly, of wages and salaries, your return will be simple enough for you to prepare yourself. Even if you have substantial interest and dividend income you most likely will not need professional tax help, but if you have such income, it is not subject to withholding and hence you will need to report your estimated income quarterly and pay a tax quarterly.

Only if your tax return is truly complex will you need professional help. If, for example, you have income property subject to depreciation, if you have made investments and qualify for the investment tax credit, or if you have other complex tax shelters, then you should consider a professional tax preparer.

In such a case, get a qualified certified public accountant (CPA) who has had tax experience, and one who does tax work on a regular basis. This latter point is important because only an accountant who is involved in tax matters at all times will be able to keep up with all the complex changes in the tax laws which take place constantly. Not only does Congress change the law frequently, but court decisions and IRS rulings result in changes.

"Your return was neat and accurate and indicated that you understood the forms completely . . . what we want to know is how?" (Source: Permission Cartoon Features Syndicate; from *The Wall Street Journal*.)

It is also suggested that once you have established a relationship with a competent tax advisor, stick with the same one. After he or she has done your return once or twice, he will become familiar with your unique problems and conditions. This will save time (and hence money) when he prepares your return and also will enable him to do a better job.

If You Are Audited

If you have filled out your tax return correctly, the chances of being audited are remote. But if you are audited, don't panic. If you have kept good records and can prove every deduction, you have nothing to fear. Even if there are some gray areas and the IRS auditor absolutely won't allow a given deduction, all you need do is to pay the extra tax, with interest of 12 percent from the time the taxes were due (normally April 15) until the audit. If the IRS feels you were negligent in making out your tax return (as opposed to having made an honest mistake), they can assess a 5 percent penalty over and above the 12 percent noted above. If you disagree with the auditor, you may appeal to the next higher level within the IRS which is the Appeals Office of the IRS. After that you have to go to court if you cannot agree.

There are two kinds of audits. First, the simple audit where several items might be questioned. These don't usually take much time. If the items are in a gray area, there may be some bargaining. The IRS may compromise and allow some but not others.

The Taxpayer Compliance Measurement Program (TCMP) is a more thorough audit. This may be an item-by-item examination of your return. There is a general feeling that if you are picked for this it is because the IRS believes there is something drastically wrong with your tax return. This is not usually true. Many of the people picked for the TCMP are picked at random. The purpose of the TCMP is to give the IRS a feeling for the various legitimate expenses, etc., of the various income groups in order to update their computer, which scans millions of tax forms to spot irregularities.

If you are audited, all you have to do is to prove your tax return. Experts do not agree on whether you should take your tax preparer with you to an audit. If it is a simple audit and only a few items are questioned, many feel your tax accountant is not needed. However, if it is a TCMP, you should probably take your tax preparer along. If you are audited, abide by the following rules:

1. Be on time.
2. Dress neatly and conservatively.
3. If your tax accountant accompanies you, let him or her do most of the talking. You should only fill in details the accountant may have overlooked in your personal affairs.
4. Come armed with all your records.
5. Don't volunteer any information and supply only that which is requested.
6. Sit silently unless spoken to.
7. Don't make small talk or be overly chatty.
8. Never lose your temper or raise your voice.
9. Smile, and be polite and courteous, but not overly friendly; that is, act very professional.

The Tax Forms

There are two forms from which individuals may choose when filing their taxes. They are the 1040 form and the so-called short form 1040A. If the taxpayer is eligible to use the so-called short form (1040A), and elects to do so, the Internal Revenue Service will calculate the tax if requested to do so. The IRS will then automatically send any refund, or bill the taxpayer for any deficiency.

The 1040 consists of a two-page form and may be used without any attachments by many taxpayers. For example, if a person had income solely from wages, salaries, and tips; interest and dividends; or certain miscellaneous income and does not itemize deductions, the basic two-page form is all that need be completed. If the taxpayer had income from other sources, wishes to itemize deductions, or wishes to claim certain credits (such as the investment tax credit mentioned above), supplementary schedules must be filled out and attached to the 1040.

If the taxpayer has an adjusted gross income of more than $20,000 ($40,000 if married and filing jointly), he or she cannot use the tax tables, but must use the appropriate tax rate schedule (either Schedule X, Y, or Z) furnished by the IRS and included in the 1040 tax form instruction booklet. You calculate your taxes from these schedules, which have the zero bracket amount built into them but not the exemptions.

If your adjusted gross income is $20,000 or less ($40,000 if filing jointly), then you must use the tables, not the rate schedules. This is true even if you itemize and use the 1040 Form. The tables, as we noted above, have both the exemptions and the zero bracket amount built into them. If your itemized deductions are in excess of the zero bracket amount ($2,300 for singles and $3,400 for joint returns), you simply take the difference between the two and subtract it from your adjusted gross income before going to the tax tables.

An example of one of these tax tables is shown below. Shown, too, are the tax forms 1040 and 1040A, and the Tax Rate Schedule X and Y, one for single taxpayers and one for married taxpayers.

TABLE 17–8

1979 Tax Table A—SINGLE (Filing Status Box 1)

For single persons with income of $20,000 or less on line 34, Form 1040, or line 11, Form 1040A, who claim 3 or fewer exemptions.

To find your tax: Read down the income column until you find your income as shown on line 34, Form 1040, or line 11, Form 1040A. Read across to the column headed by the total number of exemptions claimed. The amount shown where the two lines meet is your tax.

The $2,300 zero bracket amount and your deduction for exemptions have been taken into account if figuring the tax shown in this table. **Do not take a separate deduction for them.**

Caution: If you can be claimed as a dependent on your parent's return AND you have unearned income (interest, dividends, etc.) of $1,000 or more AND your earned income is less than $2,300, you must use Form 1040.

If line 34, Form 1040, or line 11, Form 1040A, is— Over	But not over	And the total number of exemptions claimed is— 1	2	3
		Your tax is—		
If $3,300 or less your tax is 0				
3,300	3,350	4	0	0
3,350	3,400	11	0	0
3,400	3,450	18	0	0
3,450	3,500	25	0	0
3,500	3,550	32	0	0
3,550	3,600	39	0	0
3,600	3,650	46	0	0
3,650	3,700	53	0	0
3,700	3,750	60	0	0
3,750	3,800	67	0	0
3,800	3,850	74	0	0
3,850	3,900	81	0	0
3,900	3,950	88	0	0
3,950	4,000	95	0	0
4,000	4,050	102	0	0
4,050	4,100	109	0	0
4,100	4,150	116	0	0
4,150	4,200	123	0	0
4,200	4,250	130	0	0
4,250	4,300	137	0	0
4,300	4,350	144	4	0
4,350	4,400	151	11	0
4,400	4,450	158	18	0
4,450	4,500	166	25	0
4,500	4,550	174	32	0
4,550	4,600	182	39	0
4,600	4,650	190	46	0
4,650	4,700	198	53	0
4,700	4,750	206	60	0
4,750	4,800	214	67	0
4,800	4,850	222	74	0
4,850	4,900	230	81	0
4,900	4,950	238	88	0
4,950	5,000	246	95	0
5,000	5,050	254	102	0
5,050	5,100	262	109	0
5,100	5,150	270	116	0
5,150	5,200	278	123	0
5,200	5,250	286	130	0
5,250	5,300	294	137	0
5,300	5,350	302	144	4
5,350	5,400	310	151	11
5,400	5,450	319	158	18
5,450	5,500	328	166	25
5,500	5,550	337	174	32
5,550	5,600	346	182	39
5,600	5,650	355	190	46
5,650	5,700	364	198	53
5,700	5,750	373	206	60
5,750	5,800	382	214	67
5,800	5,850	391	222	74
5,850	5,900	400	230	81

Continued next column

If line 34, Form 1040, or line 11, Form 1040A, is— Over	But not over	And the total number of exemptions claimed is— 1	2	3
		Your tax is—		
5,900	5,950	409	238	88
5,950	6,000	418	246	95
6,000	6,050	427	254	102
6,050	6,100	436	262	109
6,100	6,150	445	270	116
6,150	6,200	454	278	123
6,200	6,250	463	286	130
6,250	6,300	472	294	137
6,300	6,350	481	302	144
6,350	6,400	490	310	151
6,400	6,450	499	319	158
6,450	6,500	508	328	166
6,500	6,550	517	337	174
6,550	6,600	526	346	182
6,600	6,650	535	355	190
6,650	6,700	544	364	198
6,700	6,750	553	373	206
6,750	6,800	562	382	214
6,800	6,850	571	391	222
6,850	6,900	580	400	230
6,900	6,950	589	409	238
6,950	7,000	598	418	246
7,000	7,050	607	427	254
7,050	7,100	616	436	262
7,100	7,150	625	445	270
7,150	7,200	634	454	278
7,200	7,250	643	463	286
7,250	7,300	652	472	294
7,300	7,350	661	481	302
7,350	7,400	670	490	310
7,400	7,450	679	499	319
7,450	7,500	688	508	328
7,500	7,550	697	517	337
7,550	7,600	706	526	346
7,600	7,650	716	535	355
7,650	7,700	725	544	364
7,700	7,750	735	553	373
7,750	7,800	744	562	382
7,800	7,850	754	571	391
7,850	7,900	763	580	400
7,900	7,950	773	589	409
7,950	8,000	782	598	418
8,000	8,050	792	607	427
8,050	8,100	801	616	436
8,100	8,150	811	625	445
8,150	8,200	820	634	454
8,200	8,250	830	643	463
8,250	8,300	839	652	472
8,300	8,350	849	661	481
8,350	8,400	858	670	490
8,400	8,450	868	679	499
8,450	8,500	877	688	508

Continued next column

If line 34, Form 1040, or line 11, Form 1040A, is— Over	But not over	And the total number of exemptions claimed is— 1	2	3
		Your tax is—		
8,500	8,550	887	697	517
8,550	8,600	896	706	526
8,600	8,650	906	716	535
8,650	8,700	915	725	544
8,700	8,750	925	735	553
8,750	8,800	934	744	562
8,800	8,850	944	754	571
8,850	8,900	953	763	580
8,900	8,950	963	773	589
8,950	9,000	972	782	598
9,000	9,050	982	792	607
9,050	9,100	991	801	616
9,100	9,150	1,001	811	625
9,150	9,200	1,010	820	634
9,200	9,250	1,020	830	643
9,250	9,300	1,029	839	652
9,300	9,350	1,039	849	661
9,350	9,400	1,048	858	670
9,400	9,450	1,058	868	679
9,450	9,500	1,067	877	688
9,500	9,550	1,077	887	697
9,550	9,600	1,088	896	706
9,600	9,650	1,098	906	716
9,650	9,700	1,109	915	725
9,700	9,750	1,119	925	735
9,750	9,800	1,130	934	744
9,800	9,850	1,140	944	754
9,850	9,900	1,151	953	763
9,900	9,950	1,161	963	773
9,950	10,000	1,172	972	782
10,000	10,050	1,182	982	792
10,050	10,100	1,193	991	801
10,100	10,150	1,203	1,001	811
10,150	10,200	1,214	1,010	820
10,200	10,250	1,224	1,020	830
10,250	10,300	1,235	1,029	839
10,300	10,350	1,245	1,039	849
10,350	10,400	1,256	1,048	858
10,400	10,450	1,266	1,058	868
10,450	10,500	1,277	1,067	877
10,500	10,550	1,287	1,077	887
10,550	10,600	1,298	1,088	896
10,600	10,650	1,308	1,098	906
10,650	10,700	1,319	1,109	915
10,700	10,750	1,329	1,119	925
10,750	10,800	1,340	1,130	934
10,800	10,850	1,350	1,140	944
10,850	10,900	1,361	1,151	953
10,900	10,950	1,371	1,161	963
10,950	11,000	1,382	1,172	972
11,000	11,050	1,392	1,182	982
11,050	11,100	1,403	1,193	991

Continued on next page

(*Source:* U.S. Department of the Treasury—Internal Revenue Service.)

TABLE 17–9

| Form **1040** | Department of the Treasury—Internal Revenue Service
U.S. Individual Income Tax Return | **1979** | |

| For Privacy Act Notice, see page 3 of Instructions | For the year January 1–December 31, 1979, or other tax year beginning | 1979 ending | 19 |

Use IRS label, Other- wise, please print or type.	Your first name and initial (if joint return, also give spouse's name and initial)	Last name		Your social security number
	Present home address (Number and street including apartment number or rural route)			Spouse's social security no.
	City, town or post office, State and ZIP code		Your occupation ▶ Spouse's occupation ▶	

Presidential Election Campaign Fund

▶ Do you want $1 to go to this fund? . . . . Yes ☐ No ☐

If joint return, does your spouse want $1 to go to this fund? . . . Yes ☐ No ☐

Note: Checking "Yes" will not increase your tax or reduce your refund.

Filing Status

Check only one box.

1 ☐ Single
2 ☐ Married filing joint return (even if only one had income)
3 ☐ Married filing separate return. Enter spouse's social security number above and full name here ▶
4 ☐ Head of household. (See page 7 of Instructions.) If qualifying person is your unmarried child, enter child's name ▶
5 ☐ Qualifying widow(er) with dependent child (Year spouse died ▶ 19   ). (See page 7 of Instructions.)

Exemptions

Always check the box labeled Yourself.
Check other boxes if they apply.

6a ☐ Yourself	☐ 65 or over	☐ Blind	Enter number of boxes checked on 6a and b ▶ ☐
b ☐ Spouse	☐ 65 or over	☐ Blind	
c First names of your dependent children who lived with you ▶			Enter number of children listed ▶ ☐

d Other dependents: (1) Name	(2) Relationship	(3) Number of months lived in your home	(4) Did dependent have income of $1,000 or more?	(5) Did you provide more than one-half of dependent's support?	Enter number of other dependents ▶

Add numbers entered in boxes above ▶ ☐

7 Total number of exemptions claimed . . . .

Income

Please attach Copy B of your Forms W–2 here.

If you do not have a W–2, see page 5 of Instructions.

8	Wages, salaries, tips, etc.	8	
9	Interest income (attach Schedule B if over $400)	9	
10a	Dividends (attach Schedule B if over $400) . . . . . . , 10b Exclusion		
c	Subtract line 10b from line 10a	10c	
11	State and local income tax refunds (does not apply unless refund is for year you itemized deductions—see page 10 of Instructions)	11	
12	Alimony received	12	
13	Business income or (loss) (attach Schedule C)	13	
14	Capital gain or (loss) (attach Schedule D)	14	
15	Taxable part of capital gain distributions not reported on Schedule D (see page 10 of Instructions)	15	
16	Supplemental gains or (losses) (attach Form 4797)	16	
17	Fully taxable pensions and annuities not reported on Schedule E	17	
18	Pensions, annuities, rents, royalties, partnerships, estates or trusts, etc. (attach Schedule E)	18	
19	Farm income or (loss) (attach Schedule F)	19	
20a	Unemployment compensation. Total amount received . .		
b	Taxable part, if any, from worksheet on page 10 of Instructions	20b	
21	Other income (state nature and source—see page 10 of Instructions) ▶	21	
22	**Total income.** Add amounts in column for lines 8 through 21 . . . . ▶	22	

Please attach check or money order here.

Adjustments to Income

23	Moving expense (attach Form 3903 or 3903F)	23	
24	Employee business expenses (attach Form 2106) . .	24	
25	Payments to an IRA (see page 11 of Instructions) . .	25	
26	Payments to a Keogh (H.R. 10) retirement plan . . .	26	
27	Interest penalty on early withdrawal of savings . . .	27	
28	Alimony paid (see page 11 of Instructions)	28	
29	Disability income exclusion (attach Form 2440) . . .	29	
30	**Total adjustments.** Add lines 23 through 29 . . . . ▶	30	

Adjusted Gross Income

| 31 | **Adjusted gross income.** Subtract line 30 from line 22. If this line is less than $10,000, see page 2 of Instructions. If you want IRS to figure your tax, see page 4 of Instructions . . . . ▶ | 31 | |

☆ U.S. GOVERNMENT PRINTING OFFICE : 1979—O-283-337 58-040-1110

Form **1040** (1979)

TABLE 17–9
(continued)

Form 1040 (1979)   Page 2

Tax Computation (See Instructions on page 12)	32	Amount from line 31 (adjusted gross income)	32		
	33	If you do not itemize deductions, enter zero . . . . ⎫	33		
		If you itemize, complete Schedule A (Form 1040) and enter the amount from Schedule A, line 41 . . . ⎬			
		Caution: If you have unearned income and can be claimed as a dependent on your parent's return, check here ▶ ☐ and see page 12 of the Instructions. Also see page 12 of the Instructions if: ⎭			
		• You are married filing a separate return and your spouse itemizes deductions, OR			
		• You file Form 4563, OR			
		• You are a dual-status alien.			
	34	Subtract line 33 from line 32. Use the amount on line 34 to find your tax from the Tax Tables, or to figure your tax on Schedule TC, Part I	34		
		Use Schedule TC, Part I, and the Tax Rate Schedules ONLY if:			
		• Line 34 is more than $20,000 ($40,000 if you checked Filing Status Box 2 or 5), OR			
		• You have more exemptions than are shown in the Tax Table for your filing status, OR			
		• You use Schedule G or Form 4726 to figure your tax.			
		Otherwise, you MUST use the Tax Tables to find your tax.			
	35	Tax. Enter tax here and check if from ☐ Tax Tables or ☐ Schedule TC	35		
	36	Additional taxes. (See page 12 of Instructions.) Enter here and check if from ☐ Form 4970, ⎫	36		
		☐ Form 4972, ☐ Form 5544, ☐ Form 5405, or ☐ Section 72(m)(5) penalty tax . . ⎬			
	37	**Total.** Add lines 35 and 36 . . . . ▶	37		
Credits	38	Credit for contributions to candidates for public office . . .	38		
	39	Credit for the elderly (attach Schedules R&RP)	39		
	40	Credit for child and dependent care expenses (attach Form 2441) .	40		
	41	Investment credit (attach Form 3468)	41		
	42	Foreign tax credit (attach Form 1116)	42		
	43	Work incentive (WIN) credit (attach Form 4874)	43		
	44	Jobs credit (attach Form 5884)	44		
	45	Residential energy credits (attach Form 5695)	45		
	46	**Total credits.** Add lines 38 through 45	46		
	47	**Balance.** Subtract line 46 from line 37 and enter difference (but not less than zero) . ▶	47		
Other Taxes (Including Advance EIC Payments)	48	Self-employment tax (attach Schedule SE)	48		
	49a	Minimum tax. Attach Form 4625 and check here ▶ ☐	49a		
	49b	Alternative minimum tax. Attach Form 6251 and check here ▶ ☐	49b		
	50	Tax from recomputing prior-year investment credit (attach Form 4255)	50		
	51a	Social security (FICA) tax on tip income not reported to employer (attach Form 4137) . .	51a		
	51b	Uncollected employee FICA and RRTA tax on tips (from Form W–2)	51b		
	52	Tax on an IRA (attach Form 5329)	52		
	53	Advance earned income credit payments received (from Form W–2)	53		
	54	**Total.** Add lines 47 through 53 . . . . ▶	54		
Payments Attach Forms W–2, W–2G, and W–2P to front.	55	Total Federal income tax withheld . , , ...	55		
	56	1979 estimated tax payments and credit from 1978 return .	56		
	57	Earned income credit. If line 32 is under $10,000, see page 2 of Instructions	57		
	58	Amount paid with Form 4868	58		
	59	Excess FICA and RRTA tax withheld (two or more employers)	59		
	60	Credit for Federal tax on special fuels and oils (attach Form 4136 or 4136–T)	60		
	61	Regulated Investment Company credit (attach Form 2439)	61		
	62	**Total.** Add lines 55 through 61 . . . . ▶	62		
Refund or Balance Due	63	If line 62 is larger than line 54, enter amount **OVERPAID** . . . . ▶	63		
	64	Amount of line 63 to be **REFUNDED TO YOU** . . . . ▶	64		
	65	Amount of line 63 to be credited on 1980 estimated tax . . . . . ▶	65		
	66	If line 54 is larger than line 62, enter BALANCE DUE. Attach check or money order for full amount payable to "Internal Revenue Service." Write your social security number on check or money order . . ▶ (Check ▶ ☐ if Form 2210 (2210F) is attached. See page 15 of Instructions.) ▶ $	66		

Under penalties of perjury, I declare that I have examined this return, including accompanying schedules and statements, and to the best of my knowledge and belief, it is true, correct, and complete. Declaration of preparer (other than taxpayer) is based on all information of which preparer has any knowledge.

Please Sign Here

Your signature	Date	Spouse's signature (if filing jointly, BOTH must sign even if only one had income)

Paid Preparer's Information

Preparer's signature and date ▶		Check if self-employed ▶ ☐	Preparer's social security no.
Firm's name (or yours, if self-employed) and address ▶		E.I. No. ▶	
		ZIP code ▶	

(*Source:* U.S. Department of the Treasury—Internal Revenue Service.)

TABLE 17–10

| Form **1040A** | Department of the Treasury—Internal Revenue Service | 19**79** |
| U.S. Individual Income Tax Return | | |

Use IRS label. Otherwise, please print or type.	Your first name and initial (if joint return, also give spouse's name and initial)	Last name	Your social security number
	Present home address (Number and street, including apartment number, or rural route)		Spouse's social security no.
	City, town or post office, State and ZIP code	Your occupation ▶
		Spouse's occupation ▶

Presidential Election Campaign Fund

▶ Do you want $1 to go to this fund? . . . . Yes ▨ No
If joint return, does your spouse want $1 to go to this fund? Yes ▨ No

Note: Checking "Yes" will not increase your tax or reduce your refund.

Filing Status
Check Only One Box.

1 ___ Single
2 ___ Married filing joint return (even if only one had income)
3 ___ Married filing separate return. Enter spouse's social security number above and full name here ▶ ....
4 ___ Head of household. (See page 8 of Instructions.) If qualifying person is your unmarried child, enter child's name ▶ ....

For Privacy Act Notice, see page 14 of Instructions

Exemptions
Always check the box labeled Yourself. Check other boxes if they apply.

5a ___ Yourself   ___ 65 or over   ___ Blind
 b ___ Spouse   ___ 65 or over   ___ Blind

Enter number of boxes checked on 5a and b ▶ ___

c First names of your dependent children who lived with you ▶ ....

Enter number of children listed ▶ ___

d Other dependents: (1) Name	(2) Relationship	(3) Number of months lived in your home.	(4) Did dependent have income of $1,000 or more?	(5) Did you provide more than one-half of dependent's support?

Enter number of other dependents ▶ ___
Add numbers entered in boxes above ▶ ___

6 Total number of exemptions claimed . . . .

7 Wages, salaries, tips, etc. (Attach Forms W–2. If you do not have a W–2, see page 10 of Instructions) **7**
8 Interest income (See pages 4 and 10 of Instructions) **8**
9a Dividends .... (See pages 4 and 10 of Instructions) 9b Exclusion .... Subtract line 9b from 9a **9c**
10a Unemployment compensation. Total amount received ....
 b Taxable part, if any, from worksheet on page 11 of Instructions **10b**
11 Adjusted gross income (add lines 7, 8, 9c, and 10b). If under $10,000, see page 2 of Instructions on "Earned Income Credit" **11**
12a Credit for contributions to candidates for public office. (See page 11 of Instructions) **12a**

IF YOU WANT IRS TO FIGURE YOUR TAX, PLEASE STOP HERE AND SIGN BELOW.

 b Total Federal income tax withheld (If line 7 is more than $22,900, see page 12 of Instructions) **12b**
 c Earned income credit (from page 2 of Instructions) **12c**
13 Total (add lines 12a, b, and c) **13**
14a Tax on the amount on line 11. (See Instructions for line 14a on page 12; then find your tax in the Tax Tables on pages 15–26.) **14a**
 b Advance earned income credit payments received (from Form W–2) **14b**
15 Total (add lines 14a and 14b) **15**
16 If line 13 is larger than line 15, enter amount to be **REFUNDED TO YOU** . . . . . . ▶ **16**
17 If line 15 is larger than line 13, enter **BALANCE DUE.** Attach check or money order for full amount payable to "Internal Revenue Service." Write your social security number on check or money order . ▶ **17**

Under penalties of perjury, I declare that I have examined this return, including accompanying schedules and statements, and to the best of my knowledge and belief it is true, correct, and complete. Declaration of preparer (other than taxpayer) is based on all information of which preparer has any knowledge.

Your signature _____ Date ▶ Spouse's signature (if filing jointly, BOTH must sign even if only one had income)

Paid Preparer's Information

Preparer's signature and date ▶
Firm's name (or yours, if self-employed) and address ▶

Check if self-employed ▶ ___
Preparer's social security no.
E.I. No. ▶
ZIP code ▶

☆ U.S. GOVERNMENT PRINTING OFFICE 1979—283-319 52-0237640

Form **1040A** (1979)

(*Source:* U.S. Department of the Treasury—Internal Revenue Service.)

TABLE 17–11

SCHEDULE X—Single Taxpayers

If the amount on Schedule TC, Part I, line 3, is: Not over $2,300........ Enter on Schedule TC, Part I, line 4: —0—

Over—	But not over—		of the amount over—
$2,300	$3,400	14%	$2,300
$3,400	$4,400	$154+16%	$3,400
$4,400	$6,500	$314+18%	$4,400
$6,500	$8,500	$692+19%	$6,500
$8,500	$10,800	$1,072+21%	$8,500
$10,800	$12,900	$1,555+24%	$10,800
$12,900	$15,000	$2,059+26%	$12,900
$15,000	$18,200	$2,605+30%	$15,000
$18,200	$23,500	$3,565+34%	$18,200
$23,500	$28,800	$5,367+39%	$23,500
$28,800	$34,100	$7,434+44%	$28,800
$34,100	$41,500	$9,766+49%	$34,100
$41,500	$55,300	$13,392+55%	$41,500
$55,300	$81,800	$20,982+63%	$55,300
$81,800	$108,300	$37,677+68%	$81,800
$108,300		$55,697+70%	$108,300

SCHEDULE Y—Married Taxpayers and Qualifying Widows and Widowers

Married Filing Joint Returns and Qualifying Widows and Widowers

If the amount on Schedule TC, Part I, line 3, is: Not over $3,400........ Enter on Schedule TC, Part I, line 4: —0—

Over—	But not over—		of the amount over—
$3,400	$5,500	14%	$3,400
$5,500	$7,600	$294+16%	$5,500
$7,600	$11,900	$630+18%	$7,600
$11,900	$16,000	$1,404+21%	$11,900
$16,000	$20,200	$2,265+24%	$16,000
$20,200	$24,600	$3,273+28%	$20,200
$24,600	$29,900	$4,505+32%	$24,600
$29,900	$35,200	$6,201+37%	$29,900
$35,200	$45,800	$8,162+43%	$35,200
$45,800	$60,000	$12,720+49%	$45,800
$60,000	$85,600	$19,678+54%	$60,000
$85,600	$109,400	$33,502+59%	$85,600
$109,400	$162,400	$47,544+64%	$109,400
$162,400	$215,400	$81,464+68%	$162,400
$215,400		$117,504+70%	$215,400

Married Filing Separate Returns

If the amount on Schedule TC, Part I, line 3, is: Not over $1,700........ Enter on Schedule TC, Part I, line 4: —0—

Over—	But not over—		of the amount over—
$1,700	$2,750	14%	$1,700
$2,750	$3,800	$147.00+16%	$2,750
$3,800	$5,950	$315.00+18%	$3,800
$5,950	$8,000	$702.00+21%	$5,950
$8,000	$10,100	$1,132.50+24%	$8,000
$10,100	$12,300	$1,636.50+28%	$10,100
$12,300	$14,950	$2,252.50+32%	$12,300
$14,950	$17,600	$3,100.50+37%	$14,950
$17,600	$22,900	$4,081.00+43%	$17,600
$22,900	$30,000	$6,360.00+49%	$22,900
$30,000	$42,800	$9,839.00+54%	$30,000
$42,800	$54,700	$16,751.00+59%	$42,800
$54,700	$81,200	$23,772.00+64%	$54,700
$81,200	$107,700	$40,732.00+68%	$81,200
$107,700		$58,752.00+70%	$107,700

(*Source:* U.S. Department of the Treasury—Internal Revenue Service.)

QUESTIONS FOR REVIEW

1. Discuss the ability to pay and the benefit principle of taxation.

2. How are state and local taxes on real estate calculated? Is the property tax a good or a poor tax in your opinion?

3. Why is it that two individuals with the same income and the same dependents do not necessarily pay the same amount of taxes?

4. Mark Twain is alleged to have said, "The rich worry about taxes and the poor about the rent." What did he mean? Does the statement still make sense today?

5. Differentiate between the cash and the accrual basis.

6. Who must file a federal income tax return? Who might want to file even if they do not have to?

7. What is the dividend exclusion?

8. What are the major items that can be deducted from gross income to arrive at adjusted gross income?

9. How does filing a joint return save you money?

10. How could you calculate the burden of taxes? What is the effective tax rate?

11. It is said that capital gains receive special tax treatment. Can you explain how this works?

12. Why is it that most people who do not own a home are better off to take the zero bracket amount rather than to itemize?

13. Make a list of all the deductions and loopholes in the tax law that apply to you but which you did not know about before.

CASES

1. Joe and Bette Madox earn $28,000 per year and have one child. They are buying a house and pay interest of $4,800 on their $50,000 mortgage. In addition, their property taxes are $1,100. The Madoxes have certain other expenses that were deductible on their tax form to the extent of $633. If they were renting, they would have taken the zero bracket amount as they always have in the past, but this year their expenses will be greater than the $3,400 zero bracket amount. Calculate their taxes on a nonitemized deduction basis. Do the same with all their allowable deductions itemized. What is their tax saving from owning a house?

2. Bob and Joan Rider are a young couple with no dependents. Bob works as a salesman for a local manufacturer and earns $20,000 per year. Joan is a law student. They rent a modest apartment for $175 per month. They have never been able to itemize their deductions and get more than the zero bracket amount. Calculate the tax liability of the Riders using the zero bracket amount.

    Bob would like to have you calculate his friend Jim's taxes for this year. He made the same income but had to pay more taxes. He was single but does not believe that one more exemption should make that much difference. What is the difference in the tax liability between the two men? How can you explain it other than by additional exemptions?

3. Kevin and Eleanor Kelley, aged sixty-seven and sixty-six respectively, live in a large midwestern city where Kevin is a tool and die maker earning $395 per week. They have no other income and no dependents. Their home is completely paid for, but the property taxes on it are $885. They also had expenses during the year as follows: $392 for medical bills; $189 for drugs; $325 for medical insurance; and $329 of traveling expense for Kevin when he went to the tool and diemakers' convention in Miami, Florida. What are their deductions? Explain. Calculate their tax liability.

4. During his summer vacation, Joe worked for nine weeks at the Super Service Station. His total wages were $1,440 and his employer withheld $105 in income tax. He had no other income. What is the simplest return form Joe may file, and how much refund will he receive?

5. Jan, who is twenty and a student, worked for the Paragon Builders, Inc., for twelve weeks during her summer vacation. She earned $2,150 and her employer withheld $465 for income tax. She had $300 interest income and her parents contributed more than half her support. What is the simplest return form Jan may file, and what is the amount of her income tax refund?

6. John Rivers has an annual salary of $19,500. In addition, he received a $1,500 bonus just before Christmas. His employer withheld $3,950 for income tax and $1,296.75 for social security tax. John was ill for one week and did not work during that time, but his employer has a qualified sick-pay plan and John received his regular salary that week.

    John's wife Mary works as a waitress and earned $125 per week for the 40 weeks she worked. Her employer withheld income taxes of $1,073 and social security taxes of $333. Mary also received tips at the restaurant totaling $2,041.50. Mary received $180 of dividend income on stock that she owned individually, and $60 of interest income. During the year Mary had an auto accident in which she hit a man and caused $600 damages to the front end of her car. Her insurance policy has a $300 deductible clause. John and Mary also spent $610 in insulating their attic and weatherstripping all windows. They filed an estimated tax return and made four quarterly payments of $100 each on their estimated tax.

    In addition to their own exemptions, they are entitled to claim an exemption for their daughter, Jean. These are their other deductible items:

Contributions	$ 240
Interest	5,422
Taxes	824
Medical expenses paid (including $125 for medicine & drugs)	500
Professional dues	60
Medical Insurance	310

Compute John and Mary's additional tax or refund.

7. John and Bette Pasmack live on the West Coast, and John earned $17,500 last year. In addition, he received a bonus of $2,500 just before Christmas. His employer withheld $2,269 for income taxes and $1,163 for social security tax. John and Bette each had $60 of dividend income and, in addition, Bette received $170 interest income from a trust.

   In addition to their own exemptions, John and Bette are entitled to exemptions for son, Jack, daughter, Jean, and Bette's seventy-year-old widowed mother. Their deductible items are:

Contributions	$ 510
Interest	2,876
Taxes	989
Loss on their summer cottage damage by fire ($900 minus $100 limitation)	800
Dues to professional societies	55

Medical expenses paid (including $225 for medicine and drugs and $220 for hospitalization insurance) 1,120

Compute their additional tax or refund.

8. Peter and Julie are considering marriage but have heard that their taxes would be much higher as a married working couple than if they were both single and would like you to compute their tax liabilities under both assumptions.

   Both are lawyers. His salary is $21,000 and hers is $23,000. Pete owns a home on which he will pay $4,200 in interest and $1,100 in taxes. They both have professional dues of $180 and medical insurance expense of $288. Julie lives in an apartment and has no other itemized deductions. Pete's interest income from CDs is $750.

SUGGESTED READINGS

Anderson, William H. *Financing Modern Government*. Boston: Houghton Mifflin Co., 1973.

Bittker, Boris. *Federal Income Taxation*. Boston: Little, Brown and Co., 1980.

Bittker, Boris, and Stone, Lawrence. *Federal Income Estate and Gift Taxation*, 5th ed. Boston: Little, Brown and Co., 1977.

"The Federal Budget: Its Impact on the Economy." New York: National Industrial Conference Board, Inc., 1976.

"Federal Tax Course." Chicago: Commerce Clearing House, published annually.

"Federal Tax Courses." Englewood Cliffs, New Jersey: Prentice-Hall, Inc. Published annually.

Internal Revenue Service. "Employer's Tax Guide, Circular E." Published annually by the Internal Revenue Service.

———. "Instructions for Preparing Form 1040." An annual IRS publication which can be obtained at any post office during tax time and at any regional IRS office at other times.

———. "Instructions for Preparing Form 1040A." An annual IRS publication which can be obtained at any post office during tax return time and at any regional IRS office at other times.

———. *Tax Guide for Small Business, 1981 Edition*. Washington, D.C.: U.S. Government Printing Office, 1981. Published annually.

———. *Your Federal Income Tax*. An annual IRS publication which gives a far more detailed explanation than the "Instructions for Preparing Form 1040." It can be obtained at any IRS regional office.

Levy, Michael E., et al. *The Federal Budget: Its Impact on the Economy*. New York: The Conference Board, 1978.

"The National Debt." Philadelphia: Federal Reserve Bank of Philadelphia.

"1981 M.S. Master Tax Guide." Chicago: Commerce Clearing House. Published annually.

Pechman, Joseph A. *Federal Tax Policy*, revised ed. Washington, D.C.: Brookings Institution, 1977.

Sommerfeld, Ray M.; Anderson, Hershel M.; and Brock, Horace R. *An Introduction to Taxation*, 2nd ed. New York: Harcourt, Brace & World, 1979.

United States Budget in Brief: Fiscal Year 1981. Washington, D.C.: U.S. Government Printing Office. This is an annual publication.

Chapter Eighteen

The Tools of Estate Planning

No one is asked when he wishes to enter the world; no one is asked when he wishes to leave.

KIERKEGAARD

The objectives of this chapter are to

1   Outline the information you need to assemble to engage in estate planning

2   Introduce the document known as a will and show what it can do

3   Note what happens to property upon death in the absence of a will

4   Present trusts and show how they are of value in estate planning

5   Discuss gift and estate taxes and show how these taxes may be minimized

No one cares to discuss his or her own death. However, it is inevitable. Consequently, you should think about the disposition of your estate, and with some sort of deliberate plan or method. Why bother with a plan? The major reason is inheritance, estate, and gift taxes. Suppose a small business owner or a farmer desires to leave property to a son or daughter. Without a plan of some sort it might be necessary to dispose of the business or the farm to pay taxes. The simplest sort of plan would call for a will passing the business or the farm to the offspring and a life insurance sufficiently large to cover the tax. If the individual failed to make a will, the property possibly would not pass as wished but instead in a manner prescribed by the state's statutes. Even in the absence of taxes, it might be desirable, in the light of certain state statutes, to set up means of providing for a surviving husband or wife in order to prevent the business or the farm from being liquidated, which would defeat the intention to pass the property on to others. Additionally, if the son or daughter were a minor, one would want to designate the person who would act as a guardian for the child and for the estate.

Grateful acknowledgement is extended to Stephen R. Lindemood and Jack W. London—then students at the University of Texas School of Law, now practicing attorneys—for their assistance in the preparation of this chapter.

GATHERING THE FACTS

Since every individual and every family is unique, each estate plan will be unique to the needs of the individual. There are, however, some basic spheres of information that are important to every estate plan and your attorney must have the information to plan the best estate for your needs.

Residence and Domicile

Your residence and domicile are important to your plan. Domicile is the name given to a person's permanent home, and residence is the place where one lives without the intention of making a permanent home. They may be the same place, but if not, the site of the domicile is where the person's will is to be probated. In addition, any marital rights that may attach to the property, such as dower or community-property rights, are determined by the domicile, as are state inheritance taxes.

Family Status

Your family status is very important. A prior marriage or a separation from your present spouse can have an effect on your legal ability to make gifts of property in your will. For example, a prior spouse may have a claim against an estate. Your attorney will want to know whether you plan to have more children and whether your children are dependent on you. Your attorney will also want to know whether you have other living relatives from whom you may expect an inheritance. This is very important in developing an estate plan that will best conserve your assets, since inheritances often constitute a large portion of the assets of an estate.

Safe Deposit Box

If you have a safe deposit box, where are the box and the key? This is important information because upon your demise it is necessary for the attorney to obtain a court order to open the box, and it simplifies things if the whereabouts of the box is immediately known.

Beneficiaries

Your attorney will want to know about your beneficiaries, their names, addresses, their relationship to you, their financial needs, and their character traits. The reason for wanting to know their financial needs is that you may wish to provide financial means to enable them to live at the same standard as at present, or even at a better living standard. The character traits of the proposed beneficiaries are also important. It may be that one of the proposed beneficiaries gambles or indulges in some sort of vice; in such an event the attorney may begin thinking of establishing a trust that would provide funds over time rather than funds in a lump sum that might be gambled away or spent in loose living.

THE BALANCE SHEET

Following these questions there will be another series of questions with the major purpose of determining your net worth by means of constructing a balance sheet. Such a balance sheet will be constructed like any other balance sheet, namely, assets minus liabilities equal net worth. It will look something like that which follows, with more or fewer details depending upon the individual.

Assets
    Cash $

    Personal Property (car, jewelry, stamp collection, etc.)
    Real Estate
    Insurance
    Business Interest (value of business, if any)
    Securities (stocks and bonds, mortgages, etc.)
    Pension Rights
    Social Security Benefits
    Inheritances (possible)
    Miscellaneous (copyrights, patents, etc.)   _____

                                                               Total $

Liabilities
    Accounts Payable $
    Notes Payable
    Real Property Mortgages
    Installment Debts Owed
    Conditional Bills of Sale
    Obligations Under Contract   _____

                                                               Total $

    Net Worth   _____
    Estimated Administration Expenses (cost of handling
      estate) (subtract)   _____
    Estimated Taxes (federal and state) (subtract)   _____

                                                               Total   _____

    Anticipated Income (annual)   _____

The attorney will then probably ask your annual income. This is important, as we shall later see, because of taxes. The annual income can also be conveniently shown on the balance sheet, as illustrated.

The balance sheet will vary to some degree depending on whether you are domiciled in a community-property state or a common-law property state. In a community-property state, your attorney will want to know which property was brought into the marriage as each spouse's separate property, whether any of the rents or income from this separate property were ever commingled with funds of the marital community, and which assets were purchased with community funds. This information is necessary to determine the total value of each spouse's estate, which assets can be placed in a trust, and the probable estate tax liability of each spouse.

In any state, the attorney will want to examine your insurance policies very carefully. Assume, for example, that the individual seeking advice shows his attorney a homeowner's policy such as one described in chapter 10. It may be that the policy covers items of jewelry that are clearly owned by the wife, even though the policy is in the husband's name. If the husband dies before the wife, the tax commissioner may argue that since the policy was taken out in the husband's name, the items of jewelry must be included in the husband's estate. Suppose, too, that money has been borrowed against life insurance policies held by the husband with the wife as the beneficiary. It will make a difference whether the loan against the policy was made by the life insurance company, with the policy as the collateral for the loan, or whether the loan was made by a bank. In the former case, the beneficiary is entitled only to the net proceeds and that amount is paid to the beneficiary directly and is not included in the estate. On the other hand, if the loan was made by a bank with the policy as collateral for the loan, the courts have held that the insured's estate is primarily liable for the debt.[1] For tax purposes, this makes an important difference with regard to the so-called marital deduction, as will be explained later in the chapter.

MODERN WILLS

There are a number of different types of wills and a number of things that wills can accomplish. There are also, of course, a good many legal technicalities one should know with respect to wills. While this book will not make you an expert able to draw up your own will, it will, I hope, give you an appreciation for the problems involved and hence convince you to see an experienced and competent attorney when drawing up your will.

General Definitions

A will is ordinarily a writing that provides for the distribution of property upon the death of the writer but confers no rights prior to that time. In short, the will is ineffective prior to the death of the writer of the will. Moreover, the writer may destroy or cancel the will at any time. The person making the will is known as the testator, if a male, or the testatrix, if a female. If a person dies leaving a will, he or she is said to have died testate. One who dies without a will is said to have died intestate. A gift of land by way of a will is known as a devise, and the person receiving the gift, a devisee. A bequest, or legacy as it is sometimes called, is a gift of personal property, and the person to whom the personal property has been given is called a legatee. To be valid, a will must satisfy the requirements as to both the *intention* of the testator and the *formality* of expression of the intention.

Intention

There can be no will unless the testator manifests an intention in writing and in the will to make a provision that will be effective upon his death. This is called a testamentary intent. There likewise can be no will unless the testator has testamentary capacity. This is generally the requirement that the testator must be of sound mind. He need not possess superior or even average intelligence. He is only required (1) to plan conceptually the distribution of his property, (2) not to execute the will as a fraud, and (3) not to be under the undue control of some other person in the execution of the will.

Formality

In 1667 by the act of the British Parliament, 29 Car. II, it was enacted that "all devises and bequests of any lands or tenements . . . shall be in writing, and signed by the party so

1. *Connelly v. Wells,* 142 Conn 529.

devising the same, or by some other person in his presence and by his express directions, and shall be attested and subscribed, in the presence of said devisor by three or four credible witnesses, or else they shall be utterly void and of no effect." The laws of the United States are largely based on English legal theory, and with minor variations the above statute has been the basis of the law of wills in all of the United States. For example, the legislative bodies of the various states have said that there must be a writing. The will generally recites that the testator is of a certain age, is or is not married, and is of sound mind. The will must also be signed, the signature being as a general rule at the bottom or at the end of the will. Ordinarily this means that it must be signed at the physical end of the will. The reason is to prevent litigation in the event unsigned extra pages have been added to the will.

The act of witnessing the will, known as attestation, generally includes the signing of the will by the witnesses after a clause that states that the witnesses have observed the testator sign the will. Publication is the act of the testator's informing the attesting witnesses that the document he is signing before them is his will. The person making the will need not inform the witnesses of its contents. He merely announces that the document is his will and that he requests the witnesses to attest to his signature. This constitutes the publication. In a few states, witnesses are not required but as a general rule two or three witnesses are necessary. In those states where witnesses are required, it is generally specified that they are credible or competent and that they have no interest in the will.

Probating the Will; the Executor

Upon the death of the testatrix, the will must be probated. Probate by definition means to prove. It is the job of the executor named in the will to go into court, prove that the will is valid, and carry out its terms. When specific pieces of property are to go to named persons, the executor transfers the property to those persons. Where specific property is not designated to go to named persons, it is the function of the executor to obtain a court order, sell the property, and distribute the proceeds. The first thing that the executor is bound to do is to pay off the debts of the estate and settle taxes.

Executors are paid a fee for their services. If the testatrix appoints an executor, the fee is generally agreed upon in advance. Since probating a will is a highly complex and technical operation, probably an attorney experienced in this line of work should be appointed. If no executor has been designated by the testatrix, the court will appoint one, and then his or her fees will be determined in accordance with state law. They vary from state to state and with the size of the estate. Generally, however, executor's fees vary from 4 or 5 percent of the first $5,000 or $10,000 of the estate and are then scaled down in a series of steps to about 1 or 2 percent of that portion of an estate in excess of $200,000 or $250,000.

The probation of the validity of the will is not always a simple matter. Most states require the witnesses who attested the execution of the will to testify at probation the validity of the execution. Frequently, the witnesses are dead or for some other reason unable to testify. To forestall the possibility of preventing the probation of many wills, most states permit a will to include a self-proving clause. The will is signed and attested in the usual manner. The testatrix and witnesses then execute an affidavit before a notary public acknowledging their acts. The affidavit is appended to the will, which may then be admitted to probate without the testimony of these witnesses.

Property Subject to Disposal by Will

Any property that can be transferred by the owner during his or her lifetime generally can be transferred by will upon his or her death. The testator by his will may in addition exercise any power possessed by him to appoint by will. For example, he may have been left a parcel of real property as a life estate with the provision that upon his death it shall go to a person or persons named by him in his will.

The General Contents of a Will

No one should attempt to draw a will without the assistance of an experienced attorney except under extraordinary circumstances. And even lawyers sometimes cause a certain amount of confusion, as was expressed by Mr. Justice Cullen in *Moneypeny v. Moneypeny*, 202 NY 90: "The will is drawn with a prolixity of language and confusion in thought and in expression approximating to genius." The good judge, it seems, also had difficulty with words. However, in general, wills contain the following items:

1. A statement of the domicile of the testator or testatrix.
2. A statement revoking prior wills: "I hereby revoke all wills and codicils by me at any time heretofore made."
3. A provision for payment of debts and funeral expenses. This may read, "I direct that all my just debts and funeral expenses be paid as soon after my death as may be practicable or as they come due." The testator should communicate to the attorney his idea of the just debts he intends the executor to pay or add the clause as they become due. A simpler "just debts" clause may be interpreted as "all debts." Consider the plight of the widow who learns that the residence she expects to live in for the rest of her life must be sold for its equity value to pay off a mortgage on it—a just debt. The experienced attorney will draft this clause carefully.
4. Funeral and burial directions may sometimes be included but need not be; they may read, for instance, "I direct that my body be cremated."
5. A provision for the disposition of real property. This may read, "I devise my dwelling house and residence described as No. 4518 Martin Drive, Boulder, Colorado, to my beloved husband, John DeFoe."
6. A provision for the disposition of personal property and household effects. This may read, "I give and bequeath to my beloved wife Jane DeFoe all furniture, clothing, jewelry, pictures, works of art, silver plate, ornaments, bric-a-brac, tapestry, household goods, books, linens, glass, automobiles, boats (if any), horses (if any), and all implements and tools that may be in or upon my said real estate at the time of my death."
7. A statement about legacies. These are generally of two types: the general legacy and the specific legacy. The general legacy is a gift of money to an individual, paid out of the general assets of the estate. It is not a bequest of a particular thing or a particular fund designated from all others of the same kind.[2] The general legacy may read, "I give and bequeath to my dear friend Howard G. Jensen the sum of $1,000." The specific legacy is a bequest of a particular thing, which is a specified part of the testator's estate, distinguished from all other property of the same kind.[3] If there were inadequate assets to pay all the bequests, the general legacy would be scaled down, but a specific legacy may read, "I give and bequeath to my dear friend James G. Richardson my entire stamp collection."
8. Charitable or religious bequests. Such a statement may read, "I give and bequeath the sum of $1,000 to the Lord Nelson Home for Wayward Boys."
9. A statement concerning the residual estate. This includes all of the remaining items that have not yet been effectively disposed of by the will and is dealt with by means of a

2. *Armstead v. Union Trust Co.*, 61 F2d 677.
3. *Byrne v. Hume*, 86 Mich. 546.

so-called residuary clause giving away or disposing of all that remains in the testator's estate. This may read, "All the rest, residue, and remainder of my estate, of whatsoever kind and nature, and wheresoever situated, of which I may be seized or possessed or to which I may be entitled at the time of my death, not hereby otherwise effectually disposed of (including any property over which I have the power of appointment), I direct my Executor, herein-after named, to devise and bequeath to my beloved wife, Jane DeFoe."

10. A statement of appointment of the executor. Generally anyone not specifically disqualified by statute will be permitted to act as the executor of an estate. Often the will designates the wife as executor. Since probating a will is a technical process, however, which many persons are not qualified to carry out, often joint executors are appointed. The second executor presumably is an attorney experienced in probate matters. Although the executors of an estate are ordinarily required to furnish a bond to ensure that they will faithfully carry out their duties, in most instances the testator places a statement in the will requesting that no bond be furnished. The statement with regard to the appointment of an executor ordi-narily reads as follows, "I hereby nominate, constitute, and appoint as Executor of this my Last Will and Testament my beloved wife Jane DeFoe and my friend William V. Wilmot. In the event any of the persons named herein as Executors shall decline to act or predecease me, or for any cause shall cease or fail to act, then I nominate, constitute, and appoint as Executor of my said will in the place and stead of any or one of said persons named herein, the First National Bank, of Denver, Colorado. It is my will and I direct that my Executors and their successors, shall not be required to furnish bond for the faithful performance of their duties in any jurisdiction, any provision of the law to the contrary notwithstand-ing."

11. A statement of appointment of a guardian. Generally speaking, a surviving parent is the guardian of an infant, if there is one. When a will is involved, however, it is sometimes appropriate specifically to appoint a guardian. Frequently the surviving parent is appointed guardian under the will with a provision that if the spouse predecease the testator, then a substitute guardian will be appointed. This may read, "I hereby appoint my beloved wife Jane DeFoe guardian of the person and estate of my infant son Roger DeFoe. In the event that my wife predecease me, or shall fail to qualify, shall resign or be removed, I appoint my friend William M. Howard, guardian of the person and the estate of my infant son, Roger DeFoe. It is my will and I direct that neither my said wife nor William H. Howard shall be required to furnish any bond for the faithful performance of their offices as such guardian, any provision of the law to the contrary notwithstanding."

The Joint Will

A joint will is defined as a single testamentary instrument, which contains the wills of two or more persons, is in common, or in severalty, by them.[4]

Typically, it is executed by husband and wife and typically each leaves his or her property to the other. Many authorities feel that the joint will should not be used because it can lay the ground work for future litigation, and it can deprive the surviving spouse of the marital deduction.[5]

Essentially the joint will contains the same general type of clauses with regard to burial instructions and appointments of executors as does the will made by an individual. How-ever, the residuary clause in a joint will gives the residue of the estate to each other. Another important clause in this joint or mutual will is the following:

4. 57 Am Jur Wills Sec. 910.
5. Homer I. Harris, *Family Estate Planning Guide*, Mount Kisco, N.Y.: Baker, Voornis & Co., Inc., 1957, pp. 642–643.

We do hereby declare that the mutual and reciprocal dispositive provisions[6] herein for the benefit of the other have been made pursuant to an understanding and agreement that each has made the provisions herein in consideration of the other similarly providing, and upon condition that neither of us will during our lives alter, amend, or revoke such provisions without the written consent of the other, nor will the survivor alter, amend, or revoke the same, after the death of the first of us to die.

The importance of such a statement arises from the fact that it expresses the intent of the parties that neither will revoke or alter the will without notice to the other. In the absence of this clearly expressed intent, it may be held that the execution of the joint will without reference to the terms of instrument is not sufficient evidence of an enforceable contract to devise between the testator and testatrix. In short, either of the parties may subsequently make another will that is likely to take precedence over the joint will.

The Common Disaster Clause

All wills should have a common disaster clause. This is needed because otherwise if a husband and wife have an automobile accident and both are killed, there might be litigation to determine which died first. If the wife died first and the wife had a will leaving the property to her husband, her property, together with what he owned, would pass according to the terms of his will. However, with his wife dead, the property could not pass to her. If there were no catastrophe clause and if the wife died first, all the property might go to the husband's relatives and the wife's kin would receive nothing. To provide against this there is a common catastrophe clause, which is also frequently inserted in a will. This clause may read as follows:

In the event that we die in a common accident or disaster, we do give, devise, and bequeath all of the rest, residue, and remainder of our property, of whatsoever kind and nature, of which we may be seized or possessed or to which we may be entitled, to our children.

Protection of Dependents

The corollary to the joint will testator is the all-time legal villain who would disinherit his wife or children. Every state has some method by which it attempts to protect widows. Forty-two states retain a facet of medieval England called the right of dower. The disappointed or disinherited widow can elect to take the bounty provided in her spouse's will, can elect to receive the share of the estate that would have been hers if her spouse had died without a will, or can elect to take her right of dower. Dower simply means that she has the use for life of one-third of all that was her husband's. In the eight remaining states, the law generally provides that one-half of all property that she and her husband acquired after marriage is hers in her own right. Her husband cannot deprive her of her ownership, even if he attempts to do so by distributing more than his one-half of the community property in his will.

No state requires that children must be provided for in a parent's will. There are two types of relevant laws, however, and each state has one of them. The first requires that all children must be mentioned or acknowledged in the parent's will. This does not mean that any type of gift must be made to them. The second requires that children to be born after the

6. A dispositive provision is a clause indicating the disposition of the property, such as the general legacy, the residuary legacy, etc., as was discussed above under point 7.

execution of the will must be provided for by reference in the will. The effect of these laws is that an after-born child or one not mentioned in the will is entitled to the share that would have been his or hers if the parent had died intestate (without a will).

The Codicil

A codicil to a will is defined as an addition or change executed with the same formalities as required in the will itself. Generally speaking, it is better to draw a new will than to have a codicil. The codicil may, for instance, eliminate a person already designated as a beneficiary under the terms of the will; if so the door is left wide open for that beneficiary to contest the will—which is extremely costly to the estate and may wind up with property not being disposed of in accordance with the intention of the testator or testatrix.

The codicil refers to the will, and it is dated. It contains a dispositive provision and is attested to by the number of witnesses required in accordance with the state statute. Above the signatures of the witnesses is the following clause: "The foregoing instrument consists of one page and was on the third day of July 1981, signed and sealed at the end thereof, and at the same time published and declared by James J. DeFoe, the above named Testator, as and for a Codicil to his Last Will and Testament dated the fourth day of June 1980, in the presence of each of us, who, this attestation clause having been read to us, did at the request of said testator, in his presence and in the presence of each other sign our names as witnesses thereto."

Holographic Wills

Holographic wills are instruments that are wholly drafted by the testator as a will and meet only some of the formal requirements of a will. They must always be signed and dated, but witnesses are not necessary. Not all states recognize holographic wills and those that do may recognize them to pass property only up to a given amount of value. Typically, a holographic will is written at the time when the testator becomes aware of impending death and decides to alter completely his or her will or suddenly realizes there is none. Holographic wills written on envelopes, napkins, and even clothing have been admitted to probate in many states.

Why is not every codicil a holographic will? A codicil acknowledges the basic existence of a preexisting will and is written only to supplement that will. A holographic will supersedes an existing will and often is the only will a testator has written. Why isn't every note a person would write concerning the distribution of property designated to be a holographic will? This type of will, like any other, must meet certain minimal formal requirements. More importantly, the writing must express a testamentary intention in its author. The student can readily foresee the amount of litigation this type of instrument might cause.

What To Do with a Will

If a will cannot be found after the death of the testator, it is presumed that he or she destroyed it with the intent of revoking it. This presumption can be overcome only by proving fraudulent destruction or by showing that the testator was mentally incapable of possessing the intention to revoke.

There are generally four things that can be done with the will once it has been written:

1. In the majority of cases, the will is left with the attorney who drew it, who either puts it in an office safe or places it in a safe deposit box in a financial institution.

2. Where a financial institution has been named as one of the executors, the will is generally placed with that institution for safekeeping.

3. The will can be placed in the testator's own safe deposit box in the testator's name. This is sometimes objected to on the grounds that it takes a court order for the box to be opened after the death of the testator. However, the box must be opened anyway, and the state tax department officials who are present when the box is opened will have no objection to the removal of the will after an inventory has been taken of the contents of the box.

4. The will may be kept in the home of the testator in some sort of strongbox. This is the least recommended place to keep the will, for the reason that it is too easily accessible for purposes of destruction by persons other than the testator and that it may easily be lost or mislaid.

A sample of a modern will is shown in Figure 18-1. Figure 18-2 is a sample of the oldest known will in existence today. It was written by the Egyptian Pharaoh, Uah, and was executed in 2548 B.C. We have also found what is believed to be the shortest will ever probated. It contained just ten words: "Being of sound mind and body, I spent it all."

FIGURE 18-1. SAMPLE OF A MODERN WILL.

KNOW ALL MEN BY THESE PRESENTS:

That I, _____ of Travis County, Texas, being of sound and disposing mind and memory, and above the age of eighteen years, do make and publish this my last will and testament, hereby revoking all wills heretofore made by me.

I.

I direct that all my just debts shall be paid.

II.

Should my beloved wife, _____, survive me, I give to her all property which I shall own or be entitled to at my death.

III.

Should my said wife not survive me, I give all property which I shall own or be entitled to at my death to my son, _____.

I hereby appoint my wife, _____, independent executrix of this my last will and testament, and I direct that no bond shall be required of her as such executrix, and I further direct that no action shall be had in the County Court or any other court in relation to the administration and settlement of my estate other than the probating and recording of this my last will and testament and filing of an inventory and list of claims in the manner provided by law.

If my said wife does not survive me, I appoint my son _____, independent executor of my will without bond

FIGURE 18–1. *CONTINUED*

under the same terms and conditions which would have obtained had my wife served as independent executrix.

IN TESTIMONY WHEREOF, I have hereunto set my hand, this the _____ day of _____, 1981, in the present of _____ _____ and _____ , who witness my signature and attest this my last will and testament at my request as attesting witnesses.

(name) _____

The above instrument was now here on the date hereinabove set forth, subscribed by _____ , the testator, in our presence and in the presence of each other, and we, as attesting witnesses at his request and in his presence and in the presence of each other, sign our names hereto as attesting witnesses.

_____

Before me, the undersigned authority, on this day personally appeared _____ ,

_____ , and

_____ known to me to be the testator and the witnesses, respectively, whose names are subscribed to the annexed or foregoing instrument in their respective capacities, and, all of said persons being by me duly sworn, the said

_____ , testator, declared to me and to the said witnesses in my presence that said instrument is his last will and testament, and that he had willingly made and executed it as his free act and deed for the purposes therein expressed; and the said witnesses, each on his oath stated to me, in the presence and hearing of the said testator, that the said testator had declared to them that said instrument is his last will and testament, and that he executed same as such and wanted each of them to sign it as a witness; and upon their oaths each witness stated further that they did sign the same as witnesses in the presence of the said testator and at his request; that he was at that time nineteen years of age or over and was of sound mind; and that each of said witnesses was then at least fourteen years of age.

Testator _____

Witness _____

Witness _____

Subscribed and acknowledged before me by the said _____ , testator, and subscribed and sworn to before me by said _____ and _____, witnesses, this the _____ day of _____, 1981.

_____
Notary Public, Travis County, Texas

FIGURE 18–2. WILL
DATED 2548 B.C.,
TRANSLATED BY
THE AMERICAN
UNIVERSITY AT
CAIRO

AMENEMHAT IV,

Year 2, Month Paophi, Day 18

I, Uah, am giving a title to property to my wife SHEFTU, the woman of Gesab who is called Teta, the daughter of Sat Sepdu, of all things given to me by my brother Ankh-ren. She shall give it to any she desires of her children she bears me.

I am giving to her the Eastern slaves, 4 persons, that my brother Ankh-ren gave me. She shall give them to whomsoever she will of her children.

As to my tomb, let me be buried in it with my wife alone.

Moreover as to the house built for me by my brother Ankh-ren, my wife shall dwell therein without allowing her to be put forth on the ground by any person.

It is the deputy Gebu who shall act as guardian of my son.

Done in the presence of these witnesses:
KEMEN, Decorator of Columns.
APU, Doorkeeper of the Temple.
SENB, son of Senb, Doorkeeper of the Temple.

THE LETTER OF LAST INSTRUCTIONS

Every person should write a letter of last instructions and leave it in an easily accessible place as well as with every member of the family. A copy should also be given to the family lawyer, if there is one, and another copy should be placed in a safe deposit box. This letter should probably be rewritten and updated every year or two as the individual's assets and other conditions change.

It should be noted that a letter of last instructions is not a will or a substitute for a will; both are needed. A letter of last instructions is, in a sense, a supplementary document to a will. This letter should, among other things, include a list of all the individual's assets and liabilities and indicate where the documents are located.

As a bare minimum, it should include the following:

1. A statement of where the will, if any, may be found.
2. Funeral instructions, if that is necessary. Some people would wish to be cremated; others, buried. Some might wish to donate certain organs (e.g., eyes) to others after death. In any case all members of the family should have general knowledge in advance of future funeral arrangements.
3. A statement regarding a safe deposit box—where it and the key are located.
4. A list of all life insurance policies and their location.
5. An inventory of all stock and bonds, and where they are kept.
6. A list of all other property such as real estate, mutual funds, and business property, and their location.
7. The person's social security number should be recorded.
8. A statement indicating what benefits the deceased may have from his or her employer. There may be pension benefits, death benefits, profit-sharing plans, and other benefits to which the deceased's estate or survivors may have a claim.
9. A listing of all deposits, in banks, savings and loan associations, mutual savings banks, or credit unions.
10. A list of memberships in all unions, professional associations, lodges and fraternal organizations, and veterans groups. There may be financial benefits because of memberships in some of these organizations.
11. A list of all just debts and accounts receivable, the interest rate which they bear, the terms of their payment, and where to locate the documents to prove their validity.
12. A list of all the just debts owed by the individual, the interest rate they bear, the terms of their repayment, and the location of the pertinent documents.

Living Wills

In recent years, there has been some litigation over life support systems being used to continue the life of terminally ill people who are often in great pain or in a vegetable state. Recently, California has passed a right to die in dignity law and other states are likely to follow. This permits life support systems to be withdrawn in such cases.

Also some people have written living wills, as they are called. In a living will a person authorizes, permits, and requests that the life support system be withdrawn if he or she is in a situation such as that described above.

Sometimes the deceased wishes to become a donor of certain transplantable organs. If so, this should be spelled out in the living will, because eyes and certain other organs must be removed immediately upon death.

TRANSFER IN THE ABSENCE OF A WILL

If persons do not effectively dispose of their property by will or if they do not leave a will, their property will be distributed to certain persons related to them in accordance with state law. Since such persons acquire or succeed to the rights of the deceased, and since they do so in the absence of a will, it is said that they acquire the title to that property by intestate succession.

The right of intestate succession is not an inherent right, but exists only because the state legislatures have so provided. The legislatures of the individual states have the right to change, modify, or destroy the right to inherit property.

Plan of Intestate Distribution

Actual plans of intestate distribution vary from state to state, and the best that can be said is that they exhibit certain general patterns, which will be examined below.

Spouses

The surviving spouse, whether husband or wife, will share in the estate. The extent of the share generally depends upon the number of children and other specified heirs. In the absence of surviving blood relations, the surviving spouse customarily takes the entire estate.

Lineals

Lineals or lineal descendants are blood descendants of the decedent. The major portion of an estate not distributed to the surviving spouse is generally distributed to lineals, although sometimes parents also have a claim to part of it.

Parents

If the estate has not been exhausted by this time, the remainder is commonly distributed to the decedent's parents.

Collateral Heirs

These are persons who are not descendants of the decedent but who are related through a common ancestor. Generally they include brothers and sisters, and they are next in line after parents, although in some states they have equal claim with parents.

Administration of Estates

Administration of estates is the means of distributing property of a decedent who died intestate. When no will is left, the court or an officer designated by law appoints one or more persons who are then entitled to administer the estate of the decedent. More often than not, close relatives of the deceased make application to the court for the so-called letter of administration. Such a letter gives the administrator the obligation of gathering together the assets of the deceased, paying off the debts and taxes of the estate, and then distributing the assets in accordance with the statute pertaining to distribution of the estate. Generally, the letter of administration is granted to the first relative or person who applies. In some cases where there are creditors of the deceased and no previous application for letter of administration has been made, the letter may be granted to a creditor. In the absence of creditor, applications, or known relatives, the letter may be issued by the court to a public administrator. In any event, once the letter has been granted to the administrator, the job becomes much the same as that of the executor of an estate.

Nonprobate Property

The ownership of property can take many different forms and the distribution of one's property at death may be controlled by the form of ownership one has. It is possible to own property and distribute it as you wish after death without a will and without the trust, discussed below. This will depend on the form of ownership you have. The best illustration is the joint tenancy. This form of ownership occurs when a person conveys property to two or more other persons as equal owners and to whichever of these persons survives as the final owner. Specific language, which varies from state to state, may be placed in a deed or bill of sale to create this interest. It is usually phrased: *"To . . . . and . . . ., as joint tenants and not as tenants in common, and to the survivor of them and his or her heirs."* At the death of one joint tenant, his or her share of the property is not included in the estate or probated and the survivor is not taxed as an heir.

An individual who owns property and who might prefer it as a joint tenancy to avoid probate and taxation may have the property so converted. In order to do so, one must convey title of the property to some third person, who will reconvey it as a joint tenancy to the owner and the individual who would otherwise be the owner's intended distributee in a will. These conveyances will be necessary to comply with common-law stipulations that the joint tenants must own the same property, from the same point in time, with equal rights of use, and from the same previous owner.

A word of caution must be inserted. As mentioned above, the language of creation of the joint tenancy varies greatly from state to state and some states do not recognize the joint tenancy. Mistakes in drafting a deed could easily create a different form of ownership than the intended joint tenancy. Instead of creating this interest and acquiring its benefits, the parties might instead be required to face probate of the property and acquire tax liabilities peculiar to other forms of ownership. This description of an illustration of nonprobate property is inserted merely to inform the student that some property may be jointly owned with resulting advantages. One should consult an attorney about its application or use in one's own particular estate-planning arrangements.

In the case of real estate, ownership can also be in the form of tenancy by the entirety in common-law states. In such a case, the surviving spouse will be the sole owner upon the death of the first marriage partner. Consequently, a will need not mention property held in this form.

TRUSTS

One of the most versatile tools of estate planning is the trust. A frequently cited reason for the use of a trust is that it often reduces the tax liability of the estate. A trust created by a will will incur estate tax liability only upon the death of the creator. There will be no inheritance taxes when his or her spouse dies and none when the children die. But equally important, the use of the trust allows the creators some control over their wealth even after they die. The creation of a trust ensures that the assets of the creator or settlor can be passed on to his or her children or grandchildren without loss to the principal or corpus (its legal term). The trust can provide income and financial security to those who are inexperienced or incompetent in pecuniary transactions (such as spouse or minor children).

Creation of the Trust

The trust is an arrangement whereby title to property is transferred by the creator or settlor to another person (trustee) for the benefit of a third party (beneficiary or *cestui que trust*). The property placed in trust is called the corpus, the trust *res,* the trust fund, or the trust property. The title to the corpus is split with the trustee holding the property for an ascertainable length of time and all benefits from the corpus go to the beneficiaries.

Generally, a trust may be created for any purpose that is not against public policy. For instance, a trust created from funds obtained from the commission of a felony is void, as is a trust created to encourage divorce. There are other prerequisites that each state imposes for the creation of a valid trust. Two of the most important are *intention* and *capacity*.

There must be an intention on the part of the settlor, declared in writing, to convey property to a trust for the benefit of beneficiaries. Secret, unexpressed intentions will not effectively create a trust. There must also be a manifest intent to impose enforceable duties on the trustee to manage the property for the benefit of another.

In addition to intent, there must be capacity among all the parties involved to create a trust. The settlor must have the capacity to convey property. Thus, insane persons and minors, who cannot validly convey property, lack the capacity to create a trust. The trustee must be capable of owning property and meeting the requirements of being a fiduciary. For example, no person convicted of a felony is capable of being a fiduciary. While settlors can name themselves as beneficiaries, they cannot be their own trustee. (There are exceptions to this in some states.) Finally, a definite beneficiary who is capable of owning property is required. The beneficiary must be named or, as will be discussed later, capable of being determined under a definite standard.

The Inter Vivos Trust

The *inter vivos* trust, or so-called living trust, is one created by the grantor during his or her lifetime. The grantor also may be the beneficiary. In general, the *inter vivos* trust may be either irrevocable or revocable.

The Irrevocable Trust

An irrevocable trust occurs when the grantor gives away the corpus without any right to or control over the income and there is no possibility of reverter (any way of receiving back the corpus); further, he or she terminates any right to alter, amend, or revoke the trust.

A person might create an irrevocable trust for the benefit of a child with the idea of creating an educational fund. The income earned by the trust fund would be taxable to the trust, at a relatively low rate, and not to the father or mother, who might be at a high tax bracket. Thereby the grantor could accomplish two things: (1) reduce the total amount of tax paid and (2) provide a fund for the education of his or her child.

Not only are irrevocable trusts created for the purpose of being used as tax-saving devices but for other reasons as well. One example is the creation of a spendthrift trust by the settlor. Here a trust is used to provide a certain income to the beneficiary (who could also be the settlor) in order to limit excessive spending and, if allowed by the state in which the trust is created, to secure the corpus from creditors' demands. An irrevocable trust might be created for a specific purpose such as the education of the beneficiary. Here income from the corpus would not be vested in the beneficiary until a specified event occurs such as enrollment in a university.

The Revocable Trust

The revocable trust is just what the name implies. It can be established and can be revoked at any time or at a certain specified time. As far as the gift tax is concerned, there is no gift tax applicable at the time of the creation of the trust because the author still retains control over the corpus of the trust. In short, the grantor has not parted with the trust fund.

The Testamentary Trust

Another way a trust can be created is by making a provision for the creation of a trust through a will. Upon the death of the creator or testator, the estate of the deceased comes under the control of a testamentary trustee, who administers the trust as he or she would an *inter vivos* trust. The major reason for the creation of such a trust is to protect the beneficiary who is inexperienced. It may be undesirable, for instance, to leave a large estate consisting of investments in securities to a person lacking experience in investments. Or it may be desirable to leave property to a trustee in order to provide income for a wife for life, and at her death to provide that the corpus of the trust pass on to the children or their heirs. Often, too, property is left to a trustee to hold and to invest and to pay the income to minor children, with the corpus passing to them when they become of age. A simple testamentary trust may be included in a will by the following:

> All the rest, residue, and remainder of my estate, I give, devise, and bequeath to my Trustee, hereinafter named, IN TRUST, nevertheless for the following purposes and uses: To collect and receive the income and to pay or apply the net income therefrom not less frequently than quarter annually, to my beloved wife, Jane De-Foe, during her life. Upon her death my Trustee shall pay and distribute the principal remaining, if any, of said trust, equally share and share alike, to my children, and to my children's children *per stirpes* for those of my children who are deceased.[7]

Simple and Complex Trusts

A trust may be simple or complex. A simple trust is one in which all of the income from the trust is given to the beneficiary; a complex trust is one that retains the income at least until some predetermined time in the future, which must be spelled out in the trust agreement, if it is an irrevocable trust. The beneficiary is liable for the taxes on the income he receives from a simple trust. In the case of a complex trust, the trustee pays them, using some of the income for this purpose, and in accordance with whatever tax bracket the income of the trust indicates.

7. *Per stirpes* means that when the principal of a trust fund is disbursed, it is diluted in accordance with ancestral lines, and this is important when grandchildren are involved. The grandchildren will receive the prorated share that their parents had a claim to. For example: *A* left an estate of $100,000 for each of his two sons, *B* and *C. B* in turn has one child, while *C* has two. After *B* and *C* have died, the three children will not share *A*'s estate equally if his will calls for a *per stirpes* distribution. *B*'s child inherits all of his father's share, while *C*'s children must split their father's share. If the original fund has remained intact, *B*'s child will get $100,000 and *C*'s children, $50,000 each.

Clifford Trusts; Temporary Trusts

This is a specialized trust and could save you on personal income taxes. A Clifford trust must be a simple trust and its investment income given yearly to the beneficiary. It is irrevocable for a time and then it revokes automatically and the principal reverts to the creator. The minimum time period is ten years and one day, but it can be set up for a longer time. It also revokes automatically if the beneficiary dies prior to ten years and one day. It is useful if you are supporting (or are contributing to the support of), say, a parent or other relative. An example will make this clear. Suppose you are contributing $2,000 to supplement the social security payments of your parents. This $2,000 is not a tax deductible item to you. If you are in the 50 percent tax bracket, it takes $4,000 of your income to provide your parents with $2,000.

If you were to set up a Clifford trust today for, say, $21,000 it could earn about 10 percent or about $2,100. After trustee fees of about $100 (which is tax deductible) the beneficiary would have $2,000. The beneficiary might have to pay a tax on part of that $2,000 but presumably at a much lower rate than you. In ten years and one day or upon the death of the beneficiary, the entire $21,000 would revert to you. If after ten years and one day the trust were still needed, you would have to set up another one. Setting up a Clifford trust is a one-shot affair. You must add the entire principal sum in one payment and then cannot add to it. However, you can set up more than one such trust, and when the one you have revokes, you can establish another one. Also the beneficiary can invade the trust up to 5 percent or $5,000 per year if done on a noncumulative basis (invasion is spelled out in greater detail below).

The Life Insurance Trust

Life insurance trusts are another tool finding increased use in the overall picture of estate planning. A life insurance trust is created when the person makes a trustee, say a bank, the beneficiary of a life insurance policy. The trustee then administers the funds on behalf of someone else. To be sure, the insured can make arrangements whereby the life insurance company will make periodic payments on behalf of the beneficiaries directly, and in effect one gets a trustee through the insurance company. Moreover, this is usually cheaper than having a third party play the role of the trustee because the trustee charges a fee for these services. However, a separate trust may provide for a more flexible management of the estate than an insurance company can provide. In the case of a large estate, this flexibility may be worth the added cost.

A life insurance trust is used, as are many other trusts, to provide against speculation by the beneficiary or to prevent mismanagement of funds by an inexperienced beneficiary. In some instances, for example, if the trust is irrevocable, it will result in tax advantages to the estate; and in other instances the benefits or claims from the policies can be lent to the estate for the payment of taxes or to purchase estate assets.

Life insurance trusts are said to be either funded or unfunded. In the case of the former, the policies and other property that may be included in the trust are transferred to the trustee. The income from the other property pays the premiums on the policies while they are in force. In the case of the unfunded life insurance trust, the policies are deposited with the trustee; however, the insured pays the premiums and reserves all rights in the policies during his or her lifetime.

In both events, the trustee is named the beneficiary of the policy when it is issued or upon the death of the settlor, when the duties of the trustee begin. The company with whom the policy is taken must be consulted in any case. If one of the purposes of the life insurance trust is to effect a savings of taxes, the trust must be an irrevocable trust.

The Power of Invasion

Unfortunately, one cannot predict the future . . . even in economic terms. A man may believe that he has provided sufficient cash assets to maintain his wife and child; he has established a testamentary trust and provided that the income therefrom shall go to the support of his wife and child. However, as the years pass, the cost of living rises by far more than was anticipated. It may well be then that the income from the trust fund will be insufficient to support his wife and child. In practice, therefore, a statement is frequently inserted to provide that the trust fund may itself be used to support the beneficiaries if the need arises. This dipping into the principal is called the power of invasion. It may be unlimited, where the amount to be taken from the fund is left to the best judgment and discretion of either the beneficiary or the trustee; or it is sometimes limited to a certain percentage of the trust fund over and above the annual income per year. For example, if the fund is $100,000 and the income, say, is only $5000 in any one year, the trustee may be permitted to pay out a maximum of 3 percent, 4 percent, or even 10 percent of the principal annually, depending on how the clause is drawn.

Needless to say, the importance of the clause cannot be stressed too strongly if the purpose of the trust is for the support and maintenance of the beneficiaries. Although the courts can authorize the reformation of the trust agreement to allow dispersal of a portion of the corpus as long as no one beneficiary is deprived of his or her rightful share, this is undesirable for the beneficiaries since litigation is a costly and time-consuming process.

The Rule Against Perpetuities

In 1938, an article appeared in the *Harvard Law Review* by Professor Leach entitled "Perpetuities in a Nutshell," in which the author made as one of his points that the problem with perpetuities in a nutshell was to keep them there. The so-called rule against perpetuities is one of the most difficult and least understood principles in the law of trusts or anything else for that matter. To comprehend it at all, one must first understand that the law is opposed to a dead person guiding property forever. In short, it is not beyond the realm of possibility for persons to create trusts so that they could in effect guide their property for hundreds of years, or forever if one were to be presumptuous. Consequently, under the common law there has developed a rule that simply states that an interest must vest (finally pass to someone) not later than twenty-one years after a given number of persons named in the trust die. This is the *lives-in-being* clause. The number of lives in being permitted varies from state to state, but in all states they must be living when the trust becomes effective; unborn heirs do not count.

Today the common law still prevails in most states with variations. In New York and Minnesota, for example, title to real property cannot remain in trust for more than the lives of two persons in being. In some states, the title must vest after two lives in being, plus twenty-one years and ten months.

To give an example of a violation of the lives-in-being rule, if one provides that one's children are to have a life estate and at their death the trust property is to pass to the grandchildren, there is a violation of the rule because grandchildren may be born after the death of the testator. However, if the will creates the trust "for the duration of the life of my present wife, and upon the death of my present wife the trust is to continue for the duration of the life of the youngest child of X living at my death, with the income to be divided equally among my children and my grandchildren after my present wife's death," this is not a violation of the rule. So long as the youngest child of X, living at his death, continues to live, the children and the grandchildren will receive income even after the death of the widow. Even grandchildren not born at the time of the testator's death will receive income until the death of said child of X, after which the children and grandchildren will receive the remainder of the estate. The lives in being and the beneficiaries need not be the same individuals, although frequently they are. Moreover, while the beneficiaries may be unborn when the trust becomes effective, the lives in being may not.

The Power of Appointment

A power of appointment is defined as a device by which the owner of property grants to another person or persons the power to designate, within whatever limits he or she wishes, how the property shall be distributed after the original beneficiary passes on.

In more intelligent language, it is a device giving the beneficiary of a trust the right to alter the disposition of the trust *res* or trust fund upon his or her death through the will. For example, A by will leaves property to his son, in trust, the income from the trust fund to be paid to the son for life, and the property upon the death of the son to pass to his son's children. If the son dies before his wife, it may be that his widow will have no means of support; consequently there may be included in A's will a provision giving his son the power of appointment. This would mean that the son through his will could change the distribution of the property by providing that upon his death the income should go to his widow for life and upon her death to his children.

In the final analysis, what this does is to enable A to look into the future through the eyes of his son; for what may be considered wise today may be considered absurd tomorrow.

There are tax reasons for creating the power of appointment as well as tax problems far too complex to discuss here. One of the main reasons for including the power of appointment in a trust agreement, however, is to protect the fund for the several life beneficiaries.

The Trustee—The Role of the Fiduciary

It is the prerogative of the settlor to name the trustee for the trust. Since this person is to be responsible for the corpus of the trust for a number of years, the selection of the trustee is a critical decision. Although a private individual can be named as trustee if he or she is willing to take on the responsibilities and duties of a fiduciary for the nominal fee involved in managing the trust, the settlor generally finds it more satisfactory to name an organized trust corporation or trust department of a bank as the trustee. The settlor could expect the trust companies and banks to have a larger and more experienced staff to administer the trust and a greater willingness to take on the strict liabilities of being fiduciary than could generally be found from an individual.

Trustees owe the highest loyalty to the trust fund and the beneficiaries, and their role is spelled out by the law. As fiduciaries, they have a duty to act primarily for the benefit of the trust property. In investing or managing the property of the trust, they are held accountable, within limits, by the prudent person standard. This is to say, they must act as a reasonable and prudent person investing the funds of another. Because they cannot be engaged in anything that resembles speculation, the trustees attempt to manage the assets of the corpus in order to preserve capital and provide income. In addition to investing the assets of the corpus, the trustees must also handle all legal disputes concerning the trust, pay any tax

"... to my nephew, Phelps Putney, who always sneered at my conservative stuffed shirt stance, I leave him my shirts." (*Source:* Permission Cartoon Features Syndicate; from *The Wall Street Journal*.)

liabilities the trust generates, and handle any other responsibility resulting from the operation of the trust. Generally speaking, for their services, the trustees will receive less than 1 percent of the assets of the corpus each year.

GIFT AND ESTATE TAXES

Two possible taxes may be imposed because of death: estate taxes and inheritance taxes. In addition, there are separate gift taxes, which are not related to death. Estate taxes, also called death taxes, may be imposed at the state as well as the federal level. The same is true of gift taxes; there is a federal gift tax, and some states also levy them. Estate or death taxes come from the estate of the deceased and hence reduce the amount a person may inherit, in theory being a tax on the privilege of leaving an estate. There are both state and federal taxes on estates.

Gift taxes are imposed on the giver, and the recipient need not pay a tax on the gift. These are taxes on the privilege of giving something away, and the federal government as well as some states levy gift taxes.

Inheritance taxes are different from estate taxes in that they are a tax imposed on the privilege of inheriting something, imposed, that is, on the person receiving property. However, there are no federal inheritance taxes; only certain states impose them. There is some confusion between estate and inheritance taxes because both are often referred to as death taxes. Inheritance taxes, however, are not that. Most states have either an inheritance tax or an estate tax, but not both; only a few states do have both. In those states having both taxes, if a person died and left an estate of, say $200,000, it would be reduced by the estate tax and then the reduced amount would be further taxed because of the inheritance tax. However, there are both exemptions and deductions regarding both of these taxes.

Practices vary so much from state to state that little can be said about them except for two general comments. First, most state taxes of this sort are less severe than the federal taxes, and even the federal estate and gift taxes do not bring in vast sums. For example, in fiscal 1979, total gift and estate tax receipts at the federal level were just over $5.4 billion.[8] Second, the severity of the state taxes and exemptions varies with the closeness of the kin. Spouses are taxed less severely than children, and children less severely than other relatives. Moreover, the Federal Tax Code allows a tax credit for a large proportion of all state inheritance and estate taxes. Therefore, for all practical purposes one need pay in net terms the amount the federal government demands.

Gifts and Gift Taxes

A gift is defined as: "a voluntary transfer of property by one to another without any consideration or compensation therefor."[9] There are two major categories of gifts. One is the gift *causa mortis,* which is to take effect upon the death of the donor and which may be revoked at any time prior to death. The second is gift *inter vivos* or lifetime gift. For the latter to be effective, there must be an intent to make the gift, a delivery of the gift, and an acceptance of the gift.

In 1976, Congress changed drastically the law affecting estate and gift taxes. The new law increases the amount a person can give away or leave tax-free. However, the new law combined the estate and gift tax rates into one common rate structure and in so doing raised the rates. Before, gift tax rates were lower than estate taxes. Also, both rates were progressive. Hence, there was a double (and substantial) tax savings possible by giving assets away prior to death. This is no longer possible. Nevertheless, more modest tax savings can still be obtained by giving assets away prior to death, as we shall see below.

In short, while the dollar amounts you can give away or leave to your heirs before taxes are due is now larger, once they are due the tax bite is bigger. Congress did this by raising the exemption level. Actually, the gift tax exemption and the estate tax exemption were combined and then converted into one unified tax credit. Gifts and estates are now taxed the same way. Indeed, dying and leaving an estate is now looked upon as one final gift.

The new tax rates range from 18 percent on the first $10,000 in taxable transfers (either gifts or through an estate) up to 70 percent of taxable transfers of above $5,000,000. The exemptions as noted above were converted to a tax credit effective in 1977 for the first time. The dollar amount of this credit was $30,000 in 1977 and is scheduled to rise over the years through 1981 as shown in Table 18-1. Since the tax rates range from 18 to 70 percent, this tax credit can be converted to what an exemption would have to be to give you the equivalent tax-free transfer. It, too, is shown in Table 18-1.

Gift Tax Exclusion

It should be noted that in addition to the tax credit, there is a $3,000 annual tax exclusion insofar as gifts are concerned. Moreover, that is $3,000 per year per recipient. This $3,000 can be given tax-free. A person with five children could give them each $3,000 per year tax-free for a total of $15,000 per year. Hence it is still possible to make modest tax savings by giving assets away prior to death.

8. Federal Reserve Bulletin, November 1979, p. 31.
9. Commissioner v. *A. G. Montague,* 126 F2d 948.

TABLE 18–1. *Gift and estate tax unified credit through 1981*

YEAR	UNIFIED CREDIT	EQUIVALENT EXEMPTION
1977	$30,000	$120,666
1978	34,000	134,000
1979	38,000	147,333
1980	42,500	161,563
1981	47,000	175,625

Split Gifts

The split gift is sometimes referred to as a joint gift made by the husband and wife. It, too, can result in tax savings. The law provides among other things that a gift made by one person to any person other than his or her spouse shall be considered as having been made one-half by him and one-half by her. In order to comply with the statute, however, each spouse has to consent to the gift in writing and has to signify such consent on or before April 15 of the following year.

The net effect of all this is that the annual exclusion may be doubled. Therefore, a husband and wife may make an annual gift of $6,000 times the number of donees without paying any gift tax whatsoever.

The Marital Deduction and the Gift Tax

Not only is the marital deduction useful in the estate tax, which will be discussed below, but it is also useful with regard to gift taxes. The marital deduction permits a married donor to transfer tax-free 100 percent of the first $100,000 of gifts to a spouse. The next $100,000 of gifts would be taxed, but on gifts in excess of $200,000, the marital deduction is 50 percent. This is an overall or lifetime deduction. But it does permit wealthy individuals to transfer substantial sums tax-free to their spouses. This marital deduction is over and above the $3,000 annual exemption per recipient. A husband could therefore give his wife $103,000 in one year and then $3,000 in every year after that before he had to pay a gift tax.

Gifts Made in Contemplation of Death

Prior to 1977, gifts made less than three years prior to death were included in an estate and subject to the estate tax unless it could be proven they were *not* made in contemplation of death. This clause caused much litigation and, consequently, the phrase "unless it could be proven" was removed from the law. Now all gifts are included in the decedent's estate regardless of why or when they were made. Gift and estate taxes are now the same. Nevertheless, gifts made more than three years prior to death are important because they can reduce taxes, as we shall see below.

The Gift Tax Calculation

The gift tax is calculated by applying the proper tax rate to the cumulative lifetime taxable gifts (taxable gifts are total gifts less the $3,000 annual exclusion less also the marital deduction) and then subtracting gift taxes paid on previous gifts. This always puts future gifts in higher and higher tax brackets. For example, if a person makes a taxable gift of $150,000 and pays the tax on it and then a year or two later makes another $150,000 taxable gift, the tax on the second gift is calculated as if it were $300,000. Then when the tax on the $300,000 taxable gift is ascertained, it is reduced by the amount of the gift tax paid last year on the first $150,000 given away.

Gifts can then still reduce total (gift and estate) taxes for three reasons: (1) the $3,000 annual exclusion per recipient, (2) *gift taxes* on gifts made more than three years prior to death are not included in the taxable estate while *taxes* on gifts made less than three years before death are and (3) gifts freeze the value of appreciable assets at the value at the time of the gift for later estate tax evaluation. Consequently, the taxable estate is smaller and hence a lower tax rate is applicable. That is, all gifts are included in the taxable estate but only the tax paid on gifts made less than three years prior to death are so included. This will become clearer when I explain the estate "gross up" below.

Nontax Reasons for Making Gifts

In addition to tax reasons for making gifts, there are perfectly valid nontax reasons. In the event there is some doubt on the part of the donor that his or her will can stand an attack by a disappointed relative or heir apparent, it may be better to give away part of the estate to someone prior to death.

Furthermore, it might be desirable to give away part of an estate before death because such a reduction might lower the costs of probating the will, and also the time needed to probate the will.

Finally, it might be that a wealthy donor will give a gift to an offspring with the idea of observing how this person handles the funds. On the basis of the management of these funds, the donor may reach a decision regarding a method of testamentary disposition of the estate.

The Federal Estate Tax

As was pointed out earlier in the chapter, one of the principal objectives of estate planning is to minimize the federal estate tax. The gross estate of the decedent is defined as the total value of all property, whether real or personal, tangible or intangible, except real property situated outside the United States. Included are all taxable gifts given during the lifetime of the decedent. It should also be noted that the estate tax is levied only on the taxable estate. The actual assets in the estate are reduced by the marital deduction and administrative expenses. These latter include the cost of the funeral, probating the will, and the like.

The Marital Deduction and Estate Taxes

The marital deduction refers to that portion of an estate that may pass tax-free to a surviving spouse; that is, it reduces the taxable estate and hence the estate tax.

The marital deduction is 100 percent of the first $250,000 of the adjusted gross estate (gross estate less administrative expenses). It is nothing on the next $250,000, and 50 percent on the adjusted gross estate in excess of $500,000. On an estate of $1,000,000 then, the marital deduction reduces it to $500,000.

Calculating the Estate Tax

The amount of the estate tax is calculated by applying the new unified tax rate to the taxable estate, which includes all cumulative lifetime taxable transfers; that is, to the estate is added all previous taxable gifts, which results in the estate tax being calculated at a higher bracket because of the progressive nature of the tax (rates range from 18 to 70 percent). To be sure, there is a credit for previous gift taxes paid, but this cumulative feature does increase the burden of taxes.

The Gross Up

Taxable gifts made within three years of death (less the $3,000 annual exclusion per recipient) are included in the gross estate. So, too, are the *taxes* paid on this gift (gifts). This is referred to as "the gross up." Gifts made more than three years prior to death are also added in later to obtain the tentative taxable estate. But here is the difference; the taxes paid on earlier gifts are not included in the tentative base and hence they don't contribute to pushing it up to a higher tax bracket. After the gross estate is obtained, administrative expenses are deducted to obtain the adjusted gross estate; then the marital deduction is taken to obtain the taxable estate. Then all previous taxable gifts made are added (except those made within three years of death, which are already in). (But the taxes paid on these gifts are not picked up.) This brings us to the tentative tax base. The estate tax is then calculated by applying the proper tax bracket rate. Then a credit is subtracted from the tentative estate tax for all gift taxes paid during the lifetime. That gives us the tax before the unified gift and estate tax credit, which, when deducted, results in the final estate tax liability that must be paid. Table 18-2 illustrates both gift and estate tax calculations. Since the new tax law is being phased in over a number of years, the calculations would be slightly different than shown until 1981. It also assumes that the first two gifts were made more than three years prior to death while the third gift was not; the hypothetical individual had assets of $5,000,000 and had made gifts to his wife totaling $1,800,000.

Table 18-3 shows the unified gift and estate tax rates. While the above example in Table 18-2 is complex, it is actually a simplified version. In the real world it may be even more complex, and hence the services of a qualified attorney or tax accountant should be retained.

How a Trust Can Reduce Estate Taxes

One of the major reasons for setting up a trust is to reduce the federal estate tax. An estate tax is, technically speaking, not a property tax even though it is imposed on the property (the estate of a deceased person) before it may pass to someone else. It has been referred to as a death tax; technically, it is a tax on the privilege of passing property to someone else upon death.

You have learned above that gifts can be used to reduce estate taxes somewhat; they do this, however, by reducing the size of the estate.

Setting up a trust, on the other hand, does not reduce the size of the estate but does lessen the estate tax, as we shall see below.

It should be noted that estate taxes on certain small estates (primarily farms and businesses) can be spread over ten years but there is an interest charge on the deferred payments.

How a trust can reduce estate taxes can perhaps best be illustrated by an example.

TABLE 18–2. COMPUTATION
OF GIFT AND ESTATE
TAXES

Gift Tax

The computation of the gift tax is as follows:

Gift No. 1 (made in 1981)

Gross amount of gift	$450,000
Less:	
Annual exclusion	3,000
Marital deduction	225,000
	228,000
Taxable gift	222,000
Gift tax on gift No. 1	61,840
Less: Unified Credit	47,000
Gift tax paid on gift No. 1	14,840

Gift No. 2 (made in 1982)

Gross amount of gift	450,000
Less:	
Annual exclusion	3,000
Marital deduction	225,000
	228,000
Taxable gift	222,000
Gift tax paid on gift No. 2	74,920

Gift No. 3 (made in 1986)

Gross amount of gift	900,000
Less:	
Annual exclusion	3,000
Marital deduction	450,000
	453,000
Taxable gift	447,000
Gift tax paid on gift No. 3	166,530
Tax paid on gift No. 1	14,840
Tax paid on gift No. 2	74,920
Tax paid on gift No. 3	166,530
Total gift taxes paid	$256,290

Suppose a married couple has $500,000 of assets invested in income-yielding securities. To simplify the case, we will also assume that the gross estate and the adjusted gross estate will be the same.

Without a Trust

1. First spouse dies in 1981 and $250,000 is taxed as it passes to the survivor; $250,000 already belongs to the survivor in community property states and the marital deduction applies in the others.

2. Hence, the tax is on $250,000 and this tax is $70,800, but after the unified gift and estate tax credit of $47,000, it amounts to $23,800.

3. Second spouse dies in 1982 and leaves an estate of $500,000 (roughly).

TABLE 18–2. *(Continued)*

Estate Tax

Because the decedent paid gift taxes of $256,290 in addition to the gifts to his wife, his remaining estate at his death is $2,943,710. The computation of the estate tax is as follows:

Actual estate	$2,943,710
Gift within 3 years of death (gift No. 3 less $3,000 annual exclusion, plus the tax paid on that gift— "gross-up")	1,063,530
Gross estate	4,007,240
Less: Administration expenses	292,651
Concise Explanation	
Adjusted gross estate	3,714,589
Less: Marital deduction	1,857,295
Taxable estate	1,857,294
Plus: Adjusted taxable gifts (gifts #1 and #2)	444,000
Tentative tax base	2,301,294
Estate tax on tentative tax base	928,434
Less: Credit for gift taxes paid during life	256,290
Tax before Unified Credit	672,144
Less: Unified Credit	47,000
Estate tax payable	625,144

TABLE 18–3. *Unified gift and estate tax*

AMOUNTS SUBJECT TO TAX		TAX ON AMOUNT IN COLUMN A	TAX RATE ON AMOUNT IN EXCESS OF COLUMN A (%)
A exceeding	B But not exceeding		
$ 0	$ 10,000	—	18%
10,000	20,000	$ 1,800	20
20,000	40,000	3,800	22
40,000	60,000	8,200	24
60,000	80,000	13,000	26
80,000	100,000	18,200	28
100,000	150,000	23,800	30
150,000	250,000	38,800	32
250,000	500,000	70,800	34
500,000	750,000	155,800	37
750,000	1,100,000	248,300	39
1,100,000	1,250,000	345,800	41
1,250,000	1,500,000	448,300	43
1,500,000	2,000,000	555,800	45
2,000,000	2,500,000	780,800	49
2,500,000	3,000,000	1,025,800	53
3,000,000	3,500,000	1,290,800	57
3,500,000	4,000,000	1,575,800	61
4,000,000	4,500,000	1,880,000	65
4,500,000	5,000,000	2,205,800	69
5,000,000	—	2,550,800	70

4. The estate tax now is on $500,000 and amounts to about $155,800 because the tax is quite progressive. After the unified tax credit, this tax becomes $108,800. However, there is a second credit of $23,800 because of the estate tax paid when the first member of the marriage died. Consequently the estate tax becomes $85,000.

5. Total tax is $108,800 ($85,000 + $23,800).

With Trust

The same couple now use a trust to lessen their estate taxes.

1. First spouse dies and leaves nothing to the survivor. Rather, the $250,000 goes into an irrevocable trust established by the deceased's will and the survivor gets the income from it.

2. There is, however, a $23,800 tax on this $250,000 going into trust, because it is an estate tax. That is, it is on the estate (property) of the deceased for the privilege of passing property to, in this case, the trust.

3. Second spouse dies and leaves an estate of $250,000, not $500,000. The $250,000 in trust on her behalf is not hers.

4. Second partner's estate tax after the unified credit is also $23,800.

5. Total tax is $47,600.

6. Tax savings is $108,800 − $47,600 or $61,200.

The tax savings may be even larger if the surviving spouse lives more than two years, because the credit for the tax on prior transfers (the $23,800 when the first member of the marriage died) phases out over a ten-year period. Thus, if the surviving spouse dies more then ten years later, the estate tax in the situation without the trust is $132,600 and the tax savings is $85,000.

State Inheritance and Estate Taxes

In addition to federal estate taxes, there are state inheritance taxes and state estate taxes. An inheritance tax (the federal government does not impose an inheritance tax) is a tax on the right of a beneficiary to inherit property and it is paid by the recipient. An estate tax, as noted before, is a tax on the privilege of transferring property upon death and is imposed upon the property itself. These state taxes vary from state to state but generally their rates are lower than the federal estate taxes. However, exemptions are also generally lower. Because of this, state death taxes could be higher than the federal estate tax, but this is rarely the case. Inheritance taxes may vary not only with the size of the inheritance, but also with the degree of closeness of the beneficiary to the deceased. While these state taxes vary from state to state, the differential washes out when paying federal estate taxes. This is because the federal estate tax allows a credit for all state inheritance and estate taxes.

QUESTIONS FOR REVIEW

1. How may a person's domicile and residence differ, and what is the importance of this distinction from the point of view of estate planning?

2. Why is it important to draw up a personal balance sheet and record of annual income when planning a will?

3. What is the major purpose of a will?

4. What are the adverse possibilities of dying intestate? Would a person ever want to die intestate?

5. Why is it important to have an experienced attorney draft a will or trust arrangement? Why should the executor of a will also be experienced?

6. What are the relative merits of appointing a private individual to act as trustee as opposed to a trust corporation or trust department of a bank?

7. List what you think are the most important contents of a will.

8. Differentiate between the *inter vivos* trust, the irrevocable trust, the revocable trust, and the testamentary trust.

9. How does a *per stirpes* distribution of an estate differ from a *per capita* distribution?

10. When is a joint tenancy a desirable form of property distribution?

11. What is the idea behind the power of invasion? Do you think it is wise? Why?

12. Differentiate between a gift *causa mortis* and a gift *inter vivos*.

13. Explain how gifts can reduce total taxes.

14. What is the marital deduction and how does it work?

15. Can you think of any nontax reasons for making gifts?

16. What are the advantages of a life insurance trust to an estate with limited assets? How is it created?

CASES

1. Jack McCarthy and his wife Bette are in their early thirties and have two children, four and six. Jack earns $10,000 per year. He has $25,000 worth of life insurance. Bette earns $14,000 per year. They have $10,000 equity in their $25,000 house, $3,000 in cash in a savings and loan association, and $3,000 worth of personal assets including a car. Both Jack and Bette are in excellent health. A few evenings ago a lawyer friend of theirs told them everyone should have a will. Jack and Bette have always believed wills were for older people and probably for older people of means. Jack feels that because they are young and do not have many assets, they do not need a will. What do you think?

2. Peter Geldsack is an extremely wealthy man. He is a vigorous widower in his early sixties and has the following assets.

Assets	Value
1. Farm in Connecticut	$ 450,000
2. Ski Lodge in Aspen, Colorado	75,000
3. House in Bergen County, N.J.	100,000
4. Department Store in Newark, N.J.	1,600,000
5. Common Stock	3,452,000
6. Corporate Bonds	2,500,000
7. Municipal Bonds	2,000,000
Total	$10,177,000

Peter has two children to whom he would like to leave the bulk of his estate in equal parts. However, he would also like to leave approximately $100,000 to his faithful butler, and to do so in such a way that he will be well cared for during the rest of his life. The butler, moreover, knows little of investments, and Peter is afraid he might lose any outright cash grant. Peter would also like to leave his ski lodge to his dear friend and ski companion Grover Attwater of Glenwood Springs, Colorado.

Could you give Peter advice on drawing up a will that will carry out his wishes? If Peter died without a will, what would happen to his estate?

3. Wally and Dorothy Brown are in their middle sixties and have assets totaling close to one million dollars. They have two children to whom they wish to leave their estate split equally between them. They propose to do this in a will, but each wishes that the surviving spouse first get the entire estate and that the children have it only when they are both gone. How can this be arranged in a will?

Should they draw up a joint will? Why or why not?

4. Bernice Wilson inherited a substantial sum of money when her husband died last year. She has two children and has provided that they will share her estate equally when she is gone. However, she has recently become concerned over the high taxes, which will diminish the amount her children will receive. What taxes does she have in mind? Can you help her plan her affairs so as to minimize these taxes?

5. Joseph Horohan is a wealthy elderly widower, with only one child who knows nothing about investments. Joe knows his child would lose his money if he left it to him. He would also like to minimize taxes. Can you advise him?

6. Bill and Sara Smith, an elderly couple, have just over $1,000,000 of tax-exempt municipal bonds yielding 5.1 percent. They also own a home free and clear and have no other substantial assets. They have three grown children to whom they will leave their estate in equal parts in their will. Recently they have heard they can reduce taxes by giving part of their assets away prior to death. Is this true? How does it work? What is one of the pitfalls to be avoided if they decide to give some of their assets away?

7. Spencer D'Orsey, an exceptionally well-to-do man, has recently died. His will created a testamentary trust for his four children—Bob, Carol, Ted, and Alice. While he was alive, D'Orsey was an exceptionally opinionated man. For example, he detested Carol's husband Abby Rubin, a professional union organizer, and could not understand why Alice would not marry Richard Starkley, a young attorney employed as a trust officer in a local bank. Because of these situations, D'Orsey had some unusual provisions written into the trust. One of these provisions was that Carol would not receive her share as a beneficiary

unless she divorced her husband. In addition, Alice could not receive her share until she married Starkley. To complicate affairs, Starkley's bank was named trustee. Can D'Orsey do this to his daughters? What conflicts does Starkley face if he marries Alice?

8. Don Price drafted a will in which he distributed every item of property he owned, naming each piece. Several years later, Don became wealthy and held a large number of valuable stock certificates. When he reached the age of seventy, Don realized he should provide for the distribution of his stocks. Never an inefficient man, Don reached into the wastebasket and withdrew a sheet of butcher paper that had the words "Joe's Meat Market—Baloney" stamped on one side. On the other side, Don wrote a holographic will bequeathing his stocks to the local Catholic church. Don suffered a heart attack one week later and, as the local priest was administering Don's last rites, Joe (from the meat market) entered the room. Don looked at Joe and produced a small key. "Here, Joe, you take this. This key will open up a new way of life for you." Don soon died and his executors found that the key unlocks a small strongbox in which Don kept his stock certificates. Who gets what?

9. Howard Johnson is a wealthy land owner in Massachusetts. In response to his wife's obvious interest in becoming the owner of some of Howard's country mansions, Howard drafts a will that devises his property "To my loving wife, Louise Johnson, for her years of devotion to our family." When Howard learns that he has terminal cancer, he executes a deed to these estates to Robert Gunsel, a friend. Robert then executes a deed to these estates "To Howard Johnson and Dottie Carter, as joint tenants and not as tenants in common, and to the survivor of them and his heirs." What may Louise do to protect herself against Dottie, Howard's paramour of thirty years?

SUGGESTED READINGS

Ashley, Pritcher B. *You and Your Will; The Planning and Management.* New York: McGraw-Hill, 1977.

Drollinger, William C. *Tax Shelters and Tax Free Income for Everyone.* Ann Arbor, MI: Epic Publications, Inc., 1979.

Estate Planners Quarterly. Published by Farnsworth Publishing Co., Inc., New York.

Federal Estate and Gift Taxes. Chicago: Commerce Clearing House.

Guilfoyle, A. P.; Fossett, Alice W.; Thomas, William W.; and Scoville, Samuel S. *Tax Facts on Life Insurance*. Cincinnati, O: The National Underwriter Company. This is an annual publication.

Internal Revenue Service. *A Guide to Federal Estate and Gift Taxation*. U.S. Treasury Department, Internal Revenue Service. This pamphlet can be obtained from the local IRS office.

Journal of the American Society of Chartered Life Underwriters. Published quarterly by the American Society of Chartered Life Underwriters, 270 Bryn Mawr Avenue, (P.O. Box 59), Bryn Mawr, PA.

McCord, John H. *Estate and Gift Tax*. New York: Harcourt Brace Jovanovich, 1979.

————. *Estate and Gift Tax Reform*. St. Paul, Minn.: West Publishing, 1979.

Scott, Austin W. *The Law of Trusts,* 3d ed. Boston: Little, Brown, and Co., 1967.

Trusts and Estates, The Journal of Estate Planning and Administration. Published monthly by Communication Channels, Inc., 461 Eighth Ave., New York, N.Y.

Using Trusts in Estate Planning. New York: Practicing Law Institute, 1971.

TECHNICAL APPENDIX

(Glossary of Terms)

ADMINISTRATOR: One who administers a decedent's estate during probate. He or she differs from the executor in that the administrator is appointed by the judge of the probate court when no executor is named by a will or when the appointed executor is unable to perform the duties.

ATTESTATION: The witnessing of a paper's execution and a signed statement to that effect.

BEQUEST: A gift of personal property or money under a will.

CESTUI QUE TRUSTENT (called cetty for short): The beneficiaries of a trust.

CODICILS: Writings executed subsequent to a will and forming a part thereof.

COLLATERAL HEIRS: Persons who are not descendants of the decedent but who are related through a common ancestor. Generally they include brothers and sisters of the decedent.

CORPUS; TRUST RES: The body of the trust; the assets.

DECEDENT: A deceased person.

DEVISE: A gift of real property by the last will and testament of the donor. In contrast, a bequest or legacy is a testamentary gift of personalty.

DEVISEE: Person receiving a gift of land by way of will.

DOMICILE: The place of the permanent home of a person. The place of domicile is largely a matter of intention, though declarations of intention contrary to the actions of a person do not always control. A person has only one domicile at one time. It is not necessarily the same place as one's residence because domicile is the home, the fixed place of habitation, whereas residence is a transient place of dwelling. The domicile is where wills are probated.

DONOR: The person who holds the legal title to trust property for the purposes as stated by the terms of the trust. The person for whose benefit the trust is created is called a beneficiary or *cestui que* trustent.

ESCROW: An agreement under which certain executed documents, e.g., deeds, are delivered into the hands of a third person to be held until specified conditions are fulfilled and then delivered over to the person so performing or, in the case of default, returned to the person executing the document.

ESTATE: The interest that anyone has in property, being used particularly in connection with the interests owned by a person in real property. Also the total property of whatever kind owned by a decedent before the property is distributed according to the terms of a will, or by the laws of inheritance if the owner died intestate.

ESTATE IN SEVERALTY: An estate that is held by a person in his or her own right only, without any other person being joined or connected.

EXECUTOR: The personal representative of a testator, appointed by the testator and approved by the judge of a probate court to take charge of the testator's estate, pay the debts, and distribute the balance of the property to the beneficiaries of the will pursuant to the order of the probate court.

FEE SIMPLE: The highest in dignity and the greatest in extent of the estates in real property.

FIDUCIARY: The person or institution who manages the financial affairs of a trust.

GIFT CAUSA MORTIS: An unrevoked gift of personal property made in expectation of death.

GRANTEE: One to whom a conveyance is made by deed.

GRANTOR: One who makes a conveyance. Also the person who creates a trust.

HOLOGRAPHIC WILL: A will written entirely by the testator with his own hand.

INTER VIVOS GIFT: A gift among the living, in contrast to a gift by will or in anticipation of death.

INTER VIVOS TRUST: A trust created during the lifetime of the grantor.

INTESTATE: Having no will. An intestate is a decedent who left no will or a defective will. Property not included in a will is often called intestate property.

JOINT TENANCY: Two or more persons owning the

same land and having the same unity of interest, time, title, and possession together with the right of survivorship.

LEGACY: Specific legacy: a gift of personal property, generally a specific item of value, under a will

General legacy: a gift of a certain sum, but no specific asset cited.

LEGATEE: Person receiving a legacy or bequest.

LINEALS: Blood descendants of a decedent.

PER STIRPES: The method of distribution of the assets of a grant after the death of the original beneficiary. The children (grandchildren) share in the same proportions that their parents did (or would have).

PROBATE: The procedure of proving a will before a court having jurisdiction over the administration of the estate of a deceased person.

SETTLOR: The creator of a trust; also called grantor, trustor, and donor.

SPENDTHRIFT TRUST: A trust created to provide a fund for the maintenance of a beneficiary and at the same time to secure it against his or her improvidence or incapacity. Generally, the trust principal is beyond the reach of creditors.

TENANCY BY THE ENTIRETY: Title in real property held by husband and wife together; based on the common-law concept that a husband and wife are one person. Property held by the entirety can only be disposed of by the joint action of the husband and wife.

TENANCY IN COMMON: A type of coownership of property by which the owners have undivided interests in the property. The interests may be unequal in quantity, may have been created at different times, and may have been derived from different sources. The coowners are also known as cotenants. A cotenant may sell or otherwise dispose of his or her interest without consent of the other cotenants, and the new owner takes the right of the cotenant from whom he or she took interest. There is no survivorship right as between cotenants, and the undivided interest may be disposed of by will or, in the absence of a will, descends to the heirs of the deceased cotenant, as would other property of the same kind. All of the tenants, in the absence of agreement between them to the contrary, have equal rights of possession regardless of inequality in their undivided interests.

TESTAMENTARY INSTRUMENT: A legal document such as a will or trust bestowing certain rights to certain individuals after the death of the person making the instrument.

TESTAMENTARY TRUSTEE: A trustee appointed by or acting under a will in order to carry out a trust created by a will.

TESTATE: A testate is a decedent who left a will. Property included in the will is often called testate property.

TESTATOR: The term may be used to describe either a man who has made a will or a decedent who left a will.

TESTATRIX: A female form of testator.

TRUSTEE: The person who holds the legal title to trust property for the purposes as stated by the terms of the trust.

Glossary

ACCIDENTAL DEATH BENEFITS: A provision that may be put into a life insurance policy calling for the payment of double benefits in the case of death by accidental means. *See also "Double indemnity."*

ACTUARY: A person professionally trained in the mathematics and other technical aspects of life insurance.

AMORTIZATION: A method of paying off a home mortgage.

ANNUITANT: The person who has a contract with a life insurance company to receive periodic payments for a specific number of years, or perhaps for life.

ASKED PRICE: The price at which a dealer will sell a nonlisted or over-the-counter security.

BALANCED FUND: An investment company that holds varying proportions of bonds, preferred stocks, and common stocks from time to time in order to maintain relatively greater stability of both capital and income.

BALANCE SHEET: The method of showing all the assets and liabilities of a corporation.

BALLOON CLAUSE: A clause in an installment loan contract calling for a final payment substantially larger than the earlier payments.

BEAR MARKET: Technical term for a long-run downward-moving securities market.

BENEFICIARY: The person who receives certain benefits as spelled in a will or a life insurance contract.

BID PRICE: The price at which a dealer will buy nonlisted or over-the-counter securities.

BLUE-CHIP STOCKS: The common stock of large, well-known, financially strong corporations with good records of earnings and dividend payments over many years.

BLUE SKY LAWS: The laws of the various states regulating the sale of securities and the activities of security salespersons, brokers, and dealers.

BOND: A certificate of indebtedness that represents a loan from the bondholder to the corporation.

BOOK VALUE: The accounting concept of the value of a share of common stock. It is equal to assets minus liabilities divided by the number of shares outstanding.

BROKER: A person in the business of buying and selling securities for another party for which he or she receives a commission.

BULL MARKET: Technical term for a long-run upward-moving securities market.

CALL OPTION: A contract giving the holder the privilege of purchasing a given security from the option dealer at a specific price for a specific period of time.

CALL PRICE: As applied to bonds, the price at which a corporation can prematurely retire bonds.

CAPITAL: Total assets of a business.

CAPITAL GAINS: The market appreciation in the value of securities or other assets.

CAPITAL GAINS TAX: A special tax that must be paid by those who receive capital gains.

CAPITAL LOSS: The decline in the market value of securities or other assets.

CAPITAL STRUCTURE: The relative proportions of capital represented by bonds, preferred stock, and common stock.

CASH SURRENDER VALUE: The amount of cash a person may obtain by voluntarily surrendering a life insurance policy.

CERTIFICATES OF DEPOSIT: Certificates given by banks to indicate the number of dollars in savings a person has in a special long-run account.

CLOSED-END INVESTMENT COMPANY: A company that has a definite limit to the number of shares in itself it may sell.

COMMON STOCK EQUITIES: Certificates of ownership in a corporation.

COMMISSION BROKERS: Brokers who buy and sell securities for their customers, for which they receive a commission.

CONSUMER PRICE INDEX: A statistical device that measures the increase in the cost of living for consumers. Sometimes used to illustrate the extent that prices in general have risen or the amount of inflation that has taken place.

CONTACT BROKERS: Brokers who assist the commission brokers who are unable to handle the entire volume of business by themselves. Contact brokers do not deal with the public.

CONVERTIBLE: A bond or preferred stock that may be, under specific circumstances, exchanged for a certain number of shares of common stock.

CREDIT LIFE INSURANCE: Special term life insurance purchased when borrowing money on an installment loan basis, which is then used to pay off the loan in the event of the borrower's death before he or she pays it off.

DEALER: A person or firm who stands ready to buy or sell securities at given prices. Dealers differ from brokers in that they make the market in the given securities by being willing simultaneously either to buy at a given price or to sell at a different given price.

DEBENTURE: A type of bond that is secured by no specific assets but by the general credit and all assets of the corporation.

DEFENSIVE STOCK: A stock that usually declines less than most securities in a downward movement of the market because of the nature of the business it represents.

DIVERSIFICATION: Investing in the securities of a number of different firms and a number of different industries in an attempt to spread the risk and lessen the likelihood of losses.

DIVIDEND: The payment made to the owners of common stock.

DOLLAR COST AVERAGING: Buying securities at regular intervals with specific and equal dollar amounts. This results in lowering the average price of securities because more are purchased when the prices are depressed than when they are high.

DOUBLE INDEMNITY: A clause in a life insurance contract that requires a double payment in the case of an accidental death. *See also "Accidental death benefits."*

DOW-JONES AVERAGES: A statistical device that shows the general level and movement of security prices.

EARNINGS: A corporation's income after all expenses, including preferred dividend payments.

EX DIVIDEND: Without dividend. This means that the stock, if purchased, does not include the most recent dividend that has been declared.

FIDUCIARY: A person who has certain legal rights and powers relating to financial matters to be exercised for the benefit of another person.

FIXED ANNUITY: A contract with a life insurance company that provides the periodic payment of a fixed number of dollars for a specific period of time, or for life.

FIXED INCOME SECURITY: A preferred stock or a bond that has a stated or fixed percentage income return.

FLOOR TRADERS: Members of the New York Stock Exchange who buy and sell securities for their own account.

FORMULA TIMING: A method of buying securities in accordance with some formula that will tell you when to buy and when to sell. For example, a price earnings ratio of ten may be a signal to buy and one of fifteen or twenty a signal to sell.

GRACE PERIOD: The period, usually thirty days, following the premium due date of a life insurance policy during which an overdue premium may be paid without penalty.

GROWTH STOCK: A stock that has shown a better than average growth in earnings, hence, a better than average appreciation in its market price. Moreover, there are expectations that it will continue to do so.

HEDGE FUND: A mutual fund (or investment company) that hedges its market commitments by holding certain securities it believes are likely to increase in value and, at the same time, sells others short because it believes they are likely to decline in value. Its main objective is capital appreciation.

INCOME BONDS: Bonds on which the interest is paid only if earned.

INCOME STOCK: Stock of a corporation that has a historical record of above average earnings and dividends and that is likely to continue performing favorably.

INFLATION: An overall general upward price movement of all goods and services that results in the decline in the value of a dollar.

INSURANCE DIVIDEND: The payment made to owners of mutual life insurance policies. Part of this must be looked upon as a return of premiums, part of it as earnings.

INVESTMENT COMPANY: A corporation that sells stock of itself to the public and then uses the funds to buy the securities of many other firms. There is no limit to the number of shares an open-end investment company may sell of itself whereas a closed-end investment company does definitely have a limit in the number of shares it may sell.

KEOGH BILL: The bill that allows most of the self-employed to set up their own retirement programs with generous tax savings.

LEVERAGE: The use of borrowed money to increase the earnings of the common stockholder. If money is borrowed at 6 percent and the corporation earns 12 percent with it, the extra 6 percent accrues to the common stockholder.

LIMIT ORDER: An order to a broker to buy a certain stock only if its price falls to a specified level or to sell a stock only if the price rises to a specified level.

LIQUID: Anything that is easily and quickly convertible to cash without a substantial price concession. Liquidity is a relative term.

LOAD: The fees that must be paid when buying mutual funds. These generally range from 7 to 9 percent, but some are above and some are below this. And there are even some no-load funds.

LOAN SHARK: A person who makes loans and illegally charges interest rates in excess of what the law allows.

MANAGEMENT FEES: The fees charged by the managers of investment companies for their services in managing the portfolio.

MARGIN PURCHASES: Purchases of securities with money that is partially borrowed.

MARGIN REQUIREMENTS: The percentage of the price of a security that must be paid with the buyer's own money. The remainder may be borrowed.

MONTHLY INVESTMENT PLAN: An arrangement for regular purchases of stock listed on the New York Stock Exchange. These arrangements can be made with most member firms.

MORTALITY TABLE: Tables indicating the number of deaths per thousand at various ages, which have been developed from past experiences by life insurance companies.

MORTGAGE BONDS: Bonds behind which specific assets of a corporation have been pledged as collateral.

MUTUAL FUNDS: The more popular name for an open-end investment company. See also "Open-end investment company."

NET ASSET VALUE: As applied to mutual funds, this is the market value of underlying securities divided by the number of mutual fund shares outstanding.

NO-LOAD FUNDS: Mutual funds that do not charge any commissions on their sales. To buy these, you may have to contact the company directly.

NONFORFEITURE OPTION: The options available to holders of life insurance policies if they discontinue the payments of premiums. Generally the policy value is taken either in the form of cash, as extended term insurance, or as reduced paid-up insurance.

ODD-LOT: A block of stock consisting of fewer shares than the number customarily traded at one time, which is known as a round lot of one hundred shares.

ODD-LOT DEALER: A dealer who buys and sells odd lots exclusively.

OPEN-END INVESTMENT COMPANY (Also called mutual funds): A company that has no limit as to the number of shares in itself that it may sell.

OPEN ORDER: An order to buy or sell securities at a stipulated price that remains in effect until it is executed or cancelled.

OPTIONS: See "Puts" and "Call Option."

OVER-THE-COUNTER: The market for those securities not listed on any organized exchange.

PAID-UP INSURANCE: Insurance on which premiums are no longer due but which is still in force.

PAR VALUE: The face or stated value of a bond or a stock. In the case of a stock, this is meaningless. However, in the case of a bond or a preferred stock, the par value generally indicates the dollar value on which the annual interest or dividends are to be paid.

POLICY LOAN: A loan made by an insurance company to a policyholder on the cash surrender value of the policy.

PORTFOLIO: The securities owned by an individual or corporation.

PREEMPTIVE RIGHTS: The rights of existing stockholders to buy a prorated share of a new issue of common stock that a corporation may issue.

PREFERRED STOCK: Stock that receives preferential treatment over common stock both with respect to dividends and to claims on assets in the event that a corporation goes out of business.

PRICE EARNINGS RATIO: The market value of a common stock divided by its earnings.

PROSPECTUS: The official document that describes the shares of a new security being issued.

PROXY STATEMENT: The written permission that one stockholder gives to another person to vote his stock for him.

PUTS: Contracts that give a holder the right to sell a particular security to the option dealer at a specific price for a specific period of time.

REGISTRAR: The institution (usually a bank) that maintains a list of the common stockholders of a corporation and the number of shares that they hold.

ROUND LOTS: The fixed number or block of shares, usually one hundred, that is the commonly traded unit on the organized exchanges.

SECURITIES AND EXCHANGE COMMISSION (SEC): An agency of the United States government that administers the various federal security laws.

SENIOR SECURITIES: Securities such as bonds and preferred stock that have a higher claim than common stock on earnings as well as on assets upon liquidation.

SHORT SALES: Selling securities you do not own. To do this, you borrow them from a broker. Later, hopefully when the price falls, you buy them back and repay them.

SPECIALISTS: Members of the exchange who specialize in buying and selling only certain specific securities that are traded at a specific location on the exchange. The commission broker, or the contract broker, will go to whatever specialist is required to execute an order.

STOCK SPLIT: An increase in the number of shares of a corporation brought about by division of existing shares. A two-for-one split, for example, will result in two new shares for each old share that previously existed, making a total of three.

STOP ORDER: An order to a broker to sell a stock if the price reaches a certain level. Sometimes also called a stop loss order. For example, if you buy a stock at $100, it rises to $120, and it starts down again, you can guarantee yourself a profit by putting in a stop order at, say, $115.

THIN MARKET: A market in which there are few offers either to buy or sell. The term can be applied to a single security or to the entire market.

USURY: Interest that is in excess of what the law allows.

VARIABLE ANNUITY: An annuity contract with a life insurance company under which the dollar payments received are not fixed but vary (or fluctuate), usually with the price of common stock.

VESTING OF INTERESTS: Has to do with the legal ownership of certain benefits of a pension fund. Is important if persons leave their employer prior to retirement.

WARRANT: A certificate authorizing the owner to buy a specific company's stock at a specific price for a specific period of time, or perhaps in perpetuity.

YIELD: Income received on investments. Usually expressed as a percentage of the market price of the security.

Index

Acceleration clause, 65, 129
Actual cash value, 257–58, 263
Actuaries, 186
Add-on clause, 65, 139
Advertising:
   deceptive, 54
   newspaper, 51–52
Age:
   annuities and, 285, 288
   budget variation and, 33–35
   income and, 11
   insurance, 186–91
   insurance premiums and, 266–67
   pension fund benefits and, 289n
   savings and, 153
   social security benefits and, 278–79
   see also Life cycle
American Express Company, 93
American Stock Exchange (Amex), 354, 356
Annual percentage rate (APR), 104, 128, 139
Annuities, 281–88, 297
   account value, 283
   cash value of, 178–81, 282, 285–86
   classification by benefit payments
      annuity certain, 282, 284–85
      guaranteed premium refund, 284
      life with guaranteed minimum installments,
         284
      straight life, 284, 288
   cost of, 287–88
   deferred, 285
   defined, 281, 282
   fixed, 286, 287
   inflation and, 286
   joint or survivorship, 285
   payments, 283–84, 288
   premiums, 282–83, 286, 288
   principle of, 281–82
   private, 282
   taxes on, 282, 478, 484–85
   tax sheltered, 296–97
   uses of, 282
   variable, 286–87
   see also Life insurance; Pension plans
Antiques, 418, 419–20

Apartments, 413, 415, 444
Application for credit, 119, 120
Apportionment clause, 258–59
Aptitude tests, 15
Art investment, 420
Assessment valuation, 475
Assets:
   in bankruptcy, 42–43
   corporation, 306, 320
   individual, 24–25, 282n, 425, 511
Assigned risk plans, 266
Assignment of a policy, 220
Association of Home Appliance Manufacturers
   (AHAM), 70
Attorney General offices, 72, 149
Automated teller, 88–89
Automatic funds transfer (AFT), 90, 91, 118
Automatic premium loan (APL), 219
Automobile:
   costs of owning, 38–40
   financing, 96, 98, 104–6, 262
   purchasing guidelines, 66
   repair, 67
   tax deductions, 489
Automobile insurance, 260–69
   assigned risk plans, 266
   collision, 261–62, 268
   comprehensive, 262–63, 268
   financial responsibility laws, 265
   how much to buy, 267–69
   liability: bodily injury and property damage,
      261, 267–68
   medical payments, 263, 269
   no-fault, 263–65
   preferred risks, 266
   rates and costs, 266–67
   uninsured motorist endorsement, 265–66,
      269
   see also Insurance

Balanced funds, 394
Balance sheet:
   corporation, 320–21
   in estate planning, 510–12
   personal, 24–25

Balloon clause, 65, 139
Bank charters, 76
Banker's acceptances, 341–42
Banking services:
  automated teller, 88–89
  automatic bill payment, 90–91
  automatic funds transfer (AFT), 32, 90, 91
  checking accounts, 75–89
  credit cards (*see* Credit cards)
  drive-in, 88
  errors in, 83
  fees, 77, 81, 85, 87–88, 90, 93
  loans, 75, 88
    (*see also* Mortgage loans)
  nighttime depository lock, 91–92
  NOW accounts, 85, 90
  safety deposit boxes, 75, 91
  savings accounts, 89–91
  traveler's checks, 77, 92–93
  trusteeship, 75, 91, 528–29
Bank of America, 93
Bankruptcy, 41–43, 140
Banks, 75–76
  computerization in, 77–79, 85, 88, 90–91, 117, 118
  reform in, 92
  regulation of, 75–76
  see also Banking services; Commercial banks;
    Industrial banks; Mutual savings banks;
    Savings banks
Bank statements, 82–84, 90, 118
  reconciliation of, 83
Bargaining, 63, 66
Barron's, 400
Bearer bonds, 338
Bear market, 363–65
Beneficiary:
  life insurance, 220–22, 225
  trust, 524
  wills, 510, 512, 517
Better Business Bureaus (BBBs), 49, 52–53, 69–70
Bill payment:
  automatic, 90–91
  withholding of, 143–44
Bills of exchange, 76–77
Blue-chip stock, 334, 378
Blue Cross, 232, 233, 239–40
Blue Shield, 232, 233, 239–41
Boat insurance, 269
Bond, posting, 265
Bondholders, 306
Bonds, 337–50
  bearer, 338
  callable, 340

collateral trust, 338
convertible, 339–40
corporate, 306, 337–42, 347, 366–67, 409
coupon, 338, 343
credit ratings, 347–48
debentures, 339
equipment obligations, 338
income, 340
inflation and, 309
interest rate, 312, 337, 347
leverage and, 340–41
liquidity and risk, 168
market price, 312–13n
mortgage, 338
quotations, 366–67
serial, 340
small investor and, 165, 348–49
state and local, 344–47, 478
taxes and, 349–50, 478
U.S. government, 155, 312, 342, 343, 347, 349, 367
  marketable and nonmarketable, 165, 343, 367
  series E and H (savings), 165–68, 478
yield, 168, 312, 330, 349–50
see also Securities
Book value, 328
Brands, 50–51, 60
Brokerage firms, 316, 317
Brokers, 354–55, 357, 366
Budget, 1, 23–44
  categories
    expenditures, 26, 32, 36–41, 438, 440–41
    income, 26
    savings, 27, 32, 40
  defined, 27
  family, 29
  form, 29–31
  life cycle and, 33–35
  personal, 27–43
  plan, 24–43
  sample, 32
  two-income family, 31
Bull market, 363–65
Business, 5
  borrowing by, 100
  cycles, 373–75
  failure (risk), 311, 314
  trend analysis, 314
Business and trade associations, 70
Business organization, 304–7
  corporate form of, 305–7
  noncorporate form of, 305
    partnership, 305
    single proprietorship, 305

Callable bonds, 340
Callable preferred stock, 336–37
Capital assets, 495
Capital gains, 308–9, 495–97
　common stock, 328–31
　long-term, 309, 407, 495–96
　real estate, 416, 497
Capital gains tax, 282, 282n, 309, 478, 496–97
Capital loss, 495
Capital needs analysis, 211
Career choice, 14–16
Cash discounts, 63–65
Cashier's check, 81–82
Cash surrender value, 111, 196, 197, 200–1, 219,
　224, 225, 282, 285
Caveat emptor, 48, 52
Caveat venditor, 47
Certificates of deposit (CDs), 156, 157, 159–64
　types of, 160
Certified checks, 81
Certified financial planners (CFPs), 128
Certified public accountant (CPA), 499
Chain letters, 56
Charge accounts, 96, 114
Charities, 55
Checking accounts, 75–89, 155–56
　deposits, 85
　joint, 80–81
　NOW, 85, 90
　opening, 77
　overdrafts, 85
　service charges, 77, 81, 85, 87–88
　statements, 82–84, 90
Checkless society, 108, 116–18
Checks, 75–89
　cancelled, 82, 83, 85, 118
　cashier's, 81–82
　certified, 81
　clearing, 75, 77–80
　endorsing, 85–87
　money orders, 92–93
　need for, 117–18
　stopping payment, 87–88
　travelers', 77, 92–93
Child care, 494
Classified section, 52
Clifford trusts, 526
Closing costs, 455, 463–64
Close-out sales, 55
Clothing, 40
　standardization in sizes, 62
Codicil, 517
Coins, 418
Coinsurance clause, 233–34, 235, 237, 258–59
Collateral, 106, 111, 112, 113, 220, 262

Collateral heirs, 522
Collateral trust bonds, 338
Collection practices, 144–45
College funds, 208
College Placement Annual, 15
Collision insurance, 261–62, 268
Commercial banks, 75, 92, 111, 112, 125, 157,
　159, 161, 164
　savings departments of, 155–57
　trust department, 297–98
Commercial paper, 341–42, 372
Commodity markets, 406–7
Common-law property, 511, 523
Common stock. *See* Stocks, common
Community property, 511
Complaints, 69–70
Comprehensive insurance, 262–63, 268
Computers. *See* Banks, computerization
Condominiums:
　benefits of owning, 444, 445
　insurance policies, 253n, 256
Consumer credit, 95–133
　application for, 119, 120
　benefits and dangers of, 99–101
　classifications, 96–98
　　installment, 96
　　noninstallment, 96–98
　contracts, 120, 128–31
　counseling, 127–28
　credit cards (see Credit cards)
　dos and donts, 131–33
　discrimination in, 143
　interest rates, 101–7
　loans, 157
　　discounted, 102, 108
　　financial documents, 128–31
　　interest rates, 104–7
　rating reports, 119–21, 140
　reasons for use of, 98–99
　sources of, 107–18
Consumer Credit Protection Act, 139
Consumer durable, 98
Consumer education, 48–49
Consumer Federation of America (CFA), 72, 138
Consumer finance company, 109
Consumer finance laws, 106, 107, 109
Consumerism, 47–49, 63
　pre-purchase analysis, 48, 49–54
　　brand names, 50–51
　　choosing a store, 51
　　professional services, 50
　　repair services, 49
　　sources, 51–54
　　workmanship, 49
　purchasing, 48, 54–68

deceptive practices, 54–58
  money-saving tips, 58–62
  other information, 63–68
  redress procedures, 48
    letters, 69
    consumer protection agencies, 71–72
    refunds, 68–69
    small claims courts, 70–71
    voluntary action, 69–70
  spending patterns, 3–4
Consumer Leasing Act, 141, 144
Consumer movement, 48
Consumer organizations, 72
  voluntary, 137–38
Consumer price index, 8–9
Consumer-producers, 5–6
Consumer Protection Act, 104
Consumer protection agencies, 70, 71–72
Consumer protection laws, 104, 137–49
  enforcing agencies, 146–49
  federal, 138–46
Consumption, 3–4
Contracts:
  clauses, 65
  installment credit, 120, 128–31, 138
  service, 64
  see also Mortgage loans
Contributions, 40, 489, 493
Convertible bonds, 339–40
Convertible stock, 337
Co-ops, 444–45
Corporation:
  advantages, 306–7
  bonds and stock, 306, 366–67, 409
  capital, 340–41
  defined, 305
  nonprofit, 444–45
  reports, 319–23
Corpus, 524
Cost of living index, 9
Counseling:
  credit, 127
  investment, 319
Coupon bonds, 338, 343
Coupons, 55, 62
Credit, availability of, 8
  See also Consumer credit; Credit cards
Credit bureau, 119–21, 140–42
Credit cards, 67, 96, 114–16
  abuse, 122–24
  banks and, 108, 109, 116
  lost or stolen, 123, 139
  national, 115–16
Credit life insurance, 121–22, 139, 194, 202

Credit rating:
  bonds, 347–48
  personal, 95
Credit scoring, 121, 122
Credit unions, 109–10, 125, 155, 158–64
Crop insurance, 270
Customer satisfaction, 69
Cyclical stock, 333–34

Dancing instruction, 56
Dealer participation, 65–66
Dealers, 354, 355, 366, 389–90
Debentures, 339
Debt poolers, 56
Deceptive practices, 54–58
  See also Consumer protection laws
Deductibility clause, 262
Deductions from income tax, 40, 476, 487–92
Default, 311n
Default and delinquency clause, 128
Defensive stock, 334
Deliveries, neighbor's, 56
Demand, consumer, 100–1
Demand deposits, 76, 155–56
Dental care, 230, 489
Dental insurance, 235
Department of Health, Education and Welfare
    (HEW), 148
Deposits:
  interest yields on, 160, 161–63
  by mail, 85, 90
  safety and liquidity, 89, 164
  types of, 89, 155–56, 159–61
Depreciation, 322, 414–15, 416, 490–91, 498
Development companies, 411
Diamonds, 418–19, 426–30
Disability benefits, 274, 276, 280
Disability clause, 222
Disability insurance, 230, 236, 243–46
Disclosure settlement statement, 465–66
Discount loan, 102
Discounts, 58, 63
  cash, 63–64
  slightly-used-products, 58
Discount stores, 51, 63–64
Discrimination:
  in granting of credit, 143
  and inequality of income, 14
  in inflation, 8
  married couples, 278, 482–83
  minority groups, 14
  in social security law, 278
  women, 14, 143
Disinheritance, 516
Diversification, 315, 377n, 396, 425

Dividends:
  cash, 369–71, 478
  insurance, 223–25, 267, 478
  stock, 306, 308, 322, 371, 383, 478
Docutel System, 88
Dollar, value of, 6, 8, 173–77
  and price level risk, 311–12
Domicile, 510
Double indemnity, 222–23
Dow-Jones averages, 361, 363, 401
Downpayment, 66
Drafts, 76–77, 87
Drive-in banking, 88
Drugs and prescriptions, 60
Duplexes, 413

Earned income credit, 477–78, 486–87
Earnest money, 463, 464
Earnings per share, 328, 340–41
Economic environment, 4–9, 16–18, 100, 373
Economic obsolescence, 442
Education:
  budgeting, 41, 208
  income and, 11
Efficient market hypothesis (EMH), 377–78
Elderly, tax credits for, 493–94
Electronic Funds Transfer System (EFTS), 116–18
Emergency funds, 98, 156, 208
Employee Retirement Income Security Act
    (ERISA), 289–90, 292
Encyclopedia of Careers and Vocational Guidance, 15
Endorsements, check, 85–87
Energy conservation tips, 61–62
Energy-efficiency, 440–41, 447
Equal Credit Opportunity Act (ECOA), 141, 142
Equipment trust obligations, 338
Equity, 36
Estate planning, 509–36
  assets and liabilities, 510–12
  gifts (see Gifts)
  glossary of terms, 540–541
  information needed, 510
    beneficiaries, 510
    family and marital status, 510
  taxes (see Estate taxes; Gift taxes)
  trusts (see Trusts)
  wills (see Wills)
Estates:
  administration of, 522–23, 532
  claims against, 510
  settling, 208
Estate tax, 509, 529–36
  federal, 529–30, 532
    calculating, 533
  exemptions, 530
    gross estate, 532, 533
    marital deduction and, 512, 515, 532
    reducing, 220, 533–36
    taxable estate, 533
    trusts and, 533–36
  state, 529–30, 536
Exchanges. See Securities exchanges
Executor, 513, 515
Exemptions:
  federal income tax, 344, 402, 411, 478, 483–84, 488
  gift and estate tax, 530
Exepnditures, 4, 26, 32, 438
  major, 36–41
  national, 470–71
Expense accounts, 498

Fair Credit Billing Act, 141, 146
Fair Credit Reporting Act, 140–41
Fair Debt Collection Practices Act (FDCPA), 144–45
Family:
  insurance needs, 208–11
  two-income, 31, 440
Federal Credit Union Act, 109
Federal Credit Union Share Insurance, 164
Federal Deposit Insurance Corporation (FDIC), 89, 164
Federal Home Loan Bank, 158
Federal Home Loan Bank Board (FHLBB), 158
Federal Reserve System, 80, 313, 368
Federal Savings and Loans Insurance Corporation
    (FSLIC), 164
Federal taxes
  corporate income, 402, 411
  personal income, 24, 473, 475–87
    capital gains and losses, 495–97
    cash versus accrual basis, 476
    deductions, 40, 476, 477, 482n, 487–92
    earned and unearned income, 486–87
    earned income credit, 477–78
    estimated, 483
    exclusion ratio, 485–86
    filing and paying, 477
    gross income, 478–79, 481
    head of household, 483
    income averaging, 486–87
    itemized, 488–92
    joint returns, 477, 482, 483
    married couples and, 278, 477, 482–83
    maximum tax provision, 486–87
    for self-employed, 476, 483

taxable and nontaxable income, 478–79, 480–81, 486, 487–88
   withholding, 484
   see also Estate taxes; Gift tax; Taxes
Federal Trade Commission (FTC), 72, 145–46
FHA mortgage, 450–51, 455, 456, 457
Financial institutions. *See* Banks
Financial planning, 24–27
   for emergencies, 98, 156, 208
   taking inventory, 44
   see also Budget
Financial reforms, 92
Financial responsibility laws, 265
Financial risk, 313, 314
Food, 37
   brand names, 50–51, 60
   ingredients, 53, 54
Food shopping, 51, 59–60
Forbes magazine, 400, 402
Foreign currency investment, 421
Fraud, electronic, 118
"Free" merchandize, 55
Fringe benefits, 16, 238
Full disclosure, 389
Fundscope, 400, 402
Funeral expenses, 208, 514
Furs, 419
Futures market, 407, 408

Garnisheeing wages, 65, 140
Gas mileage "savers," 56
Gifts:
   budgeting for, 40–41
   in contemplation of death, 531
   defined, 530
   joint (split), 531
   nontax reasons for making, 532
   political contributions, 489, 493
   stock, 382
   in a will, 514–15
Gift tax, 509, 525, 529–36
   calculating, 531–32, 533–34
   deduction, 489, 493
   exclusion, 530–31
   federal, 530
   marital deduction and, 531
   time limits and, 533
G.I. life insurance, 194, 203
Glossary, 542–45
Gold, 420–21
Good Housekeeping seal, 53
Government expenditures, 4, 8, 470–71
Government regulation, 8
   in banking, 75–76
Grace period, 218, 225

Greeley, Horace, 13
Gross estate, 532, 533
Gross income, 478–79, 481
   adjusted, 487
Gross National Product (GNP), 16
Group insurance:
   health, 230, 238–39, 241
   legal, 270
   life, 192, 194, 201–2
Growth funds, 394, 400
Growth stock, 332–33
Guardian, appointment of, 509, 515

Health cures, 56
Health insurance, 38, 184, 202, 229–46
   applying for benefits, 239
   coinsurance clause, 233–34, 235, 237
   comprehensive medical, 234–36, 240
   coverage, 234, 237, 240, 249, 250
     complete, 237–38
     types of, 231
   deductibility clause, 233
   dental insurance, 235
   disability, 230, 236, 243–46
   doctor visits, 233
   group plans, 230, 238–39, 241
   guaranteed renewable and noncancellable, 239
   hospital expenses, 232, 248–249
   how much to buy, 243–46
   major medical, 233–34, 243
   national, 229, 242, 248–50
   nonprofit plans, 239–42
   regular medical expenses, 233
   surgical expenses, 232, 241
   see also Insurance
Health Maintenance Organizations (HMOs), 241–42
Hedging, 406
Holder-in-due-course, 145–46
Home financing:
   closing costs, 455, 463–64
   downpayment, 457, 458
   earnest money, 463, 464
   by means of trades, 456
   monthly payments, 458–60
   mortgages (*see* Mortgage loans)
   points, 462–63, 465
   selling without refinancing, 456–57
Home insurance, 252–60
   actual cash value, 257–58
   apportionment clause, 258–59
   on condominiums, 253n, 256
   costs, 257
   homeowner's policies, 252–56
   how much to buy, 260

Home insurance, *continued*
  plain-English policies, 256
  for renters, 253n, 256, 260
  selecting, 259–60
  separate individual policies, 256
  see also Insurance
Home Mortgage Disclosure Act, 141
Home ownership, 434–48
  affordable price range, 439–40
  assessing value of property, 446–48, 463
    energy efficiency, 440–41, 447
    improvements, 436, 448
    land, 448
    neighborhood, 441–42, 447
  building, 439, 440, 441, 442–44
  credit and, 121
  finance (*see* Home financing)
  inflation and, 436
  insurance and, 259–60
  making an offer: earnest money, 463, 464
  pros and cons of, 11–13, 435–37
  renting versus, 437–39
  taxes and, 36, 435, 488, 497
  types of homes
    condominiums or house, 444
    co-ops, 444–45
    mobile or motor, 96, 445–46
    new or old, 440
    prefabricated, 446
    town house, 444
    vacation, 446
  using a realtor, 441
  see also Real estate investment
Homeowner's policy, 252–56, 459
  medical payments insurance, 255–56
  personal liability coverage, 255
  personal property coverage, 255
  property insurance, 253–54, 511
Home repair, 49, 55, 436, 448
Homestead, 435–36
Hospital care, 229, 232, 248–49
Household operations, 36, 440–41
Housing, 36

Imitation products, 54
Income:
  annual, 511
  earned and unearned, 11, 486–87
  national, 16–18
  nonpecuniary, 16
  personal, 10–16
    age and, 11
    education and, 11
    future value and insurance needs, 211–16,
      245

inflation and, 6–8
  property ownership and, 11–13
  regional differences, 13
  taxes on, 475–87
real, 6, 7
see also Budget
Income bonds, 340
Income funds, 394, 398, 400
Income properties, 412–17
Income statement:
  corporation, 321–22
  individual, 25–26
Income stock, 333
Income tax. *See* Federal taxes; State and local
  taxes
Incontestibility, 218
Incorporation, 305
  tax benefits of, 294, 295
Individual Retirement Account (IRA), 295–96,
  487, 498, 499
Industrial banks, 110, 125, 155, 159–62, 164
Industries:
  classification of, 314–15, 316
  identifying growth and income, 372–73
Inflation:
  annuities and, 286
  bonds and, 309
  causes of, 100–1
  common stock and, 286–87, 307–8, 330, 369
  effect of, 6–8
  home ownership and, 436
  and insurance needs, 213, 245
  and insurance rates, 266, 267
  investment and, 309
  results of, 48, 154
  savings and, 154
Ingredients, list of, 53, 54
Inheritance search, 56
Inheritance taxes, state, 509, 510, 536
Installment credit, 96
  family life cycle and, 126
  see also Consumer credit; Contracts
Installment plan buying, 38, 65
  See also Consumer credit
Insurance:
  actual cash value, 257–58, 263
  all-risk plans, 253
  apportionment clause, 258–59
  assigned risk plans, 266
  bank deposits, 164
  claims, 68
  coinsurance clause, 233–34, 235, 237, 258–59
  compulsory, 265
  deductibility clause, 262
  dividends, 223–25, 267, 478

gambling versus, 185
inflation and, 213, 245, 266, 267
insurable interest, 185–86
loading charges, 191
loans on, 125
mortgage, 208, 450
personal property, 255
premiums (see Premiums)
securities, 382
title, 465
see also Health insurance; Life insurance;
    Property and liability insurance; Specialty
    insurance
Interest:
add-on, 65, 139
compound, 162, 169
law on, 139
simple, 169
theory of, 168–69
Interest rate. See Mortgage loans; names of
    financial institutions and securities
Interest rate ceiling, 92, 160, 161
Interest rate risk, 312–13
Interest rebate, 126–27
Internal Revenue Service (IRS), and pension
    plans, 291, 293, 297, 486
Interstate Commerce Commission (ICC), 67
Inter vivos trust, 524–25
Intestate, 522
Investment, 304–7
commodity markets, 406–7
counselors, 319
direct and indirect, 152, 304, 391
inflation and, 309
information sources, 315–23, 398–402
objectives, 308–10
priorities, 425
of retirement accounts, 297–98
risks, 310–15
    interest rate, 312–13
    reducing, 314–15
speculative, 406–7
services, 316–18
short-run versus long-run, 309–10
strategies
    cyclical swings, 373–75
    diversification, 315, 377n, 396, 425
    dollar averaging, 376
    formula timing, 376
    random selection, 377
    security analysis, 375
    what to buy, 372–73
    when to sell, 378
taxes and, 309
unusual, 418–22

diamonds, 418–19, 426–30
gold, 420–21
yield analysis, 312
see also Bonds; Investment companies (mutual
    funds); Investors; Pension plans; Real estate
    investment; Stocks; Trusts
Investment companies (mutual funds), 391–406
advantages and disadvantages, 287, 396–97
averages, 400–1
classification of
    closed-end, 392–93
    open-end, 393
earnings reinvestment, and taxation of, 297,
    402–5
evaluating, 400
information on, 398–402
legislation, 405–6
liquidation or withdrawal of funds, 398
loading fees, 393, 396, 397, 406
net asset value, 397
no-load funds, 397–98
objectives of, 393–96, 400
tailoring to the investor, 396
taxes and, 402
types of funds, 394–96
who should buy, 405
Investment Companies, Mutual Funds, and
    other Types, 400
Investment Company Acts, 405–6
Investment expenditures, 4, 5
Investment tax credit (ITC), 494
Investors:
diversification, 396–97
small, 160, 161, 165, 343, 348–49, 395
    in the stock market, 353, 378

Johnson's Investment Company Charts, 400, 401,
    402
Joint accounts, 80–81
Joint and survivorship annuity, 285
Joint tenancy, 523
Joint will, 515–16

Keogh plan, 293–94, 487, 498, 499

Labels, 53–54
Land:
assessing value of, 448
investment in, 416
selecting a building site, 442–44
Laws:
bankruptcy, 42
compulsory insurance, 265
consumer finance, 106, 107, 109, 125, 128
consumer protection, 104, 137–49

Laws, *continued*
  financial responsibility, 265
  homestead, 435–36
  on investment companies, 405–6
  on securities, 389–90
  usury, 137, 407n, 450, 453, 457
Leases, 438
Legacies, general and specific, 514
  See also Gifts
Legal counsel, 282n, 465, 523, 533
Legal insurance, 270
Letters, seeking refunds, 69
Liabilities, 25, 320–21, 511
Liability insurance, defined, 251
  See also Property and liability insurance
Life cycle variation, 33–35
  and installment credit, 126
  and savings plans, 153–54
Life expectancy, 186–91, 284, 288
Life insurance, 38, 184–226
  age, 186–91
  agents commission, 191
  borrowing on, 111, 219–20, 226
  beneficiaries, 220–21, 222, 225
  benefits of, 218–25
  cash surrender value, 196, 197, 200–1, 219,
    224, 225
  cautions for handling policy, 225–26
  for children, 216
  comparing policies, 206
  credit life, 121–22, 194, 202
  dividends, 223–25, 267
  family plans, 199
  family income plan, 199–200
  fraternal society, 194, 203
  G.I., 194, 203
  group, 192, 194, 201–2
  individual plans, 192
  industrial, 194, 202–3
  inflation and, 213
  level premium, 191–92
  medical examination, 195
  mortality tables and life expectancy, 186–91,
    200, 205
  mutual savings bank, 194, 203, 223
  modified plans, 199
  needs, 207, 208–16
    family, 208–11
    maintaining capital, 211
  on nonworking spouse, 216–18
  ordinary, 193, 194–200
    endowment, 197, 198–99
    limited pay life (LPL), 194, 197–98, 200
    straight life, 193, 194, 196–97, 207
    term, 194–96, 197, 202, 207

  whole life, 193, 194, 196–97, 207
  ownership of, 220
  personal income and, 193
  premiums, 38, 186, 191–92, 199, 204–6, 222
  pure, 191
  risk to company, 200
  renewable and convertible features, 195–96
  savings features, 197, 198, 199
  selecting, 204–7
  settlement options, 221–22, 283
  terminology, 203, 218–25
  see also Annuities; Health insurance; Insurance
Life insurance companies:
  credit, 121–22, 194, 202
  loans, 111, 219–20, 226
  pension plans, 288
  stock versus mutual, 223
Life insurance trust, 526–27
Lineals, 522
Liquidity, 89n, 156, 159, 308
  bonds, 168, 410
  deposits, 164
  mortgages, 410
  stocks, 328
List price, inflated, 57
Lives-in-being clause, 527
Lloyd's of London, 269
Loan ceilings, 107
Loan credit, 96
Loans:
  automatic bank, 11, 8
  consumer (*see* Consumer credit, loans)
  on life insurance, 111, 219–20, 226
  secured and unsecured, 106
  single repayment, 96, 112, 126, 130, 219
  see also Collateral; Mortgage loans)

Magazines, investment information in, 316–18,
  400
Magnetic ink character recognition (MICR), 77–78
Major Appliance Consumer Action Panel
  (MACAP), 70
Malpractice insurance, 270
Margin purchases, 367–68
Marital deduction, 512, 515, 531, 532
Maritime insurance, 185
Marketable bonds, 165
Market risk, 311, 314
Market value, 328
Married persons:
  estate planning, 285, 515–16, 523
  tax discrimination, 278, 482–83
Medicaid, 242, 250
Medical care, 38, 98, 489
  See also Health insurance

Medical payments insurance, 255–56
Medicare, 242, 248–50, 274
Merchandise:
  defective, 67
  "free", 55
  unordered, 56
  returning, 68–69
MEW (measure of economic welfare), 3
Minorities, 14
Mobile homes, 96, 445–46
Money, 4, 5
Money market CD, 160, 161, 297n
Money market funds, 395
Money orders, 92–93
Morris Plan, 110
Mortality tables, 186–91, 200, 205
Mortgage bonds, 338
Mortgage companies, 410–11
Mortgage loans:
  amortization, 453–54, 461
  assumption and refinancing, 455
  insurance, 208, 450
  interest rates, 407n, 408, 450, 457–58, 459,
    488
  investment in, 407–10
  payments, 36, 435, 445, 458–60
  penalties, 455–57
  sources, 157–58, 161, 448
  types of
    conventional, 448–50
    deferred interest, 454
    FHA, 450–51, 455, 456, 457
    flexible rate, 454
    graduated payment (GPM), 453–54
    price level adjusted, 454
    renegotiable, 454–55
    reverse, 455
    second, 410, 452
    single-payment straight, 451–52
    VA-guaranteed, 451, 455, 456, 457
    variable interest rate, 454
    wrap-around, 452–53
Motor homes, 445–46
Moving, 67–68
Mutual funds. See Investment companies
Mutual life insurance companies, 223
Mutual savings banks (MSB), 92, 113, 155, 157,
    159, 161, 164
  life insurance, 194, 203, 223

Nader, Ralph, 71
National health insurance, 229, 242, 248–50
National income, 16–18
Neighborhood, 441–42, 447
Net asset value, 397

Net income, 487–88
Net worth, 24, 25
  corporation, 320–21
  individual, 24, 25, 510–11
Newspapers:
  advertising in, 51–52
  investment information in, 315–16, 398–99
New York Stock Exchange (NYSE), 354–55, 357
  averages, 361–63
  historical record of, 356
  investment information, 319
  rules of, 369, 370, 390
Nighttime depository lock box, 91–92
No-fault insurance, 263–65
No-Load Mutual Fund Association (NLMFA), 398
Nonforfeiture value, 218–19
Noninstallment credit, 96–98
Non profit rating organizations, 53
NOW accounts, 85, 90, 155–56, 158, 159, 161,
    164

Obituary exploitation, 55
Occupation, income and, 11
Occupational Outlook for College Graduates, 15
Occupational Thesaurus, 15
Odd-lot transactions, 355–56
Offices of Consumer Affairs, 148
Open market, 353
Options market, 386–90
Origination fee, 465
Overdrafts, 85
Over-the-counter market, 353, 357–60, 365–66
Ownership. *See* Home ownership; Property
  ownership

Packaging, 53–54
Paintings, investment in, 420
Parimedical services, 230
Partnership, 305, 306
Par value, 328
Passbook savings accounts. *See* Savings accounts
Pawnbrokers, 113
Penalty clause, 455–56
Pension plans, 288–92
  government, 292
  individual tax-sheltered, 292–98
    after-tax contributions and, 293–94
    annuities, 296–97
    deferred compensation, 297
    Individual Retirement Account, 295–96
    investment outlets, 297–98
    Keogh plan, 293–94
    professional corporation, 294–95
    taxes and, 293, 294, 296
  private, 288–92

Pension plans, *continued*
  benefits, 290–91
  Employee Retirement Income Security Act
    (ERISA), 289–90, 292
  funding, 289, 290, 291
  management of fund, 288
  money purchase plan, 291
  savings through, 291
  tax benefits of, 288, 291–92, 478, 485–86,
    498
  vesting of interests, 288–89, 290
  qualified, 291, 293, 297, 486
Personal finance, 2–4
Personal liability insurance, 255, 269, 270
Personal property insurance, 255
Per stirpes, 525, 525n
Plain-English policies, 256
Platinum, 421
Political contributions, 493
Political risk, 313
Postal money orders, 93
Precious stones, 418–19
Preemptive rights, 383–85
Prefabricated homes, 446
Preferred risks, 266
Preferred stock. *See* Stocks
Premiums:
  annuities, 282–83
  insurance, 38, 186, 191–92, 199
    homeowner's policies, 257
    no-fault, 265n
    waiver, 222
Preventive medicine, 241
Price:
  discount, 58, 63
  list, 57
  suggested list, 66
  trade-in, 58, 65–66
  wholesale, 54
Price earnings ratio (PER), 375, 376
Price packing, 65–66, 121
Pricing:
  bait-and-switch, 58
  multiple, 58
  psychological, 57
  unit, 54
Principal:
  reduction of, 36
  security of, 309
Privacy, invasion of, 118
Private mortgage insurance (PMI), 450
Private sale offers, 55
Probate of will, 510, 513
Producers, 2, 5–6, 48
Production, factors of, 16–18

Professional services, 49, 50
Promissory notes, 85, 87
Promotions, 55
Property:
  common-law and community, 511
  estates and, 513–14, 522–23
  income-yielding, 12
Property and liability insurance, 251–70
  automobile (*see* Automobile insurance)
  home, 252–60
  miscellaneous and specialty, 269–70
  principle of, 251–52
  see also Insurance
Property ownership:
  and estate disposal, 523
  income and, 11–13
Property taxes, 459, 475, 488
Public Pension Benefit Guarantee Corporation
    (PPBGC), 290, 291

Quality of life, 3
Quotations (trading prices:
  bonds, 366–67
  commodities, 407
  diamonds, 430
  options, 387
  stocks, 360–63, 365–66

Rating systems, 53
Real estate investment, 308
  depreciation, 414–15
  development companies, 411
  direct, 412–17
  income properties, 412–17
  inflation and, 309, 416
  land, 416
  mortgage companies, 410–11
  mortgages, 407–10
  nonresidential, 412, 417
  projecting city growth, 416–17, 442
  real estate investment trusts (REIT), 395, 411–
    12
  residential, 412–17
  syndicate investing, 411
  yield on, 12, 413–15
Real estate investment trust (REIT), 395, 411–12
Real Estate Settlement Procedures Act, 141
Real income, 6, 7
Real property, 251, 255
Realtor, using a, 441
Receipts. *See* Record-keeping
Record-keeping, 24, 49
Reduction of principal, 36
Referral sales, 56
Refunds, 68–69

Regulation Q, 161, 163
Reinstatement, 218
Remedial loan societies, 110–11
Rental property, 412–17
Renting:
  affordable price range, 439
  insurance, 253n, 256, 260
  tenant's rights, 438–39
  versus owning, 435–39
Repairs:
  auto, 67
  home, 49, 55, 436, 448
Repossession, 58, 101
Residence, 510
Residential energy credit, 494–95
Residential income properties, 412–17
Retirement:
  age for, 278–79
  annuities, 281
  budgeting for, 34–35
  federal employees, 274, 292
  insurance needs, 209
  pension plans, 288
  programming, 273, 298–99
  social security benefits, 278
Returning a purchase, 68–69
Revolving charge account, 96, 114
Right of rescission clause, 139
Rights, preemptive, 383–85, 386
Right to die, 521–22
Risk, investment, 310–15, 410
Rule of 72, 169–70
Rule of 78, 126–27

Safety deposit box, 75, 91, 510
Sales, 51–52
  deceptive practices, 54, 55, 56
  how to shop, 62
Sales credit, 96
Sales finance companies, 113–14
Sales tax, 473–74, 488
Savings, 19
  budgeting, 27, 32, 40
  inflation and, 7, 154
  national, 100, 153–54
  through pension plans, 291
Savings account, 89–91, 155–56, 159, 163, 164
Savings and loan associations, 92, 112–13, 155, 157–61, 164
Savings banks, 75, 92, 158
  See also Mutual savings banks
Scotch whiskey, 421–22
Securities, 326–50
  bonds (see Bonds)

buying and selling
  brokers, 354–55, 357, 366
  cash sales, 367
  commissions, 355, 356, 357
  dealers, 357–60, 366, 389–90
  margin purchases, 367–68
  odd-lots transactions, 355–56
  securities exchanges, 354–60
  short sales, 368
  speculative, 334–35, 368
  timing of, 371–76
  types of orders, 368–69
insurance on, 382, 390
investment strategies, 371–78
laws on, 389–90
loss of, 381–82
money market instruments
  banker's acceptances, 341–42
  commercial paper, 341–42
  treasury bills, 341, 343–44
price fluctuation, 311
quotations of prices
  corporate bonds, 366–67
  Dow-Jones averages, 361, 363
  listed stocks, 360–61
  options market, 387
  other stock averages, 361–63
  over-the-counter stocks, 365–66
  treasury bonds, 367
state and local, 344–47
state and local bond trusts, 347
stocks (see Stocks)
in street name, 382
U.S. government, 155, 342–44
underlying, 391
Securities and Exchange Commission (SEC), 357, 389, 405
Securities exchanges, 354–60
  American Stock Exchange (Amex), 356
  members of, 354–55
  New York Stock Exchange (NYSE), 354–55
  regional, 356–57, 387
  seats on, 354, 356
Securities Investor Protection Corporation (SIPC), 390
Security agreement, 65, 106, 130
Self-employed:
  federal taxes, 476, 483
  retirement plans, 292
  social security tax, 274
Self-service, 63
Senior citizens, 493–94
  See also Age; Retirement
Serial bonds, 340
Service charges, 77, 81, 85, 87–88

Service contracts, 64
Service credit, 98
Servicemen's Group Life Insurance, 203
Services, 49–50
Sight draft, 77
Signature card, 78, 80–81
Signature loan, 106
Silver, 421
Single proprietorship, 305, 306
Single repayment loans, 96, 112, 126, 130, 219, 451–52
Small business investment company (SBIC), 395
Small claims courts, 70–71, 439
Small loan companies, 109, 125
Social security, 273–81
    benefits, 275, 486
        retirement, 276, 278
        student's, 280
        survivors', 280
    disability payments, 274, 276, 280
    future of, 280–81
    limits to earnings, 279
    quarters of coverage, 275–76
    trust funds, 276, 277
    wage statement request, 276–78
    who is covered, 274
Social Security Act, 248, 250, 273–74, 278
Social security taxes, 274–75, 281
Society, and consumer credit, 100
Specialty funds, 395
Specialty insurance, 269–70
    boat, 269
    crop, 270
    group legal, 270
    malpractice, 270
    trip, 269–70
    see also Insurance
Speculative stock, 334–35
Stamps and coins, 418
Standard and Poor's, 316–17, 331, 348, 361, 363, 401
Standard of living, 3, 6, 10
State consumer protection agencies, 72, 149
State and local bond trusts, 347
State and local securities, 344–47, 478
State and local taxes, 473–75
    inheritance and estate, 529–30, 536
    income tax, 475, 488
    other, 473, 475
    property tax, 459, 474–75
    sales tax, 473–74, 488
Stocks:
    averages, 361–63
    blue-chip, 334, 378
    buying and selling, 354–60, 367–69, 371–78

common, 327–35, 353, 354
    earnings, yield, capital gains, 328–31, 369–78
    inflation and, 286, 287, 307–8, 330, 369
    investment value, 286, 287, 307–8, 330, 369
    rankings or ratings of, 331
    value concepts, 328
co-ops, 444–45
corporate, 306
in credit unions, 158, 159, 160
cyclical, 333–34
defensive, 334
dividends
    cash, 306, 308, 478
    stock, 371, 383, 478
gifts to minors, 382
growth, 332–33, 372–73, 375
income, 333, 372–73, 375
option plans, 386n
options: puts and calls, 386–87
preemptive rights, 383–85, 386
preferred, 306, 312, 321, 335–37, 354
    callable or redeemable, 336–37
    convertible, 337
    cumulative and noncumulative, 335
    cumulative participating, 336
    participating, 335–36, 337
quotations, 360–63, 365–66
    over-the-counter, 365–66
speculative, 334–35, 368
splits, 361, 382–83
warrants, 385–86
see also Securities; Securities exchanges
Stockholders, 306, 307, 327, 335
    risk, 306
Stock insurance companies, 223
Stock market, 353
    bull and bear markets, 363–65
    declines, 356, 368, 376
    economic indicators, 373–75
    manipulation, 389
    see also New York Stock Exchange; Securities exchanges
Students:
    college funds, 208
    social security benefits, 280
    tax exemptions for, 484, 489–90
Suggested list price, 66
Survivorship, right of, 81, 91
Syndicate investing, 411

Taxation, principles of, 471–73
Tax(es), 470–506
    audit, 500
    avoidance, 407
        legal, 497–98

collection of, 473
credits, 492–95, 530
economy and, 7
estate (*see* Estate tax)
exemption, 344, 402, 411, 478, 483–84, 488
federal (*see* Federal taxes)
gift (*see* Gift tax)
inheritance, 510, 536
national expenditures and, 470–71
professional help with, 499–500
progressive, 472–82
refunds, 477, 479
regressive, 473
savings tips, 498–99
shelters, 498, 499
state and local (*see* State and local taxes)
Tax-exempt funds, 394
Tax forms, 500–6
  complexities, 473
  schedule G, 486
  schedules X and Y, 501, 506
  tables, 501, 502
  1040, 477, 500–1, 503–4
  1040A, 488, 500–1, 505–6
  withholding, 484
Tax-sheltered retirement plans, 292–98, 498, 499
Tax straddle or spread, 407
Tenancy by the entirety, 523
Testamentary trust, 524
Thrift institutions, 155–68
Time deposits, 155–56
Time draft, 77
Title, transferring, 524, 527
Title insurance, 465
Town house, 444
Trade-ins, 58, 65–66
Training schools, 55
Transportation, budgeting, 38–40
Travel, financing, 99
Travel insurance, 269–70
Travelers' checks, 77, 92–93
Treasury bills, 341, 343–44, 161, 161n, 372
Treasury bonds, 367
Treasury note CD, 160, 161, 162, 163, 343
Trip insurance, 269–70
Truncation, 85, 118
Trusts, 523–29
  beneficiary, 524, 525
    per stirpes, 525, 525n
  Clifford (temporary), 526
  creation of, 524
  inter vivos, 524–25
  life insurance, 526–27
  lives-in-being clause, 527–28
  power of appointment, 528

power of invasion clause, 526, 527
purpose, 523, 524, 533
revocable and irrevocable, 524–25, 527
  spendthrift trust, 524
rule against perpetuities, 527–28
simple and complex, 525
social security, 276, 277
taxes and, 479, 524, 525
testamentary, 525
trustee, 526
  bank as, 75, 91, 297–98, 528–29
Truth-in-lending law, 104, 128, 139–40, 141

Uniform Gifts to Minors Act, 382
Uninsured motorist endorsement, 265–66, 269
Unit pricing, 54
Used-product discount, 58
U.S. government bonds, 155, 312, 342, 343, 347, 349, 367
  series E (EE) and H (HH), 165–68, 478
U.S. government securities, 155, 342–44, 367
Usury laws, 137, 407n, 450, 453, 457

Vacation dream resorts, 56
Vacation homes, 446
Vacations, financing, 99
VA-guaranteed mortgage, 451, 455, 456, 457

Wage assignment clause, 65
Wall Street Journal, 315–16, 387, 398–99
"War" clauses, 203
Warranties, 64
Warrants, purchase, 385–86
Wealth, 4, 24
Welfare, 250
Wholesale price, 54
Withdrawals:
  penalties, 163
  savings accounts, 89–90, 159
Wiesenberger Services, Inc., 400
Wills, 512–22
  absence of, 522–23
  codicil to, 517
  common disaster clause, 516
  contesting of, 517
  definitions, 512–13
  executor of, 513, 515
  general contents, 514–15
  holographic, 517
  joint, 515–16
  living, 521–22
  probating, 510, 513
  property subject to disposal, 513–14
  protection of dependents, 516–17
  residuary clause, 515

Wills, *continued*
    safekeeping of, 517–18
    samples, 518–20
    trusts in, 525
Women:
    discrimination, 14, 143
    life expectancy, 284, 288
Workmen's compensation, 255, 256

Yachts, 419

Yellow Pages, 52
Yield:
    bonds, 312, 330, 349–50, 409
    common stock, 328–29, 375–76
    mortgage, 409–10
    real estate, 413–15

Zero bracket amount, 477, 482n, 488